De Gruyter Handbook of Entrepreneurial Finance

De Gruyter Handbook of Entrepreneurial Finance

Edited by
David Lingelbach

DE GRUYTER

ISBN 978-3-11-072675-6
e-ISBN (PDF) 978-3-11-072631-2
e-ISBN (EPUB) 978-3-11-072635-0
ISSN 2748-016X
e-ISSN 2748-0178

Library of Congress Control Number: 2021952434

Bibliographic information published by the Deutsche Nationalbibliothek
The Deutsche Nationalbibliothek lists this publication in the Deutsche Nationalbibliografie;
detailed bibliographic data are available on the internet at http://dnb.dnb.de.

© 2022 Walter de Gruyter GmbH, Berlin/Boston
Typesetting: Integra Software Services Pvt. Ltd.
Printing and binding: CPI books GmbH, Leck.

www.degruyter.com

Acknowledgments

I've incurred a lot of debts in putting together this book. David Repetto, the commissioning editor at De Gruyter, reached out to me in the midst of the pandemic to see if I would be interested in submitting a proposal. I was shocked – and grateful – when my proposal survived the review process and was selected. Thank you, Dave.

Once in the good hands of De Gruyter, Stefan Giesen, editorial director for business and economics, and Maximilian Gessl, content editor for economics and social sciences, provided gentle advice as the manuscript moved forward to publication. Thanks to both of them for making this first solo editor effort so painless and, can I say, enjoyable.

Of course, none of this book would have been possible without the 35 contributors who generated its content. What an amazing group of academics and practitioners! I am so grateful for what they have done. I'm proud to be associated with their efforts.

In a larger sense, none of this book would have been possible without those who have supported my development as an academic: Gordon Murray, Hans Landström, Colin Mason, Harry Sapienza, Roger Leeds, and Celso Brunetti, among others. The University of Baltimore's Merrick School of Business – my home institution since 2010 – has supported me in large ways and small. Particular thanks to Kurt Schmoke, president; Murray Dalziel, dean; and Ven Sriram, department chair, for watching out for my best interests.

As always, the love and support of my wife Jenny, daughter Catie, and soon-to-be son-in-law Jacob mean the world to me.

This book is dedicated to Vale, who inspired its opening story. The world is lucky to have you in it.

https://doi.org/10.1515/9783110726312-202

Contents

Part IV: **Emerging perspectives**

Editor and contributor biographies

Franklin Allen is Professor of Finance and Economics and Executive Director of the Brevan Howard Centre at Imperial College London. He was at the Wharton School of the University of Pennsylvania and is now Emeritus Professor there. He was Vice Dean and Director of Wharton Doctoral Programs, Co-Director of the Wharton Financial Institutions Center, Executive Editor of the Review of Financial Studies and Managing Editor of the Review of Finance. He was President of the American Finance Association, the Western Finance Association, the Society for Financial Studies, the Financial Intermediation Research Society and the Financial Management Association, and a Fellow of the Econometric Society. He received his doctorate from Oxford University. Dr. Allen's research interests are corporate finance, asset pricing, financial innovation, comparative financial systems, and financial crises. He is a co-author with Richard Brealey and Stewart Myers of the eighth through twelfth editions of the textbook *Principles of Corporate Finance*.

Jorge Arteaga-Fonseca is a Fulbright and UK-Chevening scholar from Nicaragua. Jorge has more than 15 years of industry experience in finance, management and entrepreneurship in Latin America. Currently he is pursuing a PhD in Entrepreneurship at Oklahoma State University. His main research interests are entrepreneurial finance and combining finance and organizational theories in entrepreneurship. Jorge has a MSc in Investment and Finance from University of Strathclyde in Glasgow, UK; MBA from EAE Business School in Barcelona, Spain; BPhil in Business Administration from Ave Maria College in Michigan, USA; and received a scholarship to participate in the 2019 Senior Executive Fellows program at Harvard Kennedy School.

Paul Asel is Managing Partner of NGP Capital, a global venture firm operating in Europe, China and the United States with $1.2 billion assets under management. NGP Capital was named the Fund of the Year by Global Corporate Venturing in 2016. Previously, Paul led technology investments at the International Finance Corporation. Paul is an Adjunct Professor at the George Mason Schar School of Policy and Government and earlier at the China Europe International Business School in Shanghai. He has lectured at the Stanford Graduate School of Business, Wharton at University of Pennsylvania and School of Advanced International Studies at Johns Hopkins University. He received an MBA from Stanford and BA from Dartmouth. Paul is co-author of *Upward Bound: Lessons of How Nine Leaders Achieved their Summits*. His articles have appeared in Barron's, CB Insights, Forbes, Global Corporate Venturing, Journal of Private Equity, Knowledge@Wharton, Stanford Business Magazine, TechCrunch and Venture Capital Journal.

Sofia Avdeitchikova holds a doctorate (2008) and a master's degree (2003) in social sciences from Lund University. In her doctoral thesis, she studied informal venture capital in Sweden, with focus on the role of proximity in investment decision-making. She has published extensively in international journals on the topics of venture capital, business angels and ambitious entrepreneurship. In addition, she has worked at the UN as advisor on Agenda 2030, headed the Department of Entrepreneurship and Enterprise at the Swedish Agency for Growth Policy Analysis, and conducted over 80 consulting assignments for government offices and various authorities in Sweden, European Commission, Nordic Council of Ministers, local and regional governments, science parks and universities.

Alexandra Bertschi-Michel, PhD, is a postdoctoral researcher at the University of Bern, Switzerland. She received her PhD in philosophy of management at the Center for family business, University of St. Gallen, Switzerland. Her research interests focus on advisors in family firms, family firm succession, private equity in family firms, and turnaround management in family firms

https://doi.org/10.1515/9783110726312-204

and her articles have been published, amongst others, in *Entrepreneurship Theory & Practice, Family Business Review, Long Range Planning*, and *Small Business Economics*. Besides her academic career, Alexandra Bertschi-Michel is also active as a family firm advisor in succession related matters (e-mail: alexandra.bertschi@iop.unibe.ch).

Aleia Bucci completed her PhD at the University of Pretoria's Gordon Institute of Business Science. Her thesis identified the ways social entrepreneurs in South Africa utilise informal learning to advance their knowledge while part of an incubation programme. Aleia's research interests include social entrepreneurship, entrepreneurial learning, and entrepreneurial ecosystems.

Yves Fassin (Belgium) holds a Master of Science in Engineering from Ghent University, a management degree from Vlerick Business School, and a PhD in Applied Economics from Ghent University. He combined his academic interests with an entrepreneurial career. He was director of the Industrial Liaison Office at Ghent University and Secretary-General of the European Venture Capital Association. He has been Managing Director of a small company and has also launched and participated in a few business start-ups. He followed the Executive Program for Growing Companies at Stanford Business School. He has been a member of the SME Committee of the Federation of Belgian Industries. He is a part-time professor at the Faculty of Economics and Business Administration, Ghent University, and Honorary Partner of Vlerick Business School. His research interests include corporate responsibility, business ethics, stakeholder management and corporate governance, and ethical issues in these fields of innovation and entrepreneurship.

Nadine Kammerlander is chaired professor of family business at WHU – Otto Beisheim School of Management in Germany where she also serves as co-director of the Institute of family business & Mittelstand. Prof. Kammerlander earned her PhD in management from the University of Bamberg and her master's degree in physics from the Technical University of Munich. Her research focuses on family firms and family offices and has been published in journals such as AMJ, AMR, JMS, JBV and ETP. She has also received international prizes such as the Carolyn Dexter Award. Nadine Kammerlander serves as Editor of Family Business Review. Family Capital named her as one of the Top 100 Global Family Influencers.

Judit Karsai is a Doctor of Science, Hungarian Academy of Sciences. She works as a scientific advisor at the Institute of Economics, Centre for Economic and Regional Studies, Hungary. She has published regularly on the subjects of private equity and venture capital financing, management buy-outs, enterprise behavior and business incubation. She has participated in numerous joint international research activities and has acted as coordinator and participant in several projects supported by the World Bank and the Commission of the European Union. She provided a thorough analysis of the venture capital and private equity industry in the Central and Eastern European (CEE) region in her three books: *Private Equity in CEE* (2010); *The new kings of capitalism. Venture capital and private equity in the CEE region* (2012, in Hungarian) and *The Odd Couple. Government participation in the CEE venture capital market* (2017, in Hungarian).

Jonathan Kimmitt is a Senior Lecturer in Entrepreneurship at Newcastle University Business School, UK. His research focuses on issues related to (social) entrepreneurship, international development, and poverty. In particular, his research has looked at recipients of microfinance and how this seeds entrepreneurial opportunities as well as how microfinance Institutions meet their diverse and complex goals. He is similarly interested in aspects of alternative investment, particularly Social Impact Bonds as well as social entrepreneurial behaviour. He has published in several international journals including Journal of Management Studies, Journal of Business

Venturing, International Small Business Journal, Entrepreneurship & Regional Development, Management and Organization Review, Technological Forecasting and Social Change, and Policy & Politics.

Darek Klonowski is Professor of Business Administration at Brandon University in Canada. Prior to working in academia, Klonowski was involved in the private equity and venture capital industry. He is the author and editor of six books on private equity and venture capital with Palgrave MacMillan.

Hans Landström is Professor Emeritus in Business Administration at Lund University, Sweden; Co-founder of two large research centres on innovation and entrepreneurship at Lund University: CIRCLE and Sten K. Johnson Centre for Entrepreneurship; President of the European Council for Small Business (ECSB) 1999–2001; and historian within the ENT Division of the AOM 2011–2016. Since 2010 he is ECSB Fellow, and in 2017 he was awarded as the Wilford L. White Fellow of the International Council for Small Business (ICSB). His research interests include entrepreneurial finance, venture capital and business angels, entrepreneurial education, and the history of entrepreneurship theory. His articles have been published in journals such as *Research Policy, Journal of Business Venturing, Small Business Economics, Entrepreneurship Theory and Practice, Entrepreneurship and Regional Development*, and *Journal of Small Business Management*.

Silas Lee holds an Honours Bachelor of Business Administration from Brandon University and is currently pursuing a JD/MBA at Osgoode Hall Law School and the Schulich School of Business. During his undergraduate degree, he developed an interest in social entrepreneurship and venture capital under the tutelage of Dr. Darek Klonowski. Silas previously worked as a strategy advisory intern at Ceridian HCM, a global software-as-a-service company, and will be completing his articles at Norton Rose Fulbright Canada LLP in Toronto, Ontario. He is the co-founder and CMO of ReNu Hygienics, a soap recycling startup, and is one of seven children.

David Lingelbach (B.S., M.S., Massachusetts Institute of Technology; Ph.D., University of Exeter) is an associate professor of entrepreneurship at the Merrick School of Business, The University of Baltimore. His research focuses on entrepreneurship and entrepreneurial finance in emerging and developing economies, and oligarch studies. His research has been published in journals such as *Journal of Management Inquiry, Venture Capital: An International Journal of Entrepreneurial Finance*, and *International Journal of Entrepreneurship and Innovation*. He is also co-author of *Entrepreneurship in Africa: Context and Perspectives*, the first international textbook in the discipline focused on that continent. He has founded or co-founded nine startups in the for- and non-profit sectors and previously served as CEO of Bank of America's businesses in the former Soviet Union and President of one of post-communist Russia's first venture capital funds. He has advised the World Bank, Asian Development Bank, the Asia Foundation, and the government of Indonesia on venture capital and entrepreneurship development. He was awarded a Fulbright Scholar grant to Myanmar and a Fulbright Specialist to Colombia and has been nominated twice for an Andrew Carnegie Fellowship. He is currently writing a commercial nonfiction book about oligarchs.

Wan Liu is a doctoral student at Zhejiang University. She has published papers in prestigious journals such as International Journal of Conflict Management, Journal of Engineering and Technology Management, Management Decision and others. She has also reviewed papers for management/business journals such as Technovation and others.

Antonio C, Malfense Fierro is a senior lecturer (Associate Professor) in entrepreneurship at Hull University Business School. Antonio's research focuses on large scale, entrepreneur owned business portfolios; family business & risk (Africa and other contexts). His capabilities extend to the development, design and undertaking of bespoke market research in challenging contexts, executive education in the areas of business opportunities, challenges (Africa/elsewhere), general entrepreneurship, venture creation, firm growth, entrepreneurship policy and market opportunity assessment. In the area of market opportunity assessment, Antonio has led a number of feasibility studies focused on determining markets for new technologies or exploring new markets for existing industries. These studies have been focused on EV charging, Carbon Nanofibers, Drone, remote sensing and Ph reduction technologies for agriculture. Antonio has undertaken a number of projects focused on entrepreneurial ecosystems and SMEs. Antonio has won a significant number of research grants focused on diverse areas of exploration.

Dr Jonathan Marks works at University of Pretoria Gordon Institute of Business Science in the entrepreneurship and innovation domain. His primary areas of research are high-growth entrepreneurship, entrepreneurial learning and education, and entrepreneurial finance. He is faculty lead for the MBA Entrepreneurship Focus, and is an innovative and award-winning educator, having developed courses and programmes across the higher-education spectrum. He brings a strong practitioner focus to his work, having started and exited a number of high-growth start-up ventures. He was founding director of the Ackerman Academy of Entrepreneurship at the University of Cape Town, from where he has an MBA and PhD focused on entrepreneurship education.

Dr. Jet Mboga is an Assistant Professor in the Management & International Department at Ziegler College of Business, Bloomsburg University of Pennsylvania. Her Research Interests include International Business: Sub-Saharan Africa; Entrepreneurship, Organizational Leadership Impact on Business and Society; Organizational Behavior: Ethical Decision Making; Cross-Cultural Management; and Corporate Governance (Strategy). Her education is credited to PhD, University of Bolton – United Kingdom; Doctor of Business Administration, Walden University –Minneapolis, MN.

Sussie C. Morrish is Professor of Marketing in the Department of Management, Marketing and Entrepreneurship at the University of Canterbury Business School. Sussie teaches undergraduate to post-graduate strategic marketing and entrepreneurship. She gained her PhD from the University of Canterbury while simultaneously teaching at the University of Auckland Business School. Her main research interests revolve around the marketing and entrepreneurship disciplines including various strategic approaches to internationalisation and sustainability. Her more recent research explores the effects of disasters on entrepreneurial business and ecosystems.

Rebecca Namatovu (PhD Gordon Institute of Business Science, University of Pretoria) is a post-doctoral researcher at the Department of Strategy and Innovation at the Copenhagen Business School. Her research interests lie at the intersection of entrepreneurship and development studies. She has conducted extensive research on entrepreneurship in resource-constrained and fragile environments. Her research quest is to understand the role of entrepreneurship in responding to global challenges like poverty, inequality and sustainability. Her work is published in the Journal of Business Venturing, Entrepreneurship and Regional Development and Academy of Management Learning and Education. Rebecca serves at the editorial review board of the Africa Journal of Management. Before joining CBS, Rebecca was a senior lecturer at Makerere University Business School, Uganda.

Minh-Hoang Nguyen holds an MSc in Sustainability Science from Ritsumeikan Asia Pacific University, Beppu, Japan, where he continues his Ph.D. track. He works as a researcher in the Centre for Interdisciplinary Social Research, Phenikaa University, Hanoi, Vietnam. He has published around 35 articles in journals and books by multiple publishers: Cell Press, De Gruyter, Elsevier, Emerald, MDPI, MIT Press, Nature Research, Oxford University Press, Springer, and Wiley. His research interest is psychological issues. He believes understanding human mental constructs and mechanisms is a fundamental approach for achieving sustainability in multiple disciplines.

Ana María Peredo, Ph.D., is a Social and Inclusive Entrepreneurship Professor at the Telfer School of Management, University of Ottawa. Prior to that, she was Professor of Political Ecology and Business and Sustainability (2000–2021) and Director of the Centre for Co-operative and Community-Based Economy (2008–2014) at the University of Victoria. She is a Peruvian anthropologist and critical management scholar, focusing on community alternatives, social economy, social justice and participatory action research, particularly among Indigenous peoples and disadvantaged communities. She has published in the areas of community-based entrepreneurship, poverty alleviation, commons and resistance movements. Ana María has published her research in top management and organizational journals and received numerous research, teaching and community engagement awards

Duygu Phillips is a Postdoctoral Researcher in Entrepreneurship at Oklahoma State University. She received her PhD in Business Administration with a major in Entrepreneurship from Oklahoma State University. Previously, she acquired her Master's in Marketing from the University of Birmingham, UK and her Bachelor's in Communications from Galatasaray University. Dr. Phillips has 15 years of experience in consulting start-ups as well as small and medium-sized businesses. She is the founder of a consulting firm specializing on start-up strategy and naming. She is the author of the first book on naming published in Turkey. Her research focuses on new venture strategy, institutional theory, organizational identity, cultural entrepreneurship, entrepreneurial finance, and family business.

Audrey Maria Popa is a graduate student at the University of Victoria obtaining her Master's in Environmental Studies, where her research will explore conservation finance and conservation economies in Canada. After completing a Bachelor of Commerce in Sustainability and Social Impact at the University of British Columbia, Audrey worked in sustainability advisory and social finance research positions in Vancouver, Toronto and Montreal. Most recently, Audrey has worked with the Table of Impact Investment Practitioners (TIIP) to co-develop a report on the *State of Social Finance in Canada*. Additionally, Audrey is currently a social finance researcher for the Canadian Network of Partner Research on Philanthropy (PhiLab) investigating how foundations across Canada can integrate social finance within their investment and granting strategy.

Meijun Qian is a Professor of Finance, and a Research Fellow at the Wharton Financial Institution Center. She was also a consultant economist for Asian Development Bank and a visiting scholar at the Becker and Friedman Institute at the University of Chicago. Meijun's research interests include comparative financial system, economic development in China and India, state capitalism, alternative finance, mutual funds, infrastructure and productivity, and leadership diversity. Her research has appeared in top-tier academic journals including *Journal of Financial Economics*, *Journal of Financial and Quantitative Analysis*, *Management Science*, and *Journal of Financial Intermediation*. It has also been presented to regulators including The Stock Exchange Committee, Federal Reserve Banks, People's Bank of China, The Capital Market Board of Turkey, World Economy Forum, and The Wilson Center. Meijun's work has had a high impact amongst academics, the financial industry, and policymakers and is widely cited.

Tiago Ratinho is Associate Professor in Entrepreneurship at IESEG School of Management, Univ. Lille, CNRS. He holds a PhD from the University of Twente (The Netherlands) and maintains a global profile conducting research and teaching in the USA, Brazil, and France on topics such as business incubation, effectuation, and technology entrepreneurship. His work can be read in international publications such as the Journal of Business Venturing, Technological Forecasting and Social Change, and Technovation. Google Scholar profile: shorturl.at/opDJK

Peter Rosa is the Emeritus Professor & George David Chair of Entrepreneurship and Family Business at the University of Edinburgh and held the George David Chair as a full professor before retiring in 2016. He was also the Director of the Edinburgh University Center for Entrepreneurship and Innovation and Head of the Entrepreneurship and Innovation Group. He has been a Visiting Professor at the Makerere University Business School (Uganda) and the Witten Herdecke University Institute of Family Business (Germany). He has published extensively in the field of portfolio entrepreneurship and family business groups and in 2019 co-edited a book, *The Family Business Group Phenomenon: Emergence and Complexities*.

Dr. Matthew Rutherford is Professor, Johnny Pope Chair, and Riata Entrepreneur in Residence at Oklahoma State University. Previously, Dr. Rutherford was Associate Professor of Management at Virginia Commonwealth University where he oversaw the entrepreneurship program. He has also served on faculty at Gonzaga University. He received his PhD from Auburn University. He has published 40 peer reviewed articles in top entrepreneurship and management journals, and is the author of the book: *Strategic Bootstrapping*. Additionally, he has presented over 100 manuscripts at international, national, and regional conferences. Dr. Rutherford's experience is in new and small firm consulting. He has provided consulting services to over 100 organizations of all sizes. His research foci are corporate entrepreneurship and innovation, family business, and new venture finance.

Antonia Schickinger is a manager within the Private Equity Group at Bain & Company in Berlin. Previously, she was a doctoral student with Prof. Dr. Nadine Kammerlander at the Institute of Family Business at WHU – Otto Beisheim School of Management. In her dissertation, which was supported by the Friedrich Naumann Foundation, Antonia focused on "Private Equity Investments of Family Firms and Family Offices". Amongst others, her research was published in the Journal of Family Business Strategy as well as in Small Business Economics. Before starting her dissertation, Antonia studied Business Administration at the University of Mannheim and worked several years as an analyst at Goldman Sachs in Frankfurt.

Dr. Bettina Schneider is the Associate Dean of Community, Research & Graduate Programs at the First Nations University of Canada (FNUniv) and is also an Associate Professor in Indigenous Business and Public Administration at FNUniv. She received her MS in community development and her PhD in Native American Studies from the University of California, Davis. She has worked at FNUniv since 2007. Dr. Schneider has also worked as a consultant for the First Nations Development Institute, First Nations Oweesta Corporation, and Opportunity Finance Network. Her research has predominantly focused on Indigenous community and economic development strategies, Native and Aboriginal financial institutions in the U.S. and Canada, Indigenous business and financial literacy curriculum, and Indigenous qualitative business research methodologies and methods.

Steven X. Si is a distinguished professor (entrepreneurship/innovation) at Zhejiang University and research professor at Bloomsburg U. of Pennsylvania. Professor Si has published about 100 peer-reviewed articles in journals such as JBV, SEJ, JAP, AMP and others. He serves/served as guest editor for seven Special Issues for the prestigious journals such as Technovation, JETM, ERD, SEJ, JBV, IJCM, APJM. Professor Si currently serves as an associate editor for the journal Technovation.

Dr Janine Swail is a senior lecturer in Entrepreneurship and Innovation at Auckland University Business School. Prior to relocating to New Zealand in 2016, Janine worked as an Assistant Professor at Newcastle University (2007–2013) and University of Nottingham (2013–2016). Her research interests focus on the impact of gender upon entrepreneurial activity, most recently in the area of entrepreneurial finance and business exit. She teaches across undergraduate and postgraduate levels and contributes to the design, delivery and coordination of courses in the area of innovation and entrepreneurship. Her recent publications can be found in *Entrepreneurship, Theory and Practice, Gender, Work and Organisation, Entrepreneurship and Regional Development* and *International Small Business Journal.* She serves on the Editorial Board of the *International Small Business Journal* and the *International Journal of Entrepreneurial Behaviour and Research.*

Quan-Hoang Vuong (Ph.D., Université Libre de Bruxelles) is Distinguished Scientist of Phenikaa University, Hanoi, Vietnam. He is also a Distinguished Associate Member of the Vietnam Institute for Advanced Study in Mathematics. He has published nearly 200 academic papers and books with many leading publishers.

Jan Warhuus is assistant professor of entrepreneurship at the School of Economics and Business Administration at St. Mary's College of California. His research interests include entrepreneurship education, entrepreneurship and gender, and new venture finance. Prior to joining St Mary's in 2018, Jan was an assistant professor of entrepreneurship at Aarhus University. From 1999 to 2013 he worked in the private sector in the San Francisco Bay Area where he was involved with several start-ups, including a role as founding management team member at GuardianEdge, a venture-capital backed data security company acquired by Symantec. Jan earned his Ph.D. from University of Southern Denmark in 2000 and his research has appeared in International Journal of Entrepreneurial Behavior and Research, Journal of Small Business and Enterprise Development, The International Journal of Management Education, Education & Training, Industry and Higher Education, and Frontiers of Entrepreneurship.

Jing Xie is an assistant professor of finance at Hong Kong Polytechnic University. He obtained his PhD of Finance from National University of Singapore. Jing's research interests include empirical corporate finance, behavioural asset pricing, institutional investor behavior, and tax avoidance. His research has appeared in top-tier academic journals including *Journal of Financial Economics*, *Journal of Financial Intermediation,* and *Journal of Corporate Finance.*

Yushan Yan is a doctoral student at Zhejiang University. She has published papers in the prestigious journals such as Management Decision, International Journal of Conflict Management and top-tier Chinese Management Journal – Management World. She has also reviewed papers for management/business journals such as Journal of Engineering and Technology Management and others.

David Lingelbach
Introduction

December 22, 2030. As her plane descended carefully through Bogotá's now-perpetually stormy cloudbank, Mu Tha readied herself for the meeting of her life. The city's rapid emergence as the new center of startup finance had caught everyone off guard, most especially the old guard on Sand Hill Road in Silicon Valley choking on that region's near-constant wildfires and the hubris and overreach of the techbro culture of the 2020s. Colombia's capital hadn't been the first pick as a finance center, but with New York, London, Shanghai, Hong Kong, and Singapore now underwater from rapid searise, governments and international organizations around the world had scrambled to make more resilient the global financial system, especially that part of it that would finance the only hope the globe had to get out of the now-cascading existential crises it faced.

Mu Tha was typical of the new generation of financiers that had arisen in the new world order. A member of the Kayan Padaung ethnic minority of the now-failed state of Myanmar, Daw Mu (Daw is a title of respect for women in that country) had been a leader in the resistance to the military junta that took power in 2021, suffering hideously disfiguring torture at their hands that had left her in near-constant pain. But as indigenous people like her gained power in the topsy turvy world of the late 2020s, Mu's disadvantages in the Western-, and then Chinese-dominated, world suddenly became advantages. Because neither the Western models of neoliberal capitalism nor Chinese models of state capitalism were working to save the planet. And as global warming accelerated, and vaccine-resistant pandemics became an annual event, ancient ways of thinking were coming to the fore again. And people like Daw Mu – indigenous people, women, people of color, marginalized people in general – were the key actors in getting financial resources to innovative startups that could save the planet.

Mu's meeting in Bogotá was with the board of the UN's Fund to Save the Planet (UNFSP). Established by UN Secretary General Greta Thunberg and inspired by Kim Stanley Robinson's *The Ministry for the Future*, UNFSP had been capitalized at $100 trillion through the confiscation of wealth of the world's wealthiest people. The fund had one purpose: to fund innovations to arrest climate change, pandemics, and any other existential threats facing the planet, and to do so as quickly and efficiently as possible.

As UNFSP's chief executive, Mu's meeting today was the most important of her life. For she would be proposing a massive investment in the only startup she and her team felt could stop the world from spinning out of control. Afterward, she was looking forward to celebrating the 30th birthday of her best friend Vale at a cozy vegetarian restaurant. Until then, the bumps she felt as her plane navigated Bogotá's turbulence were only a taste of what was to come.

******

https://doi.org/10.1515/9783110726312-001

In reality, will things turn out the way that this fictional story suggests? Who knows! But this story helps to open the mind to some of the themes that motivated this new Handbook of Entrepreneurial Finance. First, the sense that the ground is shifting under the feet of both researchers and practitioners. Next, that existential questions like climate change are increasingly shaping the opportunity set with which these practitioners and those who study them work. And, finally, that previously marginalized voices are coming quickly to the fore, as are aspects of entrepreneurial finance that didn't exist a decade ago.

Dear readers! Welcome to entrepreneurial finance, and to the De Gruyter Handbook of Entrepreneurial Finance. The aim of this book is to provide readers with an up-to-date survey about what we know about entrepreneurial finance in all its forms, and to suggest where our knowledge about this field might head next. The book is very much an academic survey, but one informed by practice. Its nineteen chapters are authored by a diverse, global body of thirty-five contributors including leading researchers, emerging voices, and practitioners. These contributors are currently based at universities or organizations located in sixteen countries and one indigenous people's land: Australia, Belgium, Canada, China, Denmark, France, Germany, Hong Kong, Hungary, New Zealand, South Africa, the Star Blanket Cree Nation Urban Indian Reserve, Sweden, Switzerland, United Kingdom, United States, and Vietnam. These colleagues have research agendas or work programs that take them across the world.

The field of entrepreneurial finance studies how new ventures obtain and manage external financial resources. Entrepreneurial finance employs theoretical insights from entrepreneurship and finance. Initial interest in the field was driven by the venture capital (VC) phenomenon and the startups funded by its participants, a phenomenon that continues to evolve (The Economist, 2021). For example, as of January 26th, 2022 seven of the ten largest companies in the world by market capitalization were funded by VCs: Apple, Microsoft, Amazon, Alphabet, Meta, Tencent, and Tesla. At that date those companies had a cumulative market capitalization of USD 10.2 trillion. Some observers contend that VC is one of the three great institutions of modern capitalism, alongside markets and companies (Mallaby, 2022).

More recently, academic and practitioner interest in entrepreneurial finance has shifted to financial innovations such as accelerators and crowdfunding. Even so, the fundamentals of startup financing have not changed. Most startups, in most of the world, and most of the time, obtain funding mainly from their founders and other individuals and businesses to which they are close.

And thus the problem that this book takes on. The bulk of the academic research on entrepreneurial finance has focused to date on phenomena that most entrepreneurs have found largely irrelevant or, at best, aspirational – VC and angel financing. Most entrepreneurs in the world, today and in the past, will never access VC, angel financing, or even more democratized forms of finance such as crowdfunding. As the editor of this Handbook, I am as guilty as many others in this discipline for focusing mainly on popular, sexy, and data-rich phenomena such as venture capital, at the expense of the distinctly much less sexy and considerably more opaque financial reality faced by founders around the world.

And yet, entrepreneurial finance is maturing as a field. This Handbook – one of several published over the past decade – is one evidence of that maturity. Another evidence is the number of literature reviews, editorials, and special issues seeking to make sense of where the field is at present, and where it might and should head.

Table I.1 indicates how early-stage scholarly work on the field has evolved since the 1950s.

Table I.1: Ph.D. Dissertations and Theses on Topics Related to Entrepreneurial Finance.

Decade	Entrepreneurial finance	Venture capital	Business angels	Crowdfunding	Corporate venturing	Total
1950–1959		2				2
1960–1969						0
1970–1979		11			1	12
1980–1989		15			2	17
1990–1999	2	46	2		1	51
2000–2009	3	448	5		11	467
2010–2019	22	229	4	91	6	352
2020–present*	26	88	8	38	3	163

Source: ProQuest Dissertations & Theses Global.
Note: *Through September 23, 2021.

Entrepreneurial finance has been fortunate to attract the interest of some of the leading researchers in entrepreneurship and finance. As is true in many other academic fields, some of these colleagues have a disproportionate impact on the field's development, as Table I.2 indicates:

Table I.2: Some Impactful Publications in Entrepreneurial Finance, Ranked by Total Citations.

Author(s)	Institutional Affiliation (at time of publication)	Date	Total Citations (a/o 9/24/21)	Citations/year
Sahlman	Harvard	1990	4,087	132
Mollick	Louvain	2015	4,065	678
Gompers & Lerner	Harvard	2004	3,566	210
Belleflamme, Lambert & Schwienbacher (2014)		2014	3,118	445

Table I.2 (continued)

Author(s)	Institutional Affiliation (at time of publication)	Date	Total Citations (a/o 9/24/21)	Citations/year
Kaplan & Stromberg	Chicago	2003	2,870	159
Kortum & Lerner	Chicago, Harvard	2001	2,833	142
Gompers & Lerner	Harvard	2001	2,290	114
Gompers	Harvard	1996	1,868	75
Bygrave & Timmons	Babson	1992	1,686	58
Ahlers et al.	MTI North America, York, WHU, Concordia	2015	1,572	262
Lerner	Harvard	1994	1,554	58
Cochrane	Chicago	2005	1,260	79

Note: Ranked by total citations (greater than 1000 total citations)

What is entrepreneurial finance? A discipline? A field? A phenomenon?

At a bare minimum, entrepreneurial finance is an established phenomenon. Depending on how one defines a new venture, entrepreneurial finance has been observed as far back as ancient Greece.

And there is little doubt that entrepreneurial finance is a proper academic field. Bird, Welsch, Astrachan, and Pistrui (2002) define three criteria for an academic field: a professional association, career opportunities through Ph.D. or certification programs, and a systematic theory and an established body of literature, evidenced by an academic journal, annual conferences, or bibliographies. Entrepreneurial finance has some of these elements. Two professional associations have been established in the field. The ENTFIN Association was formally established in 2018 by seven leading researchers in the field and have been holding annual meetings since 2016.

There is no doctoral degree program in entrepreneurial finance, but there are certificate programs in venture capital. Entrepreneurial finance has three established academic journals. *Venture Capital: An International Journal of Entrepreneurial Finance*, founded in 1999, is Scopus and Web of Science-indexed, and ranked 2 (on a scale from 4* to 1) in the 2021 Academic Journal Guide (AJG) and ranked B (on a scale of A* to C) in the 2019 Australian Business Deans Council (ABDC) Journal Quality List. *The Journal of Private Equity*, founded in 1997, publishes some academic studies on venture capital and is ranked C on the ABDC list. *The Journal of Entrepreneurial Finance*, established in 1991, is not indexed by either Scopus or Web of Science and is not ranked on either the

AJG or ABDC lists. The Academy of Entrepreneurial Finance has been organizing academic conferences since 1989 and is now associated with the Academy of Behavioral Finance and Economics. The Emerging Trends in Entrepreneurial Finance conference has been organized twice since 2017. The Institute for Small Business and Entrepreneurship has a special interest group dedicated to entrepreneurial finance.

In determining the extent of an academic field, Plaschka and Welsch (1990) put forward some guiding questions. Table I.3 provides a brief assessment along the dimensions suggested by these questions.

Table I.3: Assessing the boundaries of entrepreneurial finance as a field.

Dimension	Assessment
Boundaries	Clearly defined
Major forces	Entrepreneurship, finance
More sophisticated research designs, methods, and analyses	Yes
Shift to larger samples and datasets	Yes
Moving from exploratory to causal research	Yes

Various forces work to contribute to an academic field's institutional infrastructure (Aldrich, 2012). These include social networking mechanisms, publication opportunities, collective training and mentoring, major foundations and smaller funding sources, new mechanisms to recognize and reward individual scholarship, and globalizing trends. Some of these forces can be observed in entrepreneurial finance, such as social networking, publication opportunities, and globalizing trends. Others, such as collective training and mentoring, funding sources, mechanisms to reward scholarship, are less visible.

What are the field's proudest accomplishments?

Entrepreneurial finance's proudest accomplishment has been to define carefully the causes and processes of venture capital, which has been described as the single greatest contributor to economic efficiency (Arrow, 1995). We have a good understanding of 1) how investors evaluate prospective deals, 2) why some new ventures are funded while others are not, 3) how VCs and entrepreneurs interrelate, 4) how VCs mitigate risk, 5) the effects of VC intermediation on their portfolio companies, 6) how VC certification impacts firms, 7) how market factors shape VC organizational-level decisions and outcomes, and 8) the country-level outcomes associated with VC (Drover et al., 2017). We also understand that only a very narrow range of technological innovations are amenable to VC investment, and that a relatively small number of VCs shape the capital funding radical technological change (Lerner and Nanda, 2020). And we have identified the principal theoretical perspectives that will help us to better understand the VC phenomenon, including agency theory, resource-based theory, institutional theory, and transaction cost economics (Bellavitis et al., 2017).

What are the basic assumptions? What are valid criticisms of these assumptions?

In entrepreneurial finance the principal existing assumptions reflect the ongoing struggle between the effectual and causal worldviews (Sarasvathy, 2001), with the entrepreneurship part of the field generally informed, directly or indirectly, by effectuation and the finance part of the field by causation. Initially, the field was largely driven by assumptions reflecting the uncertainty associated with financing innovation. However, as entrepreneurial finance practice has become institutionalized, the assumptions have become increasingly causal. One valid criticism of these assumptions relates to when effectual versus causal worldviews should be utilized.

What are the main puzzles, challenges, and controversies in the field?

The main theoretical puzzle in entrepreneurial finance is derived from the main puzzle in entrepreneurship: despite our increasing knowledge, why does entrepreneurship remain so uncertain? How can we reduce that uncertainty? Should we? So for entrepreneurial finance, that puzzle translates to this: how to finance start-ups in ways that go beyond just a few gazelles or home runs? Or are those wins enough for entrepreneurial finance to have served its purpose?

Writing from an American perspective, Nicholas (2019) identified five challenges facing VC: 1) the systematic achievement of out-sized investment returns, 2) the limitations of the limited partnership organizational structure, 3) the sustainability of Silicon Valley's dominance in VC investing, 4) the influence of government on the industry in the future, and 5) the industry's truly awful diversity record. Globally, the key challenge is to marshal entrepreneurial finance using institutionally appropriate mechanisms to continue poverty reduction and, as signaled at the start of the introduction, begin tackling the multiple global existential crises through entrepreneurship and innovation.

The main controversy in the field relates to the criticism of the social utility of tech-enabled startup activity funded by entrepreneurial financing mechanisms, including corporate frauds such as WeWork (Brown and Farrell, 2021) and Theranos (Carreyrou, 2018); a hypergrowth exit mindset (Lam and Seidel, 2020); and the broader criticism of technology firms such as Google and Facebook and their impact on privacy and human agency (Zuboff, 2019). Entrepreneurial finance has served a significant role as a supporting actor in tech-enabled startups.

How is the handbook organized?

The Handbook is organized differently than earlier efforts to sum up this field. We start with the fundamental premise that entrepreneurial finance needs to be studied now and going forward from the entrepreneur's perspective. So we begin at THE INDIVIDUAL LEVEL (Part I), examining what we know and want to know about how entrepreneurs finance themselves without looking externally. These forms include founder financing (Jan Warhuus from St. Mary's College of California), bricolage and bootstrapping (Matthew Rutherford, Duygu Phillips, and Jorge Arteaga-Fonseca from Oklahoma State), effectuation (Sussie Morrish from University of Canterbury), and portfolio entrepreneurship (Antonio Malfense Fierro and Peter Rosa from University of Edinburgh).

In Chapter 1 on founder financing, Jan Warhuus discusses what we know about the role of founders' tangible resources in founding new ventures. He shows how these resources are difficult to study using positivist frameworks favored in disciplines such as corporate finance and suggests different paths forward. Chapter 2 by Matthew Rutherford, Duygu Phillips, and Jorge Arteaga-Fonseca looks at the interface between two leading theoretical perspectives on founder financing – bricolage and bootstrapping – and identifies similarities and divergences between these frameworks. Sussie Morrish takes on another theoretical perspective of use in understanding the individual level of entrepreneurial finance – effectuation – in her Chapter 3, showing how this perspective may influence our understanding of entrepreneurial financing decisions. Chapter 4 by Antonio Malfense Fierro and Peter Rosa focuses on portfolio entrepreneurship and how entrepreneurs use this approach to control risk.

Then we move to THE INNER CIRCLE (Part II), looking at those close-in financing forms that entrepreneurs are most likely to turn to when they need more than they currently have. These include informal financing (Franklin Allen from Imperial College London, Meijun Qian from Australian National University, and Jing Xie from Hong Kong Polytechnic University), startup funding within business groups (Jonathan Marks and Aleia Bucci from University of Pretoria), and incubators and accelerators (Tiago Ratinho from IESEG School of Management).

In Chapter 5, Franklin Allen, Meijun Qian, and Jing Xie map out the terrain of informal entrepreneurial financing, showing how this form is a complement (rather than a substitute) for formal entrepreneurial financing. Then Jonathan Marks and Aleia Bucci show us what we know about how business groups in emerging markets create internal capital markets to fund startup ventures. The role of incubators and accelerators in startup financing is elaborated by Tiago Ratinho in Chapter 8, identifying an important gap in our knowledge about the financial aspects of these actors.

Next we consider THE WIDER WORLD (Part III), which are all of the external financing instruments that the field has studied predominantly over the past few decades. These instruments include formal debt (Steven Si and Jet Mboga from Bloomsburg University of Pennsylvania and Wan Liu and Yushan Yan from Zhejiang University), microfinance (Jonathan Kimmitt from Newcastle University), venture capital (Darek Klonowski and Silas Lee from Brandon University), corporate venture capital (Paul Asel from NGP Capital), angel financing (Sofia Avdeitchkova from Oxford Research and Hans Landström from Lund University), government financing (Judit Karsai from the Hungarian Institute of Economics), and family offices (Antonia Schickinger from Bain & Co., Nadine Kammerlander from the WHU – Otto Beisheim School of Management, and Alexandra Bertschi-Michel from the University of Bern). We also briefly consider other instruments in this space – crowdfunding and initial coin offerings – in the Handbook's conclusion.

Chapter 8 by Steven Si, Wan Liu, Yushan Yan, and Jet Mboga complements Chapter 5, noting that formal debt is a double-edged sword with both risks and benefits for startups. Jonathan Kimmitt shows in Chapter 9 how the study of microfinance can provide new insights into entrepreneurial behavior, pointing out future research directions at the micro-, meso-, and macro levels. The important role of venture capital in entrepreneurial finance is developed in Chapter 10 by Darek Klonowski and Silas Lee, who identify several promising directions for future research. Paul Asel, a leading corporate venture capitalist, maps out the intellectual landscape of corporate venture capital in Chapter 11, pointing out how the benefits of this significant phenomenon remain hotly contested. Chapter 12 by Sofia Avdeitchikova and Hans Landström addresses another major source of external startup funding, business angels, calling attention to the changing role of these actors in the new financial landscape. Judit Karsai takes on government financing of startups in Chapter 13, correcting the misperception that this funding source is unimportant in the entrepreneurial financing world. Family offices as a source of startup finance is discussed by Antonia Schickinger, Alexandra Bertschi-Michel, and Nadine Kammerlander in Chapter 14, where the conditions under which these actors are appropriate as entrepreneurial financing sources are elaborated.

Having looked at these three levels of funding, the final section of the Handbook considers EMERGING PERSPECTIVES (Part IV). This is a somewhat edgier and more divergent section than the others, and its contributors have taken license to explore how the field might be shaped by perspectives that have been relatively neglected to date. These perspectives include non-Western worldviews (Minh-Hoang Nguyen and Quan-Hoang Vuoung from Phenikaa University), gender (Janine Swail from University of Auckland), indigenous entrepreneurship (Ana Maria Peredo from University of Ottawa, Bettina Schneider from First Nations University, and Audrey Maria Popa from University of Victoria), disaster and conflict zones (Rebecca Namatovu from Copenhagen Business School), and ethics (Yves Fassin from University of Ghent University).

Minh-Hoang Nguyen and Quan-Hoang Vuong take on a scoping review of entrepreneurial financing studies set in developing countries in Chapter 15, calling attention to the ideological homogeneity in the field of entrepreneurial finance. Chapter 16 by Janine Swail begins to redress the imbalance in the literature around gender. Rebalance is also the topic of Chapter 17 on indigenous entrepreneurial finance by Ana Maria Peredo, Bettina Schneider and Audrey Maria Popa, who use Canadian data to explore how the broader field might benefit from this perspective and practice. Chapter 18 by Rebecca Namatovu looks at the difficult-to-research activity of entrepreneurial financing in post-conflict and disaster zones, asking how the broader field can benefit from the extreme uncertainty faced by actors in these settings. Ethics and its underappreciated role in entrepreneurial finance is elaborated by Yves Fassin in Chapter 19.

At its best, entrepreneurial finance provides a bridge from a past in which capital has been accumulated to a future that is more productive and liveable. At its worst, entrepreneurial finance focuses exclusively on short-term returns on invested capital to a small group of already-wealthy investors, and makes the future more nasty and unequal. Our expanding knowledge of this important economic and social phenomenon can help us to avoid dystopian futures like the one faced by Mu Tha at the beginning of this introduction.

Can entrepreneurial finance help bring all of us a better future? The readers of this Handbook may help to answer that question in the affirmative. On behalf of the contributors, I wish each of you fair winds on your intellectual journey.

References

Ahlers, G.K.C., Cumming, D., Günther, C. & Schweizer, D. (2015). Signaling in equity crowdfunding. *Entrepreneurship Theory & Practice*, *39*(4), 955–80.

Aldrich, H.E. (2012). The emergence of entrepreneurship as an academic field: A personal essay on institutional entrepreneurship. *Research Policy*, *41*(7), 1240–48.

Arrow, K. (1995). *Interview with Kenneth Arrow, Federal Reserve Bank of Minneapolis*. https://www.minneapolisfed.org/article/1995/interview-with-kenneth-arrow.

Bellatvitis, C., Filatotchev, I., Kamuriwo, D.S. & Vanacker, T. (2017). Entrepreneurial finance: New frontiers of research and practice. *Venture Capital: An International Journal of Entrepreneurial Finance*, *19*(1/2), 1–16.

Belleflamme, P., Lambert, T. & Schwienbacher, A. (2014). Crowdfunding: Tapping the right crowd. *Journal of Business Venturing*, *29*(5), 585–609.

Bird, B., Welsch, H., Astrachan, J.H. & Pistrui, D. (2002). Family business research: The evolution of an academic field. *Family Business Review*, *15*(4), 337–50.

Brown, E. & Farrell, M. (2021). *The cult of we: WeWork, Adam Neumann, and the great startup delusion*. Crown.

Bygrave, W.D. & Timmons, J.A. (1992). *Venture capital at the crossroads*. HBS Press.

Carreyrou, J. (2018). *Bad blood: Secrets and lies in a Silicon Valley startup*. Vintage.

Cochrane, J.H. (2005). The risk and return of venture capital. *Journal of Financial Economics*, *75*(1), 3–52.

Drover, W., Busentiz, L., Matusik, S., Townsend, D., Anglin, A. & Dushnitsky, G. (2017). A review and road map of entrepreneurial equity financing research: Venture capital, corporate venture capital, angel investment, crowdfunding, and accelerators. *Journal of Management*, *43*(6), 1820–53.

The Economist. (2021). The bright new age of venture capital. *The Economist*, November 27.

Gompers, P.A. (1996). Grandstanding in the venture capital industry. *Journal of Financial Economics*, *42*(1), 133–56.

Gompers, P. & Lerner, J. (2001). The venture capital revolution. *Journal of Economic Perspectives*, *15*(2), 145–68.

Kaplan, S.N. & Stromberg, P. (2003). Financial contracting theory meets the real world: An empirical analysis of venture capital contracts. *The Review of Economic Studies*, *70*(2), 281–315.

Kortum, S. & Lerner, J. (2001). Does venture capital spur innovation? In Libecap, G.D. (Ed.), *Entrepreneurial inputs and outcomes: New studies of entrepreneurship in the United States (Advances in the study of entrepreneurship, innovation and economic growth, vol. 13)*, 1–44. Emerald.

Lam, L. & Seidel, M. (2020). Hypergrowth exit mentality: Destroying societal wellbeing through venture capital biased social construction of value. *Journal of Management Inquiry*, *29*(4), 471–74.

Lerner, J. (1994). The syndication of venture capital investments. *Financial Management*, *23*(3), 16–27.

Lerner, J. and Nanda, R. (2020). Venture capital's role in financing innovation: What we know and how much we still need to learn. *Journal of Economic Perspectives*, *34*(3), 237–61.

Mallaby, S. (2022, January 27). Behind the 'power law': How a forgotten venture capitalist kick-started Silicon Valley. *The Washington Post*, Opinions section.

Mollick, E.R. (2014). The dynamics of crowdfunding: An exploratory study. *Journal of Business Venturing*, *29*(1), 1–16.

Nicholas, T. (2019). *VC: An American history*. Harvard University Press.

Plaschka, G.R. & Welsch, H.P. (1990). Emerging structures in entrepreneurship education: Curricular designs and strategies. *Entrepreneurship Theory and Practice*, *14*(3), 55–71.

Robinson, K.S. (2020). *The ministry for the future*. Orbit.

Sahlman, W.A. (1990). The structure and governance of venture-capital organizations. *Journal of Financial Economics*, *27*(2), 473–521.

Sarasvathy, S.D. (2001). Causation and effectuation: Toward a theoretical shift from economic inevitability to entrepreneurial contingency. *Academy of Management Review*, *26*(2), 243–63.

Zuboff, S. (2019). *The age of surveillance capitalism: The fight for a human future at the new frontier of power*. PublicAffairs.

Part I: **The individual level**

The contributions in Part I consider the most under-researched part of the field: the individual level. Most startups around the world and over time are financed primarily from their founders' resources. What those resources may be and how they are gathered are the subject of this part's four chapters.

In Chapter 1 Jan Warhuus takes on the role of founders' financial resources in the startup process. He finds that our knowledge about this important topic is constrained somewhat by the theoretical frameworks from corporate finance and data collection challenges in part imposed by editors and reviewers.

In Chapter 2 Matthew Rutherford, Duygu Phillips, and Jorge Arteaga-Fonseca examine two leading theoretical perspectives of relevance to the individual level of entrepreneurial finance: bricolage and bootstrapping. They suggest that the nexus of these perspectives may be a useful focus for future research.

Chapter 3 by Sussie Morrish looks at another individual level theoretical perspective – effectuation – and considers how it may influence a startup's financing decisions.

Finally, in Chapter 4 Antonio Malfense Fierro and Peter Rosa discuss how entrepreneurs construct portfolios of businesses to manage risk.

Taken together, these four chapters help to rebalance the entrepreneurial finance field.

https://doi.org/10.1515/9783110726312-002

Jan P. Warhuus

1 The role of founders' tangible resources in founding new ventures

Abstract: This chapter explores our knowledge and lack thereof about the role of founders' resources in new venture emergence. We focus on early-stages entrepreneurship because it is here that the founders' resources play the most important role as the venture typically does not yet have assets of interest to investors. We know that is the situation for most founders and because of the raw number of founders, their resource commitment is likely to be sizable and thus important. However, we know little about the actual size or the role these resources play in the process or in acquiring outside resources and financing. This lack of knowledge is in part because early-stage new ventures do not lend themselves well to corporate finance frameworks and partly because the micro-foundational actions of interest are hard to investigate based on the positivist stance that the field of finance and its reviewers and editors typically favor.

Keywords: founders' resources, insider financing, early-stage entrepreneurship, micro-foundational actions, context

Introduction

Driving over the San Francisco Bay Bridge towards Oakland on her way home from work at a leading medical trials center, Chanel, age 33, had tears in her eyes – tears of anger, frustration, and disappointment. That same afternoon she had cheerfully gone to her boss' office with an idea for a medical trial that could potentially lead to a cure of one of the cancers they were working on combatting; only to be lectured on that "we are part of the pharmaceutical industry" and, as such, "not really interested in cures." Rather, her boss wanted to focus on treatments that required the purchase of drugs. Three years earlier, Chanel had been diagnosed with Crohn's disease. In the period since, she had experienced the limitations of pharmaceuticals and the benefits of supplementary alternatives. Combining traditional treatments with detoxing body and mind through yoga, meditation, dieting, breath work, and

Acknowledgements: Many thanks to editor David C. Lingelbach and to my colleagues and dear friends Casey J. Frid, Claus Thrane, and William B. Gartner for great conversations, insightful comments, and moral support in drafting this manuscript. Without their valuable contributions during different parts of the process, this chapter would not have been what you have in front of you today.

Jan P. Warhuus, Department of Management and Entrepreneurship, St. Mary's College of California

https://doi.org/10.1515/9783110726312-003

other tools had been her only narrow path to remission. In the process, not only had she earned an MBA and become a certified yoga teacher and wellness coach; she had also been telling her story to her family, friends, and her broad and active network within the volunteering community in Oakland and helping those of them interested in healing alternatives. She knew, firsthand, that aiming for the singular approach of providing pharmaceuticals to people was rarely the right solution to complex illness and trauma.

Over dinner that night at their house in the Laural district of Oakland, Chanel shared her frustration with her boyfriend and their two friends and roommates. After a while, her two roommates, Kimi and Jacob, looked at each other, smiled and Jacob said "do you want to, or shall I?" to Kimi. Kimi replied "Let me give it a go" and turned to Chanel: "This is not the first time. You clearly do not see yourself in that line of work forever. Why don't you take the yoga and wellness clients that you already have on the side and team up with Jill and Char? They need a place for their breathwork and meditation clients as well. You could get a studio together. There is nothing affordable like that in Oakland for the 99%. I saw this great place today down on 33rd Avenue next to my chiropractor, it's for rent. You can totally do it!" Now it was Chanel's turn to smile. She could see that she had subconsciously been begging her friends to tell her just that for quite some time.

"If you are in, I'm signing the lease!" she texted Jill and Char after the three of them had toured the space on 33rd Ave. and met a very enthusiastic chiropractor earlier the same Saturday morning. She instantly got more happy emojis back from both than anyone would ever need. After three low-key years focused on recovery and school, combined with a very well-paid job, she had about $40k in the bank, and Chanel was thinking that with the space already booked by the three of them about 30–40%, the risk was limited to the remaining capacity, and she could always cover part of that with her savings. She figured that she would need about $5k for equipment and materials – they could paint it themselves, but the space needed some TLC to work out right – and probably the same for a website with a reservation system. Even if it would take a bit of time for business to pick up and more practitioners to join them, with her current living situation and existing clients, she would be able to make the one-year lease payments, cover the startup costs, and live within the means of her savings. "What better way to spend the money?" she thought. "If it doesn't work out, I can always go back and get a six-figure pharma-job" she said out loud to herself as she took a deep breath and opened the DocuSign lease agreement.

Today, four years later, 33&Rising is a striving wellness center for the 99% with about 20 participating practitioners, a large and growing loyal following and a business model that has allowed the venture to establish itself and to grow without external financing.

The subject of this chapter is important because practically all entrepreneurs are likely to use their own personal financial and other tangible resources in the attempt to start their new venture (Gartner et al., 2012). In addition to the immediate effect of injecting funds and other resources into the startup, the ability and willingness of founders to commit resources to their startups has been shown to affect new ventures' trajectories in a number of other short- and long-term ways, including survival, growth, and the ability to get buy-in from stakeholders such as potential team members and outside financiers (Ang, 1991; Bhidé, 2000; Frid et al., 2015; Hechavarría et al., 2016).

This chapter will focus on the early stages of new venture emergence, because it is during these stages that other sources are not typically readily available and thus it is here that founder resources play the most important role (Winborg & Landström, 2001). As the firm establishes itself and grows, informal and formal sources of external financing become more readily available and both the founder's ability to match the needs of the firm and the importance of their own resources are reduced. It is important to specify the situation and context of early-stage founders because both are remarkably different from that of established businesses (Ang, 1991; Bellavitis et al., 2017; Waleczek et al., 2018; Weigand, 2016). There are many ways to define the emergence of a new venture and little practical or theoretical agreement on how best to define such events (Reynolds, 2017). In this chapter, I borrow from the U.S. Panel Study of Entrepreneurial Dynamics II (PSEDII) in defining when someone becomes an entrepreneur. Through this lens, a person is an entrepreneur if they: 1) consider themselves to be creating a new business, 2) have been active in firm creation over the past 12 months, and 3) are expected to own at least part of the new firm (Reynolds & Curtin, 2008, 2011). In the same manner, I am inspired by the Global Entrepreneurship Monitor (GEM) in defining the difference between an entrepreneur and an established business owner-manager as three and a half years after the startup becomes operational by paying wages to owners for at least six out of the last 12 months and breaking even for at least three months in a row (GEM, 2021; Kelley et al., 2016; Reynolds & Curtin, 2008). We acknowledge that the founder of the firm remains the founder forever, a founder-manager remains the founder-manger until they step down, and many ventures remain entrepreneurial and transformative past the startup phase. However, in this chapter, we will mainly focus on research on the nature and effects of founders' resource commitments during the nascent (pre-operational) and startup phases (first three and a half years after becoming operational). Finally, we differentiate founder's resources from other resources by simply considering whether the resources are controlled and owned by founder(s) prior to committing them to the startup. All other resources are considered external – below I will discuss this definition further and we will see why this is not quite as simple as it may seem.

This chapter proceeds as follows. In the first section of the literature review, we discuss the challenges in defining founder(s) resources and the importance of these resources to the economic vitality of entrepreneurship. We then discuss how the nascent-and-startup phase is unique in comparison with later stages of venturing and the corporate financial frameworks we typically use to describe and understand established companies' finances. I proceed by accounting for the typical need for founder resources and how it may impact the nascent-and-startup phase; followed by an account of what we know about the impact of founders' resource commitments on firm survival, success, and growth. Based on the literature review, we then discuss research gaps and future research directions and conclude by highlighting the most important elements of the chapter.

Literature review

Challenges in defining insider financing and the importance of founder resources: What do we know?

By the definitions outlined in the introduction, all founders commit resources towards the startup; at a minimum with intangible assets such as providing access to their network, volunteering time, and in a social and intellectual capacity. In this chapter, we will mainly focus on resources in the form of cash (including money from founding team members and/or their ability to go without pay) and other tangible assets, such as office space, production and storage facilities, materials, and vehicles. While these delimitations may sound straight forward, there are at least three grey areas of overlap with other chapters in this book: First, in the use of the entrepreneurs' private assets as collateral for external debt financing; with the definition of bootstrapping and how entrepreneurs use it; and, third, the use of bricolage and social cooptation.

The use of private assets as collateral is complicated because making an investment and acquiring financing are not separated in the early startup phases. For example, an entrepreneur with a net worth of $250k may be willing to invest $50k in their startup, but $225k of their net worth is tied up in a house, two cars, and a recreational vehicle (RV) and only $25k is currently available as "cash" in a savings account. If the entrepreneur sells the RV to free up an additional $25k and invests it along with the savings in the startup, that is clearly internally sourced financing. If the entrepreneur uses a personal credit card to come up with the additional $25k, then we enter a grey area. Since the charge only amounts to 10% of the entrepreneur's net worth, no external party is involved in the decision making, and the funds could have been sourced in other ways, many scholars would consider the use of a credit card internal funds; but the funds do flow to the emerging business from the private banking arm of a financial institution. A third equally grey option would be for the entrepreneur to take out a $25k second mortgage on their house, and most scholars and practitioners would probably classify this option the same way they would classify the credit card option. A fourth option may be to reach out to a relative for a loan – which does not involve any "outsiders," but resources not controlled by the entrepreneur. Finally, the entrepreneur may approach the commercial arm of a financial institution with a request for a $25k business loan for the startup and since the bank is actively deciding to fund the startup, this is clearly a case of external debt financing. However, that clarity erodes quickly (because of the lack of separation of investment and financing) if, for example, the entrepreneur personally co-signs for the business loan, or their house or vehicle is used as collateral, which is quite common (Frid et al., 2016). In all these cases the entrepreneur is personally liable, and from their perspective, it would make sense that they simply regard these scenarios as strategic alternatives to selling the RV – a resource fully owned and controlled by the entrepreneur beforehand.

We can leverage the discussion and scenarios in the previous paragraph to discuss founder resources vis-à-vis bootstrapping. According to Winborg and Landström (2001, p. 235–236), bootstrapping consists of "methods for meeting the need for resources without relying on long-term external finance from debt holders and/ or new owners". By this definition, founder resource commitment is one type of bootstrapping, and the authors find empirical support for this as one of five distinct types of bootstrapping. Leaning on the implicit delimitation that bootstrapping is not giving up ownership or putting debt positions on the books of the new venture, Harrison et al. (2004, p. 307) define bootstrapping "as access to resources not owned or controlled by the entrepreneur" and Block et al. (2021, Abstract) talk about "measures that entrepreneurial ventures undertake to preserve liquidity." By these two definitions, the use of founders' resources is not bootstrapping. Winborg and Landström (2001) is one of the most cited papers on bootstrapping and thus their definition has been brought forward by other researchers. However, upon closer examination, many would probably question the inclusion of founders' resources in bootstrapping. Bhide (1992, p. 110) talks about bootstrapping as "having the wits and hustle to do without" external funding. Lahm and Little (2005, p. 61) describe bootstrapping as "the transformation of human capital into financial capital" through a "highly creative process" and Waleczek et al. (2018, p. 535; my emphasis) see bootstrapping research as concerned with how entrepreneurs "acquire *new* resources creatively at minimal costs." Committing existing resources already under the control of the entrepreneur is hardly hustling, transformational, creative, or new. The situation gets even more complicated when we dig further into the Winborg and Landström definition and find that, in their definition of founder resources, they include resources from "relatives"; that is, resources actually not owned and controlled by the entrepreneur.

On another interesting dimension, Harrison et al. (2004, p. 308) divide bootstrapping into two types of "creative ways of acquiring finance" and "minimising or eliminating the need for finance by securing resources at little or no cost." With both types we see that the entrepreneur's intellectual and social capital are in play to be creative and to make the cost of resources go away. However, it is especially the latter type that does not involve traditional financing that is of interest in this chapter. There are at least two ways to make the need for, or cost of, resources go away, namely: a) making do with and repurposing what you've already got, and b) gaining access (not ownership!) (as emphasized by Stevenson & Gumpert (1985)) to resources when they are needed. Making do with and repurposing what you got has been termed "bricolage." Bricolage, conceptualized in the 1960s to aid in understanding certain human behaviors, made its way into the management literature in the 1990s, and was succinctly and firmly adopted by the field of entrepreneurship by Baker and Nelson (2005). Bricolage can be defined as the act of "making do by applying combinations of the resources at hand to new problems and opportunities" (Baker and Nelson, 2005, p. 333). Five types of bricolage can be observed in the entrepreneurial process, including seeing artifacts as resources where others overlook or undervalue them (Baker & Nelson, 2005; Clough et al., 2019). Here, many acts of upcycling serve as illustrative examples (Wegener, 2016). This type of bricolage overlaps with social recourse cooptation – an unappreciated concept with strong explanatory power, first presented in a seminal paper by Starr and MacMillan back in 1990, in which entrepreneurs use social contracting and social assets (such as friendships, trust, and reciprocity) that exist *independently* of the venture (Rawhouser et al., 2017) in coopting underutilized resources.

The importance of founder resources is hard to overstate because founders make many of these resource investments very early on in the entrepreneurial process under true "Knightian uncertainty" (Knight, 1921; Sarasvathy, 2008) before the venture represents value to formal or informal investors (Bhidé, 1992). We can use data from Aldrich and Ruef (2018) to illustrate the power of these normal and everyday investments in new venture emergence. The 12,100,000 people who were involved *as owners* in 2005 in 7,000,000 startup attempts resulted in approximately 500,000 new ventures that started hiring within a year, they *all* made investments under uncertain, unpredictable circumstances to make these hires happen. All this against a backdrop where there is no actual market for entrepreneurs (Klein, 2008; Sarasvathy, 2004) and yet young firms (zero to five years) contribute nearly all net new job creation in the U.S. economy (Kauffman Foundation, 2015). An appreciation for the commitment of those founder resources cannot be overemphasized.

Corporate finance and early-stage entrepreneurial finance

Entrepreneurial finance is different from corporate finance on several dimensions, including risk profiles, expectations and information asymmetries (including entrepreneurs not knowing what financial options may be available to them (Seghers et al., 2012)), and the way adverse selection plays out. Pecking order theory (Myers, 1984) serves as an excellent example of how early-stage entrepreneurs escape the "logic" of corporate finance. Pecking order theory suggests that firms first use internal financing, then external financing with debt followed by equity (Barclay & Smith, 2020; Myers, 1984). Based on information asymmetry, tax codes, and transaction costs this selection order makes theoretical, practical, and intuitive sense. However, some studies question whether it applies to entrepreneurs (Blaseg et al., 2021). Some find that the pecking order theory may be altered or extended by at least the entrepreneur's industry, age, and experience (Minola & Cassia, 2013) and wealth (Barclay & Smith, 2020; Frid, 2014). Other studies have found the pecking order theory to apply at least to operational SMEs (Sogorb-Mira, 2005). We recently found that the theory may not apply to wealthy founders of early-stage nascent startups (Warhuus et al., 2021); in that entrepreneurs with wealth actually tend to ask for and acquire external financing earlier in the process than entrepreneurs with less wealth, who otherwise, everything-else-equal should have a greater needs. Finally, the advent of crowdfunding and private and public incubator resources (see chapter 7) over the past couple of decades further blur the pecking order for early-stage ventures.

Aside from pecking order theory there are several other ways in which early-stage entrepreneurs escape the logic of corporate finance and these are mainly related to friction stemming from the nature of early-stage startups. Where, for example, high levels of uncertainty makes it impossible to calculate rates of return and compare investment across different investment targets, especially combined with high portions of human/intangible assets and with historically extremely skewed returns on investments. These topics are covered in other chapters in this book. However, one topic regarding founder's resources and very early-stage entrepreneurial finance that is especially at odds with corporate finance theory, and thus of particular importance to this chapter, is the lack of separation of investment and financing discussed in the *RV* example above about how to free up $25k of net worth to invest in a startup. Based on the Fisher-Separation Theorem (Fisher, 1930) and Modigliani-Miller's Theorem (Modigliani & Miller, 1958, 1963), modern financial paradigms are based on a separation between investment and finance decisions, which does not exist in early-stage entrepreneurial financing (Weigand, 2016). The separation does not exist, because the entrepreneur cannot bring about the new venture instantaneously (Gartner, 1985) and thus the separation of the person from the new organization is a slow process (Dimov, 2020). Therefore, applying a corporate finance framework to early-stage startups ignores this issue, which in turn has consequences for how we interpret the data we generate in our research. This should also have ramifications for future research, which I discuss in the Future Research section below.

Financing requirements during nascent and startup phases and the prevalence of founder financing

In popular media and in the classroom, we often meet the belief that entrepreneurs marshal resources as one of their first acts – only a fool would venture out on a project that one does not have the means to see through, right? However, the literature does not support this. In a recent study of a representative sample of 1,214 nascent (pre-operational) entrepreneurs, only 12 had external financing ready from day one and 72% did not even attempt to attract external financing during their nascent phase – a level supported by other studies (Miao et al., 2017). The 20% who asked for external financing and obtained it were, on average, about two-thirds of the way through their journey as nascent entrepreneurs (in terms of number of actions tracked and time spent in the pre-operational nascent phase) before seeking and obtaining external funding (Warhuus et al., 2021). Even exceptionally successful ventures often start with founder's resources. In a study interviewing 100 of the *Inc* 500 entrepreneurs, Bhidé (2000) found that the majority of initial funding for these companies came from the founder's personal savings and only 6% originated from venture capital and angel investors, combined. Further, Welter et al. (2017) examined the Inc. 5,000 from 2010 to 2013 and found that most of these highly successful firms did not even operate in industries associated with venture capital.

Capital intensity of industries varies greatly and is linked to lead-time. For example, you can start a consulting/service sector business "tomorrow" with very little capital investment and practically no lead time between resource commitment and billing of customers. In contrast, a startup in agriculture requires much larger initial investments in land and equipment and, for multi-year crops, significant lead time between resource commitment and billing of customers (for example, asparagus has a three-year time to yield, while almond trees need seven years). For these reasons, average numbers can be deceiving. However, Seghers *et al.* (2012, p. 69) reported that in their Belgium-based sample "[a]lmost half of the ventures (44.7 percent) were founded with less than €20,000 start-up capital" and, in the U.S. in 2018, 53% of the Inc. 5,000 companies were founded with less than $20,000 (Inc. Magazine, 2018). This certainly illustrates that starting even highflying ventures, in certain industries, is feasible within the personal savings of a successful employee, especially someone working in a high-paying industry, like Chanel in the opening case. The reality that many ventures can get off the ground with less than $20,000 in initial capital has held surprisingly stable over the last 20 years is interesting. One plausible explanation for why this number has withstood inflation over time may be that starting a business has become significantly less resource intensive in general. Many components do not any longer require hiring a professional or the purchase of expensive equipment. Rather, taxes, human resources, customer relationship management, and accounting systems, and Internet presence, can be purchased on a pay-as-you-go basis as cloud-based offerings. Another plausible contributing factor may be that the nature of the companies entrepreneurs start has changed and that entrepreneurs start more resource-light companies in information and services industries today than they did 20+ years ago. As one illustration, Zacharakis *et al.* (2017) draw on GEM reports to suggested that the *average* amount required to start a business in the US is $63,000, while Zacharakis *et al.* (2020), still using GEM data, suggest that the *median* is now $18,000. Aside from the industry and lead-time issues, an often overlooked point in discussions about the need for resources to launch a business is the fact that you rarely need the same amount of resources to *try* to launch a venture as you do to actually launch an operational business. In another study, based on the same national (U.S.) representative sample of 1,214 nascent (pre-operational, still trying) entrepreneurs as mentioned above, Gartner et al. (2012) found that these *nascent* entrepreneurs invested a median of $5,500 in their start-up *attempts*.

Effects from founders' resource commitments

There are reasons to believe that the paths to become operational, grow, and achieve success are so plentiful that no single action is required to achieve these objectives (Arenius et al., 2017). However, as we have seen, there are also reasons to believe that the entrepreneur's willingness to commit resources toward their ventures ranks very high on the list of actions taken by early-stage founders. As Bird and Schjoedt (2009) remind us, thoughts, passion, motivation, and intelligence will not create entrepreneurial value without action. These actions have to come from the entrepreneur, or nothing is founded, and these actions require allocation of resources, initially from the entrepreneurs' themselves in by far the most cases, and certainly in everyday, low-budget launch attempts of the 99% (Welter et al., 2017). We will now briefly discuss what effect such commitments can have on the emergence of the new venture.

Of great relevance to this chapter and this book is that founder resource commitments impact their ability to attract and acquire further external resources. As mentioned above, entrepreneurs who do acquire external funding first invest in taking about two-thirds of the tracked actions and spend about two-thirds of their time in the nascent phase before acquiring outside resources. There is also some support for a "mini" or "embedded" pecking order, where nascent entrepreneurs tend to initiate resource-light actions before funding and resource-heavy actions after funding (Warhuus et al., 2021). However, there are notable exceptions to this order. We suggest that this may be because the willingness of entrepreneurs with high levels of wealth to commit their own resources increases over time, especially when they regard an external funding event more as a *when* than an *if*. This all indicates that the entrepreneur must commit quite some time and resources to take these actions and, through them, gain the level of legitimacy needed to attract external funding.

In this situation, one question immediately comes to mind: What about entrepreneurs with low wealth? Frid *et al.* (2016, p. 531) found that "low-wealth business founders . . . are less likely to get external funds, and they receive lower amounts when they do," which means that entrepreneurs with low wealth are more likely to experience resource constraints during business formation and to have to rely on their existing resources. From a social constructionist vantage point, that situation means that what may look like an opportunity to an individual with wealth may not look at all like an opportunity for an individual with low wealth. Potential entrepreneurs with lower wealth may gravitate toward industries and types of business that are less capital intensive and/or where options for bricolage and social cooptation are more prevalent. There is a silver lining here that may counter this trend, as Frid *et al.* (2015) found that the amount the entrepreneur needs to invest to acquire external funding is not an absolute amount, but a matter of "skin-in-the-game" relative to individual annual income. Investing what amounts to 80% of one year's income, instead of 40%, significantly increases the chance of acquiring external financing, wealthy or not. This finding is important because the entrepreneur's relative resource commitment, rather than their wealth, can lead to commitment from other stakeholders, and these financial commitments have been shown to correlate with survival, performance, and growth (Frid et al., 2016; Gartner et al., 2012; Hechavarria et al., 2016; Reynolds, 2016).

Many studies have found, and many experts have argued, that resorting to internal funding can hinder the development of the emerging or young firm and thus impact performance and growth. Hustling and being creative to marshal enough resources internally can take time and attention away from product and market development efforts, stifling growth and threatening survival. We will not discuss or advance this intuitively obvious correlation but warn that one should not take this as a sign of any simple causation. We do not know if that is because capital injections strengthen the firm, or if it is because weaker start-ups do not self-identify as investment targets (Eckhardt et al., 2006), or if it is because financiers are able to pick winners. More important to this chapter and less frequently advanced in the literature is the opposite argument, that *not* resorting to internal funding can be a distraction and hinder the development of the emerging firm (Bhidé, 1992) as " . . . many entrepreneurs waste a lot of valuable time by prematurely seeking seed capital from business angels and even from formal venture capitalists – searches that come up empty-handed almost every time" (Bygrave, Hay, Ng, & Reynolds, 2003, p. 113). Timing is everything, they say, also in the entrepreneur's judgement about when to and when not to rely on internal resources to fund their startups.

Finally, if we use Gartner *et al.'s* (2012) finding (that entrepreneurs invested $5,500) in concert with the Aldrich and Ruef (2018) finding (that 12,100,000 people a year attempt to start a business), by simple multiplication we can start to get a sense of the combined effect of founders' mundane, everyday resource commitments:

12,100,000 times $5,500 equals roughly $66,5 billion – more than double the size of the yearly US angel investments.

Future research

From the early part of the Introduction of this chapter, I've raised the issue of definitions. Defining "founders," "resources," and "entrepreneurship" remain challenging and affect coherent knowledge development in many areas of entrepreneurship research, including finance. For example, whether we define entrepreneurship as risk taking, opportunity pursuit, or organizing impacts future research.

We then saw those definition issues spill over into understanding founders' resources vis-à-vis bootstrapping, where those resources do not fit the description of the concept of bootstrapping yet are included in some widely adopted definitions. So we can perhaps place funders' resources at the edge of bootstrapping (depending on how the resources are applied and what definition we use) but a more accurate description may be that it is in the grey area around something fuzzy; as Miao et al. (2017, p. 1) remind us "[h]owever, after nearly three decades since the seminal publication of Van Auken and Carter (1989) we know far too little about bootstrapping and its antecedents and outcomes. To make matters worse, the extant empirical literature is exceedingly confusing." Here is a clear call for a better understanding of founder's resources versus bootstrapping and, as I will argue further below, this research probably needs to be informed by what it feels like to the entrepreneur (Welter et al., 2016). For example, in the case of a loan from a relative discussed in the *RV* example above, some entrepreneurs may regard that loan founders' resources (if it comes from, for example, a parent or spouse) or as bootstrapping (if it originates from a more distant relative with a more transactional perspective on making the loan). From the *RV* example we have also seen that our knowledge about loans based on some sort of collateral/personal liability versus founder resources comes up short and calls for further research. Again, this research probably needs to be driven less by objective, one-reality definitions and more by subjective, multi-reality experiences by entrepreneurs and the resource holders, as I elaborate upon in the next paragraph.

Entrepreneurial finance research has very much fallen victim to the tendency of much scientific research to value what can be measured, rather than figuring out how to measure what we value. As Welter and colleagues (2017, p. 315) eloquently express it, "we systematically devalue entrepreneurship as a whole, by failing to see the pleasures and benefits of entrepreneurship unless they can be accounted for in wealth accumulation and job creation." Yet, within early-stage entrepreneurial finance, Sahlman (1994) argued for a broader scope and Bhide (2000, p. 39) noted that "most start-ups, however, don't have the assets that an objective investor would consider valuable." Despite that, to this day, the easier-to-observe-and-investigate (but also very rare and the exception-to-the-rule) venture capital events and angel network investments are receiving by far the most attention from researchers and editors alike (Aldrich & Ruef, 2018; Welter et al., 2017); and to such an extent where other normal and everyday sources of resources have quite consistently been labeled an "alternative" part of the new venture's resource environment (Churchill & Thorne, 1989; Cumming et al., 2019; Seghers et al., 2012; Wardrop et al., 2015). And yet "[t]his big-money model has little in common with the traditional low-budget start-up" (Bhidé, 1992, p. 109). So, I want to join the early 1980s and 1990s pioneers' in this field and the more recent 2017/2018 distinguished contributions' calls for future research to challenge the scope of the field and the labels we use (Welter et al., 2016) – in a world where everything but the exception (angel and VC financing) is labeled "alternative," it is hard for even the most critical and seasoned person to think straight.

This issue is further exacerbated by the fact that financial research typically comes from a positivist tradition. From this ontological and epistemological vantage point, because entrepreneurs have to venture out and "pursue opportunities without regard to the resources they currently control" (Stevenson, 1983, p. 23) they are consequently objectively resource constrained and there is an objective funding gap out there (see also Lam, 2010). Because these "facts" "objectively" exist in a positivist world, we need an outside force to help resolve the situation, and thus entrepreneurial finance has had a strong bias of focusing on the supply side and has regarded the demand side as static, objectively true, and given. This double whammy of strong bias toward the measurable and strong positivistic supply-side bias, means that today we know quite a bit about the extreme exceptions (for example, gazelles, VCs, and IPOs) but much less about the resource mobilization of everyday entrepreneurs who are driving the vitality of our economy and creating nearly all new jobs. This relentless bias in research input and output is so strong that it is easily observable in public policies and entrepreneurship education and textbooks (Aldrich & Ruef, 2018; Bhatia & Levina, 2020; Lahm & Little, 2005; Lam, 2010). So, as we broaden the scope, I call for a future focus on the demand side of the equation, including founder's resources. And for that to include a better understanding of founder's use of social cooptation strategies and addressing such questions as "What role do 'helpers' make in the emergence of a new venture?" and "When should 'helpers' contributions be considered or not be considered a founder resource?"

The double whammy of the past has consequences for current and future researchers (and their output) on the demand side of early-stage entrepreneurship finance, where founders' resource commitments are most important. There are probably many ripple effects of these biases, but I will limit this discussion to three main points concerning ontological stance, methodology, and research outlets. Baker and Nelson (2005) drew on Penrose (1959) to bring forward her point that inputs do not define outputs of a firm "because of differences in their ability to grasp possible uses and combinations of those inputs" (Baker and Nelson, 2005, p. 330) and conclude that an enactment approach (Gartner, 2008; Weick, 1979, 1993) based on a social constructionist stance serves us better in these types of investigations (Pittaway et al., 2018). Along this line of thought, Gartner and Baker (2010) revise Stevenson's definition of entrepreneurship to demonstrate how the definition of an opportunity is intertwined with resources owned and/or controlled by the entrepreneurs (because available resources have an effect on their assessment of the feasibility of the opportunity.) Finally, effectuation theory argues that the *means* of the entrepreneur and their sense of what their individual *affordable loss* might be, set limitations on what they imagine they can do, which in turn frames how they understand what is and what is not an opportunity (Sarasvathy, 2001). From this vantage point, not only is there a lack of separation of investment and finance, there is also a lack of separation of resources from opportunities. In other words, resources and opportunities shape each other, and, so, no objective finance gap can automatically exist. For us to really gain an understanding of these dynamics and map their micro-foundational patterns, combinations of Cartesian detachment and quantitative methodologies are not likely to be the most productive vectors of attack. As you may begin to see, we have a perfect storm on our hands: we are researching the "wrong" side of finance (supply rather than demand), based on the "wrong" ontological and epistemological stance (positivism rather than critical realism or social constructionism), with the "wrong" methodological approach (quantitative rather than qualitative or mixed methods), and accepting the relaxation of the "wrong" assumptions (ignoring lack of separation of investment vs. financing and resources vs. opportunities). I believe that the gatekeepers who decide what gets published and what does not can play an important role in driving future research in the right direction. Outlets for such research and editors willing to listen do exist, but I posit that this is a challenge for most individual researchers. To counter this, I believe we need more special issues that openly solicit contributions that ask the questions we care about (Sarasvathy, 2004) and accept explorations of these questions through other vectors of attack than a positivistic stance and quantitative methods (Welter & Gartner, 2016). Questions such as "How do founder resources shape opportunities?" "What is a resource commitment by a nascent entrepreneur?" "How do entrepreneurs convert their social and emotional assets to real assets?" need to be addressed head-on in meaningful ways.

I want to return to the notion of valuing what can be measured rather than figuring out how to measure what we value, because measuring what we value in entrepreneurial finance can indeed be very hard; so much so that it is not always a matter of falling victim to the biases discussed above but rather a very practical matter. Simply put, data is hard to gather, "because smaller and emerging firms are not required to share as much information as publicly traded companies, they are information opaque (Ang, 1991)"(Gartner et al., 2012, p. 746) and "[p]erhaps the most important characteristic defining small business finance is informational opacity." (Berger & Udell, 1998, p. 616). Even when asked, small and new ventures do not seem to want to have their financial stories told. For example, Nofsinger and Wang (2011) examined a mixed dataset of 8,277 nascent and early-stage (operating) entrepreneurs and found that only 23% reported funding data. And when it comes to asking entrepreneurs about the relationships forged to acquire funding, the response rates are even lower. For example, in an investigation of entrepreneur-banker relationships, Saparito and Coombs (2013) reported a 12% response rate, which is consistent with other studies of the entrepreneur-banker relationship (Lange et al., 1999). One can only expect even lower response rates for detached surveys about insider financial relationships with entrepreneurs themselves, life partners, friends, etc. This lack of information is evident even when we ask rather simple, objective, quantifiable questions. For example, the topic of capital structure in nascent and young ventures is not well understood in terms of level of insider/founder financing versus outside funding. Even for established, operational new businesses it can be hard to determine the level of external financing. Some authors suggest that operational entrepreneurs rely so heavily on bootstrapping that only about 25% use formal external financing (Miao et al., 2017), while others argue that new ventures are highly capitalized and that up to 75% may use some kind of debt finance (Bellavitis et al., 2017). So while the Saparito and Coombs (2013) paper may not be the exception to the rule (that lower response rates preclude you from high-end journals), I posit that these response rates may give some researchers pause, especially younger, pre-tenured professionals. Again, I call for editors and senior researchers to solicit and create more spaces for more in-depth investigations and for future researchers to answer these calls and develop the knowledge we need to consult, advocate, and educate about these important topics.

When we regard the choice of early-stage entrepreneurship as judgement under true uncertainty (Klein, 2008) and from a social constructionist vantage point, the context gets increasingly important in understanding the micro-foundational judgement and actions that entrepreneurs take (Welter, 2011; Welter et al., 2017). As Welter (2011, p. 165) notes "context is important for understanding when, how, and why entrepreneurship happens and who becomes involved" and this is especially true in the early stages of venturing. For this chapter it means, for example, that how entrepreneurs legally organize their venture and which options are available to them locally to separate (or not) the entrepreneur from the venture in different cultures and legal traditions around the world will challenge the generalizability of our findings (Rawhouser et al., 2017). The same is true for differences in tax codes, the general appreciation for entrepreneurs across communities and regions, variations in age (Ngo et al., 2021), gender differences (Neeley & Van auken, 2010; Tillmar et al., 2021), disparities in market conditions (Block et al., 2021), single- vs. multi-ethnic communities (Nguyen & Canh, 2020), and for financing options that may or may not be available to the entrepreneur – especially informal options, including options for the entrepreneur to leverage their own resources, act as bricoleurs, and leverage social cooptation strategies (Aktas et al., 2011; Lam, 2010; Nguyen & Canh, 2020). "Firms exist not only to economize on transaction costs, but also as a means for the exercise of entrepreneurial judgment, and as a low-cost mechanism for entrepreneurs to experiment with various combinations of heterogeneous capital goods" (Klein, 2008, p. 185). As one specific example of how context matters to the importance of founders' resources and future research, today service value added makes up 77% of GDP in wealthy North America, meaning that there are many opportunities for starting resource-light businesses in that region, while in less wealthy South Asia service value added makes up only 50% of the economy (World Bank, 2021). This clearly calls for regional studies with the richness to capture these contextual dimensions in understanding the role and impact of founders' resources (Ngo et al., 2021; Welter & Gartner, 2016).

I was recently reminded that "we need more in-depth studies of individuals starting out, and, observations of what resources they actually use – both tangible resources, and, also 'intangible' resources" (W.B. Gartner, personal communication, 2021). This sums up succinctly the overall message of this section of the chapter. And, interestingly, it also touches upon the discussion earlier in this section, in that it challenges the labels we use when Gartner puts *intangible* in quotation marks. When entrepreneurs constantly transform intangible resources into tangible resources (and vice versa!) these are not strong concepts in this field, and we should not adopt them from other fields of inquiry without reflection. We need future research that can help develop internally consistent language for what entrepreneurs do with their resources and how we research that.

Conclusion

In this chapter, we have explored the role of founders' tangible resources in starting up a new venture. We have focused on the nascent (pre-operational) and early-stage startup (first three and a half years as an operational business), because this is where funds and other tangible resources originating from the founders play by far the largest role.

The definition of the founder's tangible means (as resources that are owned and controlled by the entrepreneur) is clear and straight forward, however, only when the resources are readily available in the form of, for example, cash or bank deposits. Because of the lack of separation of investment and financing at the early stages of the emerging venture, the clarity erodes quickly if the founder's assets are less current, as the entrepreneur has many options for how to commit such resources to the new venture. In addition, the definition is challenged by how scholars defined bootstrapping and when intangible founder assets are used to provide for tangible assets or reduce the need for them through bricolage and social cooptation.

Despite these definitional challenges, the huge number of small commitments from founders during the early stages of new venture emergence are critical and impactful to entrepreneurial activity, jobs, and economic vitality.

The complexities in defining founder resources influence researching the phenomenon and how such research is regarded in the field of entrepreneurial finance. Despite early calls and recent support, acknowledging a lack of separation of investment and finance and a focus on the supply rather than the demand side is at odds with most research activity and publications in past decades. Positivistic-based research on the easy-to-observe, larger, much celebrated but very rare supply-side angel, VC and IPO events have had a much easier time getting through the gate guarded by journal editors than social-constructionist-based research of the mundane, everyday, smaller, incremental commitments made by a large contingent of founders embedded in the myriad of micro-foundational actions that make the emergence of new organizations happen. I presume these circumstances may give some researchers pause, and rightfully so.

In the opening case, we were reminded that in certain industries and with certain business models, external financing is not required to establish and grow a new venture. Even when external financing is required at some point, most businesses are started with initial capital of less than $20k – an amount within the reach of personal savings for many successful working professionals. This number has been surprisingly stable over at least the past couple of decades. This may be because entrepreneurs start more resource-light service businesses and due to the advent of cloud-based pay-as-you-go services, which has brought down the cost of starting a new business and especially the cost of trying – with most attempts accomplished for less than $6,000. The more the cost of attempting to start a new venture comes down, the more the importance of founder's finite resources goes up.

By definition, one must take actions toward establishing a viable venture to be a founder, and no amount of planning and passion on their own will bring about a new venture without action. These actions require resources and, in most cases, in the very early stages, the resources needed for these actions comes from the founders themselves. While founder resources are very important in and of themselves, they also impact the entrepreneur's ability to attract external resources to the venture. This gives entrepreneurs with high wealth an advantage over entrepreneurs with low wealth, as they have the ability to commit more resources. However, financiers do not only look at the nominal amount invested but also the commitment made relative to the wealth of the entrepreneur.

The challenging research environment for insightful knowledge development in early-stage entrepreneurship finance about founder resource commitments should give some researchers pause. But also, because of this situation, the major knowledge gap is primarily demand-side and micro-foundational. So, with the fair warning to fellow researcher and following other recent calls (e.g., Aldrich and Ruef, 2018; Clough *et al.*, 2019; Pittaway *et al.*, 2018; Welter *et al.*, 2017), I call for future research to take on this challenge and for editors, especially guest editors of special issues, to solicit and support those future efforts.

References

Aktas, N., Bellettre, I., & Cousin, J.-G. (2011). Capital Structure Decisions of French Very Small Businesses. *Finance*, *32*(1), 43–73. https://doi.org/10.3917/fina.321.0043

Aldrich, H. E., & Ruef, M. (2018). Unicorns, Gazelles, and Other Distractions on the Way to Understanding Real Entrepreneurship in the United States. *Academy of Management Perspectives*, *32*(4), 458–472. https://doi.org/10.5465/amp.2017.0123

Ang, J. S. (1991). Small Business Uniqueness and the Theory of Financial Management. *The Journal of Entrepreneurial Finance*, *1*(1), 1–13.

Arenius, P., Engel, Y., & Klyver, K. (2017). No particular action needed? A necessary condition analysis of gestation activities and firm emergence. *Journal of Business Venturing Insights*, *8*(June), 87–92. https://doi.org/10.1016/j.jbvi.2017.07.004

Baker, T., & Nelson, R. E. (2005). Creating Something from Nothing: Resource Construction through Entrepreneurial Bricolage. *Administrative Science Quarterly*, *50*(3), 329–366. https://doi.org/10.2189/asqu.2005.50.3.329

Barclay, M. J., & Smith, C. (2020). The Capital Structure Puzzle: Another Look at the Evidence. *Journal of Applied Corporate Finance*, *32*(1), 80–91. https://doi.org/10.1111/jacf.12390

Bellavitis, C., Filatotchev, I., Kamuriwo, D. S., & Vanacker, T. (2017). Entrepreneurial finance: new frontiers of research and practice. *Venture Capital*, *19*(1–2), 1–16. https://doi.org/10.1080/13691066.2016.1259733

Berger, A. N., & Udell, G. F. (1998). The economics of small business finance: The roles of private equity and debt markets in the financial growth cycle. *Journal of Banking & Finance*, *22*(6–8), 613–673. https://doi.org/10.1016/S0378-4266(98)00038-7

Bhatia, A., & Levina, N. (2020). The Diverse Rationalities of Entrepreneurship Education: Epistemic Stance Perspective. *Academy of Management Learning & Education*, *19*(3), 323–344. https://doi.org/10.5465/amle.2019.0201

Bhidé, A. (1992). Bootstrap Finance: The Art of Start-ups. *Harvard Business Review*, Vol. 70 No. 6, pp. 109–117.

Bhide, A.V., 2000. The Origin and Evolution of New Businesses. Oxford University Press, New York.

Bird, B. and Schjoedt, L. (2009), "Entrepreneurial Behavior: Its Nature, Scope, Recent Research, and Agenda for Future Research", in Carsrud, A. and Brännback, M. (Eds.), Understanding the Entrepreneurial Mind, Springer New York, New York, NY, pp. 327–358. DOI: 10.1007/978-1-4419-0443-0_15.

Blaseg, D., Cumming, D., & Koetter, M. (2021). Equity Crowdfunding: High-Quality or Low-Quality Entrepreneurs? *Entrepreneurship: Theory and Practice*, *45*(3), 505–530. https://doi.org/10.1177/1042258719899427

Block, J. H., Fisch, C., & Hirschmann, M. (2021). The determinants of bootstrap financing in crises: evidence from entrepreneurial ventures in the COVID-19 pandemic. *Small Business Economics*, *45*(3), 505–530. https://doi.org/10.1007/s11187-020-00445-6

Bygrave, W. D., Hay, M., Ng, E., & Reynolds, P. (2003). Executive forum: A study of informal investing in 29 nations composing the Global Entrepreneurship Monitor. *Venture Capital*, *5*(2), 101–116. https://doi.org/10.1080/1369106032000097021

Churchill, N. C., & Thorne, J. R. (1989). Alternative Financing for Entrepreneurial Ventures. *Entrepreneurship Theory and Practice, 13*(3), 7–9. https://doi.org/10.1177/104225878901300302

Clough, D. R., Fang, T. P., Vissa, B., & Wu, A. (2019). Turning Lead into Gold: How do Entrepreneurs Mobilize Resources to Exploit Opportunities? *Academy of Management Annals, 13*(1), 240–271. https://doi.org/10.5465/annals.2016.0132

Cumming, D., Deloof, M., Manigart, S., & Wright, M. (2019). New directions in entrepreneurial finance. *Journal of Banking and Finance, 100*, 252–260. https://doi.org/10.1016/j.jbankfin.2019.02.008

Dimov, D. (2020). Entrepreneurial process: mapping a multiplicity of conversations. In W. B. Gartner & B. T. Teague (Eds.), *Research Handbook on Entrepreneurial Behavior, Practice and Process* (pp. 56–80). Edward Elgar Publishing. https://doi.org/10.4337/9781788114523.00011

Eckhardt, J. T., Shane, S., & Delmar, F. (2006). Multistage Selection and the Financing of New Ventures. *Management Science, 52*(2), 220–232. https://doi.org/10.1287/mnsc.1050.0478

Fisher, I. (1930). *The Theory of Interests*. The Macmillan Co.

Frid, C. J. (2014). Acquiring financial resources to form new ventures: the impact of personal characteristics on organizational emergence. *Journal of Small Business & Entrepreneurship, 27*(3), 323–341. https://doi.org/10.1080/08276331.2015.1082895

Frid, C. J., Wyman, D. M., & Gartner, W. B. (2015). The influence of financial "skin in the game" on new venture creation. *Academy of Entrepreneurship Journal, 21*(2), 1–14.

Frid, C. J., Wyman, D. M., Gartner, W. B., & Hechavarria, D. H. (2016). Low-wealth entrepreneurs and access to external financing. *International Journal of Entrepreneurial Behavior & Research, 22*(4), 531–555. https://doi.org/10.1108/IJEBR-08-2015-0173

Gartner, W. B. (1985). A Conceptual Framework for Describing the Phenomenon of New Venture Creation. *Academy of Management Review, 10*(4), 696–706. https://doi.org/10.5465/amr.1985.4279094

Gartner, W. B. (2008). Variations in entrepreneurship. *Small Business Economics, 31*(4), 351–361. https://doi.org/10.1007/s11187-008-9139-5

Gartner, W. B., & Baker, T. (2010). A plausible history and exploration of Stevenson's definition of entrepreneurship. *Frontiers of Entrepreneurship Research, 30*(4), 142–156.

Gartner, W. B., Frid, C. J., & Alexander, J. C. (2012). Financing the emerging firm. *Small Business Economics, 39*(3), 745–761. https://doi.org/10.1007/s11187-011-9359-y

GEM. (2021). *How GEM defines entrepreneurship*. http://gem-consortium.ns-client.xyz/wiki/1149

Harrison, R. T., Mason, C. M., & Girling, P. (2004). Financial bootstrapping and venture development in the software industry. *Entrepreneurship and Regional Development, 16*(4), 307–333. https://doi.org/10.1080/0898562042000263276

Hechavarría, D. M., Matthews, C. H., & Reynolds, P. D. (2016). Does start-up financing influence start-up speed? Evidence from the panel study of entrepreneurial dynamics. *Small Business Economics, 46*(1), 137–167. https://doi.org/10.1007/s11187-015-9680-y

Inc. Magazine, A. (2018). *Inc. 5000 annual survey*. https://www.youtube.com/watch?v=BhdSk3-gkos

Kauffman Foundation. (2015). *The Importance of Young Firms for Economic Growth*.

Kelley, D., Singer, S., & Herrington, M. (2016). Global Entrepreneurship Monitor – 2015/2016 Global Report. In *Global Entrepreneurship Monitor*.

Klein, P. G. (2008). Opportunity discovery, entrepreneurial action, and economic organization. *Strategic Entrepreneurship Journal, 2*(3), 175–190. https://doi.org/10.1002/sej.50

Knight, F. H. (1921). *Risk, Uncertainty and Profit*. Houghton Mifflin.

Lahm, R. J., & Little, H. T. (2005). Bootstrapping business start-ups: entrepreneurship literature, textbooks, and teaching practices versus current business practices? *Journal of Entrepreneurship Education, 8*, 61–74.

Lam, W. (2010). Funding gap, what funding gap? Financial bootstrapping: Supply, demand and creation of entrepreneurial finance. *International Journal of Entrepreneurial Behaviour & Research, 16*(4), 268–295. https://doi.org/10.1108/13552551011054480

Lange, J. E., Warhuus, J. P., & Levie, J. (1999). Entrepreneur/banker interaction in young growing firms: A large scale international study. In P. D. Reynolds, W. D. Bygrave, S. Manigart, C. Mason, G. D. Meyer, H. J. Sapienza, & K. Shaver (Eds.), *Frontiers of Entrepreneurship Research 1999* (pp. 368–379). Babson College.

Miao, C., Rutherford, M. W., & Pollack, J. M. (2017). An exploratory meta-analysis of the nomological network of bootstrapping in SMEs. *Journal of Business Venturing Insights, 8*(April), 1–8. https://doi.org/10.1016/j.jbvi.2017.04.002

Minola, T., & Cassia, L. (2013). Financing patterns in new technology-based firms: An extension of the pecking order theory. *International Journal of Entrepreneurship and Small Business, 19*(2), 212–233. https://doi.org/10.1504/IJESB.2013.054964

Modigliani, F., & Miller, M. H. (1958). The Cost of Capital, Corporation Finance and the Theory of Investment. *The American Economic Review, 48*(3), 261–297. https://doi.org/www.jstor.org/stable/1809766

Modigliani, F., & Miller, M. H. (1963). Corporate Income Taxes and the Cost of Capital: A Correction. *American Economic Review, 53*(3), 433–443. https://doi.org/10.2307/1809167

Myers, S. C. (1984). The Capital Structure Puzzle. *The Journal of Finance, 39*(3), 574–592. https://doi.org/10.1111/j.1540-6261.1984.tb03646.x

Neeley, L., & Van auken, H. (2010). Differences Between Female And Male Entrepreneurs' Use Of Bootstrap Financing. *Journal of Developmental Entrepreneurship, 15*(1), 19–34. https://doi.org/10.1142/S1084946710001439

Ngo, V. D., Evansluong, Q., Janssen, F., & Nguyen, D. K. (2021). Social capital inequality and capital structure of new firms in a developing country: the role of bank ties. *International Journal of Entrepreneurial Behaviour and Research, 27*(7), 1649–1673. https://doi.org/10.1108/IJEBR-11-2020-0754

Nguyen, B., & Canh, N. P. (2020). Formal and informal financing decisions of small businesses. *Small Business Economics.* https://doi.org/10.1007/s11187-020-00361-9

Nofsinger, J. R., & Wang, W. (2011). Determinants of start-up firm external financing worldwide. *Journal of Banking and Finance, 35*(9), 2282–2294. https://doi.org/10.1016/j.jbankfin.2011.01.024

Penrose, E. (1959). *The Theory of the Growth of the Firm* (4th ed.). Basil Blackwell Ltd.

Pittaway, L., Aïssaoui, R., & Fox, J. (2018). Social Constructionism and Entrepreneurial Opportunity. In A. Fayolle, S. Ramoglou, M. Karatas-Ozkan, & K. Nicolopoulou (Eds.), *Philosophical Reflexivity and Entrepreneurship Research* (1st ed.). Routledge.

Rawhouser, H., Villanueva, J., & Newbert, S. L. (2017). Strategies and Tools for Entrepreneurial Resource Access: A Cross-disciplinary Review and Typology. *International Journal of Management Reviews, 19*(4), 473–491. https://doi.org/10.1111/ijmr.12105

Reynolds, P. D. (2016). Start-up Actions and Outcomes: What Entrepreneurs Do to Reach Profitability. *Foundations and Trends® in Entrepreneurship, 12*(6), 443–559. https://doi.org/10.1561/0300000071

Reynolds, P. D. (2017). When is a Firm Born? Alternative Criteria and Consequences. *Business Economics, 52*(1), 41–56. https://doi.org/10.1057/s11369-017-0022-8

Reynolds, P. D., & Curtin, R. T. (2008). Business Creation in the United States: Panel Study of Entrepreneurial Dynamics II Initial Assessment. *Foundations and Trends® in Entrepreneurship*, 4(3), 155–307. https://doi.org/10.1561/0300000022

Reynolds, P. D., & Curtin, R. T. (2011). *PSED I, II Harmonized Transitions, Outcomes Data Set*. University of Michigan.

Sahlman, W. A. (1994). "Don't Fix What Isn't Broken", in Beltz, C. A. (Ed.), *Financing Entrepreneurs*, The AEI Press, Washington, D.C., pp. 61–65.

Saparito, P. A., & Coombs, J. E. (2013). Bureaucratic Systems' Facilitating and Hindering Influence on Social Capital. *Entrepreneurship: Theory and Practice*, 37(3), 625–639. https://doi.org/10.1111/etap.12028

Sarasvathy, S. D. (2001). Causation and Effectuation: Toward A Theoretical Shift From Inevitability to Economic Entrepreneurial Contingency. *The Academy of Management Review*, 26(2), 243–263. https://doi.org/10.2307/259121

Sarasvathy, S. D. (2004). The questions we ask and the questions we care about: reformulating some problems in entrepreneurship research. *Journal of Business Venturing*, 19(5), 707–717. https://doi.org/10.1016/j.jbusvent.2003.09.006

Sarasvathy, S. D. (2008). Effectuation: Elements of Entrepreneurial Expertise. In *Effectuation: Elements of Entrepreneurial Expertise*. Edward Elgar Publishing. https://doi.org/10.4337/9781848440197

Seghers, A., Manigart, S., & Vanacker, T. (2012). The impact of human and social capital on entrepreneurs' knowledge of finance alternatives. *Journal of Small Business Management*, 50(1), 63–86. https://doi.org/10.1111/j.1540-627X.2011.00344.x

Sogorb-Mira, F. (2005). How SME uniqueness affects capital structure: Evidence from a 1994-1998 Spanish data panel. *Small Business Economics*, 25(5), 447–457. https://doi.org/10.1007/s11187-004-6486-8

Starr, J., & MacMillan, I. (1990). Resource cooptation via social contracting: resource acquisition strategies for new ventures. *Strategic Management Journal*, 11(Special issue), 79–92. https://doi.org/10.2307/2486671

Stevenson, H. H. (1983). A Perspective on Entrepreneurship. In *Harvard Business School Working Paper* (No. 9-384–131).

Stevenson, H. H., & Gumpert, D. E. (1985). The heart of entrepreneurship. *Harvard Business Review*, 63(2), 85–94.

Tillmar, M., Ahl, H., Berglund, K., & Pettersson, K. (2021). The gendered effects of entrepreneurialism in contrasting contexts. *Journal of Enterprising Communities: People and Places*, ahead-of-p(ahead-of-print), ahead-of-print. https://doi.org/10.1108/JEC-12-2020-0208

Van Auken, H., & Carter, R. (1989). Acquisition of Capital by Small Business. *Journal of Small Business Management*, 27(2), 1–9.

Waleczek, P., Zehren, T., & Flatten, T. C. (2018). Start-up financing: How founders finance their ventures' early stage. *Managerial and Decision Economics*, 39(5), 535–549. https://doi.org/10.1002/mde.2925

Wardrop, R., Zhang, B., Rau, R., & Gray, M. (2015). *The European Alternative Finance Benchmarking Report* (Issue February).

Warhuus, J. P., Frid, C. J., & Gartner, W. B. (2021). Ready or not? Nascent entrepreneurs' actions and the acquisition of external financing. *International Journal of Entrepreneurial Behaviour and Research*, 27(6), 1605–1628. https://doi.org/10.1108/IJEBR-09-2020-0586

Wegener, C. (2016). Upcycling. In V. P. Glăveanu, L. Tanggaard, & C. Wegener (Eds.), *Creativity: A New Vocabular* (1st ed., pp. 181–188). Palgrave Macmillan.

Weick, K. E. (1979). *The Social Psychology of Organizing* (2nd ed.). Addison-Wesley.

Weick, K. E. (1993). The Collapse of Sensemaking in Organizations: The Mann Gulch Disaster. *Administrative Science Quarterly*, 38(4), 628. https://doi.org/10.2307/2393339

Weigand, C. (2016). Theorizing about Financing Behavior of New Ventures: Towards an Effectual Logic. *ICSB World Conference Proceedings; Washington, DC, June 17–18*, 1–9.

Welter, F. (2011). Contextualizing Entrepreneurship-Conceptual Challenges and Ways Forward. *Entrepreneurship Theory and Practice*, *35*(1), 165–184. https://doi.org/10.1111/j.1540-6520.2010.00427.x

Welter, F., Baker, T., Audretsch, D. B., & Gartner, W. B. (2017). Everyday Entrepreneurship – A Call for Entrepreneurship Research to Embrace Entrepreneurial Diversity. *Entrepreneurship: Theory and Practice*, *41*(3), 311–321. https://doi.org/10.1111/etap.12258

Welter, F., & Gartner, W. B. (2016). Advancing our research agenda for entrepreneurship and contexts. In F. Welter & W. B. Gartner (Eds.), *A Research Agenda for Entrepreneurship and Context* (pp. 156–160). Edward Elgar Publishing. https://doi.org/10.4337/9781784716844.00017

Welter, Friederike, Gartner, W., & Wright, M. (2016). The context of contextualizing contexts. In Friederike Welter & W. B. Gartner (Eds.), *A Research Agenda for Entrepreneurship and Context* (pp. 1–15). Edward Elgar Publishing. https://doi.org/10.4337/9781784716844

Winborg, J., & Landström, H. (2001). Financial bootstrapping in small businesses. *Journal of Business Venturing*, *16*(3), 235–254. https://doi.org/10.1016/S0883-9026(99)00055-5

World Bank. (2021). *Services, value added (% of GDP)*. https://data.worldbank.org/indicator/NV.SRV.TOTL.ZS

Zacharakis, A., Bygrave, W., & Corbett, A. C. (2017). *Entrepreneurship* (4th ed.). John Wiley & Sons, Inc.

Zacharakis, A., Bygrave, W. D., & Corbett, A. C. (2020). *Entrepreneurship* (5th ed.). John Wiley & Sons, Inc.

Matthew Rutherford, Duygu Phillips, and Jorge Arteaga-Fonseca

2 The bootstrapping-bricolage interface

Abstract: The entrepreneurial frameworks of bootstrapping and bricolage both address the broad challenge of surviving and thriving under conditions of resource scarcity. However, while similar in this regard, these frameworks also possess distinct attributes. Bootstrapping has been traditionally more focused upon exploring issues concerned with financing choices (i.e., the avoidance of external finance), whereas bricolage considers a broader range of, mostly improvisational, activities. These improvisational activities can be considerations of financial capital, but may also include social, human, and institutional capital. In this work, we outline the similarities and divergences between the two frameworks, and cast them as opportunities for developing scholarly work in entrepreneurship.

Keywords: bricolage, bootstrapping, crowdfunding, lean startup

Introduction

Contrasted with more traditional approaches of entrepreneurship (e.g., causation), the perspectives of bricolage and bootstrapping offer insights into how entrepreneurs can take alternative routes to the identification and exploitation of opportunities (Fisher, 2012). More specifically, the perspectives more fully appreciate the fact that most new ventures launch under conditions of resource scarcity. Our goal here is to lay out the fundamentals of these two entrepreneurial approaches, and further, to compare and contrast them with one another. By doing this, we identify areas of overlap and propose the term: 'bootstrapping bricoleur'. We then outline a future research agenda that researchers may utilize to further explore this bootstrapping bricoleur.

While bricolage and related lines of process research (e.g., effectuation, causation, improvisation) have been compared and contrasted within the entrepreneurship literature (i.e., An, Rüiling, Zheng, & Zhang, 2020; Archer et al., 2009; Coudounaris & Arvidsson, 2021; Fisher, 2012; Servantie & Rispal, 2018), the relationship between bootstrapping and bricolage has not received much attention.[1] Consequently, the relation between the two is not clear. On the one hand, they seem very similar in that they both address the broad issue of launching and growing a business with limited

---

[1] For exceptions Salimath & Jones, 2011; Rutherford, 2015.

Matthew Rutherford, Duygu Phillips, Jorge Arteaga-Fonseca, School of Entrepreneurship, Oklahoma State University

https://doi.org/10.1515/9783110726312-004

resources at hand. On the other hand, each paradigm possesses unique properties, but these properties have not been made explicit. It is important to understand both the similarities and the distinctions, because each approach has been characterized as vital to our understanding of entrepreneurial processes; but so too have both been characterized as incomplete in this regard (e.g., Davidsson et al., 2017; Rutherford et al., 2017). By exploring the interface in this review our goal is to embrace the vitality of each approach's unique contribution for the entrepreneurial process while addressing some of the inadequacies of their distinctions.

What do we know about bootstrapping and bricolage?

Bootstrapping

Bootstrapping is a construct that has existed in the academic literature since the late 1980's (i.e., Van Auken & Carter, 1989). It is an essential phenomenon occurring within entrepreneurship (Grichnik & Singh, 2010) receiving a great deal of anecdotal exposure in mainstream media (i.e., Kawasaki, 2009), because it is well-accepted that entrepreneurs rely on bootstrapping to launch their start-ups (Shane 2008). It has multiple definitions, but one of the most widely used is from Freear et al. (2002): "highly creative ways of acquiring the use of resources without borrowing money or raising equity financing from traditional sources." (p. 278) In other words, bootstrapping is a method of securing startup resources without depending upon external financing (Freear, Sohl, & Wetzel, 1995; Winborg, 2009). A somewhat contrasting definition is suggestive of a more bounded characterization: "capital acquired from sources other than traditional providers of capital." (Van Auken & Neeley, 1996, p. 236)

Because of these differing definitions, there is some divergence within the literature on the appropriate conceptualization of bootstrapping. This divergence can be characterized in two ways: 1) financial bootstrapping, and 2) strategic bootstrapping. Though both converge around the notion of using internal funding only, the financial bootstrapping camp largely considers bootstrapping to be a capital structure (i.e., debt vs. equity) decision when launching (e.g., Bhide, 1992). By contrast, strategic bootstrapping proponents embrace a broader definition of bootstrapping that is more concerned with the many subsequent strategic decisions and actions that must be undertaken because of the decision to launch without external funding.

Financial bootstrapping places importance upon the antecedents to bootstrapping, which are comprised of both firm characteristics (age, size), as well as the entrepreneur characteristics (human and social capital, gender, owner's age) (cf. Miao et al., 2017). There are also demand-side reasons that entrepreneurs may forego external funding. The key demand-side antecedent is the desire for autonomy (Patel et al., 2011). Rightly or wrongly, many entrepreneurs prefer to be "lone wolves" and avoid financing. However, they may also not pursue external funding simply because they lack knowledge about the options available to them (Shane, 2006).

Strategic bootstrapping is more of a process-oriented perspective, concerned with the post-launch stage (e.g., Ekanem, 2005; Smith, 2009). Therefore, scholars place more importance upon the outcomes of bootstrapping. That is, the emphasis is on understanding what occurs after the decision has been made to eschew external finance. As an illustration, studies in this milieu (e.g., Jones & Jayawarna, 2010) have examined how social networks help new ventures acquire bootstrapped resources and how these resources influence business performance. Although strategic bootstrapping can also be traced back to the construct's early days (Thorne, 1989); it was Winborg and Landström's (2001) typology that launched research into strategic bootstrapping. This typology classified entrepreneurs that strategically bootstrap as "delaying; relationship-oriented; subsidy-oriented; minimizing; and private-owner financed bootstrappers." (Winborg & Landström, 2001) Delaying bootstrappers postpone their spending by lagging disbursements to suppliers and tax authorities, or delay investment by leasing equipment instead of buying. Relationship-oriented bootstrappers leverage personal relations as a means of securing the joint utilization of resources; thereby sharing and borrowing resources from other businesses in a narrow network circle. Subsidy-oriented bootstrappers adopt a quasi-market resource acquisition orientation and focus on obtaining subsidies from local, regional, and national government. Minimizing bootstrappers avoid external financing by implementing a relatively high use of cash management routines to minimize the amount of money tied-up in accounts receivables and inventory. Finally, private-owned bootstrappers display high dependence upon resources provided by the owner and his/her relatives (Chapter 1 explores founder financing in detail).

Bricolage

Bricolage is defined as "making do by applying combinations of the resources at hand to new problems and opportunities." (Baker & Nelson, 2005, p. 333) The degree to which an entrepreneur is a bricoleur is influenced by 1) the refusal to enact resource limitations by making do, 2) the newness of the opportunity they pursue, 3) the internal and external resources at hand, and 4) how the resources are combined. Bricolage was originally introduced by anthropologist and ethnologist Lévi-Strauss (1967) who conceptualized this action as "making do with what is at hand." (Baker & Nelson, 2005, p. 329) In his original work, Lévi-Straus discusses how the interaction between people from different cultures and their environments relates to better understanding of entrepreneurship (Stinchfield, Nelson, & Wood, 2013). Bricolage involves trying out solutions, then observing and dealing with the results (Archer, Baker, & Maurer, 2009). While it requires resources to be at hand, these resources can either be existing or available, such as materials and financial resources (Stenholm & Renko, 2016). In addition, these resources can be internal or external, but with the notable criterion that they need to be available cheaply or for free (Senyard, Baker, Steffens, & Davidsson, 2014). These resources may be tangible artifacts, or intangible skills and ideas (Baker & Nelson, 2005). Bricoleurs – or "handymen" (Fisher, 2012, p. 1026) – challenge the limitations they face by using those resources with which they are familiar, and in ways other than their original purposes (Stenholm & Renko, 2016; Westley & Mintzberg, 1989).

Bricolage has been utilized to explain entrepreneurial action in nascent firm growth (e.g., Baker et al., 2003), market creation (e.g., Baker & Nelson, 2005), innovation (e.g., Ciborra, 1996; Fisher, 2012; Garud & Karnoe, 2003), and social entrepreneurship (e.g., Janssen et al., 2018). In regard to nascence, Baker et al. (2003) discussed how improvisation and bricolage play a role in the founding process of new ventures. They introduced the concept of "network bricolage" and defined it as "dependence on pre-existing contact networks as the means at hand"; which holds some likeness to the construct of effectuation (Baker et al., 2003, p. 270). Regarding market creation, bricoleurs refuse to enact the limitations in resource-constrained environments (Baker & Nelson, 2005). This characteristic has led some scholars to label them as "less rational" by rejecting "the face value of traditional definitions of resource acquisition in favor of radical experimentation." (Stinchfield, Nelson, & Wood, 2013, p. 890) Within the context of innovation, bricolage has traditionally been viewed as a mechanism leading to innovative behavior because, while the objective may not be to innovate, the creative combination of resources often ends in the creation of an innovation: "Necessity is the mother of invention." (Janssen et al., 2018, p. 452). There is evidence that resource-constrained new firms can be more innovative than others (e.g., Bhide, 1994, 2003; Senyard et al., 2014). One of the reasons for this is the flexibility that new ventures possess allowing them to be more creative with the resources at hand (Mishina, Pollock, & Porac, 2004; Senyard et al., 2014). For instance, Garud and Karnoe's (2003) study shows how bricolage is co-shaped by various actors involved in the design and emergence of a technological product. Finally, research has explicated social ventures' use of bricolage to solve social problems (e.g., Desa & Basu, 2013; DiDomenico et al., 2010; Molecke & Pinkse, 2017). For instance, by extending bricolage into the social entrepreneurship context, Bojica et al. (2018) show that the effect of bricolage on growth is contingent upon the degree of autonomy involved in using the resources available at hand.

Although some scholars conceptualize bricolage as being synonymous with improvisation (e.g., Salimath & Jones, 2011), the preponderance of the literature suggests that bricolage can be both improvised and a deliberate, planned action (Baker & Nelson, 2005): "Improvisation increases the chances that bricolage will occur because there is less time to obtain appropriate resources in advance. They are not the same construct, however, as bricolage can occur in *nonimprovisational* contexts. Being skillful at bricolage may help produce valued improvisation" (Miner, Bassoff, &

Moorman, 2001, p. 314, emphasis added). The distinctions between these two constructs inspire our future research directions presented in latter part of this work.

Regarding the outcomes, bricolage in its two forms – parallel and selective – has equivocal findings on performance. Parallel bricolage (constant use and in every domain) leads to increased performance but not growth, while selective bricolage (occasional use) does lead to growth (Baker & Nelson, 2005). It has also been suggested that bricolage can be both beneficial and harmful for new ventures (Senyard, Baker, & Davidsson, 2009). For instance, Ciborra (1996) showed that bricolage reduced firm effectiveness. On the contrary, as noted earlier, if the creative combinations of resources and implementation lead to innovative solutions, then bricolage will likely have positive outcomes (e.g., Anderson, 2008; Senyard et al., 2009). Baker and Nelson (2005), therefore, suggest that as long as bricolage is not overdone, it would lead to positive results.

Bricolage provides a process-based model of resource combination and use that complements the resource-based view (Baker & Nelson, 2005). An early argument for this complementarity was Penrose (1959), which argued that the difference in firm performance outcomes is due to distinctive resource combining abilities. In this regard, Witell et al. (2017) find that addressing resource scarcity actively, making do, improvising when recombining resources, and networking with external partners are four critical capabilities to influence service innovation outcomes.

Bootstrapping and bricolage

The vital constructs of bootstrapping and bricolage both assume an environment where start-ups face constraints due to their innate liabilities of newness (Stinchcombe, 1965). In newness, start-ups struggle to develop internal resources (i.e., relationships, routines, logistics) and do not have well-developed external relationships with stakeholders (i.e., customers, suppliers, financiers). Moreover, they are also often challenged by liabilities of smallness, which reflect the lack of scale to compete with larger rivals (Aldrich & Auster, 1986).

With the extant definition of bricolage in mind, and within Baker and Nelson's (2005) conceptualization, not all bricoleurs are bootstrappers. While making do only with what is at hand very often necessitates eschewing external finance, these resources can be internal or external, but they must be available cheaply or free (Senyard et al., 2014). In the same way, not all bootstrappers are bricoleurs, because simply by virtue of eschewing external finance does not ensure that an entrepreneur will pursue new opportunities by combining resources. That is, though largely unplanned, bricolage can be a deliberate and purposeful strategy of exploiting new opportunities specifically by combining at hand resources (Baker et al., 2003). If either combining resources or newness (i.e., new opportunity and/or new purposes) is absent, the bootstrapper is not engaging in bricolage. Within the paradigm of brico- lage, not only must the resources be at hand, but they also must be applied – not sin- gularly – but in a combinatorial fashion. In addition, while bricolage may lead to innovation (Senyard et al., 2014) or "brilliant unforeseen results" (Baker & Nelson, 2005; Lévi-Strauss, 1967, p. 17), bootstrapping (regardless of perspective) is more con- cerned with avoiding external financing.

The relation between the two frameworks, though, does depend somewhat upon which conceptualization of bootstrapping is under consideration. Bricolage can be manifested through financial actions as well as other strategic activities (Baker et al., 2003). A financial bootstrapping view would seemingly place brico- lage as a potential outcome. That is, the choice to forego funding may trigger a bricolage process. A more strategic view of bootstrapping places the two frame- works more closely together conceptually, because it outlines specific tactics that resource-constrained entrepreneurs can employ to overcome these constraints (Salimath & Jones, 2011). Because it outlines these tactics, strategic bootstrapping adds some additional precision to the bricolage framework. This is noteworthy, because while bricolage has been widely embraced in entrepreneurial studies, it is still evolving and the machinations – actual implementation – of the strategy are still being developed.

Regarding the antecedents of bootstrapping and bricolage, both bricolage and bootstrapping can be either an outcome of necessity or a preference/choice. Speak- ing to necessity, the Bermuda Triangle of forces (i.e., information asymmetry, moral hazard, and adverse selection) may motivate entrepreneurs to bootstrap, as finan- ciers are unwilling to invest in new ventures (Rutherford & Phillips, 2021). With re- gard to preference, entrepreneurs choose to bootstrap and avoid external financing in order to preserve their autonomy (Patel et al., 2011). Bricolage can also be seen as the outcome of necessity since entrepreneurs make do with what is at hand in re- source-constrained environments. However, as bricoleurs refuse to enact resource constraints in the environment, it can be argued that bricolage is more of a prefer- ence than a necessity. Rather than requesting external funding, bricoleurs often ex- periment by gathering the resources available for free or cheap and combine them into new purposes (Garud & Karnoe, 2003). Both strategies or actions involve some degree of creativity. However, bricoleurs can be considered to be more creative, on average, than bootstrappers. The former creates new purposes out of existing re- sources by recombining them, while the latter aims at starting and growing a new venture without depending on external financing. In other words, bootstrappers may or may not engage in creative action.

In order to address the overlap between these two constructs, we propose the concept of "bootstrapping bricoleurs" which we define as *"enlightened entrepre- neurial rebels* who will not take external finance but pursue new opportunities by combining resources they already possess or that are easily available to them in order to achieve some predefined goals". In defining our agenda below, we believe that by meshing these two perspectives, substantial theoretical development can emerge.

Future research agenda

Broadly speaking, avenues for future research involve 1) integrating both paradigms into extant frameworks, and 2) an increased attention on measurement development. With regard to the first avenue, we believe that integrating with related literatures will more completely explicate the microprocesses of both bootstrapping and bricolage. Speaking to the second avenue, the research on both has been empirically rich, but generalizability has been somewhat limited. This is natural and necessary in growing fields but, speaking from a positivist view, for the field to continue to develop, researchers need more robust instrumentation and measures so that key relationships can be better understood. In the following section, we suggest some possible future research directions.

Crowdfunding and the bootstrapping bricoleur

Crowdfunding is defined as "the financing of a project or a venture by a group of individuals instead of professional parties." (Schwienbacher & Larralde, 2010, p. 4) It is a way for entrepreneurs to (1) generate pre-orders of their products; and (2) raise funds in exchange for a share in future profits (Belleflamme et al., 2014). Crowdfunding, as a strategic activity to acquire resources necessary to start a business and introduce new products and services, has been classified in different ways. One way is the classification by return type (Moritz & Block, 2016) including donation, sponsoring, pre-ordering, membership fees, crediting, lending, and profit-sharing (e.g., Belleflamme et al., 2014; Hemer, 2011). Short et al. (2017), on the other hand, categorized crowdfunding into three groups: rewards-based, equity-based, and debt-based. Rutherford (2015) treats donation-based crowdfunding as a stand-alone category, rather than within the rewards-based category.

Similar to bricolage and bootstrapping, entrepreneurs can deal with resource limitations including skills to run a project through crowdfunding (Schwienbacher & Larrade, 2010) which can be considered to be mostly creative ways to obtain financing (Sannajust et al., 2014). One major resemblance of crowdfunding with the constructs of interest here is the use of alternative resources excluding traditional external finance (i.e., debt and equity). Similar to all bootstrappers and most bricoleurs that avoid external financial resources, crowdfunders aim at acquiring external financing – not from debt and equity providers – but from the crowd.

Specifically, rewards-based crowdfunding may be a complementary technique to the bootstrapping bricoleur as it avoids dependence on external stakeholders yet allows for acquisition of the necessary funding. Based on this logic, bootstrapping, bricolage and crowdfunding research can complement each other in that the antecedents of rewards-based crowdfunding decisions may be insightful in the investigation of the antecedents of bootstrapping bricoleurs' decisions and vice versa.

Regarding the antecedents of bricolage, bootstrapping, and crowdfunding, there are notable similarities. First, they can all be the entrepreneurs' strategic choice or a necessity for the resource-poor entrepreneur to pursue. This separation is important to know as it may provide insights on why some crowdfunders are successful and some are not. Crowdfunders that lack initial resources at hand may be under more pressure and more constrained to invest in the complementary factors (i.e., prototype and website) that may be influential on the success of the campaign. On the other hand, crowdfunding may be a selected strategy for not only raising money but also raising awareness about and validation for the product before its launch (Schwienbacher & Larralde, 2010). For instance, a crowdfunding campaign can be run just to signal the market potential of the product the new venture is planning to launch (Sannajust et al., 2014). This is more in line with strategic bootstrapping.

Crowdfunding research has focused upon the antecedents of crowdfunding performance (Short et al., 2017). Type of rewards (e.g., Allison, Davis, Webb, & Short, 2017), campaign characteristics (e.g., Mollick, 2014), communication (e.g., Allison, Davis, Short, & Webb, 2015), firm orientations (Calic & Mosakowski, 2016), the abilities and motivations of the entrepreneur such as passion (e.g., Li et al., 2017), social networks (e.g., Colombo et al., 2015), and human capital (e.g., Ahlers et al., 2015; Piva & Rossi-Lamastra, 2018) have been shown to be influential on crowdfunding performance (Anglin et al., 2018). Bootstrapping, bricolage and crowdfunding share some common antecedents (e.g., social networks, human capital). For instance, human capital, specifically the entrepreneurs' business education and entrepreneurial experience, signaling good fit with the venture's quality and low ambiguity were found to be influential on equity crowdfunding outcomes (Piva & Rossi-Lamastra, 2018). In the same vein, bootstrapping research has looked into the effects of human capital on the outcomes of bootstrapping. It may be interesting to investigate the role of fit and ambiguity in the relationship between human capital and bootstrapping bricoleur. Other properties, such as firm orientations and type of rewards may also be informative for bootstrapping and bricolage research. For instance, while bootstrapping bricoleurs may avoid external funding and do not "owe" anything to outsiders, they may still earn funding and resources from their family and friends in exchange for some kind of rewards. The specific types of rewards may be influential in the performance outcomes of new ventures founded by bootstrapping bricoleurs.

There is evidence that these techniques (i.e., bootstrapping, bricolage, and crowd-funding) may generate successful outcomes and lead to the emergence and growth of new ventures. They can each serve as a signal of credibility and trust. However, if not well planned and executed, crowdfunding can send signals of distrust about the entre-preneur and the new venture. Moral hazard and information asymmetry play important roles in both crowdfunding and bootstrapping decisions and outcomes. However, in crowdfunding, "investors" often have access to even less information. In the similar vein, bootstrapping and bricolage outcomes – if failed – would be sending messages of distrust possibly leading to legitimacy and performance losses.

Similar to bootstrapping and bricolage research, crowdfunding is considered as a phenomena-driven research lacking theory and in need of a theoretical approach. These streams of research may be more beneficial and advanced if they contribute to the advancement of the existing theories in entrepreneurship. Authors may inves-tigate the past experiences of entrepreneurs on the success of these strategic actions. Understanding the entrepreneurs / stakeholders is key for crowdfunding, bootstrap-ping and bricolage as the offerings as well as the identity and the communication of the new venture can be altered based on the expectancies of the specific audience. In crowdfunding, motivations can be intrinsic (i.e., pleasure or fun) or extrinsic (e.g., monetary rewards or other benefits) (Allison et al., 2015). In bootstrapping, while the motivation of the entrepreneur (e.g., autonomy, prior experience, social and human capital) (Rutherford et al., 2017) is influential on performance, the stakeholder's motivation is also likely to affect the decision to bootstrap as well as the effects of boot-strapping on performance. In addition, since bricolage involves creative combination of resource at hand, it is key to create something that the stakeholders need and want.

In addition, these three lines of research can focus on the differences among different types of entrepreneurial ventures and their venture funding alternatives and choices. Stevenson et al. (2019) pioneering study looks at the shift in venture funding away from the traditional entrepreneurship to the "main street entre-preneurship" (p. 376) through the wider use of crowdfunding by the latter. As such, bootstrapping and bricolage researchers may direct their attention to this more ne-glected group of entrepreneurship (i.e., main street entrepreneurship). Moreover, the trends within entrepreneurs to utilize bootstrapping, bricolage, and crowdfund-ing require more attention. As Kuratko et al.'s (2017) analysis of the trends in ven-ture capital showed a shift from individuals, foundations, and families to pension institutions as sources of capital; it is worth looking into how the changes in trends to undertake bootstrapping, bricolage and crowdfunding affect each other as well as other new venture funding alternatives.

Chan and Parhankangas (2017) investigated the role of innovativeness on crowd-funding outcomes and found that incremental innovativeness of a campaign, perceived to be less risky than radical innovativeness, led to more successful crowdfunding investments. As crowdfunders "are not professional equity investors" (Chan & Parhankangas, 2017, p. 238), they are less willing to take on high risks such as venture capitalists may do. This is expected to be true for bootstrapping bricoleurs to fund their ventures and grow them strategically. More research can look into the effects of innovativeness and risk that these bootstrapping bricoleurs take on the outcomes of the two different types of bootstrapping.

Cultural entrepreneurship and the bootstrapping bricoleur

In this chapter one of our key foci is the resources at hand (i.e., bricolage) and the other is the avoidance of external financing (i.e., bootstrapping). Therefore, the paradigm of cultural entrepreneurship is a natural consideration as it provides theory-based prescriptions for entrepreneurs operating under extreme uncertainty in resource-poor environments. Cultural entrepreneurship is *"the processes by which actors draw upon cultural resources (e.g., discourse, language, categories, logics, and other symbolic elements) to advance entrepreneurship or to facilitate organizational and institutional innovation"* (Lounsbury & Glynn, 2019, p. 3, emphasis in original). Cultural resources listed in this definition are available to all entrepreneurs (i.e., at hand) and do not require external financing. As entrepreneurs operate in uncertain environments and try to create future value for their stakeholders (Garud et al., 2014), they can utilize discourse or storytelling to give sense to their audiences. In addition, the effective use of these cultural resources, as it may lead to positive judgments, could help entrepreneurs acquire more resources necessary to survive and grow as a result of increased legitimacy. Therefore, cultural entrepreneurship can be a complementary research area to bootstrapping and bricolage providing the bootstrapped bricoleurs the tools and strategies to make do with what is at hand, recombine various resources for new purposes, and avoid external financial debts to achieve their goals.

There is "little guidance as to what constitutes a resource or the means at hand" (Baker et al., 2003). Among the resources listed in the literature are tools, skills and myths (Lévi-Strauss, 1967) as well as networks as included in Baker and Nelson's (2005) network bricolage concept. We posit that there may be more resources at hand that entrepreneurs may utilize when involving in bricolage activities. Accordingly, within this literature, we highlight that the entrepreneur is defined as a "cultural bricoleur" (Lounsbury & Glynn, 2019, p. 12) and submit that these cultural resources can be utilized by these bricoleurs.

In this process, though, the entrepreneur acts as a cultural operative to utilize the cultural resources within the institutional environment, giving sense to various stakeholders in order to achieve their favorable legitimacy judgments. Through cultural bricolage, entrepreneurs have more flexibility such that while utilizing the stocks of capital – both resource and institutional – they can be creative and construct and tell stories that may not necessarily be constrained to what is at hand at the moment. As entrepreneurs generate future expectations (cognitive and pragmatic) about something that does not exist yet (Garud et al., 2014), they have the freedom to imagine and even improvise what they can achieve with what they currently possess and what they will acquire in time. However, it is important that the story generated is compelling such that it reflects the uniqueness of the new venture as well as the conformity to the institutional norms and rules (Lounsbury & Glynn, 2001). In addition, the story needs to be sensible (Lounsbury & Glynn, 2019) so that future expectations do not lead to disappointments (Garud, Schildt, & Lant, 2014). Therefore, while they can be flexible when crafting a narrative with the resources at hand, entrepreneurs must be careful about not going beyond what can be acceptable and appropriate and what will make sense to the stakeholders in order to generate positive judgments of legitimacy, and thus improve new venture performance. Here we are speaking to the cultural bricoleur that also encompasses cultural bootstrapper. Future research can provide insights on how bootstrapped bricoleurs can use cultural resources at hand to achieve legitimacy for their new ventures and improve performance.

Lean startup and the bootstrapping bricoleur

The lean startup process, aimed at alleviating the risk involved in new venture creation, has five building blocks, including market opportunity navigation, business model design, validated learning/customer development, minimally viable product (MVP) creation, and perseverance vs. pivoting decision (Blank, 2013; Gruber & Tal, 2017; Osterwalder & Pigneur, 2010; Ries, 2011; Shepherd & Gruber, 2020). Blank (2013) suggested that this process allows for risk reduction through an "outward-looking learning mindset" that prioritizes understanding customer needs and thus developing a business model that meets such needs (Shepherd & Gruber, 2020, p. 2).

Entrepreneurs following a lean startup process create a MVP to understand the market potential for their idea (Eisenmann et al. 2012). This process is more experimental (Contigiani & Levinthal, 2019) than the causation process, which focuses more on planning. In this vein, the lean startup is similar to bricolage as it is more improvisational than planned. Bootstrapping and bricolage can complement the lean startup process by providing a means to test the MVP and its likelihood to succeed in a certain market by launching a product faster to generate an early market validation (Mac an Bhaird & Lynn, 2015; Ries, 2011).

However, the founders of the movement state that lean startup is different from bootstrapping, in that "lean startups espouse the same objective as firms that embrace lean manufacturing: avoiding waste. A lean startup may eventually invest enormous amounts of capital in customer acquisition or operational infrastructure – but only after its business model has been validated through fast and frugal tests." (Eisenmann et al., 2012, p. 1) Since entrepreneurs are often urged to make quick decisions in the face of uncertainty, they acquire limited resources through bootstrapping (Ghezzi, 2020) or use whatever is at hand through bricolage. This, in turn, may potentially lead to undesired results and loss of potential success. However, when a lean startup process is in place, bootstrapping bricoleurs can achieve successful outcomes even when the model calls for adaptations and change. Therefore, lean startup process can simplify the entrepreneurs' problem solving, decisions and subsequent actions (Ghezzi, 2020).

The lean startup process is about testing and constantly updating the business model. To do so, entrepreneurs have several tools they can use (e.g., business model canvas, market opportunity navigator, build-measure-learn). All these tools help creating a viable business and facilitate making adjustments throughout the business creation and development process from idea generation to market selection to starting a new business. Bootstrapping research fails to consider how these changes in the business models would influence bootstrapping decisions as well as its outcomes (Mac an Bhaird & Lynn, 2015), and instead focuses most heavily upon avoiding external funding and the actions that are required because of this avoidance. Still, in nascence, lean startup and bootstrapping likely go hand in hand. Bootstrapping has been suggested to help the firm to become lean (Harrison et al., 2004) by maximizing internal efficiencies with limited resources (Salimath & Jones, 2011), much like a just-in-time inventory system (Bhide, 1992).

While it lacks the same scholarly underpinnings, the literature on lean startups is similar to effectuation in that it focuses more upon the stage after the capital structure decision has been made by the entrepreneur. Moreover, in both, the capital structure decision is largely a tacit one, in that external finance was never considered as an option – the venture "makes do" with what is at hand similar to bricolage. However, though it lacks a bona fide theory base, the lean startup process can be instrumental in understanding the differences in bootstrapping bricoleurs' successes. As bootstrapping and bricolage can be a choice or a necessity to begin with, in time, strategic bootstrapping as well as bootstrapping bricoleurs' activities will be influential on the success of bootstrapping decisions. These activities do not have to be static, as they can be tested and adjusted through the life cycle of the new venture. Those who claim that bootstrapping techniques are "adopted by design rather than necessity" (Mac an Bhaird & Lynn, 2015, p. 153) suggest that bootstrapping can support lean business model. Therefore, lean startup methodology is helpful to advance bootstrapping research especially with regard to understanding more practical considerations of the construct.

Towards measurement development in bootstrapping and bricolage

While most of the extant work in bricolage is qualitative and inductive grounded theory development (e.g., Garud & Karnoe, 2003), bootstrapping research has not fully emerged from its phenomenological roots. The result, for both, is a general lack of validated measures (e.g., Davidsson et al., 2017, Rutherford et al., 2017). Bootstrapping and bricolage processes need more attention from methodologists focused on instrument development, which should enable additional empirical examination and enhanced external validity. Similarly, and possibly as interim salvo, increased exploration of appropriate proxies may yield substantial fruit (e.g., Ketchen et al., 2013). The availability of acceptable surrogate measures would allow for increased testing in the near term, especially in the absence of robust instrumentation, and would likely enable higher powered samples in more varied contexts.

We can point to some exemplars here. With regard to bricolage, one robust instrument illustration is Stenholm & Renko's (2016) empirical study, which employed a validated survey to measure aspects of bricolage. This eight-item scale was initially developed by Senyard et al. (2014) and validated by Davidsson et al. (2017). While this is a laudable attempt to test bricolage empirically, the survey items are very broad and do little to inform implementation of bricolage. Therefore, ample opportunity exists for future scholars to engage in additional instrument development. Exemplars in bootstrapping are more limited, as methodological development here has been somewhat stunted since Winborg and Landstrom's (2001) seminal study. As such, this work should serve as a base from which future scholars can build to refine, but more importantly build upon to describe a more expansive list of techniques that can be employed by the bootstrapping bricoleur.

Conclusion

Bootstrapping and bricolage are two frameworks that are not synonymous but strongly related. The blurred lines between the two have deterred scholars from studying and advancing these phenomena in tandem. We set out to clarify not only the boundaries, but also the intersection, between the two constructs. To explicate this overlap, we sought to encourage future scholarship by proposing the "bootstrapping bricoleur" conceptualization. We contribute to entrepreneurship research through this newly defined construct and offer avenues for future research.

References

Ahlers, G. K., Cumming, D., Günther, C., & Schweizer, D. (2015). Signaling in equity crowdfunding. *Entrepreneurship Theory and Practice, 39(4)*, 955–980.

Aldrich, H., & Auster, E. R. (1986). Even dwarfs started small: Liabilities of age and size and their strategic implications. *Research in Organizational Behavior*, 8, 165–198.

Allison, T. H., Davis, B. C., Short, J. C., & Webb, J. W. (2015). Crowdfunding in a prosocial microlending environment: Examining the role of intrinsic versus extrinsic cues. *Entrepreneurship Theory and Practice, 39(1)*, 53–73. https://doi.org/10.1111/etap.12108

Allison, T. H., Davis, B. C., Webb, J. W., & Short, J. C. (2017). Persuasion in crowdfunding: An elaboration likelihood model of crowdfunding performance. *Journal of Business Venturing, 32(6)*, 707–725. https://doi.org/10.1016/j.jbusvent.2017.09.002

An, W., Rüling, C. C., Zheng, X., & Zhang, J. (2020). Configurations of effectuation, causation, and bricolage: implications for firm growth paths. *Small Business Economics, 54(3)*. https://doi.org/10.1007/s11187-019-00155-8

Anderson, O. J. (2008). A Bottom-Up Perspective on Innovations. *Administration & Society, 40(1)*, 54–78. https://doi.org/10.1177/0095399707311775

Anglin, A. H., Short, J. C., Drover, W., Stevenson, R. M., McKenny, A. F., & Allison, T. H. (2018). The power of positivity? The influence of positive psychological capital language on crowdfunding performance. *Journal of Business Venturing, 33(4)*, 470–492. https://doi.org/10.1016/j.jbusvent.2018.03.003

Archer, G. R., Baker, T., & Mauer, R. (2009). Towards an alternative theory of entrepreneurial success: Integrating bricolage, effectuation and improvisation. *Frontiers of Entrepreneurship Research, 29(6)*, 1–23.

Baker, T., Miner, A. S., & Eesley, D. T. (2003). Improvising firms: Bricolage, account giving and improvisational competencies in the founding process. *Research Policy, 32(2)*, 255–276. https://doi.org/10.1016/S0048-7333(02)00099-9

Baker, T., & Nelson, R. E. (2005). Creating something from nothing: Resource construction through entrepreneurial bricolage. *Administrative Science Quarterly, 50(3)*, 329–366. https://doi.org/10.2189/asqu.2005.50.3.329

Belleflamme, P., Lambert, T., & Schwienbacher, A. (2014). Crowdfunding: Tapping the right crowd. *Journal of business venturing, 29(5)*, 585–609.

Bhide, A. (1992). Bootstrap finance: The art of start-ups. *Harvard Business Review, 70(6)*, 109–117.

Bhide, A. (1994). How entrepreneurs craft strategies that work. *Harvard Business Review, 72(2)*, 150–161.

Bhide, A. (2003). *The origin and evolution of new businesses*. Oxford University Press.

Blank, S. (2013). Why the lean start-up changes everything. *Harvard Business Review, 91(5)*, 63–72.

Bojica, A. M., Ruiz Jiménez, J. M., Ruiz Nava, J. A., & Fuentes-Fuentes, M. M. (2018). Bricolage and growth in social entrepreneurship organisations. *Entrepreneurship & Regional Development, 30(3–4)*, 362–389. https://doi.org/10.1080/08985626.2017.1413768

Calic, G., & Mosakowski, E. (2016). Kicking off social entrepreneurship: How a sustainability orientation influences crowdfunding success. *Journal of Management Studies, 53(5)*, 738–767. https://doi.org/10.1111/joms.12201

Chan, C. R., & Parhankangas, A. (2017). Crowdfunding innovative ideas: How incremental and radical innovativeness influence funding outcomes. *Entrepreneurship Theory and Practice, 41(2)*, 237–263. https://doi.org/10.1111/etap.12268

Ciborra, C. U. (1996). The platform organization: Recombining strategies, structures, and surprises. *Organization Science, 7(2)*, 103–118.

Colombo, M. G., Franzoni, C., & Rossi-Lamastra, C. (2015). Internal social capital and the attraction of early contributions in crowdfunding. *Entrepreneurship Theory and Practice, 39(1)*, 75–100. https://doi.org/10.1111/etap.12118

Contigiani, A., & Levinthal, D. A. (2019). Situating the construct of lean start-up: adjacent conversations and possible future directions. *Industrial and Corporate Change, 28(3)*, 551–564. https://doi.org/10.1093/icc/dtz013

Coudounaris, D. N., & Arvidsson, H. G. (2021). How effectuation, causation and bricolage influence the international performance of firms via internationalisation strategy: a literature review. *Review of International Business and Strategy*.

Davidsson, P., Baker, T., & Senyard, J. M. (2017). A measure of entrepreneurial bricolage behavior. *International Journal of Entrepreneurial Behavior & Research*.

Desa, G., & Basu, S. (2013). Optimization or bricolage? Overcoming resource constraints in global social entrepreneurship. *Strategic Entrepreneurship Journal*, *7(1)*, 26–49. https://doi.org/10.1002/sej.1150

Di Domenico, M., Haugh, H., & Tracey, P. (2010). Social bricolage: Theorizing social value creation in social enterprises. *Entrepreneurship Theory and Practice*, *34(4)*, 681–703. https://doi.org/10.1111/j.1540-6520.2010.00370.x

Eisenmann, T. R., Ries, E., & Dillard, S. (2012). *Hypothesis-driven entrepreneurship: The lean startup*. Harvard Business School Entrepreneurial Management Case, (812–095).

Ekanem, I. (2005). "Bootstrapping": The investment decision-making process in small firms. *British Accounting Review*, *37(3)*, 299–318. https://doi.org/10.1016/j.bar.2005.04.004

Fisher, G. (2012). Effectuation, causation, and bricolage: A behavioral comparison of emerging theories in entrepreneurship research. *Entrepreneurship Theory and Practice*, *36(5)*, 1019–1051. https://doi.org/10.1111/j.1540-6520.2012.00537.x

Freear, J., Sohl, J. E., & Wetzel, W. (2002). Angles on angels: Financing technology-based ventures – A historical perspective. *Venture Capital: An International Journal of Entrepreneurial Finance*, 4(4), 275–287. https://doi.org/10.1080/1369106022000024923

Freear, J., Sohl, J. E., & Wetzel Jr, W. E. (1995). Angels: personal investors in the venture capital market. *Entrepreneurship & Regional Development*, *7(1)*, 85–94. https://doi.org/10.1080/08985629500000005

Garud, R., & Karnøe, P. (2003). Bricolage versus breakthrough: distributed and embedded agency in technology entrepreneurship. *Research Policy*, *32(2)*, 277–300. https://doi.org/10.1016/S0048-7333(02)00100-2

Garud, R., Schildt, H. A., & Lant, T. K. (2014). Entrepreneurial storytelling, future expectations, and the paradox of legitimacy. *Organization Science*, *25(5)*, 1479–1492. https://doi.org/10.1287/orsc.2014.0915

Ghezzi, A. (2020). How Entrepreneurs make sense of Lean Startup Approaches: Business Models as cognitive lenses to generate fast and frugal Heuristics. *Technological Forecasting and Social Change*, *161*, https://doi.org/10.1016/j.techfore.2020.120324.

Grichnik, D., & Singh, L. (2010). Resource bootstrapping of nascent entrepreneurs: Conscious entrepreneurial decision or forced reaction?. *Frontiers of Entrepreneurship Research*, *30(12)*, 3.

Gruber, M., & Tal, S. (2017). *Where to play: 3 steps for discovering your most valuable market opportunities*. Pearson.

Harrison, R. T., Mason, C. M., & Girling, P. (2004). Financial bootstrapping and venture development in the software industry. *Entrepreneurship & Regional Development*, *16(4)*, 307–333. https://doi.org/10.1080/0898562042000263276

Hemer, J. (2011). *A snapshot on crowdfunding* (No. R2/2011). Arbeitspapiere Unternehmen und Region.

Janssen, F., Fayolle, A., & Wuilaume, A. (2018). Researching bricolage in social entrepreneurship. *Entrepreneurship & Regional Development*, *30(3–4)*, 450–470. https://doi.org/10.1080/08985626.2017.1413769

Jones, O., & Jayawarna, D. (2010). Resourcing new businesses: social networks, bootstrapping and firm performance. *Venture Capital*, *12(2)*, 127–152. https://doi.org/10.1080/13691061003658886

Kawasaki, G. (2009). 10 tips for successful bootstrapping. *Entrepreneur*. Retrieved from http://www.entrepreneur.com/article/201102

Ketchen Jr, D. J., Ireland, R. D., & Baker, L. T. (2013). The use of archival proxies in strategic management studies: castles made of sand?. *Organizational Research Methods*, *16(1)*, 32–42. https://doi.org/10.1177/1094428112459911

Kuratko, D. F., Fisher, G., Bloodgood, J., & Hornsby, J. S. (2017). The paradox of new venture legitimation within an entrepreneurial ecosystem. *Small Business Economics*, *49(1)*, 119–140. https://doi.org/10.1007/s11187-017-9870-x

Lévi-Strauss, C. (1967) *The Savage Mind*. Chicago: University of Chicago Press.

Li, J. J., Chen, X. P., Kotha, S., & Fisher, G. (2017). Catching fire and spreading it: A glimpse into displayed entrepreneurial passion in crowdfunding campaigns. *Journal of Applied Psychology, 102(7)*, 1075–1090. https://doi.org/10.1037/apl0000217

Lounsbury, M., & Glynn, M. A. (2001). Cultural entrepreneurship: Stories, legitimacy, and the acquisition of resources. *Strategic Management Journal, 22(6–7)*, 545–564. https://doi.org/10.1002/smj.188

Lounsbury, M., & Glynn, M. A. (2019). *Cultural entrepreneurship: A new agenda for the study of entrepreneurial processes and possibilities*. Cambridge University Press.

Mac an Bhaird, C., & Lynn, T. (2015). Seeding the cloud: Financial bootstrapping in the computer software sector. *Venture Capital, 17(1–2)*, 151–170. https://doi.org/10.1080/13691066.2015.1021030

Miao, C., Rutherford, M. W., & Pollack, J. M. (2017). An exploratory meta-analysis of the nomological network of bootstrapping in SMEs. *Journal of Business Venturing Insights, 8, 1–8*. https://doi.org/10.1016/j.jbvi.2017.04.002

Miner, A. S., Bassoff, P., & Moorman, C. (2001). Contours of organizational improvisation and learning. *Administrative Science Quarterly, 46(2)*, 304–337. https://doi.org/10.2307/2667089

Mishina, Y., Pollock, T. G., & Porac, J. F. (2004). Are more resources always better for growth? Resource stickiness in market and product expansion. *Strategic Management Journal, 25(12)*, 1179–1197. https://doi.org/10.1002/smj.424

Molecke, G., & Pinkse, J. (2017). Accountability for social impact: A bricolage perspective on impact measurement in social enterprises. *Journal of Business Venturing, 32(5)*, 550–568. https://doi.org/10.1016/j.jbusvent.2017.05.003

Mollick, E. (2014). The dynamics of crowdfunding: An exploratory study. *Journal of business Venturing, 29(1)*, 1–16. https://doi.org/10.1016/j.jbusvent.2013.06.005

Moritz, A., & Block, J. H. (2016). Crowdfunding: A literature review and research directions. *Crowdfunding in Europe, 25–53*. https://doi.org/10.1007/978-3-319-18017-5_3

Osterwalder, A., & Pigneur, Y. (2010). *Business model generation: A handbook for visionaries, game changers, and challengers* (Vol. 1). John Wiley & Sons.

Patel, P. C., Fiet, J. O., & Sohl, J. E. (2011). Mitigating the limited scalability of bootstrapping through strategic alliances to enhance new venture growth. *International Small Business Journal, 29(5)*, 421–447. https://doi.org/10.1177/0266242610396622

Penrose, R. (1959, January). The apparent shape of a relativistically moving sphere. In A. Pelczynski & S. J. Szarek *Mathematical Proceedings of the Cambridge Philosophical Society* (Vol. 55, No. 1, pp. 137–139). Cambridge University Press.

Piva, E., & Rossi-Lamastra, C. (2018). Human capital signals and entrepreneurs' success in equity crowdfunding. *Small Business Economics, 51(3)*, 667–686. https://doi.org/10.1007/s11187-017-9950-y

Ries, E. (2011). *The lean startup: How today's entrepreneurs use continuous innovation to create radically successful businesses*. Currency.

Rutherford, M. W. (2015). *Strategic bootstrapping*. Business Expert Press.

Rutherford, M., & Phillips, D. (2021, June). Bootstrapping: Complementary Lines of Inquiry in Entrepreneurship. In *Oxford Research Encyclopedia of Business and Management*. Retrieved from https://oxfordre.com/business/view/10.1093/acrefore/9780190224851.001.0001/acrefore-9780190224851-e-309.

Rutherford, M., Pollack, J. M., Mazzei, M. J., & Sanchez-Ruiz, P. (2017). Bootstrapping: Reviewing the literature, clarifying the construct, and charting a new path forward. *Group & Organization Management, 42(5)*, 657–706. https://doi.org/10.1177/1059601117730574

Salimath, M. S., & Jones III, R. J. (2011). Scientific Entrepreneurial Management: Bricolage, Bootstrapping, and the Quest for Efficiencies. *Journal of Business & Management, 17(1)*.

Sannajust, A., Roux, F., & Chaibi, A. (2014). Crowdfunding in France: a new revolution?. *Journal of Applied Business Research (JABR)*, *30(6)*, 1919–1928. https://doi.org/10.19030/jabr.v30i6.8947

Schwienbacher, A., & Larralde, B. (2010). Crowdfunding of small entrepreneurial ventures. *Handbook of Entrepreneurial Finance, Oxford University Press, Forthcoming*. http://dx.doi.org/10.2139/ssrn.1699183

Senyard, J., Baker, T., & Davidsson, P. (2009). Entrepreneurial bricolage: Towards systematic empirical testing. *Frontiers of Entrepreneurship Research*, *29(5)*, 5.

Senyard, J., Baker, T., Steffens, P., & Davidsson, P. (2014). Bricolage as a path to innovativeness for resource constrained new firms. *Journal of Product Innovation Management*, *31(2)*, 211–230. https://doi.org/10.1111/jpim.12091

Servantie, V., & Rispal, M. H. (2018). Bricolage, effectuation, and causation shifts over time in the context of social entrepreneurship. *Entrepreneurship & Regional Development*, *30(3–4)*, 310–335. https://doi.org/10.1080/08985626.2017.1413774

Shane, S. (2006). Introduction to the focused issue on entrepreneurship. *Management Science*, *52(2)*, 155–159. https://doi.org/10.1287/mnsc.1050.0484

Shane, S. A. (2008). *The illusions of entrepreneurship*. Yale University Press.

Shepherd, D. A., & Gruber, M. (2021). The lean startup framework: Closing the academic–practitioner divide. *Entrepreneurship Theory and Practice*, *45*(5), 967–998. https://doi.org/10.1177/1042258719899415

Short, J. C., Ketchen Jr, D. J., McKenny, A. F., Allison, T. H., & Ireland, R. D. (2017). Research on crowdfunding: Reviewing the (very recent) past and celebrating the present. *Entrepreneurship Theory and Practice*, *41(2)*, 149–160. https://doi.org/10.1111/etap.12270

Smith, D. (2009). Financial bootstrapping and social capital: How technology-based start-ups fund innovation. *International Journal of Entrepreneurship and Innovation Management*, *10*, 199–209.

Stenholm, P., & Renko, M. (2016). Passionate bricoleurs and new venture survival. *Journal of Business Venturing*, *31(5)*, 595–611. https://doi.org/10.1016/j.jbusvent.2016.05.004

Stevenson, R. M., Kuratko, D. F., & Eutsler, J. (2019). Unleashing main street entrepreneurship: Crowdfunding, venture capital, and the democratization of new venture investments. *Small Business Economics*, *52(2)*, 375–393. https://doi.org/10.1007/s11187-018-0097-2

Stinchcombe, A. (1965). Organization-creating organizations. *Society*, *2(2)*, 34–35.

Stinchfield, B. T., Nelson, R. E., & Wood, M. S. (2013). Learning from Levi–Strauss' legacy: Art, craft, engineering, bricolage, and brokerage in entrepreneurship. *Entrepreneurship Theory and Practice*, *37(4)*, 889–921. https://doi.org/10.1111/j.1540-6520.2012.00523.x

Thorne, J. (1989). Alternative financing for entrepreneurial ventures. *Entrepreneurship Theory and Practice*, 13(3), 7–9. https://doi.org/10.1177/104225878901300302

Van Auken, H. E., & Carter, R. B. (1989). Acquisition of capital by small business. *Journal of Small Business Management*, *27(2)*, 1.

Van Auken, H. E, & Neeley, L. (1996). Evidence of bootstrap financing among small start-up firms. *Journal of Entrepreneurial and Small Business Finance*, *5(3)*, 235–249.

Westley, F., & Mintzberg, H. (1989). Visionary leadership and strategic management. *Strategic Management Journal*, *10(S1)*, 17–32.

Winborg, J. (2009). Use of financial bootstrapping in new businesses: A question of last resort?. *Venture Capital*, *11(1)*, 71–83. https://doi.org/10.1080/13691060802351248

Winborg, J., & Landström, H. (2001). Financial bootstrapping in small businesses: Examining small business managers' resource acquisition behaviors. *Journal of Business Venturing*, 16(3), 235–254. https://doi.org/10.1016/S0883-9026(99)00055-5

Witell, L., Gebauer, H., Jaakkola, E., Hammedi, W., Patricio, L., & Perks, H. (2017). A bricolage perspective on service innovation. *Journal of Business Research*, *79*, 290–298. https://doi.org/10.1016/j.jbusres.2017.03.021

Sussie Morrish

3 Effectuation and entrepreneurial finance

Abstract: Financial assets are critical to the performance of any venture and financing is one of the most significant decisions an entrepreneur has to make. While studies show that ventures need adequate financial resources to survive and grow, many successful ventures have been spawned with very scant resources. Entrepreneurs launch ventures using creative ways to start generating revenue and cash flow quickly. The means that one possesses can dictate their ability to gather and allocate much needed resources. This activity is at the heart of effectuation. Effectuation is centered in a logic of control rather than prediction. It has gained popularity among researchers in understanding the entrepreneurial decision-making process. This chapter explores effectuation and how it influences entrepreneurial financing decisions with a focus on the core principles that guide the practice. A set of future research agenda to advance the field is proposed.

Keywords: effectuation, affordable loss, causation, entrepreneurial decision-making, start-up ventures

Introduction

Financing decisions are a crucial element of venture success and an "important component of business strategy as they deal with the means of acquiring resources needed to realise the strategy" (Kotey, 1999, p. 12). Without adequate financial resources, business growth is constrained and is often a major cause of business failure. Finance is a contentious issue for entrepreneurs, not least because to many, it means a loss of control, yet with inadequate finance, ventures may never reach their full potential.

In comparison to corporate finance, entrepreneurial financing literature is still very much underdeveloped (Denis, 2004). The existing literature is largely dominated by venture capital and private equity, and more recently, crowdfunding (Cumming & Johan, 2017). Findings from small business studies are often generalised to entrepreneurs implying that small business owners share similar characteristics as start-up entrepreneurs. For example, small firm entrepreneurs prefer to use internal sources (i.e. cash savings and retained earnings) as their most preferred funding source (Hamilton & Fox, 1998) since this inhibited owner independence the least. Yet in contrast, Gundry and Welsch (2001) found that high-growth oriented entrepreneurs are significantly more likely to search for financing. Although

Sussie Morrish, Business School, University of Canterbury

https://doi.org/10.1515/9783110726312-005

there is an abundance of studies in venture financing, only few specifically investigated the financing preferences of specific types of entrepreneurs such as novice, serial and portfolio entrepreneurs. However, there is evidence that in comparison to others, portfolio entrepreneurs are not averse to shared ownership (Morrish, 2008), therefore may not be too concerned about control. For example, in comparison to novice and serial entrepreneurs, they are more likely to take on partners when establishing and owning businesses (Kolvereid & Bullvag, 1993). They are also likely to use multiple sources for finance during the launch of their businesses (Westhead & Birley 1993; Westhead and Wright (1998). These sources ranged from personal savings, to family, friends and even from suppliers and customers. These are also likely to continue on an ongoing basis as an operational strategy.

Kotey (1999) argues that entrepreneurial values and goals influence strategic financing decisions and suggests that debt users are low in entrepreneurial values and unaware of the risk of losing control at high debt levels. In contrast, debt avoiders pose low risk but fear loss of control of their business. She suggests that debt and equity users are cautious risk calculators, therefore pose the lowest risk to lenders. They also have the highest level of financial planning which probably accounts for them being low risk borrowers. Given this argument, debt users as opposed to debt avoiders would be attractive borrowers to finance institutions if there was preference for external financing. Based on this argument, entrepreneurs come with different financing-preference profiles and best positioned along a continuum where debt avoiders occupy one end and users the other. An entrepreneur can be at any point on this continuum as determined by the proportion of their debt use at any given situation. Moreover, the question is – what are the bases for an entrepreneur's financial decision-making?

The answer to this question may be explained by effectuation, a concept that has gained popularity in the last two decades (Sarasvathy, 2001). The inverse of causation, effectuation is a collection of non-predictive strategies that are primarily means (instead of goal) driven. Based largely on the work of Sarasvathy (2001) and originally developed with Simon (Sarasvathy & Simon, 2000), effectuation logic was originally conceptualized based on data from 27 expert entrepreneurs. These data demonstrated that 75% of the time, 63% of the participants preferred to use effectual (instead of causal) reasoning to create markets for new products. Where causation focuses on the specific end-goal that guides the accumulation of means, effectuation focuses on the means that may result in any one of the many probable ends (Sarasvathy, 2001). This chapter specifically looks at the role of effectuation in entrepreneurial financial decision-making.

Literature review

Effectuation logic

Effectuation is a dynamic and interactive process of creating new artifacts in the world. Effectual reasoning is a type of human problem solving that takes the future as fundamentally unpredictable, yet controllable through human action; the environment as constructible through choice; and goals as negotiated residuals of stakeholder commitments rather than as pre-existent preference orderings.[1]

Effectuation is a problem-solving logic in a fundamentally unpredictable future where decision makers draw on their given means (such as attributes, skills, and networks) in order to shape or control an outcome (Morrish, 2009). Entrepreneurs constantly operate in uncertain environments where it is not usually possible to predict the future. This is especially true with highly innovative offerings where demand for a product is almost impossible to ascertain. Effectuation logic offers an alternative course to the widely taught causation thinking, where decision makers start with pre-determined goals (for example, specific rate of return, number of units to sell, and market share targets) and gather needed resources (e.g., seek financial input) to achieve that goal.

In effectual thinking, the entrepreneur starts with resources available to them where goals are not pre-determined and initial envisioned outcomes may be just be one of multiple possibilities. Sarasvathy (2001) explains the difference with the metaphor of the chef. An artifact (in this case a meal) can be created through one of two processes. In causal thinking, the chef could decide on specific dish/es (pre-determined goal) and gather the ingredients to prepare it/them. By contrast, in effectual mode, the chef starts with what is available in the pantry and sets out to make the meal that could be anything but pre-determined (i.e. based on the ingredients that they find in the pantry). Using Sarasvathy's argument, the available ingredients will dictate the design of the meal. For example, having a roast dinner will depend largely on a combination of meat and vegetables and the cooking appliances available. On the other hand, pasta or rice would result in either a Mediterranean or Asian meal and would require different ways of preparation. Thus, the possibilities are many, but a meal (i.e. product) is still produced.

Entrepreneurs constantly operate in spaces with high levels of uncertainty and where opportunities can materialize. Entrepreneurship "involves the study of sources of opportunities; the processes of discovery, evaluation, and exploitation of opportunities; and the set of individuals who discover, evaluate, and exploit them" (Shane & Venkataraman, 2000, p. 218). Beyond identification of opportunities, entrepreneurs evaluate and decide whether to exploit opportunities (Keh et al., 2002;

---

1 *Source:* http://www.effectuation.org/ retrieved 9/1/2007.

Wood & Williams, 2014). Because entrepreneurs differ in their human capital, this were found to affect their decision-making (Shepherd et al., 2015). They pursue opportunities with consideration for the financial requirements and an assessment of uncertain elements. Where causation would try to eliminate or minimize uncertainty, effectuation makes an asset of uncertainty, thereby eliminating the need to overcome it (Sarasvathy, 2003). Entrepreneurial opportunity is the core of entrepreneurship where the future is still "to be" (Shane, 2000, p. 451) and is evolving (Alvarez, et al., 2010), therefore, this opportunity carries an element of uncertainty.

Many scholars suggest that entrepreneurs rely on biases and heuristics (Busenitz & Barney, 1997; Hayward, et al., 2006; Kahneman, et al., 1982). As such, they are unable to apply rational decision-making models (Kahneman, et al., 1982). However, Alvarez, et al., (2010) suggest that they can adopt decision-making processes that identifies informational bounds so that rational decisions can develop over time. These potentially incremental decision-making approaches can range from bricolage (Baker & Nelson, 2005) to Bayesian updating (Bayes, 1764). They may also apply the Linblomian science of "muddling through" (Johnston, et al., 2012) or use effectuation logic (Sarasvathy, 2001). All these approaches have implications in entrepreneurial financial decision-making and could be the difference between getting ventures off the ground or not.

Effectuation vs. causation logic

Causal logic provides useful decision criteria to achieve given goals subject to environmental selection in the face of an uncertain future. Effectual logic provides useful design principles for transforming extant environments into new futures in the face of ambiguous goals.
Sarasvathy (2008, p. xvii)

How do firms come to be conceived in someone's mind? Sarasvathy (2001) suggests that before there are products, there is human imagination and before firms and markets, there is human aspiration. Based on effectuation logic, she contends that firms come to be as an outcome of effectual (as opposed to causal) processes. This logic suggests that firm designs are reflections of the entrepreneur's individual situation. In particular, who the entrepreneurs are, what they know and whom they know. In this context, research would bear useful results, if, instead of searching for the ultimate prescription of how to build successful firms or become successful entrepreneurs, researchers asked *"Given who you are, what you know and whom you know, what types of economic and/or social artifacts can you, would you and should you create?"* (Sarasvathy, 2001, p. 258–259). These three categories are the 'means' or resources that entrepreneurs start with, the combination of which determines what types of ideas and opportunities they should pursue. These so-called 'means' reflect the entrepreneur's "own traits, tastes and abilities; the knowledge corridors they are in, and the social networks they are a part of" (Sarasvathy, 2001, p. 250).

These 'means' in another stream of entrepreneurship research are also referred to as human and social capital (Gimeno, et al., 1997; Ucbasaran, et al., 2003a; 2003b). In the effectuation realm, one may argue that these means become the bases for entrepreneurial motivation to gather the required financing resources that leads to venture creation.

To explain what effectuation is, it is necessary to explain what it is not. Put simply, it is the inverse of causation. Where causation is based on the logic of prediction that purports "to the extent that we can predict the future, we can control it," effectuation thinking is based on the logic of control – "that is to the extent that you can control the future, you do not need to predict it" (Sarasvathy, 2001, p. 252). Effectual logic holds that the future is shaped by human action (the entrepreneur's) and is concerned with controlling the future rather than predicting an uncertain one. Sarasvathy argues that human life after all is not easily analyzed or predicted, rather it is seized and exploited. Where causal logic would drive the entrepreneur to predict how it will capture the market space, effectual logic sees many different outcomes – one of which could become reality depending on how the actors play it.

Effectuation processes therefore provide a valuable means to analyze the spheres of human action, while also affecting business decisions (such as financing) in a positive way, allowing for one or more possible effects irrespective of the generalised goal with which one started. In addition, the adoption of effectuation within entrepreneurial settings means the decision-maker can change goals and even shape and construct them over time, making use of contingencies as they arise, hence that ability to control the future rather than predict it and this includes a firm's financial position.

As developed by Sarasvathy (2001), the core principles of effectual logic embody this logic of control. The notions of affordable loss (rather than expected gains), partners rather than competitive analyses and leveraging contingencies rather than avoiding them are subsumed in the five basic effectuation principles that distinguish causal from effectual reasoning.

Affordable loss (Risk a little, fail cheap)

Whereas causal rationality focuses on expected returns, effectuation generally emphasizes affordable loss in a 'zero resources to market' attitude such that given a new product idea, effectuators try to find the customers first instead of setting returns-related goals such as market shares or return on investments. This principle is directly relevant to entrepreneurial financing as it concerns financial considerations that could determine the future of the venture.

"Affordable loss involves decision-makers estimating what they might be able to put at risk and determining what they are willing to lose in order to follow a course of action" (Dew et al., 2009, p. 105). This principle relates to the concept of opportunity cost in economics and highlights what the entrepreneur can afford and willing to lose instead of the causal approach of potential return. When the opportunity cost of an action is low, entrepreneurs tend to engage in entrepreneurial activities (Amit et al., 1995). Further, they note that those earning less than the average salaries in bigger firms, quickly find it attractive to leave their job for a business start-up. Surprisingly, this is consistent with a proposition from Dew et al. (2009, p. 116) that "[w]eakly-coupled forms of payment will raise a potential entrepreneur's level of affordable loss and, therefore, increase both the likelihood of taking the plunge and the ability to take it." When an employee is earning low, it is easier to leave that paid job because the potential entrepreneur regards leaving that job with its income as an affordable loss.

Martina (2019) found that affordable loss is at the interface of ability and willingness with loss aversion acting as the mechanism that activates change from abilities to willingness. The loss aversion literature suggests that people are more concerned with wealth reduction than making gains (Thaler et al., 1997). Loss aversion from prospect theory provides another perspective that could also help to illuminate the rationale behind the principle of affordable loss. For example, social structure loss resulting from shocks can trigger a behavioural search for reasonable gain, which could eventually lead to the initiation of a new business (George et al., 2016). As stressed by Sarasvathy (2014), the two components of affordable loss are ability and willingness, which are connected to the concept of loss aversion from prospect theory (Martina, 2019).

There is literature that measures affordable loss as sub-dimension of effectual decision-making. For example, when projects are executed with a high level of innovation, Brettel et al. (2012) found that affordable loss is positively related to R&D output or efficiency. There are mixed outcomes with respect to the relationship between affordable loss and venture performance. While Smolka et al. (2018) found that affordable loss exerts a negative influence on venture performance, others found a significant positive relationship between affordable loss and venture performance (Cai et al., 2016; Roach et al., 2016). Having analysed 94 variables from 48 articles, Read et al. (2009) report a strong relationship between all effectuation sub-constructs and firm performance except affordable loss. In another study, Deligianni et al. (2017) report that except for affordable loss, all other effectuation sub-dimension have a positive interaction effect on the relationship between product diversification and performance. Of all the effectuation principles, affordable loss appears to be the most relevant to entrepreneurial financing such that effectual entrepreneurs are more likely to start ventures in innovative and creative ways without fear of financial loss. This could lead to entrepreneurs trialling multiple pathways that they would otherwise not take for fear of loss.

Bird-in-hand principle (Means-driven)

This principle originated from the notion that a bird-in-hand is worth more than a thousand in the bush. This tenet emphasises that entrepreneurs can create an effect from the resources already within their reach. Every entrepreneur has three kinds of means (Sarasvathy, 2001) to draw on when making decisions. Their behaviour is embedded in their characteristics, traits and abilities, formed through societal interactions (Sarasvathy, 2008) and in a manner relevant to their identity (Gruber & MacMillan, 2017). "Founders' identities adjust as they experience periods of pragmatic deference, contestation and domination by an in-group that moves increasingly towards identity homophily" (Baker et al., 2017, p. 2381). "Who I am" can be a ladder that connects the aspiring entrepreneur to the point of "who I want to be" that could be realized if they are able to gather the financial requirements for their venture.

Some scholars argue that entrepreneur's primary concern is raising fund (Cowling et al., 2012; Fraser et al., 2015) to achieve their pre-determined goals. Effectual entrepreneurs prioritise the resources they have and tailor their business in accordance with means readily available to them. Thus, a start-up entrepreneur may decide to start small and generate revenue quickly instead of seeking external investors. They may do this by leveraging their knowledge and experience (what I know). Sarasvathy (2008) argues that the identity of the entrepreneur depends on and is transformed by their knowledge. Knowledge and experience comprise intellectual capital and positively impacts organisational performance (Ulrich, 1997). The ability to recognise opportunity depends on the level of information that is already possessed (Shane, 2000) influenced by prior knowledge and experience. Knowledge in particular is essential to innovation and creativity, which in return are necessary to entrepreneurship (Caiazza et al., 2019; Qian, 2018) with formal or informal knowledge linked to entrepreneurial success (Alvarez & Busenitz, 2001). This success may be attributed to education as it equips and enhances entrepreneurs' cognitive skills used in the evaluation of entrepreneurial opportunities (Jiménez et al., 2015) and the subsequent assessment of financial requirements and where and how they can be sourced.

These sources may come from the entrepreneur's network (whom I know). During venture initiation and development 'whom I know' denotes the entrepreneur's social capital (Sarasvathy, 2008). There is a large body of literature on the role of social and business network in entrepreneurship (Chetty et al., 2015; Ciszewska-Mlinaric et al., 2016; Engel et al., 2017; Fernández-Pérez et al., 2016; Galkina & Chetty, 2015; Kalinic et al., 2014; Laine & Galkina, 2017; Vasilchenko & Morrish, 2011;). Indeed, networks are vital to the entrepreneurial process where personal and extended networks (e.g. friends, family, investors, suppliers, creditors, business partners, and trade associations) could be helpful in the pursuit of opportunities outside the reach of the entrepreneur's resources (Dubini & Aldrich,1991). An entrepreneur's networks can provide information, access to skills, knowledge and social legitimacy, reputation and credibility, and most important of all, access to finance (Klyver et al., 2008). These resources are essential at every stage of the entrepreneurial process. For example, Jenssen & Koenig (2002) found that the strength of network ties will determine what kind of resources the entrepreneur gets suggesting that strong ties are important channels for crucial information while weak ties provide access to funding at the start-up stage. In the same vein, Ostgaard & Birley (1996) note that access to finance is not only useful for venture initiation but also the growth and development of the firm. Thus, their findings confirmed a positive relationship between networks and venture growth.

Lemonade principle (Acknowledging the unexpected)

Meaning one should make the most out of the unexpected, the principle is inspired by the well-known saying "If life throws you lemons, make lemonade" "[T]he lemonade principle is at the heart of entrepreneurial expertise – the ability to turn the unexpected into the valuable and the profitable" (Sarasvathy, 2008, p. 90). Instead of wasting valuable time thinking about overcoming unexpected events, entrepreneurs should take advantage of these surprise occurrences as a window of opportunity. This principle encourages the entrepreneur to focus on the situation at hand rather than thinking about how to overcome unexpected occurrences in the future (Sarasvathy, 2008). For example, the venture initiation process is complex and filled with uncertainty (Packard et al., 2017). The key to successfully launching a business venture is flexibility and adapting to events as they occur (Fisher, 2012). By not holding tightly to pre-set goals, the entrepreneur can use his/her set of means to create something from evolving opportunities (Duening et al., 2012) including financing opportunities that may arise from serendipitous events (Vasilchenko and Morrish, 2011)

   This principle proposes leveraging contingencies rather than avoiding them. Causation centers on the exploitation of existing knowledge (of firms, markets, customers, etc.) and using this to pursue pre-determined goals. In effectuation, entrepreneurs explore contingencies such that new business ideas are launched before worrying about who the customer is. In a 'surprise me' attitude, entrepreneurs leverage off the contingencies that arise from a business venture believing that not all surprises are bad. It is built on the acceptance that one will never know what could become of an idea unless it is out there. Many great entrepreneurial firms are in fact a product of contingencies – behind which are individuals forging ahead despite early setbacks. Nowhere is this perhaps more pronounced than in the current pandemic setting. Despite putting contingency plans in place, a significant number of businesses were surprised by the magnitude of the event. Moreover, while many businesses struggle, others are surviving, thriving and generating significant revenue in the process. In these settings, alert entrepreneurs are starting up new ventures or adopting new business models. The availability of online platforms coupled with the readiness of markets to adapt to the digital landscape has facilitated the proliferation of online-based ventures that do not require massive financing.

Crazy quilt principle (Alliances and pre-commitments)

Contrary to the conventional way of detailed competitive analyses, the effectual entrepreneur seeks ways to form strategic alliances with stakeholders, thereby reducing or eliminating the uncertainty at the point of entry (Sarasvathy, 2008). These stakeholders are seen as co-creators of value (Brodie et al., 2019). Effectuators are able to partner with willing stakeholders within their network because they have no predetermined goals (Sarasvathy et al., 2014). Forming partnerships with stakeholders such as suppliers, customers or investors, reduces risk as the burden is shared with effectual partnerships. Notwithstanding, they also share success and the benefit with them (Chandler et al., 2011). They show their commitment by bringing their capabilities, skills, resources and experience to the business resulting in access to low-cost resources and new means (Sarasvathy 2008). Effectual entrepreneurs manage contingencies and opportunities with information gathered from stakeholders (Brettel et al. 2012). Knowing fully well that the environment is dynamic with unexpected contingencies, stakeholders prepare for the worst by investing only resources that they can afford to lose (Read et al., 2016). Effectuation reasoning is built on strategic alliances and partnerships with the entrepreneur's networks (i.e. customers, suppliers, and business partners). These networks can be potential sources of entrepreneurial finance. For example, the founder of a New Zealand start-up company 42 Below Vodka (Geoff Ross) relied on his network in the music and fashion industry to invest in his venture that led to an IPO within eight years from start-up before eventually selling to Bacardi International (Morrish & Deacon 2011).

Pilot in the plane principle (Non-predictive)

A causal model tries to predict the future by obtaining and analysing market information whereas effectuation encourages the concept of control. Effectuation highlights the non-predictive focus on the controllable parts of an uncertain future. As Sarasvathy (2008, p. 91) points out: "to the extent that entrepreneurs can control the future, the future does not need to be predicted". To mitigate uncertainty, effectuators concentrate on controlling the future by embracing a logic that refuses to centre on prediction. Another key feature of this principle is flexibility. An effectual entrepreneur can exercise control in a dynamic environment by adapting their resources to the current reality, much like the pilot in the plane can better manage turbulence with his knowledge and skills than the pre-programmed auto-pilot. In the 42 Below Vodka example, critics argued that New Zealand does not have a reputation in producing vodka but Ross exploited New Zealand's clean and green image to produce a product that while not usually associated with New Zealand, is made from ingredients (wheat and water) that New Zealand can supply in the highest quality. The founder exerted control throughout the process from originally distilling in the couple's garage and hand delivering cases to local bars to handpicking the investors. Much like a pilot, he took control of the journey from start-up until the venture was sold to one of the largest liquor companies in the world.

Effectuation and expertise

Perry et al. (2012) suggest that our understanding of entrepreneurial principles witnessed a dynamic shift with the introduction of effectuation that presents a more pragmatic view of the entrepreneurial process including financing. In contrast to the conventional understanding of entrepreneurship from the trait perspective, effectuation likened the entrepreneurial process to the development of expertise (Dew et al., 2015; Sarasvathy, 2001). Effectual logic promotes the co-creation of non-existing market in alliance with relevant stakeholders. Effectuation is a suitable theoretical basis for investigating entrepreneurial finance because it relates well to expertise. For example, habitual entrepreneurs (i.e. portfolio and serial) can be regarded as experts having repeatedly formed and created business ventures. Read and Sarasvathy (2005) found four approaches to the development of expertise that are also driven by effectual processes: *individual differences, knowledge structures, experience and deliberate practice.*

In particular, the deliberate practice approach creates an interesting facet to entrepreneurial finance since the repeated act of creating additional ventures can be regarded as such. According to the deliberate practice view, individuals that engage in deliberate practice acquire superior knowledge structures, and from that, derive superior expert performance (Ericsson, et al., 1993). Literature on deliberate practice identifies five necessary requirements that together form the foundation upon which one can build superior expert performance. These are a) *motivation* (a larger and instrumental objective to motivate themselves as deliberate practice itself is not inherently motivating), b) *understandability* (decomposing into component pieces to be completely understood), c) *feedback* (in order to upgrade performance), d) *repetition* (dedication and motivation is what separates experts from those with mere experience) and e) *fit* (with ability). From an entrepreneurial finance perspective, expert entrepreneurs develop a set of financing strategies both at the individual, firm and industry levels over time. In these scenarios, habitual entrepreneurs (e.g. serial and portfolio entrepreneurs (Macmillan, 1986) acquire experience and in a position to judge what worked and potentially ensure superior venture performance for subsequent ventures. In most cases, they would have created networks (e.g. entrepreneurial teams) that they can pull together as sources of financing thereby bypassing established and formalized financial institutions.

Read and Sarasvathy (2005) developed a set of observations based on theoretical parallels between 'experts in general' and 'expert entrepreneurs' and propose that it takes 10 years for a novice to ascend to the rank of an expert, a phenomenon referred to as the 10-year rule. In exploring the expert literature, they made four basic observations to parallel effectuation. Firstly, *experts eschew prediction* (expert entrepreneurs reject the use of predictive information) and secondly, *experts focus on can* (expert entrepreneurs prefer to do the things they can to control those parts of the environment they deem controllable). Thirdly, *experts employ means-based action* (experts are tethered to their means and flexible on goals) and finally, *experts leverage contingencies* (contingency, as opposed to planning, provides expert entrepreneurs with a wider range of viable strategy choices). Experts generally make decisions based on their own unique expertise. Experts like portfolio entrepreneurs engage in effectual decision-making that is more creative and innovative because it looks at the means one has and allows that to decide the end goal which may change several times (Morrish, 2009). An entrepreneur of 10 years will be guided by heurestics drawn from experience. When they need to raise additional capital or start a new venture, they draw on this collective experience. The strategies may be fluid and can flex as and when the opportunity presents. Instead of inviting angel investors or seeking venture capital, they may opt to release equity through profit sharing schemes with key employees or suppliers and customers.

Effectuation and venture performance

Over a decade ago, Read et al. (2009) conducted a meta-analysis to connect some of the principles of effectuation with venture performance. At that time, none of the effectual principle constructs were direct measures of any elements of effectuation. Since then, some studies have examined venture performance with respect to effectuation designed measures (An et al., 2019; Brettel et al., 2012; Cai, et al., 2016; Ciszewska-Mlinaric et al., 2016; Matalamäki et al., 2017).

Originally launched to reduce the uncertainties in the start-up process, Sarasvathy's effectuation logic has evolved, having been applied to venture performance (Cai et al., 2016; Read et al., 2009; Roach et al., 2016). A recent systematic literature review concluded that there are preliminary pieces of evidence that confirm a positive relationship between effectuation and venture performance (Grégoire & Cherchem, 2020). In the same vein, Read et al. (2009), note that three effectuation principles (means, partnerships and leverage contingency) have a significant positive impact on venture performance. Some of these empirical studies examined venture performance in relation to other firms (Smolka et al., 2018), while others measured entrepreneurs' perception of their performance in areas like sales, profit and market share growth over time (Cai et al., 2016; Deligianni et al., 2017; Laskovaia et al., 2017). Other studies measured performance indices such as sales growth, profitability and employment growth (Futterer, et al., 2017; Roach et al., 2016).

Overall, there appears to be a clear relationship between effectuation and venture performance from all of the studies mentioned above, no matter how performance was measured. For example, Smolka et al. (2018) surveyed 1,453 respondents from 25 countries and discovered that effectual logic exerts a positive impact on venture performance. Similarly, Laskovaia et al. (2017) found the same when they examined the relationship from a sample of 3411 of new venture created by student entrepreneurs from 24 countries.

Given the above findings, how does effectuation influence venture performance? It appears that effectual entrepreneurs achieve superior performance in much the same way as traditional venture investors. In extrapolating to the effectuation and financing argument, we can assume that effectuators do not necessarily need external investment. Using their own funds and leveraging their knowledge, experience and networks are suitable substitutes to overcome inadequate financial resources.

Effectuation and start-up venture financing

Entrepreneurial activities such as financing involve the acquisition and allocation of money resources, do not (and should not) necessarily affect venture-outcomes. At the start-up stage of new ventures, there is typically little or "[no] regard to resources they currently control" (Stevenson & Jarillo, 1990, p. 23). At this stage, bootstrapping is often practised and new ventures have very limited resources to 'start' with. If at all, financing activities are secondary variables that can be used to explain deviations in venture performance after the fact. For instance, the lack of money resources may affect the range and urgency of activities when gathering the necessary means to pursue a business prospect. It may affect the predisposition to the affordable loss principle (Sarasvathy, 2001), thereby affecting the speed and extent by which the intended outcome for the venture is attained.

As the venture enters a growth phase, it is often constrained by lack of resources. In the hotel industry for example, the financing requirement is substantial and meeting growth targets can be very challenging. How should entrepreneurs finance this phase? Growth can slide back when external shocks (disasters and crises) occur. Financing can be sought from institutions or by bringing in equity partners from their networks. This is usually the case at the early stages of entrepreneurial careers or when seeking to grow faster. More established entrepreneurs who have built wealth tend to structure their business so that a holding company owns the other businesses and when finance is required, the holding company provides this (Morrish, 2008). Thus, some form of internal financing is preferred.

Future research agenda

First introduced in 2001, effectuation is now a well-established concept in entrepreneurial decision making. While much theorizing has been attempted, some scholars argue against effectuation's elevation to a theory. For example, Arend, et al. (2015; 2016) suggest revisiting and tightening the units, laws and bounds of effectuation. Before it can evolve to a theory, they propose the 3E framework (experience, explain, establish) be applied to effectuation research.

In the context of this chapter, the "affordable loss" principle is very relevant. One of the most critical decisions an entrepreneur has to make relate to financing. However, while a good body of literature is forming, there is still much that is not well- articulated by the effectuation logic in terms of entrepreneurial finance. Much of this relates to what the most useful sources of entrepreneurial finance are beyond general bootstrapping. Effectuation holds that start-up entrepreneurs should "come up with the cheapest option or come up with creative ways of doing things at little cost and risk to themselves" (Read, et al., 2016, p. 112). Further investigation into this practice will widen our understanding of what these options might look like. With the notion that investment is tightly coupled with what one can afford to lose, the question of "affordable loss threshold" is an important line of investigation. At what point does an entrepreneur take financial risk to see the potential of the venture materialize? In the same vein, what are the different contexts by which financing risk can be realistically absorbed and tolerated by entrepreneurs and would be investors?

Entrepreneurial decision-making is the core of entrepreneurial action. Entrepreneurship researchers have focused on the human element of the entrepreneurial process that is beset with uncertainty (Leyden & Link, 2015). Entrepreneurs assume decision-making responsibilities in the face of these uncertainties (Packard et al., 2017). Much of previous research into entrepreneurial decision-making has focused on entry decisions (Engel et al., 2017; Reymen et al., 2015) and exit decisions (DeTienne, 2010; Hsu et al., 2016). Additionally, there is myriad of literature on opportunity assessment and exploitation decisions (Maine et al., 2014; Wood & Williams, 2014). Yet other scholars advocated for investigation of decisions beyond entry such as growth as the "first and foremost strategic decision all entrepreneurs must make" (Wright & Stigliani, 2013, p. 5). Matalamäki et al. (2017) found that effectuation is the main decision-making logic that affects the growth process in established businesses. A better understanding of growth decisions at various stages of the entrepreneurial process and how to finance this activity will help in our understanding of the interplay between financing and effectuation. Finally, a critical exploration of all the effectuation principles as they relate to entrepreneurial financing decisions would greatly enhance theory building and provide practical actions for entrepreneurs grappling with entrepreneurial finance.

Conclusion and discussion

In this chapter, we explore the ways in which effectuation logic impacts entrepreneurial finance decision-making. As an alternative decision-making logic to causation, effectuation and its underlying principles offer a practical guide to the accumulation and use of resources necessary at the various stages of the entrepreneurial process.

At the start-up phase, financing decisions can be guided by the means-driven bird in hand principle where entrepreneurs' identity (who I am), knowledge (what I know) and networks (whom I know) are leveraged to secure much needed requirements where constraints are in place. For example, Morrish (2009) found strong evidence that effectuation was applied by expert entrepreneurs at the early stages of the venture more predominantly than the later stages.

The chapter explored other strategies that entrepreneurs use to finance their ventures. A key issue is financing operations and growth of individual businesses. Entrepreneurs that are in the advanced stages of their careers no longer have the burden of debt and have the luxury of being able to finance internally. Those that still need external financing prefer to either release some shareholding by bringing in partners and co-investors or borrow from banks if necessary. With the proliferation of incubators and dragon's den events, we see entrepreneurs seeking investments to finance the next stage (often growth) of their business. While this appears to be a phenomenon for early stage entrepreneurs and founders, Morrish (2009) did find that more established entrepreneurs have an aversion to venture capital despite having connections with venture capitalists. The same can be said for borrowing money from family. It appears that debt, whether from the bank or family debt is to avoided and if cannot, should be paid off as soon as possible.

In conclusion, financing is a decision entrepreneurs do not take lightly. How and when they take on external finance are contingent on their ability to control the future they imagine for their venture. Using effectuation logic to control rather than predict the future ensures that entrepreneurs and their ventures are able to manage uncertainties and navigate turbulence.

References

Arend, R. J., Sarooghi, H., & Burkemper, A. (2015). Effectuation as ineffectual? Applying the 3E theory-assessment framework to a proposed new theory of entrepreneurship. Academy of management Review, 40(4), 630–651.

Arend, R. J., Sarooghi, H., & Burkemper, A. C. (2016). Effectuation, not being pragmatic or process theorizing, remains ineffectual: Responding to the commentaries. *Academy of Management Review*, 41(3), 549–556.

Alvarez, S. A., & Busenitz, L. W. (2001). The entrepreneurship of resource-based theory. *Entrepreneurship: Concepts, Theory and Perspective, 27*, 207–227.

Alvarez, S. A., Barney, J. B., & Young, S. L. (2010). Debates in entrepreneurship: Opportunity formation and implications for the field of entrepreneurship. In *Handbook of entrepreneurship research* (pp. 23–45). Springer, New York, NY.

Amit, R., Muller, E., & Cockburn, I. (1995). Opportunity costs and entrepreneurial activity. *Journal of Business Venturing, 10(2)*, 95–106.

An, W., Rüling, C. C., Zheng, X., & Zhang, J. (2019). Configurations of effectuation, causation, and bricolage: Implications for firm growth paths. *Small Business Economics.* 1–22.

Baker, T., & Nelson, R. E. (2005). Creating something from nothing: Resource construction through entrepreneurial bricolage. Administrative science quarterly, 50(3), 329–366.

Baker, T., Grimes, M., Hamann, R., Hmieleski, K., Kim, P., Kim, S., Pollock, T. (2017). In the beginning: Identity processes and organizing in multi-founder nascent ventures. *Academy of Management Journal, 60(6)*, 2381–2414.

Bayes, T. (1764). An Essay toward solving a Problem in the Doctrine of Chances. In *Philosophical Transactions of the Royal Society of London, 53*, 370–418. Offprint unchanged, but with title page giving the title as "A Method of Calculating the Exact Probability of All Conclusions founded on Induction."

Brettel, M., Mauer, R., Engelen, A., & Kupper, D. (2012). Corporate effectuation: Entrepreneurial action and its impact on R&D project performance. *Journal of Business Venturing, 27(2)*, 167–184.

Brodie, R. J., Löbler, H., & Fehrer, J. A. (2019). Evolution of service-dominant logic: Towards a paradigm and metatheory of the market and value cocreation? *Industrial Marketing Management, 79*(March), 3–12.

Busenitz, L. W., & Barney, J. B. (1997). Differences between entrepreneurs and managers in large organizations: Biases and heuristics in strategic decision-making. *Journal of business venturing, 12*(1), 9–30.

Cai, L., Guo, R., Fei, Y., & Liu, Z. (2016). Effectuation, exploratory learning and new venture performance: evidence from China. *Journal of Small Business Management, 55(3)*, 388–403.

Caiazza, R., Belitski, M., & Audretsch, D. B. (2019). From latent to emergent entrepreneurship: the knowledge spillover construction circle. *Journal of Technology Transfer*, 1–11.

Chandler, G. N., DeTienne, D. R., McKelvie, A., & Mumford, T. V. (2011). Causation and effectuation processes: A validation study. *Journal of Business Venturing, 26(3)*, 375–390.

Chetty, S., Ojala, A., & Leppäaho, T. (2015). Effectuation and foreign market entry of entrepreneurial firms. *European Journal of Marketing, 49(9–10)*, 1436–1459.

Ciszewska-Mlinaric, M., Obloj, K., & Wasowska, A. (2016). Effectuation and causation: Two decision-making logics of INVs at the early stage of growth and internationalisation. *Journal of East European Management Studies, 21(3)*, 275–297.

Cowling, M., Liu, W., & Ledger, A. (2012). Small business financing in the UK before and during the current financial crisis. *International Small Business Journal, 30(7)*, 778–800.

Cumming, D., & Johan, S. (2017). The problems with and promise of entrepreneurial finance. Strategic Entrepreneurship Journal, *11(3)*, 357–370.

Deligianni, I., Voudouris, I., & Lioukas, S. (2017). Do effectuation processes shape the relationship between product diversification and performance in new ventures? *Entrepreneurship: Theory and Practice, 41(3)*, 349–377.

Denis, D. J. (2004). Entrepreneurial finance: an overview of the issues and evidence. Journal of corporate finance, *10(2)*, 301–326.

Dew, N., Read, S., Sarasvathy, S. D., & Wiltbank, R. (2009). Effectual versus predictive logics in entrepreneurial decision-making: Differences between experts and novices *Journal of Business Venturing, 24(4)*, 287–309.

Dew, N., Read, S., Sarasvathy, S. D., & Wiltbank, R. (2015). Entrepreneurial expertize and the use of control. *Journal of Business Venturing Insights*, 4, 30–37.

DeTienne, DR (2010). Entrepreneurial exit as a critical component of the entrepreneurial process: Theoretical development. *Journal of Business Venturing*, 25 (2), 203–215.

Dubini, P., & Aldrich, H. (1991). Personal and extended networks are central to the entrepreneurial process. *Journal of Business Venturing*, 6(5), 305–313.

Duening, T., Shepherd, M., & Czaplewski, A. (2012). How entrepreneurs think: Why effectuation and effectual logic may be the key to successful enterprise entrepreneurship. *International Journal of Innovation Science*.

Engel, Y., Burg, E. van, Kleijn, E., & Khapova, S. N. (2017). Past career in future thinking: how career management practices shape entrepreneurial decision making. *Strategic Entrepreneurship Journal*, 11(2), 122–144.

Ericsson, K. A., Krampe, R. T., & Tesch-Römer, C. (1993). The role of deliberate practice in the acquisition of expert performance. *Psychological review*, 100(3), 363.

Fernández-Pérez, V., García-Morales, V. J., & Pullés, D. C. (2016). Entrepreneurial decision-making, external social networks and strategic flexibility: The role of CEOs' cognition. *European Management Journal*, 34(3), 296–309.

Fisher, G. (2012). Effectuation, causation, and bricolage: A behavioral comparison of emerging theories in entrepreneurship research. *Entrepreneurship: Theory and Practice, 36(5)*, 1019–1051.

Fraser, S., Bhaumik, S. K., & Wright, M. (2015). What do we know about entrepreneurial finance and its relationship with growth? *International Small Business Journal: Researching Entrepreneurship, 33(1)*, 70–88.

Futterer, F., Schmidt, J., & Heidenreich, S. (2017). Effectuation or causation as the key to corporate venture success? Investigating effects of entrepreneurial behaviors on business model innovation and venture performance. *Long Range Planning, 51(1)*, 64–81.

Galkina, T., & Chetty, S. (2015). Effectuation and networking of internationalizing SMEs. *Management International Review*, 55(5), 647–676.

George, G., Reddi Kotha, Parikh, P., Alnuaimi, T., & Bahaj, A. S. (2016). Social structure, reasonable gain, and entrepreneurship in Africa. *Strategic Management Journal*, 37(6), 1118–1131.

Gimeno, J., Folta, T. B., Cooper, A. C., & Woo, C. Y. (1997). Survival of the fittest? Entrepreneurial human capital and the persistence of underperforming firms. *Administrative science quarterly*, 750–783.

Grégoire, D. A., & Cherchem, N. (2020). A structured literature review and suggestions for future effectuation research. *Small Business Economics, 54(3)*, 621–639.

Gruber, M., & MacMillan, I. (2017). Entrepreneurial behavior: A reconceptualization and extension based on social identity theory. *Strategic Entrepreneurship Journal*, 286 (special), 271–286.

Gundry, L. K., & Welsch, H. P. (2001). The ambitious entrepreneur: High growth strategies of women-owned enterprises. *Journal of business venturing*, 16(5), 453–470.

Hamilton, Robert T., and Mark A. Fox. "The financing preferences of small firm owners." *International Journal of Entrepreneurial Behavior & Research* (1998).

Hayward, M. L., Shepherd, D. A., & Griffin, D. (2006). A hubris theory of entrepreneurship. *Management science, 52*(2), 160–172.

Hsu, D. K., Wiklund, J., Anderson, S. E., & Coffey, B. S. (2016). Entrepreneurial exit intentions and the business-family interface. *Journal of Business Venturing*, 31(6), 613–627.

Jenssen, J. I., & Koenig, H. F. (2002). The effect of social networks on resource access and business start-ups. *European Planning Studies*, 10(8), 1039–1046.

Jiménez, A., Palmero-Cámara, C., González-Santos, M. J., González-Bernal, J., & Jiménez-Eguizábal, J. A. (2015). The impact of educational levels on formal and informal entrepreneurship. *BRQ Business Research Quarterly*, 18(3), 204–212.

Johnston, W., Low, B., & Wilson, T. L. (2012). Scientific muddling: Decision making through a Lindblomian lens. *Journal of Business Research*, *65*(6), 717–719.

Kahneman, D., Slovic, S. P., Slovic, P., & Tversky, A. (Eds.). (1982). *Judgment under uncertainty: Heuristics and biases*. Cambridge university press.

Kalinic, I., Sarasvathy, S. D., & Forza, C. (2014). 'Expect the unexpected': Implications of effectual logic on the internationalization process. *International Business Review*, *23*(3), 635–647.

Keh, H. T., Foo, M. Der, & Lim, B. C. (2002). Opportunity evaluation under risky conditions: The cognitive processes of entrepreneurs. *Entrepreneurship Theory and Practice*, *27*(2), 125–148.

Klyver, K., Hindle, K., & Meyer, D. (2008). Influence of social network structure on entrepreneurship participation-a study of 20 national cultures. *International Entrepreneurship and Management Journal*, *4*(3), 331–347.

Kolvereid, L. & Bullvag, E. (1993). Novices versus experienced business founders: An exploratory investigation. *Entrepreneurship Research: Global Perspectives*. I. MacMillan and S. Birley. Amsterdam, Elsevier Science: 275–285.

Kotey, B. (1999). "Debt financing and factors internal to the business." International Small Business Journal *17*(3): 11–26.

Laine, I., & Galkina, T. (2017). The interplay of effectuation and causation in decision making: Russian SMEs under institutional uncertainty. *International Entrepreneurship and Management Journal*, *13*(3), 905–941.

Laskovaia, A., Shirokova, G., & Morris, M. H. (2017). National culture, effectuation, and new venture performance: global evidence from student entrepreneurs. *Small Business Economics*, *49*(3), 687–709.

Leyden, D. P., & Link, A. N. (2015). Toward a theory of the entrepreneurial process. *Small Business Economics*, *44*(3), 475–484.

Maine, E., Soh, P.-H., & Dos Santos, N. (2014). The role of entrepreneurial decision-making in opportunity creation and recognition. *Technovation, 39–40*, 53–72.

Martina, R. A. (2019). Toward a theory of affordable loss. *Small Business Economics*, 1–24.

Matalamäki, M., Vuorinen, T., Varamäki, E., & Sorama, K. (2017). Business growth in established companies: Roles of effectuation and causation. *Journal of Enterprising Culture*, *25*(2), 123–148.

MacMillan, I.C. (1986). To really learn about entrepreneurship, let's study habitual entrepreneurs *Journal of Business Venturing, 1*(3) (1986), pp. 241–243

Morrish, S. C. (2008). *Portfolio entrepreneurs: Pathways to growth and development*. [Doctoral thesis] University of Canterbury. https://ir.canterbury.ac.nz/handle/10092/878

Morrish, S. (2009). Portfolio entrepreneurs: an effectuation approach to multiple venture development. *Journal of Research in Marketing and Entrepreneurship*.

Morrish, S. C. & Deacon, J. H. (2011) A Tale of Two Spirits: Entrepreneurial Marketing at 42 Below Vodka and Penderyn Whisky, Journal of Small Business & Entrepreneurship, *24*(1), 113–124, DOI: 10.1080/08276331.2011.10593529

Ostgaard, T. A., & Birley, S. (1996). New venture growth and personal networks. *Journal of Business Research*, *36*(1), 37–50.

Packard, M. D., Clark, B. B., & Kleinc, P. G. (2017). Uncertainty types and transitions in the entrepreneurial process. *Organization Science*, *28*(5), 840–856.

Perry, J. T., Chandler, G. N., & Markova, G. (2012). Entrepreneurial Effectuation: A Review and Suggestions for Future Research. *Entrepreneurship: Theory and Practice*, *36*(4), 837–861.

Qian, H. (2018). Knowledge-based regional economic development: A synthetic review of knowledge spillovers, entrepreneurship, and entrepreneurial ecosystems. *Economic Development Quarterly*, *32*(2), 163–176.

Knowing what to do and doing what you know: Effectuation as a form of entrepreneurial expertise. *The Journal of Private Equity, 9(1)*, 45–62.

Read, S., & Sarasvathy, S. D. (2005). Knowing what to do and doing what you know: Effectuation as a form of entrepreneurial expertise. *The Journal of Private Equity, 9(1)*, 45–62.

Read, S., Song, M., & Smit, W. (2009). A meta-analytic review of effectuation and venture performance. *Journal of Business Venturing, 24*, 573–587.

Read, S., Sarasvathy, S., Dew, N., Wiltbank, R., & Ohlsson, A. V. 2010. Effectual entrepreneurship. London: Taylor & Francis.

Read, S., Sarasvathy, S., Dew, N., & Wiltbank, R. (2016). *Effectual entrepreneurship*. Routledge.

Reymen, I. M. M. J., Andries, P., Berends, H., Mauer, R., Stephan, U., & van Burg, E. (2015). Understanding dynamics of strategic decision making in venture creation: A process study of effectuation and causation. *Strategic Entrepreneurship Journal, 9(4)*, 351–379.

Roach, D. C., Ryman, J. A., & Makani, J. (2016). Effectuation, innovation and performance in SMEs: An empirical study. *European Journal of Innovation Management, 19(2)*, 214–238.

Sarasvathy, S. D., & Simon, H. A. (2000). Near decomposability, effectuation, and the speed of growth of entrepreneurial firms. Presented at *"The first annual technology entrepreneurship research policy conference"*, May 19 and 20, 2000. Robert H. Smith School of Business, University of Maryland. Available at www.effectuation.org

Sarasvathy, S. D. (2001). Causation and effectuation: Toward a theoretical shift from economic inevitability to entrepreneurial contingency. *The Academy of Management Review, 26(2)*, 243–263.

Sarasvathy, S. D. (2003). Entrepreneurship as a science of the artificial. Journal of Economic Psychology, 24(2), 203–220.

Sarasvathy, S.D. (2008). *Effectuation: Elements of entrepreneurial expertise*. Cheltenham, England: Elgar

Sarasvathy, S. D. (2014). The downside of entrepreneurial opportunities. *Management, 17(4)*, 305–315.

Sarasvathy, S., Kumar, K., York, J. G., & Bhagavatula, S. (2014). An effectual approach to international entrepreneurship: Overlaps, challenges, and provocative possibilities. *Entrepreneurship Theory and Practice, 38(1)*, 71–93.

Shane, S. (2000). Prior Knowledge and the Discovery of Entrepreneurial Opportunities. *Organization Science, 11(4)*, 448–469.

Shane, S., & Venkataraman, S. (2000). The Promise of Entrepreneurship as a Field of Research. *The Academy of Management Review, 25(1)*, 217.

Shepherd, D. A., Williams, T. A., & Patzelt, H. (2015). Thinking about entrepreneurial decision making: Review and research agenda. *Journal of Management, 41(1)*, 11–46.

Smolka, K. M., Verheul, I., Burmeister–Lamp, K., & Heugens, P. P. (2018). Get it together! Synergistic effects of causal and effectual decision–making logics on venture performance. *Entrepreneurship Theory and Practice, 42(4)*, 571–604.

Stevenson, H.H. and Jarillo, J.C. (1990) A paradigm of entrepreneurship: Entrepreneurial management, *Strategic Management Journal, 11*, 17–27.

Thaler, R. H., Tversky, A., Kahneman, D., & Schwartz, A. (1997). The effect of myopia and loss aversion on risk taking: an experimental test. *The Quarterly Journal of Economics, 112(2)*, 647–661.

Ucbasaran, D., Wright, M., Westhead, P., & Busenitz, L. (2003a). "The impact of entrepreneurial experience on opportunity identification and exploitation: Habitual and novice entrepreneurs." *Cognitive Approaches to Entrepreneruship Research, Advances in entrepreneurship, Firm Emergence and Growth, 6*, 231–263

Ucbasaran, D., Westhead, P., & Wright, M (2003b). "A longitudinal study of habitual entrepreneurs: starters and acquirers." *Entrepreneurship and Regional Development 15*, 207–228.

Ulrich, D. (1997). HR of the future: Conclusions and observations. *Human Resource Management, 36(1)*, 175–179.

Vasilchenko, E., & Morrish, S. (2011). The role of entrepreneurial networks in the exploration and exploitation of internationalization opportunities by information and communication technology firms. *Journal of International Marketing, 19(4)*, 88–105.

Westhead, P., & Birley, S. (1993). "A comparison of new business established by 'novice' and 'habitual' founders in Great Britain." *International Small Business Journal* 12(1): 38–60.

Westhead, P., & Wright, M. (1998b). "Novice, portfolio and serial founders: Are they different?" Journal of Business Venturing 13: 173–204.

Wiltbank, R., Read, S., Dew, N., & Sarasvathy, S. D. (2009). Prediction and control under uncertainty: outcomes in angel investing. *Journal of Business Venturing, 24(2)*, 116–133.

Wood, M. S., & Williams, D. W. (2014). Opportunity evaluation as rule-based decision making. *Journal of Management Studies, 51(4)*, 573–602.

Wright, M., & Stigliani, I. (2013). Entrepreneurship and growth. *International Small Business Journal, 31(1)*, 3–22.

Antonio Malfense Fierro and Peter Rosa

4 Portfolio entrepreneurs: The role of risk

Abstract: Financial portfolio theory suggests that diversifying through establishing a group of businesses may be an important mechanism to manage and spread risk, but empirical entrepreneurship research on portfolio entrepreneurship has failed to adequately identify how this relates to entrepreneurs' actual behaviour. This chapter evaluates the current literature and suggest a future research agenda for exploring the interplay or risk and portfolio entrepreneurship.

Keywords: risk, portfolio entrepreneurship, business groups, diversification, opportunity, uncertainty

Introduction

At its most basic, a business group is defined broadly as a collection of legally independent entities that are bound by formal and informal ties (Granovetter, 1994; Yiu, Lu, Bruton & Hoskisson, 2007), but it usually refers more specifically to a collection of firms linked through common ownership and control (Almeida & Wolfenzon, 2006; Iacobucci, 2002). The group structure, most commonly associated with large corporate firms, has been explained by a diversity of factors (Khanna & Palepu 2000). The business group structure confers advantages through alleviating transaction costs (Leff, 1976, 1978, Rocha 2012); helps provide common norms and integrative codes of behaviour (Granovetter, 1994); offers mechanisms for accruing disproportionate wealth in to the hands of a handful of families through rent-seeking and interlocking directorships based on kinship (Scott, Hughes & Mackenzie, 1980; Encarnation, 1989; Gill, 1999). Business groups can help control diversification, the management and spreading of risk, and provide means to leverage minority shareholders to finance growth (Morck & Young, 2003, 2004; Almeida & Wolfenzon, 2006).

Business groups, however, are also common in the small firms sector (Birley & Westhead, 1993; Kolvereid & Bullvag 1993; Scott & Rosa, 1996; Loiseau, 2001; Lechner & Leyronas, 2009) and they emerge frequently from the growth activities of portfolio entrepreneurs (Rosa, 1998; Westhead & Wright, 1998; Lechner & Leyronas, 2009). A parallel literature on business groups linked with portfolio entrepreneurship has emerged from the 1980s that has not been integrated into the mainstream business group literature, and which suggest entrepreneurial diversification is an important factor linked to the creation and existence of business groups. These studies, unlike in

Antonio Malfense Fierro, Business School, University of Hull
Peter Rosa, Business School, University of Edinburgh

https://doi.org/10.1515/9783110726312-006

most of the research in the management literature, focus on the entrepreneur rather than the firm as the unit of analysis (Rosa, 1998; Iacobucci & Rosa, 2010).

The economic importance of business groups and portfolio entrepreneurs[1] has been gaining recognition in the last two decade (Ucsbasaran, Alsos, Westhead & Wright 2008, Malfense Fierro et al., 2017). Interest in business groups has been focused especially on emerging and developing countries, where entrepreneur or family led business groups are regarded as mechanisms which arise from deficiencies in market mechanisms (Colpan, Hikino & Lincoln, 2010), and which allow large scale entrepreneurs and families to emerge and assume dominant positions in such countries (Balunywa & Rosa, 2009). Although many of the factors associated with business group formation (Khanna & Palepu, 2000), particularly those associated with transaction costs in imperfect capital markets (Leff, 1978), have arisen from research in developing country contexts, financial explanations linked to the spreading and management of risk have been mostly suggested by research into listed corporate firms in developed countries. The role of risk in the formation of business groups in entrepreneur or family led firms, particularly smaller firms, and in developing countries has yet to be explored in any depth.

For the purposes of this chapter we will consider risk in the Knightian sense. That risk is measurable and that uncertainty is not:

> The practical difference between the two categories risk and uncertainty, is that in the former the distribution of the outcome is known (either through calculation a priori or from statistics or past experience), while in the case of uncertainty this is not true, the reason being in general that it is impossible to form a group of instances, because the situation dealt with is in a high degree unique. The best example of uncertainty is in connection with the exercise of judgement or the formation of those opinions as to the future course of events, which opinions (and not scientific knowledge) actually guide most of conduct.   (Knight, 1921, p. 233)

Spreading risk is perhaps the most widely recognised financial factor thought to influence the formation of business groups. Spreading, reducing and minimising risk is a core element of financial management and is particularly relevant where portfolio of products, services and enterprises are being managed. This is often linked with diversification strategies where firms engage in diversification of products and services predominantly to spread and minimise risk. Financial portfolio theory provides a long-standing explanation of why some entrepreneurs decide to organise their business as a group of firms rather than as a single firm (e.g. Rugman, 1976; Amihud and Baruch, 1981; Amit and Wernerfelt, 1990; Haavisto and Hansen, 1992). It also underpins a widespread and plausible anecdotal view that the reasons why portfolio entrepreneurs start additional new ventures, and build business groups, is that they are "spreading risk", or "not putting all their eggs in one basket".

---

1 Portfolio entrepreneurs are entrepreneurs that have a minority or majority equity stake in two or more independent businesses (Westhead, Ucsbasaran, Wright and Martin, 2003).

Despite the prevalence and importance of financial theories of risk mitigation through portfolio management in the financial and management research domains, however, the explanation that portfolio entrepreneurs start new ventures to spread risk hardly figures in the literature on portfolio entrepreneurship. In a 130-page review of research on habitual (serial and portfolio) entrepreneurs, Ucsbasaran, et al., (2008) cite and discuss 45 academic articles on habitual entrepreneurship. Not a single one had the word "risk" in the title. In the same 130-page review, there is no sub-section discussing any forms of risk and portfolio entrepreneurship.

The issue of "spreading risk" is signposted briefly as a possible issue in a number of studies on portfolio entrepreneurship (Rosa, 1998; Ucsbasaran, et al., 2008, Iacobucci & Rosa, 2010), but has not been developed further in subsequent research. Most of empirical studies on portfolio entrepreneurship cited by Ucsbasaran, et al., (2008) have been exploratory, and little evidence was found in these studies that "spreading risk" was an important motive for creating new additional ventures, or was linked to processes of risk management. In contrast a diversity of other motives and strategies was discovered linked with portfolio formation. The most important of these were linked to entrepreneurial processes of diversification, (Rosa, 1998) and the need to manage the establishment of new diversifications and entrepreneurial teams (Wiklund & Shepherd, 2008; Iacobucci and Rosa, 2010).

Why did risk not appear to be a prominent issue in these exploratory studies? First, the exploratory studies mentioned above, while aware of risk issues, did not specifically focus on them. More focused and sensitive studies might reveal more subtle relationships between risk and entrepreneurship.

Second, the studies were conducted in the UK and Europe in the 1990s and 2000s when the economic and political climates were relatively stable, economies were growing, and there was a regular supply of loan and equity finance for growing ventures. Starting a new venture is always risky, so starting a new one from a well-established business is, it could be argued, far more of a risk than might be gained from the benefits of "spreading risk" through a new venture. Only when the external conditions threaten the existence of the established business would one expect "spreading risk" to become an issue. Hence, by changing the research context to less developed countries, where external conditions are less stable, the issue of spreading risk might become more relevant in assessing the motivations and strategies of portfolio entrepreneurs.

Third, all the data gathered so far on the way portfolio entrepreneurs form their business groups is based on cross-sectional interviews relying on the recall and post-rationalisation of portfolio entrepreneurs being interviewed. It is likely that a different picture might emerge in a longitudinal study examining the motives and processes of portfolio business formation.

Finally, most studies on portfolio entrepreneurs have been on small scale entrepreneurs, many of whom have only just started to evolve their business groups. There have hardly been any studies on larger scale portfolio entrepreneurs with well-established groups. It is likely that portfolio risk management might become more prominent where business groups are larger and more complex, as is predicted by the literature on large corporate business groups.

This chapter seeks to address some of these gaps by evaluating the literature pertaining to risk and portfolio entrepreneurship. The importance of such a review is that risk is an important factor in the formation of business groups by portfolio entrepreneurs, but the relationship between risk and portfolio entrepreneurship is more complex than theories of portfolio risk management predict. These factors have so far been neglected in the current literature on portfolio entrepreneurship and business groups.

Moreover, entrepreneurship theories associating entrepreneurs as "risk-takers" may not fully appreciated how opportunity-seeking entrepreneurs can be taking considerable risks by establishing new ventures, yet at the same time still be risk-averse in the formation of such ventures. Interestingly, this view has also been explicated by Gladwell (2010) who cites prominent portfolio entrepreneurs such as Ted Turner, Gianna Agnelli and Ingvar Kamprad in his analysis.

Forming groups thus may reflect processes simultaneously associated with both opportunity-led and risk-aversion led strategies. Finally, we highlight that the role of the entrepreneur is critical in the formation and development of business groups, a factor mostly absent in the management literature on business groups. Thus, the entrepreneur and the individual level of analysis should complement firms level analysis, when investigating portfolio entrepreneurship and risk.

Literature review

In the finance literature, risk is considered to be the dispersion of returns on an investment as measured by the variation of returns on the investment over time (Dickson and Giglierano, 1986). The capital asset pricing model (CAPM) is used to determine appropriate rates of return of an asset when added to a well-diversified portfolio. The two elements of risk in this process are what are commonly referred to as systematic risk and unsystematic risk. Systematic risk refers to the effects of the fluctuating performance of the general economy on the assets or securities value. This is also known as un-diversifiable risk. Unsystematic risk refers to specific risk associated with assets, for example venture specific factors such as competitor reaction, consumer acceptance and managerial competence. Unsystematic risk is diversifiable, meaning that it can be evened out or reduced through the purchase of multiple assets (in different sectors for example).

The basic premise of portfolio theory is thus that with a large enough portfolio of varying assets and securities, the portfolio's overall unique risk will be reduced by a process of combining all the assets. The risk of the portfolio will then consist of the average of the systematic risk elements of the portfolio, weighed by the value of the asset or security (Dickson & Giglierano, 1986). When applied to the firm, this theory suggests that diversified strategic business units (SBUs) can reduce overall venture risk (Naylor & Tapon, 1982). This might explain why portfolio entrepreneurs undertake a business group structure.

In this process it is important to explain how firms diversify and reduce their risk through strategic business units as this has obvious implications for understanding how portfolio entrepreneurs might use diversification of business units to diversify risk. Dickson & Giglierano (1986, p. 60), point out that *"a firm may vertically integrate forward or backward to ensure distribution channels or sources of supply and integrate horizontally to gain entry into new geographic markets, other specialist market niches, or to benefit from economies of scale in production and marketing"*. This in effect reduces the risk of the enterprise. However, they also point out that a risk exists in diversification or the purchase of strategic business units, in finding management that have the sufficient knowledge and skills of different markets to make sound decisions when confronted with a portfolio of many different firms with varying functions existing in different markets.

Thus the portfolio entrepreneur is, in essence, a super manager of a type needed to ensure that the risks of diversified businesses are mitigated. Hence there are two stages of risk mitigation in portfolio theory. First, diversification is used to spread and reduce risk. Second, the knowledge and techniques are developed to overcome the risks associated with the management of a diversity of products, services and markets. In both stages it is managerial rather than creative or entrepreneurial opportunity-seeking competencies that lead to success. Hence entrepreneurship, as an opportunity-seeking strategy and behaviour (Shane & Venkataramen, 2000), in terms of financial portfolio theory, is not a relevant factor in explaining the creation and expansion of business groups.

The empirical research on portfolio entrepreneurs, however, as mentioned earlier, has not reported any evidence that portfolio entrepreneurs set up additional new ventures to spread risk. Rosa (1998), and Rosa & Scott, (1999) in case studies of Scottish entrepreneurs, found that risk did not figure strongly in a diverse range of entrepreneurial and non-entrepreneurial motives and strategies associated with the establishment of new ventures. Rather entrepreneurs displayed a diversity of "non risk spreading" motives for establishing a new additional venture, and in many cases each new venture was started with a different motive than other previous ones. These motives included (a) "pull diversification" – the challenge of a new opportunity, serendipitous opportunity, to exploit new markets to avoid restrictions in existing one, boredom, to further a hobby; (b) "push diversification" – the need to diversify from an ailing or failing business by establishing new more profitable lines of business; and (c) a range of non-entrepreneurial reasons such as to establish a family trust, provide a living for a family member, or protecting a trade mark. Similarly, Low and MacMillan (1988), Carter (2001), Westhead et al. (2003), and Alsos et al. (2006)

provide evidence that portfolio entrepreneurs are motivated by opportunity and become adept, with experience, at the identification of opportunities and the establishment of new businesses following processes of opportunity recognition.

This literature appears to show that entrepreneurship rather than risk spreading is the prevalent motive for portfolio entrepreneurs to start additional businesses in the non-corporate sectors. However, this is not necessarily incompatible with the idea that risk spreading or risk-mitigation is also a consideration. Later studies have revealed that though entrepreneurial motives are primary drivers of business group formation by portfolio entrepreneurs, the effect of entrepreneurship may be less direct.

Wiklund & Shepherd, (2008) make the point that it is diversification that is the entrepreneurial event. Wiklund & Shepard (2008), show that 59%, of their sample of portfolio entrepreneurs use their existing firm as the mode of organising or exploiting a new opportunity. Their conclusions therefore, are that the entrepreneurship literature which focus on opportunity exploitation being the creation of a new distinct firm, is problematic in understanding the process of opportunity exploitation for portfolio entrepreneurs/entrepreneurs, in that it has reduced explanatory power in explaining opportunity exploitation through diversification.

Entrepreneurship opportunity theory consequently cannot account for why an entrepreneur decides to pursue the diversification within an existing firm, or whether he or she chooses to pursue it by establishing a new venture separate from the existing firm. Iacobucci & Rosa, (2005, 2010) on a sample of Italian manufacturing firms shed light on this by showing that the decision to create a new venture for the new entrepreneurial opportunity is driven by managerial rather than entrepreneurial motives: the need to 1) focus resources on the new firm without endangering that assets of other firms owned by the entrepreneur (to ring fence it), and 2) incorporate, by giving them a share of ownership, outside partners into the new venture (employees who may have suggested the idea, outside investors, bought in managers, joint venture partners) who might otherwise take the idea somewhere else. The new shareholders are given a stake without risking or compromising ownership in the other firms in the group. In both cases the need to control risk is an important component of the decision to start a new venture to incorporate the diversification rather than accommodate it in house.

The portfolio entrepreneurship literature shows that related diversification leading to the establishment of a new additional venture is the most common entrepreneurial expansion strategy by successful opportunity-seeking portfolio entrepreneurs (Rosa, 1998). This is associated with "pull diversification" strategies. Unrelated diversification is less common and linked rather with "push diversification," the need to diversify out of trouble when the main businesses are not thriving, or where the new venture is small scale and associated with a hobby interest.

The preference for related diversification by portfolio entrepreneurs in these studies reinforces the benefits of vertical and horizontal strategies of diversification (Dickson and Giglierano, 1986). By tending to limit diversification to their existing knowledge and competencies through "related diversification", portfolio entrepreneurs reduce the risk of having to manage unrelated and unfamiliar products, services and processes. This supports research in the 1980s that starting a business that is related to another is less risky than starting a wholly new unrelated business (Bettis & Hall, 1982, Michel & Shaked, 1984, Bettis & Mahajan, 1985).

Where unrelated diversification is required (for example having to move away from a business in an ailing or declining industry, where a new related diversification would be throwing good money after bad) the entrepreneur, lacking the knowledge and skills of the new sector he or she is entering, is commonly advised to buy in expertise by hiring outside managers with the necessary competencies. In such cases, establishing the new venture may be an appropriate mechanism for buying in competency and thus lowering the risk inherent in unrelated diversification.

Research agenda

How risk and opportunity-seeking behaviour interact to produce successful venturing by entrepreneurs has been inadequately explored in past research. It has been assumed by entrepreneurship researchers that risk-seeking is positively associated with successful opportunity-seeking behaviour (Lumpkin and Dess, 1996, 2001; Kreiser and Davis, 2010). Every new venture carries a risk, so it follows that if you are seeking to start a new venture, the ability to successfully take risks is an essential entrepreneurial quality.

Thus, there has been a tendency to view opportunity-seeking entrepreneurship and risk-aversion as incompatible. Yet the financial and strategic management literature is full of research on how risk can be mitigated by good management based on accessing insurance and better governance based on reducing moral hazard; and uncertainty reduced by careful strategic management. While these calculated remedies reduce risk that can be anticipated and calculated, they do little to protect entrepreneurs from "uncertainty", adverse events which cannot be foreseen or easily insured against.

Consequently, financial portfolio risk theory predicts that by spreading risk, adverse effects from uncertain or uninsured events can be mitigated. Hence in the context of portfolio entrepreneurship, we might conclude that the main reason entrepreneurs diversify their business into separate business entities or units, is to spread risk. The literature on portfolio entrepreneurship; however, as the chapter shows, has not found any evidence that portfolio entrepreneurs diversify to spread risk. Instead they diversify for a number of reasons, of which opportunity related diversifications (push or pull) are particularly common.

Exploring portfolio entrepreneurship in more extreme contexts where risk and uncertainty is high (such as the emerging and developing world) should yield insights into the interplay between risk, the portfolio of businesses owned by the entrepreneur and the entrepreneur. than previous European studies on portfolio entrepreneurship. In the developing and emerging world opportunities for entrepreneurs are considerable, and rising, yet the conditions for pursuing these opportunities are much riskier and uncertain. Consequently, the existing literature is insufficiently clear to advance our understanding on the relationship between successful entrepreneurs and risk. Future work could evaluate whether risk-aversion strategies are a necessary and vital complement of successful opportunity-seeking strategies for successful entrepreneurship in high-risk and uncertain environments.

Undertaking longitudinal research to assess how risk and uncertainty change and how entrepreneurs' behaviours may change over time in adapting to their particular contexts is essential to more fully understand the role of risk for portfolio entrepreneurs.

In a wider context, future studies should approach the study of business groups using the entrepreneur as well as the firm as the unit of analysis. Many of the factors associated with the formation of business groups in developing countries (e.g. Khanna and Palepu, 2000) tend to be macro factors and are researched in macro contexts. By focusing on the entrepreneur, light can also be shed on how these factors unpack at the micro-level of the entrepreneur who is the primary driver of business group formation in such countries.

How the entrepreneurship of risk interfaces with the management of risk is a complex issue that has exciting implications for future research in both developed and developing country contexts.

References

Almeida, H., & Wolfenzon, D. (2006). A theory of pyramidal ownership and family business groups. *Journal of Finance, 61*(6), 2637–2680. https://doi.org/10.1111/j.1540-6261.2006.01001.x

Alsos, G.A., Kolvereid, L., & Isaksen, E. (2006). New business early performance: Differences between firms started by novice, serial and portfolio entrepreneurs. In Christensen, P. and Poulfeldt, F. (Eds.), *Managing Complexity and change in SMEs*. Frontiers in European Research, Cheltenham: Edward Elgar, 35–49. DOI:10.4337/9781847202857.00008

Amihud, Y., & Baruch, L. (1981). Risk reduction as a managerial motive for conglomerate mergers. *The Bell Journal of Economics, 12*(2), 605–617. http://dx.doi.org/10.2307/3003575

Amit, R., & Wernerfelt, B. (1990). Why do firms reduce business risk? *Academy of Management Journal, 33*(3), 520–533. https://doi.org/10.2307/256579

Balunywa, W., & Rosa, P. (2009), The contribution of portfolio entrepreneurs to economic development and growth: the Ugandan laboratory case[conference paper], AGSE Conference, Adelaide Australia.

Bettis R. A., & Hall, K.W. (1982). Diversification strategy, accounting determined risk, and accounting determined return. *Academy of Management Journal*, *25*(2), 254–264. https://doi.org/10.5465/255989

Bettis, R. A., & Mahajan, V. (1985). Risk/return performance of diversified firms. *Management Science*, *31*(7), 785–799. https://doi.org/10.1287/mnsc.31.7.785

Birley, S., & P. Westhead (1993). A Comparison of new businesses established by `novice' and `habitual' founders in Great Britain. *International Small Business Journal*, *12*(1), 38–60. https://doi.org/10.1177/0266242693121003

Carter, S. (2001). Multiple business ownership in the farm sector- differentiating monoactive, diversified and portfolio entrepreneurs. *International Journal of Entrepreneurial Behaviour and Research*, *7*(2), 43–59. https://doi.org/10.1108/13552550110695552

Carter S., & Ram M. (2003). Reassessing portfolio entrepreneurship. *Small Business Economics*, *21*(4), 371–380. https://doi.org/10.1023/A:1026115121083

Chandler, G.N., & Lyon D. W. (2001). Issues of research design and construct measurement in entrepreneurship research: the past decade. *Entrepreneurship Theory and Practice*, *25*(4), 101–113. https://doi.org/10.1177/104225870102500407

Colpan, A. M., Hikino, T., & Lincoln, J. R. (2010). *The Oxford handbook of business groups*, Oxford, Oxford University Press DOI:10.1093/oxfordhb/9780199552863.001.0001

Dickinson, P. R., & Giglierano, J. J. (1986). Missing the boat and sinking the boat: a conceptual model of entrepreneurial risk. *Journal of Marketing*, *50*(3), 58–70. https://doi.org/10.2307/1251585

Encarnation, D. J. (1989). *Dislodging Multinationals: India's Strategy in Comparative Perspective*. Ithaca, New York/London: Cornell University Press.

Gill, S. (1999). *The Pathology of Corruption*. New Delhi: Harper/Collins.

Gladwell, M. (2010, January 18). The sure thing: how entrepreneurs really succeed. *The New Yorker*. January 18, 2010 Issue.

Granovetter, M. (1994). Business Groups, in Smelser, N.J. & Swedborg, R. (eds.) *Handbook of Economic Sociology*, Princeton, NJ: Princeton University Press

Haavisto, T., & Hansson B. (1992). Risk reduction by diversification in the Nordic stock markets. *Scandinavian Journal of Economics*, *94*(4), 581–588. https://doi.org/10.2307/3440370

Iacobucci, D. (2002). Explaining business groups started by habitual entrepreneurs in the Italian manufacturing sector. *Entrepreneurship and Regional Development*, *19*(1), 31–47. https://doi.org/10.1080/08985620110096636

Iacobucci, D., & Rosa P. (2005). Growth, diversification and business group formation in entrepreneurial firms. *Small Business Economics*, *25* (1), 65–82. DOI:10.1007/s11187-005-4258-8

Iacobucci, D., & Rosa P. (2010). The growth of business groups by habitual entrepreneurs: The role of entrepreneurial teams. *Entrepreneurship: Theory and Practice*, *34*(2), 351–377. https://doi.org/10.1111/j.1540-6520.2010.00378.x

Khanna, T., & Palepu, K. (2000). The future of business groups in emerging markets: Long- run evidence from Chile. *Academy of Management Journal*, *43(3)*, 268–285. https://doi.org/10.2307/1556395

Knight, F. H. (1921). *Risk, Uncertainty and Profit*, Reprint 2002, Beard Books, Washington DC.

Kolvereid, L., & Bullvag, E. (1993). Novices vs. experienced founders: an exploratory investigation. In Birley S., MacMillan I., & Subramony S. (Eds). *Entrepreneurship Research, Global Perspectives*, Amsterdam, Elsevier Science Publishers, 275–285.

Kreiser, P., & Davis, J. (2010). Entrepreneurial orientation and firms performance: the unique impact of innovativeness, proactiveness and risk taking. *Journal of Small Business and Entrepreneurship, 23*(1), 39–35. https://doi.org/10.1080/08276331.2010.10593472

Lechner, C., & Leyronas, C. (2009). Small-business group formation as an entrepreneurial development model. *Entrepreneurship: Theory & Practice, 33(3)*, 645–667. https://doi.org/10.1111/j.1540-6520.2009.00320.x

Leff, N. (1976). Capital markets in the less developed countries: The group principal. In R. McKinnon (Ed.), *Money and Finance in Economic Growth and Development*, New York; Dekker, 97–122.

Leff, N. (1978). Industrial organization and entrepreneurship in the developing countries; The economic groups. *Economic Development and Cultural Change, 26(4)*, 661–675.

Loiseau, H. (2001). Des groupes de la taille d'une PME. Un phenomen en plein essor *INSEE Première*.

Low, M. B., & MacMillan, I. C. (1988). Entrepreneurship: past research and future challenges. *Journal of Management, 14*(2), 139–161. https://doi.org/10.1177/014920638801400202

Lumpkin, G.T., & Dess, G.G., (1996), Clarifying the entrepreneurial orientation construct and linking it to performance. *Academy of Management Review, 21(1)*, 135–172.

Lumpkin, G. T. & Dess, G. G. (2001). Linking two dimensions of entrepreneurial orientation to firm performance: the moderating role of environment and industry life cycle. *Journal of Business Venturing, 16*(5): 429–451. https://doi.org/10.2307/258632

Mahajan, V. (2008). *Africa Rising*, Wharton Publishing.

Malfense Fierro, A.C., Noble, D., Hatem, O. & Balunywa, W. (2017). African portfolio entrepreneurship and the creation of jobs. *Journal of Small Business and Enterprise Development, 25*(5), 730–751. https://doi.org/10.1108/JSBED-02-2017-0074

Michel, A., & Shaked, I. (1984). Does business diversification affect performance? *Financial Management, 13*(4), 18–25. https://doi.org/10.2307/3665297

Morck, R., & Yeung, B. (2003). Agency problems in large family business groups, *Entrepreneurship: Theory & Practice, 27*(4), 367–382. https://doi.org/10.1111/1540-8520.t01-1-00015

Morck, R., & Yeung, B. (2004). Family control and the rent-seeking society. *Entrepreneurship: Theory & Practice, 28*(4), 391–409. https://doi.org/10.1111/j.1540-6520.2004.00053.x

Naylor, T. H., & Tapon, F. (1982). The capital asset pricing model: an evaluation of its potential as a strategic planning tool. *Management Science, 28*(10), 1166–1173. https://doi.org/10.1287/mnsc.28.10.1166

Rocha, J. M. (2012). Business groups as hierarchical clique: structures: A conceptual and methodological discussion as it applies to the mexican experience. *British Journal of Management, 23*, 291–306. http://doi.org/10.1111/j.1467-8551.2011.00740.x

Rosa, P. (1998). Entrepreneurial processes of business cluster formation and growth by 'habitual' entrepreneurs. *Entrepreneurship: Theory & Practice, 22*(4), 43–62. https://doi.org/10.1177/104225879802200403

Rosa, P. & Scott, M. (1999). Entrepreneurial diversification business cluster formation and growth. *Environment and Planning C, 17*(5), 527–548. https://doi.org/10.1068/c170527

Rugman, A. M. (1976). Risk reduction by international diversification. *Journal of International Business Studies, 7*(2), 75–80. https://doi.org/10.1057/palgrave.jibs.8490702.

Scott, J., Hughes, M., & Mackenzie, J. (1980). *The Anatomy of Scottish Capital: Scottish Companies and Scottish Capital 1900–1979*. London: Croom Helm.

Scott, M., & a Rosa, P. (1996). Has firm level analysis reached its limits? *International Small Business Journal, 14*(4), 81–89. https://doi.org/10.1177/0266242696144006

Shane, S., & Venkataraman, S. (2000). The promise of entrepreneurship as a field of research, *Academy of Management Review, 25*(1), *217–226*. https://doi.org/10.2307/259271

Ucsbasaran, D., Alsos, G. A., Westhead, P., & Wright M (2008). *Habitual Entrepreneurship*, Foundations and Trends in Entrepreneurship, 4(4),309–450. http://dx.doi.org/10.1561/0300000014

Westhead, P., & Wright, M. (1998). Novice, portfolio and serial founders: are they different? *Journal of Business Venturing*, 13(3), 173–204. https://doi.org/10.1177/104225879802200404

Westhead, P., Ucsbasaran, D., Wright, M., & Martin, F. (2003), *Habitual entrepreneurs in Scotland, characteristics, search processes, learning and performance*, Report- Scottish Enterprise www.scottish-enteprise.com, Research and Publications section.

Wiklund, J., & Shepherd D. A. (2008). Portfolio entrepreneurship: habitual and novice Founders, new entry, and mode of organizing. *Entrepreneurship, Theory & Practice, 32* (4), 701–725. https://doi.org/10.1111/j.1540-6520.2008.00249.x

Yiu, D.W., Lu, Y., Bruton, G. D., & Hoskisson, R. E. (2007). Business groups: An integrated model to focus future research. *Journal of Management Studies*, 44(8), 1551–1579. https://doi.org/10.1111/j.1467-6486.2007.00735.x

Part II: **The inner circle**

Part II expands our understanding of entrepreneurial finance by examining where entrepreneurs turn first after considering their own financial resources: the inner circle of individuals and organizations that are closest to them.

In Chapter 5 Franklin Allen, Meijun Qian, and Jing Xie look at informal financing based on social relationships and business networks. Interestingly, they find that this type of startup financing complements, rather than substitutes for, more formal financing sources.

Chapter 6 by Jonathan Marks and Aleia Bucci takes an explicit emerging markets perspective in considering how entrepreneurs are funded within business groups, a common organizational form in these institutional settings. They call attention to the need for more research on corporate governance and disclosure within these groups, relating these activities to group performance.

Tiago Ratinho in Chapter 7 takes a look at incubators and accelerators as sources of startup funding. He finds that the literature on these phenomena has underappreciated the financial role that they provide.

Other sources of financing in the inner circle might include supply chain finance, including supplier credit; and factoring (the purchase of a startup's accounts receivable at a discount).

https://doi.org/10.1515/9783110726312-007

Franklin Allen, Meijun Qian, and Jing Xie

5 Informal financing of entrepreneurs

Abstract: Financing based on social relationships and business networks provides informational and incentive advantages for entrepreneurs and lenders. The utilization of these mechanisms contributes to supporting entrepreneur activities, firm growth, and economic advancement. However, informal financing is not necessarily a substitute but likely complementary to financing through formal institutions. The practice is prevalent worldwide in developing and developed countries, in small and large firms, involving formal and informal financial institutions. Further explorations are in need to re-evaluate the dichotomy and examine cross-country/industry patterns and the selection of informal financing. The understanding of interactions among informal financing, entrepreneurship, and firm dynamics is still insufficient. The importance of relationships and networks in financing is further amplified by fintech advancement. More research is in need to understand its development and to meet new regulatory challenges.

Keywords: informal financing, entrepreneurship, information and incentives, growth, fintech

Introduction

The term "informal finance" has not been clearly defined by the academia; rather it was used vaguely to refer to financing from a variety of sources apart from banks. Generally, it includes but is not restricted to: trade credit, interpersonal borrowing (money from friends or families), private money house, pawn house, etc. (e.g., Tsai, 2004, Allen, Qian, and Qian, 2005, Ayyagari, Demirguc-Kunt and Maksimovic, 2010). However, these broadly defined informal financing mechanisms include different sources that may result from a particular institutional environment, economic development stages, and work under particular mechanisms. In differentiating informal financing from a formal financial intermediary, Diamond (1984) and Berger and Udell (1998) emphasize the existence of a delegated monitor, and Kandori (1992) and Udry (1994) emphasize the nature of self-enforcing contracts as opposed to social sanctions for repayment to differentiate formal from informal financing. These dimensions are insufficient to provide further detailed differentiation among various informal financing sources, their operating environment, and their effectiveness in promoting economic growth, respectively.

Franklin Allen, Meijun Qian, Jing Xie, Imperial College London, Australian National University, and Hong Kong Polytechnic University

https://doi.org/10.1515/9783110726312-008

We define informal financing as financing sources that rely on social relationship and business networks rather than formal institutions such as from banks, stock markets, and government. These sources include trade credits, family lending, credit cooperatives, private equity and debt, online financing platform such as P2P and crowdfunding etc. These financing sources are particularly important for entrepreneurs of start-ups when the size and risk of their business make it difficult to draw on banks, markets, and government contracts (e.g., Cumming and Groh, 2018, Elston and Audretsch, 2010). These financing sources are also prevalent in mature firms, small and medium entreprises (SMEs), and large corporations. For example, SMEs' asymmetric information imposes disadvantages for accessing formal institutions, and large firms commonly use trade credits (e.g., Giannetti, Burkart, and Ellingsen, 2011; Allen, Qian, and Xie 2019).

This chapter explores what we know and are yet to know about informal financing of entrepreneurs. It consists of two parts. The first part reviews the theoretical and empirical studies on these issues. Our key findings include the following: (1). Informal financing based on social relationships and business networks provides many informational and incentive advantages over the equity market and bank-based financing. (2). The role and contribution of financing in supporting entrepreneurship and economic growth are related to the mechanisms that utilize the features associated with social relationships and business networks. While some informal financing sources are constructive, others could be destructive to the entrepreneurs and firms. (3). The usage of informal financing is prevalent around the world. They exist in both developing countries and developed countries that have advanced equity markets and the banking industry. For example, trade credits have always been important for firms in the US and Europe. Family lending in the UK has been increasing for entrepreneurial finance despite the advanced nature of formal banks and markets.

In the second part, we discuss future research agendas in this field and their potential significance. We direct the discussion in three dimensions. (1). The conventional view that informal financing is the second-best choice when funding through formal markets and banks is not available contradicts practical developments worldwide. Considering pricing and repayment mechanisms shows that financing based on relationships and networks offers better outcomes for both entrepreneurs and lenders. This new perspective calls for revisiting some classic studies and regulatory choices. It also calls for studies to understand the cross-country industry variations while controlling for the formal institutions in place. (2). There is limited understanding of the interactions among entrepreneurs, financing sources, and firm dynamics. We need to understand more about the influences of entrepreneur preferences, the value creation of informal financing over formal financing, and their interaction with firms' life cycles. (3). Developments in Fintech and new lending trends in formal financial institutions illustrate the critical benefits of relationships and networks in financing. We need more understanding on the co-evolution of formal and informal financing. Technology advancement also provides a large volume of data to do so. It will benefit policymaking in this fin-tech new era.

The rest of the chapter provides a detailed review of studies and discusses potential future research on informal financing for entrepreneurs and firms. Evidence is elaborated to support the conclusions above.

Literature review

A rich strand of literature has studied the advantages of informal financing in overcoming information asymmetry and providing joint collateral and liquidity. This section reviews these advantages and discusses their mechanisms and consequently informal financing's contribution to entrepreneurship, firms' growth, and consequently economic growth.

Informational and incentive advantages

Karlan et al. (2009) model social relationships between individuals as collateral to secure a loan, facilitating informal contracts. For example, when an agent would like to borrow to purchase a car from another agent, a common friend could play the role of intermediary, providing both the guarantee and facilitation of the transaction if there is no formal contract enforcement mechanism in the economy. In the case of default, the borrower loses friendship, trust, and reputation with the guarantor, lender, and network. The model is empirically tested with survey data showing a strong positive correlation between social collateral and borrowing primarily driven by strong ties.

Lee and Persson (2016) develop an external financing model that considers relatives' or friends' standard altruistic preferences with respect to each other that are lacking with outsiders. The social preferences make family finance cheap but also create shadow costs that discourage its use. For example, using family finance as risk capital undermines the natural familial insurance arrangement. Therefore, the entrepreneur relies on outside funds whenever they are available. However, when the entrepreneur is capital constrained, altruism makes family investors willing to provide funds at possibly negative expected returns if this makes the project realizable.

Trade credits are the most typical example of informal financing based on business networks. Smith (1987) argues that the prevalence of non-salvageable investments made by sellers in buyers enables the seller to generate private information about customer quality and take actions to protect their investments. Biais and Gollier (1997) argue that trade credit can mitigate the information asymmetry between the borrower and the lender by incorporating the private information held by suppliers. Burkart and Ellingsen (2004) argue that suppliers may be less susceptible to the risk of strategic default than banks because inputs are less liquid and thus less easily diverted than cash by opportunistic borrows. These models predict that producers of differentiated goods, which are typically harder to divert, should extend more trade credit.

Petersen and Rajan (1997) argue that suppliers lend to customers because they have a comparative advantage in getting information about customers. Wilner (2000) suggests that a dependent supplier may help a customer with temporary financial problems because his own prospects are positively related to those of the customer. Trade creditors, desiring to maintain an enduring product-market relationship, grant more concessions to a customer in financial distress than would be granted by lenders in a competitive credit market. However, the optimal pricing in Wilner (2000) suggests that anticipating these more considerable renegotiation concessions, the debtor firm agrees to pay a higher interest rate to a trade creditor than to a credit market lender. McMillan and Woodruff (1999) emphasize the importance of networks in verifying customers' reliability and as a means of sanctioning customers who renege on deals in offering trade credits. Using survey data from Vietnam, they show that the supplier tends to offer trade credits to the customer when it is hard for the customer to find an alternative supplier and when the customer is identified through a business network.

Cunat (2007) models two characteristics of suppliers as lenders that are advantageous compared to banks. First, suppliers are better able to enforce debt repayment compared to banks. Second, suppliers may act as liquidity providers to their customers. On the repayment, Cunat (2007) argues that the entrepreneur has a stronger incentive to strategically default on the bank than on the supplier because the supplier is vital for the entrepreneur's future business due to the lack of alternative producers (the switching cost hypothesis). With regard to the provision of liquidity, as the suppliers and customers split surplus, the suppliers have an incentive to support customers during temporary liquidity shocks.

Mechanisms and contributions

There has been a wide debate on the role of informal financing in entrepreneurial finance and how this supports firms' growth and economic growth. A strand of literature shows that informal finance played an important role in firms' growth (e.g., Bias and Gollier 1997, Tsai 2004, Allen, Qian, and Qian 2005). For example, Bias and Gollier (1997) advocate that trade credit can solve the asymmetric information problem associated with bank financing, which precludes small or young firms from bank credit because trade credit usage incorporates private information between suppliers and their customers. They also report that firms without a relationship with banks resorted more to trade credit. However, another strand of literature argues that informal financing is a suboptimal substitute when formal financing is unavailable. For example, Cull, Xu, and Zhou (2009) and Ayyagari, Demirguc-Kunt and Maksimovic (2010) suggest that informal financing plays no or limited role in firm growth.

Under the perspective that the advantages of informal financing channels are to overcome asymmetric information and moral hazard issues, it makes sense to classify informal financing sources, ex-ante, based on the mechanisms they rely on for information production and repayment enforcement. The contribution and effectiveness of these informal sources in supporting entrepreneurs and firm operation largely depends on how they overcome the asymmetric information, moral hazard, adverse selection, etc.

Allen, Qian and Xie (2019) offer a general framework to classify informal financing. They adopt two criteria to separate constructive informal financing from underground financing: (a) information technology for monitoring, risk control, and pricing, and (b) the coercion and violence mechanism in case of delinquency. Although their specific form may change over time or across countries, the constructive informal financing should essentially share such mechanisms – to address the difficulty in information production and risk control that cause formal financing through banks and markets to fail. This approach of classification will be able to predict ex-ante whether a specific informal source will effectively help entrepreneurs or support firm growth.

Using the practice in China as the example, Allen, Qian, and Xie. (2019) include the following in constructive informal financing: trade credit, small loan companies, banks' credit extension arms, registered pawnshops or financing companies, direct informed lending between immediate family members and close relatives. These informal sources use personal, community, or business relationships to reduce asymmetric information and reduce risk through economic collateral. The price of funding reflects both the risk and the closeness of the relationship – the value of social bonding. In the case of delinquency or default, there are sufficient economic and social connections that facilitate renegotiation and resolutions. For example, Biais and Gollier (1997) and Petersen and Rajan (1997) argue that trade credits can solve the asymmetric information problem associated with bank financing, which precludes small or young firms from bank credits. The usage of trade credits incorporates private information between suppliers and their customers.

Constructive informal financing, which Allen, Qian and Xie (2019) call underground financing, has a coercion mechanism and includes loan sharks, unregistered pawnshops, lending agencies and loan brokers. These informal sources have little information technology to rely on. They are less concerned about the risk of the project and even less about risk monitoring or control. This type of financing is often made to speculative activities, charges extremely high interest rates or fees, and employs violence rather than legal recourse to collect payments or renegotiate in the case of delinquency. In terms of pricing, contract, and enforcement, these financing channels operate within a grey area or beyond legal boundaries, e.g., loan sharks.

Based on this classification, Allen, Qian and Xie (2019) find that informal financing is more popular in smaller, younger, and less audited firms. Constructive informal financing is positively associated with firm growth, but underground financing is not. This evidence reconciles the contradictory evidence in the empirical literature on the economic role of informal financing. In particular, while Allen, Qian, and Qian (2005) document that informal financing is the driving force in supporting the private sector in China, Ayyagari, Demirgüç-Kunt, and Maksimovic (2010) show that bank financing, not informal financing, is associated with the growth of Chinese firms. Allen, Qian and Xie (2019) demonstrate that the difference in results is driven by how uncategorized "other financing" is treaded. While the former treats it as informal financing, the latter treats it as internal financing.

The prevalence of informal financing around the world

While China provides a rich paradigm to study informal finance, it is neither the only country nor an outlier that features these financing channels. Giannetti, Serrano-Velarde, and Tarantino (2021) identify trade credit as the most important source of short-term funding for firms around the world. Allen, Qian and Xie (2019) examine informal financing in 12 emerging countries covered by the World Bank survey (Brazil, Chile, China, Egypt, Indonesia, Pakistan, Philippines, South Africa, Sri Lanka, Thailand, Turkey, and Vietnam). These 12 countries are either among the top 10 largest emerging economies or the top 10 fastest growing emerging economies in the world (Allen et al. (2019)). The percentage of informal financing, based on the categorization of constructive financing (trade credit + personal lending) and underground financing (other informal), on average accounts for 13.02% (median) or 13.16% (mean) of the total financing of working capital. It is the lowest at 4.25% in Egypt and the highest at 20.42% in Brazil. China at 9.87% actually falls in the lower middle part of the range. Please refer to Table 5.1.

The usage and positive effect of informal financing have also been documented for firms in developed countries (e.g., Cunat, 2007; Garcia-Appendini and Montoriol-Garriga, 2013). Studies on informal financing in developed countries focus on discussing the determinants and consequences of trade credit, a major form of informal financing. They emphasize specific trade-related features to support product differentiation or liquidity provision. Giannetti, Burkart, and Ellingsen (2011) argue that trade credit is an instrument to facilitate the sales of differentiated goods and services. A majority of firms in their sample, (small nonfinancial, nonfarm U.S. businesses with less than 500 employees that were in operation as of December 1998 and surveyed in 1999–2001 by the Board of Governors of the Federal Reserve System and the U.S. Small

Table 5.1: Financing sources by country.

Country	Year of Survey	# of firms	Bank Financing	Equity Financing	Government Fund	Retained Earnings	Operation Financing	Trade Credit	Inter-personalloan	Other Informal	Other	Constructive +Underground (TC, IPL, OI)
Panel A: Financing in working capital (%)												
Bangladesh	2002	974	33.21	0.51	0.48	55.82	0.51	4.17	4.26	0.46	0.58	8.90
Brazil	2003	1,505	26.95	3.03	2.26	43.99	1.50	15.37	2.52	2.53	1.84	20.42
Chile	2004	922	27.35	0.48	1.76	52.16	1.82	6.80	0.97	0.36	8.31	8.13
China	2003	1,902	26.51	11.54	0.38	13.13	NA	2.29	5.76	1.82	38.57	9.87
Egypt	2004	704	6.05	2.66	0.20	85.62	0.28	1.67	2.49	0.09	0.94	4.25
Indonesia	2003	482	17.74	1.61	0.94	39.93	1.18	3.63	8.89	6.61	19.47	19.13
Pakistan	2002	936	4.92	12.87	1.28	65.27	1.43	4.70	6.99	1.29	1.26	12.98
Philippines	2003	650	8.48	5.99	0.29	61.87	0.62	11.54	8.25	1.09	1.87	20.89
South Africa	2003	505	15.64	0.65	0.15	66.94	1.03	11.68	1.14	0.21	2.57	13.02
Sri Lanka	2004	369	22.69	12.76	1.89	32.15	1.44	10.24	2.67	0.35	15.81	13.26
Thailand	2004	1,385	45.69	11.04	0.58	24.82	NA	13.61	1.48	1.11	1.38	16.19
Turkey	2005	599	19.65	10.23	6.40	49.25	3.72	6.57	3.56	0.16	0.46	10.29
Vietnam	2005	1,096	27.60	26.36	0.84	27.23	0.72	7.43	5.30	0.65	3.04	13.38
Total		12,029	24.36	8.43	1.21	42.72	1.26	7.75	4.10	1.31	9.10	13.16

(continued)

Table 5.1 (continued)

Panel B: Financing in new investments (%)

	Year	N										
Bangladesh	2002	884	29.60	0.38	0.26	60.04	1.77	2.64	4.31	0.35	0.65	7.30
Brazil	2003	1,248	14.24	4.27	8.61	56.26	3.52	8.69	1.12	1.05	2.25	10.85
Chile	2004	655	30.74	1.21	2.55	47.48	6.08	3.51	0.60	0.23	7.60	4.34
China	2003	1,331	20.53	12.35	0.48	15.29	NA	1.04	5.93	1.78	42.60	8.75
Egypt	2004	523	6.63	3.70	0.19	87.03	0.08	0.80	0.95	0.00	0.62	1.75
Indonesia	2003	203	19.61	1.72	2.35	39.53	3.43	2.44	10.78	7.76	12.37	20.99
Pakistan	2002	222	6.70	15.95	1.28	56.97	3.50	1.96	10.20	2.71	0.72	14.87
Philippines	2003	179	13.29	4.34	0.20	57.96	1.52	7.96	10.17	0.59	3.97	18.73
South Africa	2003	462	16.12	0.09	0.50	59.51	16.25	0.62	0.84	0.22	5.86	1.68
Sri Lanka	2004	252	15.16	2.66	2.17	50.84	4.54	2.13	1.58	0.28	20.63	3.99
Thailand	2004	1,382	58.33	13.45	0.35	19.33	NA	3.53	1.82	0.68	1.95	6.03
Turkey	2005	402	23.24	9.56	5.67	46.82	7.09	4.40	2.62	0.17	0.42	7.20
Vietnam	2005	930	28.04	26.97	3.23	30.41	0.55	1.01	4.64	0.54	3.82	6.19
Total		8,673	26.52	8.96	2.39	42.13	3.98	3.23	3.34	0.93	9.58	7.50

Source: Extracted from Allen, Qian, & Xie (2019). This table presents the financing composition (percentage of the total financing) for each country. *Bank Financing* includes financing from domestic and foreign banks; *Operation Financing* includes Credit Card and Leasing arrangements. *Constructive informal financing* includes *trade credit and Interpersonal loans. Underground financing is measured with other informal financing.* In panel A and B, we report the financing composition for working capital and new investment respectively.

Business Administration), receive trade credits at low cost. Klapper, Laeven, and Rajan (2012) also support the view that trade credit may be a means for small suppliers to warrant quality to their large buyers. Using a novel set of 30,000 trade credit contracts describing buy- and sell-side characteristics, they show that the largest and most creditworthy buyers receive contracts with the longest maturities from smaller suppliers. They also show that discounts for early payment tend to be offered to riskier buyers. Ng, Smith, and Smith (1999) argue that credit terms are contractual solutions to information problems concerning product quality and buyer creditworthiness. They present evidence that financing through trade credits is extremely costly.

Garcia-Appendini and Montoriol-Garriga, (2013) find that firms with high liquidity before the 2008/2008 financial crisis increase trade credits extended to other corporations and subsequently experience better performance than ex-ante cash-poor firms. The liquidity consideration also comes into play with bankruptcy prospects. For example, Jacobson and Von Schedvin (2015) quantify the importance of trade credit chains for the propagation of corporate bankruptcy using a detailed data set on claims held by trade creditors (suppliers) on failed trade debtors (customers). They infer that both credit losses and demand shrinkage drive the trade credits to fail propagation mechanism. Costello (2020) show that suppliers exposed to a significant and exogenous decline in bank financing pass this liquidity shock to their downstream customers. Gofman and Wu (2021) study the production network and find that firms in more central or more profitable chains provide more net trade credit. They also find that more upstream firms borrow more from suppliers, lend more to customers, and hold more net trade credit. This upstream effect in trade credit is weaker for more profitable firms and longer chains.

Limitations, implications, and future research

Despite the large amount of studies that illustrate the advantage and role of informal financing in supporting entrepreneur activities, the dominant view remains dismissive. This section presents new perspectives that tackle this dismissive view, discusses their implications, and explores potentially important research topics that are yet to be conducted in this field.

Limitations of the conventional view and new perspectives

The role of financial intermediaries, such as banks and direct financing through equity markets, is to bridge the gap between economic agents with a surplus and those with a deficit of capital. However, asymmetric information between banks/markets and firms, especially small and young enterprises, may preclude financing for valuable projects. For example, small firms are more likely to resort to trade credit financing than large firms (e.g., Brandt and Li, 2003). Under this perspective, informal financing has been assumed a suboptimal choice and a substitution for bank loans when the market is incomplete due to asymmetric information or undeveloped markets (e.g., Petersen and Rajan, 1997). They are more costly or riskier (e.g., Wilner, 2000). They are used only when entrepreneurs have exhausted their wealth and liquidity (Burkart and Ellingsen, 2004, Cunat, 2007).

A recent study by Allen, Qian and Xie (2021) challenge this conventional view. By allowing direct competition among various financing channels under the same market conditions, their model predicts that informal financing can often offer Pareto improvement (better payoffs for both lenders and entrepreneurs) over bank financing even when there is no market incompleteness. The key results derive from entrepreneurs and lenders caring about their implicit benefits associated with the other party's payoff. In most cases, informal financing offers a lower financing cost and results in better project performance, as the entrepreneurs exert more effort and cash flow for the projects.

In fact, there has long existed empirical evidence in entrepreneurial financing that counters the dismissive second-best view. Despite the development of banks and markets, alternative financing remains strong in the economy, and the family lending has increased in entrepreneurial finance in Britain and the US (e.g., Dunn and Holtz-Eakin, 2000). Large or monopoly firms have used more trade credits than small firms, despite the former having better access to bank loans (e.g., Lehar et al., 2020). Allen, Qian and Xie (2019) find that constructive informal financing is more popular in regions where access to bank loans is extensive, suggesting a complementary relation between informal financing and bank financing rather than that they are substitutes. After addressing selection bias, firms that use informal financing perform better than those that use bank loans, and their financing costs are similar. This perspective is severely under-researched.

The mechanism-based categorization of informal financing in Allen, Qian and Xie (2019 and 2021) also calls for revisits of some classic studies. First, it brings more financing practices to attention. For example, corporate insider debt underscores the relationship-specific investment and monitoring mechanism (e.g., Dass, Kale and Nanda, 2015) that was originally studied only in trade credits. Sundaram and Yermack (2007) find that CEOs to whom the firm owes high debt, manage their firms conservatively. Cassell, Huang, Sanchez and Stuart (2012) find a negative association between CEO inside debt holdings and the volatility of future firm stock returns, R&D expenditures, financial leverage, and a positive association between CEO inside debt holdings and the extent of diversification and asset liquidity. Revisiting these studies will provide synergies in perspective and knowledge that allow us to understand both fields better.

The new perspective also calls for revisiting Udry's (1994) framework that differentiates informal financing with social sanction versus criminal penalty. Given regulators' concern about social impacts of informal financial institutions, the classification based on this mechanism is naturally correlated, however, not necessarily aligned, with these financing channels' legal status and lending targets. For example, some of the legally registered pawnshops may lend to gamblers rather than entrepreneurs. Indigenously organized informal institutions, such as credit cooperatives, rotation savings, credit organizations, rural cooperative foundations, and mutual benefit funds played a vital role in the early stage of China's reform until the late 1990s. They supported rural households' transition from agriculture to entrepreneurship (Qian and Huang, 2016). However, they were declared illegal by the People's Bank of China in the late 1990s and were banned. Informal financing research, focusing on mechanisms that monitor, price, reduce risk, and facilitate recourse, may provide policy-making with reliable underpinnings. It can address when and in which direction the regulated shift between these two punishments, social sanction vs legal sanctions, is beneficial to the entrepreneurs and the economy.

The evidence that informal financing is prevalent worldwide calls for new research on their cross-sectional variations. Cultural values play an essential role that has not been explored much. Here, we provide a few indicative results. Table 5.2 reports the results from regressions that use World Values Survey culture indices, one-by-one, to explain the usage of constructive informal financing, underground financing, interpersonal loans, trade credits, and others, respectively. As the table shows, constructive informal financing, trade credits, and interpersonal borrowing are significantly and positively associated with interpersonal trust and happiness. Underground financing is significantly negatively associated with happiness. These results point to some interesting linkages between people's happiness and trust and usage of types of informal financing. More detailed and in-depth studies are needed to have a thorough understanding of these issues.

Table 5.2: Culture (measures from World Value Survey) and the usage of informal financing.

	(1)	(2)	(3)	(4)	(5)
Dependent =	Constructive Informal Financing	Interpersonal Loan	Trade Credit	Underground Financing	Other
Interpersonal Trust	0.101***	0.047***	0.077***	−0.006	−0.026**
	(5.14)	(3.90)	(4.29)	(−0.90)	(−2.47)
Happiness	0.395***	0.103***	0.387***	0.121***	−0.046*
	(8.49)	(3.47)	(9.30)	(6.61)	(−1.76)

Source: The funding sources data are from the World Bank Investment Climate Survey. Observations interpersonal trust and happiness indices are from the World Value Survey (the 1999–2004 wave) conducted by the World Value Survey Association. The control variables in the regression include log(Assets), age, number of competitors, ownership, financing constraints, and bank loan access, and industry fixed effects. Each coefficient is from an independent regression.

Relatedly, there is also a large literature that studies the influence of law, accounting, industry competition, and product markets on the development of informal financing (e.g., Li, Ng and Saffar, 2021; Costello, 2019; Beck, Demirguc-Kunt and Maksimovic, 2008, Casey and O'Toole, 2014; Lehar, Song and Yuan, 2020). While these studies show country or industry preferences in using trade credits, industries with higher dependence on trade credit financing exhibit higher growth rates in countries with weaker financial institutions (Fisman and Love, 2003). Therefore, the full picture is ambiguous because of selection and causality issues. Similarly to the studies on cultural influence, academia needs more careful and in-depth investigations on these issues.

Gaps in entrepreneurial financing research

There is limited understanding of interactions among entrepreneurs, financing sources, and firm dynamics. Using survey data on small firms, Rebel and Sokolyk (2016) sort small privately held firms based on their credit needs. They find that the owners of firms that report no need for credit are older, more likely to be white, more creditworthy, and have fewer bank and nonbank relationships. Moreover, they find that about one in three discouraged borrowers would have received credit had they applied for credit. The usage of informal financing, amount and type, by start-ups also varies with entrepreneurs' personal traits (e.g., Elston and Audretsch, 2010). However, there is little exploration on how those differences result from business types, availability of networks, demographics, and latent traits that affect their social relationship and business network access. Future research along these lines could add understanding of entrepreneurship and estimate the economic value of personal traits, social relationships, and business networks.

It is not surprising that start-ups and young firms rely more on informal finance than mature and well-established firms. However, a clear picture of the dynamics, in which entrepreneurs, the firm's growth, industry, and institutional environment jointly determine the business model after the firm becomes mature and large is lacking. Will founding entrepreneurs step down and pass the power to professional managers or the business financing or retain the same previous model? Why? How does the choice influence the future path, controlling for selection?

Other intriguing and important questions in this dimension include what happens to entrepreneurs who do not secure the capital in the way they desire? Do they or who will respond by using more expensive financing channels or reducing their capital expenditures? How are stakeholder welfares affected if firms fail in the desired financing? Answers to these questions adds to our understanding of the role and value of financing in the firm life cycle.

New development and related research questions

The technological advancement with the internet has enormously affected our so-cial structure and network. It has inevitably impacted financing models based on social relationships and business networks. A variety of financing channels boomed in the past 20 years, such as crowd funding, Person-to-Person (P2P) lending, and online banking and wealth management, etc. Academic research in this area has been mainly descriptive for the practices and participants' behavioral patterns. Few studies have examined the mechanisms behind the rise, boom, selection and sur-vival of these practices with technology changes. With an overall upward trajectory, there has been also adverse events in these areas, and regulatory sluggishness has been blamed. For example, there were over 2000 P2P lending platforms in China at the peak. However, they were all declared illegal in the late 2010s, a crude regula-tory approach that China has repeatedly enforced on several community-, relation-ship-, or network-based financing practices.

Allen, Gu and Jagtiani (2021) provide a comprehensive survey on recent studies about the impact of fintech. The survey covers how credit scoring uses artificial in-telligence and machine learning, digital payment, blockchain and other distributed ledger technologies that underly crypto-assets and initial coin offerings, central bank digital currency development, cybersecurity, etc. They show that the dramatic growth of fintech has changed the financial industry landscape, creating regulatory gaps and loops. It changes the dynamics of competition, imposes new ethic chal-lenges, and potentially disrupts the entire financial system. In all the aspects men-tioned above, further explorations are necessary to understand, guide, and regulate the fast changes.

The regulatory lack of sophistication reflects a long-stood incomprehension on the co-evolution of formal and informal financing. Allen, Qian and Qian (2005) show that the sector that relies on informal mechanisms has provided the most sig-nificant growth in China. What is the counterfactual development if China had not suppressed these informal financial institutions? The second-best choice assump-tion has thwarted attention to research on informal financing. Until recently, the assumption is questioned (Allen, Qian and Xie, 2021). Meanwhile, fintech develop-ment has also generated an unprecedented volume of data and new methods that could be applied to gain insights. Countries that understand the essence of relation-ship- and network-based mechanisms, their roles for entrepreneurial financing and in the future of fintech, and their influences on household and entrepreneurial de-cisions will gain a critical advantage in this new era.

The contrast between dismissing its significance and the flourish of financing practices based on relationships and networks also manifests in the new trend of formal institutions: bank lending with joint ownership of equity and debt of firms. Jiang, Li and Shao (2010) show that these debts require a smaller risk premium and reduce investment risks. Further research on network advantages through business arrangements and the fintech development will be academically interesting and practically valuable for financial institutions, entrepreneurs, and corporations.

Concluding remarks

A large strand of literature studies the usage, mechanism, costs and role of informal financing in support entrepreneurship. The first part of this chapter reviews both theoretical and empirical studies, highlighting the following three results. First, there are informational and incentive advantages of financing based on social relationships and business networks. Second, the role and contribution of informal financing in supporting entrepreneur activities and firm growth depend on the mechanisms through which the relationships and networks are utilized. Third, the practice of informal financing is prevalent worldwide in both developing and developed countries.

The second part of the chapter discusses the future research agenda in three dimensions. First, a new perspective questions the conventional dismissive view that informal financing is a second-best choice when banks and markets are incomplete. We suggest a re-evaluation of the social sanction vs. legal sanction in repayment dichotomy, to examine cross-country/industry patterns of informal financing, and to address selection and causality issues in these studies. Second, we propose several research questions about interactions among entrepreneurs, financing choice, and firm dynamics. Finally, we note that the joint ownership of equity and debt by formal financial institutions and a variety of financing channels arising from the fintech advancement both utilize relationships and networks. This new trend provides intriguing questions and a large volume of data to understand relationship/network based informal financing for entrepreneur activities and economic growth.

References

Allen, F., Gu, X., and Jagtiani, J. (2021). A Survey of Fintech Research and Policy Discussion. *Review of Corporate Finance*, *1*, 259–339

Allen, F., Qian, J., and Qian, M. (2005). Law, Finance, and Economic Growth in China. *Journal of Financial Economics*, *77*, 57–116.

Allen, F., Qian, M., and Xie, J. (2019). Understanding Informal Financing. *Journal of Financial Intermediation*, *39*, 19–33.

Allen, F., Qian, M., and Xie, J. (2021). Implicit Benefits and Financing. Working paper, SSRN 3379442.

Ayyagari M, Demirgüç-Kunt, A., and Maksimovic, V. (2010). Formal versus Informal Finance: Evidence from China. *Review of Financial Studies*, *23*, 3048–3097

Beck, T., Demirguc-Kunt, A., and Maksimovic, V. (2008). Financing Patterns around the World: The Role of Institutions. *Journal of Financial Economics*, *89*, 467–487

Berger, A., and Udell, G. F. (1998). The Economics of Small Business Finance: The Roles of Private Equity and Debt Markets in the Financial Growth Cycle. *Journal of Banking and Finance*, *22*, 613–673.

Besley, T., Coate, S., and Loury, G. (1993). The Economics of Rotating Savings and Credit Associations. *American Economic Review*, *83*, 792–810.

Bias, B., and Gollier, C. (1997). Trade Credit and Credit Rationing. *Review of Financial Studies* 10: 903–37.

Brandt, L., and Li, H. (2003). Bank Discrimination in Transition Economies: Ideology, Information, or Incentives? *Journal of Comparative Economics*, *31*, 387–413.

Burkart, M., and Ellingsen, T. (2004). In-kind Finance: A Theory of Trade Credit. *American Economic Review*, *94*,569–590.

Cassell, C. A., Huang, S. X., Sanchez, J. M., and Stuart, M. D. (2012). Seeking safety: The relation between CEO inside debt holdings and the riskiness of firm investment and financial policies. *Journal of Financial Economics*, *103*, 588–610.

Casey, E., and O'Toole, C. M. (2014). Bank Lending Constraints, Trade Credit and Alternative Financing During the Financial Crisis: Evidence from European SMEs. *Journal of Corporate Finance*, *27*(8), 173–193.

Cole, R., and Sokolyk, T. (2018). Debt Financing, Survival, and Growth of Start-up Firms. *Journal of Corporate Finance*, *50*, 609–625.

Costello, A. (2019). The Value of Collateral in Trade Finance. *Journal of Financial Economics*, *134*, 70–90.

Costello, A. (2020). Credit Market Disruptions and Liquidity Spillover Effects in the Supply Chain. *Journal of Political Economy*, *128* (9), 3434–3468.

Cull, R., Xu, L. C., and Zhu, T. (2009). Formal Finance and Trade Credit during China's Transition. *Journal of Financial Intermediation*, 18, 173–92.

Cumming, D., and Groh, A. P. (2018). Entrepreneurial Finance: Unifying Themes and Future Directions. *Journal of Corporate Finance*, *50*, 538–555

Cunat, V. (2007). Trade Credit: Suppliers as Debt Collectors and Insurance Providers. *Review of Financial Studies*, *20*, 471–527.

Dass, N., Kale, J. R., and Nanda, V. (2015). Trade Credit, Relationship-specific Investment, and Product Market Power. *Review of Finance*, *19*, 1867–1923.

Diamond, D. (1984). Financial Intermediation and Delegated Monitoring. *Review of Economic Studies*, *51*,393–414.

Dunn, T., & Holtz-Eakin, D. (2000). Financial Capital, Human Capital, and the Transition to Self-Employment: Evidence from Intergenerational Links. Journal of Labor Economics, 18, 282–305.

Elston, J. A., and Audretsch, D. B. (2010). Risk Attitudes, Wealth and Sources of Entrepreneurial Start-up Capital. *Journal of Economic Behavior & Organization, 76* (1), 82–89.

Fisman, R., and Love, I. (2003). Trade Credit, Financial Intermediary Development, and Industry Growth. *Journal of Finance*, *58*, 353–374.

Garcia-Appendini, E., and Montoriol-Garriga, J. (2013). Firms as Liquidity Providers: Evidence from the 2007–2008 Financial Crisis, *Journal of Financial Economics*, *109* (1), 272–291

Ghatak, M., and Guinnane, T. (1999). The Economics of Lending with Joint Liability: Theory and Practice. *Journal of Development Economics*, *60*, 195–228.

Giannetti, M., Serrano-Velarde, N., and Tarantino, E. (2021). Cheap Trade Credit and Competition in Downstream Markets. *Journal of Political Economy*, forthcoming.

Giannetti, M., Burkart, M., & Ellingsen, T. (2011). What You Sell Is What You Lend- Explaining Trade Credit Contracts. Review of Financial Studies, 24, 1261–1298.

Gofman, M., and Wu, Y. (2021). Trade credit and profitability in production networks. *Journal of Financial Economics*, Forthcoming.

Jacobson, T., and Von Schedvin, E. (2015). Trade Credit and The Propagation of Corporate Failure an Empirical Analysis. *Econometrica, 83* (4), 1315–1371.

Jiang, W., Li, K. & Shao, P. (2010). When shareholders are creditors: Effects of the simultaneous holding of equity and debt by non-commercial banking institutions. The Review of Financial Studies, 23(10), 3595–3637.

Kandori, M., (1992). Social Norms and Community Enforcement. *Review of Economic Studies, 59,* 63–80.

Karlan, D., Mobius, M., Rosenblat, T., and Szeidl, A. (2009). Trust and Social Collateral. *Quarterly Journal of Economics* 124:1307–1361.

Klapper, L., Laeven, L., and Rajan, R. (2012). Trade Credit Contracts. *Review of Financial Studies, 25,* 838–867.

Lee, S., and Persson, P. (2016). Financing from Family and Friends. *Review of Financial Studies, 29,* 2341–2386.

Lehar, A., Song, Y., and Yuan, L. (2020). Industry Structure and the Strategic Provision of Trade Credit by Upstream Firms. *Review of Financial Studies, 33,* 4916–4972.

Li, X, Ng, J., and Saffar, W. (2021). Financial Reporting and Trade Credit- Evidence from Mandatory IFRS Adoption. *Contemporary Accounting Research, 38* (1), 96–128.

McMillan, J., and Woodruff, C. (1999). Interfirm Relationships and Informal Credit in Vietnam. *Quarterly Journal of Economics, 114,* 1285–1320.

Montgomery, R., Bhattacharya, D. and Hulme, D. (1996). Credit for the Poor in Bangladesh: The BRAC Rural Development Programme and the Government Thana Resource Development and Employment Programme. In D. Hulme and P. Mosley (eds.), *Finance Against Poverty,* Vol. 2, Routledge, London.

Ng, C.K., Smith, J.K., & Smith, R. L. (1999). Evidence on the Determinants of Credit Terms Used in Interfirm Trade. Journal of Finance, 54 (3), 1109–1129.

Petersen M., and Rajan. R. (1997). Trade Credit: Theories and Evidence. *Review of Financial Studies, 10,* 661–697.

Qian, M., and Huang. Y. (2016). Political Institutions, Entrenchments, and the Sustainability of Economic Development – A Lesson from Rural Finance. *China Economic Review, 40,* 152–178.

Rebel C., and Sokolyk, T (2016). Who Needs Credit and Who Gets Credit? Evidence From the Surveys of Small Business Finances. *Journal of Financial Stability, 24,* 40–60.

Smith, J. K. (1987). Trade Credit and Informational Asymmetry. *Journal of Finance, 42,* 863–872.

Sundaram, R. K., and Yermack, D. L. (2007). Pay Me Later: Inside Debt and Its Role in Managerial Compensation. *Journal of Finance, 62,* 1551–1588.

Tsai, K. (2004). Imperfect Substitutes: The Local Political Economy of Informal Finance and Microfinance in Rural China and India. *World Development, 32,* 1487–507.

Udry, C. (1994). Risk and Insurance in a Rural Credit Market: An Empirical Investigation in Northern Nigeria. *Review of Economic Studies, 61,* 495–526.

Wilner, B. S. (2000). The Exploitation of Relationships in Financial Distress: The Case of Trade Credit. *Journal of Finance, 55,* 153–178.

Jonathan Marks and Aleia Bucci

6 Funding entrepreneurs within business groups: An emerging market view

Abstract: Business groups, especially in emerging markets, overcome institutional voids and failure by creating internal capital markets. Business groups offer a range of membership benefits including market access, relational and financial capital, and competitive barriers to entry. This chapter examines the institutional, relational, and resource-based perspectives from which business groups consider funding decisions. This is contextualised within an emerging market environment with an emphasis on sub-Saharan Africa. Several areas for future research are suggested, based on recent research on this field. These research domains suggest an important move toward understanding the nature of corporate governance and disclosure within business groups, and the relationship between this and performance.

Keywords: business groups, emerging economies, institutional voids, governance, relational capital

Introduction

Emerging markets are often characterized by institutional voids which business groups overcome through the creation of their own internal markets (Chari & Dixit, 2015; Poczter, 2018), replicating the functions of missing institutions (Khanna & Palepu, 2000a) and acquiring the capability to repeatedly enter a variety of industries (Guillén, 2000). Firms can secure access to goods and services with more certainty and at a lower cost when they join or form a business group as opposed to obtaining them directly through the market (Granovetter, 1994). This chapter discusses the underlying theory that drives research into business groups, particularly in emerging markets, and offers three lenses through which to examine funding issues that relate to entrepreneurs in business groups. The chapter concludes with an agenda for future research, suggesting that areas of governance and firm performance within emerging market business groups is both an important and timely area for future research.

Jonathan Marks, Aleia Bucci, Gordon Institute of Business Sciences, University of Pretoria

https://doi.org/10.1515/9783110726312-009

Literature review

Business groups are broadly defined as "confederations of legally independent firms sharing multiplex economic and social ties"' (Poczter, 2018, p. 1150). These groups are "bound by administrative, financial, family, ethnic, society, religion and regional ties" (Mishra & Akbar, 2007, p. 23). Research into business groups has covered a varied landscape and we draw on seminal works to offer three perspectives from which to understand business group research in emerging market contexts: institutional (macro), relational (meso) and resource (micro).

Institutional perspective (Macro Level)

Research on business groups emerges from the perspective of market failure, market imperfection, and institutional voids (Carney et al., 2018; Castellacci, 2015; Guillén, 2000; Yiu et al., 2007). These features are common in an emerging market context where structural inadequacies and institutional failures that support organized economic activity are often missing (Khanna & Palepu, 2000b). It is common to find business groups with diverse business operations, offering inputs, structures and services to compensate for the lack of a country-level organizational framework (Fisman & Khanna, 2004).

Institutional voids offer both impetus and opportunity to business groups. Business groups navigate these voids through inter-firm transactions and internal markets, including professional know-how, managerial skill, labor, capital, information, and technology (Guillén, 2000; Ramaswamy et al., 2017). Business groups address institutional inadequacies associated within the normative, socio-cognitive, and regulative pillars in emerging contexts and use these inadequacies to build stronger relational capital (Pennings & Lee, 1999) and reduce high transaction costs (Khanna & Rivkin, 2001; King, 2007). However, while business groups can be important contributors to the institutional fabric of a country, they can also be exploiters of the opportunities created by structural voids (Khanna & Yafeh, 2007).

Relational perspective (Meso Level)

Business group structure, often a cue to the relational structure, is a function of social setting and intergroup connectedness (Yiu et al., 2007). The structure of business groups varies (Lensink et al., 2003) – diversified or focused, vertically or horizontally integrated, level of intragroup trade, involvement in financial services, and relationships with government (Khanna & Yafeh, 2007). The relational perspective gives rise to two dimensions of connectedness: horizontal and vertical. Horizontal refers to the manner in which firms engage among themselves as independent, interlinked, and interdependent entities (Yiu et al., 2007) and is achieved through internal transactions (Khanna & Palepu, 2000b). Interlocking directorships and cross shareholding or other horizontal mechanisms are used to create interdependency and non-ownership control (Choi et al., 2018; Hussain & Safdar, 2018; Sapinski & Carroll, 2018). This recreates an external market within business groups, overcoming institutional voids, albeit with some risk of market dominance and excessive market power (Pattnaik et al., 2018). Vertical linkages are the mechanism of control exercised by the dominant owner through the hierarchy of the business group (Yiu et al., 2007). This vertical system of control, commonly seen in Korean *chaebols*, makes use of 'central firms' to acquire younger firms with greater growth potential (Almeida et al., 2011). Also common among business groups is a pyramidal structure where firm control is exercised through a chain of ownership relationships (Almeida & Wolfenzon, 2006). These structures are used to avoid dual-share classes while still exercising control over voting rights, decision making, and cash flow (Bertrand et al., 2008). However, this structure has varying impact on firm performance (Bertrand et al., 2008; Gomez-Mejia et al., 2001).

Resource perspective (Micro Level)

Entrepreneurs need capital and labor, knowledge, and market access to successfully enter an industry (Guillén, 2000). From a resource-based view, business groups are created when firms are uniquely capable of combining foreign and domestic resources in order to repeatedly enter industries quickly and efficiently; however, they can only develop their unique capability when foreign trade and investment are asymmetric and thus limit who can access resources (Guillén, 2000). The adoption of a resource-based view, especially in emerging economies, is similar to the entrenchment/exploitation perspective suggested by Carney et al. (2018) who argue that business groups develop and grow through the exploitation of intangible resources.

Funding, investment, and capital in business groups

Given the macro, meso, and micro context facing business groups in emerging economies, there are unique funding models and issues that pertain to these groups. In the following section, we examine funding and capital in emerging market business groups from two perspectives: structure, control and performance; and constraints and internal capital markets.

Structure, control, and performance

Prior research has shown that structure within business groups emerges as a function of both growth aspirations and shareholder control as well as a mechanism to alleviate financial constraints at the firm and country level (Keister, 1998; Lo, 2021; Masulis et al., 2011). A mechanism used in entrepreneurial business groups to facilitate firm growth is incentivizing entrepreneurs within the group through minority shareholding, thereby not compromising control (Iacobucci & Rosa, 2010). In order to further the rights of shareholders and to avoid the risk of cash flow appropriations common in pyramidal business group structures, stricter control of disclosed information and market regulation from intra-group loans has been found to be an effective measure among Chilean business groups (Buchuk et al., 2014). However, the appropriations of cash flow and voting rights within family business groups raises concerns about the separation between ownership and control (Almeida et al., 2011). While diversification has been seen as a strategy to enable growth and financial performance (Lu & Beamish, 2004), this is not always the case within business groups; a study of family-controlled Spanish firms showed they have little impact on value creation through diversification (Hernández-Trasobares & Galve-Górriz, 2017). Vertical systems of control also give rise to instances of tunneling, the process by which controlling shareholders move assets and resources from companies with low cash flow rights to one with greater cash flow rights, a phenomenon observed among Indian business groups (Bertrand et al., 2002) but also within the other business group communities (Carney et al., 2018).

Constraints and internal capital markets

While member firms of business groups are able to raise external funding independently, they also have the benefit of internal capital markets to provide support (Carney et al., 2011; Korotkova, 2020; Santioni & Supino, 2018). During times of economic crisis, business groups are able to mitigate potential losses and exploit opportunities through capital reallocation (Almeida et al., 2015; Masulis et al., 2021); this is also achieved through higher retained earnings, a feature of pyramidal group structures (Almeida & Wolfenzon, 2006). Although these financing approaches are strongly favored during times of constrained external financial markets, prior research points to conflicts of interest related to intra-group capital flows (Fan et al., 2016). While external capital and market constraints may drive business group firms to seek capital from internal markets, the allocation of capital from internal capital markets does not improve the overall efficiency of capital allocation (Shin & Park, 1999). Though there is a paucity of research regarding business groups internationalizing to find financial resources, this is a common strategy among entrepreneurial multi-national corporations who overcome domestic resource and capital constraints through their internationalization efforts (Gammeltoft et al., 2010). Funding decisions under conditions of constraint within business groups are also impacted by measures of investment-cash flow sensitivity (George et al., 2011). Research within Indian business groups compared investment-cash flow sensitivity with stand-alone firms and found that stand-alone firms were more sensitive to changes in cash flow than business group firms (Lensink et al., 2003).

Business groups in emerging markets

Business groups are common in emerging markets, often dominating the economic landscape (Khanna & Yafeh, 2007; Poczter, 2018). Examples of emerging market business groups include *chaebols* in Korea, business houses in India, family holdings in Turkey, and *grupos* in Latin America (Guillén, 2000). Due to their dominance, business groups often shape the economic and socio-cultural environments in which they operate (Pattnaik et al., 2018), playing a role in facilitating development (Fisman & Khanna, 2004). However, when an emerging market advances as a result of reforms, the resources available through its markets increases (Chari & Dixit, 2015) and the role of market intermediary that business groups play diminishes (Yaprak & Karademir, 2010).

Emerging market conditions

Businesses in emerging markets often go unfunded because of low access to capital due to poor financial infrastructure and regulations (Khanna & Rivkin, 2001). Business groups use their reach to overcome these challenges, bypassing inefficient external financing in favor of accessing more advantageous financing internally (Khanna & Palepu, 2000b; Masulis et al., 2020). Some business groups include banks which provide affiliated companies with access to loans, lines of credit, and financing (Poczter, 2018). Business groups can also move money to new ventures when needed (Khanna & Palepu, 2000b) and they utilize debt financing more frequently than independent companies (Carney et al., 2011). For entrepreneurs in emerging markets, access to this level and diversity of capital is often not attainable alone and affiliation with business groups can aid in securing the necessary funding to continue operations.

Affiliation with a business group can also help entrepreneurs unlock access to external capital while reducing financing costs. This is done by providing inter-firm loans, mutually guaranteeing debt (Lensink et al., 2003), reducing opportunistic behavior, resolving disputes (Khanna & Palepu, 2000b), participating in risk-sharing practices, and obtaining mutual insurance (Khanna & Yafeh, 2007). When business groups invest in other affiliates' projects, it sends a strong signal to banks and financial institutions that the project is credible (Lensink et al., 2003). Additionally, when obtaining capital in external markets, business groups can use existing business success as guarantees and negotiate access to capital on preferential terms and without disclosing as much information (Chari & Dixit, 2015). Business group affiliation gives banks and other financial institutions more confidence in providing access to capital (Lensink et al., 2003), often leading to restricted access to capital, especially in emerging markets, for firms that are not part of business groups.

By continually entering new business verticals, business groups amass considerable experience in the entrepreneurial process (Guillén, 2000) as well as in adapting imported products to local market needs (Chari & Dixit, 2015). They exchange this information and share knowledge between members (Khanna & Rivkin, 2001), further strengthening the group. Business groups also utilize their success to provide credibility and when dealing with resource providers, continually building their networks to leverage in the future (Chari & Dixit, 2015). Affiliation with a business group provides a competitive advantage over independent firms, especially when entering a new international market (Yaprak & Karademir, 2010). Business groups enjoy economies of scale and preferential access to resources (Khanna & Rivkin, 2001; Khanna & Yafeh, 2007) mainly because their substantial size gives them immense bargaining power (Pattnaik et al., 2018). In some emerging markets, many businesses that scale to the level of an initial public offering are supported by business groups (Masulis et al., 2020). Scaling a business in an emerging market is a difficult endeavor, but entrepreneurs affiliated with business groups can leverage the networks, resources, and experience business groups provide to navigate these complexities. Entrepreneurs within business groups are often able to achieve superior growth as compared to operating independently (Chari & Dixit, 2015).

Negative consequences

Though business groups solve problems of inefficient and underdeveloped market conditions in emerging economies, their dominant market power can create barriers to entry for both small businesses and unaffiliated firms (Pattnaik et al., 2018). This is done though collusion, predatory pricing, increasing consumer switching costs, restricting access to distribution, and stalling the development of external capital markets (Pattnaik et al., 2018). In certain situations, business groups leverage offshore tax havens to evade taxes and hide illegal activities (Su & Tan, 2018). Though initially encouraging innovation by creating infrastructure, the entry barriers business groups ultimately create end up stifling innovation (Mahmood & Mitchell, 2004). These negative consequences can render business groups economically counterproductive in the long term (Pattnaik et al., 2018) as well as make it more difficult for entrepreneurs not affiliated with business groups to survive, however small medium enterprises that form part of these business groups often enjoy the positive implications of these negative market consequences.

Sub-Saharan Africa context

The sub-Saharan context is driven by high levels of uncertainty, an increasing shift to capitalism, diverse organizations across sectors, and the duality of formal and informal economies (Zoogah et al., 2015). Further, both modern and traditional contexts coexist; while the modern context is similar to the Western context, the traditional context differs significantly and is characterized by collectivism, shared values, and interdependence (Zoogah et al., 2015). Emerging markets are influenced by many sociological and cultural factors (Khanna & Rivkin, 2001; Khanna & Yafeh, 2007) and African culture places a high importance on community through the communalist philosophy of ubuntu (Venter, 2004). Ubuntu centers around the concept that a person is a person through their relationships with others (Mangaliso, 2001), contrasting the individualistic tendencies seen in Western societies (West, 2014). In many parts of sub-Saharan Africa, community and family are central influences on the socio-cultural institutional context, with diverse tribal groups providing influence through their values, beliefs, and practices (Murithi et al., 2019). For example, in Kenya, elders or tribal leaders organize a *harambee* when a member of the community needs support (monetary or otherwise) and in South Africa, community members pool and lend money through *stokvels*.

While it is more difficult to be an entrepreneur in sub-Saharan Africa than in other parts of the world (Rivera-Santos et al., 2015), community and family networks support and enable entrepreneurial activities across the continent (Khavul et al., 2009; Khayesi et al., 2014). As in other markets, African business groups build and utilize social relationships to circumvent institutional voids, but what makes them unique is their ability to leverage family and community embeddedness to increase entrepreneurial activity (Murithi et al., 2019). However, as informal businesses are prominent in Africa (Khavul et al., 2009), business groups must navigate both formal and informal domains (Murithi et al., 2019).

Research agenda

Research into business groups, especially in the emerging market context remains a vibrant area for ongoing study. Consistent with the structure presented in the previous sections, we offer areas and themes to inform a future research agenda based upon the macro, meso and micro perspectives. These are detailed below and structured along the thematic framework of institutional, relational and resource perspectives.

Institutional Perspective: recent research into internationalization of business groups has yielded the need for a typology of business; this supports work that has found that rates of growth in one period as a result of internationalization may have a negative knock-on effect on growth rates in following periods (Lin et al., 2020). This aligns with research into Indian family business groups and their internationalization strategies; there is a strong relationship between board composition and the degree of family concentration in ownership and the risk appetite of business groups (Shanmugasundaram, 2020). These findings, while consistent with a small group of Indian busines groups, need to be tested and considered in other emerging market contexts.

Relational Perspective: a necessary and growing area of study relates to the role of corporate governance within business groups. Prior research has shown the relationship between performance and governance of business groups, and the manner in which these impacts capital structures and board formation (Lin et al., 2019). To this research we can add future fields of study related to the role of external independent directors and the manner in which shareholders can and should censure and discipline business group promotors (Sanan et al., 2019). Data on business groups in emerging markets typically only capture affiliate companies that are publicly traded, providing only a partial view of the overall picture (Poczter, 2018). Business groups in emerging markets often operate under complicated ownership structures, making it difficult to determine affiliate control and ownership as well as develop an understanding of the bounds of each business group (Poczter, 2018). There is also an absence of group-level evidence as studies mainly focus on affiliates (Carney et al., 2011). Further, most analyses of business groups draw from ideologies embedded in a Western perspective which may not be valid in emerging markets (Poczter, 2018).

Resource Perspective: An area that has the potential for greater empirical research is the role of private equity funding within business groups. Investment by venture capital and private equity investors has bene shown to be associated with increased governance structures, especially post-IPO, as well as better long-term performance and profitability (Gogineni & Upadhyay, 2021). These findings correlate with research conducted with African business groups raising private equity funding, with external investors retaining their post-IPO investments in business groups for longer than unaffiliated companies (Hearn et al., 2018). Further to this, and linked to issues of corporate governance, is research into related party transactions. While prior research has shown the link between information and disclosure and financial decisions in business groups (Marchini et al., 2019), this area could benefit from more in-depth empirical study. Archival research into firm capabilities and business group performance (Wang et al., 2020) gives rise to potential areas of research using types of form performance data, in particular innovation and diversification data.

Conclusion

This chapter provided a broad theoretical lens to understand current and future areas of research into business groups in emerging economies. We offer three dimensions across which to examine the phenomenon of business groups – institutional, relational, and resource-based. We also offer insights into funding challenges that face business groups in emerging markets, as well as details of constraints and internal capital markets. These research dimensions can be understood against the backdrop of the emerging market context and the conditions, challenges, and consequences that face business groups in these market environments.

The opportunities for new and follow-on research among business groups, especially in sub-Saharan Africa are both substantial and urgent. While the phenomenon of business groups faded in America, their growth in Asia and Latin America has driven much of the theory and conceptualization. The research agenda proposed in this chapter shows substantial areas for future research in the relational and resource domain, with a particular focus on issues of governance and their relationship to strategy, growth, internationalization and firm performance. The need to test this theory in the rapidly growing context of the African continent, a geographic and cultural heterogeneity, has never been more opportune.

References

Almeida, H., Kim, C. S., & Kim, H. B. (2015). Internal capital markets in business groups: Evidence from the Asian financial crisis. *Journal of Finance*, *70*(6), 2539–2586. https://doi.org/https://doi.org/10.1111/jofi.12309

Almeida, H., Park, S. Y., Subrahmanyam, M. G., & Wolfenzon, D. (2011). The structure and formation of business groups: Evidence from Korean chaebols. *Journal of Financial Economics*, *99*(2), 447–475.

Almeida, H., & Wolfenzon, D. (2006). A theory of pyramidal ownership and family business groups. *The Journal of Finance*, *61*(6), 2637–2680. https://doi.org/https://doi.org/10.1111/j.1540-6261.2006.01001.x

Bertrand, M., Johnson, S., Samphantharak, K., & Schoar, A. (2008). Mixing Family With Business: A study of Thai business groups and the families behind them. *Journal of Financial Economics*, *88*(3), 466–498.

Bertrand, M., Mehta, P., & Mullainathan, S. (2002). Ferreting out tunneling: An application to Indian business groups. *The Quarterly Journal of Economics*, *117*(1), 121–148.

Buchuk, D., Larrain, B., Muñoz, F., & Urzúa I., F. (2014). The internal capital markets of business groups: Evidence from intra-group loans. *Journal of Financial Economics*, *112*(2), 190–212. https://doi.org/https://doi.org/10.1016/j.jfineco.2014.01.003

Carney, M., Gedajlovic, E., Heugens, P., Van Essen, M., & Van Oosterhout, J. (2011). Business group affiliation, performance, context, and strategy: A meta-analysis. *Academy of Management Journal*, *54*(3), 437–460. https://doi.org/10.5465/AMJ.2011.61967812

Carney, M., Van Essen, M., Estrin, S., & Shapiro, D. (2018). Business groups reconsidered: Beyond paragons and parasites. *Academy of Management Perspectives, 32*(4), 493–516. https://doi. org/10.5465/amp.2016.0058

Castellacci, F. (2015). Institutional voids or organizational resilience? Business groups, innovation, and market development in Latin America. *World Development, 70*, 43–58. https://doi.org/ 10.1016/j.worlddev.2014.12.014

Chari, M. D. R., & Dixit, J. (2015). Business groups and entrepreneurship in developing countries after reforms. *Journal of Business Research, 68*(6), 1359–1366. https://doi.org/10.1016/j. jbusres.2014.12.006

Choi, J. J., Jo, H., Kim, J., & Kim, M. S. (2018). Business groups and corporate social responsibility. *Journal of Business Ethics, 153*(4), 931–954. https://doi.org/10.1007/s10551-018-3916-0

Fan, J. P. H., Jin, L., & Zheng, G. (2016). Revisiting the bright and dark sides of capital flows in business groups. *Journal of Business Ethics, 134*, 509–528. https://doi.org/https://doi.org/ 10.1007/s10551-014-2382-6

Fisman, R., & Khanna, T. (2004). Facilitating development: The role of business groups. *World Development, 32*(4), 609–628. https://doi.org/10.1016/j.worlddev.2003.08.012

Gammeltoft, P., Barnard, H., & Madhok, A. (2010). Emerging multinationals, emerging theory: Macro- and micro-level perspectives. *Journal of International Management, 16*(2), 95–101. https://doi.org/10.1016/j.intman.2010.03.001

George, R., Kabir, R., & Qian, J. (2011). Investment-cash flow sensitivity and financing constraints: New evidence from Indian business group firms. *Journal of Multinational Financial Management, 21*(2), 69–88. https://doi.org/10.1016/j.mulfin.2010.12.003

Gogineni, S., & Upadhyay, A. (2021). Venture capital and private equity investors, governance and success of IPOs – Evidence from India. *SSRN*. https://doi.org/https://dx.doi.org/10.2139/ ssrn.3837449

Gomez-Mejia, L. R., Nuñez-Nickel, M., & Gutierrez, I. (2001). The role of family ties in agency contracts. *The Academy of Management Journal, 44*(1), 81–95. https://doi.org/https://doi. org/10.2307/3069338

Granovetter, M. (1994). Business groups. In N. Smelser & R. Swedberg (Eds.), *The Handbook of Economic Sociology* (pp. 453–475). Princeton University Press.

Guillén, M. F. (2000). Business groups in emerging economies: A resource-based view. *Academy of Management Journal, 43*(3), 362–380. https://doi.org/https://doi.org/10.2307/1556400

Hearn, B., Oxelheim, L., & Randøy, T. (2018). The institutional determinants of private equity involvement in business groups – The case of Africa. *Journal of World Business, 53*(2), 118–133. https://doi.org/10.1016/j.jwb.2016.02.002

Hernández-Trasobares, A., & Galve-Górriz, C. (2017). Diversification and family control as determinants of performance: A study of listed business groups. *European Research on Management and Business Economics, 23*(1), 46–64. https://doi.org/https://doi.org/10.1016/j.iedeen.2016.04.001

Hussain, S., & Safdar, N. (2018). Tunneling: Evidence from family business groups of Pakistan. *Business & Economic Review, 10*(2), 97–122. https://doi.org/dx.doi.org/10.22547/BER/10.2.5

Iacobucci, D., & Rosa, P. (2010). The growth of business groups by habitual entrepreneurs: The role of entrepreneurial teams. *Entrepreneurship Theory and Practice, 34*(2), 351–377. https://doi. org/https://doi.org/10.1111%2Fj.1540-6520.2010.00378.x

Keister, L. A. (1998). Engineering growth: Business group structure and firm performance in China's transition economy. *American Journal of Sociology, 104*(2), 404–440. https://doi.org/https:// doi.org/10.1086/210043

Khanna, T., & Palepu, K. (2000a). Is group affiliation profitable in emerging markets? An analysis of diversified Indian business groups. *Journal of Finance, 55*(2), 867–891. https://doi.org/ 10.1111/0022-1082.00229

Khanna, T., & Palepu, K. (2000b). The future of business groups in emerging markets: Long-run evidence from Chile. *Academy of Management Journal*, *43*(3), 268–285. https://doi.org/10.2307/1556395

Khanna, T., & Rivkin, J. W. (2001). Estimating the performance effects of business groups in emerging markets. *Strategic Management Journal*, *22*(1), 45–74. https://doi.org/10.1002/1097-0266(200101)22:1<45::AID-SMJ147>3.0.CO;2-F

Khanna, T., & Yafeh, Y. (2007). Business groups in emerging markets: Paragons or parasites? *Journal of Economic Literature*, *45*(2), 331–372. https://doi.org/10.1257/jel.45.2.331

Khavul, S., Bruton, G. D., & Wood, E. (2009). Informal family business in Africa. *Entrepreneurship Theory and Practice*, *33*(6), 1219–1238. https://doi.org/10.1111/j.1540-6520.2009.00342.x

Khayesi, J. N. O., George, G., & Antonakis, J. (2014). Kinship in entrepreneur networks: Performance effects of resource assembly in Africa. *Entrepreneurship Theory and Practice*, *38*(6), 1323–1342. https://doi.org/10.1111/etap.12127

King, A. (2007). Cooperation between Corporations and Environmental Groups: A Transaction Cost Perspective. *Academy of Management Review*, *32*(3), 889–900.

Korotkova, Y. (2020). Internal capital markets in Russian business groups: Evidence from corporate investments. *Journal of Corporate Finance Research*, *14*(2), 58–71. https://doi.org/https://doi.org/10.17323/j.jcfr.2073-0438.14.2.2020.58-71

Lensink, R., Van der Molen, R., & Gangopadhyay, S. (2003). Business groups, financing constraints and investment: The case of India. *Journal of Development Studies*, *40*(2), 93–119. https://doi.org/10.1080/00220380412331293787

Lin, C., Nguyen, H.C., & Tran, H.H. (2019). Comprative review of business group affiliates and firms' performance. *Baltic Journal of Management*, *14*(4), 616–640.

Lin, W.T., Chen, Y.Y., Ahstrom, D., & Wang, L.C. (2020). Does international expansion constrain growth? Business groups, internationalization, institutional distance, and the Penrose effect. *Multinational Business Review*, 29(1), 70–95.

Lo, F.-Y. (2021). Co-alignment of resources and diversification strategy on business groups. *European Journal of International Management*, *15*(4), 615–627. https://doi.org/https://dx.doi.org/10.1504/EJIM.2021.114626

Lu, J. W., & Beamish, P. W. (2004). International diversification and firm performance: The S-curve hypothesis. *The Academy of Management Journal*, *47*(4), 598–609. https://doi.org/https://doi.org/10.2307/20159604

Mahmood, I. P., & Mitchell, W. (2004). Two faces: Effects of business groups on innovation in emerging economies. *Management Science*, *50*(10), 1348–1365. https://doi.org/10.1287/mnsc.1040.0259

Mangaliso, M. P. (2001). Building competitive advantage from ubuntu: Management lessons from South Africa. *Academy of Management Executive*, *15*(3), 23–33. https://doi.org/10.5465/AME.2001.5229453

Marchini, P.L., Andreei, P., & Medioli, A. (2019). Related party transactions disclosure and procedures: a critical analysis in business groups. *Corporate Governance*, 19(6), 1253–1273.

Masulis, R. W., Pham, P. K., & Zein, J. (2011). Family business groups around the world: Financing advantages, control motivations, and organizational choices. *Review of Financial Studies*, *24*(11), 3556–3600. https://doi.org/10.1093/rfs/hhr052

Masulis, R. W., Pham, P. K., & Zein, J. (2020). Family business group expansion through IPOs: The role of internal capital markets in financing growth while preserving control. *Management Science*, *66*(11), 5191–5215. https://doi.org/10.1287/mnsc.2019.3418

Masulis, R. W., Pham, P. K., Zein, J., & Ang, A. E. S. (2021). Crises as opportunities for growth: The strategic value of business group affiliation. *UNSW Business School Research Paper Forthcoming*. https://doi.org/https://dx.doi.org/10.2139/ssrn.2517810

Mishra, A., & Akbar, M. (2007). Empirical examination of diversification strategies in business groups: Evidence from emerging markets. *International Journal of Emerging Markets*, 2(1), 22–38. https://doi.org/10.1108/17468800710718877

Murithi, W., Vershinina, N., & Rodgers, P. (2019). Where less is more: Institutional voids and business families in sub-Saharan Africa. *International Journal of Entrepreneurial Behaviour and Research*, 26(1), 158–174. https://doi.org/10.1108/IJEBR-07-2017-0239

Pattnaik, C., Lu, Q., & Gaur, A. S. (2018). Group affiliation and entry barriers: The dark side of business groups in emerging markets. *Journal of Business Ethics*, 153, 1051–1066. https://doi.org/10.1007/s10551-018-3914-2

Pennings, J. M., & Lee, K. (1999). Social capital of organization: Conceptualization, level of analysis, and performance implications. In L. R.T.A.J. & G. S.M. (Eds.), *Corporate Social Capital and Liability*. Springer. https://doi.org/https://doi.org/10.1007/978-1-4615-5027-3_3

Poczter, S. (2018). Business groups in emerging markets: A survey and analysis. *Emerging Markets Finance and Trade*, 54(5), 1150–1182. https://doi.org/10.1080/1540496X.2017.1286587

Ramaswamy, K., Purkayastha, S., & Petitt, B. S. (2017). How do institutional transitions impact the efficacy of related and unrelated diversification strategies used by business groups? *Journal of Business Research*, 72, 1–13. https://doi.org/10.1016/j.jbusres.2016.11.005

Rivera-Santos, M., Holt, D., Littlewood, D., & Kolk, A. (2015). Social entrepreneurship in sub-Saharan Africa. *Academy of Management Perspectives*, 29(1), 72–91. https://doi.org/10.5465/amp.2013.0128

Sanan, N.K., Jaisinghani, D., & Yadav, S. (2019) Corporate governance, firm performance, and business group affiliation: evidence from India. *Management Decision*, 59(8),1863–1876.

Santioni, R., & Supino, I. (2018). Internal capital markets in Italian business groups: Evidence from the financial crisis. *Questioni Di Economia e Finanza (Occasional Papers)*, 421.

Sapinski, J. P., & Carroll, W. K. (2018). Interlocking directorates and corporate networks. In A. Nölke & C. May (Eds.), *Handbook of the International Political Economy of the Corporation* (pp. 45–60). Edward Elgar Publishing.

Shanmugasundaram, S. (2020). Internationalization and governance of Indian family-owned business groups. *Journal of Family Business Management*, 10(1), 76–94.

Shin, H.-H., & Park, Y. S. (1999). Financing constraints and internal capital markets: Evidence from Korean "chaebols." *Journal of Corporate Finance*, 5(2), 169–191.

Su, W., & Tan, D. (2018). Business groups and tax havens. *Journal of Business Ethics*, 153, 1067–1081. https://doi.org/10.1007/s10551-018-3910-6

Venter, E. (2004). The notion of ubuntu and communalism in African educational discourse. *Studies in Philosophy and Education*, 23(2/3), 149–160. https://doi.org/10.1023/b:sped.0000024428.29295.03

Wang, S.H., Chen, C.J., Guo, A.R.S., & Lin, Y.H. (2020). Strategy, capabilities, and businss group peformance. *Manageemnt Decision*, 58(1), 76–97.

West, A. (2014). Ubuntu and business ethics: Problems, perspectives and prospects. *Journal of Business Ethics*, 121(1), 47–61. https://doi.org/10.1007/s10551-013-1669-3

Yaprak, A., & Karademir, B. (2010). The internationalization of emerging market business groups: An integrated literature review. *International Marketing Review*, 27(2), 245–262. https://doi.org/10.1108/02651331011037548

Yiu, D. W., Lu, Y., Bruton, G. D., & Hoskisson, R. E. (2007). Business groups: An integrated model to focus future research: Review paper. *Journal of Management Studies*, 44(8), 1551–1579. https://doi.org/10.1111/j.1467-6486.2007.00735.x

Zoogah, D. B., Peng, M. W., & Woldu, H. (2015). Institutions, resources, and organizational effectiveness in Africa. *Academy of Management Perspectives*, 29(1), 7–31. https://doi.org/10.5465/amp.2012.0033

Tiago Ratinho

7 How business incubators and accelerators finance startups

Abstract: Business incubators (BI) and business accelerators (BA) are hallmarks of entrepreneurship support. By providing a mix of infrastructure, business assistance, and access to professional networks, BIs and BAs increase startups' chances of survival, growth, and longevity. The growing body of scholarly research of BI and accelerators has so far largely overlooked the financial aspects of their intervention in startups. This chapter explores how BIs and accelerators finance indirectly startups using two common theoretical frameworks: service provision and incubation mechanisms. I finalize with implications for policy makers, business incubation and acceleration managers, prospective startups, and investors.

Keywords: business incubation, entrepreneurship support, entrepreneurial finance

Introduction

Business incubators (BI) are fundamental tools of entrepreneurship policy. Vigorous support for new business creation unleashed a host of private and public organizations to assist aspiring entrepreneurs in recent decades. The promise of local and regional economic prosperity had led governments to build new or repurposed space to house startups. Universities have established incubation programs as means to support both faculty (to commercialize technology) and students (to further their new business ideas). Private initiatives have sprung up to encourage aspiring entrepreneurs to develop professional entrepreneurial competencies.

Despite being globally ubiquitous, scholarly research often cast doubts about the benefits of BIs to startups. Broadly focused on to the general effects of BI in performance, survival, and longevity, or the internal mechanisms that govern incubation, studies fall short of finding generalizable conclusions about BI design and operation. The main reason behind this is possibly the multitude of models, missions, and environmental factors that may contribute more or less to incubation outcomes, making it difficult to disentangle the net effects on each incubated startup (Barbero et al., 2012; Bergek & Norrman, 2008; Hackett & Dilts, 2004; Ratinho et al., 2020). One largely overlooked aspect of BIs intervention is financial support. Due to its relative rarity in population surveys of BIs (Knopp, 2012), few if any empirical studies focus on BI's direct or indirect financial support to startups.

Tiago Ratinho, IESEG School of Management, Univ. Lille, CNRS, UMR 9221 - LEM - Lille Economie Management, F-59000 Lille, France

https://doi.org/10.1515/9783110726312-010

This chapter analyses the financial support given by BIs/BAs by making use of two prevailing conceptualizations of BIs. Firstly, I look at *service portfolios* (e.g. Bruneel et al., 2012; Von Zedtwitz & Grimaldi, 2006), a perspective conceptualizing incubation as a bundle of resources flowing from the BI to the startup. This stream of literature sees BAs as a subtype of BIs, a novel generation differentiated from previous incubation models by a different configuration of services provided (Pauwels et al., 2016). Secondly, I look at *incubation mechanisms* (e.g. Amezcua et al., 2013, 2020; Mian, 2014), a perspective that sees incubation/acceleration as a process consisting of more or less tailored infusion of resources in startups and heavily relying on the ability of BIs/BAs to manage external local or distant networks. In both perspectives, financial support is seen as being facilitated through brokerage with external professional network rather than directly provided. While in the service portfolio perspective, the role of finance is in the incubation/acceleration is very succinctly analyzed, the incubation mechanisms stream of literature takes a more general stance and largely omits financial support altogether.

What are BIs?

BIs are "property-based organizations with identifiable administrative centers focused on the mission of business acceleration through knowledge agglomeration and resource sharing" (Phan et al., 2005, p. 166). The first BI was created in Batavia, NY (Adkins, 2002) and since then the idea of concentrating young companies under a single roof garnered support, so much so that BIs are currently ubiquitous. Particularly during the 1980s, we have witnessed an exponential growth of BIs; in the US alone, there were 12 BIs in 1980 and estimates point to about 1400 in 2005 (Knopp, 2012). The incubation model spread to other parts of the world with some regional adaptations such as business innovation centres, incubateur and pepiniéres d"entreprises (French model), venture laboratories, and more recently business accelerators (Cohen, 2013). Comprehensive studies are lacking in the past decade but older estimates point to the presence of BIs in nearly every EU member state with over 900 BIs on the European continent (EC, 2002). During the dot-com bubble, there were as many as 350 new incubators founded to support internet startups (Hansen et al., 2000).

This extraordinary popularity and rapid dissemination of the incubator concept are the result of purposeful support by governments, regional authorities, and universities, among others, as well as a general perception of BIs' efficacy in supporting aspiring entrepreneurs and startups. But while practitioners often tout the universal benefits of BIs (e.g. Lewis, 2010), academics have had difficulty in finding everlasting effects of being incubated. Studies have found that BIs can essentially serve as a kind of artificial support to firms which will inexorably perish after graduation (Schwartz, 2008, 2011, 2013). Little support was found for the role of BIs in promoting university-industry interaction (Ratinho & Henriques, 2010; Rothaermel & Thursby, 2005), promoting academic entrepreneurs and high-tech companies birth (Benneworth & Ratinho, 2014), or regional innovation activity (Colombo & Delmastro, 2002). However, other perspectives have emerged more recently, providing alternative (and more charitable) explanations for these less positive aggregate results.

BIs are extremely heterogeneous (Knopp, 2012) and new models under the incubation umbrella increasingly emerge. Perhaps the largest industry association – the US-based National Business Incubator Association – changed its name to International Business Innovation Association to expand overseas but also to welcome among its members other related organization much as shared workspaces or entrepreneurship centers (InBIA, 2021). Academic research followed suit. Given the multitude of models, missions, promoters, and regional characteristics, BIs should not be assessed against an universal standard (Bergek & Norrman, 2008).

I now turn our attention to two of the common conceptualizations of BIs: service portfolios (e.g. Bruneel et al., 2012; Von Zedtwitz & Grimaldi, 2006); and incubation mechanisms (e.g. Amezcua et al., 2013, 2020; S. A. Mian, 2014).

Service portfolios: Incubators as service providers

The conceptualization of BIs as service providers is the most pervasive in the academic literature. Since the 1980s when the phenomenon of incubation appeared on the radar of researchers, BIs have been investigated as organizations that provide a bundle of services designed to assist aspiring entrepreneurs to establish to launch their ventures and allow them to thrive (Smilor & Gill, 1986). The underlying theoretical rationale of this conceptualization is the resource-based view of the firm (RBV) popularized by Barney (1991), according to which firm's sustained competitive advantage is due to valuable, rare, inimitable, and non-substitutable bundles of resources. Logically, as startups lack the resources or otherwise do not meet the VRIN conditions, the BI's intervention is geared towards ensuring the flow of such resources alongside their development (Soetanto, 2006). This perspective also gave way to the debate about the impact of selection process as well as the potential detrimental effects of a potential mismatch between the service portfolio and tenant companies (Aerts et al., 2007).

In their study of historical generations of BIs, Bruneel and colleagues (2012) identify three fundamental service types traditionally provided by BIs: infrastructure, business assistance, and access to networks. The most visible service provide by BIs is *infrastructure*. In fact, despite the advent of virtual incubators (Carayannis & von Zedtwitz, 2005; Durão et al., 2005), BIs remain essentially a property-based organization. Either built from scratch or established in repurposed older buildings usually as part of regional economic revitalization, BIs concentrate geographically aspiring entrepreneurs, startups, and sometimes more established companies which guarantee a more stable bottom line (these latter often called anchor companies). The physical infrastructure dimension is directly associated with income. These BIs charge lease tenants based on square footage.

Business assistance consists of any service oriented towards helping the startup to accelerate its learning curve. The most common form of business assistance is coaching (Bruneel et al., 2012): individual support initiatives geared towards accelerating tenants' learning and skills development processes, generally involving tenant firms being assigned coaches or mentors, either for a fee or free of charge (e.g. Barrow, 2001; Knopp, 2012). General training is also often available within these BIs (Aerts et al., 2007; Barrow, 2001).

Finally, *access to networks* allows BIs to provide tenants services they do not necessarily have in-house. BIs' networks can be more or less specialized and facilitate tenants' access to potential customers, suppliers, technology partners or investors (Hansen et al., 2000; Scillitoe and Chakrabarti, 2010). Networking is in fact what differentiated BIs models in the beginning of the 2000s and was heralded as the most determinative factor for long term impact in startups (Hansen et al., 2000) and company development while being incubated (McAdam & Marlow, 2008). As BIs institutionalize their networks, that networking is no longer dependent on individuals' personal networks or contacts but rely on the active BIs' network management. One example of access to networks is venture capital (Bruneel et al., 2012). In fact, the same authors describe a particular BI that has strong institutional linkages to seed and venture capital funds by way of their common promoter (a university). This example illustrates what this service dimension describes: a host of preferential access to services that do not exist and are not directly provided by the BI.

Mechanisms of incubation: Incubators as resource scouts

More recently, research in BIs used a different theoretical conceptualization to understanding BIs' intervention in startups predicated in mechanisms rather than service provision (Amezcua et al., 2013, 2020). Although also inspired by the RBV of the firm, this theoretical view of incubation allows for a more refined view of the resource provision to startups as well as a better understanding of the BIs' expertise. For instance, business support services such as mentoring are seen and interpreted according to their impact on the startup and ability to provide resources that are harder for the startup to find without assistance. In a way, this perspective expands the networking aspect of the service provision we have discussed above introducing nuanced functions for the BIs to intervene in startup that re depended on the geographical location.

The three mechanisms identified in this conceptualization are buffering, bridging, and curating. *Buffering* consists of providing resources that intend to shelter the startup from potential adverse conditions of the external environment. This mechanism allows BIs to provide resources to the startup at lower nominal costs when compared to external alternatives. For instance, BIs often lease key-in-hand offices or other similar kinds of workstations bundled with general administrative services such as internet connection, meeting rooms, kitchen, etc.

Bridging consists of services that aim to connect the startup to resource providers. These may be associated with the BI to provide resources at lower costs or not be easily available in the immediate surroundings. Startups often have both general and industry-specific needs. For instance, all startups can benefit from preferential arrangements with professionals such as lawyers, accountants, or web designers as well as training in general business topics such marketing, sales, or human resources. Other industry-specific resources may include consultants or investors specialized in the startup's given industry.

Curating resources is a particular kind of the bridging mechanism. Rather than a mere listing of professionals or general agreements for resource provision, BIs can guide an entrepreneur to the best possible (or best match) provider. This mechanism is the most selective and idiosyncratic. It aims at facilitating the most appropriate relationships that nurture the development of unique capabilities in the startup. For instance, while all startups may benefit from legal advice at one point of their existence, a biotech/pharma new venture needs a lawyer experienced in patents, clinicals trials, among others.

It is noteworthy to emphasize that these mechanisms are not necessarily tied to one specific type of resource (financial, managerial, strategic, . . .). For instance, buffering can be enacted to lower the nominal costs of accountants in the region where the BI is located. This follows from the theoretical distinction between the two conceptualizations of BIs; each mechanism's value is analyzed through the prism of the startup and its surroundings as opposed to the service portfolio perspective that mostly espouses a "one size fits all" approach to the BIs' intervention.

BI's indirect financial support

In this section, I wish to explore the indirect financial support given by BIs. Regardless of which perspective we use, it is rather elementary that BIs intervention has both direct and indirect financial advantages. While rare, the former do exist in the form of direct cash allowances usually given in competitive contests, stipends given in cash or goods (i.e. specialized training sessions) as part of the incubation model

(Ratinho & Mitsopoulos, 2021). However, the indirect financial support is hardly mentioned in the literature.

Take the example of coaching, an integral part of business support. If the startup would not have a coach assigned by the BI it could presumably find one by itself. Besides the hourly rate of the rate, the startup would have to factor in the search and selection costs which may be more or less time-consuming. Thus, a BI-assigned coach is a substantial indirect financial support in that it saves the startup the coach's fee as well as the burden associated with finding one. But what if the coach provided by the BI is unreachable by standard methods and only accept referrals?[1]

Coaching can be associated with three incubation mechanisms:

- Buffering, if the coach is provided for free or at a more advantageous rates than it would generally be accessible in the market for other non-incubated startups.
- Bridging, if the coach is specialized in a given industry and does not usually offer her services in the geographical region in which the startup operates in.
- Curating, if the coach is not specialized but also a crucial element that can unleash a whole new host of opportunities.

Let's consider another example, that of infrastructure. Key-in-hand offices represent substantial indirect financial support for startups. Even if not leased at lower than market rates, the unnecessary burden of contracting utilities, the added value of reception services, and access to private meeting rooms already makes the choice of a BI location attractive. However, the relative value of infrastructure varies according to the startup's sector of activity. A service startup has less to gain from a key-in-hand office than a food startup benefits from a kitchen incubator.

Industry effects and benefits to startups

The value of the BI's intervention strongly depends on the sector of activity of the startup. For that reason, BIs often adapt to local environmental conditions, weighing diversification of tenant portfolios against specialization (Schwartz & Hornych, 2008, 2012). However, since the overwhelming majority of BIs are generalist, understanding the relative impact of (financial) support in startups can be the key to better ascertain the impact of BI.

To assess the relative impact of indirect financial support on startups, I use as example four archetypical startups:

---

[1] Randy Komisar, a famous tech attorney and virtual CEO based in Silicon Valley, reputedly abides by this rule.

- Technology-intensive – startups whose value proposition depends on a tangible product with a relatively long development cycle. For instance, biotech/pharma, robotics, or similar products.
- Service oriented startups are those developing a value proposition based on selling a service rather than a product (e.g, web services, SaaS, and fintech).
- Micro-manufacturing startups are those whose value proposition involves a product that need to be manufactured at a small scale. Small crafts businesses, or any small scale manufacturing business are good examples of this category.
- Finally, food companies are those developing value propositions associated to food such as new innovative restaurants or food products.

These four startups archetypes differ substantially in their patterns of innovation, scale potential, and development cycles. Similarly, the relative impact of indirect financial support services is disparate.

Technology intensive startups stand to gain the most out of infrastructure where to develop their products. If we consider the example of biotech/pharmaceutical startups, we see that without access to a proper laboratory where to conduct the necessary experiments and further clinical trials if needed, the startup is incapable to plausibly engage in product development. For these kind of startups, business assistance has a relatively reduced impact and access to networks is almost negligible when compared to infrastructure (see Table 7.1). Service oriented startups, on the contrary, gain little from having access to infrastructure as their gestation activities depend much more on business assistance and to an even higher degree on access to networks. BIs can lend their institutional weight to signal the legitimacy of the startup in the critical phases of accessing pools of customers, skilled labor, specialized suppliers, or investors.

Table 7.1: Indirect financial support of BI and sectors of activity.

	Technology intensive	Service	Micro-manufacturing	Food
Infrastructure	$$$$$	$	$$$$	$$$$$$
Business assistance	$$	$$	$$	$
Networks	$	$$$$$	$$	$

Note: $ = estimate of relative value of each service to startups.

Similarly to technology-intensive new ventures, micro-manufacturing startups are very dependent of infrastructure but have more to gain from access to networks for the same motives listed above for service companies: external legitimacy. Finally, food startups are very much dependent on infrastructure but gain relatively less from business assistance. A common configuration for incubating food business is what is known as kitchen incubator. Kitchen incubators provide commercial kitchens space so startup under a common roof usually with a taste room to welcome general public at designated hours. At least when housed there, food startup do not gain much from business assistance or access to networks since the common room is the main selling channel.

Regional effects and value of being incubated

In their empirical analysis on a comprehensive longitudinal database of US-based BIs, Amezcua and colleagues (2020) reveal that BIs are most effective in increasing startup longevity in three regional configurations: rural locations, low industry concentration areas, and urban areas with startups' high industry concentration. The mechanisms behind the successful BI intervention in each case differ slightly (see Table 7.2) and for the purposes of this book chapter those will be the basis for the discussion of the relative value for the startup.

Implicit to the conceptualization of BI's intervention presented by Amezcua and colleagues (2020), is the notion of relative expertise to enact each of the three mechanisms. Buffering by means of providing services at lower costs involves less expertise than bridging resources to startup to valuable resources present in the region or distant. For instance, buffering may depend on available funding or endowments of BI's parent institution; take the example of university-based incubator which provide offices at low or no cost on campus; or private incubators that tinker with lease costs to create economies of scale and scope.

Bridging, however, is less dependent on tangible resources and contingent on social and political capital residing in the BIs' personal and/or parent institutions. It involves sourcing, creating, and maintaining networks of professionals, investors, and industry leaders in order to be able to provide startups with both generic resources when their nominal costs are high; or industry specific resources that are easily obtainable.

Lastly, the mechanism of curating services is the most complex, idiosyncratic, and the one requiring most expertise from the BI's personnel. Usually salient in BIs located in urban regions with high industry concentration, curating resources involves knowing in detail what a particularly startup needs. Contrary to bridging services that cater to the population (general resources) or to a significant portion (industry specific resources) of incubatees, curating implies being familiar with the idiosyncrasies of each startup such as stage of development, internal processes, internal capabilities, personality and management styles to ensure a good match between startups and resources providers.

I build on Table 7.2 theoretical conceptualization of BIs and their impact on startups' longevity according to geographical location to derive the relative impact of BIs' indirect financial support (Table 7.3). In rural areas with low industry concentration, the mechanism of *bridging* provides the bulk of the indirect financial support. These regions are characterized by a paucity of both generic resources such as commercial

Table 7.2: Dominant BI mechanism per type of regional environment.

	Low Urbanization (Rural regions)	High Urbanization (Urban areas)
Low Industry Concentration	**Bridging to generic and specific resource providers**	**Buffering of generic resources; Bridging to specific resources**
	Generic resources: low Specialized resources: low Nominal costs: low	Generic resources: high Specialized resources: low Nominal costs: moderate (specific) to high (generic)
	Likely conditions for a venture located in an extra-urban area (e.g., small municipality or township);	Likely conditions for a venture in a city, but outside that region's dominant industry;
	Example of organizations in this type of region: . . . company: Gateway 2000 Computers outside Sioux City, Iowa . . . incubator: Startup Sioux City (provides access to "essential" services plus tech industry-specific assistance.)	Example of organizations in this type of region: . . . company: Microsoft in Redmond (Seattle), Washington (at the time, Seattle was known for aerospace) . . . incubator: i2E in Oklahoma (provides primarily tech industry assistance)
	Incubator's primary function: Bridging to generic and specific resources	Incubator's primary functions: Buffering against high nominal-costs of generic resources
High Industry Concentration	**Bridging to generic resources; curating of specific resources**	**Curating all resources**
	Generic resources: low Specialized resources: high Nominal costs: low (generic) to moderate (specific)	Generic resources: high Specialized resources: high Nominal costs: very high
	Likely conditions for a venture started in a small municipality or township, but within the region's dominant industry;	Likely conditions for a venture started in a city and within the region's dominant industry;
	Example of organizations in this type of region: . . . company: Contec Inc. in Spartanburg, South Carolina (provides engineering services and products to SC's automotive industry) . . . incubator: Spark Center (provides general resources, but not industry specific assistance)	Example of organizations in this type of region: . . . company: Facebook in Menlo Park, CA . . . sponsor example: BOLT (provides and facilitates access to manufacturing and design services specifically to tech hardware companies)

Table 7.2 (continued)

	Low Urbanization (Rural regions)	High Urbanization (Urban areas)
	Incubator's primary function: *Bridging* to generic resources and *curating* of specific resources	Incubator's primary functions: *Curating* of generic and specific resources

Source: Adapted from Amezcua et al. (2020)

banks, business services, office space, etc., as well as specialized industry-specific resources. There are few local competitors for resources thus lowering nominal costs relatively to urban areas (for instance, lower wages are practiced in these areas). BIs' indirect financial support against this environmental context is more pronounced when the mechanism of bridging is enacted. If nominal costs of resources are lower and those are relatively rare in any case, it means that any startup can acquire those by themselves easily thus making buffering less relevant. Similarly, there is less need for curation of resources since it is relatively affordable in time and cost for to startup to survey the environment for both generic and industry-specific resources. Bridging, however, by connecting the startup with resources that are not available in the regions are where the most value lies.

If urbanization is low (rural areas) but the BI is now located in an area with high industry concentration, its indirect financial support to startups in that industry is more salient when the three mechanisms are enacted simultaneously. Such regions are characterized by low to moderate nominal costs of resources: generic resources may still be available at a lower cost relatively to more urban areas (as seen in the previous archetypical region) but industry specific resources are more costly due to the increased industry concentration and ensuing local competitiveness. For instance, accounting services or general legal counsel is available at a low cost while highly skilled labor or first tier suppliers are more expensive. *Bridging* remains important particularly for distantly located industry specific resources but *buffering* against high costs of locally available similarly resources becomes more salient. Similarly, BIs may provide more indirect financial support by doing *curation* of local resources, particularly industry-specific ones.

In areas where urbanization is high and the startup's industry concentration low, the indirect financial support is maximized when the BI focusses on the mechanism of *buffering*. In such geographical locations, the cost of generic resources is high compared to rural areas while specialized resources are available at a relatively low cost. Thus, BIs' indirect financial support will be higher when the mechanism of buffering is enacted as means to lower the costs and easiness of access to generic resources. Curation of local generic resources may also be of value for the startup.

Table 7.3: Relative value of each BI mechanism in each regional configuration.

	Rural areas Low industry concentration	Rural areas High industry concentration	Urban areas Low industry concentration	Urban areas High industry concentration
Buffering	$	$$	$$$$	$
Bridging	$$$$$	$$$	$	$
Curation	$	$$	$$	$$$$$

Note: $ = estimate of relative value of each service to startups

Finally, in regions where both urbanization and startup industry concentration is high, BIs should focus on *curation* of resources to provide the most indirect financial support to startup. In such areas, usually world class cities or industrial clusters, all types of resources are available but at high costs. Further, the sheer abundance of resources makes any search and selection expensive for a startup. Curation is therefore the mechanism more likely to yield the most indirect financial support to startup.

Research agenda

There are a few possible avenues for research to advance our understanding about direct and indirect financial support of BIs/BAs to startups. In this section, I outline the three most prominent ones that emerge from the discussion above as well as from the latest academic research on incubation and acceleration.

The impact of the intervention: When incubation helps

BIs/BAs intervention has been under academic scrutiny for the most part of the last four decades. And while many studies have investigated the role of BIs/BAs in startups survival and performance, researchers agree that the heterogeneity of incubation/acceleration models provides a substantial challenge to ascertain their positive or negative impact (Albort-Morant & Oghazi, 2015; Hackett & Dilts, 2004; Ratinho et al., 2020). An often issue is that of mismatch between startup's needs and the BIs/BAs intervention that can emerge due to tenant selection criteria (Bruneel et al., 2012) or as a result of the incubation process over the years (McAdam & McAdam, 2008). In the case of financial support, this raises questions that merit further research:

- What happens when the service portfolio is not the most needed by the startup? For instance, startups access capital through an internal competition before gaining access to professional network while it would be wiser to dedicate time to acquire industry knowledge and engage in customer development with the assistance of an experienced entrepreneur. Would this mean that the direct support is wasted? Or less impactful? Should the company save it for later?

- What is the impact of enacting mechanisms that are misaligned with the environmental conditions experienced by the startup? Could direct finance support compensate for this misalignment? For instance, an incubator dedicated to the curation of resources in a location where startups could find them anyway (rural areas with no industry concentration) could somehow compensate this misalignment with seed investments?

Syndicate direct/indirect support

After establishing the rarity of direct financial support, I outlined the relative impact of the indirect financial support given by BIs/BAs. However, incubation and acceleration are constantly evolving and new models of entrepreneurship support designed with different combinations of direct and indirect support are likely possible. For instance, some of the most popular BAs (e.g., Y Combinator) often offer a stipend to startups and/or invest in startup at the end of the program in exchange for startup's equity. Highly competitive, these BAs are perhaps the most prominent example of a mix of direct (stipend, investment) and indirect (educational program, networking) financial support. There is also record of other organizations provide commercial real estate to specialized startups (e.g. biotech firms) taking equity of rental payments.[2]

These examples show that academic research has barely scratched the surfaced of entrepreneurial finance that includes indirect as well as direct support. And while there are studies showing that, for instance, VCs have a positive effect in professionalizing management teams (Hellmann & Puri, 2002), the magnitude of these effects remain largely overlooked. Further, we still lack evidence about the impact of the mixed direct and indirect support to be able to adequately design and operate this kind of support purposefully. a few possible questions are ripe for research:

- What is the optimal mix of direct and indirect financial support BIs/BAs should deploy? Is there a difference between providing them simultaneously or sequentially? Does it make more sense to provide firstly indirect support in the form of access to professional network before grating access to seed capital? Or are there startups that can benefit more capital before they are ready to reap the benefits of an extended professional network?

---

2 I gratefully thank the editor for having provided such a case-in-point example of this form of financial support.

– Are there strong industry effects of providing direct, indirect, or both kinds of financial support? Startups operating in industries with long development cycles may benefit more from indirect financial support in the form of labs before being able to profit from capital injections to manufacture.

Looking at the entrepreneurial ecosystem

A substantial amount of attention has been dedicated to entrepreneurial ecosystems and its role in designing entrepreneurial support mechanisms. For instance, in fairly under-developed ecosystems, BIs challenge existent archetypes and provide rather unique service portfolios eroding the boundaries between blurring the boundaries between angel investors, property-based incubation, acceleration, and entrepreneurship education (Ratinho & Mitsopoulos, 2021). In their study made in Greece – a resource-constrained economy which lost a third of its wealth in one decade – multiple intriguing combinations of entrepreneurship support were found: co-location of all angel investments combined with periodical compulsory monitoring; co-working space provision conditional to mentoring and participation in frequent pitch competitions; and an educational program with curated interactions with investors (Ratinho & Mitsopoulos, 2021, pp. 310–311). Further, studies have shown that BIs in emerging markets can operate as systemic intermediaries not only support (in)directly startups but essentially modifying the environment in which the startups operates (Dutt et al., 2015). Against this backdrop, several research questions emerge:

– Are BIs/BAs the best suited entrepreneurship support mechanism to be able to provide a higher share of direct financial support? The opposite is also worth asking: are VCs and other financiers able to operate entrepreneurship support mechanisms that rely more substantially in indirect financial support?

– What are the boundary conditions for BIs/BAs to engage in more systemic interventions? For instance, should incubation in well-functioning markets include this function or is the effect only substantial in resource-constrained environments?

Implications

In this chapter, I have taken a novel perspective of looking at BIs/BAs intervention as a mix direct and, for the most part, indirect financial support. Taken together, this exercise has implications for investors, startups, incubation/acceleration managers, and policy makers.

Implications for investors: Investors should be more aware of the possibility of syndicate investments by mixing direct and indirect financial support. For instance, financial investments can be accompanied by indirect financial support. The BIs' intervention in terms resources obtained through their services and mechanisms could be a condition to access capital. When coupled with direct financial investment (angel funding or seed capital), the BI's indirect financial support can be an asset and represent a considerable amount of the investment depending on sector of activity and geographical location.

Implications for startups: Financial resources are of utmost importance to startups (Clarysse & Bruneel, 2007). My assessment of BIs' intervention as indirect financial support should help startups in the gestation phase to look more carefully to each BIs service portfolios and available incubation mechanisms before seeking our other complementary formal financial investments The choice of a BIs should be made wisely and according to local environmental conditions and sector of activity of the startup.

Implications for BI managers: Perhaps it is rather trivial for BI managers to associate their intervention as indirect financial support given from their point of view service provision or mechanism deployment has costs. However, the costs in which in the incubator incurs to provide services other than infrastructure (usually has high fixed costs) are not directly proportional to the value those have on startups. Take the example of access to networks through bridging or curating. The value for startups is extremely high while for BIs the marginal costs of adding one more professional contact to their rolodex is low.

Implications for policy makers: it may a truism to say the incubation is much more than the shiny new infrastructure. My assessment of the indirect financial support of BIs can inform policy makers and those involved in designing entrepreneurial support policies that include BIs to consider further the issue of BI expertise. Providing services as well as establishing and managing professional incubation mechanisms requires specialized expertise.

References

Adkins, D. (2002). *A Brief History of Business Incubation in the United States*. National Business Incubation Association.

Aerts, K., Matthyssens, P., & Vandenbempt, K. (2007). Critical role and screening practices of European business incubators. *Technovation, 27*(5), 254–267. Scopus. https://doi.org/10.1016/j.technovation.2006.12.002

Albort-Morant, G., & Oghazi, P. (2015). How useful are incubators for new entrepreneurs? *Journal of Business Research*. https://doi.org/10.1016/j.jbusres.2015.12.019

Amezcua, A. S., Grimes, M. G., Bradley, S. W., & Wiklund, J. (2013). Organizational sponsorship and founding environments: A contingency view on the survival of business incubated firms, 1994–2007. *Academy of Management Journal, 56*(6), 1628–1654.

Amezcua, A. S., Ratinho, T., Plummer, L. A., & Jayamohan, P. (2020). Organizational sponsorship and the economics of place: How regional urbanization and localization shape incubator outcomes. *Journal of Business Venturing*, *35*(July), 105967. https://doi.org/10.1016/j.jbusvent.2019.105967

Barbero, J. L., Casillas, J. C., Ramos, A., & Guitar, S. (2012). Revisiting incubation performance. *Technological Forecasting and Social Change*, *79*(5), 888–902. https://doi.org/10.1016/j.techfore.2011.12.003

Barney, J. (1991). Firm Resources and Competitive Advantage. *Journal of Management*, *17*(1), 99–120.

Barrow, C. (2001). Incubators: A Realist's Guide to the World's New Business Accelerators. Wiley.

Benneworth, P., & Ratinho, T. (2014). Reframing the Role of Knowledge Parks and Science Cities in Knowledge-Based Urban Development. *Environment and Planning C: Government and Policy*, *32*(5), 784–808. https://doi.org/10.1068/c1266r

Bergek, A., & Norrman, C. (2008). Incubator best practice: A framework. *Technovation*, *28*(1–2), 20–28. https://doi.org/10.1016/j.technovation.2007.07.008

Bruneel, J., Ratinho, T., Clarysse, B., & Groen, A. (2012). The evolution of business incubators: Comparing demand and supply of business incubation services across different incubator generations. *Technovation*, *32*(2), 110–121. https://doi.org/10.1016/j.technovation.2011.11.003

Carayannis, E. G., & von Zedtwitz, M. (2005). Architecting gloCal (global–local), real-virtual incubator networks (G-RVINs) as catalysts and accelerators of entrepreneurship in transitioning and developing economies: Lessons learned and best practices from current development and business incubation practices. *Technovation*, *25*(2), 95–110. https://doi.org/10.1016/S0166-4972(03)00072-5

Clarysse, B., & Bruneel, J. (2007). Nurturing and growing innovative start-ups: The role of policy as integrator. *R&d Management*, *37*(2), 139–149.

Cohen, S. (2013). What Do Accelerators Do? Insights from Incubators and Angels. *Innovations*, *8*(3–4), 19–25.

Colombo, M. G., & Delmastro, M. (2002). How effective are technology incubators?: Evidence from Italy. *Research Policy*, *31*(7), 1103–1122.

Durão, D., Sarmento, M., Varela, V., & Maltez, L. (2005). Virtual and real-estate science and technology parks: A case study of Taguspark. *Technovation*, *25*(3), 237–244. https://doi.org/10.1016/S0166-4972(03)00110-X

Dutt, N., Hawn, O., Vidal, E., Chatterji, A. K., McGahan, A. M., & Mitchell, W. (2015). How Open System Intermediaries Address Institutional Failures: The Case of Business Incubators in Emerging-Market Countries. *Academy of Management Journal*, amj. 2012.0463. https://doi.org/10.5465/amj.2012.0463

EC. (2002). *Benchmarking of Business Incubators*. European Commission.

Hackett, S. M., & Dilts, D. M. (2004). A systematic review of business incubation research. *The Journal of Technology Transfer*, *29*(1), 55–82.

Hansen, M. T., Chesbrough, H. W., Nohria, N., & Sull, D. N. (2000). Networked incubators. *Harvard Business Review*, *78*(5), 74–84.

Hellmann, T., & Puri, M. (2002). Venture capital and the professionalization of start-up firms: Empirical evidence. *The Journal of Finance*, *57*(1), 169–197.

InBIA. (2021). *Business Incubation FAQs*. https://www.inbia.org/

Knopp, L. (2012). *2012 State of the Business Incubation Industry*. NBIA Publications.

Lewis, D. (2010). *Business Incubators and Their Role in Job Creation*. U.S. House of Representatives Committee on Small Businesses.

McAdam, M., & Marlow, S. (2008). A preliminary investigation into networking activities within the university incubator. *International Journal of Entrepreneurial Behaviour & Research*, *14*(4), 219–241. https://doi.org/10.1108/13552550810887390

McAdam, M., & McAdam, R. (2008). High tech start-ups in University Science Park incubators: The relationship between the start-up's lifecycle progression and use of the incubator's resources. *Technovation*, *28*(5), 277–290. https://doi.org/10.1016/j.technovation.2007.07.012

Mian, S. (2014). Business incubation mechanisms and new venture support: Emerging structures of US science parks and incubators. *International Journal of Entrepreneurship and Small Business*, *23*(4), 419–435. Scopus. https://doi.org/10.1504/IJESB.2014.065682

Pauwels, C., Clarysse, B., Wright, M., & Jonas Van Hove. (2016). Understanding a new generation incubation model: The accelerator. *Technovation, 50–51*, 13–24. https://doi.org/10.1016/j.technovation.2015.09.003

Phan, P. H., Siegel, D. S., & Wright, M. (2005). Science parks and incubators: Observations, synthesis and future research. *Journal of Business Venturing*, *20*(2), 165–182. https://doi.org/10.1016/j.jbusvent.2003.12.001

Ratinho, T., Amezcua, A. S., Honig, B., & Zeng, Z. (2020). Supporting entrepreneurs: A systematic review of literature and an agenda for research. *Technological Forecasting and Social Change*, *154*, 119956. https://doi.org/10.1016/j.techfore.2020.119956

Ratinho, T., & Henriques, E. (2010). The role of science parks and business incubators in converging countries: Evidence from Portugal. *Technovation*, *30*(4), 278–290. https://doi.org/10.1016/j.technovation.2009.09.002

Ratinho, T., & Mitsopoulos, M. (2021). New forms of entrepreneurship support in a growing entrepreneurial ecosystem: The case of business incubation in Greece. In S. Mian, M. Klofsten, & W. Lamine, *Handbook of Research on Business and Technology Incubation and Acceleration* (pp. 299–315). Edward Elgar Publishing. https://doi.org/10.4337/9781788974783.00026

Rothaermel, F. T., & Thursby, M. (2005). University–incubator firm knowledge flows: Assessing their impact on incubator firm performance. *Research Policy*, *34*(3), 305–320. https://doi.org/10.1016/j.respol.2004.11.006

Schwartz, M. (2008). Beyond incubation: An analysis of firm survival and exit dynamics in the post-graduation period. *The Journal of Technology Transfer*, *34*(4), 403–421. https://doi.org/10.1007/s10961-008-9095-x

Schwartz, M. (2011). Incubating an illusion? Long-term incubator firm performance after graduation. *Growth and Change*, *42*(4), 491–516. Scopus. https://doi.org/10.1111/j.1468-2257.2011.00565.x

Schwartz, M. (2013). A control group study of incubators' impact to promote firm survival. *The Journal of Technology Transfer*, *38*(3), 302–331. https://doi.org/10.1007/s10961-012-9254-y

Schwartz, M., & Hornych, C. (2008). Specialization as strategy for business incubators: An assessment of the Central German Multimedia Center. *Technovation*, *28*(7), 436–449. https://doi.org/10.1016/j.technovation.2008.02.003

Schwartz, M., & Hornych, C. (2012). Specialisation versus diversification: Perceived benefits of different business incubation models. *International Journal of Entrepreneurship and Innovation Management*, *15*(3), 177–197. Scopus. https://doi.org/10.1504/IJEIM.2012.046599

Scillitoe, J. L., & Chakrabarti, A. K. (2010). The role of incubator interactions in assisting new ventures. Technovation, 30(3), 155–167. Scopus. https://doi.org/10.1016/j.technovation.2009.12.002

Smilor, R. W., & Gill, M. D., Jr. (1986). *The New Business Incubator: Linking Talent, Technology, Capital and Know-How.* Lexington Books.

Soetanto, D. P. (2006). Nurturing technology-based firms: The resources-based perspective in the incubation process. *International Journal of Management and Enterprise Development*, *3*(6), 534–547.

Von Zedtwitz, M., & Grimaldi, R. (2006). Are Service Profiles Incubator-Specific? Results from an Empirical Investigation in Italy. *The Journal of Technology Transfer*, *31*(4), 459–468.

Part III: **The wider world**

Part III contains seven chapters that address the most researched phenomena in entrepreneurial finance. These activities are typically more arms length than those considered in Parts I and II. They have also been more heavily researched than the activities in those Parts.

In Chapter 8, Steven Si, Wan Liu, Yushan Yan and Jet Mboga present what we know about formal debt as a source of entrepreneurial finance. Their chapter can be read as a bookend to Chapter 5 on informal financing. Their chapter points out rightly that formal debt is a double-edged sword, bringing benefits and risks to startups.

Chapter 9 by Jonathan Kimmitt looks at microfinance and entrepreneurial finance, examining research and future research opportunities at the micro, meso, and macro levels. It demonstrates how this research stream offers insights into entrepreneurial behavior, microfinance dynamics, and financial inclusion tensions.

Venture capital is addressed in Chapter 10 by Darek Klonowski and Silas Lee. This topic has been the subject of entire academic handbooks in the past, so the effort to compress our knowledge in this central research domain has been challenging. The chapter provides an overview of venture capital with a special focus on its characteristics, global fundraising and investing statistics, its advantages to entrepreneurs, the VC investment process, VC performance, and VC in emerging markets. It is also the first chapter in this Handbook to explicitly addresss the impact of the COVID-19 pandemic.

Chapter 11 by Paul Asel addresses a phenomenon related to venture capital: corporate venture capital. Although written by a leading practitioner, this chapter delves deeply into the research, while also casting a skeptical eye on the efficacy of some of the research findings for practice.

Sofia Avdeitchkova and Hans Landström take on the business angel research literature in Chapter 12. They propose that this research be reframed around value creation, distinguishing between business, situational, and system aspects.

Judit Karsai examines the government's role in financing startups in Chapter 13. She identifies how governments can best support entrepreneurial finance, reaffirming the research that has found indirect support to work most effectively.

Finally, this part concludes with a discussion by Antonia Schickinger, Alexandra Bertschi-Michel, and Nadine Kammerlander in Chapter 14 on an interesting emerging research stream: family offices as sources of entrepreneurial finance. They present original research that provides suggestions about the most effective family office practices in financing startups.

https://doi.org/10.1515/9783110726312-011

Steven Si, Wan Liu, Yushan Yan, and Jet Mboga

8 Formal debt as a source of entrepreneurial finance

Abstract: Financing forms can be classified into two categories: formal financing and informal financing. Formal finance obtains funds from formal financial intermediaries such as banks or private lenders. Formal debt is defined as a loan that is sourced from banks and other formal financial intermediaries (Elston et al., 2016; Coleman et al., 2016). The fundamental difference between formal and informal debt lies with creditors. Formal debt is generally assumed to be borrowed from official formal financial sources. In reality of debt business,formal debt is an essential part of developing debt financing for startups or venture enterprises. Therefore, it is imperative for startups or venture enterprises to understand and choose the formal debt mode correctly. However, formal debt is a double-edged sword, which meets the capital needs of a startup and brings financial benefits, and brings risks to startup, which may lead to financial crisis and make the startups face the risk of bankruptcy.

Keywords: formal financing, formal debt, benefits, risks, startups management

Introduction

A startup is a young company founded by one or more entrepreneurs to develop a unique product or service and bring it to market. By its nature, the typical startup tends to be a shoestring operation, with initial funding from the founders or their friends and families. As a part of the economy, startups play an increasingly important role in employment, innovation, and new product development. The literature on startup finance has recognized that capital decisions about which source of financing to use can have important implications for a firm's operations, including failure risk, firm performance, and sustainability (Denis, 2004; Hall et al., 2010). The funding sources of startups can be divided into internal financing and external financing. The primary source of internal financing is internal owner capital, friend capital, and interest-free loans from affiliated companies. Entrepreneurs often do not have sufficient internal resources to finance a new venture and seek external sources. How startups obtain external capital is one of the most fundamental issues in entrepreneurship research (Cassar, 2004). External financing mainly includes banks, relationship lending, angel investors, venture capital, trade credit, leasing,

Jet Mboga, Bloomsburg University of Pennsylvania
Steven Si, Bloomsburg University of Pennsylvania; Zhejiang University
Wan Liu, Yushan Yan, Zhejiang University

https://doi.org/10.1515/9783110726312-012

etc. Debt is considered the focus of small business research (Wright et al., 2016) and is usually described as owing money, owed money that is past due or the feeling as if you owe someone something.

Financing forms can be classified into two categories: formal financing and informal financing. General laws and regulations govern formal finance. Common forms include banking, venture capital, and government capital (Ledgerwood, 1999). Formal finance obtains funds from formal financial intermediaries such as banks, while informal finance receives funds from friends, family, relatives, or private lenders (Elston et al., 2016). Informal finance is a source of capital that is not subject to legal infrastructure and is not protected by legal infrastructure. Based on this principle, we can distinguish between formal and informal debt.

Formal debt is defined as a loan that is sourced from banks and other formal financial intermediaries (Elston et al., 2016; Coleman et al., 2016). The fundamental difference between formal and informal debt lies with creditors. Formal debt is generally assumed to be borrowed from official formal financial sources. How to understand formal debt? In general, talking about "debt" is from the perspective of "borrower," so if we look at "lender," we can see "credit" relative to "debt." Formal credit is defined as the extension of credit operated by government-regulated financial institutions within the regulatory framework of the financial system (Campero & Kaiser, 2013). Formal sources include banks, savings banks, and government credit programs; Informal sources are money lenders, pawnbrokers, family, or friends. Formal debt is processed based on complex information and independence principles, while informal debt decisions are made using soft (private) information and relationship-based principles (Nguyen & Canh, 2020; Coleman et al., 2016). Given this difference between the two, entrepreneurs face tradeoffs in determining the appropriate source of debt for their businesses. Wu et al. (2016) suggest that informal funding and formal funding differ in the provisions of the financing contracts. Specifically, informal debt is attractive to entrepreneurs because it is relatively fast, has low initial transaction costs, and does not require collateral (Wu et al. 2016; Coleman et al., 2016). While the lower interest rates of formal bank lending may make it the preferred route, a longer loan processing time may not align with the required time frame. Table 8.1 lists the definitions, sources, characteristics, and examples of formal and informal debt.

Table 8.1: The difference between formal and informal debt.

Formal sources of debt	Informal source of debt
The formal sources of debt that laws and regulations follow are the government registers.	The informal sources include all small and scattered units beyond the government's control; they must obey its laws and regulations.
Social welfare is the primary motive for formal sources.	Profit-making is the primary motive for informal sources.

Table 8.1 (continued)

Formal sources of debt	Informal source of debt
Formal debt usually charges lower interest rates.	They charge much higher interest rates for informal sources.
Examples: Banks and cooperatives	Examples: Moneylenders, merchants, workers, relatives, and friends.

Literature review

The role of formal debt in financing

Startups have some unique characteristics of capital structure. First, there is no track record for investors to judge a startup. This opacity makes it harder for startups to secure outside investment in their nascent stages (Bruno & Tyebjee, 1985). Outside equity investors will demand a higher stake because of the potential risk of opacity (Berger & Udell, 1995). For the startup owner, internal financing is the first choice, followed by external debt such as bank financing and expensive equity investments (Sanyal & Mann, 2010). Secondly, compared with large or mature listed companies, the financing choices of startups are more influenced by individuals or specific circumstances (Sanyal & Mann, 2010), for example, owner attributes, regional factors, and local conditions related to the financial structure of startups, social resources. The capital structure of startups can be explained by static trade-off options or pecking order framework (Cassar, 2004). Static trade-off choices mainly include the risk of bankruptcy for the firm (Harris & Raviv, 1991) and agency costs arising from external financing such as debt (Myers, 1977). Due to information asymmetry between companies and their potential financiers, researchers believe that startups follow the pecking order theory when choosing a capital structure (Coleman et al., 2016). When the risk exposure caused by information asymmetry is greater, the new equity holders expect a higher return on capital. In this context, companies prefer internal rather than external financing when obtaining financing, preferring to choose any debt over external equity (Myers & Majluf, 1984). Thirdly, size is also an essential factor in a startup's decision to use debt and bank financing. The larger the scale, the significant the proportion of these two types of external financing (Cassar, 2004). Based on the theory of asset specificity, existing studies have found that startups with more tangible assets as potential collateral are more likely to use external liabilities in their financial structure because of the higher liquidation value of these assets (Sanyal & Mann, 2010). From the perspective of dynamic capital structure, the different development stages of startups also affect financing decisions due to the life-cycle theory. For example, the same company's initial and subsequent financing decisions of the same company may lead to additional securities selection due to the phase of control of subsequent bondholders (Fluck, 2000).

Conventional wisdom holds that startups rely primarily on equity financing, either through the entrepreneur's equity or through external equity financing, such as venture capital, angel financing (BA), or an initial public offering (IPO). This view assumes that the startup is a company that is about to go public or is the result of venture capital financing (Chemmanur & Fulghieri, 2014). However, most startups may not want or need venture capital. They wish to avoid excessive investor interference with company management or conflict with company strategy (Hellmann & Puri, 2000). They are reluctant to weaken their control or encounter problems in evaluating the transaction or exclusive rights that constitute the transaction. Another conventional view is that informal capital dominates the capital structure of startups. Startups are considered the opaquest companies in the economy (Cassar, 2004) and lack formal capital markets. Therefore, they are forced to rely on informal networks such as family and friends and other sources of financing such as credit cards for initial funding (Peterson & Rajan, 1994).

Unlike the above two views, in the field of startup research, numerous studies reported that startups are heavily dependent on bank debt financing (Cassia & Vismara, 2009; DeLoof et al., 2019). Robb and Robinson (2014) found that newly formed companies rely heavily on formal debt financing: owner-backed bank loans, commercial bank loans, and commercial credit lines. Even the smallest startups rely on formal credit channels more than personal credit cards and informal loans (Robb & Robinson, 2014).

Formal debt is part of debt financing that borrows cash from lenders at a fixed interest rate and a predetermined maturity date. The principal must be repaid in full on the due date, but regular repayment of the principal may be part of the loan arrangement. Debt may take the form of loans or the sale of bonds. The form of the loan itself does not change the principle of the transaction: the lender retains the right to the loan and may claim the loan back under the conditions set out in the facility. However, the significant characteristics of debt obscure the critical role that debt plays in entrepreneurial finance. The share of debt in the capital structure of US startups is similar to the 50% of total debt in the capital structure of most US firms (Kashyap & Stein, 2007). Perhaps surprisingly, the same is true of America's youngest firms (those less than two years old), which have a debt of about 52% of their capital structure (Derrien et al., 2019). Even for high-growth startups where private equity financing dominated early growth, debt financing played an essential role in the firms' capital structure as they went public (Brav, 2009).

While the ratio of debt capital structure for small firms is like that of large firms (Jõeveer, 2013), debt financing itself is entirely different from the types of bonds, contracting tools used, lending techniques, and intermediary roles. Much of the debt is tradeable for large firms, such as commercial paper, syndicated loans, and public bond issues. For startups, almost all the debt is non-tradable, with the most considerable portion being non-syndicated commercial loans (Acharya et al., 2018).

Approaches of formal debt

Approaches of formal debt: The primary sources of formal debt of startup enterprises are commercial credit loans, bank loans, government loans, and leasing companies. Of course, it is more difficult for a startup to borrow money than an established one. However, for a startup entrepreneur, if the entrepreneur has some work experience, owns a substantial stake in the firm, and can submit a good business plan, he/she can borrow money from one or more sources. However, if the entrepreneur's equity is small or secured, there is little hope that the startup will receive formal debt. Formal debt availability is due partly to the startup location; America's entrepreneurial hot-beds, such as eastern Massachusetts and California's Silicon Valley, have debt, lease, and equity capital readily available than in the Midwest. In addition, there is a close relationship between the venture capital firm and the loan manager of the bank. This connection makes it easier for startups and early-stage companies to borrow money.

Commercial credit loan: Commercial credit is the primary source of short-term funds for startup enterprises. If a startup pays a 30 -, 60 – or 90-day fee for goods or services, it is in effect getting a 30 – to 90-day loan. Many small startups have access to such commercial credit without other forms of debt financing resources. Suppliers obtain such commercial credit loans to gain new customers, and it usually includes the risk of bad debts not paying the price of their goods.

Whether a new enterprise can obtain commercial credit depends on the quality and credibility of its entrepreneurs and the relationships it establishes with its suppliers. There are two caveat points for entrepreneurs. First, late or non-payment may cause suppliers to suspend deliveries or to ship only on cash on delivery. Second, the actual cost of using commercial credit can be very high. Since the cost of commercial credit is unlikely to be expressed in one-year costs, the startup needs to carefully analyze the advantages and disadvantages of this debt to find the most favorable debt terms to purchase the product.

Bank loans: Formal debt comes in many forms, but the most common is a bank loan or bank overdraft. A bank loan provides longer-term financing for a startup, with the bank specifying the fixed term of the loan (say five years), the interest rate, when and how much the loan will be paid. Banks typically require the startup to provide some guarantee for loans, although this usually comes in the form of a personal guarantee from the entrepreneur. Bank loans are conducive to the financing of fixed asset investment, and the interest rate is usually lower than the bank overdraft rate. However, they do not offer much flexibility. Bank overdraft is a short-term debt that is also widely used by startups and small businesses. An overdraft is, in effect, a loan instrument – when the bank balance is below zero, the bank lets the business "have the money," and in return, it charges a higher interest rate. As a result, overdrafts can be an excellent way to help a business deal with seasonal fluctuations in cash flow or when the business has short-term cash flow problems (for example, a significant customer cannot turn in on time).

Government loan: Regional, state and federal agencies have programs to provide loans to startups. These projects are usually part of the economic development plans of the municipal government or the Ministry of Commerce. Some government loans are attractive because their interest rates are well below market rates. Small Business Administration (SBA) and Capital Acquisition Program (CAP) loans are usually made at market prices. The main target of government loans is solvent companies located in administrative areas. These companies will either keep existing jobs or create new ones. For instance, entrepreneurs sign an agreement to receive such debt: the local government provides $20 000 for each loan. The company has promised to create one new job over the next 18 to 24 months. The downside of this formal loan is that it usually takes a long time to reach the company.

Chattel mortgage and equipment leasing loan: A common way to provide a secured long-term loan is to designate suitable property (chattel) as collateral. Movables used as collateral are any kind of mechanical equipment or business property. Just as real property is used as security, the movable property remains the borrower's property unless the lessor fails to pay the debt. General mortgage credit is mainly limited to new machinery and equipment, or good performance of second-hand machinery and equipment can be sold. The loan terms of a chattel mortgage are usually from one year to five years, but there are some longer terms.

Table 8.2 lists the primary forms of formal debt for startups and how difficult it is for startups to obtain formal debt. The type of formal debt chosen by a startup depends on clear measures such as the interest rate or cost of the loan capital, key terms, covenants, and how appropriate it is to the owner's situation and the company's needs at the time. How good a deal an entrepreneur can strike depends on his relative negotiating skills and ability to compete with rivals.

Table 8.2: Formal debt sources of a startup business.

Formal debt sources	lenders	The difficulty level for a startup business to obtain it
Commercial credit loan	Suppliers	Accessible
Bank loans	Commercial banks or state-owned banks	Sometimes to access, depends on entrepreneurs' equity proportion
Government loan	Government	Accessible
Chattel mortgage and equipment leasing loan	Leasing companies	Sometimes to access, if there are assets available

Pros and cons of formal debt

Formal debt is borrowed from a formal institution, government, or nongovernmental (NGOs) organization (such as a leasing company) within an agreed repayment period. The amount of repayment depends on the loan size, term, and interest rate. Startups prefer formal debt to informal debt for several reasons. First, borrowing from an institution such as a bank or government can send a good signal to other potential lenders. Signals sent by formal institutions are considered credible by other lenders because the bank or government has sufficient resources and comparative advantage to evaluate the borrower and may effectively liquidate the enterprise compared to other lenders. This is especially true because formal institutions have a comparative advantage in mitigating information asymmetry. Second, startups opt for formal debt hoping that formal institutions will provide investment capital in difficult times and negotiate the rollover of existing debt. Companies also want banks to invest resources and monitor them, not liquidate them if the timing is terrible (Hadlock & James, 2002). Third, it is cheaper and perhaps more prudent for companies to give proprietary information to fewer lenders than make it public since competitors could use it. Fourth, a long-term relationship with an established institution also benefits startups. This can result in little or no need for collateral since formal institutions can build profiles of clients' companies over time. Such filings can serve as a collateral substitute that can lead to attractive lending rates for companies. In addition, this familiarity allows companies to avoid credit rationing under challenging times when most credit providers are reluctant to lend.

A borrower who surrenders a portion of his profits over to the lender above the standard interest rate on loans may end up exerting less than optimal effort in production. Another disadvantage of using formal debt is that such loans may be from one bank with which the firm may have established an exclusive long-term relationship, which implies that if the bank encounters hard times, the firm may face difficulties accessing loans elsewhere. Furthermore, bank loans may be more expensive than public debt, as a premium of banks' obligations to put aside reserves in support of deposits they use to create loans–a cost which Fama (1985) terms an implicit tax on loans.

On the contrary, many factors discourage companies from using formal debt and lead a startup to prefer informal debt. A startup can opt for informal debt rather than formal debt to avoid the paperwork and waiting time to get the funding they need (Coleman et al., 2016). The use of informal debt will also reduce monopoly rent payments, leading to a long-term relationship between a firm and a formal institution. If borrowers pay lenders a percentage of their profits (higher than standard lending rates), they may end up using less than optimal productive efforts. Another drawback to using formal debt is that the loan may come from a bank with which the company may have an exclusive long-term relationship, meaning that if the bank hits hard times, the company may find it difficult to obtain credit elsewhere.

In addition, bank loans can be more expensive than public debt because banks are obligated to set aside reserves to support the deposit they use to create the loans; Fama (1985) calls this cost an implicit tax on loans. In general, the pros and cons of formal debt can be summarized in Table 8.3.

Table 8.3: Pros and Cons of formal debt.

Pros	Cons
Low-interest rates	Lengthy paperwork
Predictable monthly payments	Longer wait time
May help build business credit	Requires strong credit
Professional banker relationship	Usually requires specific collateral
Lending is available for many entrepreneurs	More expensive than public loans

Startup's difficulties and preparations in applying for formal debt

Startups, especially high-tech businesses, account for almost all net employment growth and have a fundamental impact on overall economic productivity as the economy evolves. However, startups have many weaknesses. One of them is the lack of startup capital and financing support. Formal debt is not inexhaustible. Commercial banks have a rigorous review of loans, so it is not easy for a startup to obtain formal loans for internal and external reasons. The main reasons are as follows:

There exist complex internal factors in applying for formal debt. Startups tend to be small and lack financial support. When many startups are founded, they often rely heavily on informal debt for funding. Due to the limited financial resources of startups, it is easy for them to experience cash flow difficulties in operation, especially during economic downturns. In addition, in general, the operation and management of startups are in their infancy, and many startups have not established a sound financial system, which makes it difficult for them to get support from financial institutions, leading to the situation of capital shortage. In addition, startups are weak in market competitiveness and can avoid market risks, so startups can quickly go bankrupt.

The external factors that make it difficult for startups to obtain formal debt are mainly the high risk of startup loans and the difficulty in providing appropriate loan guarantees and finding loan guarantors. So most commercial banks are afraid to lend money to startups easily. Secondly, large and medium-sized enterprises have many loans, and the bank pays a lower unit cost of loans. However, many startups and the amount of individual loans applied for are small, so the cost of loans for startup enterprises is relatively high. According to the World Bank, the operating costs of large loans are about 0.3% to 0.5% of total loans, while the administrative costs of start-up loans are as high as 2.6% to 2.7%.

The next question is how do startups prepare to apply for formal debt? It includes: 1) Establishing a good relationship with formal institutions is the key for a startup enterprise to cooperate reasonably with banks and obtain bank loans smoothly. How to build a good relationship between a formal institution (such as a bank) and a business? First, enterprises should pay attention to the construction of integrity. Banks are regarded as the primary source of formal debt for startups. Since banks cannot understand startups' production and operation activities, they often start using funds, turnover, financial accounting, and other aspects when investigating enterprises. Whether the financial accounting of an enterprise is standardized, the quality of accounting personnel, and whether the financial management of an enterprise pays attention to compliance are essential standards for banks to measure the level of enterprise management. If an enterprise wants to win the bank's trust and leave a good impression on the bank, it must do an excellent job managing funds. Second, the enterprise should often take the initiative to report the company's operation to the bank. This is a psychological skill to maintain public relations, from which the bank will feel the respect of the entrepreneurs for the company, and through regular contact and communication with the enterprise, strengthen the trust of the enterprise, change the potential prejudice, reduce the distrust of the startup enterprise, and gradually establish a good relationship with the enterprise. Finally, entrepreneurs should also improve their management level and build a good reputation through efforts. The credit construction of enterprises is the primary operating income of enterprises, and the economic income of enterprises depends on the management level of enterprises to a large extent. Therefore, improving the management level of the enterprise also helps to increase the favorable impression of startup enterprises towards formal institutions. 2) Preparation of commercial investment project feasibility report. The feasibility study report of investment projects plays a vital role in obtaining the preferential support of project loan scale and bank loan. Startups should pay attention to solving the following problems when writing reports: First, project reports should conform to relevant national policies and focus on advanced technology development, economic contribution, and feasibility. Second, it is necessary to clarify the key issues, including the company's current situation, development prospects, technical capabilities, production capacity, infrastructure and inventory of raw materials, product sales. 3) Choose the right time to take out the loan. For loan opportunity selection, attention should be paid to ensuring that the funds needed by the startup enterprises are in place in time, and it is also necessary to facilitate the bank to arrange credit funds and standardize the credit scale. The bank credit scale shall be granted once at the beginning of the New Year and shall be used quarterly and shall not be suspended without authorization. Therefore, in general, if a startup needs to apply for multiple loans, the submission application of loans at the end of the year and each quarter is not appropriate. Formal institutions should be informed of their plans to use funds in advance so that they do not become passive in terms of funds in advance to not become passive in loan size and equity. In addition to maintaining a good relationship with formal institutions, enterprises can also establish interactive relationships with other potential lenders. In this way, when an enterprise needs a large number of funds for a project, and a bank (such as a commercial bank) cannot solve the problem in time due to various reasons, it can adopt the way of a syndicated loan to solve the problem, but also can fight for bank funds for the enterprise to turn to the next production. 4) Strive for the support of SMEs guarantee institutions. As mentioned above, when selecting loan projects, commercial banks often require enterprises to provide good loan guarantees or mortgages to guarantee their credit. Startup enterprises have limited capital and a small operation scale, so it is difficult to obtain bank loans. Therefore, startups should strive for the responsibilities of small and medium-sized enterprises and get support from insurance institutions as much as possible.

Future research agenda

Firstly, it is potential to study the financing structure of startups in specific industries, especially the role of formal debt. Due to the online databases mainly covering high-tech industries, there are abundant empirical studies in this industry (Cassar, 2004). If the research can be supplemented by empirical research from different industries, the capital structure theory can be further developed. For example, what are the differences in the capital structure of startups in five major industries (manufacturing/mining/construction/service/service/gene industry)? Whether the attitude towards debt financing also changes with different industries?

Secondly, in the research of venture financing, context, especially the institutional context, researchers have concerned (Wright et al., 2016). Existing studies have found that formal finance in emerging economies is more limited compared with mature economies, so informal finance plays a vital role in startups. However, the value of informal debt promoting innovation is weak (Wu et al., 2016). In the future, researchers can further explore the role of informal debt in other institutional contexts (Wright et al., 2016; Coleman et al., 2016) and how formal and informal debt can cooperate in different institutional environments to promote the development of startups better.

Thirdly, the development of emerging Internet technology promotes the development of debt financing, including point-to-point loans in crowdfunding and venture debt (Wright et al., 2016). Venture debt is located at the intersection of venture capital and traditional debt (De Rassenfosse & Fischer, 2016), which can accelerate growth through leverage without diluting shares (Hong et al., 2020). New financing methods and traditional forms may overlap, a complement or replace each other

(Wright et al., 2016). What is the impact of these new financing forms on formal debt? How do startups choose or combine several of them? Will the formal debt itself change with the financing environment? These issues need to be further studied.

Conclusion

To sum up, a formal debt agreement is a simple way to pay startups' debts, it's legally binding and allows startups to settle their debts over a short period of time at an affordable rate for supporting startups survive and development. In reality of debt business, formal debt is an essential part of developing debt financing for startups or venture enterprises. Therefore, it is imperative for startups or venture enterprises to understand and choose the formal debt mode correctly. In financing, enterprises should make reasonable financial plans according to their conditions and raise financing risk awareness. At the same time, a startup should improve its ability, establish a sense of integrity, gain trust through formal institutions to get a better future. In addition, the formal debt of a startup enterprise refers to the financial behavior of a startup enterprise to raise funds through bank loans, commercial credit, government assistance, and leasing companies. Through formal debt, it can solve the liquidity problem of startups and diversify the sources of capital. However, formal debt is a double-edged sword, which meets the capital needs of a startup and brings financial benefits, and brings risks to startup, which may lead to financial crisis and make the startups face the risk of bankruptcy. Therefore, it is vital for startups, especially those innovative and technology-based startups, to correctly understand and choose the formal debt model. Efficient in formal debt, enterprises should pay attention to improving the awareness of financing risk and, according to their situation, develop suitable financial plans and controllable formal debt, and effectively use formal debt to promote the development of startup enterprises. At the same time, besides the relevant knowledge about formal debt approaches and technology-based skills, startup entrepreneurs should improve and continually improve their ability, establish a sense of integrity, and gain trust through formal institutions to have a better future.

References

Acharya, V. V., Eisert, T., Eufinger, C., & Hirsch, C. (2018). Real effects of the sovereign debt crisis in Europe: Evidence from syndicated loans. *The Review of Financial Studies*, *31*(8), 2855–2896.
Berger, A. N., & Udell, G. F. (1995). Relationship lending and lines of credit in small firm finance. *Journal of business*, 351–381.

Brav, O. (2009). Access to capital, capital structure, and the funding of the firm. *The journal of finance, 64(1), 263–308.*

Bruno, A. V., & Tyebjee, T. T. (1985). The entrepreneur's search for capital. *Journal of business Venturing, 1(1),* 61–74.

Campero, A., & Kaiser, K. (2013). *Access to credit: awareness and use of formal and informal credit institutions* (No. 2013–07). Working Papers.

Cassar, G. (2004). The financing of business startup. *Journal of business venturing, 19(2),* 261–283.

Cassia, L., & Vismara, S. (2009). Firms' trade credit and the local level of development of the banking system in Europe. *Investment Management and Financial Innovations,* (6, Issue. 4), 46–58.

Chemmanur, T. J., & Fulghieri, P. (2014). Entrepreneurial finance and innovation: An introduction and agenda for future research. *The Review of Financial Studies, 27(1),* 1–19.

Coleman, S., Cotei, C., & Farhat, J. (2016). The debt-equity financing decisions of US startup firms. *Journal of Economics and Finance, 40(1),* 105–126.

De Rassenfosse, G., & Fischer, T. (2016). Venture debt financing: Determinants of the lending decision. *Strategic Entrepreneurship Journal, 10(3),* 235–256.

Deloof, M., La Rocca, M., & Vanacker, T. (2019). Local banking development and the use of debt financing by new firms. *Entrepreneurship Theory and Practice, 43(6),* 1250–1276.

Denis, D. J. (2004). Entrepreneurial finance: an overview of the issues and evidence. *Journal of corporate finance, 10(2),* 301–326.

Derrien, F., Mesonnier, J. S., & Vuillemey, G. (2019). Startup Costs and the Capital Structure of Young Firms. In *Funding Stability and Financial Regulation Workshop.* Banque de France.

Elston, J. A., Chen, S., & Weidinger, A. (2016). The role of informal capital on new venture formation and growth in China. *Small Business Economics, 46(1), 79–91.*

Fama, E. F. (1985). What's different about banks? *Journal of monetary economics, 15(1), 29–39.*

Fluck, Z. (2000). Capital structure decisions in small and large firms: a life-cycle theory of financing.

Hadlock, C. J., & James, C. M. (2002). Do banks provide financial slack? *the Journal of Finance, 57(3), 1383–1419.*

Hall, J. K., Daneke, G. A., & Lenox, M. J. (2010). Sustainable development and entrepreneurship: Past contributions and future directions. *Journal of business venturing, 25(5),* 439–448.

Harris, M., & Raviv, A. (1991). The theory of capital structure. *the Journal of Finance, 46(1),* 297–355.

Hellmann, T., & Puri, M. (2000). The interaction between product market and financing strategy: The role of venture capital. *The review of financial studies, 13(4),* 959–984.

Hong, J. S., Na, S., & Park, J. J. (2020). The Possibility and the Way to Introduce of Venture Debt to Encourage Growth of Ventures. *Asia-Pacific Journal of Business Venturing and Entrepreneurship, 15(4),* 17–25.

Jõeveer, K. (2013). What do we know about the capital structure of small firms? *Small Business Economics, 41(2),* 479–501.

Kashyap, A. K., & Stein, J. C. (2007). *7. Monetary Policy and Bank Lending* (pp. 221–262). University of Chicago Press.

Ledgerwood, J. (1999). Sustainable banking with the poor microfinance handbook.

Myers, S. C. (1977). Determinants of corporate borrowing. *Journal of financial economics, 5(2),* 147–175.

Myers, S. C., & Majluf, N. S. (1984). Corporate financing and investment decisions when firms have information that investors do not have. *Journal of financial economics, 13(2),* 187–221.

Nguyen, B., & Canh, N. P. (2020). Formal and informal financing decisions of small businesses. *Small Business Economics, 1–23.*

Peterson, M. A., & Rajan, R. G. (1994). The Benefit of Firm Creditors Relationship: Evidence from Small Business Data. *Journal of Finance*, *49*(1), 337–341.

Robb, A. M., & Robinson, D. T. (2014). The capital structure decisions of new firms. *The Review of Financial Studies,27*(1), 153–179.

Sanyal, P., & Mann, C. L. (2010). *The financial structure of startup firms: The role of assets, information, and entrepreneur characteristics (No. 10–17). Working Papers.*

Wright, M., Lumpkin, T., Zott, C., & Agarwal, R. (2016). The evolving entrepreneurial finance landscape. *Strategic Entrepreneurship Journal, 10(3), 229–234.*

Wu, J., Si, S., & Wu, X. (2016). Entrepreneurial finance and innovation: Informal debt as an empirical case. *Strategic Entrepreneurship Journal, 10(3), 257–273.*

Jonathan Kimmitt

9 Microfinance and entrepreneurial finance: A review and future research agenda

Abstract: Research on microfinance and entrepreneurship has grown significantly in recent years, offering insight into entrepreneurial behaviour, microfinance dynamics and various tensions concerning financial inclusion. This chapter provides an overview of prior research in this space, specifically analysing micro, meso and macro levels of research. Whilst this has been insightful for both theory and practice, further opportunities exist across these three levels. At a micro-level, research should adopt a more holistic view of poverty and process. At a meso-level, more research is required analysing entrepreneurs and new models of microfinance such as individual lending and micro-equity. At a macro level, further empirical work is needed into the sources of microfinance failure and the role of financial institutions within complex systems. The chapter offers a set of perspectives and research questions around these three levels.

Keywords: microfinance, group lending, poverty, financial inclusion, debt

Introduction

In the last two decades, the volume of microfinance research has grown exponentially. Microfinance refers to the provision of financial services to the (entrepreneurial) poor, mainly in developing and emerging markets (Yunus, 1999). In such contexts, entrepreneurs lack access to formal financial systems because they typically operate ventures in the informal economy, have limited or no credit history and/or formal assets. This lack of formal market presence or record of performance makes lending risky and challenging for formal banks to offer services to entrepreneurs. Thus, microfinance institutions (MFIs) emerged to tackle this specific problem and as a way of integrating the entrepreneurial poor into the financial system.

The purpose of this chapter to delve deep into how MFIs approach this integration as well as how it relates to entrepreneurial finance and poverty. As the microfinance industry emerged, prominent research stemmed from experts in development studies and economics (e.g. Morduch, 1999). But more recently, entrepreneurship scholars have become increasingly interested in understanding how microfinance seeds entrepreneurship (Bruton, Khavul, Siegel, & Wright, 2015; Newman, Schwarz & Ahlstrom, 2017) and stimulates a variety of entrepreneurial behaviours such as

Jonathan Kimmitt, Business School, Newcastle University

https://doi.org/10.1515/9783110726312-013

recursive practices (Kimmitt & Dimov, 2021) whilst enabling social outcomes such as increased freedoms (Chliova, Brinckmann, & Rosenbusch, 2015).

In this chapter, I will provide an overview of current research at the intersection of microfinance and entrepreneurial finance. This will combine some of our understanding of microfinance from other disciplinary areas alongside more recent insights from entrepreneurship research. The review will be divided into three areas: micro, meso and macro. At the micro level, the review will assess prior research at the level of the individual entrepreneur and the relationship between microfinance provision, entrepreneurial behaviour, and outcomes. At the meso level, the chapter will discuss research which emphasises the relational side of microfinance and how entrepreneurial behaviour relates to group behaviour, loan officer relationships and the broader context. At the macro level, the chapter will discuss the role of MFIs as the providers of financial services and how they nurture systems and complex institutional environments to seed micro entrepreneurship. This same structure will subsequently be used to map out future research directions at micro, meso and macro levels.

Literature review

The underlying logic of microfinance

Microfinance refers to a range of financial services provided to the entrepreneurial poor in developing countries.[1] Research has mainly focused on "microcredit" as one of the sub-components of financial offerings. Microcredit refers to the provision of (usually) small amounts of credit to the entrepreneurial poor. One logic of this method is a move away from initiatives that are seen as hand-outs and may ultimately engender a kind of dependency. In theory, the commitment of entering this kind of financial transaction creates the 'right' kind of incentives for entrepreneurs to invest efficiently and effectively.

To achieve this, the classic microfinance model aimed to supplant traditional collateral (e.g. assets) with relational collateral. To reduce information asymmetry associated with lending, many MFIs drew upon social capital within communities to establish groups of entrepreneurs (i.e. often several micro-traders). Ranging from anywhere between 5 and 20 members, entrepreneurs would borrow and be collectively responsible for repayment (Ghatak, 1999). This risk sharing approach would allow many MFIs to permeate communities at a large scale whilst minimising institutional risk and, crucially, give entrepreneurs access to financial resources.

---

1 This review acknowledges that microfinance can also be provided for non-entrepreneurial reasons (e.g. smoothing household consumption) but it focuses on how it used for entrepreneurs and small business owners as this is the aim of the chapter.

The underlying logic behind this rests on the principal that the entrepreneurial poor are willing to invest to grow their (often) micro-firms. By growing their ventures, in theory, they can improve their incomes which will ultimately provide further options over important life choices such as access to healthcare, transportation, the education of children and so forth (Gries & Naudé, 2011; Yunus, 1999). There are further potential externalities in terms of stimulating local and national economic development and being able to offer jobs to support business development (Chliova et al., 2015).

Although group-lending has been a dominant method of entrepreneurial finance for several years, MFIs have also started to shift their lending method towards traditional individual liability approaches. This ties in with the idea of dynamic incentives whereby successful repayment of a loan is tied to accessing the next larger loan (Tedeschi, 2006). Individual liability was introduced to allow for greater flexibility so that finance could be provided to more established, less risky ventures that could demonstrate business growth yet are still not regarded as being sufficiently developed for mainstream banks or investors. This cohort of entrepreneurs are often regarded as the "missing middle" (Kimmitt, Scarlata & Dimov, 2016) for whom group lending may be too restrictive because of lower loan amounts and the risk of joint liability.

Overall, microfinance has grown exponentially in the last few decades as a potential tool for tackling poverty through entrepreneurship. According to MIX Market, as of 2017, there were 120 million borrowers globally with a gross loan portfolio of $112 billion. Whilst this can vary by region, the trend continues to show industry growth (MIX Market, 2018).

Current research

Whilst the previous section outlined the "nuts and bolts" of how microfinance operates, this section will delve deeper and offer a review of research at the intersection of microfinance and entrepreneurial finance. The review is broken up between micro, meso and macro level perspectives. At the micro-level, this section will review research that primarily focuses on the behaviour of the individual and the outcomes associated with entrepreneurial behaviour and microfinance. At the meso level, the review will focus on microfinance in a more relational sense and how entrepreneurs interact with group members, their local context and loan officers. At the macro level, the focus will shift towards reviewing the MFIs themselves as hybrid organizational forms that operate within complex institutional environments.

Micro level: Entrepreneurial attributes, skills, and capacities

Scholars have increasingly argued for a growing recognition of entrepreneurship as a crucial ingredient for economic growth and poverty reduction across developing countries (Easterly, 2001; Acs & Virgill, 2010). From a micro individual perspective, research has characterised the relationship between poverty and entrepreneurship as being dependent on the presence or absence of individual qualities or abilities. Yessoufou et al. (2018) highlight the role of personal motivations, attributes, and networking as central ingredients of opportunity exploitation in conditions of poverty, whilst Alvarez and Barney (2014) stress human capital as a central feature of opportunity development and poverty reduction. This has been particularly prevalent in development studies with the growing interest in self-help initiatives such as microfinance and the notion that the route out of poverty is through individual hard work (Yunus, 1999).

Therefore, at this micro level, prior research on microfinance has continued this trend by assessing the degree to which the provision of credit can enable business growth and reduce poverty. This perspective primarily focuses on individual agency to explain successful entrepreneurial behaviour. Bradley et al. (2012) argue that variations in performance may be due to an entrepreneurial 'idea problem' and a blend of different capitals (human and social) is required in addition to the financial capital that microfinance provides. Bruton et al. (2011) go further by looking at the cognitive processes of entrepreneurs investing microfinance, suggesting that the successful deployment of financial resources requires entrepreneurs to have a planning and future orientation.

One point of departure in this literature is how authors conceptualise poverty and the role that microfinance may have in enabling its reduction. Whilst there is consensus that business growth and development is important, some authors conceptualise it as the most relevant outcome and often with inadequate proxies of repayment as a measure (e.g. Bourlès & Cozarenco, 2018), whilst others take a more holistic approach to understanding these outcomes. Most notably, one of the most comprehensive analyses pertains to the meta-analysis by Chliova et al. (2015) which draws from the development framework put forward by Sen (1999). In Sen's understanding, one should assess poverty reduction initiatives such as microfinance by looking at the freedoms that ensue; this requires a more holistic view of the individual's situation.

For an entrepreneur investing a microfinance loan, this requires not just assessing whether the business has grown but the extent to which it allows the individual to enjoy other freedoms. Chliova et al. (2015) find that microfinance seems to enable venture profitability and other vital outcomes such as access to education, healthcare, and women's empowerment. The latter is also an important thread in microfinance research, although less evidence exists within the entrepreneurship literature. Women's empowerment has been one of the notable aims of microfinance, particularly through the Grameen Bank where 97% of borrowers are female. Research points towards the importance of business success through larger loan amounts (Weber & Ahmad, 2014) but when one considers household dynamics and the role of patriarchy in some countries, this may dampen the effect of such financial interventions (Ngo & Wahhaj, 2012).

However, complex and often counterintuitive relationships have been identified within the literature. Kimmitt et al. (2020) draw from Sen's (1999) capabilities approach to critique current entrepreneurship research that takes a primarily hedonistic view whereby individual entrepreneurs are assumed to flourish when their resource requirements are remediated (Sutter, Bruton, & Chen, 2019). Instead, in moving away from this perspective we see that entrepreneurs' well-being may indeed improve even if the business has made limited progress financially; alternate conditions such as family health and community dynamics are just as important as improved income. Similarly, Kimmitt and Dimov (2020) adopt this capabilities perspective to illustrative how, despite the presence of microfinance input, entrepreneurs follow different practice paths depending on whether their "process freedom" is inhibited or not.

In summary, to date, the entrepreneurship literature has thus far taken a relatively conventional approach that has tested and explored the different facets of microfinance on its underlying logic at a micro-level, as per second section of this chapter. But more recently, scholars have sought to pick apart this underlying logic drawing from theoretical perspectives in development studies as well as the knowledge of heterogeneous entrepreneurial behaviour. Building upon McMullen (2011), entrepreneurship scholars would benefit from asking more critical questions regarding microfinance, as a tool that indebts entrepreneurs, and the multi-dimensional aspect of poverty it relates to.

Meso level: Group relationships

The micro level perspective on entrepreneurship and microfinance represents a dominant aspect of research in this space. However, such an individualistic approach is overly simplistic (and often punitive) in the sense that entrenched poverty is presumed to persist because an individual entrepreneur does not make the "right" decision or have the necessary commercial acumen when investing loans (Bradshaw, 2007). At the meso-level, research offers a more nuanced understanding of the interplay between individual entrepreneurs and relational aspects of their context.

Prior research has looked at the relationships between entrepreneurs and other members of lending groups. What is notable in the approaches from traditional entrepreneurial finance theory is that everything hinges on the quality of the entrepreneur and thus on the initial selection (Macmillan, 1985). Indeed, prior studies have shown that the quality of the management team is an essential criterion used by external investors (Haines, Madill, & Riding, 2003). MFIs operate no such strict criteria for selection. One function of joint liability is that it reduces institutional risk but there are downsides for entrepreneurs such as some increased risk-taking in groups formed of individuals less well known to each other (Gine et al., 2010). This could have deleterious consequences in terms of indebting entrepreneurs as well as passing on repayments and causing tension with other group members. It is for this reason that experimentation with the risks and liability of group lending have been discussed in a way to optimise institutional outreach but minimise issues of moral hazard (Allen, 2016).

Thus, trust between members is seen as being crucial to an effective group and MFIs lean on social capital to smooth the process. But this is an overly optimistic view of most communities where the glue that social capital provides may be less apparent (Postelnicu & Hermes, 2018). Therefore, entrepreneurs must deal with group conflict and changes in membership; this is a source of uncertainty. Inevitably, this involves bringing in group members who may be less well known to the group, requiring time and effort to build trust or have it eroded further. And whilst groups that have a close bond and are relatively homogenous may be more likely to repay loans (Godquin, 2004), the lack of diversity from homogenous groups may be less useful for entrepreneurial learning.

Further group tensions can arise when entrepreneurs begin to outgrow what group-liability can offer. Often, groups share risk with a sizeable loan amount spread between multiple entrepreneurs (e.g. £1000 split between 10 entrepreneurs equating to £100 each). But as a business develops then financial capital needs can increase for some but not others. This is one of the reasons that individual-liability has been introduced by many MFIs (Khavul et al., 2013), so that a more flexible alternative exists which can accommodate higher loan amounts and, from the institution's point of view, lower risk entrepreneurs (Frankiewicz & Churchill, 2011).

In mainstream entrepreneurship theory, entrepreneurial finance is portrayed the uncertainty of exchange which is managed by a careful selection process (Haines, Madill & Riding, 2003). Fiet (1995) identifies the mechanisms whereby initial uncertainty is subsequently translated into two types of risk: market and relationship (or agency) risk. In the former, risk is judged by the financier through a consideration of the nature of the market in which the venture is positioned and whether the company can realistically achieve its financial objectives. Therefore, market risk is a consequence of the company's competitive conditions, the growth and potential of the market, and the need for the company's product/service within that marketplace (Fiet, 1995). At the meso-level, what is interesting within the microfinance domain is the hitherto underexplored relationship between entrepreneurs and their loan officers. Research has demonstrated that the purpose of the role of the loan officer is to empower by selecting client entrepreneurs, distributing loans, and managing repayments yet they often just become de facto debt collectors (Siwale & Richie, 2012). A large volume of research has focused on the group lending mechanism yet the decision-making processes of loan officers, their perceived risks and biases in selection are less well understood (Bruns, Holland, Shepherd & Wiklund, 2008).

Macro level: Organisational dynamics

At the macro level, microfinance research has focused on understanding the organizational dynamics of MFIs and their relationship with the wider institutional context. Often categorised as a form of social enterprise, MFIs are complex organizational forms because they exhibit dual behaviours in that they strive to alleviate poverty yet must be financially sustainable. Research has drawn from the framing of institutional logics to help understand this duality (Kent & Dacin, 2013). These represent the organizing principles, informal rules of action and interaction that guide a particular field (Thornton & Ocasio, 1999). In this perspective, the relationship between institutional logics, organizational fields and institutional change intertwines.

Prior research has positioned MFIs as a form of "institutional entrepreneur" i. e., the organization driving institutional change. Mair and Marti (2009) emphasize how MFIs position themselves as actors able to change normative, cognitive, and regulative institutions by empowering women entrepreneurs. But MFIs can also be subject to the imposition of new logics from actors such as regulators or other dominant field members (DiMaggio & Powell, 1983; Siwale & Kimmitt, 2019). In other industry contexts, the idea of strategically managing conflicting logics so they can co-exist has been identified (Reay & Hinings, 2009). MFIs have been shown to exhibit both "development" and "banking" logics (Battilana & Dorado, 2010; Khavul, Chavez & Bruton, 2013). In the former, the purpose of MFIs is to reduce poverty through financial inclusion (Mair & Martí, 2006; Zahra et al., 2009). In the latter, they must meet their business requirements by ensuring financial sustainability through client outreach, loan distribution, low rates of portfolio-at-risk as well as considering how to grow. For many MFIs, they use market based approaches of revenue maximization and cost reduction to address their development logic in a way that is assumed to be more financially sustainable (Battilana & Dorado, 2010; Zahra et al., 2009).

Given the presence of such institutional logics, MFIs exhibit dual identities (Moss et al., 2011) and the pro-active management of these identities is considered key to their performance and survival. The literature conceives of MFIs as being a form "hybrid organization" whereby these identities and conflicting logics are combined into organizational life (Smith & Besharov, 2019). Battilana and Dorado (2010) specifically show the value of workplace (e.g. loan officers) socialisation into these dual logics as being an effective method for organizational improvement. Canales (2014) demonstrates the value of loan officer discretion in managing these tensions.

However, the literature is somewhat divided on the extent to which these conflicts can be harmoniously remedied to allow MFIs to perform effectively. Mersland

and Strøm (2009) identify the value of local rather than international board of directors in facilitating organizational performance; Randøy et al. (2015) emphasise the relevance of entrepreneur managed MFIs in achieving social impact, whilst Galema et al. (2012) look at the decision-making freedom of MFI CEOs whereby increased power may increase financial risk. Despite the risks taken, very little is known about MFI performance and particularly about failure. In one such effort, Siwale et al. (2021) highlight the story of MFI failure in Zambia through a hybrid organizing framing. They show that external legitimation efforts can skew organizational identity and ultimately lead to the demise of the MFI which is perhaps a more extreme example of the "mission drift" reported elsewhere (Cornforth, 2014). Yet, alternatively, research has indicated that social and economic logics may combine to elicit financial performance (Muñoz & Kimmitt, 2019).

Aside of the institutional logics framing, research has also linked MFI behaviour and performance with their broader institutional environment. Most studies of this nature are cross-national comparisons aimed at understanding how and why microfinance performs in certain countries. Kimmitt and Muñoz (2017) use an institutional complexity approach to illustrate how various combinations of instrumental freedoms can unusually lead to financial inclusion. In particular, the presence of a sound political environment in Latin America seems crucial. Similarly, Kimmitt et al. (2016) identify higher levels of microfinance penetration in Sub-Saharan African contexts where the political environment is more stable. Drori et al. (2018) emphasise how the role of institutions and language can enable or inhibit financial inclusion amongst women entrepreneurs. This points us towards a more nuanced understanding of institutions and microfinance performance beyond an institutional logics perspective that simply lays out organizational tensions between social and economic performance.

Future research

Micro level: New perspectives on poverty and microfinance

This chapter reviewed the literature at the micro level of entrepreneurial finance and microfinance research. To date, most of this research follows an individual agency explanation of this relationship i.e., the success of microfinance provision is dependent upon individual attributes, skills and/or capacities then enables business development. However, there is significant scope for furthering our understanding at the micro-level. This requires refreshing our understanding of entrepreneurship and poverty to be able to unpick microfinance's role.

One fruitful area for future research is to widen our understanding of poverty and agency more broadly. In most prior research, there is a chain of logic that positions microfinance as something that seeds entrepreneurial development, initiates an improvement in individual income which subsequently lifts the individual and their family away from the poverty line. However, this view has more recently been questioned by Kimmitt et al. (2020) who show a disconnect between improvements in income poverty and individual life satisfaction. This is because we tend to view entrepreneurship as primarily having a remediation function (i.e. it addresses lost income and access to financial resources).

Thus, current research in this space mainly takes a hedonic view of poverty with an over emphasis in the role of income, financial capital, and life satisfaction. In this respect, poverty is conceptually related to well-being yet most research focuses on this hedonic aspect rather than a broader eudaimonic perspective (Ryff, 2019). Factors like life purpose, goal pursuit, self-determination, and personal growth, all central to understanding how wellbeing can be achieved, are inherently future-oriented (Ryan & Deci, 2001). For example, hope has emerged as an interesting concept for entrepreneurship researchers, whereby people hope for a (better) future through continuous reflection and self-appraisal for their capacities and pursuit of certain life goals (Arend, 2020; Snyder, 2002). Thus, the multi-dimensionality of the well-being concept has been neglected within the literature which would allow us to ask important questions about the link (or lack thereof) between microfinance, entrepreneurship, and poverty. At this micro-level, there is value in following recent advances into understanding the cognitive processes of hope in conditions of poverty and indebtedness of microfinance (Kimmitt et al., 2020).

By expanding our understanding of poverty outcomes at the micro-level, we can also build upon prior research in entrepreneurship from a capabilities perspective. Whilst several scholars have drawn from Sen's (1999) seminal work to understand entrepreneurial outcomes, in most research "capabilities" are being used as something that it is synonymous with any and all poverty related outcomes. Further, most research only partially uses this development framework with some misuse or misunderstanding of concepts (e.g. Naminse et al., 2019). Thus, we need to adopt the capabilities approach in a more holistic manner to better understand the relationship between entrepreneurship, poverty, and microfinance.

To achieve this, I argue here, future research should move away from cross-sectional research designs towards a more process-oriented approach. The persistence of poverty can be explained in several ways, but one lesser-known understood approach is through process as a complex interaction of factors across individuals, contexts and time (Bradshaw, 2007). This approach offers significant value because it emphasises how problems or progress are cumulative and explained by the linkage between events that mark the 'spirals' of the process. The power of this approach lies in its ability to understanding that these linkages are difficult to break, typically reinforced over time and inherently complex.

Such a process approach, in combination with the capabilities perspective, has been adopted by Kimmitt and Dimov (2021) in their study of microfinance entrepreneurs. By opening-up the role of "process freedom" as a central input into the entrepreneurial process it identifies the differing entrepreneurial practices that can emerge under similar contextual conditions. Process oriented research has long been advocated for in entrepreneurship and management research more broadly (Van de Ven & Engleman, 2004) and this resonates with a more holistic approach to the capabilities approach whereby decision-making processes and the freedom attached to them are seen as being central to understanding poverty, and therefore the impact of microfinance on decision-making. Similarly, this prospective approach to entrepreneurial decision-making is regarded as important to understanding opportunity development process (Dimov, 2011).

In summary, future research at the micro-level of entrepreneurship and microfinance research requires a renewed conceptualisation of poverty beyond simple income and life satisfaction measures. A more eudaimonic perspective of poverty is needed to advance the conversation. Complementary to this is the need to advance an improved understanding of Sen's (1999) capabilities approach within entrepreneurship research. This will require a renewed effort around different research designs to incorporate a more process-oriented understanding of poverty to help us understanding entrepreneurial decision-making in the context of entrepreneurial micro investments.

Meso level: New investment models

The review of the literature highlighted how research at the meso-level typically focuses on relationships that the entrepreneur has with the financial institution but mainly through interactions with group members. This research certainly demonstrates a mixed picture with some perspectives pointing to the value of social capital developed within communities with counter views emphasizing the deleterious consequences of a break down in relationships (Rankin, 2002). Ultimately, the microfinance industry has recognised that a one-size-fits-all approach around group lending is unlikely to be productive given the diverse range of entrepreneurial needs and economic structures across emerging economies.

In this context, more research needs to focus on the alternative financing mechanisms that MFIs provide. First, research would benefit from looking at individual lending as something which can be used to target the "missing middle" (Kimmitt et al., 2016) but also offered as an incentive to group members who wish to progress away from the limits of group membership. In group-liability, risk is shared between group members allowing MFIs to lend to entrepreneurs through a group guarantee. In individual lending, the risk is pushed back onto the MFI in much the same way that traditional bank lending operates.

Therefore, future research would benefit from examining the association between entrepreneurs in individual lending mechanisms and their relationship with loan officers. Prior research portrays loan officers primarily as enforcers of group liability and as debt collectors (Siwale, 2012). But for loan officers distributing to individual entrepreneurs a more thorough assessment of the business venture and the entrepreneur behind is likely required because of the institutional risk. Future research should examine the decision-making criteria adopted by loan officers as they evaluate both agency and market risk. What informal signals are important to loan officers? What formal procedures do MFIs put in place to filter entrepreneurs that are suitable for individual or group lending?

Consistent with research at the micro-level, future research should examine the long-term dynamics between entrepreneurs and their loan officers, using a process approach. The benefit of this is to be able to identify, at a granular level, how entrepreneurs and financiers negotiate with one another and how they build relationships. Given the crucial role of building trust between institutions and the local population (Zhang et al., 2017), understanding how trust is enabled (or not) between entrepreneurs and their financiers would be a valuable future research direction.

To extend this perspective, research should also involve looking more closely at the role of loan officers. In traditional entrepreneurial finance research, lenders are portrayed as being rather risk averse and adopting certain criteria based on their prior experience and background e.g. bank finance. But from an organizational point of view, MFIs follow social purpose logics of poverty reduction and empowerment. Therefore, we would expect this ethos to shine through in all lending approaches and differ somewhat from traditional theory. But loan officers and the workforce of the microfinance industry varies with regards to skills, expertise, and knowledge whilst also operating in contexts where social and cultural norms create barriers for the workforce of MFIs (Siwale, 2016). This is likely to have ramifications for the selection, distribution, and development of trust between entrepreneur and financier.

Therefore, at a meso-level, we need to better understand the relationship between the entrepreneur and those working on the ground within the financial institution. In this respect, future research should also look at the role of micro-equity and entrepreneurial outcomes. The emergence of this financing phenomena is relatively recent and indicates a move away from the indebtedness model that is currently provided by MFIs. It is particularly interesting because it provides a new financial option for entrepreneurs based on access to a larger and more involved forms of investment. Further, this points to a limitation in the traditional lending approaches currently afforded by most MFIs.

There is very limited volume of research on micro-equity. Ayayi (2012) emphasizes the potential complementarities of micro-equity to current microcredit programmes for growing entrepreneurial firms. But several interesting research questions emerge from this phenomenon. Estapé-Dubreuil et al. (2012) describe "micro-angels" as investors who are much more aligned to an angel investor approach to investment which is typically wealthy individuals looking to invest in promising entrepreneurs and their ventures. However, micro-equity investment could also be managed through MFIs themselves as part of a broader financial portfolio. In this respect, they may behave like a venture capitalist firm with a more stringent set of requirements such as a formal business plan, financial figures and projections, formal auditing and so forth.

Therefore, a variety of interesting research questions emerge here regarding selection criteria, deal structuring and post-investment management. Given the social purpose of MFIs, how are these incorporated into the investment process? Given the institutional contexts, what are the barriers to micro-equity investment where legal arrangements may be opaquer? How do MFIs train or recruit staff for equity-investment in addition to loan distribution? What does an entrepreneur do to build legitimacy to equity investors as opposed to lenders? At this meso-level, this research should aim to understand the relational dynamics between micro investors and entrepreneurial behaviour.

In summary, future research at the meso-level should build upon prior studies investigating the relationship between entrepreneurs and their group members. There is scope for future research on entrepreneurs who adopt for or migrate into individual lending. This will require more research into the loan officers whose individual judgment, backgrounds, skills, and expertise now become more critical to distributing loans. Whilst we have a sense of what signals may be relevant for lending on microfinance lending platforms (Moss et al., 2015) we know far less about how this works for loan officers in the field. Similarly, future research should investigate micro-equity and the relationships between this new form of investor and entrepreneurial outcomes.

Macro level: Nuancing the role of MFIs

Research at the macro-level has primarily focused on organizational dynamics of MFIs and the interface between financial inclusion and the institutional environment. Although this has shone on a light on the complex dynamics of managing social and economic tensions whilst enabling community change, it seems to be a somewhat misrepresentation of what is experienced by most MFIs. In particular, the theoretical framing of institutional entrepreneurship (Mair & Marti, 2009) implies high levels of ability to instigate social change. Evidence indicates that most MFIs operate as lenders guided by microfinance's underlying logic but not all are necessarily as immersed in trying to transform institutional structures as prior research suggests (Siwale & Kimmitt, 2019). This section outlines the need for a more realistic and nuanced understanding of MFI performance and for understanding their role more broadly in the context of complex systems.

There is an inherent success bias in this strand of research at the macro level. Recently, Siwale et al. (2021) offer one of the first detailed accounts of MFI failure, based on the de-legitimation processes of the most well-known MFIs in Zambia. Their research indicates how MFI actors can associate the organization with stakeholders for whom their interests' mis-align with its social goals. A large body of research exists on the topic of organizational failure defined as "a deterioration in an organization's adaptation to its microniche and the associated reduction of resources within the organization" (Cameron et al., 1988, p.9). Failure is associated with negative consequences such as downsizing or death. In this definition, the source of failure can also be internal to the organization and/or because of external factors (Mellahi et al., 2002).

Therefore, research at the macro-level needs a better understanding of the drivers of MFI failure. This will help to enable a more nuanced conversation regarding MFI performance more broadly. Although studies such as those by Battilana and Dorado (2010) have importantly emphasised how organisations mitigate the challenging and competing institutional logics within firms, the reality for most MFIs is likely an ongoing debate regarding how social and economic logics translate into practices and achieving social outcomes (i.e. poverty reduction). For example, following Sun and Liang's (2021) scrutiny of the affordability of microfinance depending on the presence or absence of dominant social or economic logics.

One promising avenue for a more nuanced understanding of MFI performance would be for future research to adopt a systems perspective, drawing from complexity theory. In this view, there are a range of inter-dependent factors, conditions and contexts that help us to understand the role of MFIs within the local economy. The poverty experienced by micro-entrepreneurs is driven by multiple factors, some of which may be within the control of the MFI but most which are unlikely to be (e.g. decisions around local infrastructure, the quality of schooling etc.). From a complexity perspective, these factors at play in other parts of the system are likely to be just as relevant to entrepreneurial outcomes as the provision of microcredit or micro-equity.

The language of complexity theory resonates with the idea of the "entrepreneurial ecosystem" which has cultural, social, and material properties (Spigel, 2017). These are entrepreneurial-related factors which are regarded as being interdependent and can combine to enable or hinder entrepreneurs to start and grow new ventures. Yet, MFIs are only likely to enable one aspect of the ecosystem through access to investment. More research should be conducted to help understand the relationship between MFIs and the broader ecosystem, building on co-creation perspective work from Sun and Im (2015). Rather than assuming inevitable institutional change, the concept of institutional work helps us to understand how systems and institutions are changed, maintained, or disrupted (Lawrence et al., 2011). By seeding entrepreneurial activities, do MFIs help to improve the entrepreneurial culture? Do some of the lesser-known support services (i.e. financial literacy training) help to improve skills and facilitate the ecosystem's development? Do the actions of MFIs to enable unhelpful features of a system to persist?

In summary, future research needs to take a more nuanced perspective of MFI performance. This involves looking beyond the obvious success cases that dominate a lot of the literature to date and examining under-performance more closely. This could also involve taking a closer ethical examination of the suitability of MFIs in local contexts where entrepreneurial support may not be the most appropriate intervention (Kimmitt & Muñoz, 2018). Further, one such theoretical lens for examining this would be complexity theory which brings together the collection of factors that enable or hinder entrepreneurial development.

Conclusion

This chapter has provided an overview of current understanding at the intersection of entrepreneurial finance and microfinance research. It sets out three levels of research – micro, meso, macro – and sets out a research agenda around these levels. These are categories designed to help analyse and organise the chapter fluently, but research would also benefit from adopting a multi-level perspective. In addition, there are areas of further research and discussion that are beyond the scope of this chapter, such as the role of entrepreneurial/financial literacy training offered by some MFIs. These are also important discussions but are perceived to be a subdimension of the broader, and arguably more pertinent issues identified within the chapter.

In this chapter, I set out the three levels of current and future research about how we frame poverty within entrepreneurship research (micro), the role of different lending mechanisms and relationships in the microfinance space (meso), and the performance and role of MFIs in the context of a broader (eco) system. I hope that this may help elicit refreshed conversations in this space and provide entrepreneurship researchers with improved theoretical and practical ideas as to how to contribute to our understanding of the role of microfinance in facilitating entrepreneurship, and ultimately poverty reduction.

References

Acs, Z. J., & Virgill, N. (2010). Entrepreneurship in developing countries. In *Handbook of entrepreneurship research*, 485–515. Springer, New York, NY.

Allen, T. (2016). Optimal (partial) group liability in microfinance lending. *Journal of Development Economics*, *121*, 201–216.

Alvarez, S. A., & Barney, J. B. (2014). Entrepreneurial opportunities and poverty alleviation. *Entrepreneurship theory and practice*, *38*(1), 159–184.

Arend, R. J. (2020). The roles of thought and affect on entrepreneurship–A new hope. *Journal of Business Venturing Insights*, *14*.

Ayayi, A. G. (2012). Micro-credit and Micro-equity: The David and the Goliath of Micro-enterprise Financing. *Economic Papers: A journal of applied economics and policy*, *31*(2), 244–254.

Battilana, J., & Dorado, S. (2010). Building sustainable hybrid organizations: The case of commercial microfinance organizations. *Academy of Management Journal*, *53*(6), 1419–1440.

Bourlès, R., & Cozarenco, A. (2018). Entrepreneurial motivation and business performance: evidence from a French microfinance institution. *Small Business Economics*, *51*(4), 943–963.

Bradshaw, T. K. (2007). Theories of poverty and anti-poverty programs in community development. *Community Development*, *38*(1), 7–25.

Bradley, S. W., McMullen, J. S., Artz, K., & Simiyu, E. M. (2012). Capital is not enough: Innovation in developing economies. *Journal of Management Studies*, *49*(4), 684–717.

Bruns, V., Holland, D. V., Shepherd, D. A., & Wiklund, J. (2008). The role of human capital in loan officers' decision policies. *Entrepreneurship Theory and Practice*, *32*(3), 485–506.

Bruton, G. D., Khavul, S., & Chavez, H. (2011). Microlending in emerging economies: Building a new line of inquiry from the ground up. *Journal of International Business Studies*, *42*(5), 718–739.

Bruton G, Khavul S, Siegel D, Wright M. (2015) New Financial Alternatives in Seeding Entrepreneurship: Microfinance, Crowdfunding, and Peer-to-Peer Innovations. *Entrepreneurship Theory and Practice*. 39 (1), 9–26.

Canales, R. (2014). Weaving straw into gold: Managing organizational tensions between standardization and flexibility in microfinance. *Organization Science*, 25(1), 1–28.

Cameron, K. S., Sutton, R. I., & Whetten, D. A. (Eds.). (1988). *Readings in organizational decline: Frameworks, research, and prescriptions*. Ballinger Publishing Company.

Chliova, M., Brinckmann, J., & Rosenbusch, N. (2015). Is microcredit a blessing for the poor? A meta-analysis examining development outcomes and contextual considerations. *Journal of Business Venturing*, 30(3), 467–487.

Cornforth, C. (2014). Understanding and combating mission drift in social enterprises. *Social enterprise journal*. 10 (1), 3–20.

DiMaggio, P. J., & Powell, W. W. (1983). The iron cage revisited: Institutional isomorphism and collective rationality in organizational fields. *American Sociological Review*, 147–160.

Dimov, D. (2011). Grappling with the unbearable elusiveness of entrepreneurial opportunities. *Entrepreneurship Theory and Practice*, *35*(1), 57–81.

Drori, I., Manos, R., Santacreu-Vasut, E., Shenkar, O., & Shoham, A. (2018). Language and market inclusivity for women entrepreneurship: the case of microfinance. *Journal of Business Venturing*, *33*(4), 395–415.

Easterly, W. (2001). *The elusive quest for growth: economists' adventures and misadventures in the tropics*. MIT press.

Estapé-Dubreuil, G., Ashta, A., & Hédou, J. P. (2012). Micro-equity and social entrepreneurship from a venture capital perspective. *Strategic Change*, *21*(7-8), 355–368.

Fiet, J. O. (1995). Risk avoidance strategies in venture capital markets. *Journal of Management Studies*, *32*(4), 551–574.

Frankiewicz, C., & Churchill, C. (2011). Making microfinance work. Geneva: International Labour Office.

Galema, R., Lensink, R., & Mersland, R. (2012). Do powerful CEOs determine microfinance performance?. *Journal of Management Studies*, *49*(4), 718–742.

Ghatak, M. (1999). Group lending, local information and peer selection. *Journal of Development Economics*, *60*(1), 27–50.

Giné, X., Jakiela, P., Karlan, D., & Morduch, J. (2010). Microfinance games. *American Economic Journal: Applied Economics*, *2*(3), 60–95.

Godquin, M. (2004). Microfinance repayment performance in Bangladesh: How to improve the allocation of loans by MFIs. *World Development*, *32*(11), 1909–1926.

Gries, T., & Naudé, W. (2011). Entrepreneurship and human development: A capability approach. *Journal of Public Economics*, *95*(3–4), 216–224.

Haines Jr, G. H., Madill, J. J., & Riding, A. L. (2003). Informal investment in Canada: financing small business growth. *Journal of Small Business & Entrepreneurship*, *16*(3–4), 13–40.

Kent, D., & Dacin, M. T. (2013). Bankers at the gate: Microfinance and the high cost of borrowed logics. *Journal of Business Venturing*, *28*(6), 759–773.

Khavul, S., Chavez, H., & Bruton, G. D. (2013). When institutional change outruns the change agent: The contested terrain of entrepreneurial microfinance for those in poverty. *Journal of Business Venturing*, *28*(1), 30–50.

Kimmitt, J., & Dimov, D. (2021). The recursive interplay of capabilities and constraints amongst microfinance entrepreneurs. *International Journal of Entrepreneurial Behavior & Research*, *27*(3), 600–628.

Kimmitt, J., & Munoz, P. (2017). Entrepreneurship and financial inclusion through the lens of instrumental freedoms. *International Small Business Journal*, *35*(7), 803–828.

Kimmitt, J., & Muñoz, P. (2018). Sensemaking the 'social' in social entrepreneurship. *International Small Business Journal*, *36*(8), 859–886.

Kimmitt, J., Muñoz, P., & Newbery, R. (2020). Poverty and the varieties of entrepreneurship in the pursuit of prosperity. *Journal of Business Venturing*, *35*(4), 105939.

Kimmitt, J., Scarlata, M., & Dimov, D. (2016). An empirical investigation of the interplay between microcredit, institutional context, and entrepreneurial capabilities. *Venture Capital*, *18*(3), 257–276.

Lawrence, T., Suddaby, R., & Leca, B. (2011). Institutional work: Refocusing institutional studies of organization. *Journal of Management Inquiry*, *20*(1), 52–58.

MacMillan, I. C., Siegel, R., & Narasimha, P. S. (1985). Criteria used by venture capitalists to evaluate new venture proposals. *Journal of Business Venturing*, *1*(1), 119–128.

Mair, J., & Marti, I. (2006). Social entrepreneurship research: A source of explanation, prediction, and delight. *Journal of World Business*, *41*(1), 36–44.

Mair, J., & Marti, I. (2009). Entrepreneurship in and around institutional voids: A case study from Bangladesh. *Journal of Business Venturing*, *24*(5), 419–435.

McMullen, J. S. (2011). Delineating the domain of development entrepreneurship: A market–based approach to facilitating inclusive economic growth. *Entrepreneurship Theory and Practice*, *35* (1), 185–215.

Mersland, R., & Strøm, R. Ø. (2009). Performance and governance in microfinance institutions. *Journal of Banking & Finance*, *33*(4), 662–669.

MIX Market (2018), *Global Outreach & Financial Performance Benchmark Report* https://www.the mix.org/publications/global-outreach-and-financial-performance-benchmark-report-2017–2018 (Accessed 11th June, 2021)

Mellahi, K., Jackson, P., & Sparks, L. (2002). An exploratory study into failure in successful organizations: The case of Marks & Spencer. *British Journal of Management*, *13*(1), 15–29.

Morduch, J. (1999). The microfinance promise. *Journal of Economic Literature*, *37*(4), 1569–1614.

Moss, T. W., Short, J. C., Payne, G. T., & Lumpkin, G. T. (2011). Dual identities in social ventures: An exploratory study. *Entrepreneurship Theory and Practice*, *35*(4), 805–830.

Moss, T. W., Neubaum, D. O., & Meyskens, M. (2015). The effect of virtuous and entrepreneurial orientations on microfinance lending and repayment: A signaling theory perspective. *Entrepreneurship Theory and Practice*, *39*(1), 27–52.

Muñoz, P., & Kimmitt, J. (2019). Social mission as competitive advantage: A configurational analysis of the strategic conditions of social entrepreneurship. *Journal of Business Research*, *101*, 854–861.

Naminse, E. Y., Zhuang, J., & Zhu, F. (2019). The relation between entrepreneurship and rural poverty alleviation in China. *Management Decision*. 57 (9), 2593–2611.

Newman, A., Schwarz, S., & Ahlstrom, D. (2017). Microfinance and entrepreneurship: An introduction. *International Small Business Journal*, 35(7), 787–792.

Ngo, T. M. P., & Wahhaj, Z. (2012). Microfinance and gender empowerment. *Journal of Development Economics*, 99(1), 1–12.

Ocasio, W., & Thornton, P. H. (1999). Institutional logics and the historical contingency of power in organizations: Executive succession in the higher education publishing industry, 1958–1990. *American Journal of Sociology*, 105(3), 801–843.

Postelnicu, L., & Hermes, N. (2018). Microfinance performance and social capital: A cross-country analysis. *Journal of Business Ethics*, 153(2), 427–445.

Randøy, T., Strøm, R. Ø., & Mersland, R. (2015). The impact of entrepreneur–CEOs in microfinance institutions: A global survey. *Entrepreneurship Theory and Practice*, 39(4), 927–953.

Rankin, K. N. (2002). Social capital, microfinance, and the politics of development. *Feminist economics*, 8(1), 1–24.

Reay, T., & Hinings, C. R. (2009). Managing the rivalry of competing institutional logics. Organization studies, 30(6), 629–652.

Ryan, R. M., & Deci, E. L. (2001). On happiness and human potentials: A review of research on hedonic and eudaimonic well-being. *Annual review of psychology*, 52(1), 141–166.

Ryff, C. D. (2019). Entrepreneurship and eudaimonic well-being: Five venues for new science. *Journal of Business Venturing*, 34(4), 646–663.

Sen, A. (1999). Development as Freedom. *Oxford University Press*.

Siwale, J. (2016). Microfinance and loan officers' work experiences: Perspectives from Zambia. The Journal of Development Studies, 52(9), 1289–1305.

Siwale, J. N., & Ritchie, J. (2012). Disclosing the loan officer's role in microfinance development. *International Small Business Journal*, 30(4), 432–450.

Siwale, J., & Kimmitt, J. (2019). The discourse of institutional change in the Zambian microfinance sector. *Africa Journal of Management*, 5(1), 47–78.

Siwale, J., Kimmitt, J., & Amankwah-Amoah, J. (2021). The Failure of Hybrid Organizations: A Legitimation Perspective. *Management and Organization Review*. 17(3), 452–485.

Spigel, B. (2017). The relational organization of entrepreneurial ecosystems. *Entrepreneurship Theory and Practice*, 41(1), 49–72.

Smith, W. K., & Besharov, M. L. (2019). Bowing before dual gods: How structured flexibility sustains organizational hybridity. *Administrative Science Quarterly*, 64(1), 1–44.

Snyder, C. R. (2002). Hope theory: Rainbows in the mind. *Psychological Inquiry*, 13(4), 249–275.

Sun, S. L., & Im, J. (2015). Cutting microfinance interest rates: An opportunity co–creation perspective. *Entrepreneurship Theory and Practice*, 39(1), 101–128.

Sun, S. L., & Liang, H. (2021). Globalization and affordability of microfinance. *Journal of Business Venturing*, 36(1), 106065.

Sutter, C., Bruton, G. D., & Chen, J. (2019). Entrepreneurship as a solution to extreme poverty: A review and future research directions. *Journal of Business Venturing*, 34(1), 197–214.

Tedeschi, G. A. (2006). Here today, gone tomorrow: Can dynamic incentives make microfinance more flexible?. *Journal of Development Economics*, 80(1), 84–105.

Van de Ven, A. H., & Engleman, R. M. (2004). Event-and outcome-driven explanations of entrepreneurship. *Journal of Business Venturing*, 19(3), 343–358.

Weber, O., & Ahmad, A. (2014). Empowerment through microfinance: The relation between loan cycle and level of empowerment. *World Development*, 62, 75–87.

Yessoufou, A. W., Blok, V., & Omta, S. W. F. (2018). The process of entrepreneurial action at the base of the pyramid in developing countries: a case of vegetable farmers in Benin. *Entrepreneurship & Regional Development*, 30(1–2), 1–28.

Yunus, M. (1999). Banker to the Poor: Micro-lending and the Battle. *Against World Poverty*.

Zhang, Y., Zhou, X., & Lei, W. (2017). Social capital and its contingent value in poverty reduction: evidence from Western China. *World Development, 93*, 350–361.

Zahra, S. A., Gedajlovic, E., Neubaum, D. O., & Shulman, J. M. (2009). A typology of social entrepreneurs: Motives, search processes and ethical challenges. *Journal of Business Venturing, 24*(5), 519–532.

Darek Klonowski and Silas Lee

10 Venture capital as a source of entrepreneurial finance

Abstract: Venture capital (VC) focuses on the provision of capital and know-how to the most promising young entrepreneurial firms by institutional investors. This chapter provides an overview of VC with a special focus on its characteristics, global fundraising and investing statistics, its advantages to entrepreneurs, the VC investment process, VC performance, and VC in emerging markets. Moreover, due to recent events surrounding COVID-19, this chapter briefly notes the initial dislocations occurring in the VC industry. In the context of these challenges, this chapter ends with suggestions for future research.

Keywords: venture capital, definitions, characteristics, key numbers, process, performance, COVID-19

Introduction

Venture capital (VC) is an act of investing that focuses on the most promising start-ups and young businesses (Amit, Brander, and Zott, 1998; Gorman and Sahlman, 1989).[1] It is also a mechanism that combines equity capital with know-how to identify attractive investment opportunities in the marketplace and ultimately accelerate entrepreneurial development (Klonowski, 2013a). In exchange for their provision of capital and know-how, VC expects to generate above-average returns. The *Oxford Dictionary* identifies VC as an investment that "may involve a lot of risk" (Oxford Dictionary, 2021), while *Investopedia*, on the other hand, defines it as financing provided to "startup companies and small businesses that are believed to have long-term growth potential" (Chen, 2020).

Although the terms "venture capital" and "private equity" are often used interchangeably, the two differ in theory and practice. VC is a subset of private equity, referring more to investments made in a company's early development phases; this definition may vary from one geographic region to another. For example, Invest Europe defines VC as "private equity that is focused on startup companies" (Invest Europe, 2021). Additionally, the National Venture Capital Association (NVCA) in the United States (U.S.) describes VC as "investments made by professional, institutional

---

1 We would like to thank Marissa Stelmack for editing this chapter.

Darek Klonowski, Silas Lee, Department of Business Administration, Brandon University

https://doi.org/10.1515/9783110726312-014

managers of risk capital that enable and support the most innovative and promising companies" (NVCA, 2021a).

VC fund managers (i.e., general partners; GPs) do not manage their own money, but instead raise cash from investors (i.e., pension funds, endowments, insurance firms, etc.) and wealthy individuals; these investors are called limited partners (LPs). The investments made by venture capitalists (VCs) are held until a liquidity event, otherwise known as an exit, occurs, which could include a purchase by a strategic investor or an initial public offering (IPO). As a result of the liquidity event, the VC firm realizes it profits (or losses) from the initial investment in its portfolio firms. VCs typically invest in emerging and innovative products and technologies that are often highly scalable but may not yet be profitable. Although these investments can be highly lucrative when successful, they can also lead to partial or complete losses, which is why this form of investing is characterized by high risk.

In contrast to VC, private equity predominantly refers to equity capital investments in a private firm that is further advanced in its entrepreneurial development. While VC and private equity firms pursue the same goals, the primary of which is a focus on increasing the value of investee businesses and selling their equity stake for a profit, both forms of investing are distinct in several ways. Key differences between VC and private equity include the types of firms they support, the amount of capital expended, the percentage of ownership obtained, the investee's maturity, and the composition of debt and equity used in the investment process. VC firms also tend to seek out young, technology-oriented companies that are rapidly growing. The active management that VCs furnish in their portfolio companies may help their businesses to become more successful with robust revenue growth, increased profitability, and improved exit prospects (Chemmanur, Krishnan, and Nandy, 2011; Hellmann and Puri, 2002). In contrast, private equity firms are generally interested in mature ventures that may operate in more traditional industries, such as manufacturing or transportation. Private equity investors often invest in established businesses that may desire a rapid expansion or suffer from some underlying operational inefficiencies.

Geographical factors have also influenced the usage of the terms "venture capital" and "private equity" (Sorenson and Stuart, 2001). Historically, investors in the U.S. have gravitated towards investing in early-stage firms, while European investors instead favored later-stage expansion deals. This dichotomy led U.S. investors to regard their investments as "venture capital," whereas their European counterparts preferred the term "private equity."

Academics have long described VC as a distinctive asset class due to its strong emphasis on governance by VCs through staged financing, contractual provisions, and active involvement with their portfolio companies (Lerner and Nanda, 2020). For example, follow-on investments may be provided as the investee firm grows, which can typically be expected every year or two. These follow-on rounds of investing are also equity-based, with shares allocated under an agreed valuation. In the words of American economist and Nobel laureate Kenneth Arrow, "Venture capital has done much more, I think, to improve efficiency than anything".[2]

VCs are full-time professional investors who support innovations that cannot be financed through traditional banks or other forms of entrepreneurial finance, occupy nascent industries, and require three to five years (or longer) to come to fruition (Klonowski, 2013a; Hellmann and Puri, 2000). Thus, VC is a long-term investment that allows investee firms sufficient time for value creation, generation, and perpetuation. Before investing, VCs conduct due diligence on the founders and their business concepts to evaluate the potential of an investment opportunity, which results in one or two investments out of every one hundred business plans they review (Klonowski, 2013a). When structuring a deal, VCs contribute financial expertise and set appropriate incentives and compensation systems (Hellmann, 2006; Florin, 2005; Casamatta, 2003). Following the initial investment, VCs' role is to raise additional funds for their portfolio companies and actively monitor them both formally, through participation on the board level (Gabrielson and Huse, 2002), and informally (Klonowski, 2021; Klonowski, 2013a). VCs also provide strategic advice and play a vibrant role in corporate governance and the exit decision, such as influencing an investee firm's public offering (Chemmanur, Krishnan, and Nandy, 2011; Gabrielson and Huse, 2002). Although discussed briefly here, the specifics of the VC investment process will be outlined in more detail further in this chapter.

One of the main objectives of VCs is to create value for LPs, which firm-level studies suggest is done through the careful selection, and advising, of portfolio firms. For example, research shows that entrepreneurial firms backed by VCs are more likely to grow faster in terms of sales and employment (Chemmanur, Krishnan, and Nandy, 2011; Jain and Kini, 1995). Furthermore, and contrary to popular belief, VC creates value not only for its institutional investors, but also to the economy generally by encouraging the development of high-growth firms that create jobs and generate wealth (Davis et al., 2014; Samila and Sorenson, 2011). Among publicly traded firms worldwide, seven of the top eight firms by market capitalization in 2020 were financed by VC before going public; they include Alphabet, Amazon, Apple, Facebook, and Microsoft in the U.S., and Alibaba and Tencent in China (PWC, 2020). In the U.S., which may be considered an epicenter of the global VC industry, firms financed by venture funds comprise less than 0.5% of firms founded each year, and yet represent nearly half of entrepreneurial companies promoted on the stock exchange (Lerner and Nanda, 2020). Although academics and business leaders have widely attributed economic growth resulting from VC to specific areas within the U.S., such as the San Francisco Bay Area and the Boston-New York-Washington corridor, the entire country

---

2 Arrow, Kenneth. 1995. Interview with Kenneth Arrow. Federal Reserve Bank of Minneapolis. www.minneapolisfed.org.

has benefited from this growth to some degree (Bottazzi and Da Rin, 2002; Sorenson and Stuart, 2001).

The roots of VC can be traced back to the late 1400s when Queen Isabella of Spain backed Christopher Columbus with capital (money, ships, supplies, etc.) for his venture (voyages across the Atlantic), which was characterized by an asymmetrically high pay-off compared to her at-risk capital (Zarco, 2016). However, the practice was not recognized until Georges Doriot, a Harvard professor commonly referred to as the "Father of Venture Capital," put the industry on the map. In 1946, Doriot established the American Research and Development Corporation in Boston, Massachusetts, for the purpose of investing in young businesses during World War II. Many of the practices envisioned by Doriot are still utilized today, including the intense scrutiny of business plans before financing, the provision of oversight and capital, the staged funding of investments, and the ultimate return of capital and profits to the outside investors who provided the initial funding (Lerner and Nanda, 2020). Three decades after Doriot's visionary idea, VC firms had invested approximately $750 million in startups (Prive, 2013).

The industry's evolution since these humble beginnings is associated with repeated waves of technological innovation: the invention of the microprocessor in the 1970s, the widespread use of personal computing in the early 1980s, the emergence of biotechnology in the mid-1980s, and the birth of the Internet and ecommerce in the 1990s (Lerner and Nanda, 2020). VC investments appear to be driven by technological changes (Ewens, Nanda, and Rhodes-Kropf, 2018). Due to the promise of high returns, the risks VCs were willing to take to secure these returns ballooned in the early 2000s. The oversaturation of cash in Silicon Valley, for example, led VC firms to "spray and pray" their capital at firms with even a small chance of success (Ewens, Nanda, and Rhodes-Kropf, 2018). Following the burst of the "dot com" bubble, VC firms hit the news headlines again in the 2000s because of their integral role in the ascension of smartphones, mobile applications, and cloud computing (Lerner and Nanda, 2020; Kortum and Lerner, 2000). Today, most VC firms desire to invest in firms that are developing novel ways of applying information and communications technology or improving the efficiency of existing services at much lower price points, such as Uber Technologies and Groupon (CB Insights, 2019). For example, the software sector in the U.S. has received more than one-third of total VC investments (34%) in 2020, followed by commercial services (10%) (NAVCA, 2020).

Literature review

Global statistics: Key numbers

Before discussing the key characteristics and features of VC, it is important to understand the two key numbers that characterize the global VC industry: fundraising and investing. Fundraising activity is often indicative of the attractiveness of a specific market as perceived by investors. Investing activities reflect the amount of capital directed to investment opportunities, which VC firms have been able to identify, evaluate, and secure with suitable legal and financial terms.

Figure 10.1a presents fundraising and investing statistics in the total private equity industry between 2007 and 2020 (note these numbers also include buyout activities). Since 2007, the total cumulative amount of global fundraising has equaled $7.2 trillion, while cumulative investing is equal to $5.5 trillion. The difference between these amounts, equal to $1.7 trillion, represents the value of "dry powder", or un-invested capital, available to VCs. Growth in investing generally outpaced

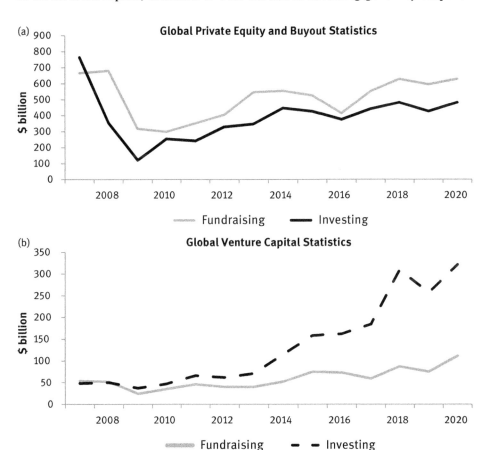

Figure 10.1: Key statistics in the global venture capital and private equity industry a) Annual global statistics for private equity and buyouts between 2007 and 2020 (Source: Compiled from various sources, including Prequin, Bain, Cambridge Associates, and EMPEA) b) Annual global statistics for venture capital between 2007 and 2020 (Source: Based on NVCA, 2021b).
Note: There may be some overlap between fundraising and investing figures in parts a and b of the graph due to different definitions of private equity and venture capital in different geographic regions.

fundraising, although this trend changed dramatically with the onset of the 2008 financial crisis. Since then, the industry has struggled to reach pre-2008 levels of fundraising and investing; fundraising has exceeded investing activities. The industry has also found it increasingly difficult to locate suitable investment opportunities to generate above average returns, which is a negative trend that continues today (Klonowski, 2018). Figure 10.1b presents investing and fundraising statistics in VC. Between 2007 and 2020, the total cumulative amount of VC global fundraising amounted to $0.8 trillion, while cumulative investing was equal to $1.9 trillion. It is important to note that investing has outpaced fundraising since 2008 in the VC industry.

Characteristics of venture capital

Startups generally have two options when seeking capital for growth or new major expenses: raise money from an external source of entrepreneurial finance or rely on internal sources of financing (Block et al., 2018; Klonowski, 2013a). Internal financing (also known as "bootstrapping") occurs when a business employs its savings, revenues, or a liquidation of other assets to fund a new strategy. When a firm is fundraising internally, it is not reliant on creditors, so advantages of this type of financing include the lack of underwriting timelines or credit reports, and its ready availability. However, if a firm is cash-strapped, it may turn to external financing; this entails debt financing from creditors or financial institutions such as banks, government assistance programs (i.e., grants and subsidies), business angels (i.e., funding from wealthy individuals, retired executives, serial entrepreneurs), corporate VCs, and VCs.

VC is distinguishable from other entrepreneurial financing forms in several ways. VC finances new ventures through equity and quasi-equity participation, which means that VCs offer capital in exchange for an ownership stake or a right or option to convert debt into ownership. However, VC is generally subordinate to other financing sources because, unlike commercial loans, it is not secured through any personal assets of the entrepreneur or the investee firm. In other words, venture funds have a lower priority than traditional financiers in the event of default, liquidation, or orderly windup of the venture. If an investee firm goes bankrupt, for example, VCs may receive cents on the dollar or even nothing from their investment.

As mentioned earlier in this chapter, VC is highly selective by nature. A VC's mission is to find the "needle in the haystack" by choosing the greatest potential winners. Effective capital allocation is critical because the risk of investment losses and the potential for a future payout are both very high. VC is best suited for firms that are highly profitable, hold above-average growth potential, maintain a substantial market share and superiority over their rivals, and are well managed. To recruit such candidates, VCs scrupulously investigate each prospect in the due diligence phase, which can take months to complete because it aims to address the risks associated with each enterprise. Once funding is approved, the VC firm will hold its investment for a period of three to five years, or until peak value is achieved, before disposing of its shares. During this time, the investment is illiquid.

Financial returns in VC investing are derived from the realization of investee firms' value upon exit. Dividends are rarely paid out during the investment period, although this may occur if the investee firm is extraordinarily cash generative. All of the startup's profits are instead reinvested into operations, plant expansions, product or service development, business acquisitions, or distribution structures. Return expectations are proportional to the financial, operational, and political risks undertaken by VCs (VC performance will be highlighted later in this chapter).

In addition to cash, however, VCs also contribute both operational and financial knowledge and expertise; these investors are known for their active participation in the management of portfolio firms. Put simply, VC is the "business of building businesses" by means of active involvement, although this approach may have been more accurate in the early stages of the VC industry's development (Hayes and Scott; 2021; Klonowski, 2013a). Accordingly, a fund manager who does not understand the business will impede rather than improve it, which is a critical trait that distinguishes VC from other financing alternatives (De Bettignies and Brander, 2007).

The most important characteristic of VC is its exit orientation. Before commencing any deal, VCs must be reasonably confident that they can cash out their shares at the end of the holding period. There are two preferred exit routes, the first of which is the sale of the venture fund's ownership stake in a portfolio firm to a strategic investor, such as a holding company or buyout firm. Alternatively, the public markets can step in and provide liquidity through an IPO, which is a considerably more expensive and time-consuming avenue. If the exit opportunity of a business appears weak, and there is doubt as to whether the venture could achieve either route, VCs may choose not to invest, even if the business initially appears attractive.

Finally, VC is a cyclical business; this asset class boom-bust is powered by a medley of high-risk appetites, bullish optimism, and lemming-like behavior that manifests when the market appears desirable (Gompers and Lerner, 2004). Since the supply of VC is dictated by investors' willingness to provide funds to venture firms, the expectation of higher returns naturally results in a greater desire to participate in risk-equity investing. New venture funds are formed as the excitement builds, and just like any investment, competition intensifies, and deals become increasingly more expensive as the amount of available capital grows (Klonowski, 2013a; Gompers and Lerner, 2002). In turn, this propulsion puts downward pressure on potential returns, causing venture funds to complete transactions at inflated valuations, gamble on asset liquidity, and establish weak legal protections. These unattractive prospects eventually force VC firms to abandon the market, although over time, the supply of VC contracts and the VC cycle begins anew (Klonowski, 2013a; Gompers and Lerner, 2004).

Venture capital: Advantages and disadvantages to entrepreneurs

Entrepreneurs are a critical part of the VC ecosystem; without them, the entire VC ecosystem would cease to exist. For entrepreneurs, VC represents a number of distinct advantages and disadvantages. With regard to advantages, these can include access to permanent capital, the possibility of further leverage (and financing), increased credibility in the marketplace, and valuable know-how to benefit and improve the valuation of their entrepreneurial venture. These four main advantages will be briefly extrapolated upon below.

Firstly, by allowing VCs to hold an ownership position in the entrepreneurial venture, the entrepreneurial firm will receive "permanent" capital that does not require repayment, the provision of collateral, or personal guarantees. There are also no expectations of dividends paid to VCs, since their primary objective is to enhance the value of the firm through a combination of internal growth and external means of expansion; in short, cash flow generated by the firm is used for reinvestment purposes.

A positive consequence of additional equity provided to entrepreneurial firms by VC is an improvement to the balance sheet of the investee firm and a further possibility of leverage access (i.e., debt), which is set at a reasonable level in terms of debt-to-equity composition. It is commonly understood that further debt can enhance the value of the firm if management is capable of producing projects that are value generative (i.e., capital budgeting projects with positive net present values). The involvement of VCs in the firm can also improve the entrepreneur's ability to raise extra equity, which may be important for entrepreneurial firms exhibiting high growth trajectories (note that robust growth is one of the key characteristics of VC-backed entrepreneurial firms). Although VCs expect that subsequent rounds of financing may occur at higher valuations, this often confirms that the investee firm is on the right, and perhaps accelerated, value creation trajectory. Of course, an increase in value is also welcome to entrepreneurs who are keen to continue growing their business.

The presence of VCs in the entrepreneurial firm is often interpreted as a further confirmation of the entrepreneurial firm's credibility in the eyes of their clients, suppliers, business partners, and other stakeholders; this participation may also be received with some envy. Evidence suggests that the reputation and involvement of some VCs may even act as guarantors and verifiers of the underlying quality of the entrepreneurial firm, although this may not always be true. In the case of an IPO, entrepreneurial firms are likely to receive a "certification premium" (i.e., higher valuation), outperform non-VC-backed firms in the market, and suffer underpricing to a lesser degree (Megginson and Weiss, 1991).

Finally, the last distinguishing feature of venture capitalism is the provision of know-how to entrepreneurial firms. VCs participate on the board of directors of the investee firm and can act as a useful sounding board for all critical decisions. VC activism may not only enhance the performance of the investee firm, but can also minimize failure, since portfolio firms are closely monitored (Jackson, Bates, and Bradford, 2012; Chemmanur, Krishnan, and Nandy, 2011; Large and Muegge, 2008; Busenitz, Fiet and Moesel, 2004; Davila, Foster, and Gupta, 2003; Lerner, 1995). En-trepreneurial firms can rely on VCs' participation in strategic planning and business plan revisions, the recruitment of senior management, the raising of future capital, and the execution of acquisitions. Additionally, VCs contribute to the professionali-zation and corporatization of entrepreneurial firms.

The key disadvantages of venture capitalism include dilution of ownership (which makes it one of the most expensive forms of entrepreneurial finance), long-term partnerships without the chance of business "divorce", the requirement of ex-tensive approvals and veto rights, and the necessity of an exit (Klonowski, 2013a; Hsu, 2004).

The venture capital investment process

The completion of a successful VC transaction requires the deal to progress through a number of specific stages (Tyebjee and Bruno, 1984). This is no easy task for en-trepreneurs and VCs because of the many unique challenges they will face. Entre-preneurs, for example, must prepare themselves for effective interactions with VCs; they need to become investment-ready by preparing business plans (Mason and Stark, 2004; Mason and Harrison, 2003), understanding the basic finance and legal language used during the negotiating process, and comprehending VCs' expecta-tions. VCs, on the other hand, play a dual role of educator and negotiator (Ber-glund, Hellstrom, and Sjolander, 2007) while simultaneously maintaining fiduciary responsibility to their own financiers (i.e., LPs).

Since the mid-1990s, academics have attempted to succinctly describe the nu-ances and details of the VC investment process. One of its early descriptions in-volved its definition as a five-stage process consisting of deal origination, screening, evaluation, deal structuring, and post-investment activities (Tyebjee and Bruno, 1984). Subsequent research of the investment process portrayed the same step-by-step process, although further details were provided, each stage was more clearly de-lineated, and specific attention was paid to various forms of due diligence (Fried and Hisrich, 1994). Within these more comprehensive depictions, six stages of the VC in-vestment process were defined, including origination, the VC firm's generic screen, the generic screen, first-phase evaluation, second-phase evaluation, and closing. A further understanding of the VC process led to its more detailed analysis, which aimed to unpack VC activities post-closing (Klonowski, 2013a). Yet another model captured eight stages, which consist of deal generation, initial screening, due diligence phase I and internal feedback, pre-approval completions, due diligence phase II and internal approvals, deal completion, monitoring, and exit (Klonowski, 2013a). However, the most intuitive model of VC investing is a five-stage model consisting of deal generation, due diligence, financial contracting, monitoring, and exiting; these five phases of the investment process cover all key VC activities throughout the investment. This flow is represented in Figure 10.2, and the following section will describe each of these stages in more detail.

Figure 10.2: The key components of the venture capital investment process.
Source: Authors compilation

Stages of the venture capital investment process

Below, we describe each phase of the VC process in detail. It is along this process that value creation or destruction occurs (Klonowski, 2018).

Strong deal flow is the lifeblood of VC investing and the entire VC ecosystem (Manigart et al., 2006; Sorenson and Stuart, 2001). VC firms rely on a wide network of relationships and contacts in the deal generation process, which may include professionals such as bankers, accountants, lawyers, investment bankers, consultants, and advisors. These important stakeholders of the VC ecosystem are effective sources of deals. Ways in which VCs can enhance their existing networks may consist of belonging to professional associations, visiting trade fairs, attending and speaking at conferences, making "cold calls", and maintaining a strong internal registry of contacts. However, VCs not only rely on existing relationships, but also engage in strategies of direct marketing by attempting to identify profitable segments of the economy, and then invest in attractive firms within these potentially lucrative sections. These marketing strategies include developing a "pitch book" and brochure, launching an informative website, establishing a strong social media presence, and writing newspaper articles (Klonowski, 2013a).

Furthermore, a strong deal flow is important for three primary reasons. Firstly, a suboptimal set of opportunities is likely to lead to poor investment decisions. In other words, poor deal flow may lead to problems with investee firms, compromised exits, and subprime returns. Secondly, since the VC industry is competitive, access to strong deal flow ensures that VC firms are able to secure the right investment opportunities, conduct due diligence in a slow but deliberate manner, and agree to a suitable legal deal. Thirdly, deal flow is critical to the long-term existence of VC firms, as strong deal flow is a fundamental pre-requisite of any future successful fundraising.

The second critical stage of the VC process is due diligence, during which the VC firm aims to understand the underlying strengths and weaknesses of potential investee firms (see, for example, Zacharakis and Shepherd, 2005; Zacharakis and Shepherd, 2001; Muzyka, Birley, and Leleux, 1996; Tyebjee and Bruno, 1984; Hall and Hofer, 1993). The vast majority of investment proposals that VCs receive are rejected during this stage, and in fact, a small percentage of reviewed opportunities are converted into actual deals. Due diligence consists of at least three separate forms of investigations, which are characterized by increasing levels of scope, depth, and intensity. During initial stages of the due diligence process, VCs attempt to identify any obvious "deal breakers" on the commercial side of the potential investee business and ascertain the likelihood of closing a deal by discussing the main terms they would likely require, should the deal persist any further. Next, a more intense stage of due diligence is performed in the context of the firm's financial projections and business valuation through in-depth investigations of the market, management, competitive dynamics, business models, historical financials, and future financial forecasts (Knockaert and Vanacker, 2013; Kaplan, Sensoy, and Stromberg, 2009; Mason and Stark, 2004; MacMillan, Siegel, and Narasimha, 1985). A thorough discussion in these areas provide the basis for the establishment of a proper valuation range for the underlying venture. Once this stage of due diligence is completed, VCs involve external advisors, whose key areas of investigation relate to accounting, legal, environmental, and operational matters.

Financial contracting, the next step in the VC investment process, is one of the most complex phases (Hellmann, 2006; Casamatta, 2003; Kaplan and Stromberg, 2003; Kirilenko, 2001). In essence, after having thoroughly understood the underlying strengths of the potential investee firm, reviewed its financial forecasts multiple times, and established strong foundations for ascertaining business valuation, VCs proceed to negotiate a basic structure for the deal. Continuous and more complex discussions between founders and VCs eventually culminate in the signing of a foundational and legally non-binding document called a term sheet, heads of terms, or letter of intent. This milestone document is used as a template to develop more complex legal documentation.

Active, hands-on involvement in portfolio firms has historically been one of the most distinguishing features of VC (Chemmanur, Krishnan, and Nandy, 2011; Hellmann and Puri, 2002; Lerner, 1995; Gorman and Sahlman, 1989). While some VCs are more proficient at providing this service than others, the industry understands that investee firms (especially those in early stages of development) require a robust strategic plan, strong financial acumen, and the ability to raise subsequent rounds of financing. However, the most critical considerations for VCs during this stage of the investment process are whether the firm is developing according to its original business plan (Klonowski, 2013a) and if the investee firm is still progressing towards an anticipated exit (Hellmann, 2006). If the firm has deviated from its business plan (which may or may not influence exit alternatives), the firm may develop a revised budget, amend its expansion plans, and postpone the execution of specific projects. However, it is natural within VC investing that several portfolio firms underperform, become insolvent, and even go bankrupt; the cause of these challenges may include poor management, reckless expansion, forceful competition, weak market growth, or excessive debt. In these worst-case scenarios, VCs need to consider if a turnaround, sale, merger, or orderly wind-up of the troubled firm's affairs is the best option for their circumstances.

The VC investment process ends with the achievement of an exit or divestment, which represents the monetization of the VCs' illiquid investments and a transfer of realized cash to LPs (Klonowski, 2018; Lerner, 1994). As noted previously, VCs seek to monetize their investment through the two most common exit routes, namely an IPO or a sale to a strategic investor (Bock and Schmidt, 2015; Cochrane, 2005; Cumming and MacIntosh, 2003); both of these options have advantages and disadvantages to VCs. It is widely understood that an IPO is often the most preferred exit modes (Bock and Schmidt, 2015; Cochrane, 2005) due to the highest exit potential (Bayar and Chemmanur, 2011; Phallipou and Gottschalg, 2009). There are also other avenues to achieve an exit, such as a merger, sale to financial investors, sale to founder or management, or liquidation, although these forms may result in compromised returns to VCs and LPs alike (Klonowski, 2013a; Cumming and MacIntosh, 2003). Significantly, an exit does not occur automatically, but it is preceded by an intense focus on achieving key strategic objectives (i.e., increasing market share, securing market leadership, improving distribution structures, etc.) and financial milestones (Cumming, 2008; Mason and Harrison, 2006). Of course, the existence of viable exit routes and legal infrastructure are critical components of VC development (Armour and Cumming, 2006; Black and Gilson, 1998; Murray, 1995).

Venture capital performance

Of the numerous contentious and complex issues in the VC industry, financial performance, particularly in the context of the above average and outsized returns that GPs promise to generate for LPs, is one of the most important. For example, it is on the basis of this promise that GPs are able to charge substantial management fees, which are known in the industry as a "2/20" arrangement (i.e., 2% fixed fee and a 20% performance-based reward) (Ivashina and Lerner, 2019; Metrick and Yasuda, 2010; Litvak, 2009; Gompers and Lerner, 1999). These fees represent one of the most lucrative compensation schemes in the entire financial services sector (Klonowski, 2018). To ensure their compensation, GPs promise to deliver returns in excess of those available in public equities markets by some percentage, which is broadly recognized to be equal to 3% (Applebaum and Batt, 2014). One of the most recognized measures to distinguish if financial returns are in excess of returns from public equities markets is the public market equivalent (PME; defined as GPs' actual financial returns in comparison to returns which would have been generated by investing the same amount in public equities markets); this excess return is called an "illiquidity premium" in this chapter (Klonowski, 2018). Other common measures utilized to determine financial returns in the industry are internal rates of return (IRR), distributions to paid-in capital (DPI), cash-on-cash (C-on-C), or multiples of invested capital (MOIC).

Over the years, academics have attempted to investigate the VC ecosystem to understand the industry's financial performance (see, for example, Robinson and Sensoy, 2016; Phalippou, 2014; Kaplan and Schoar, 2005). There are multiple observations that can be made about these studies, such as their illustration of inconsistent financial outcomes. However, the financial returns mentioned in academic studies reflect and depend on the time period, the source of information, the length of observation, and access to relevant information. For example, reports from GPs operating in the 1980s and 1990s confirm significant above average annual returns, which were often in excess of 30–50% (see Figure 10.3). Secondly, while academics disagree about the long-term financial outcomes of VC, they are more consistent in their perception of a declining trajectory in VC returns over the last 30 years. Further evidence also confirms that GPs have problems repeating their performance from fund-to-fund; in other words, there is a limited persistence of returns. Lastly, returns vary region-to-region, which is verified by the higher VC returns that are typically seen in the U.S. when compared to Europe even though they have recently been converging.

Studies on financial returns from the VC industry can be broadly broken into three categories. In the first instance, there are numerous academic investigations (see, for example, Phalippou, 2014; Phalippou and Gottschalg, 2009) that suggest VC returns are worse than returns from public equities markets. One of the most negative studies on VC performance came from the Kauffman Foundation, which outlined that only about 25% of GPs were able to beat the equities market, while nearly 50% of GPs analyzed in the study did not provide any returns at all (Mulcahy, Weeks and Bradley, 2012). The second broad category includes studies which confirm that returns from VC and public equities markets are about equal (see, for example, Kaplan and Schoar, 2005; Moskowitz and Vissing-Jorgensen, 2002). There is also a third category of academic inquiry, which proposes that VC can effectively and consistently beat returns from public equities markets (see, for example, Robinson and Sensoy, 2016; Harris, Jenkinson, and Kaplan, 2014). These studies, however, reinforce the idea that VC is only able to exceed returns from public equities markets by less or equal to 3%; thus, these returns are below or equal to LP expectancies. Limited academic papers confirm returns in excess of 3% (see, for example, Ljungqvist and Richardson, 2003).

Figure 10.3 illustrates the financial performance of the VC industry in the context of the U.S. Returns from VC (i.e., investing in firms at early stages of development) and private equity (i.e., supporting firms at later stages of expansion) are differentiated in this graph. Furthermore, Figure 10.3 presents historical perspectives on these returns over a period of over 40 years (1986 and 2019); there are four characteristics included in the graph, namely nominal returns from VC and private equity, as well as illiquidity premiums from these same two categories.

There are multiple conclusions that can be drawn from the graph and associated data, such as that long-term average nominal returns from VC and private equity are equal to 25.0% and 15.4%, respectively. These returns are driven by an extraordinary financial performance of the asset class between 1990 and 1997 that VC has not been able to replicate since this period. Secondly, over the 40-year period outlined by Figure 10.3, the volatility of returns has also varied between the two categories of private investing; expressed in the form of standard deviation, the volatility of returns between VC, which was equal to 25.0%, and that of private equity, equal to 6.5%, represents a substantial difference. A third observation from this graph illustrates a significant convergence of returns from VC and private equity following the "dot com" era. This convergence is visible in the flat line of nominal returns from VC and private equity post-2000, which were equal to 14.4% and 13.2%, respectively. Furthermore, illiquidity premiums for VC were equal to 3.9% and 3.3% for private equity in the post-dot com era; this is less than 1% above the LP minimum expectation threshold. Finally, there are numerous periods when returns from both categories were outright negative.

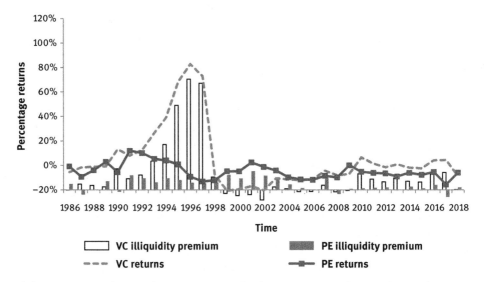

Figure 10.3: Financial returns from venture capital and private equity in the United States between 1986 and 2018.
Source: Compiled on the basis of data from Cambridge Associates

Venture capital in emerging markets

Emerging markets have become a major force in the global economy over the last two decades, and their course of economic development is expected to continue in the foreseeable future (Dabrowski, 2020). As an example, China is expected to surpass the United States as the world's foremost economic titan in the next few years. Economic growth in these markets is founded on strong manufacturing and service capabilities, a rapidly expanding and more wealthy middle class, substantial investments in local infrastructure, high rural-to-urban migration, accountable public finance decisions, prudent levels of public debt, and a diminished reliance on export activities (Klonowski, 2019). Emerging markets have also shown resilience to financial crises, successfully dealt with economic declines, demonstrated flexibility when adjusting economic structures, and confirmed a desire to expand outwardly to other countries. The economic miracle of many emerging markets is not only rooted in mass entrepreneurship, but also in technological innovations, access to natural resources, and vigorous human capital (including relying on returnees); these components are yet to be fully manifested on the international scale (Reid, 2020).

Although still imperfect, there has been significant improvement to institutional development in emerging markets (see for example, Johan and Zhang, 2016; Lingelbach, 2015; Klonowski, 2013b, Humphrey-Jenner and Suchard, 2013, Scheela and Jittrapanum, 2012; Bruton, Ahlstrom, and Puky, 2009). One of the most important components of this development relates to systemic and institutional infrastructure, including laws and regulations, intellectual property protection, taxation, corporate governance orientation, legal infrastructure (including the court system), and bureaucratic mechanisms. Thus, many countries in emerging markets systematically focused on the development of strong legal (i.e., property rights, ownership laws, and arbitration laws), accounting (i.e., merging own standards with international ones), and fiscal infrastructure (i.e., preferred taxation, economic zones, and fiscal policies) (Gruenhagen, 2020). Further attempts to improve institutional infrastructure is driven by local politicians' desire to improve their systemic competitiveness in the international arena and attract international investors. However, international investors, including VC financiers, are naturally attracted to the general storyline of emerging markets because it is underpinned by strong fundamentals. These international investors are similarly enticed by the opportunity to employ capital at higher increments in key sectors of the economy (such as infrastructure, banking, power generation, distribution, natural resources, and so on), therefore achieving premium financial returns (Quinlan, 2020; Klonowski, 2019).

Although VC has made a relatively small contribution to the development of the entrepreneurial ecosystem in emerging markets thus far, evidence nevertheless suggests that VC firms have assisted entrepreneurial firms in their managerial processes, operational efficiencies, corporate governance structures, management capabilities, and their ability to obtain requisite finance (Klonowski, 2011). There is additional evidence to suggest that VC firms have contributed to growing the economy, enhancing local employment prospects, and perpetuating innovation in emerging market countries as well (Klonowski, 2011).

However, the provision of VC in emerging markets have continued with a number of developmental problems (Klonowski, 2011; Ahlstrom, Bruton, and Yeh, 2007; Ahlstrom and Bruton, 2006). Most significantly, some emerging market countries are seen to represent a geopolitical risk related to political stability, the rule of law, corporate governance structures, corruption, and so on. Secondly, financial returns from VC have been volatile and unpredictable, which reflects relative instability in public equities markets and an inconsistent flow of foreign direct investment. There is also evidence to suggest that it may be difficult to process deals in some emerging market countries; challenges to deal completion may be due to complex legal infrastructure, imperfect accounting regulations, or a lack of preparation on the part of capital demanders (Klonowski, 2011). Furthermore, exit opportunities have been lopsided and skewed either towards public equities markets or trade sale. In China, for example, evidence indicates that the regulatory framework to achieve an IPO is challenging for all stakeholders (i.e., issuers, underwriters, and investors) (Chen, 2020). Lastly, there is also corruption within some emerging market countries, therefore creating an adverse impact on economic activity, international credibility, and country attractiveness (Puffer and McCarthy, 2020).

Venture capital and COVID-19

In early March of 2020, the World Health Organization (WHO) declared the existence of novel coronavirus, which was termed "COVID-19". The initial predictions noted that, in the absence of significant intrusions, there would be about 40 million deaths worldwide in 2020 alone. Following this announcement, the vast majority of governments moved to implement a number of restrictive public measures, mandates, and orders that most commonly included closures of public spaces, stay-at-home orders, travel restrictions, and border closures. As a result, most small and medium-sized enterprises (SMEs) were not allowed to operate or were forced to operate on a restrictive basis. Since these government decisions can effectively make or break SMEs, many businesses were detrimentally impacted by the added restrictions, regulations, and requirements. On the other hand, many governments have also aimed to provide some assistance to SME firms, such as payroll protection, wage subsidies, tax deferral schemes, loan guarantee programs, commercial eviction bans, rent payment assistance, and interest payment deferrals.

These restrictive measures have caused negative economic, social, and psychological consequences on populations, economies, and businesses. SMEs around the globe were one of the most affected sectors of the economy, experiencing this negative impact both profoundly and unequally. Firstly, restrictions have affected SMEs operating in different market segments to varying degrees; for example, those operating in retail, hospitality, transportation, leisure, recreation, and various forms of manufacturing have been the most negatively impacted. Secondly, research confirms that over three quarters of SMEs were affected, of which up to 50% were affected in a severe manner. The vast majority of firms continue to question their short- and medium-term survival. Thirdly, due to rapidly decreased revenue and high fixed costs, many firms only had enough cash to last for a few weeks or months.

The VC industry has also been affected by COVID-19 restrictions (Klonowski, 2021; Gompers et al., 2020; Arundale and Mason, 2020). Due to the industry's heavy reliance upon it, the most important area of impact has been in-person interactions. These interactions are critical throughout the VC investment process, including during networking, due diligence, financial contracting, and working with firms. In the initial stages of the outbreak, evidence indicates that the VC industry went into its own lockdown, resulting in limited face-to-face interactions, work-from-home arrangements, and a reduction in the number of deals closed. Furthermore, there were fewer deals being done because the key focus of the VC industry was on portfolio firms, many of which were disproportionately affected by restrictions; deal volume subsequently fell by 50 or 60%. In their assessment of investee firms, VC firms predominantly focused on trading, EBITDA (earnings before interest, taxes, depreciation, and amortization), and liquidity. Other efforts in relation to portfolio firms focused on cutting costs, finding new revenue streams, revising business plans, and arranging finance facilities.

By the end of the summer of 2020, VC activities returned to face-to-face meetings, office-based work (on a regular or rotational basis), and more active networking. External advisors were also more willing to engage in the provision of due diligence services. However, many of these positive trends were again interrupted by another wave of restrictions in the fall. While it is unclear at the moment what the VC industry will look like in the future, it is certain that VCs will undoubtedly experience significant difficulties when returning to their normal patterns of operation.

Future research in venture capital

In recent years, academics have attempted to analyze the field of VC and chart areas of research that are newly emerging, uninvestigated, or under-researched (see for example, Bonini and Capizzi, 2019; Cumming et al., 2019; Cumming and Groh, 2018; Bellavitis et al., 2017). While the importance of many of these contemplations should not be understated, the impact of COVID-19 is anticipated to create a significant disruption to the VC industry, to the point where a significant portion of previous academic contemplations could become either more or less relevant in at least the short-to medium-term. While there are perhaps too many uncertainties at the moment to significantly narrow the field of research in VC, the three critical areas that will most likely be fundamental pillars of the VC industry in the future have been selected for further analysis.

The first area of potential academic research that is critical to the overall perpetuation of the flourishing VC ecosystem relates to the entrepreneurial sector. It is clear that many entrepreneurial firms have struggled with issues related to operations and staffing, decreased market demand, financial management, supply chain, and access to finance, just to note a few prevalent concerns. These challenges not only disrupt new business formation, but also prevent the migration of preexisting businesses to new levels of development. These disruptions are likely to severely limit the number of investable projects the VC industry can pursue, which, in turn, would effectively freeze a significant part of the industry that is focused on the sectors most affected by COVID-19. The key research questions in this area include: What new financial and operational challenges will entrepreneurial firms face in the years to come? How will the survival rate of young firms be impacted? Are there any new forms of entrepreneurial finance that are likely to emerge in the COVID-19 era? Could crowdfunding platforms, business angels, debt providers, and equity providers play a more important role in the future of entrepreneurial finance?

Secondly, the VC community prides itself on active hands-on interaction with entrepreneurial firms. Since the emergence of COVID-19, initial evidence confirms that the relationship between founders and VCs is being redefined in new ways. The key questions in this research theme may relate to the following areas: Are new ways of communicating between entrepreneurs and VCs (i.e., rooted in online interactions) effective? Are these new channels of communication likely to create more conflicts, stresses, and strains between the two parties? How are new modes of communications likely to influence mutual trust? Will VCs need to increase their level of hands-on assistance to investee firms in the COVID-19 era? How can VCs re-tool and re-adjust their business models in order to effectively assist entrepreneurial firms in addressing new challenges?

Finally, it is also important to focus on VC's financial performance, which is a motivational engine of the entire industry. It may be noted that the financial sustainability of the entire VC ecosystem is grounded in three inter-linked financial components: monetary and non-monetary rewards to entrepreneurs, returns to LPs, and returns to GPs. If the VC ecosystem is likely to prosper, it is essential that these three components are stable, balanced, and equalized. Hence, the key questions surrounding VC's financial viability relate to the following concerns: Will LPs' financial performance (in terms of net returns) continue to fall in the future? How could GPs improve financial returns? What are the main adjustments that GPs need to make on the operational side to reduce cost? What broad-based structural adjustments can be made throughout the entire VC ecosystem to enhance financial performance? What are the key changes to LP-GP partnership agreements that need to be addressed in the future?

Conclusion

VC, which focuses on the provision of capital and know-how to entrepreneurial firms by institutional investors, may be an important contributor to entrepreneurship. In the U.S, for example, VC has contributed to the success of firms such as Google, Groupon, Twitter, Instagram, Zynga, Dell, Intel, and Microsoft, among many others. And yet, VC has a relatively small impact on entrepreneurial development, as only one in about fifteen hundred entrepreneurial firms receive VC financing in the United States; this represents less than 0.1% of entrepreneurial firms in the U.S. (Klonowski, 2019). The remaining 99.9% of U.S. entrepreneurial firms must raise capital from other financial sources.

Prior to 2020, the VC industry developed a pre-orchestrated, well designed, and robustly tested system of investing its capital into entrepreneurial firms. This investment scheme involves a number of phases through which financial and non-financial value is either created or destroyed, including deal generation, due diligence, financial contracting, monitoring, and exiting. However, due to the events surrounding COVID-19, the VC industry's deal processing system has been dislocated and redefined. In order to be effective, the VC industry must revive and reinvent itself in some new meaningful way, which will likely take place over the next five to ten years.

References

Ahlstrom, D., Bruton, G. D., & Yeh, K. S. (2007). Venture capital in China: Past, present, and future. Asia Pacific Journal of Management, 24(3), 247–268.

Ahlstrom, D., & Bruton, G. D. (2006). Venture capital in emerging economies: Networks and institutional change. Entrepreneurship Theory and Practice, 30(2), 299–320.

Amit, R., Brander, J., & Zott, C. (1998). Why do venture capital firms exist? Theory and Canadian evidence. Journal of Business Venturing, 13(6), 441–466.

Applebaum, E., & Batt, R. (2014). Private equity at work: When Wall Street manages Main Street. Russell Sage Foundation.

Armour, J., & Cumming, D. (2006). The legislative road to Silicon Valley. Oxford Economic Papers, 58(4), 596–635.

Arundale, K., & Mason, C. (2020). Private equity & venture capital: Riding the COVID-19 crisis. Innovation in Business, Economics & Finance 1. Monica Billio and Simone Varotto (eds.). Ca' Foscari University Press.

Bayar, O., & Chemmanur, T. (2011). IPOs versus acquisitions and the valuation premium puzzle: A theory of exit choice by entrepreneurs and venture capitalists. Journal of Financial and Quantitative Analysis, 46(6): 1755–1793

Bellavitis, C., Filatotchev, I., Kamuriwo, D. S., & Venacker, T. (2017). Entrepreneurial finance: New frontiers of research and practice. Venture Capital: An International Journal of Entrepreneurial Finance, 19(1–2), 1–6.

Berglund, H., Hellstrom, T., & Sjolander, S. (2007). Entrepreneurial learning and the role of venture capitalists. Venture Capital: An International Journal of Entrepreneurial Finance, 9(3), 165–197.

Black, B. S., & Gilson, R. J. (1998). Venture capital and the structure of capital markets: banks versus stock markets. Journal of Financial Economics, 47(3), 243–277.

Block, J., Colombo, M., Cumming, D., & Vismara, S. (2018). New players in entrepreneurial finance and why they are there. Small Business Economics, 50(January), 239–250.

Bock, C., & Schimdt, M. (2015). Should I stay, or should I go? – How fund dynamics influence venture capital exit decisions. Journal of Financial Economics, 27(1), 68–82.

Bonini, S., & Capizzi, V. (2019). The role of venture capital in the emerging entrepreneurial finance ecosystem: Future threats and opportunities. Venture Capital: An International Journal of Entrepreneurial Finance, 21(2–3), 137–175.

Bottazzi, L., & Da Rin, M. (2002). Venture capital in Europe and the financing of innovative companies. Economic Policy, 17(34), 229–269.

Bruton, G. D., Ahlstrom, D., & Puky, T. (2009). Institution difference and the development of entrepreneurial ventures: A comparison of the venture capital industries in Latin America and Asia. Journal of International Business Studies, 40(5), 762–778.

Busenitz, L. W., Fiet, J. O., & Moesel, D. (2004). Reconsidering the venture capitalists' "value added" proposition: An organizational learning perspective. Journal of Business Venturing, 19(6), 787–807.

Cambridge Associates. (2020). U.S. Private Equity Index and Selected Benchmark Statistics. June 3.

Cambridge Associates. (2014). U.S. Private Equity Index and Selected Benchmark Statistics. March 31.

Cambridge Associates. (2020). U.S. Venture Index and Selected Benchmark Statistics. June 30.

Cambridge Associates. (2014). U.S. Venture Index and Selected Benchmark Statistics. March 31.

Casamatta, C. (2003). Financing and advising: Optimal financial contracts with venture capitalists. Journal of Finance, 58(5), 2059–2085.

CB Insights. (2019). From Alibaba to Zynga: 40 of the best VC bets of all time and what we can learn from them. CB Insights. https://www.cbinsights.com/research/best-venture-capital-investments/#Qualtrics

Chemmanur, T. J., Krishnan, K., & Nandy, D. K. (2011). Does venture capital financing improve efficiency in private firms? A look beneath the surface. Review of Financial Studies, 24(12), 4037–4090.

Chen, J. (2020).Venture Capital. Investopedia. https://www.investopedia.com/terms/v/venturecapital.asp

Chen, S. (2020). The development venture capital in China. Entrepreneurial Finance in Emerging Markets: Exploring Tools, Techniques, and Innovative Technologies. Klonowski, D. (ed.). Palgrave MacMillan.

Cochrane, J. (2005). The risk and return of venture capital. Journal of Financial Economics, 75(1), 3–52.

Cornelli, F., & Yosha, O. (2003). Stage financing and the role of convertible securities. Review of Economic Studies, 70(1), 1–32.

Cumming, D. (2008). Contracts and exits in venture capital finance. Review of Financial Studies, 21(5), 1947–1982.

Cumming, D., Deloof, M., Manigart, S., & Wright, M. (2019). New directions in entrepreneurial finance. Journal of Banking and Finance, 100(C), 252–260.

Cumming, D., & Groh, A. P. (2018). Entrepreneurial finance: Unifying themes and future directions. Journal of Corporate Finance, 50(50), 538–555.

Cumming, D., & MacIntosh, J. (2003). A cross-country comparison of full and partial venture capital exits. Journal of Banking and Finance, 27(3), 511–548.

Dabrowski, M. (2020). Emerging markets and their role in a global economy. Entrepreneurial Finance in Emerging Markets: Exploring Tools, Techniques, and Innovative Technologies. Klonowski, D. (ed.). Palgrave MacMillan.

Davila, A., Foster, G., & Gupta. M. (2003). Venture capital financing and the growth of startup firms. Journal of Business Venturing, 18(6), 689–708.

Davis, S. J., Haltwanger, J., Handley, K., Jasrmin, R., Lerner, J., & Miranda, J. (2014). Private equity, jobs, and productivity. American Economic Review, 104(12), 956–990.

De Bettignies, J-E, & Brander, J. (2007). Financing entrepreneurship: Bank finance versus venture capital. Journal of Business Venturing, 22(6), 808–832.

Ewens, M., Nanda, R., & Rhodes-Kropf, M. (2018). Cost of experimentation and the evolution of venture capital. Journal of Financial Economics, 128(3), 422–442.

Florin, J. (2005). Is venture capital worth it? Effect on firm performance and founder returns. Journal of Business Venturing, 20(1), 113–135.

Fried, V. H., & Hisrich, R. D. (1994). Toward a mode of venture capital investment decision making. Financial Management, 23(3), 28–37.

Gabrielson, J., & Huse, M. (2002). The venture capitalist and the board of directors in the SMEs: roles and processes. Venture Capital: An International Journal of Entrepreneurial Finance, 4(2), 125–146.

Gompers, P., Gornall, W., Kaplan, S., & Strebulaev, I.A. (2020). Venture capitalists and COVID-19. Working paper.

Gompers, P. A., & Lerner, J. (2004). The Venture Capital Cycle. MIT Press.

Gompers, P. A., & Lerner, J. (2002). Money chasing deals? The impact of fund inflows on private equity valuation. Journal of Financial Economics, 55(2), 281–325.

Gompers, P. A., & Lerner, J. (1999). An analysis of compensation in the U.S. venture capital partnerships. Journal of Financial Economics, 51(1), 3–44.

Gorman, M., & Sahlman, W. A. (1989). What do venture capitalists do? Journal of Business Venturing, 4(4), 231–248.

Gruenhagen, H. J. (2020). China's institutional environment for entrepreneurship. Entrepreneurial Finance in Emerging Markets: Exploring Tools, Techniques, and Innovative Technologies. Klonowski, D. (ed.). Palgrave MacMillan.

Hall, J., & Hofer, C. (1993). Venture capitalists' decision criteria and new venture evaluation. Journal of Business Venturing, 8(1), 25–42.

Harris, R. S., Tim Jenkinson, T., & Kaplan. S. N. (2014). Private equity performance: What do we know? Journal of Finance, 69(5), 1851–1882.

Hayes, A., & Scott, G. (2021). Venture capital. Investopedia.https://www.investopedia.com/terms/v/venturecapital.asp

Hellmann, T. (2006). IPOs, acquisitions, and the use of convertible securities in venture capital. Journal of Financial Economics, 81(3), 649–679.

Hellmann, T., & Puri, M. (2002). Venture capital and professionalization of start-ups firms: Empirical evidence. Journal of Finance, 57(1), 167–197.

Hellmann, T., & Puri, M. (2000). The interaction between product market and financing strategy: The role of venture capital. Review of Financial Studies, 13(4), 959–984.

Hsu, D. (2004). What do entrepreneurs pay for venture capital affiliation? Journal of Finance, 59(4), 1505–1844.

Humphrey-Jenner, M., & Suchard, J-A. (2013). Foreign VCs and venture capital success: Evidence from China. Journal of Corporate Finance, 21, 16–35.

Invest Europe. (2021). About private equity. Invest Europe. https://www.investeurope.eu/about-private-equity/

Ivashina, V., & Lerner, J. (2019). Pay now or pay later? The economics within private equity partnerships. Journal of Financial Economics, 131(1), 61–87.

Jackson, W., Bates, T., & Bradford, W. D. (2012). Does venture capitalist activism improve investment performance? Journal of Business Venturing, 27(3), 342–257.

Jain, B., & Kini, O. (1995). Venture capitalist participation and post-issue operating performance of IPO firms. Managerial and Decision Economics, 16(6), 593–606.

Johan, S. & Zhang, M. (2016). Private equity exits in emerging markets. Emerging Markets Review, 29, 133–153.

Kaplan, S. N., Sensoy, B., & Stromberg. P. (2009). Should investors bet on the jockey or the horse? Evidence from the evolution of firms from early business plans to public companies. Journal of Finance, 64(1), 75–115.

Kaplan, S., & Schoar, A. (2005). Private equity performance: Returns, persistence and capital flows. Journal of Finance, 60(4), 1791–1823.

Kaplan, S., & Stromberg, P. (2003). Financial contracting theory meets the real world: An empirical analysis of venture capital contracts. Review of Economic Studies, 70(2), 281–315.

Kirilenko, A. (2001). Valuation and control in venture finance. Journal of Finance, 56(2), 564–587.

Klonowski, D. (2021). Venture Capital Redefined: The Economic, Political, and Social Impact of COVID on the VC Ecosystem. Palgrave MacMillan.

Klonowski, D. (2019). Mature and not mature enough: Comparing private equity in developed and emerging markets. Journal of Private Equity, 22(2), 9–18.

Klonowski, D. (2018). The Venture Capital Deformation: Value Destruction throughout the Investment Process. Palgrave MacMillan.

Klonowski, D. (2013a). The Venture Capital Investment Process: Principles and Practice. Palgrave MacMillan.

Klonowski, D. (2013b). Private equity in emerging markets: The new frontiers of international finance. Journal of Private Equity, 16(2), 20–37.

Klonowski, D. (2011). Private Equity in Poland: Winning Leadership in Emerging Markets. Palgrave MacMillan.

Knockaert, M., & Vanacker, T. (2013). The association between venture capitalists' selection and value adding behavior: evidence from early stage high tech venture capitalists. Small Business Economics, 40(3), 493–509.

Kortum, S., & Lerner, J. (2000). Assessing the contribution venture capital to innovation. RAND Journal of Economics, 31(4), 674–692.

Large, D., & Muegge, S. (2008). Venture capitalists' non-financial value-added: an evaluation of the evidence and implications for research. Venture Capital: An International Journal of Entrepreneurial Finance, 10(1), 21–53.

Lerner, J., & Nanda, R. (2020). Venture capital's role in financing innovation: What we know and how much we still need to learn. Journal of Economic Perspectives, 34(3), 237–261.

Lerner, J. (1995). Venture capitalists and the oversight of private firms. Journal of Finance, 50(1), 301–318.

Lerner, J. (1994). Venture capitalists and the decision to go public. Journal of Financial Economics, 35(3), 293–316.

Lingelbach, D. (2015). Developing venture capital when institutions change. Venture Capital: An International Journal of Entrepreneurial Finance, 17(4), 327–363.

Litvak, K. (2009). Venture capital limited partnership agreements: Understanding compensation arrangements. University of Chicago Law Review, 76(1), 161–218.

Ljungqvist, A., & Richardson, M. (2003). The cash flow, return, and risk characteristics of private equity. NBER working paper.

MacMillan, I. C., Siegel, R., & Subba Narasimha, P.N. (1985). Criteria used by venture capitalists to evaluate new venture proposal. Journal of Business Venturing, 1(1), 119–128.

Manigart, S., Lockett, A., Meulman, M., Wright, M., Landstrom, H., Bruining, H., Desbrieres, P., & Hommel, U. (2006). Venture capitalists' decision to syndicate. Entrepreneurship Theory and Practice, 30(2), 131–153.

Mason, C. M., & Harrison, R. T. (2006). After the exit: Acquisitions, entrepreneurial recycling, and regional economic development. Regional Studies, 40(1), 55–73.

Mason, C. M., & Stark, M. (2004). What do investors look for in a business plan? A comparison of the investment criteria bankers, venture capitalists, and business angels. International Small Business Journal, 22(3), 227–248.

Mason, C. M., & Harrison, R. T. (2003). "Auditioning for money": What do technology investors look for at the initial screening stage? Journal of Private Equity, 6(2), 29–42.

Megginson, W. L., & Weiss, K. A. (1991). Venture capitalist certification in initial public offerings. Journal of Finance, 46(3), 879–903.

Metrick, A., & Yasuda, A. (2010). The economics of private equity. Review of Financial Studies, 23(6), 2303–2341.

Moskowitz, T. J., & Vissing-Jorgensen, A. (2002). The returns to entrepreneurial investment: A private equity premium puzzle? American Economic Review, 92(4), 745–778.

Mulcahy, D., Weeks, B., & Bradley. H. S. (2012). We have met the enemy . . . and it is us: Lessons from twenty years of the Kauffman Foundation's investments in venture capital funds and the triumph of hope over experience. Ewing Marion Kauffman Foundation.

Murray, G. C. (1995). Evolution and change: An analysis of the first decade of the UK venture capital industry. Journal of Business Finance and Accounting, 22(8), 1077–1106.

Muzyka, D., Birlely, S., & Leleux, B. (1996). Trade-offs in the investment decisions of European venture capitalists. Journal of Business Venturing, 11(4), 273–287.

North America Venture Capital Association. (2021a). What is Venture Capital? NVCA. https://nvca.org/about-us/what-is-vc/

National Venture Capital Association. (2021b). NVCA Yearbook. NVCA. https://nvca.org/wp-content/uploads/2021/03/NVCA-2021-Yearbook.pdf

National Venture Capital Association. (2020). NVCA Yearbook. NVCA. https://nvca.org/wp-content/uploads/2020/03/NVCA-2020-Yearbook.pdf

Oxford Dictionary. OxfordLearnersDictionaries.com dictionary. www.oxfordlearnersdictionaries.com/definition/american_english/venture-capital

Phalippou, L. (2014). Performance of buyout funds revisited? Review of Finance, 18(1),189–218.

Phalippou, L., & Gottschalg, O. (2009). The performance of private equity funds. Review of Financial Studies, 22(4), 1747–1776.

Prive, Tanya. (2013). The biggest threat to venture capitalists. Forbes (March 20). https://www.forbes.com/sites/tanyaprive/2013/03/20/the-biggest-threat-to-venture-capitalists/?sh=1301e55955a7

Puffer, S. M., & McCarthy, D. J. (2020). Economic growth, institutions, and corruption in emerging markets. Entrepreneurial Finance in Emerging Markets: Exploring Tools, Techniques, and Innovative Technologies. Klonowski, D. (ed.). Palgrave MacMillan.

PWC. (2020.) Global Top 100 Companies – June 2020 Update. June.

Quinlan, J. (2020). Promise and peril in the age of turbulence in emerging markets: Implications for private equity investors. Entrepreneurial Finance in Emerging Markets: Exploring Tools, Techniques, and Innovative Technologies. Klonowski, D. (ed.). Palgrave MacMillan.

Reid, D. 2020. China, an emergent innovator? A competence misplaced, capability regained. Entrepreneurial Finance in Emerging Markets: Exploring Tools, Techniques, and Innovative Technologies. Klonowski, D. (ed.). Palgrave MacMillan.

Robinson, D. T., & Sensoy, B. A. (2016). Cyclicality, performance measurement, and cash flow liquidity in private equity. Journal of Financial Economics, 122(3), 521–543.

Samila, S., & Sorenson, O. (2011). Venture capital, entrepreneurship, and economic growth. Review of Economics and Statistic, 93(1), 338–349.

Scheela, W., & Jittrapanum. T. (2012). Do institutions matter for business angel investing in emerging markets? Venture Capital: An International Journal of Entrepreneurial Finance, 14(4), 289–308.

Sorenson, O., & Stuart, T. E. (2001). Syndication networks and the spatial distribution of venture capital investments. American Journal of Sociology, 106(6), 1546–1588.

Tyebjee, T. T., & Bruno, A. V. (1984). A model of venture capitalist investment activity. Management Science, 30(9), 1051–1066.

Zacharakis, A. L., & Shepherd, D. A. (2005). A non-additive decision-aid for venture capitalists' decisions. European Journal of Operational Research, 162(3), 673–689.

Zacharakis, A. L., & Shepherd, D. A. (2001). The nature of information and overconfidence on venture capitalists' decision making. Journal of Business Venturing, 16(4), 311–332.

Zarco, Juan Ramon. (2016). Was Queen Isabella of Span the first and how would Columbus fare under 5 T's? https://jrzarco2001.wordpress.com/2016/04/06/was-queen-isabella-of-spain-the-first-vc-and-how-would-columbus-fare-under-5-ts/

Paul Asel

11 Corporate venture capital: A literature review and research agenda

Abstract: The study of corporate venture capital (CVC), which involves equity stakes from corporations in startup technology companies, spans more than fifty years and draws extensively from financial, organizational and entrepreneurship theory. While the CVC industry has grown substantially in the past two decades, the benefits for corporate sponsors and startups are still hotly debated in boardrooms. CVC structures and practices are rapidly evolving offering a rich tapestry for further study. CVC literature has progressed significantly, yet many topics remain unexplored with potential impact on CVC practices, finance, innovation and the corporation. This work is timely as technology increasingly impacts traditional industries rendering questions on the applicability of CVC across these sectors. This literature review surveys 238 CVC studies citing over 100 seminal CVC studies from the past two decades as well as their intellectual antecedents and theoretical perspectives that inform CVC research.

Keywords: corporate venture capital, corporate venturing, innovation, venture capital, literature review, bibliographic analysis

Introduction

Corporate venture capital (CVC) refers to "equity investments made by non-financial corporations in young, early-stage companies, not made solely for financial gain" (Chesbrough, 2002). CVC lies within the broader field of corporate venturing (CV), which includes all internal and external new business development activity. External CV involves new business creation through interfirm activities such as CVC, alliances, joint ventures, acquisitions or spin-offs (Keil, 2002). Internal CV refers to entrepreneurial efforts to create new business within companies (Van de Vrande et al., 2006).

 CVC has a long history with 25% of the Fortune 500 sponsoring programs in the 1960s. Firms increase CVC activity in intensely competitive industries experiencing rapid technology change (Basu et al., 2011). The four waves of CVC have been driven by the advent of semiconductors in the 1960s, personal computers in the 1980s, the Internet in the 1990s and mobile devices in the 2010s (Munce, 2018). As technology transforms traditional industries, CVC investment has grown six-fold

Paul Asel, NGP Capital

https://doi.org/10.1515/9783110726312-015

since 2010 with over 2126 firms globally participating in 14% of global venture deals in 2020 (Andonov, 2021).

CVC has changed considerably in the past two decades. CVC programs have matured from an average lifespan of 2.5 years (Gompers & Lerner, 2000) to nearly ten years (Yang et al., 2016), of which 26% were founded over ten years ago (Ma, 2020). Eli Lilly, Nokia, Novartis, Qualcomm, and SAP have sponsored continuous CVC programs for over 20 years, while those at Intel and GlaxoSmithKline exceed 30 years. CVC investments at Google and Tencent exceed $1 billion annually. CVC has emerged as a field distinct from traditional venture capital (VC) practices (Mason et al., 2019). New global entrants have adapted to local industry conditions infusing CVC with new ideas and practices (Weber & Weber, 2005, Meng et al., 2020).

Literature review

Corporate innovation and corporate venture capital

Corporate sponsor support and, thus, alignment with corporate strategy are essential to CVC success and survival (Gompers & Lerner, 2000). March (1991) describes two essential tasks for an innovative business: exploiting existing business assets and exploring future opportunities. Exploitation optimizes near term results while exploratory activities seek to maximize long term potential. Yet exploitation tends to drive out exploration in corporate contests for scarce resources, so CVC survival requires ambidexterity serving both near and long-term corporate objectives (Hill & Birkinshaw, 2014).

Chesbrough (2003) espoused Open Innovation to balance internal exploitative tendencies and leverage external resources where knowledge and skills are widely distributed. Open Innovation and the rise of digital platforms have expanded the role of CVC. As digital platforms enabled by the Internet and smartphones require robust partner ecosystems, ecosystem building has replaced technology gap filling as the dominant form of CVC investing (Fulghieri & Sevilir, 2009, Pinkow & Iverson, 2020). The largest CVC programs today – Alibaba, Google, Salesforce and TenCent – are ecosystem investors.

Real option theory (Hellman, 2002, Van de Vrande et al., 2006) integrates CVC into a corporate innovation framework through a build, buy, partner/invest model as shown in Figure 11.1. During periods of uncertainty, companies deploy reversible, exploratory strategies such as alliances and CVC investments. Studies show that CVC augments alliances (Dushnitsky & Lavie, 2010, Van de Vrande & Vanhaverbeke, 2013), complements R&D (Dushnitsky & Lenox, 2005b) and increases acquisition success rates (Benson & Ziedonis, 2009).

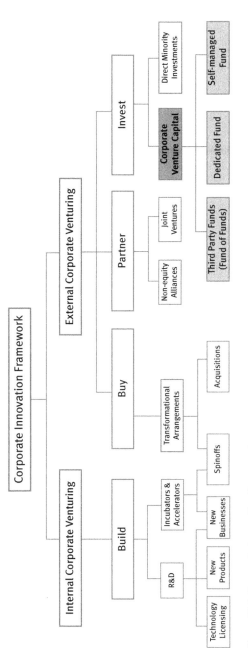

Figure 11.1: Corporate Innovation Framework.
Source: Adapted from Keil (2002) and Mason (2019)

Review methodology

CVC studies draw extensively from financial, organizational and entrepreneurship theory. CVC may be viewed through the financial lens of real options and transaction cost frameworks. The corporate perspective interjects organizational structure and behavior, business strategy, ambidexterity and resource theory. Entrepreneurship promotes open innovation to tap new technologies and business models. CVCs much engage effectively with entrepreneurs, investors and corporate sponsors introducing isomorphism and agency theory as they balance different interests, structures, incentives and timelines. Table 11.1 shows how these theoretical perspectives have influenced CVC literature.

Table 11.1: Theoretical Perspectives Influencing CVC Studies.

Theoretical Perspectives	Key Concepts	Early Proponents	Usage in Studies[1]	Leading CVC Proponents
Strategic Positioning	Competitive threats, five forces	Schumpeter, Porter	83	Birkinshaw, Dushnitsky, Hill, Lerner, Rossi
Resource Dependence Theory	Absorptive capacity	Pfeffer/ Salancik	61	Dushnitsky, Wadhwa, Zahra
Institutional Theory	Ambidexterity, structure & incentives	Coase, Drucker, March	48	Keil, Rossi, Titus, Wadhwa
Social/ Behavioral Theory	Isomorphism, influence, social capital	DiMaggio	45	Birkinshaw, Dokko, Gaba, Hill, Maula, Souitaris, Weber, Yang
Open Innovation	Platforms, ecosystem, network effect	Chesbrough, Gawer/ Cusumano	31	Anokhin, Meng, Van Angeren, Pinkow
Real Options Theory	Managing uncertainty, window on innovation	Black Scholes, Dixit, Amram	31	van de Vrande, Basu, Wadhwa, Sahaym
Agency Theory	Balancing multiple allegiances	Arrow, Eisenhardt	21	Basu, Katila

[1]Based on self-attribution, prevailing logic evident in studies, bibliographic reference analysis, keyword searches.

This literature review offers a glimpse into the complexity and nuance these multiple perspectives bring to CVC studies. This CVC review covers 208 academic and 30 practitioner studies cited in scholarly papers. While prior CVC literature reviews have focused on studies in top journals, this review is broader covering 86 academic journals published in English selected from Google Scholar, forward and backward citations of CVC studies, plus reviews of selected journals and scholars. The bibliographic and literature analyses include all 208 academic studies, while the discussion cites seminal CVC studies.

This literature review conducted extensive analysis across these 238 CVC studies. Applying bibliographic methods consistent with those used by Rohm (2018), this review traces how CVC literature evolved over the past fifty years and identify thought leading studies. Each study was analyzed across 163 indices summarizing research objective and methods, applied schools of thought, data sets used, hypotheses tested and validated, dependent and key independent variables and sentiment analysis. This indexing relied primarily on author self-attribution supplemented by textual and keyword analysis and commentary by other scholars in their literature reviews relevant to their research. Analyses and figures in this literature review summarize salient observations from this analytical exercise.

This review focuses on CVC studies since 2000. As anthropologists observe a full life cycle when studying new cultures, this review starts from the end of the third CVC wave and covers the fourth wave. The dotcom bubble burst in 2000 wiping out over 50% of CVC programs (Chesbrough, 2002). The CVC industry has matured in the past two decades as many fledgling programs that survived the dotcom bust have grown into global organizations investing as much or more than large VC firms.

While focusing on recent studies, this CVC review also honors seminal contributions from thought leaders in other fields. Figure 11.2 connects studies using citations among the CVC studies reviewed illustrating how Resource Dependence Theory (Pfeffer & Salancik, 1978), Strategic Positioning (Porter, 1980), isomorphism (DiMaggio, 1983), Agency Theory (Eisenhardt, 1989) and Organizational Theory (March, 1991) have influenced CVC literature. Studying direct citations and second order impact, including subsequent studies that cited studies that had referenced seminal works, Schumpeter has most widely influenced CVC literature among early scholars. His books on creative destruction were directly cited or indirectly referenced by 62% of CVC studies reviewed.

Table 11.2 shows the most frequently cited CVC studies as a percentage of all subsequent CVC studies in this review. Studies published from 2000–2009 represent eight of the ten most frequently cited studies, of which Dushnitsky coauthored four.

CVC literature has evolved as both the industry and supporting theory have matured. Scholars have shifted from theory and case study to archival studies as richer data sets become available. Figure 11.3 shows that archival studies have increased from 31% to 76% of all CVC studies over the past twenty years.

As Table 11.3 indicates, Dushitsky, Maula and Keil are the most widely published CVC scholars and most widely cited within CVC literature. Chesbrough, Gompers and Lerner are more widely cited overall as their research and influence extend beyond CVC. Gompers and Lerner discuss CVC within the broader VC context, while Chesbrough, Birkinshaw and Zahra cover CVC within CV.

Among recent studies, Chesbrough, 2002; Dushitsky & Lenox, 2005a; Dushnitsky & Lenox, 2005b; and Dushnitsky & Lenox, 2006 were each cited over fifty times

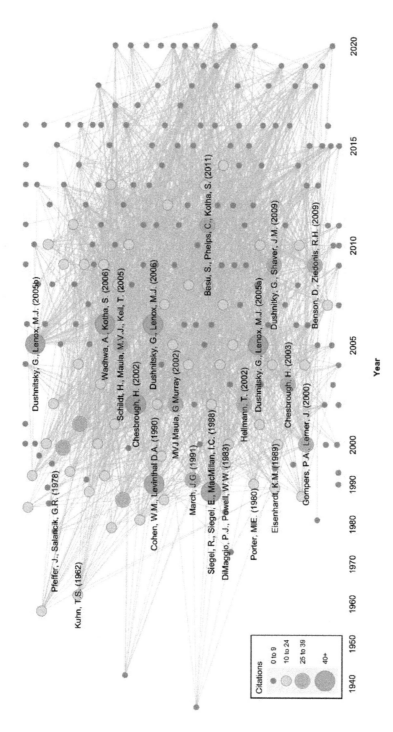

Figure 11.2: Bibliographic analysis of CVC literature.

Table 11.2: Most frequently cited studies among CVC literature reviewed.

Study	Direct Citations	Second Order References
Dushnitsky & Lenox (2006)	44.9%	63.0%
Dushnitsky & Lenox (2005a)	42.6%	65.6%
Chesbrough (2002)	38.2%	68.2%
Dushnitsky & Lenox (2005b)	37.2%	68.6%
Benson & Ziedonis (2009)	34.2%	60.3%
Wadhwa & Kotha (2006)	30.4%	56.5%
Basu et al. (2011)	28.7%	40.2%
Dushnitsky & Shaver (2009)	27.9%	59.4%
Siegel et al. (1988)	25.4%	61.5%
Schildt et al. (2005)	25.0%	52.0%

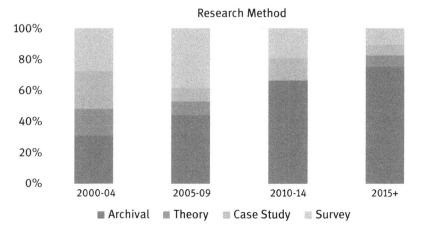

Figure 11.3: Shift in CVC Studies from Case Study to Archival Research.

by CVC studies in this literature review. Studies by Dushnitsky were cited by 57% of reviewed CVC studies since 2000; Chesbrough, Gompers and Maula received citations from over 40%.

Three academic journals published nearly 20% of CVC studies from 2000–2020. That CVC studies appear in 86 academic journals underscores the breadth of CVC literature. Figure 11.4 and Table 11.4 show that coverage diversified in the past decade with major publications accounting for 33% of CVC studies from 2016–2020 during which non-US studies represented 24% of all CVC articles versus 15% in the prior fifteen years.

Table 11.3: Analysis of CVC Publications by Scholar.

CVC Publications: Citations						
Citations: CVC Studies				Citations: All Studies		
Author	# Studies	Citations	Annual Avg	Author	# Studies	Citations	Annual Avg
Dushnitsky	12	274	1.7	Chesbrough	6	25,921	257.1
Maula	12	181	1.1	Gompers	5	5,377	57.9
Keil	9	143	1.1	Lerner	5	5,135	50.5
Chesbrough	6	131	1.2	Dushnitsky	12	2,830	17.8
Gompers	5	108	1.1	Maula	12	2,774	16.6
Lerner	5	89	0.9	Keil	9	1,795	14.4
Kotha	5	88	1.6	Zahra	5	1,185	20.2
Schildt	2	59	2.0	Birkinshaw	8	1,043	11.5
Wadhwa	5	58	1.0	Schildt	2	971	33.8
Birkinshaw	8	51	0.5	Kotha	5	867	16.3
Zahra	5	35	0.7	Wadhwa	5	764	14.8

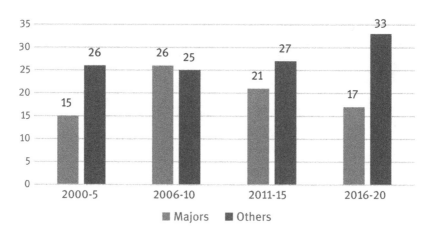

Figure 11.4: CVC Studies, Publications 2000–20.

Review of studies

CVC programs serve four stakeholders. Successful CVC programs gain acceptance among entrepreneurs, venture firms and corporate sponsors while attracting and retaining talent credible in each community. Active investors have fiduciary roles

Table 11.4: Journals Publishing CVC Studies 2000–20.

Journal	Studies	Annual Citations	
		Average	Median
Journal of Business Venturing	16	15.3	11.6
Strategic Management Journal	15	17.9	16.0
Entrepreneurship Theory and Practice	9	13.5	8.8
Venture Capital, An International Journal of Entrepreneurial Finance	7	8.6	8.4
Harvard Business School Press	5	305.3	67.1
Academy of Management Journal	5	18.4	15.8
Strategic Entrepreneurship Journal	5	7.4	7.5
Research-Technology Management	5	4.9	5.5
Journal of Finance	4	70.1	60.1
Journal of Management	4	33.6	27.5
Journal of Financial Economics	4	25.1	18.6
Other Journals	109	13.0	5.5

both with their corporate sponsors and portfolio companies. Most studies evaluate CVC programs in relation to one or more of these stakeholders. This review reflects CVC literature and discusses these four relationships sequentially in this section.

As Table 11.5 shows, a majority of the 208 academic CVC studies focus on the corporate sponsor relationship, including 35% which focus on CVC benefits to corporate sponsors. CVC relations with startups and the venture community receive comparable treatment. Over 25% of studies explore CVC best practices. Among corporate sponsor studies, 69% affirmed the role of CVC and 85% were either affirmative or neutral. Studies were more wary on the benefits and risks of CVC engagement for startups: 43% were affirmative and 23% were cautionary.

Scholars tend to apply consistent theoretical frameworks across their studies. While most scholars explain CVC adoption based on strategic and institutional considerations, Gaba ascribes social factors as a key factor across three studies (Gaba & Meyer, 2008, Gaba & Bhattacharya 2012, Gaba & Dokko, 2016). Van de Vrande applied open innovation and real options across five studies to illuminate CVC's role in corporate innovation. Strategic intent informs CVC structure, yet institutional and behavioral factors also intervened at Xerox and General Electric (Lerner, 2012). Agency theory explains how CVCs engage with startups (Hellman, 2002, Katila et al., 2008, Park & Steensma, 2012).

Table 11.5: CVC Topics and Notable CVC Studies.

CVC Studies: Areas of Inquiry	Number of Studies	Prominent Schools of Thought	Selected CVC Studies
CVC & Corporate Sponsor Relationship			
Corporate Sponsor Benefits	73	Strategic Positioning, Resource Theory, Open Innovation	Anokhin et al. (2016), Benson & Zeidonis (2009, 2010), Dushnitsky & Lenox (2005a, 2005b), Keil (2002, 2004), Wadhwa & Kotha (2006)
CVC Role in Corporate Innovation	24	Real Options, Open Innovation	Chesbrough (2003), Ivanov & Xie (2010), Schildt et al. (2005), Tong & Li (2011), Van de Vrande et al. (2009)
Reasons CVC Programs Start/ Stop	23	Strategic, Social, Institutional, Agency Theory	Chesbrough (2000), Gaba & Meyer (2008), Gaba & Dokko (2016), Hill & Birkinshaw (2008, 2014)
CVC & Entrepreneur/Startup Relationship			
CVC Benefits/Risks for Startups	32	Resource Theory, Agency Theory	Hellmann (2002), Ivanov & Xie (2010), Katila et al. (2008), Maula et al. (2009), Panhke et al. (2015), Park & Steensma (2012)
CVC & Venture Industry			
CVC Performance	26		Chemmanur et al. (2014), Gompers & Lerner (2000), Gompers (2002), Hochberg et al. (2007)
CVC Operations & Personnel			
CVC Best Practices	34	Institutional, Behavioral	Birkinshaw et al. (2002), Dokko & Gaba (2012), Keil (2010), Mason et al. (2019), Miles & Covin (2002)
CVC Structure & Incentives	22	Strategic, Institutional, Behavioral	Asel et al. (2015), Birkinshaw & Hill (2005), Dushnitsky & Shapira (2010), Miles & Covin (2002), Pinkow & Iverson (2020)

Role of CVC in corporate venturing

Studies suggest that CVC is best applied within a broader corporate innovation strategy (Chesbrough 2003). As Figure 11.5 shows, CVC involves modest commitments and higher optionality offering flexibility in periods of rapid technology change (Van de Vrande et al., 2009). CVC investment and alliances add more value when paired (Dushnitsky & Lavie, 2010) and enable deeper engagement than alliances alone (Schildt et al., 2005). Weiblen and Chesbrough (2015) counter that CVC is best for fewer, deeper relationships while non-equity arrangements better reinforce broader ecosystem plays.

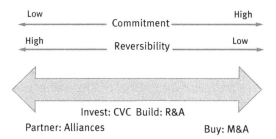

Figure 11.5: Comparison of selected corporate venturing modes.

Corporate benefits from CVC activity

Scholars have debated the corporate benefits of CVC investing more than any other CVC topic as corporate support is essential for survival and growth. Studies are overwhelmingly affirmative with 59% of studies ascribing value to CVC programs and only 4% expressing substantial skepticism. Studies cite several benefits: 89% refer to its role in enhancing strategic positioning, 79% in bolstering innovation, 63% for exploring new opportunities or exploiting existing assets, and 31% as a window on technology.

CVC investment positively correlates with corporate R&D spending (Dushnitsky & Lenox 2005b, Sahaym et al., 2010) and corporate patent production (Wadhwa et al., 2010) suggesting they are complements, though corporations can substitute CVC for R&D to fill technology gaps (Ma, 2020) or accelerate innovation in highly competitive markets (Fulghieri & Sevilir, 2009, Kim et al., 2016). Other studies found a positive relationship between CVC investment and corporate innovation holds only at moderate CVC investment rates (Lee & Kang 2015) and with active CVC portfolio engagement to facilitate knowledge transfer (Wadhwa & Kotha, 2006).

Alignment of CVC investment and corporate strategy is a prerequisite for relevant learning (Zahra & Hayton, 2008). CVC can provide early signals for disruptive technologies in core or adjacent businesses (Maula et al., 2013). Adjacent investments are more impactful than either alliances or joint ventures (Keil, Maula, Schildt & Zarha, 2008) as they expand the search space and develop new cognitive maps (Keil, 2002). Adjacent knowledge is up to six times more valuable than distant knowledge, which is harder to embed in the corporate lexicon (Keil, Autio, & George, 2008).

Absorptive capacity is vital for knowledge transfer. Insight is only useful if corporations can absorb and leverage the knowledge (Dushnitsky & Lenox 2005a, 2005b), and companies can get locked out from emerging markets if they do not invest enough early (Cohen & Levinthal, 1990). CVC investments are associated with higher patent production for tech leaders but not for laggards (Kim et al., 2016). CVC investment promotes exploratory learning in nascent technologies to alleviate lockout risk (Wadhwa & Basu, 2013) and engage lead users for user generated innovation (Smith & Shah, 2013). Anokhin et al. (2016) emphasizes the value adding role of active, adjacent investments observing that 80% of CVC activity adds little strategic value as investments are either passive, too early or too distant to be impactful. Others indicate that portfolio diversity can unlock corporate mental maps and pattern recognition subject to coordination costs (Lee & Kang, 2015) and adequate corporate linkages (Lin & Lee, 2011). These findings reinforce studies that identify a U-shaped relationship between portfolio diversification and knowledge transfer (Yang et al., 2014, Yang et al., 2016).

CVC inception and discontinuation

Venture capital funding is highly cyclical, and CVC commitments have been particularly volatile. In the aftermath of the dotcom bubble, Chesbrough ruminated, "The general pattern is a cycle that starts with enthusiasm, continues into implementation, then encounters significant difficulties, and ends with eventual termination of the initiative. Yet, within a few years, another generation of businesses undertakes the effort anew, and the cycle occurs again." (Chesbrough, 2000, p. 31).

A strategic view suggests that companies launch CVC activity in intensely competitive industries experiencing rapid technology change (Basu et al., 2011) and switch to CV activity with lower reversibility like acquisitions when technology stabilizes (Titus et al., 2017, Tong & Li, 2011).

From an institutional resource perspective, companies may increase CVC to bolster technology (Ma, 2020) when companies underperform but suspend CVC investment when performance rebounds (Gaba & Bhattacharya, 2012, Titus et al., 2020).

Gaba explains CVC cyclicality as a social phenomenon. Described as contagions, firms adopt new practices (Gaba & Meyer, 2008) and stop them (Gaba & Dokko, 2016) in response to social and institutional pressure. Brigl et al. (2016) found in a study of

180 companies across six sectors that CV practices are consistent within industries but distinct across industries reinforcing a pattern of corporate mimicry.

Corporate alignment with well-defined, shared objectives are vital for CVC success and longevity (Gompers, 2002). CVCs with a consistent strategic focus are as stable as VCs (Gompers & Lerner, 2000).

CVC impact on startups

CVCs have a fiduciary duty to both their corporate sponsors and startups in which they invest. CVCs intermediate engagement between startups and corporate sponsors, which raises agency concerns if objectives differ. Dushnitsky and Shaver (2009) highlight this as the paradox of CVC: the most valued startup partners may be those most reluctant to engage for fear of misappropriation. As a result, studies are mixed in their assessment of CVC influence on startups.

CVCs potentially confer many advantages to startups. CVCs outperform VCs in helping startups build commercial credibility and capacity, providing technical support, attracting customers and partners, and entering foreign markets (Maula et al., 2005). A survey by Macmillan et al. (2008) found that 74% of CVCs offer R&D support, 55% sales support and 19% operational support. CVC-backed companies are more innovative (Chemmanur et al., 2014), more likely to go public and perform better in the aftermarket (Gompers, 2002, Park & Steensma, 2012), obtain higher IPO valuations (Ivanov & Xie, 2010) and acquisition prices (Janney et al., 2021) than their VC-backed counterparts.

But competitive threats and misappropriation risk may impede CVC engagement with startups. Suggestively titled "Swimming with Sharks," Katila et al. (2008) highlights the tension between startup's need for partner resources and potential misuse of resources by corporate "sharks." Reputational risk is an effective deterrent if the threat of lockout in future syndicates outweighs the value of misappropriation (Hallen et al., 2014, Kim et al., 2016). Intel has alleviated potential concerns by garnering a good reputation with startups established over thirty years (Sears et al., 2020).

Startups consider CVC investments differently in complementary and competitive situations. CVCs have more access and influence in complementary investments (Masulis & Nahata, 2009, Maula et al., 2009). CVCs may pay premia to invest in competitive situations or earn discounts in complementary cases when corporate endorsement is highly valued (Hellman, 2002). Startup perceptions of corporate sponsors may explain differential treatment as CVCs typically pay premia in the US but are offered discounts in China.

CVC performance: Measuring financial and strategic value

CVC serves a dual mandate to deliver both financial returns and strategic benefits. Evaluating performance is thus more complex than for VCs, which focus solely on financial returns. Studies have consistently found that most CVCs pursue mixed financial and strategic objectives. In a survey of 158 global CVCs, 23% pursue primarily strategic goals, 9% financial goals, and 67% mixed objectives (Andonov, 2021). CVCs with clear strategic or financial orientation have performed better and proven as stable as VCs (Gompers & Lerner, 2000, Rohm et al., 2018, Weber & Weber, 2005).

Both fiduciary and strategic mandates have challenges within a corporate setting as illustrated in Figure 11.6. Financial performance is ascertainable over five to ten years, and early returns may be misleading as losses are often realized before gains (Asel, 2021). CVC must therefore deliver early strategic wins to demonstrate value within the "corporate patience cycle", typically within three years during which CVC programs are assessed (Mason et al., 2019).

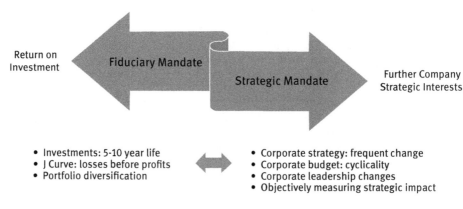

Figure 11.6: Dual Mandate for CVC Activity.
Source: Asel (2021)

Strategic mandates pose further challenges. Strategic value defies ready definition and objective measurement. In dynamic markets with evolving strategic initiatives, perceived relevance in long lived assets often differ at entry and exit. Tightly defined strategic objectives may undermine the exploratory benefits in which CVCs excel (Asel, 2021).

Since companies rarely disclose CVC activity, studies use crude proxies for financial returns (IPO performance) and strategic value (corporate patent filings). Industry data citing annual CVC investment refers to total funding in rounds with CVCs participation, which substantially overstates actual CVC annual investment.

Nevertheless, scholars have developed creative approaches to assess CVC performance. Using 10-K footnotes for 90 corporations from 1990–2002, Allen and

Hevert (2007) found that 39% of CVCs met or exceeded VC industry benchmarks, but pooled CVC IRRs were 2% compared with 26% for their US VC peers. Hamm et al. (2018) analyzed sparse financial statement data for 115 US firms and found that CVC programs complement R&D spending, substitute for capital expenditures and launch during periods of slowing corporate growth.

CVC structure and operating practices

Structure moderates CVC performance and objectives (Dushnitsky & Shapira, 2010). As Figure 11.7 shows, higher CVC autonomy aligns with exploratory orientation (Pinkow & Iversen, 2020). Higher CVC autonomy is associated with higher portfolio diversification and financial focus (Yang, 2012). CVC activity may be structured internally within the corporation; directly and externally in a dedicated, company sponsored fund; or indirectly and externally through a multi-investor fund. External CVC funds offer more autonomy and alignment with financial performance, while internal corporate funds integrate better with strategic objectives (Asel et al., 2015, Miles & Covin, 2002). In a global survey of 158 CVCs, 44% of CVCs invest from separate fund structures of which 20% operate with high autonomy (Andonov, 2021).

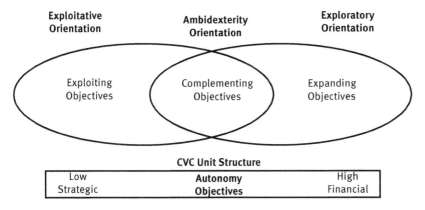

Figure 11.7: Framework for Corporate Objectives and CVC Unit Orientation.

CVC financial or strategic orientation is influenced by where management seeks legitimacy among VCs or corporate executives (Dokko & Gaba, 2012, Souitaris et al., 2012). Corporate objectives inform CVC structure, which predicates CVC staffing, who then mold CVC practices (Asel et al.,2015). CVC have adapted VC governance, incentives and process to fit the corporate context (Souitaris et al., 2012). Financially oriented CVCs can adopt VC practices with less variation than strategically oriented CVCs (Hill et al., 2009). Basu et al. (2016) highlighted the entrepreneurial nature of

CVC managing dynamic markets, changes in corporate strategy and leadership, and needs of startups.

High powered incentives and autonomy are positively associated with CVC performance and longevity (Maula et al., 2009). Yet equity incentives may distract from strategic objectives (Ernst et al., 2005, Lerner, 2012, Yang, 2012) without materially improving financial performance (Birkinshaw et al., 2002). Birkinshaw and Hill (2005) warn against using financial incentives to derive strategic returns.

Key CVC success factors include high level corporate support, a mix of CVC personnel with venture and corporate experience, and active engagement with portfolio companies (Basu et al., 2016, Birkinshaw & Hill, 2005, Mason et al., 2019). Weber (2009) describes the CVC as a bridge between the startup and corporate sponsor initially as a matchmaker and later as a facilitator, mediator and troubleshooter. Strategic value exchanges should be bidirectional between the startup and corporate sponsor with CVCs securing business unit support prior to investment (Napp & Minshall, 2011).

Better networked CVCs have access to better deal flow and perform better (Keil et al., 2010, Hochberg et al., 2007). Recognizing the centrality of deal flow, 89% of VCs and 62% of CVCs consider deal sourcing very important (Macmillan et al., 2008). Proprietary deal flow and limited disclosure of CVC activity avoid telegraphing strategic interests to competitors (Anokhin et al., 2011).

As the CVC industry has matured, recent research explores the CVC lifecycles. Studies observe that CVC investment varies inversely with corporate R&D performance (Gaba & Bhattacharya, 2012, Ma, 2020, Titus et al., 2020). Mason et al. (2019) identifies three phases in the CVC lifecycle: startup, expansion and resiliency. Mason also highlights how industry dynamics, shifts in corporate strategy and management changes require adjustments and can be existential for CVCs.

Future research agenda

Methodological challenges

CVC literature pronates positively. An affirmative tilt is consistent with practice in many professions. Public market investors have potent long instruments but limited short options. Stock analysts disproportionately weight toward buy rather than sell recommendations. Scholars, like research analysts, are to be neutral arbiters, yet studies that do not illuminate go unpublished, so incentives predispose a positive outlook. Future research would do well to validate some seminal studies on which the foundational premises for CVC are based.

This literature review categorized each study based on the nature of hypotheses tested, conclusions reached, and keyword searches that reflected tone and substance across studies. Studies were rated as affirmative if the conclusions and tone were favorable to CVC, skeptical if studies were cautionary on CVC, and balanced if not decidedly favorable or skeptical. Across all studies in this review, 45% were affirmative of CVC, 47% were neutral and 8% skeptical. As Table 11.6 shows, case studies and surveys had higher ratios of affirmative to skeptical reviews than archival studies. Selection bias in surveys and case studies is a potential factor in affirmative tilt as half of all surveys relied exclusively on views from CVC practitioners while only 25% received views from corporate sponsors. Affirmative studies are more frequently cited than negative studies, though balanced studies are most frequently cited.

Table 11.6: Posture of CVC Studies.

	Posture of Study on CVC			Affirmative to Skeptical Ratio
	Affirmative	Neutral	Skeptical	
All CVC Studies	45%	46%	9%	5.1x
Archival Studies	45%	41%	13%	3.5x
Surveys & Interviews	37%	61%	2%	15.0x
Case Studies	50%	44%	6%	8.0x
Average annual citations	13.6	15.1	11.1	
Median annual citations	8.4	8.5	3.7	

Most studies yielded conclusive results as 85% of all hypotheses tested were validated and 62% of studies validated all hypotheses tested. Studies with mixed results often enriched the discussion, and most scholars referred to unverified hypotheses as matters for further study. Studies yielding internally inconsistent results posed greater challenges. Corporations with active CVC investment programs had better overall acquisition performance (Benson & Ziedonis, 2009) but fared poorly on acquisitions in which they had made a prior CVC investment (Benson & Ziedonis, 2010). Splitting the studies yielded a cleaner narrative but leaves the reader to reconcile the results.

Case studies are more poignant but also more susceptible to narrative bias, especially when companies are identified in the study. CVC brands mirror those of their corporate sponsor. CVC case studies risk seeming outdated when future events are unkind to the corporate sponsor (Birkinshaw et al., 2002, Mason & Rohner, 2002). It is particularly troubling when CVC narratives alter with the status of the corporate sponsor as with Nokia where disparaging case studies (Lerner, 2012) followed laudatory ones (Chesbrough, 2003, Birkinshaw et al., 2002, Mason & Rohner, 2002, Zarha & Hayton, 2008) after Nokia faltered. Anonymized case studies encourage more balanced assessments and are less susceptible to later reevaluation (Keil, 2002, Keil, 2004, Keil et al., 2008; Basu et al., 2016).

Data methods – availability heuristic

Patents were used as the dependent variable in 27% of the archival studies. Of 25 patent-oriented studies, 24 affirmed a positive impact of CVC investment on corporate innovation. No case studies nor surveys have corroborated the direct impact of CVC investment on corporate patents, a limitation that most archival studies acknowledge. Practitioner literature is largely moot on patents: academic CVC studies refer to patents ten times more frequently than in practitioner literature. While it is logical that CVC and R&D spending are positively correlated, specious correlation is also possible. The CVC industry would benefit from future research that identifies best practices in capturing and transferring market and technology insight while adhering to CVC fiduciary duty to portfolio companies.

Latency – leading and lagging indicators

Studies using archival data were published on average 8.5 years after the sample research period. Survey studies were published 4.9 years on average after surveys or interviews were conducted. While latency is a common problem across business studies, issues arise amidst paradigm shifts or when findings are timely. Open Innovation (Chesbrough, 2003) presaged the emergence of platform investors such as Google and Salesforce, which founded their CVC programs in 2008 and 2009, respectively. Yet as Figure 11.8 shows, empirical work has substantially lagged the rise of platform and ecosystem CVC investors.

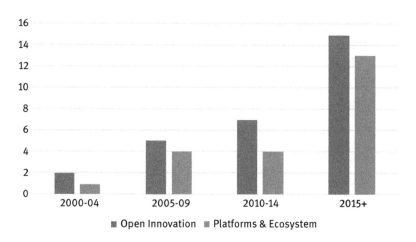

Figure 11.8: Paradigm Shift Adoption in CVC Literature.

Data reuse is one cause of long lag times. Weber published four studies from 2005 to 2016 based on 32 interviews gathered in 2001. Birkinshaw and Hill authored 7 studies from 2002 to 2014 based on 95 surveys and interviews gathered in 2001 and 2003. Progression of these studies offer a lens into theory refinement as the authors apply static data to a consistent theme. Birkinshaw and Hill study CVC structure advocating for more CVC autonomy in 2005, assessing exploratory and exploitative orientation in 2008, and ultimately making the case for ambidexterity in 2014. Nevertheless, understanding how their respondents' views evolved during a decade of considerable change could have been equally illuminating.

Latency is immaterial if studies are timeless, yet sampling in some studies seem favorable to the findings. A widely cited study suggests that CVC investment favorably impacts corporate valuations using data sample from 1990–1999, which coincides with the dotcom boom (Dushnitsky & Lenox, 2006). Earlier studies by the authors used data from 1969–1999 (Dushnitsky & Lenox 2005a, 2005b). One wonders if data from before 1990 or after 1999 would replicate the results.

Future research questions

While CVC literature has matured during the past two decades, opportunities for further CVC research are myriad, including several areas that are largely untapped. Following is a shortlist of topics worth further exploration.

Open innovation is a new paradigm that is largely unexplored in CVC literature. As Figure 11.9 shows, the largest CVCs in recent years are ecosystem investors, which is distinct from CVC programs designed for technology gap filling investments that predominate in CVC studies. Digital platforms are winner-take-most markets that rely on a vast partner ecosystem (Asel, 2021). Van Angeren and Karunakaran (2020) describe how ecosystem investing works at Salesforce Ventures. Dushnitsky and Kang (2018) propose that ecosystem-CVCs experience superior short- and long-term performance relative to CVCs with different objectives.

Many of the companies in Figure 11.9 compete in colliding markets offering a rich backdrop for future research. Future studies should evaluate the role of CVC for platform investments and alternative measures to evaluate performance.

Further research may also explore the role of CVC as part of a corporate innovation framework. Studies consistently highlight the need for CVCs to be aligned with corporate objectives and the assertion that most CVC activity adds little strategic value as investments are either passive, too early or too distant to be impactful (Anokhin et al., 2016) should be further explored. Open innovation expands the aperture as it shifts corporate orientation toward external, exploratory activity. Van de Vrande et al. (2006) claims that CVC studied alone overstates its impact on innovation. CVC studied alone may instead discount its impact on innovation as CVC

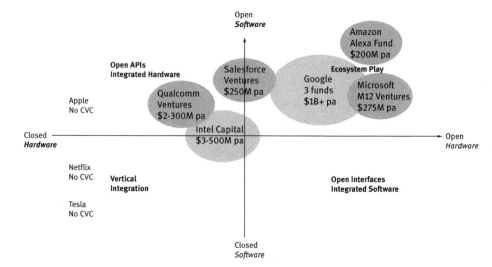

Figure 11.9: Largest CVCs are Ecosystem Investors.
Source: Asel (2021)

unleashes both exploratory and exploitative capacity while augmenting R&D, alliances, and acquisitions.

CVC has been described as an ambidextrous activity, yet research has not yet parsed how CVC balances exploratory and exploitative interests. CVC autonomy promotes exploratory activity. Tight alignment with business units serves exploitative interests. Does an ambidextrous approach require a hybrid design? Could a hybrid approach better serve dual strategic and financial objectives despite earlier findings that CVCs with a singular focus tend to perform better (Gompers and Lerner 2000)? Further research could also distinguish between radical and incremental innovation and how to best balance both within an innovation framework and CVC design.

International dimensions of CVC deserve further research. The US share of global venture capital investment is now below 50%, yet international studies are significantly underrepresented in CVC literature. Tencent, Alibaba, Legend and Xiaomi are among the largest CVC investors globally with pathbreaking ecosystem models and an outsized role in the China venture ecosystem. The norms for CVC investing in China differ markedly from that of the US, yet research on China and other international markets is formative.

Little academic work has studied the lifecycle of CVC programs and institutions. Mason et al. (2019) and their colleagues at Global Corporate Venturing offer a big leap forward from a practitioner perspective. Mason addresses the need to cohere global best practices in a heterogenous, fragmented industry. As the average CVC lifespan has increased four-fold during the past two decades, little attention has been paid to the expansion and resilience phases of CVC programs and how organizations progress from one phase to the next. The venture capital industry has grown significantly in the past decade and both VCs and CVCs have expanded their scope of operations and services to both startups and strategic partners. The institutionalization of CVC is an untapped topic.

Future research may also explore how changes in the corporate context impacts CVC. Managing CVCs is an entrepreneurial activity. In addition to operating in dynamic venture capital and technology markets, CVC leaders respond to industry downturns, management changes, corporate reorganizations, strategic shifts, acquisitions and divestitures, and fluctuating corporate performance and prospects. CVC studies highlight the need for consistency (Lerner, 2012), yet CVC programs, like their corporate sponsors and startups in which they invest, must adapt to survive and thrive. Literature is scant on how CVC programs evolve as they mature.

Further research is needed on CVC design and organizational structures, which have evolved significantly over the past two decades. In 2000 almost all CVC programs were internally managed within the corporate sponsor. Recent surveys indicate that a large minority of CVC programs are separately managed (Andonov, 2021), which understates the shift from an investment volume perspective. CVC design moderates program objectives, personnel, incentives and performance, yet only 10% of the studies reviewed here identify or discuss CVC structure. Future research may explore origins of CVC structure, alignment with financial and strategic objectives, hybrid forms, impact on program sustainability and performance, personnel choices, and conditions under which trade-offs occur.

Further research could address research limitations identified in this review. We still have a limited understanding of how CVC investments impact corporate R&D capabilities. Pahnke et al. (2015) used both archival data and surveys to help bridge this gap. Future research may augment archival studies with case studies to corroborate and explain archival findings in practice. Surveys have relied disproportionately on CVCs. Future research should incorporate the corporate perspective. Future research may replicate notable studies that relied on data from the dotcom era (Allen & Hevert, 2007, Dushnitsky & Lenox, 2006) to test if those foundational findings are still valid today.

Measuring CVC performance has been problematic given the paucity of available financial data and measures for strategic value. Researchers must devise reliable qualitative and quantitative approaches to evaluate performance. New data and analytical tools may avail new approaches as recent research has demonstrated (Hamm 2018, Rohm et al., 2018). Real-time analytics may also help reduce lag times between data collection and publication. Opensource data may also facilitate study updates and replication.

Conclusion

Do CVCs add value to their corporate sponsors? As a CVC practitioner and leader, I believe CVC programs offer a window on new technology that reinforces an open innovation culture, enhances digital ecosystems, augments internal CV activity, explores new market opportunities, bolsters alliances and foretells early threats. When done well, CVC offers low-cost options and leverages internal resources while providing shareholders with a superior financial return on investment. This view is more widely shared as the CVC industry has grown six-fold in the past decade with over 2000 active firms globally.

Yet despite the myriad studies espousing CVC program benefits for corporate sponsors in the past two decades, the composite findings are not entirely convincing. In industries with longstanding, successful CVC programs, competitors have taken alternate approaches. Among corporate executives who sponsor these longstanding CVC programs, opinions on their efficacy differ. CVC objectives and practices differ widely, which may signal the malleability of CVC or it could represent lack of acknowledged industry standards. Given the significant capital allocated to CVC annually and its impact on innovation, corporate sponsors and the startup ecosystem, there is much at stake in resolving open issues.

CVC also offers a lens into finance, entrepreneurship and organizational behavior informing theoretical perspectives in each of these fields. Theoretical frameworks established in these disciplines have informed CVC literature. As the CVC industry matures, CVC studies are increasingly impacting other fields of study. As shown in Figure 5, leading scholars such as Gompers, Lerner, Chesbrough, Birkinshaw and Zahra have drawn on CVC for insights on the venture industry, innovation and broader CV activity.

While CVC literature has progressed significantly in the past two decades, there are still many topics that remain unexplored with potential impact on CVC practices, finance, innovation and the corporation. This work is timely as technology is impacting a broadening array of traditional industries and the applicability of CVC across sectors is widely debated in boardrooms globally.

References

Allen, S.A., Hevert, K.T. (2007). Venture capital investing by information technology companies: Did it pay? *Journal of Business Venturing* 22(2): 262–282.

Andonov, K. (2021). The World of Corporate Venturing 2021: the definitive guide to the industry. Global Corporate Venturing Magazine 2021(2): 16–80.

Anokhin S., Örtqvist D., Thorgren S., Wincent J. (2011). Corporate venturing deal syndication and innovation: the information exchange paradox. *Long Range Planning* 44(2): 134–151.

Anokhin S., Wincent J., Oghazi P. (2016). Strategic effects of corporate venture capital investments. *Journal of Business Venturing Insights* (5): 63–69.

Asel, P. (2021). Corporate Venture: A Catalyst for Digital Transformation. *Global Corporate Venturing Magazine* (2): 66–72.

Asel, P., Park, H. D., Velamuri, S. R. (2015). Creating Values through Corporate Venture Capital Programs: The Choice between Internal and External Fund Structures. *The Journal of Private Equity* 19(1): 63–72.

Basu, S., Phelps, C., Kotha, S. (2011). Towards understanding who makes corporate venture capital investments and why. *Journal of Business Venturing*, 26(2): 153–171.

Basu, S., Wadhwa, A. (2013). External venturing and discontinuous strategic renewal: An options perspective. *Journal of Product Innovation Management* 30(5): 956–975.

Basu, S., Phelps, C.C., Kotha, S. (2016). Search and integration in external venturing: An inductive examination of corporate venture capital units. *Strategic Entrepreneurship Journal* 10(2): 129–152.

Benson, D., Ziedonis, R.H. (2009). Corporate Venture Capital as a Window on New Technologies: Implications for the Performance of Corporate Investors When Acquiring Startups. *Organization Science* 20(2): 329–351.

Benson, D., Ziedonis, R.H. (2010). Corporate venture capital and the returns to acquiring portfolio companies. *Journal of Financial Economics* 98(3): 478–499.

Birkinshaw, J., van Basten Batenburg, R., Murray, R. (2002). Venturing to Succeed. *Business Strategy Review* 13(4): 10–17.

Birkinshaw J, Hill SA. (2005). Corporate venturing units: vehicles for strategic success in the new Europe. *Organizational Dynamics* 34: 247–257.

Brigl, M., Hong, M., Roos, A., Schmieg, F., Wu, X. (2016). Corporate venturing shifts gear: How the largest companies apply a broad set of tools to speed in-novation. *The Boston Consulting Group*.

Chemmanur, T. J., Loutskina, E., Tian, X. (2014). Corporate Venture Capital, Value Creation, and Innovation. *The Review of Financial Studies* 27(8): 2434–2473.

Chesbrough, H. W. (2000). Designing corporate ventures in the shadow of private venture capital. *California Management Review 42 (3):* 31–49.

Chesbrough, H. (2002). Making sense of corporate venture capital. *Harvard Business Review* 80(3) 90–100.

Chesbrough, H. (2003). *Open Innovation: The New Imperative for Creating and Profiting from Technology*, Harvard Business School Press.

Cohen, W.M., Levinthal D.A. (1990). Absorptive capacity: a new perspective on learning and innovation, *Administrative Science Quarterly* 35 (1): 128–152.

DiMaggio, P.J., Powell, W.W. (1983). The iron cage revisited: Institutional isomorphism and collective rationality in organizational fields. *American Sociological Review* 147–160.

Dokko G., Gaba V. (2012). Venturing into new territory: career experiences of corporate venture capital managers and practice variation. *Academy of Management Journal* 55(3): 563–583.

Dushnitsky, G., Lenox, M.J. (2005a). When do incumbents learn from entrepreneurial ventures? Corporate venture capital and investing company innovation rates. *Research Policy* 34(5): 615–639.

Dushnitsky, G., Lenox, M.J. (2005b). When do companies undertake R&D by investing in new ventures? *Strategic Management Journal* 26(10): 947–965.

Dushnitsky, G., Lenox, M.J. (2006). When does corporate venture capital investment create firm value? *Journal of Business Venturing* 21(6): 753–772.

Dushnitsky G., Shaver J.M. (2009). Limitations to Inter-Organizational Knowledge Acquisitions: The Paradox of Corporate Venture Capital. *Strategic Management Journal* 30(10): 1045–1064.

Dushnitsky, G., Lavie, D., (2010). How Alliance Formation Shapes Corporate Venture Capital Investment in the Software Industry: A Resource-Based Perspective. *Strategic Entrepreneurship Journal* 4(1): 22–48.

Dushnitsky G., Shapira Z. (2010). Entrepreneurial finance meets organizational reality: comparing investment practices and performance of corporate and independent venture capitalists. *Strategic Management Journal* 31(9): 990–1017.

Dushnitsky, G., Kang, S., 2018). Seeding a Star or Constructing a Constellation? Corporate Venturing as an Ecosystem Strategy. *Academy of Management Proceedings* 2018(1).

Eisenhardt, K.M. (1989). Building theories from case study research. *Academy of Management Review* 14(4): 532–550.

Ernst H., Witt P., Brachtendorf G. (2005). Corporate venture capital as a strategy for external innovation: an exploratory empirical study. *R&D Management* 35(3): 233–242.

Fulghieri, P., Sevilir, M. (2009). Organization and Financing of innovation, and the choice between corporate and independent venture capital. *Journal of Financial and Quantitative Analysis* 44 (6): 1291–1321.

Gaba, V., Meyer, A.D. (2008). Crossing the organizational species barrier: how venture capital practices infiltrated the information technology sector. *Academy of Management Journal* 51(5): 976–998.

Gaba V, Bhattacharya S. (2012), Aspirations, innovation, and corporate venture capital: a behavioral perspective. *Strategic Entrepreneurship Journal* 6(2): 178–199.

Gaba, V., Dokko, G. (2016). Learning to let go: Social influence, learning, and the abandonment of corporate venture capital practices. *Strategic Management Journal* 37(8): 1558–1577.

Gompers, P.A., Lerner, J. (2000). The determinants of corporate venture capital success: organizational structure, incentives and complementarities. *National Bureau of Economic Research, Working Paper* 6725.

Gompers, P.A. (2002). Corporations and the financing of innovation: the corporate venturing experience. *Federal Reserve Bank of Atlanta Economic Review* 87(4): 1–17.

Hallen, B.L., Katila, R., Rosenberger, J.D. (2014). How do social defenses work? A resource-dependence lens on technology ventures, venture capital investors, and corporate relationships. *Academy of Management Journal* 57(4).

Hamm, S.J.W., Jung, M.J., Park, M. (2018). How Transparent are Firms about their Corporate Venture Capital Investments? *Harvard Law School Forum*.

Hellmann, T. (2002), A theory of strategic venture investing. *Journal of Financial Economics* 64: 285–314.

Hill S.A., Birkinshaw J. (2008). Strategy-organization configurations in corporate venture units: impact on performance and survival. *Journal of Business Venturing* 23(4): 423–444.

Hill, S.A., Birkinshaw, J. (2014). Ambidexterity and survival in corporate venture units. *Journal of Management* 40(7): 1899–1931.

Hill, S.A., Maula, M.V.J., Birkinshaw, J.M., Murray, G. (2009). Transferability of the venture capital model to the corporate context: Implications for the performance of corporate venture units. *Strategic Entrepreneurship Journal* 3(1): 3–27.

Hochberg, Y.V., Ljungqvist, A., Lu, Y. (2007). Whom you know matters: venture capital networks and investment performance. *Journal of Finance* 62(1): 251–301.

Ivanov, V.I., Xie, F. (2010). Do Corporate Venture Capitalists Add Value to Start-Up Firms? Evidence from IPOs and Acquisitions of VC-Backed Companies. *Financial Management* 39(1): 129–152.

Janney, J.J., Damaraju, N.L., Dess, G.G. (2021). The role of corporate venture capital on returns to acquiring firms: evidence from the biotechnology industry. *Venture Capital: An International Journal of Entrepreneurial Finance* 23(2): 111–127.

Katila, R., Rosenberger, J.D., Eisenhardt, K.M. (2008). Swimming with sharks: Technology ventures, defense mechanisms and corporate relationships. *Administrative Science Quarterly* 53(2): 295–332.

Keil T. (2002). *External Corporate Venturing: Strategic Renewal in Rapidly Changing Industries*. Quorum.

Keil, T. (2004). Building external corporate venturing capability. *Journal of Management Studies* 41 (5): 799–825.

Keil T., Autio E., George G. (2008). Corporate venture capital, disembodied experimentation and capability development. *Journal of Management Studies* 45(8): 1475–1505.

Keil, T., Maula, M.V.J., Schildt, H., Zahra, S.A. (2008). The effect of governance modes and relatedness of external business development activities on innovative performance. *Strategic Management Journal, 29:* 895–907.

Keil, T., Maula, M.V.J., Wilson, C. (2010). Unique resources of corporate venture capitalists as a key to entry into rigid venture capital syndication networks. *Entrepreneurship Theory and Practice* 34(1): 83–103.

Kim, J.Y., Steensma, H.K., Park, H.D. (2017). The Influence of Technological Links, Social Ties, and Incumbent Firm Opportunistic Propensity on the Formation of Corporate Venture Capital Deals. *Journal of Management* 45(4): 1595–1622.

Kim K., Gopal A., Hoberg G. (2016). Does product market competition drive open innovation: evidence from CVC investments in the IT industry. *Information Systems Research* 27(2): 259–281.

Kuhn, T.S. (1962). *The Structure of Scientific Revolutions*, University of Chicago Press.

Lee, S.U., Kang, J. (2015). Technological diversification through corporate venture capital investments: Creating various options to strengthen dynamic capabilities. *Industry and Innovation* 22(5): 349–374.

Lerner, J. (2012). *The architecture of innovation: The economics of creative organizations*. Harvard Business Press.

Lin, S.J., Lee, J.R. (2011). Configuring a corporate venturing portfolio to create growth value: Within-portfolio diversity and strategic linkage. *Journal of Business Venturing* 26(4): 489–503.

Ma, S. (2020). The life cycle of corporate venture capital. *The Review of Financial Studies* 33(1): 358–394.

MacMillan, I., Roberts, E., Livada, V., Wang A. (2008). Corporate Venture Capital Seeking Innovation and Strategic Growth: Recent patterns in CVC mission, structure, and investment. *National Institute of Standards and Technology*, US Department of Commerce, 8–96.

March, J.G. (1991). Exploration and exploitation in organizational learning. *Organization Science* 2: 71–87.

Mason, H., Rohner, T. (2002). *The Venture Imperative*. Harvard Business School Press.

Mason, H., Arrington, E., Mawson, J. (2019). *Corporate Venturing: a Survival Guide*. Global Corporate Venturing.

Masulis, R.W., Nahata, R. (2009). Financial contracting with strategic investors: Evidence from corporate venture capital backed IPOs. *Journal of Financial Intermediation* 18(4): 599–631.

Maula, M.V.J., Autio, E., Murray, G. (2005). Corporate venture capitalists and independent venture capitalists: what do they know, who do they know, and should entrepreneurs care? *Venture Capital* 7(1): 3–19.

Maula, M.V.J., Autio, E., Murray, G. (2009). Corporate venture capital and the balance of risks and rewards for portfolio companies. *Journal of Business Venturing* 24(3): 274–286.

Maula, M.V.J., Keil, T., Zahra, S. (2013). Top management's attention to discontinuous technological change: corporate venture capital as an alert mechanism. *Organization Science* 24(3): 926–947.

Meng, F., Tian, Z., Chang, B., Yu, H., Zhang, S. (2020). Research on the niche evolution game of ecological community innovation of corporate venture capital based on logistic extended complexity model. *Complexity* Article ID 6327218.

Miles, M.P., Covin, J.G. (2002). Exploring the Practice of Corporate Venturing: Some Common Forms and Their Organizational Implications. *Entrepreneurship Theory and Practice* 26(3): 21–40.

Munce, C.F. (2018). Corporate Venture Capital Primer. *Stanford Graduate School of Business* case study.

Napp, J.J., Minshall, T. (2011). Corporate venture capital investments for enhancing innovation: Challenges and solutions. *Research-Technology Management* 54(2): 27–36.

Pahnke, E.D., Katila, R., Eisenhardt, K.M. (2015). Who takes you to the dance? How partners' institutional logics influence innovation in young firms. *Administrative Science Quarterly* 60 (4): 596–633.

Park, H.D., Steensma, H.K. (2012). When does corporate venture capital add value for new ventures? *Strategic Management Journal* 33(1): 1–22.

Pfeffer, J., Salancik, G.R. (1978). *The external control of organizations: A resource dependence perspective*. New York: Harper and Row.

Pinkow, F., Iversen, J. (2020). Strategic Objectives of Corporate Venture Capital as a Tool for Open Innovation. *Journal of Open Innovation: Technology, Market and Complexity* 6(4): 157.

Porter, M.E. (1980). *Competitive Strategy: Techniques for Analyzing Industries and Competitors*, Free Press.

Rohm, P., Kohn, A., Kuckertz, A., Dehnen, H. (2018). A World of Difference? The Impact of corporate venture capitalists' investment motivation on startup valuation. *Journal of Business Economics* 88: 531–557.

Rohm, P. (2018). Exploring the landscape of corporate venture capital: a systematic review of the entrepreneurial and finance literature. Management Review Quarterly 68: 279–319.

Sahaym, A., Steensma, H.K., Barden, J.Q. (2010). The influence of R&D investment on the corporate venture capital: an industry-level analysis. *Journal of Business Venturing* 25: 376–388.

Schildt, H., Maula, M.V.J., Keil, T. (2005). Explorative and exploitative learning from external corporate ventures. *Entrepreneurship Theory and Practice* 29(4): 493–515.

Sears, J.B., McLeod, M.S., Evert, R.E., Payne, G.T. (2020). Alleviating concerns of misappropriation in corporate venture capital: Creating credible commitments and calculative trust. *Strategic Organization*, ISSN: 1476–1270.

Siegel R., Siegel E., MacMillan I.C. (1988). Corporate venture capitalists: Autonomy, obstacles, and performance. *Journal of Business Venturing* 3: 233–247.

Smith, S.W., Shah, S.K. (2013). Do innovative users generate more useful insights? An analysis of corporate venture capital investments in the medical device industry. *Strategic Entrepreneurship Journal* 7(2): 151–167.

Souitaris, V., Zerbinati, S., Liu, G. (2012). Which iron cage? Endo- and exo-isomorphism in corporate venture capital programs. *Academy of Management Journal* 55(2): 477–505.

Titus Jr., V.K., House, J.M., Covin, J.G. (2017). The influence of exploration on external corporate venturing activity. *Journal of Management* 43(5): 1609–1630.

Titus Jr., V.K., Parker, O., Covin, J.G. (2020). Organizational Aspirations and External Venturing: The Contingency of Entrepreneurial Orientation. *Entrepreneurship Theory and Practice* 44(4): 645–670.

Tong, T.W., Li, Y. (2011). Real options and investment mode: Evidence from corporate venture capital and acquisition. *Organization Science* 22(3): 659–674.

Van Angeren, J., Karunakaran, A. (2020). Platform Venture Capital Investments and the Introduction and Withdrawal of Complementary Products. *Academy of Management Proceedings*, 2020(1).

Van de Vrande, V., Vanhaverbeke, W., Duysters, G. (2009). External technology sourcing: The effect of uncertainty on governance mode choice. *Journal of Business Venturing* 24(1): 62–80.

Van de Vrande, V., Vanhaverbeke, W. (2013). How Prior Corporate Venture Capital Investments Shape Technological Alliances: A Real Options Approach. *Entrepreneurship Theory and Practice* 37(5): 1019–1043.

Van de Vrande, V., Lemmens, C., Vanhaverbeke, W. (2006). Choosing Governance Modes for External Technology Sourcing. *R&D Management* 36(3): 347–363.

Wadhwa, A., Kotha, S. (2006). Knowledge creation through external venturing: evidence from the telecommunications equipment manufacturing industry. *Academy of Management Journal* 49 (4): 819–835.

Wadhwa, A., Phelps, C., Kotha, S. (2010). Creating exploratory innovations by learning from entrepreneurial ventures. *New Frontiers in Entrepreneurship* 26: 147–173.

Wadhwa, A., Basu, S. (2013). Exploration and resource commitments in unequal partnerships: An examination of corporate venture capital investments. *Journal of Product Innovation Management* 30(5): 916–936.

Weber, C. (2009). Corporate Venture Capitalists with a 'Bird's-Eye View' – A Dynamic Social Network Perspective. *Schmalenbach Business Review* 61: 195–224.

Weber, C., Weber, B. (2005). Corporate venture capital organizations in Germany. *Venture Capital: An International Journal of Entrepreneurial Finance* 7(1): 51–73.

Weiblen, T., Chesbrough, H.W. (2015). Engaging with startups to enhance corporate innovation. *California Management Review* 57(2): 66–90.

Yang, Y. (2012). Bilateral inter-organizational learning in corporate venture capital activity: Governance characteristics, knowledge transfer, and performance. *Management Research Review* 35(5): 352–378.

Yang, Y., Narayanan, V.K., De Carolis, D.M. (2014). The relationship between portfolio diversification and firm value: The evidence from corporate venture capital activity. *Strategic Management Journal* 35(13): 1993–2011.

Yang, Y., Chen, T., Zhang, L. (2016). Corporate venture capital program autonomy, corporate investors' attention and portfolio diversification. *Journal of Strategy and Management* 9(3): 302–321.

Zahra, S.A., Hayton, J.C. (2008). The effect of international venturing on firm performance: The moderating influence of absorptive capacity. *Journal of Business Venturing* 23(2): 195–220.

Sofia Avdeitchikova and Hans Landström

12 The role of business angels in the new financial landscape

Abstract: Both access to and use of external sources of finance by entrepreneurial ventures have transformed significantly over the past 10–15 years, which may have induced an important shift in the role of business angels (BAs). In this chapter we elaborate on this changing role of BAs, and in particular on the value creation provided by BAs in the new financial landscape. We propose to reframe the discussion on the value creation of BAs to better capture their current and potential contribution to the economy and society, and distinguish between three aspects of value creation of BAs – *business*, that is their financial and non-financial contribution to the firms that they invest in; *situational*, that is, their role at critical points of economic and societal development, and *system*, that is, their role in strengthening regional entrepreneurial ecosystems. Further, we suggest a number of areas that we believe to be particularly fruitful over the coming years for deepening our knowledge about the role of BAs in the new financial landscape.

Keywords: business angels, entrepreneurial finance, financial landscape, value creation, entrepreneurial ecosystems

Introduction

Both access to and use of external sources of finance by entrepreneurial ventures have transformed significantly over the past 10–15 years. One might, rightfully so, argue that the nature and the context of entrepreneurial activity evolves all the time, and that the claim that "this time, it's different" may seem premature. Still, we would argue that some major developments over this period may have induced an important shift in the role of business angels (BAs). In this chapter we will elaborate on this changing role of BAs, and in particular on the value creation provided by BAs in the new financial landscape. We will define BAs in a rather narrow sense: "A wealthy individual, acting alone or in a formal or informal syndicate, who invests his or her own money directly in an unquoted business in which there is no family connection" (Avdeitchikova et al., 2008, p. 375).

Over the past decade we can identify several changes in entrepreneurial activities as well as in the financial markets for entrepreneurial ventures that are of relevance from both scholarly and policy perspectives, but also for the role that

Sofia Avdeitchikova, Hans Landström, Oxford Research and Lund University

https://doi.org/10.1515/9783110726312-016

BAs are playing in this changing landscape. Specifically, we want to emphasize the following.

First, the *nature of the entrepreneurial activity* has undergone a major transformation. The digital age has created changes in the entrepreneurial behavior, and we have seen a lot of new business models emerging. These business models are based on new forms of communication (e.g., social media), increased customization (e.g., 3D printing), online platforms, increased interest in the social and sustainable aspects of entrepreneurship, and the sharing and Gig Economy (Landström, 2017). The new trends in entrepreneurial behavior have had significant effects on the demand for resources and financial capital. In many cases entrepreneurial ventures may require fewer resources. Many new business models are less resource intensive, and entrepreneurs try "to do more with less" (Baker and Nelson, 2005). The concept of "lean start-up" has emerged as somewhat of a golden standard in entrepreneurship, partly owing to the history of very expensive start-up failures during the dot.com bubble (Ries, 2011). Indeed, both national (e.g., Swedish Agency for Economic and Regional Growth, 2021a) and EU-level surveys point towards the relatively diminished importance of access to finance as barrier for growth for young and innovative SMEs. According to a European Central Bank and European Commission survey on the access to finance of enterprises (European Commission, 2020), just under 10% of young and innovative SMEs in the EU countries perceived access to finance as the key barrier for growth in 2019, compared to close to 20% a decade earlier.

Second, the *start-up financing landscape* has changed significantly. Digitalization of the financial markets is extensive, which has affected both old financial players and created new financial instruments, and scholars are talking about a FinTech revolution (Hommel and Bican, 2020). Over the past 10–15 years, we have seen a democratization and disintermediation of financial sources, particularly through crowdfunding and initial coin offerings (ICOs), a decline in formal venture capital as source of early-stage finance, and a rise of angel groups in many countries (Mason and Harrison, 2015; Harrison and Mason, 2019). Further, business angels and venture capital funds are no longer necessarily assumed to have complementary roles in the financing landscape, or what Mason (2017) refers to as a "breakdown in funding escalator". Similarly, Bessière et al. (2018) argue that we need to reassess our understanding of the "funding trajectories" of startups, based on evolving dynamics between the old and the new financial sources.

Finally, a development of major importance from the perspective of entrepreneurial finance is the *increasing role of governments in providing risk finance* to growth-oriented SMEs. This is particularly pronounced in the EU countries, where the use of financial instruments targeting growth-oriented SMEs within the European Regional Development Fund almost doubled between the 2007–2013 and 2014–2020 program period and is expected to further increase in the coming six-year program period. The funds channeled through EU programs are often matched by national public funding, which means that the amount of risk finance available through public sources in some EU countries could currently be at an all-time high. For instance, a recent overview of government-supported financial instruments in Sweden showed that the amount of early-stage venture capital available for investment through the state system in early 2020s was almost 1.8 billion Euro, which is a historically high number (Swedish Agency for Economic and Regional Growth, 2021b). This estimate does not include other broadly used sources of public risk finance, such as public grants, soft loans and loan guarantees, the use of which have steadily increased as well.

It is in this changing landscape of entrepreneurial behavior and financial markets for entrepreneurial ventures, and the increased supply of innovation funding instruments (particularly in the EU) that we can expect a changing dynamic between existing and new financial actors, searching to position themselves in the new environment. Given the changes we have identified, we will focus on the role of BAs, and the question that is posed in this chapter is: What is the role of BAs in this new financial landscape?

In answering this question, we particularly consider three aspects of value creation by business angels. We start from a *business* aspect and discuss the role of BAs as finance providers to early-stage ventures. Next, we discuss the role of BAs from what we call a *situational* aspect, focusing on major societal developments (such as financial crises and major technological transitions) and discuss the (potential) role of BAs in those changes. Finally, we discuss the role of BAs from a *system* aspect, focusing on their (potential) significance in strengthening regional entrepreneurial ecosystems.

This chapter contributes to the literature on entrepreneurial finance by offering an updated and contextualized understanding of the role of BAs in the financial system, taking into account the recent and emerging developments in the entrepreneurial and financial landscape. When talking about developments and trends, we most often refer to examples and data from the USA, UK and Sweden. This is partially because these are contexts that are familiar to us as authors, but also because we find it interesting to look at countries where BA investing has been around for some years, and has possibly undergone a transformation over time. Nonetheless, we fully acknowledge that the entrepreneurial finance system varies significantly between countries, and that the trends that we talk about may apply to some countries/regions and not to others. Our purpose is not to give a full and comprehensive diagnosis of the state of BA investing. Instead, our aspiration is to stimulate further research and policy discussion about the role of BAs in the financial system, in a more nuanced and informed manner.

In the next section, we will make a historical review of the BAs' role in the financial landscape at different points in time, but also the knowledge development in this field of research, particularly regarding the value creation in the ventures in which the BAs invest. Finally, we will reframe the discussion of the BAs' value creation, introduce a discussion around different aspects of value creation (business, situational, and system), and discuss some suggestions for further research questions on the role of BAs in the future.

Literature review: The role of BAs in the financial landscape – a retrospective

Before we dive into our discussion of the role of BAs in the new financial landscape, it is important to understand why both scholars and practitioners have continuously emphasized the importance of BAs. Therefore, we start by a review of what the academic literature tells us until now of the role and significance of BAs. In particular, we focus on what we know so far about how BAs create value. In the next section, we examine this from a current and forward-looking perspective and discuss how and in which contexts we believe that BAs create value today and in the future.

BAs as a financial source in the financial landscape

Private individuals have always had a tendency to invest in high-risk projects and we can go as far back as the Babylonian era in the 17th and 18th centuries BC as well as early medieval Europe for examples. Perhaps the best-known example is the decision by Queen Isabella of Spain to finance the voyage of Christopher Columbus in 1492, which can be regarded as a highly profitable (for the Spanish) BA investment. It can also be argued that in many countries investments by private individuals were heavily influential in the development of the industrial revolution during the nineteenth and twentieth centuries. For example, in the US, groups of domestic and European private investors were responsible for financing the development of several new industries, such as railroads, steel, petroleum and glass (Benjamin and Margulis, 2001).

In a more modern context, wealthy private individuals tended to support different theatre productions in London and New York, maybe as an opportunity to rub shoulders with celebrities, and were regarded as 'angels' by theatre owners and producers as they were prepared to fund the set-up of a production, and as very few theatre productions were profitable, such individuals had to have angelic qualities (Storey and Greene, 2010).

In the 1950s and 1960s, interest in the BA market emerged among policymakers. In particular, the financial problems experienced by many young technology-based firms triggered this interest. For example, in the late 1950s, the Federal Reserve in the US performed a couple of studies regarding the initial financing of

new technology-based firms, which led to the creation of the Small Business Investment Company (SBIC) program in the US. And BAs were perceived as an important external source of finance for entrepreneurial ventures with a basis in new technologies.

Later, in the 1980s and 1990s, BA market had consolidated its position in the
US, and was identified as an important financial source for many new and growing
ventures. For example, Wetzel (1983) argued that BAs probably represented the
largest pool of risk capital for entrepreneurial ventures and played an essential role
in the growth of high-tech sectors in many countries. Early studies from the US and
the UK (Wetzel 1987, Mason and Harrison, 1990) showed that BAs provide at least
as much capital to firms as formal venture capital investors and financed many
more ventures than venture capital funds (for a summary, see Avdeitchikova and
Landström, 2016).

The importance of BAs triggered an increased interest from governments to introduce policy measures to stimulate the BA markets. In particular, governments
paid attention to two major market problems (Mason and Harrison, 1997): (1) the
lack of BAs in the economy, and (2) the inefficiency of the BA market. As a consequence, several interventions to increase the number of BAs in the society were introduced, aiming to improve the risk-return ratio of BA investments through tax
incentives, either by reducing the net acquisition costs using 'front-end' tax incentives, or through favorable tax rates applicable to capital gains on small business
investments, i.e., 'back-end' tax incentives (Mason and Harrison, 2000, 2002; for a
summary, see Carpentier and Suret, 2016). In order to improve the efficiency of the
BA market, many governmental initiatives have supported different forms of BA networks, which enable entrepreneurs and BAs to meet and interact (Mason and Harrison, 1999; for a summary, see Lahti and Keinonen, 2016).

The interest from governments to stimulate the BA market has continued, and
in the 2000s it was popular to introduce different forms of co-investments funds. In
this respect, the most popular role model was the Scottish Co-Investment Fund
(SCIF), introduced in 2003, and in which governmental capital (mainly provided by
EU funds) was used to scale-up the investments made by private (approved) investors (venture capitalists and BAs) (Hayton et al., 2008).

Over the last decade the BA markets still play a role as an important financial
source in emerging and growing businesses. However, as identified by Harrison
and Mason (2019) the BA markets have developed in different directions in different
countries:

– The invisible markets, which is the initial market structure that involves individual BAs making decisions to invest on their own, in which they identify potential
  investment objects through personal and social networks. We can assume that
  these markets are found in countries with a rather underdeveloped BA market.
– The network markets. Often with government support, business angel networks (BANs) have been established, which act as a "dating agency" matching
  entrepreneurs and investors. BAN-member investors still invest directly as

individuals or as part of ad-hoc deal-specific syndicates, but more formal managed angel syndicates may occur.

–   The angel-group markets. In more well-developed markets such as in the US and the UK, we can identify more visible, structured and accessible BA markets organized around BA groups, which also may mobilize passive capital, and that enable larger amounts of investments, including follow-on rounds of investments.

Thus, we can assume that differences in the characteristics of and the way the BA markets is organized will influence the role that the BA market will play in different countries.

Our knowledge about BAs

Even though equity investments made by private individuals are a very old phenomenon, and the market is of great importance in many countries, the research interest did not emerge until William Wetzel at the University of New Hampshire in the US published his seminal article "Angels and informal risk capital" in 1983. In the article he emphasized the importance of BAs in the financing of entrepreneurial ventures, and tried to put some boundaries around the phenomenon and put BAs on the 'research map' (Landström, 2007). Since then, the research interest in BAs has been rather large, and over the years many hundreds of scientific articles have been published on the characteristics and activities of BAs (see Landström and Mason, 2016a). We can divide the research on BAs in three phases:

Phase 1: In the pioneering phase of BA research it was obvious that it become interesting to get data with regards the size of the market (e.g., Ou, 1987; Short and Riding, 1988; Gaston, 1989; for a summary, see Avdeitchikova and Landström, 2016). It also become important to get an understanding of the individuals – the BAs – and a large number of studies was conducted to describe the BA's attitudes, behavior, and investment characteristics (so-called "ABC-studies"). Studies were conducted in different regions in the US (e.g., Tymes and Krasner, 1983; Gaston and Bell, 1986; Aram, 1987) as well as internationally (e.g., Riding and Short, 1987; Harrison and Mason, 1991; Landström, 1993). The studies showed that the 'typical' angel investor is a middle-aged male with a reasonable high net income and net worth; with previous start- up experiences; and who makes about one investment a year, usually close to home. It was also shown that even if the conditions differed from country to country, there were many similarities in the ABC of BAs in different countries (Kelly, 2007).

Phase 2: These pioneering studies were important, not only because they made the BA market visible for entrepreneurs, potential BA investors, and policy-makers, but also because the studies provided a basis for further research. In the 1990s the research developed in different directions, but in general remained rather descriptive in character, i.e., it was important to describe and understand what happened "out there." These studies can be grouped into three categories:

- Studies on the BAs' investment process, i.e., to understand how BAs made their investments and the investment criteria they used for selecting their investments (e.g., Riding et al., 1994; Landström, 1995, 1998; Mason and Rogers, 1997; for a summary, see Maxwell, 2016).
- Studies on the BAs' value creation in the ventures in which they invested. It was obvious that BAs not only provided financial capital in the businesses, but also added a lot of other contributions (for a summary, see Politis, 2008, 2016), such as mentorship (Freear et al., 1995) and strategic knowledge (Harrison and Mason, 1992).
- Studies on the effects of policy measures, particularly, in the UK, where a lot of measures were introduced to stimulate and improve the BA market. Several studies were conducted to describe and evaluate these initiatives (e.g., Mason, 2009).

Phase 3: A rather eclectic phase of BA research emerged in the 2000s. First, a considerable amount of research has continued to investigate the investment decision-making by BAs but with a much narrower focus. For example, studies paid attention to the trust between the entrepreneur and the BA (e.g., Bammens and Collewaert, 2014), but also to the conflicts that may arise between these actors (e.g., Maxwell et al., 2011; 2014; Mitteness et al., 2012; Parhankangas and Ehrlich, 2014). A second theme has been a focus on specific types of angels, notably founder angels (Festel and De Cleyn, 2013), super angels and women angels (Harrison and Mason, 2007; Sohl and Hill, 2007; Amatucci, 2016). As BA markets had matured in many countries, for example, in the UK and US, and the markets have become more institutionalized and visible, a particular interest has been paid to different kinds of 'angel groups' that have emerged in these contexts (Sohl, 2007). Third, some studies have sought to introduce a time dimension, examining angel investment trends over time and specifically following the global financial crisis (Månsson and Landström, 2005; Mason and Harrison, 2015; Sohl, 2006).

Interestingly, although the BA markets can be assumed to be as important as ever before for the finance of emerging ventures in different countries, the research interest declined significantly, and almost died, in the 2010s. The interest among researchers changed in favor of 'new' phenomena such as crowdfunding and initial coin offering (ICOs). In this respect, the research on BAs has significantly contributed to our understanding of the heterogeneity of the informal venture capital market – defined in a broader sense than a narrow focus on BAs – and the possibility to compare and contrast different sources of informal venture capital. In times with a lot of entrepreneurial and technological changes it is important to emphasize the broad range of different financial sources available.

BAs' value creation in the businesses in which they invest

One of the key issues in previous BA research was the value creation that BAs provide, and in this respect, most research has focused on value creation for business, rather than for industrial sectors or economic and societal development. Thus, the focus in research particularly elaborates the contributions made by BAs in the ventures in which they invest, and we can also find research on the financial value creation that BAs generates in terms of rate of return for the BAs.

BAs value creation in the ventures in which they invest

Wetzel (1986) recognized BAs as 'smart' investors who contribute added value beyond financial capital to the ventures in which they invest. Thus, BAs provide the ventures in which they invest with their business skills, experience and access to their networks. Avdeitchikova and Landström (2016) summarized BAs' contribution to the businesses in which they invest in the following ways:

- *Increasing the supply of capital.* BAs contribute directly to increasing the flow of finance to new and growing businesses. Furthermore, it is not just the *quantity* of finance that BAs provide that is important, but also the *type* of finance. BA finance primarily provides small amounts of finance in the early stages of firms' development (e.g., Mason and Harrison, 2000; Sohl, 2012).
- *Contributing to ventures' ability to attract more financing.* Since BAs predominantly invest equity capital (Landström, 2017), their investments contribute to strengthening the balance sheets of the firms, and might give positive signals to other investors and the market, reducing some of the informational asymmetry and leading to lower perceived risk for other financiers (e.g., Elitzur and Gavious, 2003; Conti, Thursby and Rothaermel, 2011). Thus, companies that have received angel funding would presumably be more likely to receive other types of funding later (e.g., Madill et al., 2005; Robb and Robinson, 2014).
- *Increasing the 'quality' of firms.* BA investing is often associated with an active involvement of the investor, which can take shape of advising, coaching, and providing access to investor's network. Further, as BAs invest their own money, it can also be assumed that BAs may add value faster and in a more flexible manner than many other investors such as venture capitalists and banks. Thus, firms that receive BA funding potentially gain access to non-financial value, which can be expected to result in better prospects for development and growth compared to firms that use more traditional sources of funding. Making a more detailed analysis of the value-added provided by BAs, Politis (2008, 2016) has summarized the benefits in the following ways:

- Sounding board and strategic role; providing strategic advice based on extensive business know-how and management experience (e.g., Politis and Landström, 2002; Madill et al., 2005; Wong et al., 2009).
- Supervision and monitoring role; safeguarding the investment from potential managerial misbehavior (e.g., Ehrlich et al., 1994; Saetre, 2003; Madill et al., 2005).
- Resource acquisition role; channeling resources through their personal networks (e.g., Brettel, 2003; Sørheim, 2005; Macht and Robinson, 2009).
- Mentoring role; being a helpful, open and trustful partner (e.g., Freear et al., 1995; Politis and Landström, 2002; Saetre, 2003).

Does the value-added contribution provided by BAs translate into effects on venture development? The results from different studies that provide insights into the subjective perceptions by the entrepreneurs indicate that a majority of entrepreneurs consider their relationship to BAs as productive (e.g., Freear et al., 1995; Lindström and Olofsson, 2001; Ardichvili et al., 2003; for a summary, see Politis, 2016). However, some studies (e.g., Ehrlich et al., 1994; Bammens and Collewaert, 2014) indicate that entrepreneurs seldom are fully satisfied with their BA relationship, particularly when the BA does not show relevant experience and expertise in the thematic area of the business. When it comes to more data-driven studies on BAs' value added effects on business performance, the number of studies is scarce (one exception is Landström, 1992). As expressed by Politis in her review of earlier research within the field (Politis, 2016), the lack of studies on BAs' impact on business performance is surprising since it may be perceived as the *sina qua non* of BA investment and something that typically motivates entrepreneurs to seek BA finance.

BAs' returns on investments

The average holding period for successful investments is four to five years. We can assume, based on Mason and Harrison (2002), that failed investments are exited earlier, likely by selling the investment back to the management team. Further, due to limited exit opportunities, moderately performing investments are likely to have the longest holding period. The typical exit route for BAs is trade sale, i.e., acquisition of the venture by an established company, whereas IPOs are rare, or as May and Simmons (2001, p. 177) put it "an IPO is to an exit strategy what a royal flush is to a poker hand. It's a rare event." However, our knowledge about the BA exit process is limited. It might be due to the fact that (1) BAs themselves historically have paid little attention to the potential exit routes (Van Osnabrugge and Robinson, 2002) and seldom appear to prepare the venture for an exit (Politis, 2008); and (2) many of the tax incentives that have been introduced in various countries are focused on stimulating BAs to make investments rather than on the returns from the investments (Mason et al., 2015).

The few studies on BA investment returns that have been conducted are fairly consistent, irrespective of time periods and geographical context (Mason et al., 2015), showing that the returns on BA investments are highly skewed, with a high proportion of losses, a few exits that generate a break-even, and a small subset of exits that generate fairly high returns. That is, around half of all investments fail to generate a return, while a small minority of investments generate more than ten times the amount of cash invested (Lumme et al., 1998; Mason et al., 2015; Mason and Harrison, 2002; Vo, 2013; Wiltbank, 2009). The conclusion is that the returns on BA investments are not very high (Shane, 2009), and for successful BAs it is important to minimize the losses as much as possible by, for example, "fast failures", i.e., quickly exiting those investments that will never generate any larger returns (the so-called "living dead"), even if the BA has an emotional commitment to the investment (Gifford, 1997).

However, we have to be aware that studies of BA returns often focus on returns on individual investments, but seldom on the overall returns on the portfolio of the BA, which for the BA might be more important (Mason et al., 2015). In addition, BAs are increasingly investing as part of more formalized angel groups (Sohl, 2007; 2012), which creates greater diversification and reduced risk, and might also increase the professionalism of the BA investment process, highlighting the need for a stronger "exit-oriented approach" in BA investments. And earlier research (Mason and Harrison, 2002) has indicated that multiple investors seem to create higher returns, but a lot more research is needed on this issue.

Future research agenda: Reframing the discussion on the significance of BAs – a three-level approach

In the previous section we reviewed the current literature on BAs, in particular what we know about the significance of BAs and how BAs create value. We have also argued that the research so far is giving limited guidance for how to understand the distinct role of BAs in the economy. One reason for this research gap is that researchers so far have been mostly interested in how BAs contribute to the firms they invest in – the business aspects of value creation – whether they chose to look at it from the perspective of individual firms, or from the perspective of the BAs.

We argue that a different view on value creation aspects might be useful to further inform the discussion on the role of BAs. Thus, we propose to reframe the discussion and separate between three partially related but yet conceptually distinct aspects of contribution of BAs to the economy (and society) – *business*, *situational* and *system*. We start from a business aspect and discuss the role of BAs as finance providers to early-stage ventures. Next, we discuss the role of BAs from what we call a situational aspect, focusing on major societal developments (such as financial crises and major technological transitions) and discuss the (potential) role of BAs in those. Finally, we discuss the role of BAs from a system aspect, focusing on their (potential) significance in strengthening the regional entrepreneurial ecosystems. Separating between these three aspects allows for a more nuanced understanding of what particular gap BAs can help to bridge, which would in turn imply quite different implications for policymakers.

In this section we go through these three aspects, discuss their importance in the context of the new financial landscape, and propose a number of research questions that need more recognition in order to increase our understanding of the role of BAs in the economy and society.

Business aspects of value creation – are BAs still important risk finance providers?

When the research on BAs took off in the 1980s, the scholars noted that BAs may be key actors in the financial system with regards to enabling and accelerating growth of ambitious, risk-taking, and often technology-based firms emerging at that point in time. Apart from BAs being high net worth individuals that could contribute risk capital to start-ups that are financially constrained, they also could provide smaller investments, addressing the needs of firms in very early stages, that were not yet interesting for venture capital funds. Further, they could make investment decisions faster and had less rigorous due diligence processes than venture capital funds, which implied higher risk appetite, broader scope of investments and lower transaction costs.

Today, some four decades later, the key argument for why BAs have an important role as risk financiers has remained pretty much the same (e.g., EBAN, 2019). But, have the changes in the nature of entrepreneurial activity and the financial landscape for entrepreneurial ventures also led to a change in the role of BAs as providers of risk finance? We believe that they might have, while acknowledging that the development of the BA market has likely been very different in different countries. Below, we formulate a number of research questions regarding BAs' business value creation that we believe are valuable to for further studies.

Have the fools, gamblers and altruists moved to the platforms, and what are their value creation functions?

The discussion about the heterogeneity of BAs has been around for almost as long as the research on BAs (e.g., Gaston, 1989; Landström, 1992; Stevenson and Coveney, 1994; Sullivan and Miller, 1996; Sørheim and Landström, 2001). While there isn't any single generally accepted categorization of BAs, the studies have quite consistently found that far from all angels are experienced, commercially and technically savvy individuals seeking to make good investments that would generate high returns. Some have other characteristics. For example, some BAs are fun-seeking, gambling, or seeking to contribute to socially beneficial products. Thus, there is a need to take this heterogeneity into consideration, and we believe that different kinds of BA investors add different kinds of value to the businesses in which they invest.

Following our argument about market heterogeneity, we assume that the professionalization of the BA market in the USA, UK and many EU-countries throughout the 2000s has contributed to a shake-out in the categories of fools, gamblers and altruist investors, who might in turn have found easier, cheaper and more accessible ways to channel their investment interest, not least through crowdfunding platforms. The fact that the average investment of a BA seems to have increased over the past decade – at the same time as the use of crowdfunding platforms expanded – is a possible indicator of this development.

Have organized angels lost their risk appetite and changed their value added?

The professionalization that we can identify in some markets (see above) will also affect the behavior and value creation of BAs. The more formal organization of the BA market has increased, bringing about more rigorous investment procedures. Increasingly, angel groups and networks are using gatekeepers to keep away investments that don't comply with certain standards. Even when potential investees get past the gatekeepers, the investment decision-making and due diligence processes are significantly more rigorous, with more critical eyes and voices involved. We believe that this may have contributed to increased risk aversion among BAs in the markets with high level of organization. Obviously, the introduction of more formalized angel groups will also have significant consequences for the contributions and value added created by BAs in the businesses in which they invest, for example in terms of larger investments, more and specialized competence and experience, but also a more efficient financial eco-system.

What value do BAs create in the ventures in which they invest?

Based on the changes that we have identified in the business and financial context, together with the fact that the behavior of BAs may be different depending on the maturity of the BA market in the country, we believe that the role of BAs as a financial source in countries with well-developed financial systems is getting *increasingly niched*. For example, due to extensive public support, expanding supply of alternative sources of funding, and increased availability of (and a strong preference for) soft money in early development stages, there are reasons to believe that BAs need to find their niches in the market. Thus, the general importance of obtaining BA finance to get through the "valley of death", i.e., the negative cash-flow in initial stages of firm development, has diminished somewhat over the last 10–15 years and is likely to continue to do so. This is especially valid in the seed stages, where BAs have to some extent been crowded out by public and alternative finance. The niche where BAs still are likely to play a major role going forward is primarily in sectors that require significant specialized competence, and, at least moderately, capital-intensive scale-up processes, where particularly angel groups are important players – often in collaboration with public sector investors. Some examples of such sectors include artificial intelligence (AI)/machine learning, digital health and fintech.

Following this line of argumentation, we also believe that the value creation to the business in which BAs invest may have changed, towards a more intense, formalized, and specialized role in business development. For example, we find more and more BAs involved in different kinds of accelerator activities. Thus, in this new landscape and in future research, it becomes important to elaborate on the characteristics and process of value that BAs provide to the businesses in which they invest.

Situational aspects of value creation – do BAs have a role at critical points of economic and societal development?

From the *situational* perspective, the current knowledge is rather limited, and the results of current studies are incoherent. With regards to the role of business angels in economic downturns, the few studies that had looked at BA investment in post-crisis years (Avdeitchikova, 2008; Mason and Harrison, 2015; Bilau et al., 2017; and British Business Bank, 2020) have pointed out a relatively high investment activity by BAs, especially compared to the slow bounce-back of formal venture capital. One of the possible reasons for that is that BAs have broader investment portfolios than venture capital funds, investing in assets such as real estate and the stock market. Thus, when other assets recover after economic crises, BAs can free up equity to invest in unquoted firms. From the situational perspective, this would indicate that BAs may have a role in strengthening resilience of the economies by providing risk capital in financial downturns, or at least early on in the recovery processes.

With regards to the role of business angels at critical points of societal development, such as much-needed technological transitions in such spheres as mobility, energy and healthcare systems, the evidence of BAs being in the forefront is rather scarce. On the contrary, studies that have looked at BA investments in clean technology show that historically, business angels have been reluctant to move into this sector, due to high technological uncertainty and unstable institutional environment, such as taxes, government support schemes and regulations (e.g., Isaksson, 2016). The same could be observed in the life science sector, that BAs mostly "stayed away from", at least until early 2010s (ERC, 2015). The limited evidence that exists indicates that the vast majority of BAs much more often follow rather than lead, when it comes to technological transitions.

However, this is not to say that all BAs are technologically conservative. We do believe that a portion of BAs might well be heavily involved in technological changing activities, for example, by identifying high potential sectors, getting involved in accelerator programs, and catalyzing follow-on funding to emerging sectors. Thus, there is an obvious need for research that elaborate on BAs' role in societal and technological changes. Below, we formulate some areas for further research with a focus on the situational aspects of BA value creation.

Has the scope of BA investing changed?

This question, that is indeed key to understanding the significance of BAs as a source of risk finance, is notoriously hard to answer. In the UK, the British Business Bank is conducting an annual study on BA activity, using data from two tax schemes that the UK government offers to UK taxpayers for their equity investment in higher-risk early-stage start-ups and small companies, Enterprise Investment Scheme (EIS) and Seed Enterprise Investment Scheme (SEIS). The data shows that between 2012 and 2019, angel investing grew by about 60%, from £1.2B in 2012 to just over £1.9B in 2019. The period, however, likely includes the post-financial crisis bounce-back, as the highest growth appeared in the period between 2012 and 2015, whereafter the development has stagnated. Also, the SEIS tax scheme was introduced in 2012, and has likely contributed to increased visibility of angel investment in the seed stage.

In the US, the annual data has been gathered from at least early 2000s by the Center for Venture Research, based on extrapolation from the "visible market". Looking at the same time period, the market has remained rather stable, from $22.9B in 2012 to $23.9B in 2019. Before that period, there are notable downturns around the IT and the financial crises, with a bounce-back period of 2–3 years. Thus, based on the available data, there is no clear trend in terms of the scope of BA investing in these countries, while there is some notable cyclicity.

The studies that attempt to estimate the scope of BA investing are few and have severe methodological limitations. Most of the estimates available are based on extrapolations of data from the "visible market" (BAs who are organized in networks, angel groups and syndicates), which poses two challenges. First, the extent of organization of BAs is difficult to know and verify. What we do know is that it varies over time and in different national contexts. The estimates of the investment volumes are therefore very sensitive to the assumptions about the level of organization of the market. The second challenge is that we know rather little about BAs who are not organized. Thus, data gathered from BAs who are organized in networks, angel groups and syndicates seem hardly representative of the "general population" of BAs in the country. Taken together, the data constraints limit both the quality and usefulness of such estimates.

Has the extensive public support crowded out angel investors?

Notably, both the financial crisis of 2008–2009 and the most recent COVID-related economic crisis have led to increase of the capitalization of the SME support system, including instruments that are particularly relevant for early-stage entrepreneurial ventures. For example, most OECD countries introduced or strengthened governmental loan guarantees as a direct policy response to the financial crisis. Further, a number of countries including Australia, Austria, UK, Denmark and Finland, increased the capital base of the governmental venture capital schemes, and an extra allocation was made from the European Commission to the EIB and EIF (OECD, 2009).

However, once the supply of public finance is increased, the funding is rarely retracted in the periods of financial stability – for bureaucratic, political or other reasons. This means that there is an increased volume of capital in the support system that is not necessarily matched by the appropriate volume of investable ventures. For instance, the European Court of Auditors (2016) report found that the disbursement rates of EU-funded innovation finance instruments under the 2007–2013 program was under 60%, indicating that several EU countries might be experiencing an oversupply of innovation finance to SMEs. While the public innovation schemes often are designed for the funding to be disbursed in collaboration between public and private partners, evidence shows that the SME finance systems may have become increasingly dependent on public participation.

System aspects of value creation – do BAs have a role in strengthening regional entrepreneurial ecosystems?

Already in late 1980s and early 1990s researchers raised the need to apply an ecosystem perspective to understand the emergence and growth of firms (Aldrich, 1990; Moore, 1993). The key argument was that businesses don't evolve in a 'vacuum', but rather in an embedded relationship with suppliers, users, financiers and human capital. The subsequent studies by Isenberg (2010), Feld (2012), Zacharakis et al. (2003), and Mason and Brown (2014) have contributed significantly to our understanding of the components of the entrepreneurial ecosystems, where both tangible dimensions (such as availability of a strong knowledge/research base) and non-tangible dimensions (such as success stories, societal norms and non-governmental institutions) were added to the model.

The main message of this literature to policymakers has been that fostering entrepreneurship – and particularly high-growth knowledge-based firms – requires investments in increasing the resources, functionality and dynamics of the system, which in turn acts as a supporting mechanism for high-growth entrepreneurship. Thus, understanding the system, its actors and dynamics is key for the design of effective support mechanisms. This is a very different perspective to the traditional entrepreneurship policy approaches, which most often are a combination of transactional measures (e.g., grants, subsidies, etc.) with attractive "framework conditions" (e.g., low taxes, stable regulations, and low administrative burdens) (Mason and Brown, 2014). One of the key features of entrepreneurial ecosystems is that they are *dynamic*, which means that they evolve over time and that actors can play multiple roles in the system (Alvedalen, 2021). Particularly, successful entrepreneurs are seen not only as output, but also as *input* to the system.

Looking at BA investing from the lens of entrepreneurial ecosystem provides a different perspective on the angels' role and contribution. We believe this perspective is more fruitful than focusing on the direct financial or non-financial contribution by angel investors to firms in which they invest, as illustrated in the review of business-level approach earlier in this chapter. From the system point of view, BAs can be seen as enablers of the development of the system, thus having a potential impact not only on the businesses that they invest in, but also on the strength and functionality of the entrepreneurial system itself.

There are several mechanisms for how BAs can contribute to the strength and functionality of entrepreneurial ecosystems – beyond the firm-level aspects of value-added – based on what we know about what BAs do and how they create value:[1]

- *Increasing capacity and professionalization of system actors.* BAs may contribute to spreading knowledge on entrepreneurial and investor practices through their contribution to regional incubators, accelerators, and case competitions.
- *Enhancing the attractiveness and visibility of the system.* An ecosystem with high level of BA investing is perceived as more attractive for start-ups with high growth ambitions, thus contributing to higher levels of entrepreneurial activity. Examples of successful investments also contribute to the visibility of the system, including towards international players.
- *Enhancing the connectedness of the system.* Based on BAs' experience and their business and social networks, we can assume that BAs may contribute significantly to the networking of the ecosystem, connecting firms to competence, customers, suppliers, investors and other partners within the ecosystem.

---

[1] Based on the taxonomy of entrepreneurial systems by Mason and Brown (2014).

- *Enhancing entrepreneurial orientation of the system.* A dynamic ecosystem with active and visible BAs will also enhance the entrepreneurial culture within the ecosystem, characterized by social norms and role models, etc., creating a virtuous cycle of entrepreneurial activities.

From the system aspect of value creation, we argue that BAs have become increasingly important in strengthening of entrepreneurial ecosystems. This is particularly relevant in the context of EU countries, where industrial policies have been emphasizing multi-core development, and investments in the regional infrastructure for entrepreneurship and high-growth firms have increased over the last 10–15 years. However, our knowledge of this value creation of BAs from a system perspective is virtually non-existent, which we believe is another fruitful path for further research.

Some concluding remarks

In this chapter, we have argued that the developments in entrepreneurial activities and the financial landscape over the past 10–15 years have induced an important shift in the role of BAs, which calls for revisiting what we know and believe about the value creation provided by BAs. We have reviewed the current literature in the field and concluded that our knowledge about BAs value creation so far has mainly been focused on the contributions that BAs provide to the individual business in which they invest, or what we call *business* aspects of value creation. While this knowledge is important, it is not sufficient to understand the contribution of BAs to the economy and society. Thus, we have proposed to reframe the discussion about the value creation of BAs to focus on additional two aspects of BAs potential contribution, namely *situational* value creation, that is, their role at critical points of economic and societal development, as well as their *system* value creation, that is, their role in strengthening regional entrepreneurial ecosystems.

Below, we suggest a number of areas that we believe to be particularly fruitful over the coming years for deepening our knowledge about the role of BAs in the new financial landscape. Those are:

- How has the role of BAs as early-stage risk finance providers evolved? In what settings has BA involvement become more (less) significant?
- How does BA investing interplay with public and alternative sources of early-stage risk finance? What does the new "funding escalator", or a variety of those, look like?
- What is the role of BAs at critical points of economic and societal development, specifically in economic downturns and in technological transitions? What are the key factors promoting (inhibiting) this involvement?

– What role do BAs play in strengthening regional entrepreneurial systems? What factors influence this value creation of BAs, and what policy instruments are likely to contribute to it?

References

Aldrich, H.E. (1990). Using an Ecological Perspective to Study Organizational Founding Rates. *Entrepreneurship Theory and Practice, 14*(3), 7–24.

Alvedalen, J. (2021). *Entrepreneurial Ecosystems in Life Science Industry: A study of start-ups, scale ups and resilience of Entrepreneurial Ecosystems* [Doctoral dissertation]. Sweden: Lund University.

Amatucci, F.M. (2016). Women business angels: theory and practice. In H. Landström & C. Mason (Eds.), *Handbook of Research on Business Angels* (pp. 92–111). Cheltenham: Edward Elgar.

Aram, J.D. (1987). *Informal Risk Capital in the Great Lakes Region*. Washington D.C.: Small Business Administration.

Ardichvili, A., Cardozo, R., & Ray, S. (2003). A theory of entrepreneurial opportunity identification and development. *Journal of Business Venturing, 18*(1), 105–123.

Avdeitchikova, S. (2008). *Close-ups from afar. The nature of the informal venture capital market in a spatial context* [Doctoral dissertation]. Sweden: Lund University.

Avdeitchikova, S. & Landström, H. (2016). The economic significance of business angels: toward comparable indicators. In H. Landström & C. Mason (Eds.), *Handbook of Research on Business Angels* (pp. 53–75). Cheltenham: Edward Elgar.

Avdeitchikova, S., Landström, H., & Månsson, N. (2008). What do we mean when we talk about business angels? Some reflections on definitions and sampling. *Venture Capital, 10*(4), 371–394.

Baker, T., & Nelson, R. E. (2005). Creating Something from Nothing: Resource Construction through Entrepreneurial Bricolage. *Administrative Science Quarterly, 50*(3), 329–366.

Bammes, Y., & Collewaert, V. (2014). Trust between entrepreneurs and angel investors: Exploring positive and negative implications for venture performance assessments. *Journal of Management, 40*(7), 1980–2008.

Benjamin, G., & Margulis, J. (2001). *The Angel Investor's Handbook: How to Profit from Early-Stage Investing*. Blomberg Press.

Bessière, V., Stephany, E., & Wirtz, P. (2018, May 31 – June 1). *Crowdfunding, Business Angels, and Venture Capital: New Funding Trajectories for Start-Ups?*. 2nd Emerging Trends in Entrepreneurial Finance Conference, Hoboken, NJ, United States. http://dx.doi.org/10.2139/ssrn.3137095

Bilau, J., Mason, C., & Botelho, T. (2017). Angel investing in an austerity economy. *European Planning Studies, 25*(9), 1516–1537.

Brettel, M. (2003). Business Angels in Germany. A Research Note. *Venture Capital, 5*(3), 251–268.

British Business Bank. (2020). *The UK Business Angel Market 2020*. https://ukbaa.org.uk/wp-content/uploads/2020/10/20201008-BBB-Business-Angels-Report-Final.pdf

Carpentier, C., & Suret, J-M. (2016). The effectiveness of tax incentives for business angels. In H. Landström & C. Mason (Eds.), *Handbook of Research on Business Angels* (pp. 327–353). Edward Elgar.

Conti, A., Thursby, M.C., & Rothaermel, F. (2011). *Show me the right stuff: signals for high tech startups*. NBER Working Paper 17050, Cambridge, MA.

EBAN. (2019). *EBAN Statistics Compendium 2019*. https://www.eban.org/wp-content/uploads/2020/12/EBAN-Statistics-Compendium-2019.pdf

Ehrlich, S.E., De Noble, T., Moore, T. & Weaver, R. (1994). After the cash arrives: a competitive study of venture capital and private investor involvement in entrepreneurial firms. *Journal of Business Venturing, 9*(1), 67–82.

Elitzur, R., & Gavious, A. (2003). Contracting, signaling, and moral hazard: A model of entrepreneurs, angels, and venture capitalists. *Journal of Business Venturing, 18*, 709–725.

ERC. (2015). *A nation of angels: Assessing the impact of angel investing across the UK.* https://centreforentrepreneurs.org/wp-content/uploads/2015/11/ERC_Nation_of_Angels_Full_Report.pdf

European Union. (2016). *Implementing the EU budget through financial instruments – lessons to be learnt from the 2007– 2013 programme period.* Special Report.

European Commission. (2020). *Access to finance for small and medium-sized enterprises since the financial crisis: evidence from survey data.* https://www.ecb.europa.eu/pub/economic-bulletin/articles/2020/html/ecb.ebart202004_02~80dcc6a564.en.html

Feld, B. (2012). *Startup Communities: Building Entrepreneurial Ecosystem in Your City.* Wiley.

Festel, G.W., & DeCleyn, S. H. (2013). Founding Angels as an Emerging Subtype of Angel Investment Model in High-Tech Businesses. *Venture Capital, 15*(3): 261–282.

Freear, J., Sohl, J.E. & Wetzel, W.E. (1995). Who Bankrolls Software Entrepreneurs. *Frontiers of Entrepreneurship Research*, 394–406.

Gaston, R.J. (1989). *Finding Private Venture Capital for Your Firms: A Complete Guide.* New York: Wiley.

Gaston, R.J., & Bell S.E. (1986). *Informal Risk Capital in the Sunbelt.* Washington D.C.: Small Business Administration.

Gifford, S. (1997). Limited attention and the role of the venture capitalist. *Journal of Business Venturing, 16*(6), 459–482.

Harrison, R.T., & Mason C.M. (1991). Informal venture capital in the UK and the USA: A comparison of investor characteristics, investment preferences and decision-making. *Frontiers of Entrepreneurship Research, 15*, 469–481.

Harrison, R. T., & Mason, C. M. (1992). International perspective on the supply of informal venture capital. *Journal of Business Venturing, 7*, 459–475.

Harrison, R.T., & Mason, C. M. (2007). Does Gender Matter? Women Business Angels and the Supply of Entrepreneurial Finance. *Entrepreneurship Theory and Practice, 31*(3), 445–472.

Harrison, R.T., & Mason, C. M. (2019). Venture Capital 20 years on: reflections on the evolution of a field. *Venture Capital, 21*(1), 1–34.

Hayton, K., Thom, G., Percy, V., Boyd, C. & Latimer, K., (2008). *Evaluation of the Scottish co-investment fund.* A Report to Scottish Enterprise. Glasgow: Hayton Consulting & GEN.

Hommel, K., & Bican, P. M. (2020). Digital Entrepreneurship in Finance: Fintechs and Funding Decision Criteria. *Sustainability, 12*(19), 8035.

Isaksson, A. (2016). Kommersialiseringsprocessen för företag inom miljöteknik och cleantech. Unpublished working paper. Chalmers University of Technology.

Isenberg, D.J. (2010). How to Start an Entrepreneurial Revolution. *Harvard Business Review*, June, 2–11.

Kelly, P. (2007). Business angel research: The road traveled and the journey ahead. In Landström, H. (Ed.). *Handbook of Research on Venture Capital* (pp. 315–331). Cheltenham: Edward Elgar.

Lahti, T., & Keinonen, H. (2016). Business angel networks: a review and assessment of their value to entrepreneurship. In H. Landström & C.M. Mason (Eds.). *Handbook of Research on Business Angels* (pp. 354–378). Cheltenham: Edward Elgar.

Landström, H. (1992). The relationship between private investors and small firms: An agency theory approach. *Entrepreneurship and Regional Development, 4*, 199–223.

Landström, H. (1993). Informal risk capital in Sweden and some international comparisons. *Journal of Business Venturing, 8,* 525–540.

Landström, H. (1995). A pilot study on the investment decision-making behavior of informal investors on Sweden. *Journal of Small Business Management, 33*(3), 67–76.

Landström, H. (1998). Informal Investors as Entrepreneurs. *Technovation, 18,* 321–333.

Landström, H. (Ed.). (2007). *Handbook of Research on Venture Capital.* Cheltenham: Edward Elgar.

Landström, H. (2017). *Advanced Introduction to Entrepreneurial Finance.* Cheltenham: Edward Elgar.

Landström, H. & Mason C.M. (2016a). Business angels as a research field. In H. Landström & C.M. Mason (Eds.). Handbook of Research on Business Angels (pp. 1–22). Cheltenham: Edward Elgar.

Landström, H. & Mason C.M. (Eds.) (2016b). *Handbook of Research on Business Angels.* Cheltenham: Edward Elgar.

Landström, H. & Olofsson, C. (1995). Informal Risk Capital in Sweden. In R.T. Harrison & C.M. Mason (Eds.). *Informal Venture Capital: Evaluating the Impact of Business Introduction Services.* London: Prentice Hall.

Landström, H., Parhankangas, A-L., & Mason, C. (2019). *Handbook of Research on Crowdfunding.* Cheltenham: Edward Elgar.

Lindström, G. & Olofsson, C. (2001). Affärsänglar och teknikbaserade tillväxtföretag [Business Angels and technology-based high-growth firms]. Stockholm: SNS Förlag.

Lumme, A., Mason, C.M., & Suomi, M. (1998). *Informal Venture Capital: Investors, Investment and Policy Issues in Finland.* Boston, MA: Kluwer.

Macht, S., & Robinson, J. (2009). Do business angels benefit their investee companies? *International Journal of Entrepreneurial Behaviour & Research, 15*(2), 187–208.

Madill, J., Haines, G. H., & Riding, A. L. (2005). The role of angels in technology SMEs. *Venture Capital, 7*(2), 107–129.

Mason, C.M. (2017, 20 June). *Financing the scale-up of the entrepreneurial businesses: beyond the funding escalator* [conference presentation], CEEDR/ISBE seminar on SME Finance, Middlesex University. https://www.mdx.ac.uk/__data/assets/pdf_file/0024/371922/Middlesex-June -2017-short-version.pdf

Mason, C. M. (2009). Public policy support for informal venture capital market: a critical review. *International Small Business Journal, 27*(5), 536–556.

Mason, C., & Brown, R. (2014). *Entrepreneurial ecosystems and growth-oriented entrepreneurship.* Report to OECD, Paris.

Mason, C.M., & Harrison, R.T. (1990). Informal Risk Capital: A Review and Research Agenda. Working Paper No 1. University of Southampton and University of Ulster.

Mason, C.M., & Harrison, R. T. (1992). The supply of equity finance in the U.K.: A strategy for closing the equity gap. *Entrepreneurship and Regional Development, 4,* 357–380.

Mason, C. M., & Harrison, R. T. (1997). Business angels in the UK: a response to Stevenson and Coveney. *International Small Business Journal, 15*(2), 83–90.

Mason, C.M. & Harrison, R.T. (1999). Public policy and the development of the informal venture capital market. In K. Cowling (ed), Industrial Policy in Europe (pp. 201–223). London: Routledge.

Mason, C. M., & Harrison, R. T. (2000). Influences on the supply of informal venture capital in the UK: an exploratory study of investor attitudes. *International Small Business Journal, 18*(4), 11–25.

Mason, C. M., & Harrison, R. T. (2002). Barriers to invest in informal venture capital sector. *Entrepreneurship and Regional Development, 14,* 271–287.

Mason, C. M., & Harrison R. T. (2008). Measuring business angel investment activity in the United Kingdom: a review of potential data sources. *Venture Capital, 10*(4), 309–330.

Mason, C. M., & Harrison, R. T. (2015). Business angel investment activity in the financial crises: UK evidence and policy implications. *Environment and Planning C: Government and Policy, 38*(1), 43–60.

Mason, C.M., & Rogers, A. (1997). Understanding the Business Angel's Investment Decision. Working Paper No. 14. Southampton University.

Mason, C.M., Harrison R.T., & Botelho, T. (2015). Business angel exists: Strategies and Processes. In J.G. Hussain & J.M. Scott (Eds.) *Research Handbook on Entrepreneurial Finance* (pp. 102–124). Cheltenham: Edward Elgar.

Maxwell, A. (2016). Investment decision-making by business angels. In H. Landström (Ed.) *Handbook of Research on Venture Capital* (pp. 115–146). Cheltenham: Edward Elgar.

Maxwell, A., Jeffrey, S. A., & Lévesque, M. (2011). Business Angels Early Stage Decision Making. *Journal of Business Venturing, 26*: 21–225.

Maxwell, A. L., & Lévesque, M. (2014). Trustworthiness: A Critical Ingredient for Entrepreneurs Seeking Investors. *Entrepreneurship Theory and Practice, 38*(5), 1057–1080.

Maxwell, A., Lévesque M., & Jeffrey S. (2014). The Non-Compensatory Relationship between Risk and Return in Business Angel Investment Decisions. *Academy of Management Proceedings* 1: 10463.

May, J., & Simmons, C. (2001). *Every Business Needs an Angel*. New York: Crown Business.

Mitteness, C., Sudek, R., & Cardon, M. S. (2012). Angel Investor Characteristics that Determine whether Perceived Passion Leads to Higher Evaluations of Funding Potential. *Journal of Business Venturing, 27*(5), 592–606.

Moore, J. (1993). Predators and Prey: A New Ecology of Competition, *Harvard Business Review*. May.

Månsson, N., & Landström, H. (2005). Business Angels in a Changing Economy: The Case of Sweden. *Venture Capital, 8*(4): 281–301.

OECD (2009). *The Impact of the Global Crisis on SME and Entrepreneurship Financing and Policy Responses*, https://www.oecd.org/industry/smes/49316499.pdf

Ou, C., 1987. Holding of Privately-held Business Assets by American Families. Washington, D.C.: Small Business Administration.

Parhankangas, A. L., & Ehrlich, M. (2014). How Entrepreneurs Seduce Business Angels: And Impression Management Approach. *Journal of Business Venturing, 29*(4), 543–564.

Politis, D. (2008). Business angels and value added: What do we know and where do we go? *Venture Capital, 10*(2), 127–147.

Politis, D. (2016). Business angels as smart investors: A systematic review of the evidence. In H. Landström & C. Mason (Eds.). *Handbook of Research on Business Angels* (pp. 147–175). Cheltenham: Edward Elgar.

Politis, D., & Landström, H. (2002). Informal Investors as Entrepreneurs – The Development of An Entrepreneurial Career. *Venture Capital, 4*(2): 78–101.

Riding, A., & Short, D. (1987). On the estimation of investment potential of informal investors: a capture/recapture approach. *Journal of Small Business and Entrepreneurship, 5*(4), 26–40.

Riding, A., Duxbury, L., & Haines, G. (1994). *Financing Enterprise Development: Decision-Making by Canadian Angels*. Ottawa: Carleton University.

Ries, E. (2011). *The Lean Startup*. New York: Crown Business.

Robb, A. M. & Robinson, D. T. (2014). The capital structure decisions of new firms. *Review of Financial Studies, 27*(1), 153–179.

Sætre, A. (2003). Entrepreneurial perspectives on informal venture capital. *Venture Capital, 5*(1), 71–94.

Shane, S.A. (2009). *Fools Gold? The Truth Behind Angel Investing in America*. New York: Oxford University Press.

Short, D. M., & Riding, A. L. (1988). On the estimation of the investment potential of informal investors. *Journal of Small Business and Entrepreneurship, 5*, 26–40.

Sohl, J. E. (2006). Angel investing: Changing strategies during volatile times. *Journal of Entrepreneurial Finance and Business Ventures, 11*(2), 27–47.

Sohl, J.E. (2007). The organization of the informal venture capital market. In H. Landström (Ed.) *Handbook of Research on Venture Capital* (pp. 347–370). Cheltenham: Edward Elgar.

Sohl, J.E. (2012). The changing nature of the angel market. In H. Landström & C.M. Mason (Eds.) *Handbook of Research on Venture Capital, Volume 2* (pp. 17–41). Cheltenham: Edward Elgar.

Sohl, J. E., & Hill, L. (2007). Women Business Angels: Insights from Angel Groups. *Venture Capital, 9* (3), 207–222.

Stevenson, H., & Coveney P. (1994). *Survey of business angels*. Henley: Venture Capital Report Ltd.

Storey, D.J., & Greene, F.J. (2010). *Small Business and Entrepreneurship*. Harlow: Pearson.

Sullivan, M. K., & Miller, A. (1996). Segmenting the informal venture capital market. *Journal of Business Research, 36*(1), 25–35.

Swedish Agency for Economic and Regional Growth (2021a). *Företagens villkor och verklighet 2020* [Fact sheet].

Swedish Agency for Economic and Regional Growth (2021b). *Utbudet av statligt capital: bidrag, lån och garantier samt riskkapital*. Unpublished report.

Sørheim, R. (2005). Business angels as facilitators for further finance: an exploratory study. *Journal of Small Business and Enterprise Development, 12*(2), 178–192.

Sørheim, R., & Landström H. (2001). Informal investors – a categorization with policy implications. *Entrepreneurship and Regional Development, 13*, 351–370.

Tymes, E., & Krasner, O. (1983). Informal Risk Capital in California. *Frontiers of Entrepreneurship Research*, pp. 347–368.

Van Osnabrugge, M., & Robinson, R.J. (2002). *Angel Investing: Matching Startup Funds with Startup Companies*. San Francisco, CA: Jossey-Bass.

Vo. D. (2013). *The Geography of Angel Investment* [Doctoral dissertation]. Canada: University of Victoria.

Wetzel, W.E. (1983). Angels and informal risk capital. *Sloan Management Review, 24*, 23–34.

Wetzel, W.E. (1986). Informal risk capital: Knowns and unknowns. In D. Sexton & R. Smilor (Eds.), The Art and Science of Entrepreneurship (pp. 85–108). Cambridge, MA: Ballinger.

Wetzel, W.E. (1987). The informal venture capital market: aspects of scale and market efficiency. *Journal of Business Venturing, 2*(4), 299–313.

Wiltbank, R.E. (2009). *Siding with the Angels: Business Angel Investing – Promising Outcomes and Effective Strategies*. London: NESTA.

Wong, A., Bhatia, M. & Freeman, Z. (2009). Angel finance: the other venture capital. Strategic Change, 18(7-8), 221–230.

Zacharakis, A.L., Shepherd, D.A., & Coombs, J.E. (2003). The development of venture capital backed internet companies: An ecosystem perspective. *Journal of Business Venturing, 18*, 217–231.

Judit Karsai

13 Government financing of startups

Abstract: Governments play a significant role in financing startups at all stages of their development. Contrary to popular belief, the vast majority of startup financing is not provided by venture capital, but by grants and lending, for which public guarantees offer support. In the case of venture capital investments, the most effective way of government support is to co-invest with private investors and leverage the capital of private funds, rather than investing directly in startups. Government guarantees available to private investors of venture capital funds can also contribute to a significant increase in the volume of venture capital financing startups. Experience has shown that the most effective way for the government to finance startups is not by providing funds directly to companies, but by acting as a catalyst for funding by encouraging private players in the market. The analysis below illustrates which of the many solutions developed worldwide to provide government support have spread in practice and with what success.

Keywords: startup, government support, loan finance, venture capital, business angel

Introduction

Startups are young, often innovative businesses with high growth potential that want to enter the market with new products or services. At the same time, they are often characterized by scalability and disruptiveness. While their growth potential is high, so is their mortality rate. For this reason, their financing involves high uncertainty which traditional financing instruments are unable to address. Startups often require considerable amounts of funding for their rapid development, which they are not yet able to raise from internal sources in the early stages of their development. Given that the emergence and breakthrough market success of promising startups has significant economic development effects, both directly and through externalities, in terms of contributing to GDP and creating new jobs and promoting the development of the local economy, it is in the interest of economic policy that these companies receive government support for their development.

Acknowledgements: This study has been implemented with support provided from the National Research, Development and Innovation Fund of Hungary, financed under the K-18 funding scheme, Project no. K 128682.

Judit Karsai, Institute of Economics, Centre for Economic and Regional Studies (KRTK)

https://doi.org/10.1515/9783110726312-017

Government financial assistance to startups can take two major forms. First, this assistance can be provided by granting budget support directly. Second, governments can forego tax and return revenues and thus encourage market players to provide financing; governments can take over part of the risk in order to increase the supply of business funds. Third, governments can regulate the function of the market in ways that are beneficial for startups (Gampfer et al., 2016; OECD, 2018).

Relatively little is known about the effectiveness and efficiency of government assistance to startups in its many forms. Governments find it difficult to select the "right" startups to support, that is, to define the target group itself, as this requires predicting ex-ante which of the many promising startups will be able to grow quickly and which will be the most successful. This is more apparent in hindsight, but what is not clear is what would have happened to the startups who had received financial support in the absence of government involvement (Greene & Rosiello, 2020).

Government support should be able to adapt to the different development phases of startups. For example, in the seed stage, non-reimbursable public grants can be provided for research and development to develop prototypes, and startups can be supported by coaching and mentoring services to help them further develop. For early-stage startups, business angels can be encouraged to take risks and make it easier to reach investable startups. The market expansion of young companies that already have new products and services can be facilitated by the government by increasing the supply of funds to venture capitalists (OECD, 2015). This can be done by investing public venture capital directly in startups, or by attracting co-investment from market players, as well as through private fund of funds. In the case of startups that already have significant revenues, the government can facilitate the use of bank loans by providing guarantees linked to the granting of loans and can also promote the use of so-called hybrid instruments that do not lead to a dilution of the ownership structure of startups (Flachenecker et al., 2020; Mason, 2020).

Bai et al. (2021) assembled the first comprehensive and detailed data on the universe of government funding programs of entrepreneurial ventures around the world active between 1995 and 2019 (755 programs in 66 countries). They illustrated the different types of financial instruments employed by governments. The most prevalent type of government instrument was grants, accounting for 44% of all programs. The second most popular financing form was equity funding, accounting for 18%. But governments utilize a host of other types of financial instruments, ranging from credit guarantees and loans, to innovation vouchers and tax credits. When accounting for the size of the programs, tax credits and government loans were more widespread, partially because they tended to be utilized by later-stage and larger companies.

The line of thought for this chapter is as follows. The analysis first addresses the issue of non-reimbursable public grants and tax incentives in the research and development phase. It then reviews government instruments to encourage investment by business angels, which play a key role in financing startups, and to facilitate their availability to startups. The chapter then analyzes the possibilities and actual practices of public participation in the field of institutional venture capital investments. The chapter next provides an overview of the instruments to facilitate debt financing. The analysis presents several examples of financing solutions in practice. The chapter concludes with a discussion of the growing importance of government support in times of crisis and general findings on government participation in startup financing.

Literature review

Government support to promote research and development

There is a wide range of possibilities for government funding to support early-stage companies with rapid growth potential. They can receive grants to cover part of the funding of R&D and innovation processes. They can benefit from soft loans, which also aim to stimulate innovative activities through more favorable market conditions, which can take the form of lower interest rates, lengthened maturities or lower collateral requirements. Finally, companies can deduct some of the costs related to R&D and innovation from their taxes, that is, they can benefit from government tax relief in this way.

The US Small Business Innovation Research (SBIR) support program has served as a model for central support for innovation-driven development in many countries. According to evaluations, the first phase of the SBIR program, which provided small amounts of support, had a very positive impact on awarded technology companies, as it doubled the likelihood of companies accessing venture capital and promoted patents and business revenue growth (Howell, 2017). However, the bulk of the funding is related to the second, much larger volume of the SBIR program, the evaluation of which is far from positive. Experience shows that a relatively small number of companies received a disproportionate number of grants, and serious lobbying was underway to win tenders for a returning group of participants. The experience of the SBIR program underscores the importance of proper design of support programs, the need for careful evaluation, and the readiness to prepare for program restructuring (Howell, 2017; Lerner, 1999; Lerner & Nanda, 2020).

Evaluations of non-reimbursable public grants mostly confirm that this form of support promotes the growth of companies, has a positive impact on R&D expenditure, performance growth and employment (Colombo et al., 2013; Dvouletý et al., 2021; Grilli & Murtinu (2012); Hottenrott & Richstein, 2020). At the same time, Muraközy and Telegdy (2020) found that the innovation impact of non-reimbursable public grants was weak.

Programs tailored to young innovative firms include tax incentives and reductions in social security spending for young firms that demonstrate an innovation focus. The size of the discounts is usually linked to the size of R&D expenditure. Over the past decade, tax incentives for R&D activities have become a key instrument for supporting R&D in many OECD countries (OECD, 2020). The rationale behind these programs is that it is not easy to deal with a lack of financing in the first years of a company's development, and tax relief can help young companies to increase cash flow during their development period, thus facilitating the next stage of development.

The different types of support granted during the development period for young companies should not be seen as an alternative but as interlinked elements of support policy. In such an approach grants and preferential loans can be managed together, as they together can reduce the burden on founders and accelerate the process leading to growth capital. A recent analysis of the two policy instruments together did not support the view that government support would crowd out private investors, and funding through a government support program is more likely to precede subsequent investments and facilitate access to venture capital (Hottenrott & Richstein, 2020). A similar approach is reflected in the European Innovation Council's EIC Accelerator program, launched in the spring of 2021 by the European Union. This initiative aims to attract new investors to broaden the scope of innovations by providing both grants and direct equity investments to startups that are selected through a rigorous selection process.

Overall, the provision of government assistance to early-stage companies to reduce financial constraints has become a popular policy tool, with some form of support scheme in almost all developed countries. However, surveys on government support to startups, including scaleups, are rare.

Government incentives for business angels to invest

Business angels typically invest in startup companies. The government can use several means to encourage business angels. On the one hand, it can make the capital investment of business angels cheaper by reducing the tax burden on business angels depending on the amount of the investment, or by allowing it to be postponed or even offset against loss-making investments. It is also possible that business angels will receive a tax deduction on their capital gains from successful investments. On the other hand, the government can also facilitate the matching of investors and those seeking capital investment, as well as the more organized cooperation and exchange of experience between business angels. In practice, the latter assistance is provided through public contributions to the establishment and operation of business angel networks. A third tool to help business angels invest is the creation and operation of public co-investment venture capital funds. These government-funded co-investment funds invest alongside business angels. They support angel investors by sharing risks and enabling them to achieve greater portfolio diversification

(Mason, 2020). The combined investment of private and public resources increases the gains available to both parties through economies of scale. To further encourage co-investment, business angels may receive a higher share of the return on the investment than their investment ratio, or they may have to cover a smaller share of the loss. (Co-investment venture capital funds are discussed in more detail in the next chapter.) The choice between a wide range of public instruments to encourage business angels to invest is mainly determined by the degree of development of the capital markets in each country.

The Enterprise Investment Scheme (EIS) and the Seed Enterprise Investment Scheme (SEIS) are two of the best-known and most generous tax relief schemes in the UK, offering 30 per cent tax relief on investments in businesses registered with the scheme (among many other tax benefits). Investors (individuals and business angels as well) are eligible for tax incentives if they invest directly or through special professional equity funds (EIS Fund or Venture Capital Trust, VCT) in companies that are registered in the scheme. Evaluations show that for every GBP1 invested, the government gets GBP4 back in tax revenue, and for every GBP1 million invested, 9 jobs are created (Dimitriu, 2020).

The most common form of tax incentive is the so-called front-end method, which reduces investment costs. The so-called back-end solution, on the other hand, offers a reduced tax rate on the return generated by the investment. The latter increases the return on successful transactions but does not give a discount to investors who suffer losses. A third solution makes it possible to deduct capital losses from the normal income of investors. Loss insurance schemes also occur in some countries. It is also possible to apply different discounts simultaneously.

There is little analyses of programs that use government funds to encourage business angel investments. However, surveys show that business angels would invest a significant part of their capital, up to 40–50 per cent, without incentives. In addition, highly skilled business angels make up a large proportion of the recipients of the discounts, although they are not the main target groups for the discounts. It is also not known whether tax incentives have a significant and lasting impact on employment, growth and productivity. The long-term effects of the programs have not yet been studied. Researchers suggest that the most advantageous incentives link discounts to yield developments and are also less costly than cost-cutting incentive modalities (Carpentier & Suret, 2014). Although the preferential tax rate applicable to capital gains increases the after-tax rate of return of successful investors, it provides nothing to investors who sustain a loss. The use of tax incentives to encourage the investment of individual business angels is also somewhat at odds with the fact that business angels increasingly decide collectively on their investments in more advanced markets. In addition, business angel groups are increasingly investing in public co-investment funds, and this scheme has become a major form of business angel investment support (Bileau et. al., 2017; Growth analysis, 2013; Harrison, 2018; Owen & Mason, 2016).

Another initiative that has become popular among policy makers worldwide is the promotion of Business Angel Networks (BANs). The role of networks includes matchmaking between business angel investors and entrepreneurs, filling the information gap, and creating links between business angels who want to invest and other actors in the local ecosystem (European Commission, 2002). In addition, the networks provide additional knowledge and support from experienced business angels to help other members of the network, provide practical training for angels, and generate transactions.

In Europe (with the exception of the UK), business angel networks are more widespread than in the Anglo-Saxon countries, but the success and investment activity of these organizations varies widely (Wilson & Silva, 2013). Lahti and Keinonen (2016) argue that there is no clear answer to the question of whether there is a need for public sector intervention to support the creation and operation of business angel networks.

At the same time, successful European networks are increasingly similar to business angel groups, where the involvement of business angel investors in group investments is essential and the role of the network is more limited. The weight of public involvement is diminishing as market forces take over the role of the government and the private sector becomes able and willing to finance services.

Government participation in the venture capital market

In the venture capital market, public intervention seeks to solve problems arising from market failure in the form of equity gaps in the financing of seed and early stage enterprises (Leleux & Surlemont, 2003). On the other hand, government intervention seeks to achieve social and national strategic interests that go beyond financial returns. These objectives include creating jobs and promoting economic growth in specific regions or sectors (Lerner, 2009; Murray et al., 2012).

The key role played by venture capital is not contradicted by the low incidence rate. Although venture capital-backed companies account for a small proportion of startups, some of them can be a breakthrough success. In the homeland of venture capital, the United States, the narrow range and significant impact of companies selected by venture capital is well illustrated by the fact that while between 1979 and 2013 only 0.1 per cent of startups received venture capital, 43 per cent of listed companies were venture capital-funded companies (OECD, 2018).

There are a number of reservations about government involvement in the venture capital market. This is partly due to questioning the expertise, objectivity and motivation required to properly select and raise companies and the possibility of crowding out private resources (Colombo et al., 2016). This is because the effectiveness of government intervention, including its impact on the companies that access finance, varies greatly depending on the mechanism through which government funds reach companies: directly or in partnership with private venture capitalists. Two basic requirements for avoiding negative impacts are the independence of governing and managing bodies from political actors and the high level of co-financing required from private investors (Bai et al., 2021; Lerner, 2020).

Among the public instruments promoting the functioning of the venture capital market less emphasis is placed on guaranteeing investments, and the supply of resources from the government budget dominates the market.

Government guarantee for venture capital investments

There are two basic types of guarantee schemes for equity investments. In one case, the guarantee is given for the loss realized by the venture capital fund on the investment, whereas in the other case the guarantee is given to the investors of the venture capital funds.

In the first case, fund managers can reclaim a certain proportion of their losses. This scheme has been experimented with in many countries in the past, with a typical guarantee for 50 per cent of the losses. The first known guarantee scheme that went wrong was the German WFG scheme (Gilson, 2003). Failures included both extensive government guarantees for losses and inadequate incentives for investors to actively participate in nascent businesses (Flachenecker et al., 2020). Such a scheme has been used in several other European countries. Experience has shown that the cost of guaranteeing projects exceeded the benefits of the programs (Avnimelech & Teubal, 2006; Gilson, 2003) and that such programs were therefore abolished in almost all the countries concerned.

Subsequently, the European Union planned to introduce guarantee schemes for fund investors rather than a guarantee scheme for capital investments, similar to those schemes already in place in the United States (Aernoudt, 2019). The government then only participates in the selection of private venture capital funds whose investors it guarantees. This solution was developed in the United States as part of the Small Business Investment Company (SBIC) program, introduced in 1958, which still operates today (Lerner, 2009). SBICs are privately owned, privately managed, for-profit funds, whose investments are partly made using the capital of their own investors and partly using additional resources which they receive at a favorable interest rate thanks to the guarantee provided by the Small Investment Administration (SBA). SBICs can raise capital on favorable terms on the public capital market by using the SBA guarantee when selling guaranteed securities on the market (Aernoudt, 2017).

In Europe, where risk aversion is much higher than in the US (Gampfer et al., 2016; Standaert, 2019), other types of public equity schemes based on direct or indirect capital investment by the government have long been set up to improve the availability of venture capital (Standaert, 2019). These investment schemes could not resolve the equity gap needed to scale up rapidly developing, promising, and innovative companies (Aernoudt, 2017). That is why, sixty years after the introduction of SBIC, a program with a similar spirit called European Scale-Up Action for Risk Capital (ESCALAR) was introduced in Europe. In fact, the ESCALAR mechanism contributes to investments in companies by mobilizing risk-averse private investors (such as pension funds or insurers) by guaranteeing investments in funds (Aernoudt, 2019).

An important common lesson from the SBIC and ESCALAR programs is that for risk capital linked guarantees to work effectively, the guarantee should be applied at the time of raising capital, rather than at the project level when capital is invested. The ratio of unguaranteed to guaranteed investors should be fixed in advance. Furthermore, only effectively managed funds should be allowed into the system after pre-screening. Representatives of the government should be kept away from the boards of the funds and decision-making at project level (Aernoudt, 2019).

Government resources in venture capital investments

As a venture capital investor, a government can play three main roles depending on its activity (Standaert, 2019). In the first case, public fund managers decide on the companies to be included in the portfolio, then carry out activities to increase their added value and monitor the development of the companies. For example, this is how the community development venture capital (CDVC) funds work in the United States, or the funds financed by the Business Development Bank in Canada, or the public capital funds financed by the Hungarian Development Bank in Hungary. Such fund management was also characteristic of the Swedish Almi Invest and the Danish Voekstfunden at the start. This role has now typically disappeared or been greatly reduced.

In the second case, the government invests in a syndicated manner with private venture capital investors. Public venture capitalists then base their investments on the activities of private investors, entrusting them with the selection and upbringing of companies. One of the basic models of co-investment funds was the Scottish Co-Investment Fund (SCF), established in 2003, which invested capital together with business angel syndicates and venture capital funds. The investing partners of the government carried out a preliminary screening of the companies, negotiated the terms of the investment and pledged the capital. The government fund only automatically added its share if the deal met the requirements. Such co-investment funds were set up by the French BPI, the German KfW, the Finnish SITRA, the Spanish Axis Participiones and the UK Innovation Investment Fund in the UK.

In the third case, in the fund-of-funds scheme, public venture capitalists participate only in the selection of private venture capital funds in which they invest capital. This solution was used in the Small Business Investment Company (SBIC) program (Lerner, 2009). A similar scheme was applied to the Israeli Yozma program, the European Investment Fund (EIF) and the British Enterprise Capital Funds (ECF) (Standaert and Manigart, 2018). Examples of public participation as a fund-of-funds (FoF) include the Norwegian Argentum Fondsinvesteringer AS, the early Korea Fund of Funds (KfoF), the Turkish Istanbul Venture Capital Initiative (iVCi), or the Multilateral Investment Fund (MIF), which finances Latin American funds, and the Dutch Venture Initiative in the Netherlands.

To attract private investors, the government applies a profit-sharing structure that increases the expected return for private investors in private funds. For example, for both SBIC and ECF programs, the return of private fund investors is increased by providing commitments in the form of interest-bearing loans/bonds. In continental Europe, on the other hand, public investors invest pari passu in funds as private investors, as required by European legislation prohibiting government support, limiting the opportunity to attract private investors (Aernoudt, 2017). An exception is when investments are made in economically underdeveloped areas or at the earliest stages of company development. In this case, private investors may receive a higher proportion of returns than they are entitled to on the basis of their investment rate or bear a smaller proportion of losses (cf. Karsai, 2018).

The impact of government venture capital investments can be assessed in two ways (Standaert, 2019). On the one hand, it is possible to examine the impact of public participation on the venture capital market itself and, on the other hand, how its presence affects the companies that have received financing. In the former case, it is expedient to analyze the crowding-out of private capital, and in the latter the impact on innovation, company growth, added value and investor exit. A well-known example of crowding-out is the Canadian LSVCC scheme, where tax relief for small investors in public equity funds led to crowding-out of private capital (Colombo et al., 2016). Another negative example is the Government Guidance Fund initiative launched in China, in which the government expected co-investment from non-private sector participants, that is, municipal or provincial government levels, or large state-owned companies. However, this has greatly degraded the quality of market information obtained from co-investors (Lerner, 2020). A positive example, however, is the Israeli Yozma program, which provided the funds with additional incentives and buy-back opportunities when they achieved positive returns.

The analysis of public investment schemes provides answers both to the characteristics of the companies selected for investment and to the impact of public investment on the post-investment performance of the selected companies. When fund managers, who are the sole investors of public capital, decide on the companies to be selected, public capital is typically allocated to sectors and geographic areas that are less popular with private investors (Bertoni et al., 2015; Kovner & Lerner, 2015). Larger, later-stage and foreign companies are less favored by public funds, which prefer to invest in local companies. Investments syndicated with private investors and companies selected by funds of funds are more similar to the portfolio of exclusive public funds in terms of their life stage and geographical location (Bertoni et al., 2017). Where the share of public funds of funds was higher, less risky companies were included in the funds' portfolios, bankruptcies were less likely to occur, while the proportion of companies promising new and unique technologies was higher among portfolio companies (Knockaert et al., 2010).

Funds funded exclusively by the government are less involved in creating added value than private funds because their incentive system does not encourage them to do so. They have to deal with many more companies at the same time than their private counterparts, thus dividing their attention (Jaaskelainen et al., 2006; Knockaert et al., 2006). Public funds are also not under the constant pressure on private funds to raise new funds. Thus, they do not have to constantly prove their competence in order to be able to attract new investors when setting up new funds after fixed-term funds (Gompers, 1996). Public funds are motivated by social or perceived utility rather than by the pursuit of a financial outcome (Manigart et al., 2002). Research has failed to show positive effects as a result of exclusive public investments, and in some cases they showed even negative effects, in terms of an increase in the number of employees in portfolio companies (Grilli & Murtinu, 2014), an increase in sales (Grilli & Murtinu, 2014, 2015), operational efficiency (Alperovych et al., 2015), patent filing (Bertoni & Tykvová, 2015) and the likelihood of exits (IPO and sale to professional investors) (Cumming et al., 2017). In Europe, the portfolio companies of sovereign public funds were less likely to receive another capital injection in the next phase of their development than their counterparts included in the portfolio of independent fund managers (Vanackert et al., 2014).

In the case of syndicated public funds, the impact on companies was overwhelmingly positive, with better results compared to companies assisted solely by private investors in several respects, including revenue growth (Grilli & Murtinu, 2014, 2015), patent filing (Bertoni & Tykvová, 2015), or the likelihood of exits (Brander et al., 2015; Cumming et al., 2017). The better performance was partly due to the higher amount of investable capital raised through syndication (Brander et al., 2015; Grilli & Murtinu, 2014). The only exception was China, where syndicated public funds did not achieve better results (Zhang, 2018). The supervision of government venture capitalists by a government agency in China increased the potential costs of coordination due to the annual evaluation of government venture capitalists' performance and a daily supervision of their investment process.

Private funds financed at a higher rate by public fund-of-funds behaved as more patient investors, their companies remained longer in the portfolio of funds, which was more favorable to achieving social goals, but had a negative impact on financial returns (Buzzacchi et al., 2013). Companies financed in this way were less likely to be successful after exits (IPOs or acquisitions) (Brander et al., 2015). The only time when the government achieved better outcomes in terms of exit values was when public capital was invested in private funds (Cumming et al., 2016).

Recent research (Alperovych et al., 2020) found that government venture capital funds are less able to close the equity gap in the venture capital market if the target companies are older and are located in a more economically backward area, and if the targets are selected locally. The negative impact will be more pronounced if both equity funds and companies are located in less developed areas, especially in countries where corruption is strong. Investing in a syndicated way with private equity investors, however, improves the chances of closing the equity gap. The expertise of public funds is explicitly improving in the sector-specific area and syndication is increasing the experience of investors. In light of this, researchers recommend that investments by government capital funds should not be limited to local investments, especially in underdeveloped regions, which reduces the possibility of attracting private investors that are not available locally. Local public investors are more likely to be exposed to collusion and inefficient investments (Bertoni & Quas, 2016, Liben-Nowell et al., 2005). That is, while distance has a negative impact on private venture capital investments (Cumming & Dai, 2010), it is beneficial for public venture capital. Another suggestion from researchers is that public venture capitalists should, whenever possible, invest in syndication with their private counterparts. This makes it possible to achieve better performance (Bertoni & Tykvová, 2015; Cumming et al., 2017).

Government participation in the credit market

For innovative young firms, commercializing unproven technologies, external debt is widely viewed as an unlikely way to fund their risky projects in the absence of tangible assets or stable cash flows to secure the loan (Hall & Lerner, 2010). They are very likely to face credit constraints because of their limited availability of collateral assets to secure borrowing and their informational opacity due to the limited financial track records, which prevents banks from evaluating their creditworthiness (Berger & Udell, 1990). Information asymmetries are particularly acute in this setting, exacerbating frictions between lenders and debtors (Leleand & Pyle, 1977; Stiglitz & Weiss, 1981). Fast-growing companies are more likely to receive higher loan rates than typical small and medium-sized enterprises (Rostamkalaei & Freel, 2016). This either indicates that these companies are more risky for banks, or reflects the fact that fast-growing companies prefer to opt for more expensive loans over equity financing in order to retain their ownership stake (Brown et al., 2017). According to a report by the European Commission (European Commission, 2016), 71 per cent of European startups identified access to finance as the most significant barrier to becoming a scaleup.

The difficulties faced by small firms, especially startups, in accessing credit have called for deeper reflection by policy makers, who have introduced different types of government programs to help these firms gain access to credit lines and loans that would otherwise be unavailable to them (Cowling, 2010; Cowling & Siepel, 2013; Marti & Quas, 2017; Ughetto et al., 2017). These public intervention programs include direct governmental credit subsidization programs, loan guarantee programs that supply government guarantees to banks, as well as programs providing hybrid finance. While direct governmental subsidization programs have rarely achieved the expected success (Zia, 2008), loan guarantee programs have been mostly successful in terms of SMEs while there is no evidence on startups (Flachenecker 2020; Ughetto et al., 2017). In recent years governments have been also stepping up efforts to address startups' growth capital gaps. For instance, the European Union, in the framework of the Programme for the Competitiveness of Enterprises and Small and Medium-sized Enterprises (COSME) supported the startups' growth through mezzanine finance funds (OECD, 2018).

Government guarantee for loans

Loan guarantees have become the most common form of government support in the credit market. The guarantee does not reduce the risk of lending, it only reduces the loss given default (LGD) for the guaranteed party in the event of a loan default. In other words, it shares the risk of lending by the guarantor reimbursing a predetermined part of the unpaid loan.

These public intervention programs differ worldwide in their pricing; risk assessment and risk management practices, in the role played by government; in the lending criteria; in the proportion of the total loan which is guaranteed; in the distribution of losses between the lender and the guarantor in case of default; and in the restrictions which typically concern the sector, type of business, or geographic area of reference (Beck et al., 2010; Honohan, 2010; Ughetto et al., 2017).

Numerous loan guarantee programs have been successfully introduced in many developed and developing countries (Beck et al., 2010; Bochi et al., 2014; Cowling & Mitchell, 2003; Honohan, 2010). Government guarantees have an overall positive impact on the growth and performance of beneficiaries (Bertoni et al., 2017). The provision of guarantees also affects the cost of lending, since if the risk of the loan is reduced, the price of the loan will generally also be lower (Ughetto et al., 2017). Most countries in the European Union have loan guarantee schemes targeting startups. The guarantee facility is also included in the 2021–2027 programming period of the EUInvest program. Guarantee programs are also financed by individual regions under the EU structural framework.

Whereas evaluations show that guarantees are very successful in leveraging private loans, there is no evidence of positive economic impact specifically on high growth innovative startups. This is, however, also because most evaluations of guarantees do not assess this question (Flachenecker et al., 2020). For the loan guarantee scheme to work effectively, a number of conditions must be met. First of all, guarantee provision should not be applied at project level. For particularly risky sub-markets such as startups, a higher coverage ratio or a longer grace period should be set.

Government assistance for hybrid finance

Hybrid instruments, such as subordinated loans or bonds, participant loans, silent partnerships, convertible loans or warrants, and mezzanine financing, combine the features of equity and debt in a single financing instrument, while having the characteristics of both (OECD, 2015). They differ from loans in that their providers take on a larger share of the risk/return sharing and are therefore more expensive for the companies to use than debt alone. At the same time, the risk and expected return are lower compared to equity. In the event of insolvency, investors in hybrid assets are ranked lower in the order of priority of claims compared to other creditors, but higher than ordinary shareholders.

Hybrid instruments are a particularly attractive form for startups approaching a turning point in their life cycle. This financing is suitable for companies that need a capital injection but cannot further increase their leverage, are not yet ready for an IPO, or the owners do not want to further transfer control of their company. However, the profitability and market position of the company using the hybrid instrument must be sufficiently stable to support debt service payments. Financing with hybrid instruments is typical of developed capital markets, but public participation is relatively low.

Hybrid instruments were particularly widespread in the field of mezzanine financing. Public participation can be achieved either through programs run by public agencies set up for this purpose or indirectly through public financing of private mezzanine funds, either directly or through a fund-of-funds. At the national level, such schemes include the Development Contract introduced by the OSEO in France and the AWS Guarantees for Mezzanine Investment guarantee scheme in Austria.

Future research agenda

Although there has been a recent wave of research on government intervention in startup financing, future research is still needed to improve our understanding of the consequences, and therefore the effectiveness, of government initiatives on the long run. There is also limited research on joint use of government financing types as it is unclear whether different types are substitutes or complements for each other. However, the availability of data presents a clear constraint for progress in government programs' evaluation (Botelho et al., 2021). The most significant challenge for empirical research is the ability to produce data covering representative samples of startups, more precisely the inability to clearly distinguish startups among SMEs in the data sources. Notwithstanding, a better understanding the role that public funding can play in startup finance will be helpful not only for startups but also for policy makers designing these programs.

Conclusion

Governments interested in promoting economic development seek to use a number of means to help finance companies that are important for economic growth to be attractive to market participants. This chapter examined the market-conforming solutions the government can use to facilitate the financing of startups. When the development of these companies is also hampered by an economic crisis, the need for government involvement becomes even stronger (Mason, 2020). While state guarantees for bank loans can already help a wide range of companies in difficulty as a result of the crisis, other types of government support may also be required for extremely risky but promising young companies that are rarely in possession of the necessary conditions for obtaining bank loans. These include, inter alia, 1) wider use of capital schemes linking public capital investment to a private capital contribution, 2) the extension of tax incentives offered to business angels, 3) the promotion of wider use of convertible loan instruments, and 4) the extension of grants and the promotion of solutions that do not result in dilution of the ownership structure of the companies concerned and do not undermine the chances of fast-growing companies to raise capital from private investors in the later stages of their development.

References

Aernoudt, R. (2017). The Scale-Up Gap and How to Address It. *Venture capital: An International Journal of Entrepreneurial Finance, 19*(4), 361–372. https://doi.org/10.1080/13691066.2017.1348724.

Aernoudt, R. (2019). Guarantee Instrument Obsolete or Future -Oriented? In A. Quas, Y. Alperovych, & C. Bellavitis, I. Paeleman, & D, S. Kamuriwo (Eds.), *New Frontiers in Entrepreneurial Finance Research* (pp. 93–117). World Scientific Publishing Co. Pte. Ltd. Retrieved April 23, 2021, from https://ideas.repec.org/b/wsi/wsbook/11344.html

Alperovych, Y., Groh, A.P., & Quas, A. (2020). Bridging the equity gap for young innovative companies: The design of effective government venture capital fund programs. *Research Policy, 49*, 104051. https://doi.org/10.1016/j.respol.2020.104051

Alperovych, Y., Hübner, G., & Lobet, F. (2015). How does government versus private venture capital backing affect a firm's efficiency? Evidence from Belgium. *Journal of Business Venturing 30*(4), 508–525. https://doi.org/10.1016/j.jbusvent.2014.11.001

Avinimelech, G., & Teubal, M. (2006). Creating Venture Capital Industries that Co-evolve with High Tech: Insights From an Extended Industry Life Cycle Perspective of the Israeli Experience. *Research Policy*, *35*(10), 1477–1498. https://doi.org/10.1016/j.respol.2006.09.017

Bai, J., Berstein, S., Dev, A., & Lerner, J. (2021): Public Entrepreneurial Finance around the Globe. NBER Working Paper No. 28744. Retrieved August 15, 2021, from https://www.nber.org/papers/w28744. http://doi.org/10.3386/w28744

Beck, T., Klapper, l.F., & Mendoza, J.C. (2010). The typology of partial credit guarantee funds around the world. *Journal of Financial Stability*, *6*(4), 10–25. http://dx.doi.org/10.1016/j.jfs.2008.12.003

Berger A.N., & Udell G.F. (1990). Collateral, loan quality and bank risk. *Journal of Monetary Economics*, *25*(1), 21–42. https://doi.org/10.1016/0304-3932(90)90042-3

Berger A.N., & Udell G.F. (1998). The Economics of Small Business Finance: The Roles of Private Equity and Debt Markets in the Financial Growth Cycle. *Journal of Banking and Finance*, *22*(6–8), 613–673. https://doi.org/10.1016/S0378-4266(98)00038-7

Bertoni, F., & Quas, A. (2016, November 1). *The Electoral Cycle of Government Venture Capital Investments*. SSRN Electronic Journal, 1–39. https://doi.org/10.2139/ssrn.2777169

Bertoni, F., & Tykvová, T. (2015). Does governmental venture capital spur invention and innovation? Evidence from young European biotech companies. *Research Policy*, *44*(4) 925–935. https://doi.org/10.1016/j.respol.2015.02.002

Bertoni, F., Colombo, M.G., & Quas, A. (2015). The patterns of venture capital investments in Europe. *Small Business Economics* *45*(3), 543–560. https://doi.org/10.1007/s11187-015-9662-0

Bertoni, F., Colombo, M.G., & Quas, A. (2017). The Role of Venture Capital in the Venture Capital Ecosystem: An Organizational Ecology Perspective. *Entrepreneurship Theory and Practice*, *43*(3), 611–628. https://doi.org/10.1177/1042258717735303

Bertoni, F., Martí, J., & Carmelo, R. (2019). The impact of government-supported participative loans on the growth of entrepreneurial ventures. *Research Policy*, *48*(1), 371–384. https://doi.org/10.1016/j.respol.2018.09.006

Bileau, J., Mason, C., Botelho, T., & Sarkar, S. (2017). Angel investing in an era of austerity: The case of Portugal. *European Planning Studies*, *25*(9), 1516–1537. https://doi.org/10.1080/09654313.2017.1328045

Boschi, M., Girardi, A., & Ventura, M. (2014). partial credit guarantees and SME financing. *Journal of Financial Stability*, *15*, 192–194. https://doi.org/10.1016/j.jfs.2014.09.007

Botelho, T.L., Fehder, D., & Hochberg, Y. (2021). Innovation-driven entrepreneurship. NBER Working Paper No. 28990. Retrieved August 15, 2021, from https://www.nber.org/system/files/working_papers/w28990/w28990.pdf

Brander, J.A., Du, Q., & Hellmann, T. (2015). The Effects of Government-Sponsored Venture Capital: International Evidence. *Review of Finance*, *19*(2), 571–618. https://doi.org/10.1093/rof/rfu009

Brown, R. C., Anyadike-Danes, M., Hart, M., & Mason, C. (2012). The growth dynamics of technology-based firms in Scotland. Fraser of Allander Economic Commentary, 36 (1),56–65. Retrieved April 23, 2021, from https://pure.strath.ac.uk/ws/portalfiles/portal/30733418/FEC_36_1_2012_BrownRAnydike_DanesMMasonCRichmondK.pdf

Brown, R., Mason, C., & Mawson, S. (2014). *Increasing 'The Vital 6 Percent': Designing Effective Public Policy to Support High Growth Firms*. Nesta Working Paper No. 14/01. Retrieved April 23, 2021, from http://www.nesta.org.uk/publications/increasing-'-vital-6-percent'-designing-effective-public-policy-support-high-growth

Brown, R., Mawson, S., & Mason, C. (2017). Myth-busting and entrepreneurship policy: the case of high growth firms. *Entrepreneurship and Regional Development*, *29*, 414–443. https://doi.org/10.1080/08985626.2017.1291762

Buzzacchi, L., Scellato, G., & Ughetto, E. (2013). The Investment Strategies of Publicly Sponsored Venture Capital Funds. *Journal of Banking and Finance*, *37*(3), 707–716. https://doi.org/ 10.1016/j.jbankfin.2012.10.018

Carpentier, C., & Suret, J.-M. (2014). *Post-Investment Migration of Candian Venture Capital-Backed New Technology-Based Firms*. Montreal: CIRANO – Scientific Publications 2014s-27. Retrieved April 23, 2021, from https://cirano.qc.ca/pdf/publication/2014s-27.pdf

Colombo, M.G., Croce, A., & Guerini, M. (2013). The effect of public subsidies on firms' investment–cash flow sensitivity: Transient or persistent? *Research Policy 42*, 1605–1623. https://doi.org//10.1016/j.respol.2013.07.003

Colombo, M. G., Cumming, D. J., & Vismara, S. (2016). Governmental Venture Capital for Innovative Young Firms. *Journal of Technology Transfer*, *41*(1)10–24. https://doi.org/10.1007/s10961-014-9380-9.

Cowling, M. (2010). The role of loan guarantee schemes in alleviating credit rationing in the UK. *Journal of Financial Stability*, *6*(1), 36–44. https://doi.org/10.1016/J.JFS.2009.05.007

Cowling, M., & Mitchell, P. (2003). Is the small firms' loan guarantee scheme hazardous for banks or helpful to small business? *Small Business Economics*, *21*(1), 63–72. https://www.jstor.org/ stable/40229278

Cowling, M., & Siepel, J. (2013). Public intervention in UK small firm credit markets: value for-for-money or waste of scarce resources? *Technovation*, *33*(8–9), 265–275. https://doi.org/10. 1016/j.technovation.2012.11.002

Cumming, D.J., Grilli, L., & Murtinu, S. (2017). Governmental and Independent Venture Capital Investments in Europe: A Firmlevel Performance Analysis. *Journal of Corporate Finance*, *42*, 439–459. https://doi.org/10.1016/j.jcorpfin.2014.10.016

Cumming, D.J., Knill, A., & Syvrud, K. (2016). Do International investors enhance private firm value? Evidence from venture capital. *Journal of International Business Studies*, *47*(3), 347–373. https://doi.org/10.1057/jibs.2015.46

Cumming, D., & Dai, N. (2010). Local Bias in Venture Capital Investments. *Journal of Empirical Finance*, *17*(3), 362–380. https://doi.org/10.1016/j.jempfin.2009.11.001

Davila, A., Foster, G., & Gupta, M. (2003). Venture Capital Financing and the Growth of Startup Firms. *Journal of Business Venturing*, *18*(6) 689–708. https://doi.org/10.1016/S0883-9026 (02)00127-1

Demir, R., Wennberg, K., & McKelvie, A. (2017). The Strategic Management of High-growth Firms: A Review and Theoretical Conceptualization. *Long Range Planning*, *50*(4), 431–456. https://doi. org/10.1016/j.lrp.2016.09.004.

Dimitriu, S. (2020). What will it take to save the UK's startups and sacaleups? *Sifted*. Retrieved April 23, 2021, from https://sifted.eu/articles/uk-startups-coronavirus-government/

Duruflé, G., Hellmann, T., & Wilson, K. (2018). From start-up to scale-up: Examining public policies for the financing of highgrowth ventures. In C. Mayer, S. Micossi, M. Onado, M. Pagano, & A. Polo (Eds.), *Finance and Investment. The European Case* (pp.179–219). Oxford University Press. https://doi.org/10.1093/oso/9780198815815.003.0011

Dvouletý, O., Srhoj, S. & Pantea, S. (2021). Public SME grants and firm performance in European Union: A systematic review of empirical evidence. *Small Business Economics*, *57*(1), 243–263. https://doi.org/10.1007/s11187-019-00306-x

EFAA (2019). Annual Report. European Federation of Accountants and Auditors for SMEs, EFAA, Brussels. Retrieved April 23, 2021, from https://www.efaa.com/cms/upload/efaa_files/pdf/ Publications/Annual_reports/Annual_Report_EFAA_2019_Final.pdf

European Commission (2002). *Benchmarking business angels*. European Commission, Enterprise Directorate-General, European Union. Retrieved April 23, 2021, from https://ec.europa.eu/ growth/content/benchmarking-business-angels-0_sv

European Commission (2021). *Study on Equity Investments in Europe: Mind the Gap*. European Commission, Directorate-General for Research and Innovation, European Union. https://doi. org/10.2777/001375

European Investment Fund (2021). *Scale-Up Financing and IPOs: Evidence From Three Surveys*. EIF Working paper No. 69, European Investment Fund, Research and Market Analysis. Retrieved April 23, 2021, from https://www.eif.org/news_centre/publications/eif_working_ paper_2021_69.pdf

Flachenecker, F., Gavigan, J. P, Goenaga Beldarrain, X., Pasi, G., Preziosi, N., Stamenov, B., & Testa, G. (2020). *High Growth Enterprises: demographics, finance and policy measures*. JRC119788, Joint Research Centre, EUR 30077 EN, Publications Office of the European Union. https://doi.org/10.2760/34219

Gampfer, R., Mitchell, J., Stamenov, B., Zifciakova, J., & Jonkers, K. (2016). Improving access to finance: which schemes best support the emergence of high-tech innovative enterprises? A mapping, analysis and assessment of finance instruments in selected EU Member States. Joint Research Centre, European Commission, Science for policy report series. Retrieved August 15, 2021, from https://doi.org/10.2791/635757

Gilson, R. (2003). Engineering a Venture Capital Market: Lessons from the American Experience. Stanford Law Review, 55 (4),1067–1103. Retrieved April 23, 2021, from http://www.jstor.org/ stable/1229601

Gompers, P. J. (1996). Grandstanding in the Venture Capital Industry. *Journal of Financial Economics*, *42*(1), 133–156. https://doi.org/10.1016/0304-405X(96)00874-4

Greene, F. J., & Rosiello, A. (2020). A commentary on the impacts of 'Great Lockdown' and its aftermath on scaling firms: What are the implications for entrepreneurial research? *International Small Business Journal*, *38*(7),583–592. https://doi.org/10.1177/ 0266242620961912

Grilli, L., & Murtinu, S. (2012). Do public subsidies affect the performance of new technology-based firms? The importance of evaluation schemes and agency goals. *Prometheus, Critical Studies in Innovation*, *30*(1), 97–11. https://doi.org/10.1080/08109028.2012.676836

Grilli, L., & Murtinu, S. (2014). Government, Venture Capital and the Growth of European High-tech Entrepreneurial Firms. *Research Policy*, *43*(9), 1523–1543. https://doi.org/10.1016/ j.respol.2014.04.002

Grilli, L., & Murtinu, S. (2015). New Technology-based Firms in Europe: Market Penetration, Public Venture Capital, and Timing of Investment. *Industrial and Corporate Change*, *24*(5), 1109–1148. https://doi.org/10.1093/icc/dtu025

Growth analysis (2013, August). *Business Angel, Coinvestment Funds and Policy Portfolios*. Tillvaxtanalys, 2009/055, Swedish Agency for Growth Policy Analysis. https://www.tillvaxta nalys.se/download/18.62dd45451715a00666f1cb35/1586366170761/Report_2013_08.pdf

Hall, B. H., & Lerner, J. (2010). The Financing of R&D and Innovation. In B. Hall & N. Rosenberg (Eds.), *Handbook of the Economics of Innovation*, Vol. 1, (pp. 609–639). Elsevier. https://doi. org/10.1016/S0169-7218(10)01014-2

Harrison, R. T. (2018). Crossing the Chasm: The Role of Co-Investment Funds in Strengthening the Regional Business Angel Ecosystem. *Small Enterprise Research*, *25*(1), 3–22. https://doi.org/ 10.1080/13215906.2018.1428910

Honohan, P. (2010). Partial credit guarantees: principles and practice. *Journal of Financial Stability*, *6*(1), 1–9. https://doi.org/10.1016/J.JFS.2009.05.008

Hottenrott, H., & Richstein, R. (2020). Start-up subsidies: does the polcy instrument matter? *Research Policy*, *49*(1), https://doi.org/10.1016/j.respol.2019.103888

Howell, S. T. (2017). Financing Innovation: Evidence from R&D Grants. *American Economic Review*, *107*(4), 1136–64. https://doi.org/10.1257/aer.20150808

Jaaskelainen, M., Maula, M., & Seppa, T. (2006). Allocation of Attention to Portfolio Companies and the Performance of Venture Capital firms. *Entrepreneurship Theory and Practice, 30*(2), 185–206. https://doi.org/10.1111/j.1540-6520.2006.00117.x

Jaaskelainen, M., Maula, M., & Murray, G.C. (2007). Profit Distribution and Compensation Structures in Public Policy and Privately Funded Hybrid Venture Capital Funds. *Research Policy, 36*(7), 913–929. https://doi.org/10.1016/j.respol.2007.02.021

Karsai, J. (2018). Government venture capital in central and eastern Europe. *Venture Capital: An International Journal of Entrepreneurial Finance, 20*(1), 73–102. https://doi.org/10.1080/13691066.2018.1411040

Knockaert, M., Lockett, A., Clarysse, B., & Wright, M. (2006). Do Human Capital and Fund Characteristics Drive Follow-up Behaviour of Early Stage High-tech VCs? *International Journal of Technology Management, 34*(1-2), 7–27. https://doi.org/10.1504/IJTM.2006.009445

Knockaert, M., Clarysse, B., & Wright, M. (2010). The Extent and Nature of Heterogeneity of Venture capital Selection Behaviour in New Technology-based Firms. *R & D Management, 40*(4), 357–371. https://doi.org/10.1111/j.1467-9310.2010.00607.x

Kovner, A., & Lerner, J. (2015). Doing Well by Doing Good? Community Development Venture Capital. *Journal of Economics and Management Strategy, 24*(3), 643–663. https://doi.org/10.1111/jems.12100

Lahti, T., & Keinonen, H. (2016). Business Angel Networks: A Review and Assessment of Their Value to Entrepreneurship. In H. Landström, & C. Mason (Eds.), *Handbook of Research on Business Angels* (pp. 354–378). Edward Elgar.

Leland, H.E., & Pyle, D.H. (1977). Information Asymmetries, Financial Structure, and Financial Intermediation. *The Journal of Finance, 32*(2), 371–387. https://doi.org/10.2307/2326770

Leleux, B., & Surlemont, B. (2003). Public Versus Private Venture Capital: Seeding or Crowding Out? A Pan-European Analysis. *Journal of Business Venturing, 18*(1), 81–104. https://doi.org/10.1016/S0883-9026(01)00078-7

Lerner, J. (1999). The Government as Venture Capitalist: The Long-Run Impact of SBIR Program. The Journal of Business, 72(3), 285–318. https://doi.org/10.1086/209616

Lerner, J. (2009). *Boulevard of Broken Dreams: Why Public Efforts to Boost Entrepreneurship and Venture Capital Have Failed – and What to do About It*. Princeton University Press. https://www.jstor.org/stable/j.ctt7t2br

Lerner, J. (2020, October 26). Government Incentives for Entrepreneurship. *Innovation and Public Policy NBER Conference*. https://www.nber.org/system/files/chapters/c14426/c14426.pdf

Lerner, J., & Nanda, R. (2020). Venture Capital's Role in Finanancing Innovation: What We Know and How Much We Still Need to Learn. Harward Business School Finance Working Paper No. 20–131, Harward Business School. http://dx.doi.org/10.2139/ssrn.3633054

Liben-Nowell, D., Novk., J., Kumar, R., Raghavan, P., & Tomkins, A. (2005). Geographic routing in societal networks. Proceedings of the National Academy of Sciences of the United States of America, 102(33),11623–11628. https://doi.org/10.1073/pnas.0503018102

Manigart, S., Baeyens, K., & Van Hyfte, W. (2002). The Survival of Venture Capital Backed Companies. *Venture Capital: An International Journal of Entrepreneurial Finance, 4*(2), 103–124. https://doi.org/10.1080/13691060110103233

Marti, R.J., & Quas, A. (2017). A bacon in the night: government certification of SMEs towards banks. *Small Business Economics, 50*(2), 397–413. https://doi.org/10.101007/s11187-016-9828-4

Mason, C. (2020, April 30). The Coronavirus Economic Crisis: Its Impact on Venture Capital and High Growth Enterprises. *Joint Research Centre, European Commission*. https://doi.org/10.2760/408017

Miller, S. M., Hoffer, A., & Wille, D. (2017). Small-business Financing After the Financial Crisis: Lessons from the Literature. *Journal of Entrepreneurship and Public Policy*, 6(3), 315–339. https://doi.org/10.1108/JEPP-D-17-00005

Muraközy, B., & Telegdy, Á. (2020). The Effects of EU-Funded Enterprise Grants on Firms and Workers. IZA Discussion Papers 13410, Institute of Labor Economics (IZA). https://www.iza.org/publications/dp/13410/the-effects-of-eu-funded-enterprise-grants-on-firms-and-workers

Murray, G., Cowling, M., Liu, W., & Kalinowska-Beszczynska, O. (2012). *Government co-financed 'Hybrid' Venture Capital programmes: generalizing developed economy experience and its relevance to emerging nations*. Kauffman International Research and Policy Roundtable, Liverpool. https://www.semanticscholar.org/paper/Government-co-financed-'Hybrid'-Venture-Capital-and-Murray-Cowling/2e24b15f50b2341bfa9d0704251bcb6c6268546c#paper-header

OECD (2015). New approaches to SME and Entrepeneurship Financing: Broadening the Range of Instruments. OECD Publishing, Paris. https://doi.org/10.1787/9789264240957-en.

OECD (2018). *Financing SMEs and Entrepreneurs 2018: An OECD Scoreboard*. OECD Publishing, Paris. https://doi.org/10.1787/fin_sme_ent-2018-en

OECD (2020). The effects of R&D tax incentives and their role in the innovation policy mix: Findings from the OECD microBeRD project, 2016-19. OECD Science, Technology and Industry Policy Papers, No. 92, OECD Publishing, Paris. https://doi.org/10.1787/65234003-en

Owen, R. (Baldock), & Mason, C. (2016). The Role of Government Co-Investment Funds in the Supply of Entrepreneurial Finance: An Assessment of the Early Operation of the UK Angel Co-Fund. *Environment and Planning C: Government and Policy*, 35 (3), 434–456. https://doi.org/10.1177/0263774X16667072

Rostamkalaei, A., & Freel, M. (2016). The cost of growth: small firms and the pricing of bank loans. *Small Business Economics*, 46(2), 255–272. https://doi.org/10.1007/s11187-015-9681-x

Rückert, D., Delanote, J., & Reypens, C. (2020). From starting to scaling: How to foster startup growth in Europe. EIB Thematic Study, European Investment Bank. https://doi.org/10.2867/42527

Standauert, T. (2019). To the Rescue: Government Intervention in Venture Capital Markets. In A. Quas, Y. Alperovych, & B. Cristiano, (Eds.), *New Frontiers in Entrepreneurial Finance Research* (pp. 51–91). World Scientific. https://doi.org/10.1142/9789811202766_0003

Standaert, T., & Manigart, S. (2018). Government as Fund-of-und and VC Fund Sponsors: Effect on Employment in Portfolio Companies. *Small Business Economics*, 50(2), 357–373. https://doi.org/10.1007/s11187-016-9831-9

Stiglitz, J.E., & Weiss, A. (1981). Credit Rationing in Markets with Imperfect Information. The American Economic Review, 71(3),393–410. https://www.jstor.org/stable/1802787

Sterk, V., Sedlacek, P., & Pugsley, B. (2021). The nature of firm growth. *American Economic Review*, 111(2), 547–579. https://doi.org/10.1257/aer.20190748.

Ughetto, E., Scellato, G., & Cowling, M. (2017). Cost of capital and public loan guarantees to small firms. *Small Business Economics, 49, 319–377*. https://doi.org/10.1007/s11187-017-9845-y

Vanacker, T., Heughebaert, A., & Manigart, S. (2014). Institutional Frameworks, Venture Capital and the Financing of European New Technology-based Firms. *Corporate Governance: An International Review*, 22(3), 199–215. https://doi.org/10.1111/corg.12046

Vanacker, T.R., & S. Manigart (2010). Pecking order and Debt capacity Considerations for High-growth Companies Seeking Financing. *Small Business Economics*, 35(1), 53–69. https://doi.org/10.1007/s11187-008-9150-x

Wilson, K., & Silva, F. (2013). Policies for Seed and Early Stage Finance: Findings from the 2012 OECD Financing Questionnaire. OECD Science, Technology and Industry Policy Papers, No. 9, OECD Publishing. http://dx.doi.org/10.1787/5k3xqsf00j33-en

Zhang, Y. (2018). Gain or pain? New evidence on mixed syndication between governmental and private venture capital firms in China. *Small Business Economics*, *51*(4), 995–1031. https://doi.org/10.1007/s11187-018-9989-4

Zhia, B. (2008). Export incentives, financial constraints, and the (Mis)allocation of credit: micro-level evidence from subsidized export loans. *Journal of Financial Economics*, *87*(2), 498–527. https://doi.org/10.1016/j.jfineco.2006.12.006

Antonia Schickinger, Alexandra Bertschi-Michel,
and Nadine Kammerlander

14 Family offices as startup investors: A synergetic relationship of the old and new economy?

Abstract: Family offices have emerged increasingly as important players in the financing market. Given their significant assets under management, they have successfully invested in various asset classes. New trends indicate that startup investments might be an attractive investment opportunity for family offices, especially in low-interest environments. Moreover, startups might benefit from family office characteristics, such as patient capital. In this book chapter, we outline the extant literature on family offices as startup financing vehicles before providing insights into the findings of an empirical study on family offices' investment behavior. Subsequently, we provide an extensive discussion on the conditions under which family offices are suitable investors for startups – and startups attractive targets for family offices. We focus on shared market experience, startup phase, and risk preferences of the family offices. This book chapter contributes to the academic discussion by integrating research on family offices and startup discussions and by outlining promising avenues for further research. Additionally, this book chapter creates value for family office and startup professionals by outlining best practices and important considerations for family office-startup corporations.

Keywords: family office, entrepreneurial family, startup investment, venture capital, private equity

Introduction

Somewhat unnoticed by the public, a new sort of player has emerged on the financial markets of many Western and Eastern economies over the last two decades: family offices. Family offices denote legal entities that administer the wealth of one or few affluent entrepreneurial families (Bierl & Kammerlander, 2019). Often the owner-families aim to reinvest their wealth after selling their family firm; family offices are an appropriate vehicle for pursuing such endeavors. In other cases, entrepreneurial families accumulate substantial wealth in addition to the money

Antonia Schickinger, Nadine Kammerlander, WHU – Otto Beisheim School of Management
Alexandra Bertschi-Michel, University of Bern

https://doi.org/10.1515/9783110726312-018

invested in the family firm – such as through continuous and generous dividend payments. Also, these families might set up or join a family office in order to re-invest their wealth into entrepreneurial projects (Schickinger et al., 2021b). While the number of family offices has steadily increased in the last two decades, there are no precise figures about the number and assets under management of these financial vehicles. The first reason is that the term 'family office' is not legally protected and there is no register of family offices; the second reason is that family offices often prefer acting in the background and avoiding (too much) publicity. Service providers estimate that there are approximately 7,000 to 11,000 family offices active around the world (World Ultra Wealth Report, 2014) and that family offices around the world currently administer wealth of USD 32.3 trillion (World Ultra Wealth Report, 2019). With a general projected population increase, the World Ultra Wealth Report (2019) forecasts a total asset class wealth of USD 43 trillion by 2023.

Most individuals associate family office investments with real estate investments, such as residential and office buildings in major cities. Yet a study by Schickinger et al. (2021b) showed that roughly half of the surveyed family offices conduct direct entrepreneurial investments, and that family offices also invest into new and existing firms in an indirect way, via VC funds for example. Indeed, there are several prominent examples of family offices' entrepreneurial investments. For instance, Athos, the family office of Hexal founders Thomas and Andreas Strüngmann, was one of the first and most substantial capital providers of BioNTech, nowadays well known for its development of a leading Covid19-vaccine.[1] The brothers' family office is also invested in the European startup IQM, active in quantum computing.[2] Specialized service providers such as Hamburg-based bridges+links connect interested family offices and hand-selected startups for potential investment opportunities.[3] Other family offices prefer indirect over direct investments. For instance, the VC Fund LaFamiglia is backed by substantial family office money and has been investing in startups since 2016.[4]

Despite those successes and developments, family offices' investment in startups is not the 'default case' yet. While the patient capital and entrepreneurial experience of some business families can help startups, many family offices are still somewhat reluctant to provide capital to new ventures due to their risk aversion as well as other impediments to such cooperation including different communication and work styles (Kammerlander & Leitner, 2018). Moreover, despite the growing interest of literature in single family offices (SFOs; e.g., Welsh et al., 2013; Wessel

---

1 https://www.tagesschau.de/wirtschaft/unternehmen/portrait-struengmann-hexal-biontech-101.html.
2 https://www.manager-magazin.de/finanzen/struengmann-brueder-investieren-in-quantencomputer-a-b0d7b35f-8de4-4d19-882a-cbf2e162663e.
3 https://bridgeslinks.vc/.
4 https://www.sueddeutsche.de/wirtschaft/wagniskapital-la-famiglia-deutsche-unternehmerfamilien-schliessen-sich-zusammen-1.3297540.

et al., 2014; Zellweger & Kammerlander, 2015) as well as startup investments in general (Davila et al., 2003), it is not entirely clear how SFOs make their investment decisions. Specifically, it so far remains unknown which criteria utilize SFOs to make their entrepreneurial investment decisions, although a recent study of Block and colleagues (2019) indicated that family offices in general place a high emphasis on a target's potential revenue growth. In particular, SFOs have been found to have very idiosyncratic investment decision-making processes (Schickinger et al., 2021a), which is why we need further knowledge on the specific processes within SFOs. As such, the following book chapter aims to shed light on questions such as whether SFOs tend to invest in startup firms or more mature firms, and what underlying reasons drive their investment decisions. Reasons that lead SFOs to invest in newly founded firms may include the possibility to actively shape the development of the firm or to pursue the family office's own business ideas. In contrast, other reasons might support SFO investment in mature firms, for instance over the course of a succession, as those firms have a more proven and stable business model with easier to estimate annual returns for investors.

In this chapter, we first review the literature on SFOs as well as that on entrepreneurial investing by focusing on venture capital and private equity. Subsequently, we analyze and discuss data from a recently conducted study by two of the authors (Schickinger et al., 2021b) on SFOs located in Germany, Austria, and Switzerland, investigating and analyzing SFOs decision criteria and investment preferences. As a takeaway from this analysis, we come up with two decision trees for family offices, visualizing the criteria based on which family offices will rather invest in early stage firms by assuming the role of a startup financing partner also called business angel vs. investments in more mature firms by assuming the role of a PE investor. Finally, we come up with a set of corresponding research gaps and provide an overview of potential avenues for future research in the field.

Literature review

Single family offices

A single family office (SFO) is defined as "a corporate structure owned by a single family and primarily dedicated to the management of family assets and the fulfillment of individual and tailored needs of family members" (Schickinger et al., 2021b), while pursuing a long-term focus (Zellweger & Kammerlander, 2015). Although the literature on SFOs is still in in an early stage (Welsh et al., 2013), SFOs have become an indispensable investment vehicle for entrepreneurial families (e.g., Rosplock, 2014; Roure et al., 2013; Welsh et al., 2013; Wessel et al., 2014; Zellweger & Kammerlander, 2015). Specifically, entrepreneurial families often establish a SFO to pool their financial resources after the sale of the original family firm (Scholes et al., 2008; Wennberg et al., 2011) or after excess profits for instance due to generous dividend payouts (Bierl & Kammerlander, 2019; Decker & Lange, 2013). Consequently, the owning family may define the SFO as their new financial (Bierl & Kammerlander, 2019) as well as entrepreneurial anchor (Zellweger et al., 2010).

Research on SFOs has primarily pointed out important characteristics along several dimensions, including family goals (e.g., Rivo-López et al., 2017; Welsh et al., 2013), governance (e.g., Zellweger & Kammerlander, 2015), and entrepreneurial investment behavior (e.g., Bierl & Kammerlander, 2019; Schickinger et al., 2021b). With regard to family goals, prior literature underlines that an SFO can be aligned in various ways: as a corporate structure (1) to manage SFO investment with a long-term and transgenerational focus (Bierl & Kammerlander, 2019; Welsh et al., 2013), (2) to preserve wealth (Block et al., 2019; Decker & Lange, 2013; Rivo-López et al., 2017; Welsh et al., 2013), or (3) to fulfill both economic and noneconomic family requirements (Rivo-López et al., 2017; Wessel et al., 2014). With regards to governance, scholars agree that governance plays a critical role within SFOs. In general, managers of SFOs are entrusted with the task to manage family (i.e., governance) issues (Rivo-López et al., 2017; Roure et al., 2013). An official governance structure and process thereby helps to mitigate agency conflicts between the owning family and the respective family office manager as well as between multiple family members (e.g., Suess, 2014; Wessel et al., 2014; Zellweger & Kammerlander, 2015). With regard to entrepreneurial investment behavior, multiple scholars highlight that a key task of an SFO management is to advise the owning family investment-wise on new as well as existing opportunities (Bierl & Kammerlander, 2019; Gray, 2005; Welsh et al., 2013; Wessel et al., 2014). Specifically, entrepreneurial families regularly invest in portfolio companies (i.e., established, profitable firms as well as digital businesses/startups; Le Breton-Miller & Miller, 2018; Schickinger et al., 2021a; Sieger et al., 2011), which they support and develop strategically as well as operationally (Naldi et al., 2011). Consequently, within the acquisition market, SFOs compete with traditional private equity and, to a lesser extent, venture capital firms.

Although most SFO scholars have so far researched in a descriptive, conceptual manner or using small qualitative samples (e.g., Rosplock, 2014, Welsh et al. 2013; Wessel et al. 2014), the first quantitative larger-scale studies have emerged (e.g., Block et al., 2019; Schickinger et al., 2021a).

Entrepreneurial investing: Venture capital and private equity

Venture capital firms (VC) generally invest in early stage startup firms. Literature thereby distinguishes between business angels investing at a very early stage, and growth investors investing after the first developments have been made in order to achieve scale effects and thus revenue growth. The underlying reason for VC investments is often to help in creating a new innovative business idea or model. Hence, such investments are frequently linked not just with financial support but also with specific knowledge, market access, network, and other sources VCs possess (e.g., Manigart et al., 2002; Sapienza et al., 1996). The overall investment aim is, thus, to help create and develop a new business and sell it afterwards either in a private sale, for example, to a bigger competitor, or by going public and listing an IPO (Gompers & Lerner, 1999). Research has found that VCs typically exit when the expected marginal costs of maintaining the investment are greater than the expected marginal benefit, meaning that business volumes begin to grow going along with increasing costs (Cumming & Johan, 2010). The time horizon thereby is typically less than five years and strongly depends also on the institutional context in which VCs operate (Zacharakis et al., 2007). The investment targets for VCs are rarely family firms, as these firms at such an early stage of their life cycle are often heavily or even solely founded by the controlling family. The family thereby also frequently follows a clear pecking-order regarding their financing, first using internally available funds, followed by debt and, finally, external equity, whereby the latter is often viewed skeptically (Poutziouris, 2001; Romano et al., 2001).

Private equity (PE) firms, in contrast, generally invest in more mature firms having an established business model and more predictable revenues. Hence, PE firms more frequently invest into family firms than VCs do. In general, PE and VCs investments seldom overlap in their investments (Dawson, 2011). Regarding their focus, PE firms primarily strive for financial (rather than strategic) investments, although they are often active financial investors providing knowledge, network access, and other support to increase the target's operating performance (Kaplan & Strömberg, 2009). As such, PE firms also increasingly invest in family firms that are for instance in need of financial support to achieve growth, internationalization, and innovation or to solve succession issues. Since the primary goal of PE firms usually is to increase the value of their portfolio firms – either to quickly sell the acquired firms at a gain or to have a stable revenue generator over time via dividend payments in order to invest in new targets – they frequently intervene in the portfolio firms' management (Barber & Goold, 2007).

Thereby, particularly PE firms invest in family firms, several issues arise. When acquiring family firms, it was found that PE firms have less bargaining power due to information asymmetries (Michel et al., 2020) and after having once acquired a family firm, tensions might arise due to different time horizons (i.e., a family firm's relatively longer-term perspective vs. a PE firm's relatively shorter-term perspective), different opinions regarding the stakeholder management (stewardship behavior of family firms vs. efficiency orientation in PE), or different performance expectations. Due to such challenges, recent academic findings indicate that family firms prefer to only collaborate with PE investors in challenging situations such as when facing turnaround, succession, or growth issues (Rottke & Thiele, 2018).

However, to date we still lack knowledge on how entrepreneurial investors of different kinds make their decisions for or against a certain investment. In fact, the investment criteria of investors only recently have been further explored by a large-scale conjoint analysis by Block and colleagues, which has analyzed according to which criteria the following investors decide for or against an investment: family offices (FO), business angels (BA), venture capital funds (VCs), and growth equity funds (GEFs). The study finds that among all these investors the following, identical pecking-order regarding their investment decision criteria applies. First, revenue growth seems to be the most important criterion, followed next by value added of the firm's product or service, and, then, third, the firms' management track record. Surprisingly, aspects such as current profitability and the business model seemed less important (Block et al., 2019).

But how about wealthy families that frequently enter equity markets for entrepreneurial investments? As families or family firms investing via family offices have been found to have idiosyncratic decision making logics (Schickinger et al., 2021a) we might assume that their decision processes regarding entrepreneurial financing are uniquely shaped. For example, research shows that, compared with PE investors, family offices have less deal experience and a less professionalized investment approach (Rottke & Thiele, 2018). However, we so far lack a profound knowledge, according to which criteria they actually make investment decisions.

Emerging research

Research design

For this book chapter, we focused on SFOs located in Germany, Austria, and Switzerland (the so called DACH region) and re-analyzed the dataset described in Schickinger et al. (2021b). Although differences in culture as well as legal and tax settings can generally influence the investment behavior and functioning of SFOs, we believe that DACH is a focal region within the SFO context. First, business-owning and wealthy entrepreneurial families have a long-standing tradition and represent the backbone of the German, Austrian, and Swiss economy (DeMassis et al., 2018). Second, from a global perspective, Germany is the third largest country in terms of Ultra-High Net Worth individuals (with a total worth of at least USD 30 million; Datastream, 2020). Thus, German-speaking countries are likely to represent a broad range of SFOs as well as an adequate level of professionalization for a valid representation of the global SFO market.

In the absence of a complete SFO database, we identified our study participants in three steps. First, we identified 86 SFOs with the help of the Listenchampion database (Listenchampion, 2017). Second, VuFO e.V. (this abbreviation stand for "Verband unabhaengiger Family Offices", an official organization for family offices located in Germany) provided us with 13 SFO members. Third, we enriched our database with prior personal contacts (105 SFOs) as well as comprehensive and manual Internet research (146 SFOs). After eliminating dissolved SFO structures, so-called multi-family offices, offshore structures, as well as outdated postal addresses, our final data set resulted in 323 German-speaking SFOs and potential study participants. After inviting all SFOs via physical mail to participate in our study and following up via phone or email, 109 SFOs responded and agreed to participate in our research (response rate: 34%). We conducted interviews with family members (71%) as well as managers of SFOs (29%) between September 2017 and June 2018. We thereby focused on personal appointments (62%) rather than phone interviews. More details on the research design of this study can be found in Schickinger et al. (2021b).

To study SFOs in an exploratory way (Yin, 1994), the interviews combined a broad range of quantitative and qualitative questions on – among other topics – goals and entrepreneurial investment behavior. Specifically, within the context of entrepreneurial investment behavior, we also focused on the investment behavior of SFOs in general (i.e., in all asset classes) and on the investment behavior of SFOs in venture capital and private equity in particular. The semi-structured nature of the interviews gave all participants the opportunity to distinctively explain their underlying intentions and perception of the key topics and thereby validating what has been said numerically. Each interview took on average up to two hours, was recorded electronically and captured in the same way, regardless of a personal or phone interview. After the interview process, we systematically processed the data in Excel (e.g., Kammerlander et al., 2015) and followed best practices regarding qualitative research (see, e.g., De Massis & Kammerlander, 2019). Each study participant was asked to answer questions on individual characteristics as well as characteristics on the SFO entity which they own (in case of owning family members) or in which they work (in case of SFO managers). The following subsection as well as Table 14.1 summarize the particularities of the 109 German-speaking SFOs and their representatives.

The SFOs in our sample show many characteristics in which they significantly differ from one another, paving the way towards nuanced profiling. For example, at the time of the interview, 55% of all SFO-owning families still owned the original family firm, whereas 45% had already exited. Moreover, most families (57%) highlighted their entrepreneurial activities lasting over multiple generations, which also led to a multi-industry background (i.e., the family firm is active in two or more sectors). Furthermore, 70% of all interviewees were in their third or later entrepreneurial family generation, going back as far as 30 generations. In terms of the SFO generation, i.e. how often the SFO had already been passed on to the next generation, the picture was clearly different. The vast majority (88%) were in the first or second generation. This is consistent with the relatively recent founding date of SFOs in the European context, as 65% of SFOs were established after 2000. Although many entrepreneurial families in Germany can look back on a family history that spans decades, if not centuries, most of them did not start founding a dedicated SFO structure until the late 1990s or earlier 2000s. Unlike German-speaking families, American entrepreneurial families – despite often having a much shorter family firm history – established a dedicated SFO structure at an earlier date. For example, the first SFOs in the USA were founded in the early 1900s, such as the House of Morgan.

Another distinguishing feature is that only half of all SFOs in our sample decided to invest in portfolio companies directly, in established firms (i.e., PE investment; 49%) and/ or directly in startups (i.e., VC investment; 45%), without investing in traditional fund vehicles of third party providers.

The SFOs in our sample were also different from one another with regard to their size (i.e., number of employees) and their management team (i.e., external vs. internal management). First, with regard to size, the SFOs in our sample employed on average ten individuals, ranging from one to 150 employees. Second, with regard to the management team, the vast majority of SFOs in our sample (78%) were managed by more family-internal managers than family-external managers. Only a small minority was managed solely by family-external managers (16%) or mixed teams with more family-external than family-internal managers (6%). Overall, depending on the personal needs as well as the financial situation of the owning family, SFOs can be established in heterogeneous dimensions regarding their professionalization and management. In particular, assets under management were often a driver for the number of employees as well as for the inclusion of external managers. However, there were also cases where assets worth billions were managed with a very small number of employees. As such, SFOs can also be set up as relatively small entities with one or two persons in charge (8% of our sample). In these cases, the management of the SFO was often tied to a single family member or a few selected family members. For example, in these settings, we often met the father together with the daughter or son in charge of the family wealth. Another prominent structure were SFOs incorporated within the family firm (28% of our sample), often also called 'embedded family offices' (Zellweger & Kammerlander, 2015). In these cases, the SFO was often part of the controller or accounting team of the family firm, where the CFO of the family firm was also the head of the SFO.

With regards to individual characteristics, the majority (71%) of our interview partners were members of the SFO-owning family, partly with an active role within the management board (58%) and partly not (13%). The remainder of our interview partners were family-external senior managers (i.e., family officer, CEO; 25%) or employees of the SFO (4%). The level of education was generally high among all interviewees, with 94% having an academic degree and 36% having a doctorate or MBA degree. The differences between family-internal- and -external interviewees were marginal. Similar to other working environments in the financial sector, almost all of our interview partners were male (94%). More details on the descriptive statistics of the 109 German-speaking SFOs can be found in Table 14.1 as well as in Schickinger et al. (2021b).

Table 14.1: Descriptive statistics of the 109 German-speaking SFOs.

	Number	%
Family member	77	71%
Gender (male)	103	94%
Academic degree	102	94%
MBA/PhD	39	36%
Family member in management	92	84%
SFO with original family firm	60	55%
SFO in first generation	52	48%
Direct PE investments	53	49%
Direct VC investments	49	45%

	Min	Max	Mean	Median
Age of interview partner	28	82	48.2	47.5
SFO founding year	1696	2018	2000	2004
SFO generation	1	20	1.9	2.0
Family generation	1	30	4.0	4.0
Number of employees	1	150	10.4	5.0

Emerging results

> In the beginning, we were almost naive – as a result, we made a lot of mistakes. [. . .] I used to think that a family office is like a bank. [. . .] After a short time I had to realize that a family office is more a reflection of the owners. And today I would say: that is so individual.
>
> (Owner family, SFO No. 6)

In the following section, we present our observations of our unique sample of 109 German-speaking SFOs in multiple steps. First, we show and explain the importance of family- and investment-related goals. Second, we explain the entrepreneurial investment behavior of SFOs in general and with regards to direct investments in VC and PE in particular. Then, we link our findings and provide two frameworks to help answer the crucial questions "The family office: a startup or PE investor?" and "When are family offices the right investors for startups?".

Goals

Despite all the significant differences among the SFOs within our interview group, we observed a general understanding of the importance of setting goals that are aligned with all (empowered) family members.[5] These goals primarily focused on the importance of asset preservation as well as the importance of a transgenerational, entrepreneurial orientation. Managers and owners of SFOs thereby often ask themselves the questions: What are our goals and motives in setting up an SFO? How risk-averse or risk-taking is our investment strategy? Do I want the next generation to benefit from the family wealth, and, if so, to what extent?

With regard to the importance of asset preservation, entrepreneurial families agree that preserving and increasing wealth is a key goal when setting up an SFO. 40% of our study participants have the primary goal to preserve their wealth, while 60% aim for a risk-adjusted wealth enhancement. The following two quotes highlight the importance of asset preservation:

> The overarching goal is definitely asset preservation. [. . .] If you look at the current interest rate environment this year, for example, you have to make certain sacrifices in terms of pure risk minimization.   (Owner family, SFO No. 91)

> I try to keep it balanced. [. . .] Maximizing returns is very important to me, but capital preservation is the basic requirement.   (Owner family, SFO No. 5)

If large parts of the family wealth are still linked to the original family firm, asset preservation and the importance of a diversified asset allocation outside the family firm is particularly important.

Furthermore, we analyzed the transgenerational, entrepreneurial orientation of the SFO-owning family in two steps: First, we analyzed the number of generations that are actively involved and empowered within the family office, which ensures a smooth transgenerational process. Second, we analyzed the intention to pass on investments to the next generation as well as the intention to hold vs. selectively quit vs. sell investments (in this case: direct equity investments in established firms or startups). With regards to the number of generations that are actively involved and empowered within the family office, our panel group already did take significant first steps. Specifically, 43% already actively involve two (on in one case even three) generations within the family office, which depends on the age of the upcoming generation.

Moreover, the vast majority (71%) aim to invest for the long-term and specifically in assets that they intend to pass on to the next generations. For a detailed analysis, we dug deeper into the investment rationales of each SFO, especially in the context of direct

---

5 Parts of this section are based on chapter "4.1. Family-related goals of SFOs" from the study Schickinger et al. (2021b) as well as on "SFOs, family equity and transgenerational entrepreneurship" from the study Bierl et al. (2018).

equity investments in established firms or startups. We distinguished between three basic types of investment strategies and underlined these with respective quotes of our interviewees. First, there are SFOs with an opportunistic, short-term orientation, where investments are regarded independently with the clear intention to sell at a given point in time. A family officer exemplified the so-called 'buy, build, and sell' strategy as follows:

> Asset preservation is important, but asset growth is more important to us. We are purely opportunistic. We are hunters and gatherers. (Family officer, SFO No. 16)

Second, there are SFOs with a semi-strategic, medium-term orientation, where each investment is only sold when an adequate price or opportunity, often also primarily for the portfolio company, arises. The following quote of a family officer presents an example of this so-called 'buy, build, and selectively quit' approach:

> We invest in companies that are either good companies today or where we say, okay, this will be a good, profitable company in three years, and I would like to be involved in it for the rest of my life. We don't buy a company with the goal of exiting within 24 months – it usually doesn't work. Those are usually the hot potatoes, that's gambling. (Family officer, SFO No. 81)

Third, there are SFOs with a pure strategic and long-term orientation, where investments are regarded as a strategic commitment with the clear intention to hold for better or worse. The following quote of a shareholder and family member of the SFO exemplifies this 'buy, build, and hold' approach:

> We've never sold anything before. We buy to hold. Selling companies would be an absolute sacrilege. (Owner family, SFO No. 8)

These statements are exemplary for the observed mix of all three investment rationales among the 109 surveyed SFOs. In line with perceived long-term orientation of SFOs, the vast majority of SFOs aim for a 'buy, build, and selectively quit' (54%) or a 'buy, build, and hold' approach (35%). Only a small minority (11%) follow the clear intention to sell investments at a given point of time, as illustrated in Figure 14.1.

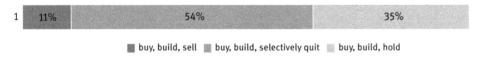

■ buy, build, sell ▨ buy, build, selectively quit ▨ buy, build, hold

Figure 14.1: Overview of the strategic orientation of the 109 SFO-owning families.

Entrepreneurial investment behavior of SFOs

> You only invest in what you really know about.

(Family officer, SFO No. 69)

Many SFOs stress the importance of diversification across various asset classes in general, and liquid and alternative asset classes in particular. We observed that all SFOs diversify within liquid asset classes such as cash and cash equivalents (i.e., foreign exchange, 68%), equities (74%), and fixed income (59%). Moreover, the importance of alternative asset classes within the investment strategy of SFOs becomes clear in Figure 14.2. The most frequently mentioned asset classes were real estate (83%), as well as direct entrepreneurial investments in startups or established firms via an own investment vehicle (45% and 49% respectively) and indirect entrepreneurial investments via an existing fund structure of a third-party provider (39%).

We also observed that the asset allocation changes over time (often over generations), but in particular once the original family firm was sold. If the original family firm is still in the hands of the family, it usually represents the family's largest single asset and strongest source of income. In comparison, families who have sold the original family firm lose the cluster risk of owning a (mid to large sized) enterprise but at the same time also lose the strongest source of income. In order to compensate for the loss of income, managers of SFOs diversify across multiple asset classes to generate return in a (low interest rate) environment (see Figure 14.3). In these cases, we specifically observe a significant shift away from so-called 'safe-haven' investments such as cash and cash equivalents (61%, previously 73%) or property (6%, previously 18%). These SFOs focus more often on riskier asset classes such as in entrepreneurial direct investments in startups (61%, previously 31%) or established firms (65%, previously 35%), but also indirect investments via PE and VC fund vehicles gain significant popularity (51%, previously 31%). Finally, almost all SFOs continue to invest in real estate even after the sale of the original family firm, which we interpret as a means of "risk insurance" against the overall portfolio.

A direct investment in innovative startups was especially successful among SFOs, if respective family members themselves had a link to or professional experience in the respective business field. If this was not the case, interviewees highlighted that they preferred indirect investments via fund vehicles or co-investments. A family officer explained:

> We've burned our hands on things of which we had little expertise.

(Family officer, SFO No. 57)

In the case of direct entrepreneurial investments in established firms, a focus on good access to qualified deal flow as well as a few selected industries appear to be crucial for success.

Although investments in startups would be feasible for almost every SFO because the initial investment amount is significantly lower than for established firms, we observe that almost the same number of SFOs invests in either one of them. An explanation for ruling out startup investments per se is that the wealth of

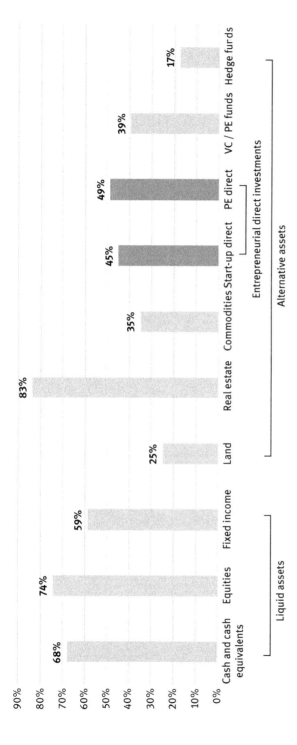

Figure 14.2: Asset class allocation of 109 German-speaking SFOs.

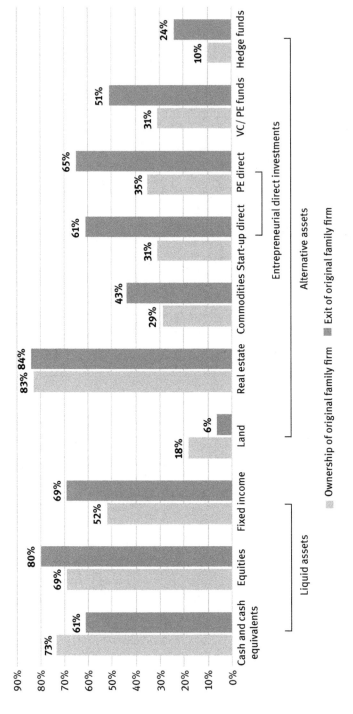

Figure 14.3: Asset class allocation of family offices who still own vs. who have sold the original family firm.

SFO-owning families has mostly been generated by entrepreneurs from the 'old economy,' who are often older in age and much more familiar with non-digital business models. These families define the SFO as an incontestable institution that will last over generations to come and as such live according to the following principle:

> Our direct investment portfolio is the learning factory for our next generation.
>
> (Owner family, SFO No. 37)

In contrast, startup investments often require a certain degree of speed as well as the clear intention to sell at a certain point in time – and not to pass on the investment to the next generation. As such, SFOs with fewer assets under management, less institutionalized structures, and younger owners tend to invest more heavily in startups. Also, entrepreneurs from the 'new economy,' who have already sold a successful startup in the past, maintain their passion for this kind of investment and often become well-known mentors and supporters within the venture scene. We also observe this clear trend toward one of the two asset classes (VC vs. PE investment) in our numerical analysis, with only 24% of all surveyed SFOs focusing on both direct investments in startups and established firms.

The family office: A startup or PE investor?

When analyzing family offices as investors a first question that arises is whether or under what circumstances family offices are suited as a startup investor or as a PE investor, investing in more mature firms. The answer is: it depends, as the decision tree visualized in Figure 14.4 shows.

Our interviews showed that some family offices as investors aim to be involved in both strategic and operational issues, meaning that the family office not just provides strategic guidance (i.e., fulfilling steering functions in the supervisory board or providing network contacts) but also aims to be actively involved into the operating business e.g., by striving to incorporate specific skills and experiences such as in distinct day-to-day financial or B2B/B2C sales processes. In this case, the family office maintains a very active, often also passionate, role as an investor. Given that early-stage companies tend to need more active operational support than later-stage companies, funding rounds are consequently lower and, in turn, the capital invested is on average less than EUR 2mn per investor per deal. The lower investment size is often in line with a risk-return perspective: First, these businesses (in case of startups) are still rather small and early-stage and as such a higher risk investment than later-stage businesses. Second, the family office also tries to mitigate its risk of losses endangering the family wealth by just investing small portions at a time. Such rather small-cap investors can be further distinguished by whether they strive to invest into a digital business or not. More precisely, if the investment is not into a digital business, the family office as investor assumes the role of a micro- or

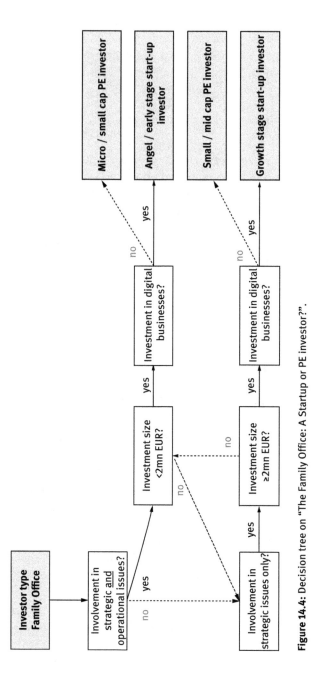

Figure 14.4: Decision tree on "The Family Office: A Startup or PE investor?".

small cap PE investor. In contrast, if the investment is into a novel digital business, the family office as investor assumes the role of an angel or early startup investor. Particularly such smaller investments frequently require active entrepreneurial and operational guidance.

In contrast to such active investors, many family offices as investors also prefer to just be involved as strategic investors without any operating involvement. Such investors mostly provide strategic guidelines and goals but mostly withdraw from any operating decisions. In this case, the family office rather maintains a passive role as investor but thereby invests on average larger amounts of more than EUR 2mn (if investment is below EUR 2mn, see decision tree above resulting in either micro- or small cap PE investors/angel or early startup investors). Furthermore, also regarding bigger investments of more than EUR 2mn, the question again arises whether the family office invests into a digital business or not. Again, if the investment is not into a digital business, the family office rather acts as a small or mid cap PE investor, whereas if the investment is into a novel digital business, the family office rather maintains the role of a growth stage startup investor. Such investments are thus particularly suitable for family offices with the capability to add strategic, rather than operational, value and with a primarily financial focus. In this case, family offices often have limited knowledge in the specific industry or business to become actively involved.

The comprehensive decision tree is visualized in Figure 14.4. Based on this summary, we can draw the conclusion that family offices in cases of investments in non-digital businesses take the role of a PE investor, while in cases of micro- and small-cap investments they take a more active role as in cases of bigger small- and mid-cap investments where they rather assume a passive role. In contrast, if the family office invests into novel digital businesses, it rather assumes the role of a startup investor, while, again, for smaller investments the role is more active in a sense of a business angel providing also operating guidance. In cases of bigger investments, the family office rather assumes a passive role of a growth investor.

When are family offices the right investors?

Another crucial question is: under which conditions are family offices the best investors? In order to answer this question, one must first distinguish between newly founded startup firms and established firms (see also Figure 14.5).

If the firm to be invested in is a startup and is in search for a solely financially driven pre-seed investment round, then most frequently angel investors are the right type of investor (Manigart et al., 2002). However, in some specific cases, it might be also a smaller-sized family office that has, for instance, a specific focus in the startup's industry or personal relations to the founders of the startup, which make them an appropriate investor.

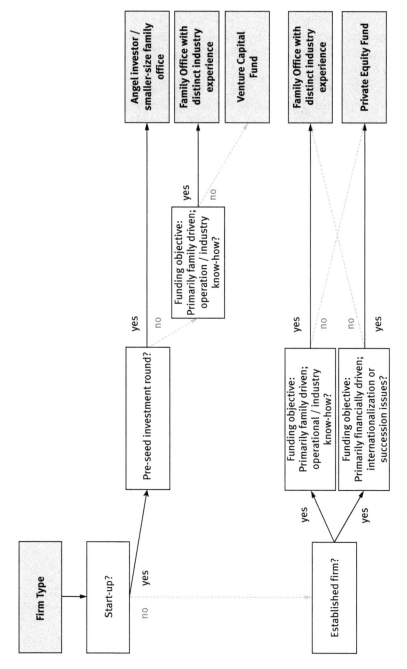

Figure 14.5: Decision tree on "When are Family Offices the right investors?".

If the firm to be invested in is a startup but with no need for a pre-seed investment round, a further question to be answered is the funding objective of the firm. When the major funding objective is primarily the need for operational or industry know-how, then a family office with a distinct industry experience will be the right investor (Block et al., 2019). The family office can provide specialist knowledge and network access to the startup firm. In contrast, when the major funding objective is financially driven (i.e., in order to achieve scale effects, internationalization and, growth), a (international) venture capital fund might be an appropriate investor (Devigne et al., 2013).

Also if the firm to be invested in is an established firm with a mature business model, it depends again on the funding objective of the firm which investor type suits best. Also in this case, when the funding objective is primarily driven by a search for operational and industry know-how, a family office having a distinct industry experience will be the appropriate investor being able to provide expertise and knowledge to the firm.

However, established firms might have particular funding objectives related to financial aspects, for example, to internationalization ambitions or unsolved ownership succession issues (Rottke & Thiele, 2018). In fact, many mature firms face challenges to either expand their established business model internationally (Dixit & Jayaraman, 2001; Wright et al., 2002), or to solve questions of ownership succession internally either within the family or via a management-buy-out (MBO) (Molly et al., 2018). In these cases, a private equity fund will most probably be the right investor as this type of investor is known to thrive on internationalization or to frequently invest, for example, in former family firms in order to solve the inherent ownership succession challenges.

The comprehensive decision tree is visualized in Figure 14.5. From this summary, we can draw the conclusion that family offices are most suitable investors in cases of startup as well as established firms, if they rather pursue a funding objective that is largely family driven with the primary aim to acquire operational or industry-specific know-how, expertise or network access.

Research gaps and future research

The growing relevance of family offices as startup investors, and the nascent stage of research on this topic, come along with interesting research questions.

As noted above, the topic of risk is key for family office decision makers. While inherently risk-averse, the low interest environments forces family offices to increasingly invest into alternative asset classes such as startups. More research is required on how family offices deal with the risk inherent to startup investments and what the decision-making process for such investments looks like. Members of entrepreneurial families often tend to make quick decisions that are based on gut feeling rather than thoughtful, in depth analyses and detailed calculations (Huang & Pearce, 2015). Still, this decision-making approach has been very successful in the past, mostly due to the deep expertise and knowledge that family members possess around their business. Startup investments, however, are a game changer for family offices. In particular when it comes to digital business models of startups, family office decision makers are often unfamiliar with the business model and might lack an intuitive understanding of promising vs. unpromising investments. Hence, future research might dig deeper into how decision making in family offices differ for PE versus VC investments (if at all) and could reveal potential best practices for family offices, especially considering that family offices often lack abundant resources that might help them in decision-making.

Furthermore, research on family resources – or 'familiness' – could conduct large-scale empirical studies in which phases family offices are the 'best (new) owners' for startups. While family support and industry knowledge might be particularly helpful in early phases, the reduced risk in later phases might smooth the family office-startup relationship. Research might also scrutinize if (and under which conditions) direct versus indirect startup investments turn out most beneficial for both – family offices as well as startups. In this regard, a deeper investigation of the role of the family office strategic and operational involvement might be a promising research arena. Members of family offices often prefer to be deeply engaged in the startup in order to follow their own entrepreneurial passion and legacy. However, to date, we lack a clear understanding of whether such 'diversity' (young startup founders with often digital experience and old economy family office owners) is beneficial or detrimental for the startups, and under what conditions. Hence, it is unclear if the family office owners and managers do or do not provide additional value going beyond 'patient capital.' Lastly, we started our theoretical and empirical discussion with family office heterogeneity. Similarly, there is much heterogeneity among startups, ranging from those with high growth and quick exit ambitions (the ones following the 'unicorn' ideal) and the so called 'zebra' startups that aim to achieve sustainable growth. Research effort should be invested in finding out what types of startups do or do not fit specific types of family office investors.

Lastly, more research is needed to understand the role of startup investments for family offices and family businesses. Classical strategy research and practice categorizes investments along the dimensions of market position and market growth, differentiating between cash cows, poor dogs, stars, and question marks (i.e., Morrison & Wensley, 1991). When comparing family-led organizations with other organizations remarkable differences emerge: First, family influence encourages organizations to 'nurture' the dogs (instead of selling or killing them). Second, family influence often goes along with a strong focus on the cash cows (indeed the core businesses are often treated as 'holy cash cows'), in which much money is re-invested despite strategical advice of not doing so. Lastly, family influenced organizations such as family businesses and family offices often miss out to pay substantial attention to, and develop, stars. Their focus on the existing businesses as well as the risk aversion and closed, non-diverse networks render family members inattentive to the growth opportunities of the future. Startup investments of family offices can be a promising first step to overcome this strategic weakness of family organizations. Employing qualitative or fsQCA methods, research might investigate the barriers, enablers, and processes of such strategic additions.

Conclusion

Family offices' investments in startups have the potential to kill several problems with one stone. Such investments might provide startups with the much needed patient capital, coupled with knowledge in the existing markets. And these investments might help family offices to diversify their portfolio, gain sustainable competitive advantages, and contribute substantially to their return on investments. Yet family office investments in startups are not no-brainers. Indeed, family offices need to clearly reflect on their risk profile, their goals, and their decision-making processes before investing in startups. And startups need to reflect on the required resources to determine their 'best future owner.' With our book chapter we aim to provide an overview of the various aspects to be considered.

References

Barber, F., & Goold, M. (2007). The strategic secret of private equity. *Harvard Business Review*, *85*(9), 53.

Bierl, P., & Kammerlander, N. (2019). Family equity as transgenerational mechanism for entrepreneurial families. *Journal of Family Business Management*, in press. http://dx.doi.org/10.1108/JFBM-09-2018-0043

Bierl, P., Schickinger, A., Leitterstorf, M.P., & Kammerlander, N. (2018). *Family Office, Family Equity und Private Equity. Unternehmerisches Investieren und generationsübergreifendes Unternehmertum*. WHU – Otto Beisheim School of Management.

Block, J., Fisch, C., Vismara, S., & Andres, R. (2019). Private equity investment criteria: An experimental conjoint analysis of venture capital, business angels, and family offices. Journal of Corporate Finance, 58, 329–352. http://dx.doi.org/10.1016/j.jcorpfin.2019.05.009

Cumming, D., & Johan, S. (2010). Venture capital investment duration. *Journal of Small Business Management*, *48*(2), 228–257. https://doi.org/10.1111/j.1540-627X.2010.00293.x.

Datastream (2020). The top 20 countries for ultra high net worth individuals. https://www.visualca pitalist.com/top-20-countries-for-ultra-high-net-worth-individuals/

Davila, A., Foster, G., & Gupta, M. (2003). Venture capital financing and the growth of startup firms. *Journal of Business Venturing*, *18*(6), 689–708. https://doi.org/10.1016/S0883-9026(02)00127-1

Dawson, A. (2011). Private equity investment decisions in family firms: The role of human resources and agency costs. *Journal of Business Venturing*, *26*(2), 189–199. http://dx.doi.org/10.1016/j. jbusvent.2009.05.004

De Massis, A., Audretsch, D., Uhlaner, L., & Kammerlander, N. (2018). Innovation with limited resources: Management lessons from the German Mittelstand. *Journal of Product Innovation Management*, *35*(1), 125–146. http://dx.doi.org/10.1111/jpim.12373

De Massis, A., & Kammerlander, N. 2019). Handbook of qualitative research methods for family business. Edward Elgar Publishing. https://doi.org/10.4337/9781788116459.

Decker, C., & Lange, K. (2013). Exploring a secretive organization: What can we learn about family offices from the public sphere? *Organizational Dynamics*, *42*(4), 298–306. http://dx.doi.org/ 10.1016/j.orgdyn.2013.07.008

Devigne, D., Vanacker, T., Manigart, S., & Paeleman, I. (2013). The role of domestic and cross-border venture capital investors in the growth of portfolio companies. *Small Business Economics*, *40*(3), 553–573. http://dx.doi.org/10.1007/s11187-011-9383-y.

Dixit, A., & Jayaraman, N. (2001). Internationalization strategies of Private Equity firms. The Journal of Private Equity, 5(1), 40–54. https://doi.org/10.3905/jpe.2001.319999.

Gompers, P., & Lerner, J. (1999). An analysis of compensation in the U.S. venture capital partnership. Journal of Financial Economics, 51(1), 3–44. https://doi.org/10.1016/S0304-405X (98)00042-7.

Gompers, P., Kaplan, S.N., & Mukharlyamov, V. (2016). What do private equity firms say they do? Journal of Financial Economics, 121(3), 449–476. http://dx.doi.org/10.1016/j. jfineco.2016.06.003

Gray, L.P. (2005). How family dynamics influence the structure of the family office. *Journal of Wealth Management*, *8*(2), 9–17. http://dx.doi.org/10.3905/jwm.2005.571004.

Huang, L., & Pearce, J. L. (2015). Managing the unknowable: The effectiveness of early-stage investor gut feel in entrepreneurial investment decisions. *Administrative Science Quarterly*, *60*(4), 634–670. http://dx.doi.org/10.1177/0001839215597270

Kammerlander, N., Dessi, C., Bird, M., Floris, M., & Murru, A. (2015). The impact of shared stories on family firm innovation: A multicase study. *Family Business Review*, *28*(4), 332–354. https:// doi.org/10.1177/0894486515607777

Kammerlander, N., & Leitner, L. (2018, September 17). When entrepreneurs raise entrepreneurs. Entrepreneur & Innovation Exchange. https://familybusiness.org/content/When-entrepreneurs-raise-entrepreneurs

Kaplan, S. N., & Stromberg, P. (2009). Leveraged buyouts and private equity. *Journal of Economic Perspectives*, *23*(1), 121–46. https://doi.org/10.1257/jep.23.1.121

Le Breton-Miller, I., & Miller, D. (2018). Beyond the firm: Business families as entrepreneurs. *Entrepreneurship: Theory and Practice*, *42*(4), 527–536. https://doi.org/10.1177/ 1042258717739004

Listenchampion (2017). Top 100 Family Offices Deutschland – Liste der größten verwalteten Familien Vermögen. Retrieved from www.listenchampion.de.

Manigart, S., De Waele, K., Wright, M., Robbie, K., Desbrières, P., Sapienza, H. J., & Beekman, A. (2002). Determinants of required return in venture capital investments: a five-country study. *Journal of Business Venturing*, *17*(4), 291–312. https://doi.org/10.1016/S0883-9026 (00)00067-7

Michel, A., Ahlers, O., Hack, A., & Kellermanns, F. W. (2020). Who is the king of the hill? On bargaining power in private equity buyouts. *Long Range Planning*, *53*(2), 1–21. https://doi. org/10.1016/j.lrp.2018.11.003

Molly, V., Arijs, D., & Lambrecht, J. (2018). Building and maintaining the family business-private equity relationship: An integrated agency-stewardship perspective. Journal of Small Business and Enterprise Development, 25(1), 41–63. https://doi.org/10.1108/JSBED-02-2017-0051.

Morrison, A., & Wensley, R. (1991). Boxing up or boxed in?: A short history of the Boston Consulting Group share/growth matrix. *Journal of Marketing Management, 7*(2), 105–129. https://doi.org/10.1080/0267257X.1991.9964145

Naldi, L., Nordqvist, M., & Zellweger, T.M. (2011). Knowledge resources and performance: The moderating role of family involvement in strategy processes. *Academy of Management Proceedings*, 2011(1), 1–38. https://doi.org/10.5465/ambpp.2011.65870497

Poutziouris, P. Z. (2001). The views of family companies on venture capital: Empirical evidence from the UK small to medium-size enterprising economy. *Family Business Review, 14*(3), 277–291. https://doi.org/10.1111/j.1741-6248.2001.00277.x

Rivo-López, E., Villanueva-Villar, M., Vaquero-Garcia, A., & Lago-Penas, S. (2017). Family offices: What, why and what for. Organizational Dynamics, 46(4), 262–270. https://doi.org/10.1016/j.orgdyn.2017.03.002.

Romano, C. A., Tanewski, G. A., & Smyrnios, K. X. (2001). Capital structure decision making: A model for family business. *Journal of Business Venturing, 16*(3), 285–310. https://doi.org/10.1016/S0883-9026(99)00053-1

Rosplock, K. (2014). *The complete family office handbook: A guide for affluent families and the advisors who serve them*. Bloomberg Press.

Rottke, O. M., & Thiele, F. K. (2018). Do family investors differ from other investors? Similarity, experience, and professionalism in the light of family investee firm challenges. *Journal of Business Economics, 88*(2), 139–166. https://dx.doi.org/10.1007/s11573-017-0871-7.

Roure, J., Segurado, J.L., Welsh, D., & Rosplock, K. (2013). Toward a conceptual model of the role of entrepreneurship in the family office. *Journal of Applied Management & Entrepreneurship, 18*(4), 42–63. https://dx.doi.org/10.9774/GLEAF.3709.2013.oc.00005

Sapienza, H. J., Manigart, S., & Vermeir, W. (1996). Venture capitalist governance and value added in four countries. *Journal of Business Venturing, 11*(6), 439–469. https://dx.doi.org/10.1016/S0883-9026(96)00052-3

Schickinger, A., Bertschi-Michel, A., Leitterstorf, M.P., & Kammerlander, N. (2021a). Same same, but different: capital structures in single family offices compared with private equity firms. *Small Business Economics*, in press. https://doi.org/10.1007/s11187-021-00448-x

Schickinger, A., Bierl, P., Leitterstorf, M.P., & Kammerlander, N. (2021b). Family-related goals, entrepreneurial investment behavior, and governance mechanisms of single family offices: An exploratory study. *Journal of Family Business Strategy*, in press. https://doi.org/10.1016/j.jfbs.2020.100393

Scholes, L., Westhead, P., & Burrows, A. (2008). Family firm succession: The management buy-out and buy-in routes. *Journal of Small Business Management and Enterprise Development, 15*(1), 8–30. http://dx.doi.org/10.1108/14626000810850829

Sieger, P., Zellweger, T.M., Nason, R.S., & Clinton, E. (2011). Portfolio entrepreneurship in family firms: A resource-based perspective. *Strategic Entrepreneurship Journal, 5*(4), 327–351. https://doi.org/10.1002/sej.120

Suess, J. (2014). Family governance – Literature review and the development of a conceptual model. *Journal of Family Business Strategy, 5*(2), 138–155. https://doi.org/10.1016/j.jfbs.2014.02.001

Welsh, D., Memili, E., Rosplock, K., Roure, J., & Segurado, J.L. (2013). Perceptions of entrepreneurship across generations in family offices: A stewardship theory perspective. *Journal of Family Business Strategy, 4*(3), 213–226. http://dx.doi.org/10.1016/j.jfbs.2013.07.003.

Wennberg, K., Wiklund, J., Hellerstedt, K., & Nordqvist, M. (2011). Implications of intra-family and external ownership transfer of family firms: Short-term and long-term performance differences. *Strategic Entrepreneurship Journal*, *5*(4), 352–372. https://doi.org/10.1002/sej.118

Wessel, S., Decker, C., Lange, K., & Hack, A. (2014). One size does not fit all: Entrepreneurial families' reliance on family offices. *European Management Journal*, *32*(1), 37–45. http://dx.doi.org/10.1016/j.emj.2013.08.003.

World Ultra Wealth Report (2014). The world ultra wealth report 2014. https://www.wealthx.com/report/the-wealth-x-and-ubs-world-ultra-wealth-report-2014/.

World Ultra Wealth Report (2019). The world ultra wealth report 2019. https://www.wealthx.com/report/world-ultra-wealth-report-2019/

Yin, R.K. (1994). Discovering the future of the case study method in evaluation research. *American Journal of Evaluation*, *15*(3), 283–290. https://doi.org/10.1177/109821409401500309

Zacharakis, A. L., McMullen, J. S., & Shepherd, D. A. (2007). Venture capitalists' decision policies across three countries: an institutional theory perspective. *Journal of International Business Studies*, *38*(5), 691–708. https://doi.org/10.1057/palgrave.jibs.8400291

Zellweger, T.M., & Kammerlander, N. (2015). Family, wealth, and governance: An agency account. *Entrepreneurship: Theory & Practice*, *39*(6), 1281–1303. http://dx.doi.org/10.1111/etap.12182.

Zellweger, T.M., Eddleston, K.A., & Kellermanns, F.W. (2010). Exploring the concept of familiness: Introducing family firm identity. *Journal of Family Business Strategy*, *1*(1), 54–63. http://dx.doi.org/10.1016/j.jfbs.2009.12.003.

Part IV: **Emerging perspectives**

Part IV consists of five chapters that explore emerging research streams in entrepreneurial finance. These chapters are more speculative in nature, but the topics they address represent several interesting paths forward, particularly for junior researchers interested in making their marks in this field.

Chapter 15 by Minh-Hoang Nguyen and Quan-Hoang Vuong lays out what we know about entrepreneurial finance in developing and emerging markets. It identifies five existing research themes: macro-environment and financial systems; finance and entrepreneurial performance; gender issues and microfinance; venture capital; and crowdfunding.

In Chapter 16 Janine Swail takes on the role of gender in entrepreneurial finance. She challenges the normative thinking and gendered assumptions that still permeate much of the entrepreneurial finance literature and calls attention to the slowness with which the extant literature has responded to gender-focused literature elsewhere in entrepreneurship.

Chapter 17 by Ana Maria Peredo, Bettina Schneider, and Audrey Maria Popa makes a strong effort to map out how the indigenous entrepreneurial finance literature might evolve. Using Canadian evidence, the chapter proposes three avenues for future research.

Chapter 18 by Rebecca Namatovu takes on how startups are financed in post-conflict and disaster zones. She looks across a broad number of literatures and identifies both research gaps and the interplay between institutions, entrepreneurial finance, and context.

Ethics and entrepreneurial finance is addressed by Yves Fassin in this part's final chapter. The dark side of investor and entrepreneur behavior has been addressed to a limited extent in the literature, and this chapter identifies a variety of paths forward.

https://doi.org/10.1515/9783110726312-019

Minh-Hoang Nguyen and Quan-Hoang Vuong

15 A scoping review of most influential entrepreneurial finance studies in developing countries

Abstract: Entrepreneurial finance research has been flourishing in recent years due in part to the significant changes in the global socio-economic situations. However, despite many reviews performed, little is known about the state-of-the-art of literature about developing countries. Therefore, this chapter aims to provide a synthesis of the research landscape and major research topics of entrepreneurial finance in developing countries, as well as some suggestions for future research directions. From 13,775 publications retrieved from the Web of Science database, 33 eligible highly-cited publications were selected for the review. The proportion of highly-cited cited publications about developing countries is minimal, constituting 6.85% of the total highly cited publications. This result can further validate the evidence of ideological homogeneity in the field of entrepreneurial finance. Even though the methodologies used are diverse (e.g., quantitative, qualitative, experimental, and mixed methods), quantitative methods (specifically, Ordinary Least Squares analysis) are still the dominant approach. By further reviewing the contents of 33 publications, we identified five major research topics: 1) macro-environment and financial systems, 2) finance and entrepreneurs' performance, 3) gender issues and microfinance, 4) venture capital, and 5) crowdfunding. The suggested research questions for further systematic review and research are also provided accordingly. Additionally, we also found that the financial activities and the impact of financial issues on entrepreneurial activities of enterprises are considerably influenced by the socio-cultural, institutional, and legal characteristics of the local countries.

Keywords: entrepreneurial finance, socio-cultural differences, institutional differences, Western ideological homogeneity, developing countries

Introduction

Entrepreneurship is a phenomenon that has been increasingly promoted in many developed and developing countries due to the benefits it generates. The benefits can be at multiple levels, from the individual level, organizational level, to national level (Luke et al., 2007). Besides the economic merits, such as profit, wealth creation, innovation, improved standard of living, increased employment rate, increased GDP

Minh-Hoang Nguyen, Quan-Hoang Vuong, Phenikaa University

https://doi.org/10.1515/9783110726312-020

and tax revenue, entrepreneurship also contributes to the pursuit of sustainable development in terms of social and environmental aspects (Dean & McMullen, 2007; Dhahri & Omri, 2018). The survival and growth rate of start-ups are greatly dependent on financial conditions (Ferrucci et al., 2021). Financial constraints are among the major causes that hinder entrepreneurial activities, especially start-ups in developing countries like Thailand, Mexico, Jamaica, and Vietnam (Honig, 1998; McKenzie & Woodruff, 2008; Paulson & Townsend, 2004; Vuong et al., 2016). Due to the development of entrepreneurship, financial markets in developing countries also become more active to meet the financing demand of entrepreneurs (Lingelbach, 2012, 2016). However, the weak institutional and legal systems remain as challenges for entrepreneurs' financing activities (Johnson et al., 2002; Li et al., 2008).

Until now, researchers have conducted many reviews on the financial issues of entrepreneurship (Block et al., 2018; Cumming et al., 2019; Mitter & Kraus, 2011; Nguyen, Pham, et al., 2021; Tenca et al., 2018), but little is known about entrepreneurial finance's state-of-the-art in developing countries. There are some reviews about entrepreneurship in developing countries, but they do not focus solely on the financial aspect. One of those works is the systematic review of Panda (2018) about the constraints faced by women entrepreneurs in developing countries. Based on the findings of 35 research articles, the author highlights that financial constraints and unstable business, economic and political environments are substantive impediments to women's entrepreneurship. However, another review only covers the entrepreneurship topic in China. Using a narrative review, Ahlstrom and Ding (2014) provide an overview of the entrepreneurship research in China and state that Chinese entrepreneurs acquire limited formal financing and greatly rely on social capital (e.g. family and social relationships). This pattern might be the result of distinct institutional and cultural characteristics embedded in Chinese societies. Therefore, this chapter aims to provide a scoping review of the most influential studies about entrepreneurial finance in developing countries.

Why should it be a scoping review? Scoping review is a systematic approach to identify the scope or coverage of a literature body on a particular topic with a clear indication of the volume of studies available and an overview of their focuses (Munn, Peters, et al., 2018). Most of the previous reviews about entrepreneurial finance are performed using the narrative approach, subject to the reviewers' prior knowledge and viewpoint. To avoid subjectivity in the narrative review, systematic and scoping reviews are two potential alternatives due to their systematic, structured, and transparent processes that reduce biases.

A systematic review has five indications: 1) uncover the international evidence, 2) validate current practice/ seek variation/ identify new practices, 3) identify and inform areas for future research, 4) identify and investigate conflicting results, and 5) produce statements to guide decision-making (Munn, Peters, et al., 2018). In other words, systematic reviews are usually employed to answer well-defined research questions and assess the quality of evidence (Munn, Stern, et al., 2018). In contrast, the scoping review does not focus much on details, but rather an overview of the landscape so that it can be used for six main purposes: 1) identify the types of available evidence in a given field, 2) identify key concepts, 3) identify the research methodology, 4) identify key characteristics related to a concept, 5) act as a precursor of a systematic review, and 6) identify and analyze knowledge gap (Munn, Peters, et al., 2018).

So, why should we focus on the core research articles (most influential studies), but not all of them? Entrepreneurial finance is a flourishing field, so reviewing an enormous number of studies can reduce the precision and efficiency of identifying major research topics. To better identify the content of major research topics (contexts, causes, methodology, results, etc.), the review should only focus on publications with the highest representativeness. The most highly cited publications can be representative samples because, regardless of how the publications have been cited, their impacts on subsequent research cannot be denied (Vuong et al., 2021). Such impacts might more or less shape the contents of subsequent studies.

Moreover, the citations in this review are from the Web of Science (WoS) database (one of the most prestigious scientific databases) so the impacts of highly cited research articles are even more substantial and reliable than those in other databases (e.g., Google Scholar). A WoS citation is only recorded when both citing and cited articles are simultaneously published in journals qualified by the database. Because of this process, the impact of the cited document is evaluated twice by qualified editors and reviewers. Therefore, we argue that the core collection of research articles can be used as representative samples for scoping review.

Overall, the current chapter attempts to provide a scoping review of core research articles (most influential studies) in the entrepreneurial finance literature about developing countries. The term "developing country" in this review refers to countries that are not included in the list of developed countries classified by the United Nations (2014). The scoping review is expected to achieve two objectives:
1. To identify major research topics
2. To identify research questions for later systematic reviews and further research in those topics

A detailed explanation of the scoping review methodology is given in the next section. The third section presents major research topics in the field and the description of their contents. Research questions for later systematic reviews and further research are also recommended in the third section. The final section provides a conclusion and indicates the limitations of the current review.

Literature review

Methodology

The current scoping review was conducted following the Preferred Reporting Items for Systematic reviews and Meta-Analyses extension for Scoping Reviews (PRISMA-ScR) (Tricco et al., 2018) with additional reference to the guidance of Peters et al. (2015). This section explains how we defined and collected the core collection of entrepreneurial finance.

In a recent study examining the ideological homogeneity of entrepreneurial finance literature, Vuong et al. (2021) suggest that any scientific field has a nucleus (or a set of ideologies/core values) that was used by editors, reviewers, and researchers to evaluate the scientific rigors and significance, or enrich the literature. The suggestion is based on the Mindsponge theoretical framework (Q.-H. Vuong, 2016; Vuong & Napier, 2015). To be included in the nucleus, a research article has to show its influence over other works in the related field, which can be measured through the citation mechanism. Therefore, it is plausible to say the nucleus of a scientific field is constructed by the most influential publications (or highly cited publications) within the field (Vuong et al., 2021). Publications that acquired 100 or more citations were considered highly-cited publications and included in the review (Fu & Ho, 2016; X. Zhang et al., 2019).

The data retrieved from the WoS database were used in the current review. We employed the search queries proposed by Nguyen et al. (2021) for search documents related to entrepreneurial finance. Nguyen, Pham, et al. (2021) generated the search keywords by referring to prior bibliometric studies about finance and entrepreneurship (Aparicio et al., 2019; Cumming & Groh, 2018; Padilla-Ospina et al., 2018; Vallaster et al., 2019; Xu et al., 2018; D. Zhang et al., 2019). However, the search queries might also be not sufficient because they did not include the common financing sources in developing countries, such as family/friend loan, microfinance, bootstrapping, Islamic finance (Abou-Gabal et al., 2011; Guangrong & Enyan, 2011; Pham et al., 2020). Thus, we decided to expand the search queries to include those keywords.

We conducted the search on 4 June 2021 through the field tag "Topic" using the following two sets of keywords.

- TS = ("entrepreneur*" OR "startup*" OR "start-up*" OR "new enterprise*" OR "new firm*")
- TS = ("financ*" OR "debt*" OR "venture capital*" OR "trade credit*" OR "crowd-fund*" OR "angel invest*" OR "private equit*" OR "IPO*" OR "family loan*" OR "friend loan*" OR "bootstrapping" OR "microfinanc*" OR "islamic financ*")

The generated data were combined employing the Boolean AND and retrieved under the Excel spreadsheet format (.xls). Then, multiple filtering steps to exclude ineligible publications were conducted following the PRISMA guideline.

First of all, we excluded all non-highly-cited publications from the initial data samples, yielding 535 highly cited publications. Next, all publications that are not research articles, such as review articles, editorial articles, books, etc., are eliminated. Then, we manually screened the eligibility of each publication using the following criteria:
- The research articles are about business activities.
- The financial issues and entrepreneurial activities are the pivotal topics of the research article.
- The research articles employ data from developing countries.

The manual eligibility screening process was conducted by two collaborators with the A.I. for Social Data Lab (AISDL) of Vuong & Associates. One author (Minh-Hoang Nguyen) supervised the screening process and double-checked the results at the end. Finally, 33 countries were included in the review (see Table A1). Even though the methodology was rigorously designed and implemented, it still holds some limitations that will be reported at the end for transparency (Vuong, 2020).

Major research topics

This section presents major research topics in entrepreneurial finance in developing countries by synthesizing the main findings of 33 eligible publications. However, 33 publications only account for 6.85% of highly cited publications in entrepreneurial finance (482 publications). Most of the remaining literature (83.82% or 404 publications) is conducted using solely developed countries' data. These statistics additionally validate the evidence of ideological homogeneity advocated by Vuong et al. (2021).

By reviewing and synthesizing the contents and findings of 33 publications, we identified five major research topics: 1) macro-environment and financial systems, 2) finance and entrepreneurs' performance, 3) gender issues and microfinance, 4) venture capital, and 5) crowdfunding. The most common research topic is macro-environment and financial systems, with nine publications (27.27%). Next, finance and entrepreneurs' performance follows, with eight publications (24.24%). Finally, gender issues and microfinance and venture capital shared the third place with six publications (18.18%; see Figure 15.1A).

The methodologies employed by 33 research studies were relatively diverse. We grouped those methodologies into four main categories: 1) qualitative method, 2) quantitative method, 3) experimental method, and 4) mixed method (see Figure 15.1B). The most frequently employed methodology is the quantitative method (60.61%). In contrast, only 3.03% of the studies used both qualitative and quantitative simultaneously. Even though there is a high variation in terms of methodology, analyses in quantitative methods were quite homogenous. Specifically, the simple Ordinary Least

Squares (OLS) regression analysis is used in 17 studies, constituting 85% of studies employing the quantitative method.

A.

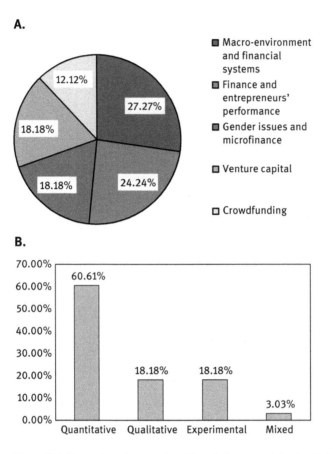

B.

Figure 15.1: Proportion of research articles. A: by research topics, B: by methodology.

Macro-environment and financial systems

The first research topic is about the macro-environment and financial systems. Nine publications in this category mainly focus on the triangle between economic growth, financial systems, and entrepreneurship. One example is the study of King and Levine (1993). Based on the endogenous growth model regarding connections between finance, entrepreneurship, and economic growth, as well as empirical evidence from 80 developed and developing countries, they suggest that financial systems can positively facilitate entrepreneurship and eventually induce productivity improvement. King and Levine (1993, p. 540) state that "a more-developed financial system fosters productivity improvement by choosing higher quality entrepreneurs and projects, by more effectively mobilizing external financing for these entrepreneurs, by providing superior vehicles for diversifying the risk of innovative activities, and by revealing more accurately the potentially large profits associated with the uncertain business of innovation."

However, two major formal institutional factors hinder the positive effects of financial systems on entrepreneurial activities: weak laws and regulations, and taxation. For example, Chinese entrepreneurs perceive inadequate laws and regulations, tax burden, and lack of access to finance as primary barriers to pursue innovation activities, as well as competitive fairness and support systems (Zhu et al., 2012). Even though financial constraints can negatively affect firm growth, insecure property rights are a more important factor (Johnson et al., 2000). Using the dataset of 1,471 entrepreneurs in post-communist countries, Johnson et al. (2002) also find that weak property rights were negatively associated with entrepreneurs' lower reinvestment from retained earnings.

Due to the inadequate protection from expropriation and policy discrimination, private entrepreneurs in regions with relatively weaker laws and regulations (e.g., China) have to use informal protection methods to increase access to bank loans. Such methods include political participation and philanthropic activities (Bai et al., 2006). Li et al. (2008) also confirm the positive impact of political participation on firm growth and access to finance from banks or other state institutions. Besides, they also note that the impact was higher in the regions with weaker market institutions and legal protections. In the region with a weaker legal system, propping and tunnelling practices are also prevalent, which helps explain why markets in developing countries grow rapidly but are subject to economic and financial crises (Friedman et al., 2003). Propping refers to the transfers of funds from a higher-level firm to a lower-level firm in the pyramidal chain, whereas tunnelling refers to the transfer that is made in the opposite direction (Riyanto & Toolsema, 2008). Nevertheless, if laws and regulations are well designed, entrepreneurial activities can be increased. Lee et al. (2011), employing a cross-national database from 29 countries during the 1990–2008 period, suggest that entrepreneur-friendly bankruptcy law was positively correlated with the rate of new firm entry.

Taxation is another major factor that hampers economic growth and entrepreneurship. Djankov et al. (2010), analyzing the data of 85 countries, of which 58 are developing countries, in 2004, find that the increase in effective corporate tax adversely influences the entrepreneurial activities and aggregate investment and foreign direct investment (FDI). The results remain the same when controlling other factors, such as quality of tax administration, property rights security, economic development level, and regulation. In China, such negative outcomes might result from the higher cost of innovation and lower innovation opportunities due to the value-added tax (VAT) system. Nonetheless, suppose a pro-innovation tax system and research and development (R&D) tax credit policy is implemented. In that case, these will lead to lower costs and risk of innovation, as well as more innovation opportunities (Zhu et al., 2012).

Finance and entrepreneurs' performance

The second major research topic of entrepreneurial finance in developing countries is finance and entrepreneurs' performance. Studies about this topic focus on the relationship between financial issues and patterns, performance, or growth of new firms from the microeconomic perspectives. Two studies were conducted using experimental design, consisting of 33.33% of the total experimental studies. The most highly-cited publication about this topic is the study of Yang (2008), which examines how the rising financial capital due to migrants' exchange rate shocks during the 1997 Asian financial crisis affects the entrepreneurship patterns in the Philippines.

To explore the relationship between financial capital and the performance of entrepreneurs, researchers have looked at two directions. First, researchers have explored the impact of financial issues, such as access to finance and financial constraints, on the patterns of entrepreneurs. Yang (2008) found that Philippines households that received extra remittance from overseas due to the sudden and heterogeneous changes in the exchange rate during the 1997 Asian financial crisis were more likely to spend more time and capital on their enterprises. In contrast, households with limited financial capital have a lower likelihood to start a business, a lower amount of investment, and more financial constraints. The effects of financial constraints are more significant in poor regions than in developed ones (Paulson & Townsend, 2004). Financial constraints also reduce entrepreneurs' chances to pursue initiatives that can improve growth and survival in the industrial sector, such as a transition to energy efficiency practices (Nagesha & Balachandra, 2006).

In the second direction, the pivotal research issues are the impacts of financial issues on new firms' performance (e.g., innovation performance, profitability, and growth). Additional start-up capital and obtaining a small business loan are found to help improve the profitability of businesses with and without employees (Honig, 1998). Open innovation also positively affects the financial performance of service-sector firms, and the effect is amplified if the firms are entrepreneurial-oriented (Cheng & Huizingh, 2014). Two experimental studies of McKenzie and Woodruff (2008) and Drexler et al. (2014) find that providing external capital and improving financial literacy through the rule-of-thumb training help increase microenterprises' profits, financial practices, and objective reporting quality. These effects are more impactful among more financially constrained and less sophisticated entrepreneurs. Furthermore, Aghion et al. (2007) discover that private credit and stock market capitalization promote both entry and post-entry growth of new small firms.

Even though the abundance of financial capital can positively affect the performance of new firms, the impacts seem to be conditional on the sector, size, and stage of the firms. For example, despite the positive impact of access to finance on the entry growth of new small firms, Aghion et al. (2007) find no or negative impacts on that of large firms. Moreover, increasing financial capital does not enhance firms' profits that belong to the high technology sector (Honig, 1998).

Gender issues and microfinance

The third major entrepreneurial finance research topic in developing countries is related to gender issues. Studies about gender issues frequently involve microfinance because microfinance empowers and improves women's subjective well-being as a vulnerable population in developing countries. Thus, we named this research topic gender issues and microfinance. This topic comprises two pivotal issues.

The first issue concerns the effect of gender on new firms' financial activities and performance. Employing the World Bank Enterprise Survey data of developing countries in three regions – Europe and Central Asia, Latin America, and Sub-Saharan Africa – Bardasi et al. (2011) find gender gaps in firm size and efficiency growth. Female entrepreneurs also face no discrimination in access to formal finance. Female entrepreneurs in Europe and Central Asia are less likely to seek formal finance than their counterparts. In micro and small family enterprises (MSEs), employing family members is positively associated with sales but negatively associated with profit. However, if the enterprise is led by a female, employing a family member increases both sales and profits (Cruz et al., 2012).

The second pivotal issue in this research topic is the relationship between microfinance lenders and female entrepreneurs. The tricky research questions of this issue are mainly related to 1) the high performance among borrowers, and 2) the failure among borrowers (Bruton et al., 2011). The experimental research of Karlan and Valdivia (2011) shows that female entrepreneurs receiving entrepreneurship training have a greater level of business knowledge, practices, and revenues. The training also helps improve loan repayment and client retention rates. Individual and joint liability loans in the experimental study of Attanasio et al. (2015) also lead to higher repayment rates among Mongolian female borrowers. Nevertheless, only the joint liability loan, under which a small group of borrowers is denied subsequent loans if any one of them does not repay the loan, helps improve the probability of business creation.

Although the impact of microfinance on female entrepreneurial activities is exhibited in several experimental studies, the result is still not validated in some circumstances. For example, Karlan and Zinman (2011)'s experiment shows that access to microfinance negatively influences the business activities and employees as well as the subjective well-being of the entrepreneurs, even when female samples are analyzed separately. They think inconsistencies of the microfinance impacts are results of the complex and disparate mechanisms that start with the household rather than with the business.

Venture capital

Venture capital is the fourth major research topic of entrepreneurial finance research in developing countries. The research topic aims to examine the relationship between entrepreneurs and venture capitalists and their activities. Venture capital financing – developed originally in the cultures and institutional systems of developed Western countries – has to adapt to the local institutional and legal systems when introduced to developing countries, many of which also have different formal and informal institutions in comparison to Western countries. Therefore, most researchers tend to concentrate on exploring the differences of venture capital among countries in terms of culture, institutional and legal systems, and how the local cultures, institutional and legal systems affect venture capital activities.

A study of venture capital activity in 68 countries during the 1996–2006 period shows that formal institutions (a.k.a. a set of political, economic, and contractual rules that regulate individual behavior and shape people interaction) are positively associated with the total number of venture capital investments within a country. However, the impact of this positive association is lessened in countries with a higher level of uncertainty avoidance and collectivism (Li & Zahra, 2012). Ahlstrom and Bruton (2006) also assert that venture capitalists in developed and developing countries have several similarities, but differences with the Anglo-American model still exist. For example, unlike VCs in developed countries, VCs in developing countries must prioritize building their networks to conduct needed activities and even employ informal institutions as substitutes due to the shortage of formal institutions.

Greater reliance on informal cultural-cognitive institutions is also an important criterion to achieve funding in developing countries (Ahlstrom & Bruton, 2006). This is because local cultural values (e.g., *guanxi*) have considerable influence over venture capital industry activities through social capital and social networks (Batjargal & Liu, 2004). In a comparative study regarding the entrepreneurial activity of venture capital, Bruton et al. (2009) find significant differences between industry practices in Latin America and Asia. However, they did not include South and West Asia samples in the study due to considerable cultural and institutional differences. The result highlights that practices of venture capital industries might be significantly distinct across developing countries due to their cultural and institutional diversity.

Besides the cultural and institutional aspects, the legal system is another factor that differentiates venture capital activities among countries. The study of Cumming et al. (2006) indicates that venture-backed companies in countries with higher legality indices have a higher probability of initial public offering (IPO) exits. The legal system quality is also observed to have a more substantial effect on IPO exit than the stock market size. The governance structure of investments in the venture capital industry is also influenced by legal issues, such as legal origin and accounting standards (Cumming et al., 2010).

Crowdfunding

The fifth major research topic is crowdfunding. Along with venture capital, crowdfunding is one of the financing sources that received the greatest attention from entrepreneurial finance researchers worldwide recently. As crowdfunding only emerged in 2010, studies are conducted more recently than those of other topics. Most of the studies employ data from global crowdfunding platforms, including both users from developed and developing countries. Here, only studies employing data from crowdfunding platforms that are specifically designed for finance provision among developing countries (e.g., Kiva) are included.

One of the crucial questions in this topic is what factors influence the effectiveness of crowdfunding campaigns. Signalling businesses' characteristics and intentions through narratives is suggested to raise the amount of funding from crowdfunding platforms. Studying over 400,000 loans made on the Kiva crowdfunding platform during 2006–2012, Moss et al. (2015) discovered that campaigns or businesses signalled as autonomous, competitively aggressive, and risk-taking receive a more significant amount of funding and receive it more rapidly. In contrast, those signalled with conscientiousness, courage, empathy, and warmth narratives are less likely to be funded (Moss et al., 2015).

Apart from funding outcomes, how the campaigns frame their narratives also influences the lenders' responses (Allison et al., 2015). It was found from the samples of 36,665 loans made on Kiva that campaigns were described as an opportunity to support others would receive more positive responses from lenders. Meanwhile, lenders would exhibit less positive responses if the campaigns were referred to as business opportunities.

One remarkable point is that despite the many similar crowdfunding patterns across countries (e.g., China and the USA), some cross-cultural differences still exist (Zheng et al., 2014). In particular, the three dimensions of social capital (e.g. structural dimension, relational dimension, and cognitive dimension) have stronger predictive power towards crowdfunding performance in China than in the USA. Therefore, besides employing global data to study crowdfunding (e.g., data from global crowdfunding platforms), exploring the crowdfunding practices using a country-specific dataset is also necessary to detect the distinctions among different cultural, institutional, and legal contexts.

Research agendas

The entrepreneurship model generated in developed countries, despite being beneficial, is not universally applicable (Bruton et al., 2018). The entrepreneurial activities in developing countries are relatively distinct from those in developed countries because they are shaped by different values, norms, and socio-cultural and institutional settings. Thus, examinations of entrepreneurial finance in developing countries will enrich our understanding of finance-related activities of entrepreneurship through a variety of lenses. Such knowledge, eventually, helps researchers develop indigenous theories that are not only effective in fostering economic development but also face less resistance from the local institutional and socio-cultural filter processes (Nguyen, Pham, et al., 2021). This section provides future research questions for each of the five major topics and research directions for entrepreneurial finance research in developing countries as a whole.

Macro-environment and financial systems. A developed financial system can improve entrepreneurs' productivity, but institutional factors usually hinder it in developing countries (Johnson et al., 2000; Zhu et al., 2012). The inadequate laws and regulation systems in developing countries can lead to the less effective financial performance of entrepreneurs, as compared to developed countries. Tunnelling and probing are more prevalent practices in developing countries than developed counterparts due to their weak legal systems (Friedman et al., 2003). Besides, taxation is also an influential macroeconomic factor contributing to entrepreneurs' financial activities and outcomes (Djankov et al., 2010). Based on these relationships between the macro-environment and financial systems in developing countries, we suggest three research questions for future systematic reviews or research lines for further research:
– How do financial systems in developing countries affect entrepreneurship (e.g., entry, survival, growth, innovation, and social-economic contribution rates)?
– How do legal systems (e.g., laws and regulations) in developing countries affect the impact of financial systems on entrepreneurship (e.g., entry, survival, growth, innovation, and social-economic contribution rates)?
– How do taxations (e.g., laws and regulations) in developing countries affect the impact of financial systems on entrepreneurship (e.g., entry, survival, growth, innovation, and social-economic contribution rates)?

Finance and entrepreneurs' performance. Investigation of the relationship between finance and new firms at the microeconomic level is the second major topic of entrepreneurial finance among developing countries. Even though it is evident that financial availability can facilitate new firms' performance (Yang, 2008), the effects are also subject to the sector, size, and stage of the firms (Aghion et al., 2007; Honig, 1998). Moreover, the socio-cultural traits of entrepreneurs are strong predictors of entrepreneurship processes (Q. H. Vuong, 2016a), so new firms' financial

activities might be different across developing countries with distinct socio-cultural values. Thus, we recommend future systematic reviews and research pay attention to the following three research questions:
-   How do financial issues affect the patterns and activities of new firms across different sectors, sizes, and stages in developing countries?
-   How do financial issues affect new firms' growth and financial performance across different sectors, sizes, and stages in developing countries?
-   How do socio-cultural values moderate the relationship between financial issues and new firms' patterns, activities, growth, and financial performance across developing countries?

Gender issues and microfinance. The involvement between microfinance and gender issues is an important research topic in developing countries because female entrepreneurs often acquire less access to formal finance (Bardasi et al., 2011). However, there remain inconsistencies among experimental studies about the effects of microfinance on female entrepreneurs' growth and performance (Attanasio et al., 2015; Karlan & Zinman, 2011). This is believed to result from complex and disparate mechanisms driven by households' characteristics (Karlan & Zinman, 2011). Such characteristics might be explained by the socio-cultural contexts where the households are residing. Considering such findings, we recommend four research questions for future systematic review and further confirmatory research:
-   What are the gender differences in terms of financial performance and access to finance among entrepreneurs in developing countries?
-   How does microfinance (under different schemes and methods) affect female entrepreneurs' growth and financial performance in developing countries?
-   How does microfinance (under different schemes and methods) affect female entrepreneurs' repayment and client retention rate in developing countries?
-   How do socio-cultural values moderate the impacts of microfinance on female entrepreneurs' performance and activities in developing countries?

Venture capital. Although venture capital financing derived from cultures and institutional systems of developed Western countries, it has been localized to adapt to the indigenous institutional and legal systems as well as socio-cultural contexts in developing countries. Due to greater influences of cultural, institutional and legal aspects on venture capital activities and patterns, we propose three potential research questions for future systematic review and further research:
-   How do the cultural values differentiate the venture capital industries' activities and patterns across different countries?
-   How does the institutional system differentiate the venture capital industries' activities and patterns across different countries?
-   How does the legal system differentiate the venture capital industries' activities and patterns across different countries?

Crowdfunding. Crowdfunding is an emerging financial approach that makes use of the internet and enables globalized microfinance. Recently, many crowdfunding platforms have been launched to support entrepreneurs in low-income countries to acquire funding internationally (e.g., Kiva). Research in this topic focuses on contributing factors of crowdfunding effectiveness. The factors are often associated with types of information that are exposed to the lenders, like the campaign's description narrative (Allison et al., 2015; Moss et al., 2015). The lenders' prior experience and socio-cultural backgrounds influence how such information is perceived, so we suggest two following research questions for future systematic reviews and research:

- What are factors contributing to crowdfunding performance and patterns of entrepreneurs across developing countries?
- How do the socio-cultural traits of the lenders affect the crowdfunding performance and patterns of entrepreneurs in developing countries?

In general, entrepreneurial finance is a multiplex topic. The relationship between finance and entrepreneurship is not similar across countries due to their distinct socio-cultural, institutional, and legal contexts. Such distinctions require researchers to pay more attention to the socio-cultural, institutional, and legal differences while conducting empirical investigations and making theoretical propositions. Moreover, the overreliance on the Western model of entrepreneurship narrows researchers' understanding and creates Western ideological homogeneity among entrepreneurial finance literature. The lack of heterogeneity in the field might result in several negative outcomes: 1) preventing the dissemination of unconventional knowledge (or indigenous theories), 2) making new or innovative ideas underevaluated, and 3) generating blind spots due to scientific uniformity (Vuong et al., 2021). Thus, besides research questions proposed above, future studies regarding entrepreneurial finance in developing countries should concentrate on the following two directions so that indigenous values can be recognized and blind spots of Western-generated theories can be avoided (Bruton et al., 2018):

- What are the fundamental differences between entrepreneurial finance practices among developing and developed countries (or non-Western and Western countries)?
- What are mechanisms and factors (e.g., socio-cultural, institutional, or legal aspects) that drive the differences between entrepreneurial finance practices among developing and developed countries (or non-Western and Western countries)?

Conclusion

This chapter employs a scoping review to provide an overview of the major research topics of the entrepreneurial finance landscape in developing countries. From 13,775 publications of entrepreneurial finance retrieved from the WoS databases, 33 eligible publications were selected for the review. First of all, the proportion of publications about developing countries (6.85%) is relatively minimal compared to those using data from developed countries (83.82%). This result can further validate the evidence of ideological homogeneity in entrepreneurial finance literature (Vuong et al., 2021). It should also be acknowledged that the lack of empirical data in developing countries is one of the major causes of ideological homogeneity (Q. H. Vuong, 2016b).

Secondly, the methodologies employed by 33 studies are relatively diverse, namely: *quantitative method*, *qualitative method*, *experimental method*, and *mixed method*. Among four approaches, the quantitative approach, specifically OLS regression analysis, is most frequently used by researchers. Thirdly and most importantly, we identified five major research topics: 1) *macro-environment and financial systems*, 2) *finance and entrepreneurs' performance*, 3) *gender issues and microfinance*, 4) *venture capital*, and 5) *crowdfunding*. Besides indicating the main contents and directions in these topics, we also proposed research questions for further systematic reviews and studies. Systematic reviews are costly (Munn, Peters, et al., 2018; Vuong, 2018), so such research questions will significantly facilitate the problem-identification processes and reduce time and effort while conducting systematic reviews.

Additionally, one prominent pattern seems to appear across several major research topics about developing countries. That is the financial activity and the impact of financial issues on the performance of new enterprises are subject to the socio-cultural, institutional, and legal characteristics of the local countries and areas (Ahlstrom & Bruton, 2006; Bai et al., 2006; Cumming et al., 2006; Yang, 2008; Zheng et al., 2014). Living in a certain area long enough, the entrepreneurs or financers are significantly influenced by the values and ways of thinking that are shaped by the socio-cultural, institutional, and legal characteristics of the given area. Those impacts might be driven by the information-processing mechanism of the individuals' mindsets (Q.-H. Vuong, 2016; Vuong & Napier, 2015). Empirically, socio-cultural factors are found to be significant determinants of entrepreneurial activity in developing countries (Q. H. Vuong, 2016a). Given that overreliance on financial resources does not necessarily lead to innovation and sustainable growth in a developing country (Nguyen et al., 2019; Vuong & Napier, 2014), we recommend future research on entrepreneurial finance to pay more attention to the impacts of interactions between financial resources and other indigenous factors (e.g., socio-cultural traits) on the innovation performance and sustainable development among new firms.

The current review is not without limitations. Despite the wide coverage, the WoS database cannot entirely cover all the high-quality publications regarding entrepreneurial finance because the journals of those publications are not indexed in the WoS database. However, the number of those publications might be few, so not including them might not affect the review's results much. Moreover, there is also the possibility that researchers in developing countries publish in journals indexed by the national database due to language barriers (Nguyen, Nguyen, et al., 2021). Also, because of the language barriers, the searched results from the WoS database might be biased towards Western countries. Nonetheless, non-Western countries are striving to standardize their evaluation systems according to the WoS and Scopus databases, so using publications downloaded from WoS is one of the optimal choices at the moment. Last but not least, performing a scoping review on the most influential studies in the field can help identify the most prominent research topics but might overlook the recently emerging topics.

Appendix

Table A1: Description of 33 eligible publications by major research topics.

Macro-environment and financial issues					
Citations	References	Geography	Sample size	Methodology	Analytical method
1159	King and Levine (1993)	Both developing and developed countries	80 countries	Quantitative	Three-stage least squares (3SLS)
653	Li et al. (2008)	China	3,258 privately owned enterprises	Quantitative	OLS regression
362	Johnson et al. (2002)	Poland, Romania, Slovakia, Ukraine, and Russia	1,471 entrepreneurs in five countries	Quantitative	Ordered probit regression
308	Friedman et al. (2003)	Both developing and developed countries	14,591 firms in the Worldscope database	Quantitative	OLS regression
219	Djankov et al. (2010)	Both developing and developed countries	85 countries	Quantitative	OLS regression
159	Zhu et al. (2012)	China	82 top managers and owners at 41 SMEs	Qualitative	Semi-structured interview
118	Bai et al. (2006)	China	3,073 private enterprises	Quantitative	Ordered logistic regression

Table A1 (continued)

Macro-environment and financial issues					
Citations	References	Geography	Sample size	Methodology	Analytical method
108	Lee et al. (2011)	Both developing and developed countries	29 countries during 1990–2008	Quantitative	Generalized estimating equations
101	Johnson et al. (2000)	Poland, Romania and Slovakia	300 manufacturing firms	Quantitative	OLS and ordered probit regressions
Financial constraints					
Citations	References	Geography	Sample size	Methodology	Analytical method
381	Yang (2008)	Philippines	1,646 households having a member (s) working overseas	Quantitative	OLS regression
186	Honig (1998)	Jamaica	215 enterprises	Quantitative	OLS regression
168	Cheng and Huizingh (2014)	Taiwan	224 service companies	Quantitative	Exploratory factor analysis and structural equation modeling
117	McKenzie and Woodruff (2008)	Mexico	207 firms	Experimental	Probit regression
117	Nagesha and Balachandra (2006)	India	Two energy-intensive clusters of foundry and brick and tile	Qualitative	Analytic hierarchy process
136	Drexler et al. (2014)	Dominican Republic	1,193 existing ADOPEM business or personal loan clients	Experimental	OLS and Tobit regressions
111	Paulson and Townsend (2004)	Thailand	2,880 households in rural and semi-urban areas	Quantitative	Reduced-form OLS regression
105	Aghion et al. (2007)	Both developing and developed countries	16 countries	Quantitative	OLS regression

Table A1 (continued)

Citations	References	Geography	Sample size	Methodology	Analytical method
Gender and microfinance					
223	Karlan and Valdivia (2011)	Peru	More than 3,000 members of the Foundation for International Community Assistance	Experimental	OLS and probit regressions
146	Karlan and Zinman (2011)	Philippines	1,601 marginally creditworthy applicants	Experimental	OLS regression
143	Cruz et al. (2012)	Dominican Republic	392 micro and small enterprises	Quantitative	Hierarchical regression
108	Attanasio et al. (2015)	Mongolia	1,148 women	Experimental	OLS and probit regressions
107	Bardasi et al. (2011)	Developing regions	27 countries in Eastern Europe and Central Asia, 13 countries in Latin America, and 22 countries in Sub-Saharan Africa	Quantitative	OLS regression
106	Bruton et al. (2011)	Guatemala and Dominican Republic	15 borrowers	Qualitative	Case study

Citations	References	Geography	Sample size	Methodology	Analytical method
Venture capital: institutional and cultural differences					
248	Batjargal and Liu (2004)	China	160 domestic venture capital firms	Mixed	Logistic regression
233	Ahlstrom and Bruton (2006)	Hong Kong, Taiwan, China, Singapore, Taiwan, and South Korea	60 venture capital fund managers and 5 government officials	Qualitative	Semi-structured, in-depth interview
156	Li and Zahra (2012)	Both developing and developed countries	Venture capital activities in 68 countries during 1996–2006	Qualitative	Generalized least squares (GLS) and two-stage least squares regressions

Table A1 (continued)

			Venture capital: institutional and cultural differences		
Citations	References	Geography	Sample size	Methodology	Analytical method
135	Cumming et al. (2010)	Both developing and developed countries	3,848 portfolio firms in 39 countries from North and South America, Europe and Asia during 1971–2003	Quantitative	Multinomial logit regressions
117	Cumming et al. (2006)	Both developing and developed countries	468 venture capital-backed companies from 12 countries in the Asia-Pacific	Quantitative	Multinomial logit regression
115	Bruton et al. (2009)	Both developing and developed countries	13 venture capitalists and four industry experts in Asia, and 13 venture capitalists and four industry experts in Latin America	Qualitative	Grounded Theory
			Crowdfunding		
Citations	References	Geography	Sample size	Methodology	Analytical method
221	Allison et al. (2015)	Both developing and developed countries	3,6000 entrepreneurs on Kiva.org crowdfunding platform	Quantitative	OLS regression
214	Zheng et al. (2014)	Both developing and developed countries	515 and 270 crowdfunding projects in China and the US, respectively	Quantitative	OLS regression
121	Moss et al. (2015)	Both developing and developed countries	Over 400,000 loans made to entrepreneurs who use the crowdfunding platform Kiva during 2006–2012	Quantitative	OLS regression
111	Burtch et al. (2015)	Both developing and developed countries	128,701 visitors that entered the studied crowdfunding platform	Experimental	OLS regression

References

Abou-Gabal, N., Khwaja, A., & Klinger, B. (2011). *Islamic finance and entrepreneurship: challenges and opportunities ahead*. Harvard University. Retrieved from https://www.belfercenter.org/sites/default/files/legacy/files/EFL%20Final.pdf

Aghion, P., Fally, T., & Scarpetta, S. (2007). Credit constraints as a barrier to the entry and post-entry growth of firms. *Economic Policy, 22*(52), 732–779.

Ahlstrom, D., & Bruton, G. D. (2006). Venture capital in emerging economies: Networks and institutional change. *Entrepreneurship Theory and Practice, 30*(2), 299–320.

Ahlstrom, D., & Ding, Z. (2014). Entrepreneurship in China: an overview. *International Small Business Journal, 32*(6), 610–618.

Allison, T. H., Davis, B. C., Short, J. C., & Webb, J. W. (2015). Crowdfunding in a prosocial microlending environment: Examining the role of intrinsic versus extrinsic cues. *Entrepreneurship Theory and Practice, 39*(1), 53–73.

Aparicio, G., Iturralde, T., & Maseda, A. (2019). Conceptual structure and perspectives on Entrepreneurship education research: A bibliometric review. *European Research on Management and Business Economics, 25*(3), 105–113.

Attanasio, O., Augsburg, B., De Haas, R., Fitzsimons, E., & Harmgart, H. (2015). The impacts of microfinance: Evidence from joint-liability lending in Mongolia. *American Economic Journal: Applied Economics, 7*(1), 90–122.

Bai, C. E., Lu, J., & Tao, Z. (2006). Property rights protection and access to bank loans: Evidence from private enterprises in China. *Economics of Transition, 14*(4), 611–628.

Bardasi, E., Sabarwal, S., & Terrell, K. (2011). How do female entrepreneurs perform? Evidence from three developing regions. *Small Business Economics, 37*(4), 417.

Batjargal, B., & Liu, M. (2004). Entrepreneurs' access to private equity in China: The role of social capital. *Organization Science, 15*(2), 159–172.

Block, J. H., Colombo, M. G., Cumming, D. J., & Vismara, S. (2018). New players in entrepreneurial finance and why they are there. *Small Business Economics, 50*(2), 239–250.

Bruton, G. D., Ahlstrom, D., & Puky, T. (2009). Institutional differences and the development of entrepreneurial ventures: A comparison of the venture capital industries in Latin America and Asia. *Journal of International Business Studies, 40*(5), 762–778.

Bruton, G. D., Khavul, S., & Chavez, H. (2011). Microlending in emerging economies: Building a new line of inquiry from the ground up. *Journal of International Business Studies, 42*(5), 718–739.

Bruton, G. D., Zahra, S. A., & Cai, L. (2018). Examining entrepreneurship through indigenous lenses. *Entrepreneurship Theory and Practice, 42*(3), 351–361.

Burtch, G., Ghose, A., & Wattal, S. (2015). The hidden cost of accommodating crowdfunder privacy preferences: A randomized field experiment. *Management science, 61*(5), 949–962.

Cheng, C. C., & Huizingh, E. K. (2014). When is open innovation beneficial? The role of strategic orientation. *Journal of Product Innovation Management, 31*(6), 1235–1253.

Cruz, C., Justo, R., & De Castro, J. O. (2012). Does family employment enhance MSEs performance?: Integrating socioemotional wealth and family embeddedness perspectives. *Journal of business venturing, 27*(1), 62–76.

Cumming, D., Deloof, M., Manigart, S., & Wright, M. (2019). New directions in entrepreneurial finance. *Journal of Banking & Finance, 100*, 252–260.

Cumming, D., Fleming, G., & Schwienbacher, A. (2006). Legality and venture capital exits. *Journal of corporate finance, 12*(2), 214–245.

Cumming, D., & Groh, A. P. (2018). Entrepreneurial finance: Unifying themes and future directions. *Journal of corporate finance, 50*, 538–555.

Cumming, D., Schmidt, D., & Walz, U. (2010). Legality and venture capital governance around the world. *Journal of business venturing*, *25*(1), 54–72.

Dean, T. J., & McMullen, J. S. (2007). Toward a theory of sustainable entrepreneurship: Reducing environmental degradation through entrepreneurial action. *Journal of business venturing*, *22*(1), 50–76.

Dhahri, S., & Omri, A. (2018). Entrepreneurship contribution to the three pillars of sustainable development: What does the evidence really say? *World Development*, *106*, 64–77.

Djankov, S., Ganser, T., McLiesh, C., Ramalho, R., & Shleifer, A. (2010). The effect of corporate taxes on investment and entrepreneurship. *American Economic Journal: Macroeconomics*, *2*(3), 31–64.

Drexler, A., Fischer, G., & Schoar, A. (2014). Keeping it simple: Financial literacy and rules of thumb. *American Economic Journal: Applied Economics*, *6*(2), 1–31.

Ferrucci, E., Guida, R., & Meliciani, V. (2021). Financial constraints and the growth and survival of innovative start-ups: An analysis of Italian firms. *European Financial Management*, *27*(2), 364–386.

Friedman, E., Johnson, S., & Mitton, T. (2003). Propping and tunneling. *Journal of Comparative Economics*, *31*(4), 732–750.

Fu, H.-Z., & Ho, Y.-S. (2016). Highly cited Antarctic articles using Science Citation Index Expanded: a bibliometric analysis. *Scientometrics*, *109*(1), 337–357.

Guangrong, M., & Enyan, Y. (2011). Social Networks, Informal Finance and Entrepreneurship. *Economic Research Journal*, *3*, 83–94.

Honig, B. (1998). What determines success? Examining the human, financial, and social capital of Jamaican microentrepreneurs. *Journal of business venturing*, *13*(5), 371–394.

Johnson, S., McMillan, J., & Woodruff, C. (2000). Entrepreneurs and the ordering of institutional reform: Poland, Slovakia, Romania, Russia and Ukraine compared. *Economics of Transition*, *8*(1), 1–36.

Johnson, S., McMillan, J., & Woodruff, C. (2002). Property rights and finance. *American Economic Review*, *92*(5), 1335–1356.

Karlan, D., & Valdivia, M. (2011). Teaching entrepreneurship: Impact of business training on microfinance clients and institutions. *Review of Economics and Statistics*, *93*(2), 510–527.

Karlan, D., & Zinman, J. (2011). Microcredit in theory and practice: Using randomized credit scoring for impact evaluation. *science*, *332*(6035), 1278–1284.

King, R. G., & Levine, R. (1993). Finance, entrepreneurship and growth. *Journal of Monetary Economics*, *32*(3), 513–542.

Lee, S.-H., Yamakawa, Y., Peng, M. W., & Barney, J. B. (2011). How do bankruptcy laws affect entrepreneurship development around the world? *Journal of business venturing*, *26*(5), 505–520.

Li, H., Meng, L., Wang, Q., & Zhou, L.-A. (2008). Political connections, financing and firm performance: Evidence from Chinese private firms. *Journal of Development Economics*, *87*(2), 283–299.

Li, Y., & Zahra, S. A. (2012). Formal institutions, culture, and venture capital activity: A cross-country analysis. *Journal of business venturing*, *27*(1), 95–111.

Lingelbach, D. (2012). Global venture capital 'hotspots': developing countries. In H. Landström & C. Mason (Eds.), *Handbook of Research on Venture Capital* (Vol. 2, pp. 251–279). Edward Elgar Publishing.

Lingelbach, D. (2016). Business angels in sub-Saharan Africa. In H. Landström & C. Mason (Eds.), *Handbook of research on business angels* (pp. 256–281). Edward Elgar Publishing.

Luke, B., Verreynne, M.-L., & Kearins, K. (2007). Measuring the benefits of entrepreneurship at different levels of analysis. *Journal of Management and Organization*, *13*(4), 312–330.

McKenzie, D., & Woodruff, C. (2008). Experimental evidence on returns to capital and access to finance in Mexico. *The World Bank Economic Review, 22*(3), 457–482.

Mitter, C., & Kraus, S. (2011). Entrepreneurial finance–issues and evidence, revisited. *International Journal of Entrepreneurship and Innovation Management, 14*(2–3), 132–150.

Moss, T. W., Neubaum, D. O., & Meyskens, M. (2015). The effect of virtuous and entrepreneurial orientations on microfinance lending and repayment: A signaling theory perspective. *Entrepreneurship Theory and Practice, 39*(1), 27–52.

Munn, Z., Peters, M. D., Stern, C., Tufanaru, C., McArthur, A., & Aromataris, E. (2018). Systematic review or scoping review? Guidance for authors when choosing between a systematic or scoping review approach. *BMC Medical Research Methodology, 18*(1), 1–7.

Munn, Z., Stern, C., Aromataris, E., Lockwood, C., & Jordan, Z. (2018). What kind of systematic review should I conduct? A proposed typology and guidance for systematic reviewers in the medical and health sciences. *BMC Medical Research Methodology, 18*(1), 5.

Nagesha, N., & Balachandra, P. (2006). Barriers to energy efficiency in small industry clusters: multi-criteria-based prioritization using the analytic hierarchy process. *Energy, 31*(12), 1969–1983.

Nguyen, M.-H., Nguyen, H. T. T., Le, T.-T., Luong, A.-P., & Vuong, Q.-H. (2021). Gender issues in family business research: A bibliometric scoping review. *Journal of Asian Business and Economic Studies, ahead-of-print.*

Nguyen, M.-H., Pham, T.-H., Ho, M.-T., Nguyen, H. T. T., & Vuong, Q.-H. (2021). On the social and conceptual structure of the 50-year research landscape in entrepreneurial finance. *SN Business & Economics, 1*(2), 1–29.

Nguyen, V.-H. T., Vuong, T.-T., Ho, M.-T., & Vuong, Q.-H. (2019). The new politics of debt in the transition economy of Vietnam. *Austrian Journal of South-East Asian Studies, 12*(1), 91–110.

Padilla-Ospina, A. M., Medina-Vásquez, J. E., & Rivera-Godoy, J. A. (2018). Financing innovation: A bibliometric analysis of the field. *Journal of Business & Finance Librarianship, 23*(1), 63–102.

Panda, S. J. G. i. M. A. I. J. (2018). Constraints faced by women entrepreneurs in developing countries: review and ranking. *Gender in Management: An International Journal, 33*(4), 315–331.

Paulson, A. L., & Townsend, R. (2004). Entrepreneurship and financial constraints in Thailand. *Journal of corporate finance, 10*(2), 229–262.

Peters, M. D., Godfrey, C. M., Khalil, H., McInerney, P., Parker, D., & Soares, C. B. (2015). Guidance for conducting systematic scoping reviews. *JBI Evidence Implementation, 13*(3), 141–146.

Pham, T.-H., Ho, M.-T., Vuong, T.-T., Nguyen, M.-C., & Vuong, Q.-H. (2020). Entrepreneurial finance: Insights from English language training market in Vietnam. *Journal of Risk and Financial Management, 13*(5), 96.

Riyanto, Y. E., & Toolsema, L. A. (2008). Tunneling and propping: A justification for pyramidal ownership. *Journal of Banking and Finance, 32*(10), 2178–2187.

Tenca, F., Croce, A., & Ughetto, E. (2018). Business angels research in entrepreneurial finance: A literature review and a research agenda. *Journal of Economic Surveys, 32*(5), 1384–1413.

Tricco, A. C., Lillie, E., Zarin, W., O'Brien, K. K., Colquhoun, H., Levac, D., . . . Weeks, L. (2018). PRISMA extension for scoping reviews (PRISMA-ScR): checklist and explanation. *Annals of Internal Medicine, 169*(7), 467–473.

United Nations. (2014). *World economic situation and prospects 2014.* Retrieved from https://www.un.org/development/desa/dpad/publication/world-economic-situation-and-prospects-2014/

Vallaster, C., Kraus, S., Lindahl, J. M. M., & Nielsen, A. (2019). Ethics and entrepreneurship: A bibliometric study and literature review. *Journal of Business Research, 99*, 226–237.

Vuong, Q.-H. (2016). Global Mindset as the Integration of Emerging Socio-Cultural Values Through Mindsponge Processes: A Transition Economy Perspective. In J. Kuada (Ed.), *Global Mindsets: Exploration and Perspectives* (pp. 109–126). Routledge.

Vuong, Q.-H. (2018). The (ir)rational consideration of the cost of science in transition economies. *Nature Human Behaviour*, *2*, 5.

Vuong, Q.-H. (2020). Reform retractions to make them more transparent. *Nature*, *582*, 149.

Vuong, Q.-H., & Napier, N. K. (2015). Acculturation and global mindsponge: an emerging market perspective. *International Journal of Intercultural Relations*, *49*, 354–367.

Vuong, Q.-H., Nguyen, T. T. H., Pham, T.-H., Ho, M.-T., & Nguyen, M.-H. (2021). Assessing the ideological homogeneity in entrepreneurial finance research by highly cited publications. *Humanities and Social Sciences Communications*, *8*, 110.

Vuong, Q. H. (2016a). Impacts of geographical locations and sociocultural traits on the Vietnamese entrepreneurship. *SpringerPlus*, *5*(1), 1189.

Vuong, Q. H. (2016b). Survey data on entrepreneurs' subjective plan and perceptions of the likelihood of success. *Data in brief*, *6*, 858–864.

Vuong, Q. H., Do, T. H., & Vuong, T. T. (2016). Resources, experience, and perseverance in entrepreneurs' perceived likelihood of success in an emerging economy. *Journal of Innovation and Entrepreneurship*, *5*(1), 1–24.

Vuong, Q. H., & Napier, N. K. (2014). Resource curse or destructive creation in transition: Evidence from Vietnam's corporate sector. *Management Research Review*, *37*(7), 642–657.

Xu, X., Chen, X., Jia, F., Brown, S., Gong, Y., & Xu, Y. (2018). Supply chain finance: A systematic literature review and bibliometric analysis. *International Journal of Production Economics*, *204*, 160–173.

Yang, D. (2008). International migration, remittances and household investment: Evidence from Philippine migrants' exchange rate shocks. *The Economic Journal*, *118*(528), 591–630.

Zhang, D., Zhang, Z., & Managi, S. (2019). A bibliometric analysis on green finance: Current status, development, and future directions. *Finance Research Letters*, *29*, 425–430.

Zhang, X., Estoque, R. C., Xie, H., Murayama, Y., & Ranagalale, M. (2019). Bibliometric analysis of highly cited articles on ecosystem services. *PLOS ONE*, *14*(2), e0210707.

Zheng, H., Li, D., Wu, J., & Xu, Y. (2014). The role of multidimensional social capital in crowdfunding: A comparative study in China and US. *Information & Management*, *51*(4), 488–496.

Zhu, Y., Wittmann, X., & Peng, M. W. (2012). Institution-based barriers to innovation in SMEs in China. *Asia Pacific Journal of Management*, *29*(4), 1131–1142.

Janine Swail

16 Conceptualizing gender in entrepreneurial finance: Past trends, current developments and future opportunities

Abstract: This chapter will illustrate how gender is intertwined in the entrepreneurial activities of raising and awarding entrepreneurial finance with a particular focus on the areas of angel and venture capital financing. The aim here is to provide a meaningful gender perspective to challenge normative thinking and gendered assumptions that still permeate much of the entrepreneurial finance literature. The chapter begins by discussing the influence of gender on broader entrepreneurial behaviour before focusing in on the specific domain of entrepreneurial finance. A mini-review of the literature is then presented spanning two time periods – 2000–2015 and 2016 to date – to illustrate how the field has developed, albeit slowly in its conceptualization of gender. We then turn our attention to the future opportunities for research and advance five different areas or 'roads less traveled' for scholars to continue on.

Keywords: gender, women entrepreneurs, venture capital, angel financing, bias

Introduction

Since the early 2000s, the concept of gender within the entrepreneurial finance (EF) literature has been elusive at best and ignored at worst. Drover, Busenitz, Matusik, Townsend, Anglin and Dushnitsky (2017) published "A Review and Roadmap of Entrepreneurial Equity Financing Research" in the Journal of Management and alluded to gender (as a variable) briefly in two separate sentences. Tenca, Croce and Ughetto (2018) argue that within the business angel research, an established subset of EF, gender (as a theme) has received scant attention despite its potential to "produce high-impact research" (p. 1403). Conversely, "access to finance" is one of the most well-trodden domains within women's entrepreneurship research (Henry, Foss & Ahl, 2016), largely because it is consistently cited as one of the most pressing challenges faced by women entrepreneurs globally (OECD/EU, 2018). Over the last two decades, a gendered critique has persistently challenged the notion that entrepreneurship is a meritocratic field of agentic activity (Marlow & Swail, 2014: Ahl, 2006; Bruni, Gherardi & Poggio, 2004) which has permitted the development of

Janine Swail, Business School, University of Auckland

https://doi.org/10.1515/9783110726312-021

more informed debates and robust theorizing that conceptualizes gender as socially constructed and "performed" by both women and men.

Thus, the EF domain could be better served by more critical analyses adopting a gender lens to facilitate new perspectives and alternative ways of thinking. However, in doing so a noteworthy starting point emphasizes that simply "adding women to the mix" in an attempt to address the dominant masculine discourse that prevails in much of the EF literature will *not* meaningfully move the field forward. As Harding (1987) argues ". . . defining what is in need of explanation for only from the perspective of the bourgeois white men leads to partial and even perverse understandings of social life" (p. 7). Leitch, Welter and Henry (2018) acknowledge that the dial has moved slightly in recent empirical studies from exploring what is visible and easily accessed towards less obvious explanations to the persistent gender finance gap per se. Therefore, the aim of this chapter is to discuss how gender has been conceptualized to date within EF through a critique of past trends, current developments and concluding with highlighting future opportunities. EF encompasses venture capital, private equity, private debt, trade credit, IPOs, angel finance, and crowdfunding, among other forms of finance (Cumming & Johan, 2017). Applying a gender lens to the gamut of EF is not within the scope of this chapter, particularly if exploring from both demand and supply side perspectives. Rather our analysis will focus first on areas that have received the most attention to date: angel finance and venture capital. For both areas we present insights from key empirical studies that have focused on both demand and supply-side of financing. The final section will build on these cumulative insights across contexts to elucidate "a road less traveled" not just for gender scholars to continue on but for EF scholars to join.

Literature review

The influence of gender upon entrepreneurial behavior

To scaffold the forthcoming analysis of gender and EF, we must first interrogate how the influence of gender upon entrepreneurial behavior is interpreted and articulated. Lindgren and Packendorff (2003) suggest that the mainstream entrepreneurship field has uncritically adopted some taken-for-granted assumptions, including normative, masculinized assumptions that have hampered its development. Therefore, the dominant discourse of entrepreneurship embodies particular forms of masculinity which have an impact on both male and female subjectivities whereby entrepreneurial identities are both contested and legitimized (Hamilton, 2014). From a feminist post-structuralist perspective, which draws attention to how knowledge is produced and "what has been obscured or made invisible" (Fletcher, 2001,

p. 23) it is argued that women's entrepreneurship has been neglected historically and there has been limited attention paid to gender dynamics (Byrne, Radu-Lefebvre, Fattoum & Balachandra, 2021). The lack of explicit feminist analysis has produced a prejudicial ontology (Marlow & Al-Dajani, 2017) that celebrates the ideal entrepreneur as an innovative, competitive and aggressive hero-type i.e., inherently male (and white) (Ahl, 2006; Gupta, Turban, Wasti & Sikdar, 2009). As a result, this unconscious bias has, "on the one hand, rendered women invisible in that all entrepreneurs are universally coded male. On the other hand, women are 'othered' as, when their entrepreneurial efforts have been recognized, they have been assessed against a mythical stereotypical male" (Marlow & Al-Dajani, 2017, p. 181). This "othering" practice has served to sustain social expectations of male/female entrepreneur difference, thereby implicitly reproducing male experience as a preferred normative value (Bruni, Gherardi, & Poggio, 2004). Consequently, this has given considerable voice to the 'underperformance thesis;' the alleged association between gender and firm performance where women-owned firms are more likely to be labelled as 'under-performing' (Marlow, Shaw and Carter, 2008; McAdam and Marlow, 2013). In response, critical feminist scholars within entrepreneurship argue that this label is a myth which has arisen, and persists, as an articulation of embedded socially situated gendered assumptions of female deficiency (McAdam and Marlow, 2013). What is produced is a feminized entrepreneurial-deficit model that questions women's ambition, competency, and risk propensity with regard to their early-stage ventures.

Critical feminist perspectives challenge these 'lack of agentic ability' assumptions by highlighting how multiple structural constraints combined with stereotypical biases regarding poor entrepreneurial 'fit' limit women's ability to accrue entrepreneurial resources (Henry et al. 2016; Marlow and Martinez Dy, 2018). Furthermore, Kelan (2009) argues that denotations of gender remain a proxy for femininity; yet the negative value associated with feminine attributes and behaviors renders women disadvantaged as gendered subject beings (Butler, 2011), particularly in entrepreneurial contexts where masculinity is the 'default setting' (Marlow and Al-Dajani, 2017). As a result, the opportunity to analytically expose how both women and men 'do' gender as well as entrepreneurship has been largely overlooked. It is therefore unsurprising that the subset of literature on EF has afforded limited attention to gender influences and practices. The following sections shed light on how EF studies have conceptualized gender and draw on literature from 2000–2021.[1]

---

[1] This chapter is not a meta-review of literature to date. Rather we employ key articles and book chapters to illustrate how gender has been conceptualised to date in the EF literature, specifically angel and VC finance. For a wider, systematic literature review see: Lindvert, Alsos and Ljunggren (2021).

Past trends – venture capital and angel finance (from 2000–2015)

The seminal research conducted by the Diana Project[2] has heavily influenced the study of venture capital funding in women-led businesses over the last 22 years, albeit with a US-centric focus. Their pioneering study in 1999, as the venture capital industry in the United States was growing rapidly, asked the question 'Is gender a factor?' with respect to patterns of venture capital (Greene, Brush, Hart and Saparito, 2001). The resounding conclusion of their study was affirmative, revealing that between 1988–1999 VC investment in companies with a woman on the executive team did not exceed 4%. Thirteen years later (in 2012), a follow up study reported an increase of from 4% to 15%. However, this is somewhat overshadowed by the fact that only 2.7% (183) of VC funded companies had a woman in the CEO role; or that 86% of all VC-funded ventures had no women at all in management positions, despite that fact there was no difference found between the performance profiles of VC funded ventures with male or female CEOs (Brush, Greene, Balachandra and Davis, 2018).

Comparable statistics for Europe and other parts of the world are limited for the earlier part of this timeframe largely due to the relative infancy of venture capital industries outside of the US. Furthermore, during this period VC markets contracted, whilst angel financing grew significantly (Brush, Greene, Balachandra and Davis, 2014). For example, in 2012 there were 412 active VC firms in the US compared to 1022 at the height of the dot.com bubble in 2000 (Brush et al. 2018). In 2014, Sohl (2015) reported angel investments in the US totaling $24.1 billion in 73,400 ventures compared to $48 billion in 4356 venture capital deals. The growth of angel financing is also evident in Europe with total investment increasing by 8.3% from 5.5 billion euros in 2012 to 6.1 billion in 2015 (European Business Angel Network, 2015, cited in Edelman, Manolova and Brush, 2017). Despite the fact that these high-net worth individuals were becoming more visible across EF ecosystems globally, only 15% of their capital investments went to women recipients and women angels represented 26.1% of the angel market in the US (Sohl, 2015).

Alternative explanations have been advanced when interpreting the above statistics that consider both demand and supply perspectives in relation to women entrepreneurs' access to finance. Turning our attention to the demand-side, it is apparent that earlier literature is underpinned by the 'underperformance hypothesis' or 'deficit model' previously discussed. First, an established body of literature recognizes that a rational explanation as to why fewer women entrepreneurs receive

---

2 The Diana Project is a multi-university longitudinal research program designed to determine and influence the factors that lead to high-growth, women-led ventures, by investigating the supply of and demand for resources for women-led ventures and by comparing growth models in male- and female-led ventures. Further details on the purpose and publications can be found at https://www. dianaproject.org.

EF is largely because their businesses do not 'fit' the typical profile (Coleman and Robb, 2009; Crosnon and Gneezy, 2009; Fairlie and Robb, 2009). The broader entrepreneurship literature defines women early-stage ventures as smaller, younger and more risk-averse (when compared to male-owned), home-based, locally-focused and operating in sectors where growth may be limited (Carter and Shaw, 2006; McAdam, 2013; Carter, Mwaura, Ram, Trehan and Jones, 2015; Leitch et al. 2018). Indeed, Brush et al. (2014) found that the majority of women-founded start-ups capitalize their ventures using personal finances as opposed to external financing. Furthermore, a recent study using data from the Panel Study of Entrepreneurial Dynamics II (PSED II) confirmed that women (nascent) entrepreneurs are considerably less likely to ask for financing and suggested that the size of an entrepreneur's support network is an important conditioning factor (Kwapisz and Hechavarria, 2018). Thus, Cowling, Marlow and Liu (2020, p. 855) explain that ". . . the picture painted by prevailing evidence regarding demand suggests a scenario where a number of factors coalesce to channel women towards dependency upon informal funding, whilst those who do seek formal funding may be more cautious in their ambitions, given feminised risk aversion."

A gendered critique requires further investigation to this current reality if we are to critically understand the structural mechanisms and hegemonic discourses at play that disable women entrepreneurs from the opportunity to grow their ventures using EF in the first instance. First, it must be acknowledged that when studying growth-oriented, early-stage ventures who pursue EF options, we are already focusing on a distinct minority. Brush et al. (2018, p. 116) described the access of venture capital in the US as a "black swan' event" because approximately a mere 1% of all businesses in the US ever receive venture financing (Lerner and Tag, 2013). With regard the performance of new and small firms, Storey (2011) argues that many small firms never experience growth, rather contraction is much more typical. Therefore, the nature of women-owned businesses as small, young and risk averse is simply a reflection of the majority of firms in any given population. Yet, women entrepreneurs are pejoratively singled out for not exploring external finance, simply reinforcing the feminised entrepreneurial-deficit discourse so prevalent in Western societies (Ahl and Marlow, 2021; Marlow and Martinez-Dy, 2018).

Second, how gender positions, benefits and disadvantages some entrepreneurs over others must be critically examined. Gendered structural challenges impede women's entrepreneurial agency often marginalizing their start-up activities into service oriented, low growth sectors (Ahl and Marlow, 2021). These sectors are not characterized by the technological and innovative advances deemed necessary to create the exit-focused business models many investors demand (Lam and Seidel, 2020). Consequently, they do not attract the attention of EF ecosystems and are financed organically, informally, or with personal finances. The proposed solution here to such embedded structural subordination is for women to simply 'step-up' and commit to launching ventures in the "'right' (male dominated) industries and produce growth trajectories matching those of male-owned and managed businesses" (Harrison, Leitch, McAdam, 2020, p. 1044), which in turn will lead to more women-owned ventures securing EF. Problem solved! Except that by individualizing the 'problem', structural discrimination, alongside occupational segregation, are masked as the very source of inequality that deny women entrepreneurs entry into EF arenas from the outset.

For those women who are able to "'make themselves over' into the preferred entrepreneurial prototypes" (Marlow, 2020, p. 44)' suitable for raising external capital, other forms of masculine hegemony present ongoing challenges. Gender role perceptions, gender stereotyping, and gendered networks have all been examined in greater depth since the mid-2000s within EF, albeit with an overwhelming methodological focus of employing 'gender as a variable' (GAV) (Cromie, 1987) to compare women against male-owned businesses (Alsos, Isaksen and Ljunggren, 2006; Brush et al. 2004; Becker-Blease and Sohl, 2007; Coleman and Robb, 2009). I acknowledge given the relative paucity of research exploring gender in EF, a GAV approach is a useful starting point to build a picture of the 'current state' of the field even if it, "simply adds women to the research agenda, in order to make women's presence and conditions visible" (Henry et al. 2016, p. 221). Nonetheless, gender is incorrectly operationalized as an equivalent 'sex' variable, underpinned by essentialist assumptions and compared against a 'male norm'. Subsequently, contextual factors affecting women's life situation are not always considered and women were (unintentionally) blamed for not being as successful in raising finance, *when compared* to their male counterparts with one study concluding "that women need to put in even more efforts on this issue than men" (Alsos et al. 2006, p. 682).

Indeed, one way for women to expend '*more effort*' was for them to step up as finance providers and support women entrepreneurs through proactively selecting their ventures to finance. During this period empirical studies began to respond to calls and extend a welcome focus on these supply-side issues of EF. However, the rationale for extending focus was premised on the assumption that the relative minority of women who operate as investors in EF ecosystems (be that as business angels or venture fund managers/partners) was potentially impacting upon women entrepreneurs' access to EF. Yet the collective evidence base is somewhat inconclusive as to whether women angels for example, are more likely to invest in women-founded ventures. Harrison and Mason (2007) reported that women angels were only *slightly* more likely to invest. However, Becker-Blease and Sohl (2011) found that predominantly or all-women angel groups will not automatically favor women entrepreneurs' proposals. Edelman et al. (2017, p. 309) suggest that such neutrality or reluctance of women angels to invest in women-led businesses is related to the need to "prove themselves in a male-dominated investment world," albeit this explanation requires further investigation. Thus, similar to the 'deficit' or 'lacking' narrative that has endured in women's entrepreneurship research, the same narrative has been used to study women as external finance providers. Studies during this period reported a declining trend among VC firms in the US, with women partners dropping from 10% in 1999 to 6% in 2013. Harrison and Mason (2007, p. 453) reported the relative invisibility of women business angels who accounted for "fewer than 5%" in the UK with estimates of between 200–500 potential and active women business angels. A compelling conclusion among these studies and others (Brush et al. 2004) was that the dominance of male networks among VC and angel landscapes and resultant gender imbalance was serving to structurally disadvantage women entrepreneurs seeking capital.

The concept of 'homophily', defined as the "tendency of individuals to associate with others based on shared characteristics" (Greenberg and Mollick, 2017, p. 341), was first introduced in this space to explain how gender homophily may result in men being more likely to prefer investing in businesses with male CEOs than female CEOs, or all male teams. Becker-Blease and Sohl (2007) confirmed strong evidence of homophily from the demand-side with entrepreneurs seeking capital from same-sex investors, but the evidence was weaker on the supply side between 2000–2004. Nonetheless, they supported ongoing public policy recommendations (Brush et al. 2004: Harrison and Mason, 2007) that a solution to address the funding gap for women entrepreneurs was to increase the participation of women in early-stage markets. This prompted a somewhat 'deja-vu' approach to researching women angels with studies again focusing on gender differences (e.g., self-confidence or self-efficacy, risk-aversion, prior entrepreneurial experience); this time between male and female investors, drawing similar 'under-performance' reasons for their lack of and/or underwhelming participation in investment ecosystems (Becker-Blease and Sohl, 2011); Harrison and Mason, 2007). More constructively, Coleman and Robb (2016) explored why women choose *not to become* angel investors, advancing five reasons, two of which chime with the under-performance narrative: (1) they do not feel prepared and; 2) are risk averse when making their first investment; however, the other three do acknowledge structural disadvantage: 3) they do not know about angel investing; 4) they do not know other angel investors in their networks and: 5) they do not see investment opportunities. Indeed, this prompted the launch of the Rising Tide Angel Training Program (in 2015) with the goal of increasing the number of women angel investors capable of investing in growth-oriented women-owned firms through a program of education, training, and hands-on experience with the angel investing process (Coleman and Robb, 2018).

Current developments and future opportunities (2015 to present)

Current research focusing on the persistent gender gap in EF is still prioritized and will likely continue to be as statistics globally report stagnating to marginal improvement in women entrepreneurs' access to EF. More concerning is that the most recent European studies suggest a worsening effect in 2020 due to the COVID-19 global pandemic (Wauters, 2021), which are likely to be corroborated as data emerges through 2021/2022. Furthermore, the 'women don't step up, or ask' explanation is questioned in one of the first studies to explore this phenomenon *in relative*, as opposed to absolute terms. Here, Cawen and Sjöberg (2021) found that out of all European companies founded by women, only 11% received Series A venture capital, compared with 20% of companies founded by men. In short, the gendered status-quo remains despite growing evidence that women-founded and women-led start-ups generate more revenue per dollar invested and outperform in capital productivity (Boston Consulting Group, 2018; Hebert, 2020). To make sense of these sobering industry statistics, the academy has shifted slightly by advancing a more nuanced, albeit small body of work that focuses on less obvious explanations for the EF gender gap. This section presents insights from these recent studies before advancing future directions to explore.

Moving beyond, 'women don't ask' and other deficit narratives, recent work interrogates more seriously the role of gender stereotypes, gender homophily, gendered language and rhetoric, emphasizing the importance of cognitions, perceptions and heuristics for financing decisions (Malmstrom, Johansson and Wincent, 2017; Balachandra, Briggs, Eddleston and Brush, 2019; Harrison, Botelho and Mason, 2020; Johansson, Malmstrom, Lahti and Wincent, 2021). Further, while research silos still operate across the supply and demand landscapes, greater attention has been afforded to understanding the role of gender and how it interacts in entrepreneur (demand) – investor (supply) relationships. Acknowledging that gender is embedded in entrepreneur-financier relationships that are inherently more complex than observed differences between men and women (Carter, Shaw, Lam and Wilson, 2007; Alsos and Ljunggren, 2017) is fundamental to the development of EF field and indeed recent work has begun to advance more critical avenues of inquiry. Alsos and Ljunggren (2017) applied signaling theory to examine the interface between demand and supply to understand gender biases related to risk capital investments by analyzing decision documents of four investment cases (archival data spanning 2005–2013). They found that investors evaluate both male and female entrepreneurs against a masculine norm and neglected signals more often presented by women. Stereotypical gender ascriptions influenced the interpretations of signals received, leading investment funds to interpret similar characteristics differently between male and females. However, rather than advancing recommendations to challenge these stereotypes, they individualize the problem and consequently default to self-improvement strategies and suggest that women entrepreneurs should signal their venture's quality more strongly using more masculine signals (Swail and Marlow, 2018). Malmstrom et al. (2017, p. 855) conducted a discourse analysis on longitudinal observations of government VC decisions to identify how gender stereotypes are socially constructed at a group level by language and rhetoric during social interactions among female and male VCs and thus activated when assessing entrepreneurs' potential. Similar to Alsos and Ljunggren (2017), they concluded "that the perceived lack of female entrepreneurs' potential occurs based on socially constructed stereotypical images applied to both men and women' lead to 'cover gender biases" that impact negatively upon women's access to finance. Edelman, Donnelly, Manolova and Brush (2018) confirmed similar gender identity stereotypes manifested in hidden and often unconscious biases among angel groups with mostly men.

However, some studies that have applied gender role congruity theory within entrepreneurial contexts *contest* suggestions that displaying more masculine characteristics will resolve sex-based biases against women (Koenig, Eagly, Mitchell and Ristikari, 2011). Gupta et al. (2009) highlighted that the very practice of pursuing high growth entrepreneurship, with aggressive funding goals and a hyper-growth mindset is considered a masculine behavior in itself. Yet, when women entrepreneurs pitch aggressively, they violate their gender stereotype, which rather than resulting in empowerment will lead to negative perceptions and undermine legitimacy (Diaz-Garcia and Welter, 2013). Conversely, if they conform to their expected femininity, they will be viewed as incompetent and emotional, not conducive to the entrepreneur stereotype. Byrne et al. (2021) discussed a more complex analogy of 'gender gymnastics' in CEO succession and argue that women CEOs need to combine various masculine and feminine identities and practices to attain legitimacy. Balachandra et al. (2019) extended this theory to the VC context and reported investor bias against both male and female entrepreneurs who display more feminine stereotyped behaviors. Albeit the context was isolated to the initial pitch stage of the capital raising process, their analysis is in line with current thinking that acknowledges all entrepreneurs perform gender through displays of both masculinity and femininity. That said, despite advancing theoretical inquiry by suggesting that the gender disparity in VC cannot be solely attributed to sex-based biases against women, a practical implication advanced is that women endeavoring to raise capital should ensure that they do not exhibit strong feminine behaviors. Indeed, in a most recent study Balachandra et al. (2021) credited women for *not* using linguistic styles traditionally attributed to women when pitching and for avoiding the use of gendered language. Yet again, the onus is on women to 'fix' themselves and adjust their behaviors accordingly, rather than contemplating initiatives that might educate or simply raise awareness among VC professionals on unconscious bias issues and other stifling structural mechanisms that are systemic in the sector.

Kanze, Huang, Conley, and Higgins (2018) expose unconscious gender bias using regulatory focus theory to analyze the questions that investors ask entrepreneurs during an annual startup funding competition (TechCrunch Disrupt New York City). Male entrepreneurs received promotion-focused questions (concerned with approaching gains and avoiding non-gains; e.g. How do you want to acquire customers?), and female entrepreneurs received prevention-focused questions (concerned with avoiding losses and approaching non-losses; e.g. How many daily and monthly active users do you have?). Entrepreneurs tended to respond with matching regulatory focus. This resulted in divergent funding outcomes for entrepreneurs, whereby those asked promotion-focused questions raised significantly higher amounts of funding than those asked prevention-focused questions. Their practical recommendations proposed a 'switching' intervention, whereby women entrepreneurs in particular develop the astute skill to first recognize when they are being asked a prevention question and then simultaneously craft a promotion answer in order to mitigate the negative consequences of gender bias. Again, the issue is individualized so that it becomes a female entrepreneur's 'problem to solve'. However, this study is one of first to also advocate for behavioral change among VCs who should learn to balance the promotion versus prevention orientation of their questions to reduce their own unconscious bias.

Revisiting the supply-side and the assumption that more female investors will increase the supply of funding to women founders, recent studies have begun to explore the complexities of homophily in this space. Indeed, Kanze et al. (2018) confirmed that implicit bias was practiced by female and male VCs alike. When female investors do back female founders, Snellman and Solal (2020) proposed that the market interprets this as an expression of diversity activism (Greenberg and Molick, 2017) as opposed to a signal of quality. They found that female-founded firms funded only by female investors were two times less likely to raise additional capital compared to those whose first-round investors included male VCs. This undermines the role of women-only capital networks but clearly further research needs to explore this phenomenon further, particularly as Harrison et al. (2020) advocated for women-only angel networks and training programmes to mitigate women-angel performance and participation pitfalls as a consequence of stereotype threat.

Future research agenda

Moving forward, we suggest the EF field needs to focus on a broader range of phenomenon to shift the focus of gender disparity in EF from a 'woman's problem' to an 'investment ecosystem problem'. Indeed, the growth and long-term sustainability of a broader entrepreneurial ecosystem (EE) depend not so much on central actors who establish framework conditions, but on the interactional processes that reproduce and transform prevailing norms and make the EE more attractive to a broader range of participants (Spigel, Kitagawa, and Mason 2020). The practical implications of much of the existing research pertaining to gender and EF are still concerned with 'fixing' women at the expense of ignoring the gendered institutional structures of investment eco-systems. Such structures serve to frame the beliefs and actions of individuals that undermine and delegitimize certain groups over others. It is now largely accepted that implicit bias is influencing the decisions and actions of finance providers (Kanze et al. 2018; Malmstrom et al. 2017; Leitch at al. 2018), but we know very little about how, and even if financial institutions (e.g., venture capital organisations and angel networks) are seriously addressing such biases. Whilst there appears to be a legitimate focus on increasing both gender and ethnic diversity in VC and private equity firms (Lewin, 2021), as well as among business angel networks (Coleman and Robb, 2018), progress is slow, and as researchers, we are still inconclusive as to whether or not addressing balance is ameliorating the gender funding gap. Brush et al (2018) suggest future research could explore how venture capital firms recruit, hire, promote, and reward investment decision-makers. Indeed, scholars could broaden their focus from the micro (individual) to more meso (organisational) and macro (EE) levels, using a wider range of methods such as longitudinal case studies, observations, and continued focus on rhetoric and language through discourse analysis (Balachandra et al. 2021) that permit more nuanced explorations. Leitch et al. (2018) suggest future research not only analyze the gendered structures of finance industries but also the extent to which gendered discourses in politics and financing industries might be reinforcing gender financing gaps.

Second, there is a growing body of evidence that strongly refutes the notion of the 'underperforming' women entrepreneur (Robb and Watson, 2012; Hebert, 2020; Goldstein, Gonzalez Martinez & Papineni, 2019). A Boston Consulting Group (2018) study, revealed that women entrepreneurs generate more revenue than their male counterparts despite receiving lower financial backing. For every $1 of investment raised, women-owned ventures generated $0.78 in revenue, in comparison to $0.31 generated by male-owned ventures. Kanze, Conley, Okimoto, Phillips & Merluzzi (2020) confirmed that investors penalize female founders for lack of 'industry fit' but reported that female founders raised significantly more (not less) funding when catering to female-dominated industries considered suitable for them. Thus, "(i)nvestor bias thwarts otherwise high potential for labor market productivity and growth" (Kanze et al., 2020, p. 7). We suggest that EF could be the first entrepreneurship research domain to "park" the 'underperforming' narrative and turn its attention to the 'outperformers'; those women-founded businesses who upon successfully raising finance build more robust and profitable businesses. What can we learn from these founders, their ventures and capital raising experiences? How do they maximize the returns on the angel/VC investments they secure – i.e. in which parts of the business do they put this investment and do they generate longer runways as a result? Do women-founded firms recruit and lead more diverse entrepreneurial teams (which is proven to result in more creative and unconventional problem solving)? What do we know about women entrepreneurs who have exited a venture and gone on to become investors in their EEs – is this a growing trend in EEs globally that can make an impact?

Third, despite a maturing debate analyzing women's entrepreneurial behavior more broadly (Jennings and Brush, 2013) and a body of work within EF that acknowledges the persistence of gender bias, Marlow and Martinez Dy (2018, p. 4) caution against "presenting gender as a one-dimensional property of women alone, rather than recognizing it as a multiplicity enacted by all human subjects in a diverse range of contexts." Within EF, there is an opportunity to build on recent work that has acknowledged the performance (through language and behavior) of both masculinities and femininities among women *and men* within investment ecosystems (Balachandra et al. 2019; Balachandra et al. 2021). To progress knowledge, a first step is recognizing the diversity and complexity of gendered performances and ascriptions, but we can broaden our discussions through analyzing the multiplicity of gender effects found in EF. Such future analysis will permit researchers to think beyond the current assumptions that entrepreneurial actors are cis-identified (gender matches that assigned at birth) heterosexuals who conform to a stereotypical gender binary, and rather explore the capital raising journeys and challenges of lesbian, gay, transgender, queer/questioning, intersex and asexual as well as non-binary and gender non-conforming individuals, who will no doubt experience gender bias as a consequence of disrupting the pervasive masculine norm of EF ecosystems.

Fourth, a limitation of this chapter was that space did not permit a discussion of newer forms of finance such as crowdfunding platforms, accelerators and incubators, proof-of-concept centers and university-based seed funds from the supply or demand-side perspective. To what extent do these newer sources present opportunities for women founders to finance their ventures, or do they experience similar challenges? Equity crowdfunding platforms, for example, have received attention for being more welcoming forums for women to raise finance, with studies reporting women, compared to men, were more successful in obtaining funding and a clear pattern of women investors supporting women-led projects (Marom, Robb and Sade, 2014; Gafni, Maron, Robb and Sade, 2021). Greenberg and Mollick (2017) offered a particularly useful theoretical perspective of 'activist choice homophily' whereby women's preference to fund women entrepreneurs stem from perceived structural barriers that come from a mutual social identity. However, cautioning against the tendency of EF scholars to research in silos, I suggest that future studies do not explore these research contexts separately but rather look at how these alternative sources of finance (crowdfunding, accelerators, incubators etc.) facilitate and enhance (or not) the likelihood of further rounds of finance using more traditional sources for women entrepreneurs.

Finally, it would be remiss not to urge future studies to specifically address the impact of the COVID-19 global pandemic on women entrepreneurs' efforts to raise capital, particularly *de novo* ventures. Globally, venture funding fell by approximately 6% in the first six months of 2019, followed by a further sharp drop of 17% in the first half of 2020 (Crunchbase, 2020). The pandemic has amplified gender and social inequalities (Blundell, Costa Dias and Joyce, 2020) and highlighted differences in male and female entrepreneurship, particularly the role of family responsibilities and care at the micro level of the entrepreneur. The home is a gendered space where traditional gender roles and relations have proved persistent. Most women in heterosexual relationships are responsible for the bulk of domestic labor and the importance of childcare has been identified as important to supporting women's entry into and continuance of self-employment (Jayawarna, Marlow and Swail, 2020). Further, a recent study in New Zealand reported that women founders often renegotiated household responsibilities with partners who often share more of the 'load[3]' which often involved stepping into a primary carer role to allow women time and energy to focus on raising capital (Swail, 2021). Thus, gender affects every sphere of home life, including physical space allocation, emotional support to family members, and the mental load of planning, scheduling and food shopping. COVID-19 forced most entrepreneurial businesses to operate from the domestic sphere. For example, capital raising entrepreneurs were delivered online pitches over Zoom and other online platforms. We currently have no insights into women founders' experiences in these challenging contexts. Further Brown, Rocha and Cowling (2020) reported that entrepreneurial ventures most affected by the crisis are early-stage start-ups featuring the greatest levels of informational opacity, with investors choosing to re-invest follow-on funds within their existing portfolio companies. How will such risk-averse investor behaviors effect the success rate of early-stage women entrepreneurs to raise finance? Only time and robust research will tell.

Conclusion

While work on gender and the broader area of finance has (rightly) oriented to the problematic politics of hegemonic/alpha men (Clarke and Roberts, 2016; Connell, 1998), these conversations have been slow to emerge in the narrower EF literature. This chapter endeavors to illustrate how gender is intertwined in the entrepreneurial activities of raising and awarding EF, but the field has only 'scratched the surface' in terms of applying a meaningful gender perspective to challenge normative thinking and gendered assumptions. This chapter began by discussing the influence of gender on broader entrepreneurial behaviour before focusing in on the specific domain of EF. I then presented a mini-review of the literature pertaining specifically to gender, angel and VC finance, split over two time periods – 2000–2015 and 2016 to present. My aim here was to illustrate how the field has developed, albeit slowly in its conceptualization of gender. We then turned our attention to the future opportunities for research and advanced five different areas or 'roads less traveled' for scholars to continue on. To conclude, I point out two cul-de-sacs to avoid in future research: 1) explaining disparities between men and women founders who access equity investment, simply as a 'women don't ask' issue. This is only a starting point and is not the explanation in itself; only by understanding *why* women don't ask can policy respond with appropriate engagement solutions and recommendations. 2) "park"

---

3 Sharing the load at home is an "umbrella" term for the variety of tasks required to run a household, and how these tasks are shared.

the 'underperforming women entrepreneur' narrative by advancing discourses that explain structural disadvantage and gendered mechanisms in EF ecosystems as opposed to those that individualize the issues, thus reducing them to problems for women to fix themselves.

References

Ahl, H. (2006). Why Research on Women Entrepreneurs Needs New Directions. *Entrepreneurship Theory and Practice*, *30*(5), 595–621. https://doi.org/10.1111/j.1540-6520.2006.00138.x

Ahl, H., & Marlow, S. (2021). Exploring the false promise of entrepreneurship through a postfeminist critique of the enterprise policy discourse in Sweden and the UK. *Human Relations*, *74*(1), 41–68. https://doi.org/10.1177/0018726719848480

Alsos, G. A., Isaksen, E. J., & Ljunggren, E. (2006). New Venture Financing and Subsequent Business Growth in Men– and Women–Led Businesses. *Entrepreneurship Theory and Practice*, *30*(5), 667–686. https://doi.org/10.1111/j.1540-6520.2006.00141.x

Alsos, G. A., & Ljunggren, E. (2017). The Role of Gender in Entrepreneur–Investor Relationships: A Signaling Theory Approach. *Entrepreneurship Theory and Practice*, *41*(4), 567–590. https://doi.org/10.1111/etp.12226

Balachandra, L., Briggs, T., Eddleston, K., & Brush, C. (2019). Don't Pitch Like a Girl!: How Gender Stereotypes Influence Investor Decisions. *Entrepreneurship Theory and Practice*, *43*(1), 116–137. https://doi.org/10.1177/1042258717728028

Balachandra, L., Fischer, K., & Brush, C. (2021). Do (women's) words matter? The influence of gendered language in entrepreneurial pitching. *Journal of Business Venturing Insights*, *15*, e00224. https://doi.org/10.1016/j.jbvi.2021.e00224

Becker-Blease, J. R., & Sohl, J. E. (2007). Do women-owned businesses have equal access to angel capital? *Journal of Business Venturing*, *22*(4), 503–521. https://doi.org/10.1016/j.jbusvent.2006.06.003

Becker–Blease, J. R., & Sohl, J. E. (2011). The Effect of Gender Diversity on Angel Group Investment. *Entrepreneurship Theory and Practice*, *35*(4), 709–733. https://doi.org/10.1111/j.1540-6520.2010.00391.x

Blundell, R., Dias, M. C., Joyce, R., & Xu, X. (2020). COVID-19 and Inequalities*. *Fiscal Studies*, *41*(2), 291–319. https://doi.org/10.1111/1475-5890.12232

Boston Consulting Group. (2018). Why Women-Owned Startups are a Better Bet. https://www.bcg.com/en-au/publications/2018/why-women-owned-startups-are-better-bet 2021 Boston Consulting Group

Brown, R., Rocha, A., & Cowling, M. (2020). Financing entrepreneurship in times of crisis: Exploring the impact of COVID-19 on the market for entrepreneurial finance in the United Kingdom. *International Small Business Journal*, *38*(5), 380–390. https://doi.org/10.1177/0266242620937464

Bruni, A., Gherardi, S., & Poggio, B. (2004). Doing Gender, Doing Entrepreneurship: An Ethnographic Account of Intertwined Practices. *Gender, Work & Organization*, *11*(4), 406–429. https://doi.org/10.1111/j.1468-0432.2004.00240.x

Brush, C. G., Carter, N. M., Gatewood, E., Greene, P. G., & Hart, M. (2004). *Clearing the hurdles: Women building high-growth businesses*. FT/Prentice Hall.

Brush, C., Greene, P., Balachandran, L., & Davis, A. E. (2014). Women Entrepreneurs 2014: Bridging the Gender Gap in Venture Capital.

Brush, C., Greene, P., Balachandra, L., & Davis, A. (2018). The gender gap in venture capital-progress, problems, and perspectives. *Venture Capital*, *20*(2), 115–136. https://doi.org/10.1080/13691066.2017.1349266

Butler, J. (2011). *Bodies that matter: On the discursive limits of "sex."* Routledge.

Byrne, J., Radu-Lefebvre, M., Fattoum, S., & Balachandra, L. (2021). Gender Gymnastics in CEO succession: Masculinities, Femininities and Legitimacy. *Organization Studies*, *42*(1), 129–159. https://doi.org/10.1177/0170840619879184

Carter, S. L., & Shaw, E. (2006). *Women's business ownership: Recent research and policy developments*. https://pureportal.strath.ac.uk/en/publications/womens-business-ownership-recent-research-and-policy-developments

Carter, S., Mwaura, S., Ram, M., Trehan, K., & Jones, T. (2015). Barriers to ethnic minority and women's enterprise: Existing evidence, policy tensions and unsettled questions. *International Small Business Journal*, *33*(1), 49–69. https://doi.org/10.1177/0266242614556823

Carter, S., Shaw, E., Lam, W., & Wilson, F. (2007). Gender, Entrepreneurship, and Bank Lending: The Criteria and Processes Used by Bank Loan Officers in Assessing Applications. *Entrepreneurship Theory and Practice*, *31*(3), 427–444. https://doi.org/10.1111/j.1540-6520.2007.00181.x

Cawen, C. & Sjöberg, A. (2021) *The outsized role of gender in European venture funding*. https://www.ngpcap.com/uploads/The-outsized-role-of-gender-in-EU-venture-funding-NGPCapital.pdf (accessed on 19/ 06/2021)

Clarke, C., & Roberts, A. (2016). Mark Carney and the Gendered Political Economy of British Central Banking. *The British Journal of Politics and International Relations*, *18*(1), 49–71. https://doi.org/10.1111/1467-856X.12062

Coleman, S., & Robb, A. (2009). A comparison of new firm financing by gender: Evidence from the Kauffman Firm Survey data. *Small Business Economics*, *33*(4), 397. https://doi.org/10.1007/s11187-009-9205-7

Coleman, S., & Robb, A. (2016). Financing high growth women-owned enterprises: Evidence from the United States. *Women's Entrepreneurship in Global and Local Contexts*. https://www.elgaronline.com/view/edcoll/9781784717414/9781784717414.00016.xml

Coleman, S., & Robb, A. (2018). Executive forum: linkingwomen's growth-oriented entrepreneurship policy and practice: Results from the Rising Tide Angel Training Program. *Venture Capital*, *20*(2), 211–231. https://doi.org/10.1080/13691066.2018.1419845

Connell, R. W. (1998). Masculinities and Globalization. *Men and Masculinities*, *1*(1), 3–23. https://doi.org/10.1177/1097184X98001001001

Cowling, M., Marlow, S., & Liu, W. (2020). Gender and bank lending after the global financial crisis: Are women entrepreneurs safer bets? *Small Business Economics*, *55*(4), 853–880. https://doi.org/10.1007/s11187-019-00168-3

Cromie, S. (1987). Motivations of aspiring male and female entrepreneurs. *Journal of Organizational Behavior*, *8*(3), 251–261. https://doi.org/10.1002/job.4030080306

Croson, R., & Gneezy, U. (2009). Gender Differences in Preferences. *Journal of Economic Literature*, *47*(2), 448–474. https://doi.org/10.1257/jel.47.2.448

Crunchbase_State_of_Funding_Covid_FINAL.pdf. (n.d.). Retrieved August 6, 2021, from http://about.crunchbase.com/wp-content/uploads/2020/08/Crunchbase_State_of_Funding_Covid_FINAL.pdf

Cumming, D., & Johan, S. (2017). The Problems with and Promise of Entrepreneurial Finance: The Problems with and Promise of Entrepreneurial Finance. *Strategic Entrepreneurship Journal*, *11*(3), 357–370. https://doi.org/10.1002/sej.1265

Drover, W., Busenitz, L., Matusik, S., Townsend, D., Anglin, A., & Dushnitsky, G. (2017). A Review and Road Map of Entrepreneurial Equity Financing Research: Venture Capital, Corporate

Venture Capital, Angel Investment, Crowdfunding, and Accelerators. *Journal of Management*, *43*(6), 1820–1853. https://doi.org/10.1177/0149206317690584

Edelman, L. F., Donnelly, R., Manolova, T., & Brush, C. G. (2018). Gender stereotypes in the angel investment process. *International Journal of Gender and Entrepreneurship*, *10*(2), 134–157. https://doi.org/10.1108/IJGE-12-2017-0078

Edelman, L. F., Manolova, T. S., & Brush, C. G. (2017). Angel Investing: A Literature Review. *Foundations and Trends® in Entrepreneurship*, *13*(4–5), 265–439. https://doi.org/10.1561/0300000051

Fairlie, R. W., & Robb, A. M. (2009). Gender Differences in Business Performance: Evidence from the Characteristics of Business Owners Survey. *Small Business Economics*, *33*(4), 375–395.

Fletcher, J. K. (2001). *Disappearing acts: Gender, power, and relational practice at work* (1. MIT Press paperback ed). MIT Press.

Gafni, H., Marom, D., Robb, A., & Sade, O. (2021). Gender Dynamics in Crowdfunding (Kickstarter): Evidence on Entrepreneurs, Backers, and Taste-Based Discrimination*. *Review of Finance*, *25*(2), 235–274. https://doi.org/10.1093/rof/rfaa041

García, M.-C. D., & Welter, F. (2013). Gender identities and practices: Interpreting women entrepreneurs' narratives. *International Small Business Journal: Researching Entrepreneurship*, *31*(4), 384–404. https://doi.org/10.1177/0266242611422829

Goldstein, M., Gonzalez Martinez, P., & Papineni, S. (2019). *Tackling the Global Profitarchy: Gender and the Choice of Business Sector* (SSRN Scholarly Paper ID 3430471). Social Science Research Network. https://papers.ssrn.com/abstract=3430471

Greenberg, J., & Mollick, E. (2017). Activist Choice Homophily and the Crowdfunding of Female Founders. *Administrative Science Quarterly*, *62*(2), 341–374. https://doi.org/10.1177/0001839216678847

Greene, P. G., Brush, C. G., Hart, M. M., & Saparito, P. (2001). Patterns of venture capital funding: Is gender a factor? *Venture Capital*, *3*(1), 63–83. https://doi.org/10.1080/13691060118175

Gupta, V. K., Turban, D. B., Wasti, S. A., & Sikdar, A. (2009). The Role of Gender Stereotypes in Perceptions of Entrepreneurs and Intentions to Become an Entrepreneur. *Entrepreneurship Theory and Practice*, *33*(2), 397–417. https://doi.org/10.1111/j.1540-6520.2009.00296.x

Hamilton, E. (2014). Entrepreneurial Narrative Identity and Gender: A Double Epistemological Shift. *Journal of Small Business Management*, *52*(4), 703–712. https://doi.org/10.1111/jsbm.12127

Harding, S. G. (Ed.). (1987). *Feminism and methodology: Social science issues*. Indiana University Press; Open University Press.

Harrison, R. T., Botelho, T., & Mason, C. M. (2020). Women on the edge of a breakthrough? A stereotype threat theory of women's angel investing. *International Small Business Journal: Researching Entrepreneurship*, *38*(8), 768–797. https://doi.org/10.1177/0266242620927312

Harrison, R. T., Leitch, C. M., & McAdam, M. (2020). Woman's entrepreneurship as a gendered niche: The implications for regional development policy. *Journal of Economic Geography*, *20*(4), 1041–1067. https://doi.org/10.1093/jeg/lbz035

Harrison, R. T., & Mason, C. M. (2007). Does Gender Matter? Women Business Angels and the Supply of Entrepreneurial Finance. *Entrepreneurship Theory and Practice*, *31*(3), 445–472. https://doi.org/10.1111/j.1540-6520.2007.00182.x

Hebert, C. (2020). *Gender Stereotypes and Entrepreneur Financing* (SSRN Scholarly Paper ID 3318245). Social Science Research Network. https://doi.org/10.2139/ssrn.3318245

Henry, C., Foss, L., & Ahl, H. (2016). Gender and entrepreneurship research: A review of methodological approaches. *International Small Business Journal: Researching Entrepreneurship*, *34*(3), 217–241. https://doi.org/10.1177/0266242614549779

Jayawarna, D., Marlow, S., & Swail, J. (2020). A Gendered Life Course Explanation of the Exit Decision in the Context of Household Dynamics. *Entrepreneurship Theory and Practice*, 104225872094012. https://doi.org/10.1177/1042258720940123

Jennings, J. E., & Brush, C. G. (2013). Research on Women Entrepreneurs: Challenges to (and from) the Broader Entrepreneurship Literature? *Academy of Management Annals*, *7*(1), 663–715. https://doi.org/10.5465/19416520.2013.782190

Johansson, J., Malmström, M., Lahti, T., & Wincent, J. (2021). Oh, it's complex to see women here, isn't it and this seems to take all my attention! A repertory grid approach to capture venture capitalists cognitive structures when evaluating women entrepreneurs. *Journal of Business Venturing Insights*, *15*, e00218. https://doi.org/10.1016/j.jbvi.2020.e00218

Kanze, D., Conley, M. A., Okimoto, T. G., Phillips, D. J., & Merluzzi, J. (2020). Evidence that investors penalize female founders for lack of industry fit. *Science Advances*, *6*(48), eabd7664. https://doi.org/10.1126/sciadv.abd7664

Kanze, D., Huang, L., Conley, M. A., & Higgins, E. T. (2018). We Ask Men to Win and Women Not to Lose: Closing the Gender Gap in Startup Funding. *Academy of Management Journal*, *61*(2), 586–614. https://doi.org/10.5465/amj.2016.1215

Kelan, E. (2009). *Performing gender at work*. Palgrave Macmillan.

Koenig, A. M., Eagly, A. H., Mitchell, A. A., & Ristikari, T. (2011). Are leader stereotypes masculine? A meta-analysis of three research paradigms. *Psychological Bulletin*, *137*(4), 616–642. https://doi.org/10.1037/a0023557

Kwapisz, A., & Hechavarría, D. M. (2018). Women don't ask: An investigation of start-up financing and gender. *Venture Capital*, *20*(2), 159–190. https://doi.org/10.1080/13691066.2017.1345119

Lam, L., & Seidel, M.-D. L. (2020). Hypergrowth Exit Mindset: Destroying Societal Wellbeing through Venture Capital Biased Social Construction of Value. *Journal of Management Inquiry*, *29*(4), 471–474. https://doi.org/10.1177/1056492620929085

Leitch, C., Welter, F., & Henry, C. (2018). Women entrepreneurs' financing revisited: Taking stock and looking forward. *Venture Capital*, *20*(2), 103–114. https://doi.org/10.1080/13691066.2018.1418624

Lewin, A. (2021, March 17). *In data: Diversity in European VC*. Sifted. https://sifted.eu/articles/diversity-data-european-vc/

Lerner, J., & Tag, J. (2013). Institutions and venture capital. *Industrial and Corporate Change*, *22*(1), 153–182. https://doi.org/10.1093/icc/dts050

Lindgren, M., & Packendorff, J. (2003). *A project-based view of entrepreneurship: Towards action-orientation, seriality and collectivity* (pp. 86–102). Edward Elgar Publishing. http://urn.kb.se/resolve?urn=urn:nbn:se:kth:diva-47899

Lindvert, M., Alsos, G.A. & Ljunggren, E. (2021) Gender and entrepreneurial financing – A systematic literature review. *Paper presented at the Diana International Research Conference, May 21–22, 2021*.

Malmström, M., Johansson, J., & Wincent, J. (2017). Gender Stereotypes and Venture Support Decisions: How Governmental Venture Capitalists Socially Construct Entrepreneurs' Potential. *Entrepreneurship Theory and Practice*, *41*(5), 833–860. https://doi.org/10.1111/etap.12275

Marlow, S. (2020). Gender and entrepreneurship: Past achievements and future possibilities. *International Journal of Gender and Entrepreneurship*, *12*(1), 39–52. https://doi.org/10.1108/IJGE-05-2019-0090

Marlow, S., & Al-Dajani, H. (2017). Critically evaluating contemporary entrepreneurship from a feminist perspective. In *Critical Perspectives on Entrepreneurship*. Routledge.

Marlow, S., Carter, S., & Shaw, E. (2008). Constructing Female Entrepreneurship Policy in the UK: Is the US a Relevant Benchmark? *Environment and Planning C: Government and Policy*, *26*(2), 335–351. https://doi.org/10.1068/c0732r

Marlow, S., & Martinez Dy, A. (2018). Annual review article: Is it time to rethink the gender agenda in entrepreneurship research? *International Small Business Journal: Researching Entrepreneurship*, *36*(1), 3–22. https://doi.org/10.1177/0266242617738321

Marlow, S., & Swail, J. (2014). Gender, risk and finance: Why can't a woman be more like a man? *Entrepreneurship & Regional Development, 26*(1–2), 80–96. https://doi.org/10.1080/ 08985626.2013.860484

Marom, D., Robb, A., & Sade, O. (2014). Gender Dynamics in Crowdfunding (Kickstarter): Evidence on Entrepreneurs, Investors, Deals and Taste Based Discrimination. *SSRN Electronic Journal.* https://doi.org/10.2139/ssrn.2442954

McAdam, M. (2013). *Female Entrepreneurship* (1st ed.). Routledge. https://doi.org/10.4324/ 9780203075487

McAdam, M., & Marlow, S. (2013). A Gendered Critique of the Copreneurial Business Partnership: Exploring the Implications for Entrepreneurial Emancipation. *The International Journal of Entrepreneurship and Innovation, 14*(3), 151–163. https://doi.org/10.5367/ijei.2013.0120

OECD (2018). *Policy Brief on Women's Entrepreneurship* (OECD SME and Entrepreneurship Papers No. 8; OECD SME and Entrepreneurship Papers, Vol. 8). https://doi.org/10.1787/dd2d79e7-en

Robb, A. M., & Watson, J. (2012). Gender differences in firm performance: Evidence from new ventures in the United States. *Journal of Business Venturing, 27*(5), 544–558. https://doi.org/ 10.1016/j.jbusvent.2011.10.002

Snellman, K. E., & Solal, I. (2020). Does Investor Gender Matter? The Signaling Effect of Gender Homophily in Entrepreneurial Finance. *Academy of Management Proceedings,* 2020(1), 21230. https://doi.org/10.5465/AMBPP.2020.21230abstract

Sohl, J.E. (2015) *The Angel Investor Market in 2014: A Market Correction in Deal Size,* 15 May, Center for Venture Research, University of New Hampshire.

Spigel, B., Kitagawa, F., & Mason, C. (2020). A manifesto for researching entrepreneurial ecosystems. Local Economy, 35(5),482–495. https://doi.org/10.1177/0269094220959052

Storey, D. J. (2011). Optimism and chance: The elephants in the entrepreneurship room. *International Small Business Journal: Researching Entrepreneurship, 29*(4), 303–321. https:// doi.org/10.1177/0266242611403871

Swail, J. (2021) *Raising Capital in Aotearoa New Zealand: Insights from Women Entrepreneurs.* https://protect-au.mimecast.com/s/_5IeCnx1ANU35EKns9zmpB?domain=cdn.auckland.ac.nz

Swail, J., & Marlow, S. (2018). 'Embrace the masculine; attenuate the feminine' – gender, identity work and entrepreneurial legitimation in the nascent context. *Entrepreneurship & Regional Development, 30*(1–2), 256–282. https://doi.org/10.1080/08985626.2017.1406539

Tenca, F., Croce, A., & Ughetto, E. (2018). Business Angels Research in Entrepreneurial Finance: A Literature Review and a Research Agenda. *Journal of Economic Surveys, 32*(5), 1384–1413. https://doi.org/10.1111/joes.12224

Wauters, R. (2021) *New research confirms: if you're a female startup founder, fat chance raising venture funding in Europe.* Tech.eu. https://tech.eu/features/37864/women-european-venture-research/

Ana María Peredo, Bettina Schneider, and Audrey Maria Popa

17 Indigenous entrepreneurial finance: Mapping the landscape with Canadian evidence

Abstract: This chapter considers the evolving landscape of financing sources available for Indigenous entrepreneurs using Canada as an example. The aim is to suggest how, in the colonial environment of Canadian financial services, Indigenous people have not only been able to lobby for access to funding, but also have found ways of marshalling their own financial resources to support entrepreneurship. An overview of the literature on Indigenous entrepreneurship and Indigenous finance brings out their distinctive character and value orientation. An outline is given of resources available for Indigenous entrepreneurship in Canada, from governmental initiatives through arrangements offered by mainstream financial institutions and government to innovative organizations assembled by Indigenous people themselves. Three vital questions for future research are identified: (1) should the institutions mobilized by Indigenous people themselves remain niche organizations, perhaps bridging entrepreneurs to mainstream options, or should these institutions seek to enlarge their role? (2) Does accessing funds from mainstream sources, or even from Indigenous organizations immersed in a profit-based, market environment, risk perpetuating dependency and undermining distinctive Indigenous interests and values? (3) What should the role of mainstream organizations be in relation to the distinctive character of Indigenous entrepreneurship?

Keywords: Indigenous entrepreneurship, finance, Canada, Indigenous values

Introduction

There is a nascent but growing literature on Indigenous entrepreneurship (Dana, 2015; Hindle & Moroz, 2010; Peredo et al., 2004; Peredo & Anderson, 2006) and a less extensive one on Indigenous finance. However, with the recognition of entrepreneurial activity among Indigenous peoples, finance programs to support entrepreneurial activities have been sprouting in different parts of the world. The aim of this chapter is to provide an overview of the financing landscape available to Indigenous entrepreneurs in Canada. We use Canada as an exemplar to show how,

Ana María Peredo, Bettina Schneider, Audrey Maria Popa, University of Ottawa and University of Victoria, First Nations University, University of Victoria

https://doi.org/10.1515/9783110726312-022

under a colonial legacy, including restricted legal and regulatory frameworks, Indigenous peoples are using entrepreneurship and financial tools to break from state dependency and rebuild their nations' autonomy and self-determination (Anderson, 1999; Peredo & Anderson, 2006)

In Canada, as elsewhere, Indigenous People have suffered the socio-economic consequences of colonization, including dispossession of land and systematic exclusion from full participation in the economy and state dependency. However, in the last three decades, Indigenous leaders and communities are increasingly able to assert control over their territories and shape their participation in the Canadian economy, with several critical milestones marking the way. For example, a 1994 report to Canada's Royal Commission on Aboriginal Peoples reported increasing pressures from Indigenous leaders to governments and business sectors demanding a voice at negotiation tables where matters concerning their territories are considered (DesBrisay, 1994). A further and notable development has been that many Indigenous communities own and successfully run their own businesses (Anderson et al., 2003; CCAB, 2020; Nelson, 2019; Sayers & Peredo, 2017). In doing so, they engage in business on their own terms and exercise innovation in solving societal challenges (Peredo et al., 2019). For example, at the time of this writing, 2021, Indigenous People are in the course of developing Vancouver's largest affordable housing project on their own reserve territory in downtown Vancouver – one of the most expensive cities in the world.

Indigenous community-owned businesses, organized by Indigenous governments and Economic Development Corporations, and family and individual businesses, led by Indigenous entrepreneurs, are growing in number, on and off-reserve in Canada. At the same time, social and environmental awareness have become central drivers in some parts of the financial sector. For example, credit unions have played a role in funding large community projects under the banner of supporting a blended value approach (Henriquez et al., 2020).

As we will see in this chapter, Indigenous organizations and the Canadian government have played a fundamental role, often as partners, in building financial infrastructure. In addition, co-operatives and credit unions have played a crucial role as a socio-economic organization, particularly in the Canadian Arctic. The private banking sector is also recognizing Indigenous governments and entrepreneurs as a valuable part of the financial market. In sum, the financial landscape oriented to Indigenous entrepreneurs is expanding in terms of the actors and the types of services offered.

In what follows, we provide a brief literature overview about what we know about Indigenous entrepreneurship and Indigenous finance; we then outline financing services available to Indigenous entrepreneurs in Canada as an example to help understand Indigenous entrepreneurial finance in practice; finally, on the basis of the literature reviews and Canadian case, we identify a research agenda before drawing some conclusions.

Literature review

Indigenous entrepreneurship

There is a nascent but growing literature on specifically *Indigenous* entrepreneurship (Dana, 2015; Hindle & Moroz, 2010; Peredo et al., 2004; Peredo & Anderson, 2006). It includes some differences of opinion as to what should, as a matter of definition, count as Indigenous entrepreneurship. Some (e.g. Dana & Anderson, 2007; Galbraith & Stiles, 2003) hold it applies to whatever, wherever, and however entrepreneurial activity is engaged in by Indigenous people. Others hold that Indigenous entrepreneurship is distinguished not just by its agents, but also by its location and cultural environment. For instance, Peredo et al. (2004, p. 12), for instance, identify Indigenous entrepreneurs, as "situated in communities of Indigenous people with the shared social, economic, and cultural patterns that qualify them as Indigenous populations."

Scholars with this latter perspective tend to see that cultural environment as contributing features that at the empirical level distinguish Indigenous forms of entrepreneurship. Indigenous cultures are diverse and intensely varied, but it is widely held, for instance (e.g., Bishop, 1999; Redpath & Nielsen, 1997; Tully, 1994), that they tend to display in various ways and to various degrees what Peredo and Chrisman (2006) call "community orientation." By this they mean that community members "experience their membership as resembling the life of parts of an organism and . . . feel their status and wellbeing is a function of the reciprocated contributions they make to their community" (p. 313). This tendency in many Indigenous cultures is borne out in two features that several scholars identify within Indigenous entrepreneurship: its characteristic goals, and its typical forms of governance. Indigenous entrepreneurship is seen as aimed not at individual economic benefit but at multiple goals (Peredo & Chrisman, 2006, 2017) that may include, for instance, social and cultural purposes such as self-determination and heritage preservation, but also immediate benefits such as medical and elder care. Berkes and Adhikari (2006) likewise see any individual profit motive in Indigenous entrepreneurship as subordinated to meeting community needs and aims. Indigenous communities, like other communities, develop sophisticated but informal ways of guiding behaviour in everything from the activities of trading to the undertakings of hunting and harvest. Commenting on Indigenous people pursuing "development" in Canada, Anderson et al. (2006, p. 61) comment: "Their goal is not economic development alone, but economic development as part of the larger agenda of rebuilding their communities and nations and reasserting their control over their traditional territories."

Hand-in-hand with this community-based goal structure goes the typical form of organization. Lindsay (2005, p. 206) sees Indigenous entrepreneurship as embodying "entrepreneurial strategies originating in and controlled by the community, and the sanction of Indigenous culture". In the Indigenous communities discussed by Peredo and Chrisman (2006), the entrepreneurs are communities acting collectively, and the enterprises they create are governed by the community organized in such a way as to protect and maintain the community goal orientation.

Standard conceptions of entrepreneurship are centred on market activity, populated by individual profit maximizers amid whom entrepreneurs occupy a special place. We have already seen reasons to loosen the restriction to individuals and profit in considering Indigenous entrepreneurship. In discussions of Indigenous entrepreneurship, Peredo and McLean (2010, p. 610) have proposed that freeing the concept of "entrepreneurship" in this way allows us to recognize a range of often-innovative ways in which transfers take place for the purpose of increasing value for both giver and receiver in Indigenous settings. Entrepreneurship can then take its place as furthering not just individual, "economic" benefits, but also social and cultural outcomes, and not just by market exchange. In considering Indigenous entrepreneurship in its Canadian setting, it is essential to consider those distinguishable characteristics.

Indigenous finance

'Indigenous finance' refers to the financial activities conducted by, or for, Indigenous people. It encapsulates both financing designed for Indigenous entrepreneurs and financing managed by Indigenous communities and individuals. This emergent field still lacks a clear definition and is just beginning to receive increasing attention in academic circles. Indigenous finance, like Indigenous communities, represents an extremely varied and diverse sector. Indigenous finance is often seen as distinct in addressing the specific needs of Indigenous entrepreneurs. In this brief review of Indigenous finance, we will discuss three main themes within the field: the challenges of mainstream entrepreneurial finance located in an Indigenous context, the similarities and differences between Indigenous finance and other forms of finance, and, most importantly, the integration of Indigenous values in Indigenous finance.

Challenges of entrepreneurial finance in an Indigenous context

In countries like Canada, it is well acknowledged that funding barriers exist for many Indigenous groups, especially those living on-reserve (Ketilson, 2014). Indigenous entrepreneurs face a variety of barriers when it comes to finance. Due to Section 89 of the *Indian Act*, land on reserve cannot be used as collateral because band members collectively hold land titles (Northern Development Ministers Forum, 2010). Therefore, individual Indigenous entrepreneurs on-reserve are often unable to leverage their homes as collateral to access capital for their businesses. However, Indigenous and non-Indigenous financial institutions are finding creative solutions around this barrier. A lack of collateral and established credit, often due to socio-economic and structural challenges, a lack of local financial institutions, and a lack of profitability limit Indigenous entrepreneurs' access to debt financing (Conference Board of Canda, 2020; Cooper, 2016). Equity financing is also hard to access due to limited personal resources, networks of family and friends able to invest in their businesses, inadequate retained earnings, a lack of community investment funds, and access to venture capital (Cooper, 2016). According to Canadian Council for Aboriginal Business (CCAB) study in 2011, Indigenous entrepreneurs tend to rely heavily on personal resources for their financing needs due to many of the barriers discussed (CCAB, 2011; Cooper, 2016). These types of barriers are a global phenomenon (Loosemore & Denny-Smith, 2016). Many Indigenous and non-Indigenous financial institutions are finding creative solutions around these barriers.

In addition to the barriers Indigenous entrepreneurs face, many report that to access entrepreneurial finance, they are required to change their behaviours and conform to externally imposed social norms to access capital. Required changes include alterations in communication styles and priorities, and values of their business to appeal to lenders and investors, which typically value the Eurocentric standards embedded in western entrepreneurship (Pinto & Blue, 2015; Peredo & McLean, 2010). A lack of understanding of Indigenous communities, their cultures, political structures, economies, and general ways of being, is believed to be central as to why mainstream financial institutions have historically been unsuccessful in conducting business with Indigenous entrepreneurs at a necessary scale (Standing Senate Committee on Aboriginal Peoples, 2007).

Despite the challenges Indigenous entrepreneurs face, Indigenous business ownership is growing at five times the rate of self-employed Canadians (Indigenous Economic Report, 2019). Currently, 1.4% of Canadian SMEs are majority-owned by Indigenous peoples. Statistics Canada's 2016 Census highlights the following numbers regarding Indigenous entrepreneurs: 54,255 Indigenous Canadians (15 years of age and older) reported being self-employed. Of these, the Métis made up 53.2% of the Indigenous self-employed population, followed by First Nations at 41.4%, and the Inuit at 1.8% (Conference Board of Canada, 2020, p. 2). Overall, Indigenous entrepreneurial finance is dynamic and driven by increased demand from Indigenous-owned and operated businesses. It is estimated that Canada's Indigenous economy is worth 30 billion dollars, with over 50,000 Indigenous-owned companies, and is expected to more than triple in size by 2025 (Indigenous Economic Report, 2019; Amato, 2020).

Indigenous finance and Indigenous values

While traditional finance in Western societies focuses on profit-maximization and wealth accumulation, Indigenous finance often integrates decision-making principles unfamiliar to traditional finance, such as community values and traditional knowledge (Bargh, 2020). An example of this is demonstrated in the integration of the Māori cultural value of *kaitiakitanga* in investment decisions by *Iwi* investors in New Zealand. *Kaitiakitanga*, prohibits *Iwi* investors from making investment decisions that could result in environmental damage – a strong Māori value (Poyser, Scott & Gilbert, 2020). Additional core financial practices integrated from Māori cultural values include *whanaungatanga*, representing social and family relationships, *mana/rangatiratanga*, community governance, *tapu*, spiritual quality, and *utu*, meaning balance (Bargh, 2020, Craig et al., 2018; Love, 2017). Māori investment management values are just one example of how Indigenous community values, histories and ways of being are integrated into financial decision making. A similar example in Canada is Raven Indigenous Capital Partners, the first Indigenous-owned and controlled social finance intermediary in the country (UBC Sauder Centre for Social Innovation & Impact Investing, 2018). Raven Indigenous Capital Partners incorporates an Indigenous culture-centred approach and invests in Indigenous social enterprise to revitalize the Indigenous economy in Canada and the United States. For the organization, the raven after it is named symbolizes rebirth and transformation, as it does in many Indigenous cultures. This focus on transformation is core to the company's mission, which centres on revitalizing the Indigenous economy in Canada by addressing the systemic barriers Indigenous entrepreneurs encounter (Raven Capital Partners, 2021). While Canada's Indigenous financial institution models vary greatly compared to *Iwi* investment firms in New Zealand, there are certainly similarities between such institutions when it comes to values and accountability; each is guided by Indigenous values and is accountable to the communities they serve. For example, Craig et al. (2013), have employed the concept of 'accountability reporting' instead of financial reporting, to capture Indigenous perspectives within Indigenous financial organizations (Poyser, Scott & Gilbert, 2020).

The integration of values is central to the concept of Indigenous finance. Indigenous financial institutions are incorporating cultural values and knowledge about their communities and aligning institutional rules and norms with the values and needs of their communities. These institutions are balancing a range of unique cultural values while participating in and transforming a westernized financial world.

Indigenous finance and social finance: The case of Canada

In Canada, Indigenous peoples are recognized under Canada's Constitution as composed of three distinct groups: First Nations, Métis and Inuit peoples. There are over 1.6 million Indigenous peoples in Canada (StatsCan, 2016), which comprises 5% of the total population.[1]

---

[1] Throughout this chapter, "Indigenous" will be used to refer to the original peoples of Canada. "Aboriginal" will be widely used when referring to different Indigenous institutions that still include "Aboriginal" in their names given that they were established at a time when the term was more commonly used.

There is abundant historical and archeological evidence that Indigenous Peoples engaged in entrepreneurial activities long before the arrival of Europeans. Those entrepreneurial activities were guided by cultural values supporting their resource-based economies and local and regional trade (AFOA BC, 2011). Hunting, trade, barter, and the redistribution of surplus goods were widely practiced to sustain community (Macleod, 2016). At the outset of contact with European settlers, the Indigenous people of present-day Canada were heavily relied upon to establish trade routes for the fur trade based on their extensive knowledge of routes, the land, and animals. Many Indigenous trade routes were used by European hunters, trappers, and traders (Macleod, 2016). According to Keith Martell, President and CEO of the First Nations Bank of Canada, "The economy of Canada in the 400 years since the first contact with Europeans was developed on the back of Indigenous people – the fur trade, the support of settlers and explorers – that was all Indigenous business" (Jansen, 2020).

The economic skills and values that Indigenous people cultivated during pre-contact times enabled them to survive colonization and its financial exclusion and systemic barriers and provided the foundations of current Indigenous business and entrepreneurship in Canada. Legislation such as *The Indian Act* (1876), with its prescriptions on Indigenous governance, land tenure, and land use, restricted economic activity and excluded Indigenous peoples from equitable participation in the economy (Dahiwale, 2007; Joseph, 2018). For example, the pass system required First Nations people to present a travel document, authorized by an Indian agent, to leave and return to the reserve and do business with outsiders on and off the reserve (Joseph, 2018; Schneider, 2018). Without a pass, one could be imprisoned for leaving the reserve or have rations or other privileges withheld. Essentially, "the pass system was used effectively by Indian agents to control the movements of Indians" (Joseph, 2018, p. 50) and restricted First Nations from trade, barter, and business activities. Under *The Indian Act*, the permit system allowed the government to "prohibit or regulate the sale, barter, exchange, or gift by an Indian or Indian band of any grain, root crop, or other produce grown on any reserve in western Canada" (Carter, 1990, p. 156). Through the permit system, First Nations trade, barter, and ability to sell products grown through farming were restricted from 1881 until 2014. Essentially, due to restrictive legislation under the *Indian Act*, Indigenous economies and entrepreneurship were highly restricted.

Growing Indigenous political activism throughout the 20th century led to the creation of the National Indian Brotherhood (NIB)[2] in 1967 and the beginning of a new political era for Indigenous Peoples in Canada. The NIB and other provincial

---

2 The National Indian Brotherhood dissolved in the late 1970s and the Assembly of First Nations became the voice of First Nations in Canada through a deliberative assembly of First Nations, represented by their Chiefs.

and regional Indigenous organizations demanded the recognition of Indigenous rights. Several important landmark court decisions throughout the 1970s advanced the recognition of the rights of First Nations in Canada. In 1973, the Supreme Court decision regarding the Calder Case, originally brought forward by the Nisga'a in 1967 to ensure continued recognition of Aboriginal title, led to the negotiation of comprehensive land claims settlements. The decision also led to the establishment of a comprehensive land claims policy that allows for self-government agreements to be negotiated and executed. Comprehensive land claims are modern-day treaties initiated by Indigenous peoples who did not sign treaties and allow for self-government agreements to be negotiated and implemented based on outstanding Aboriginal titles (Dyck & Sadik, 2016). As a result, land claim settlements and more business development opportunities began to grow. Indigenous leaders began to demand increased autonomy and self-determination, including increased control over their own institutions, finances, and economic resources. This transformational period led to the assertion of Indigenous institutional control and the birth of Aboriginal Financial Institutions (AFIs) and other types of Indigenous financial organizations to create new opportunities for Indigenous peoples and address the economic inequities and the financial exclusion of Indigenous peoples that colonization created.

Mapping the landscape of Indigenous finance in Canada

The number and kinds of sources of finance for Indigenous entrepreneurs are constantly increasing and evolving. They generally aim to support individual and community, and inter-organizational level Indigenous enterprises. Table 17.1 represents the variety of sources.

Table 17.1: Indigenous Finance in Canada: Mapping the Landscape.

Financing Mechanism	Description
Category 1: Government Of Canada Financing Support For Indigenous Entrepreneurs	
The Aboriginal Entrepreneurship Program	Capitalized by the Government of Canada and managed by the National Aboriginal Capital Corporation Association.
Business Development Bank of Canada (BDC)	A Crown corporation devoted to Canadian entrepreneurs with dedicated funding for Indigenous entrepreneurs through Indigenous banking opportunities to Indigenous communities.
Indigenous Growth Fund	A $150M investment fund launched in April 2021 that enhances the pool of capital for Indigenous SMEs through AFIs.

Table 17.1 (continued)

Financing Mechanism	Description	
The Indigenous Business Stabilization Program – Covid	The program includes two components: The Emergency Loan program and the Emergency Loan Delivery Program.	
Category 2: Indigenous-Owned National Advocacy And Financial Institutions		
Indigenous Credit Unions and Co-Operatives	Indigenous credit unions and co-operatives are Indigenous-owned financial institutions. Indigenous peoples have historically pooled resources, including financial resources, through co-operation. The first Indigenous co-op was incorporated in 1945 by the Kinoosao Fishers' Co-op.	Examples include the Me-Dian Credit Union, Caisse Populaire Kahnawake, and the Arctic Co-operative Fund.
Indigenous Banks and Trusts	Indigenous Banks and Trusts are Indigenous-owned and controlled federally regulated financial institutions.	Examples include: The First Nations Bank of Canada (FNBC) and Peace Hills Trust
Aboriginal Financial Institutions (AFIs)	Aboriginal Financial Institutions (AFIs) are Indigenous-owned and controlled developmental lending organizations.	Examples include the Aboriginal Capital Corporations, Aboriginal Community Futures Development Corporations (ACFDCs), and Aboriginal Developmental Lenders (ADLs).
Indigenous-Owned Intermediaries	Indigenous-owned intermediaries are institutions that help facilitate investment-related activities, including but not limited to entrepreneurial incubation, direct investment, and mentorship.	Raven Indigenous Capital Partners is an example of Canada's first Indigenous social finance intermediary.
Category 3: Credit Unions and Co-Operatives		
Credit Unions and Co-Operatives	Credit Unions and Co-operatives are community-owned organizations funded and governed democratically by their members.	Examples include the Vancity Credit Union and Desjardins Group.
Category 4: Commercial Banks: "The Big Five"		
The Big Five Commercial Banks in Canada	The Big Five commercial banks in Canada account for more than 90% of banking assets in Canada and conduct banking activities with Indigenous communities across Canada.	The big give includes the Bank of Montreal, the Royal Bank of Canada, the Canadian Imperial Bank of Canada, Toronto-Dominion, and Scotiabank.

Government of Canada financing support for Indigenous entrepreneurs

Beginning in the 1970s, the Government of Canada began to shift away from its policy of resisting distinctively Indigenous economic and political organization, with programs such as the Indian Economic Development Fund (Dahiwale, 2007). Since then, programs have proliferated to support Indigenous business capacity.

I.   *The Aboriginal Entrepreneurship Program (AEP)* was established and capitalized by the Government of Canada in the 1990s. In 2014, Indigenous and Northern Affairs Canada transferred its Aboriginal Business Financing Program to the National Aboriginal Capital Corporation Association (NACCA) to be distributed through the Aboriginal Financial Institutions (AFIs) network. The AEP goal is to increase the number of Indigenous-run businesses in Canada, aiming "to build capacity, reduce barriers and increase access to capital, by forging partnerships that will increase economic opportunities for First Nations, Inuit and Métis people" (Indigenous Services Canada, 2021a). Two funding streams exist under the AEP program: Access to Capital and Access to Business Opportunities.

The Access to Capital funding stream provides Indigenous small – medium-sized businesses with access to non-repayable funding up to $99,999 and to community-owned Aboriginal businesses up to $250,000. The Access to Business Opportunities funding stream provides a maximum of $500,000, reimbursed for 100% of costs, for: "institutional development, including training and development and business, supports to business development organizations; business advisory services and training; commercial ventures including business innovation and growth; market development; business development and advocacy activities" (Indigenous Services Canada, 2021b).

II. *The Business Development Bank of Canada (BDC)* is a Crown financial corporation providing direct and indirect financial services to Indigenous communities, offering Indigenous entrepreneur loans up to $350,000 for enterprises on or off-reserve (BDC, 2021). As of 2020, BDC provided $400M to Indigenous clients.

III. *The Indigenous Growth Fund* is a $150M Indigenous social impact fund launched by the federal government in April 2021 that enhances the pool of capital for Indigenous SMEs through AFIs. This fund is oriented to all the sectors with high growth potential, including agricultural export products. Lead investors in this fund include the Government of Canada and the BDC; Export Development Canada and Farm Credit Canada have also made commitments (NACCA, 2021f).

IV. *The Indigenous Business Stabilization Program* was announced in 2020, with two components: (a) The Emergency Loan Program, providing Indigenous-owned businesses impacted by COVID-19 with interest-free loans and non-repayable contributions to support their immediate working capital and operational needs; and (b) the Emergency Loan Delivery Program that covers delivery and administration costs of AFIs and NACCA. (NACCA, 2020).

Indigenous-owned and -controlled financial institutions

A promising development has been the creation of Indigenous-owned and controlled organizations dedicated to supporting its members financially. Prominent in this development has been the establishment of Indigenous banks and trusts; Aboriginal Financial Institutions under the National Aboriginal Capital Corporation Association (NACCA); Indigenous credit unions; Indigenous not-for-profits; and Indigenous Economic Development Corporations.

Indigenous-owned credit unions and cooperatives

Since time immemorial, Indigenous peoples have pooled resources, including financial resources, through co-operation. However, their approach to the formally-constituted 'cooperative' model is complicated by its association with the institutions imposing colonization (Sengupta, 2015). They have nevertheless been long-time users of the co-operative model, particularly in the fishing and agriculture sectors. The first Indigenous co-op was incorporated in 1945 by the Kinoosao Fishers' Co-op, and through the decades, there has been an increase of Indigenous co-operatives (White, 2001; Sengupta, 2015). Among the major Indigenous co-operatives:

i. *Me-Dian Credit Union* is Canada's first Indigenous credit union. It was created in 1978 through the support of the Manitoba Métis Federation, which helped to open the Métis Credit Union, and eventually changed its name to Me-Dian Credit Union (Me-Dian) to reflect the inclusion of the broader Indigenous community in its membership.

ii. *Caisse Populaire Kahnawake*, on a reserve outside Montreal, was created in the mid-1980s to develop its own financial institution for economic development purposes and decrease government dependence. The credit union model was chosen as it provides the flexibility to meet the needs of its members. Its location on reserve allows for tax benefits (Cooper, 2016).

iii. *Arctic Co-operative Fund* is owned by the Arctic Co-operative Limited, a network of 33 co-operatives across the arctic. It was created in 1986 and provides loans for working capital, infrastructure development and debt re-structuring. It has successfully built its initial capital of 10 million from various government agencies to 41 million. The fund works closely with its members, and repayment rates are high (Ketilson, 2014).

Indigenous banks and trusts

i. *First Nations Bank of Canada (FNBC)* was established through a partnership between the Saskatchewan Indian Equity Foundation (SIEF), an Aboriginal Financial

Institution established in the mid-1980s by the First Nations of Saskatchewan, the Federation of Saskatchewan Indian Nations (FSIN),[3] and Toronto-Dominion Bank (TD). SIEF, the FSIN, and TD launched FNBC in 1996 with a $2 million investment from SIEF and an $8 million-dollar investment from TD (Cooper, 2016). FNBC is 83% Indigenous-owned and controlled, with Indigenous banking representing over 90% of their business and the largest Indigenous financial services market share in the regions it serves (First Nations Bank of Canada, 2020). FNBC offers a full range of financial services, but its main focus is to provide financial assistance to the Indigenous Peoples of Canada (First Nations Bank of Canada, 2021).

ii. *Peace Hills Trust* is Canada's largest First Nations-owned, federally regulated financial institution. It is owned by the Samson Cree Nation of Maskwacis in Alberta. It has eight regional offices across the country that provide full-service banking, credit, and trust services to Indigenous governments, small- and medium-sized businesses, and individuals (Peace Hills Trust, 2021).

Métis capital corporations and entrepreneurship funds

These entities invest in Métis businesses and entrepreneurs starting up and/or growing their businesses. Examples of Métis capital corporations are Apeetogosan Metis Development Inc. in Alberta, the SaskMétis in Saskatchewan, and the Louis Riel Capital Corporation in Manitoba; all of these capital corporations are also Aboriginal Financial Institutions. The Louis Riel Capital Corporation in Manitoba focuses on "debt financing and creative financing that the big banks and credit unions usually don't do to help Métis contractors or business in general" (Metis Economic Development Strategy, 2015, p. 4). The Métis Economic Development Fund (MEDF) is a 10 million dollar fund that provides debt and equity financing of $20,000–500,000 per opportunity to Métis owned and controlled enterprises incorporated in Manitoba to support economic development (Métis Economic Development Fund, 2021).

Aboriginal Financial Institutions (AFIs)

In the mid-1980s, First Nations leaders recommended creating Aboriginal Financial Institutions (AFIs) to address systemic inequities and the lack of available capital to finance Aboriginal small-business development. These replaced the Indian Economic Development Fund in financing small and medium-sized enterprises (SMEs). AFIs are Indigenous-owned and controlled business lending organizations that the Federal

---

3 FSIN is now known as the Federation of Sovereign Indigenous Nations.

Government capitalizes. Ketilson (2014, p. 44) notes that AFIs "have their own lending criteria and a strong understanding of their communities and local economies".

"AFI" is a collective term denoting three types of Canadian Aboriginal-controlled financial institutions: Aboriginal Capital Corporations (ACCs), Aboriginal Community Futures Development Corporations (ACFDCs) and Aboriginal Developmental Lenders (ADLs). Within the last 30 years, 59 AFIs have been established throughout Canada. Annually, they provide more than "$120 million in loans to 500 Indigenous-owned start-ups and 750 existing businesses" that employ over 13,000 people (NACCA, 2020). AFIs have provided more than 50,000 loans, totalling over $3 billion, with an above average repayment rate (97.5%) for developmental loans (NACCA, 2021b).

i. *Aboriginal Capital Corporations* were first established in the mid-1980s to deliver business products and services to Indigenous entrepreneurs. They offer various services, including term loans, letters of credit, operating and working capital loans, and technical support and advice to Canadian Indigenous businesses and communities (NACCA, 2021c).

ii. Aboriginal Community Futures Development Corporations (ACFDCs) were established in the late 80s and early 90s as a federally-capitalized element in an overall community development strategy to support economic development in rural and remote areas. Specifically, ACFDCs provide financial and technical assistance and training to small business rural entrepreneurs to start, expand, franchise or sell a business (Community Futures Network, 2020).

iii. *Aboriginal Developmental Lenders (ADLs)* provide debt and equity capital and various business support services to Indigenous businesses and communities. They are capitalized either by the private sector or the provincial/territorial governments (NACCA, 2021c). Examples are the Clarence Campeau Development Fund in Saskatchewan and Manitoba's First People's Economic Growth Fund.

iv. *The National Aboriginal Capital Corporation Association (NACCA)* was created in 1997 as a third-level organization to provide a unified voice for Indigenous-led finance and business development. Its vision is to promote "thriving, prosperous, Aboriginal businesses with equitable access to capital and care" (NACCA, 2021d). NACCA is an advocate network that publishes national and regional results of AFI work and fosters partnerships. As an organizational development organization, NACCA supports AFIs in building capacity and delivering the government-funded Aboriginal Entrepreneurship Program (AEP).

v. *Indigenous-owned Intermediaries* are gaining a presence in Canada's entrepreneurial finance landscape. They play a crucial role in connecting enterprises to funding and mentorship opportunities, a particular challenge noted among Indigenous entrepreneurs in Canada. An example is Raven Indigenous Capital Partners, the first Indigenous-led and -owned social finance intermediary. It invests in Indigenous social enterprises across Canada and the United States (Raven Indigenous Capital Partners, 2021).

Mainstream credit unions and cooperatives

Mainstream Credit Unions and Cooperatives are community-owned organizations funded and governed democratically by their members. Credit unions in Canada are financial co-operatives. Vancity and Desjardin are among those that have played a significant role in funding important social infrastructure development in Indigenous communities. Vancity, for example, serves both Indigenous and non-Indigenous populations, working in partnership with Indigenous not-for-profit and First Nations government organizations to provide additional capital. Vancity has helped fund First Nations economic projects such as energy (Sayer & Peredo, 2017); on- and off-reserve housing solutions; acquiring or creating community-owned assets, such as office buildings, housing complexes, or community-based social enterprises; and small business and start-up loans (Vancity, 2021).

Commercial banks: "The Big Five"

In Canada, the Bank of Montreal, Canadian Imperial Bank of Commerce, Royal Bank of Canada, Scotiabank, and Toronto-Dominion are commonly labelled "the Big Five" and are the largest banks in Canada in terms of total assets. Each of the Big Five has on-reserve branches and offers tailored financial services to Indigenous communities, governments, and businesses. The private banks view the Indigenous market as an emerging market that could provide the banking sector with very considerable revenue, including a small business sector growing at six times faster rate than in the non-Indigenous market (Schecter, 2015).

In addition to financing services on and off-reserve, all of the Big Five offer community investment and engagement supports to Indigenous communities such as scholarships and internships, educational programs, sponsorships, community partnerships and gifts.

Indigenous Economic Development Corporations

Indigenous Economic Development Corporations (IEDCs) are Indigenous, community-owned organizations that guide economic and business development for First Nations, Métis or Inuit governments and provide revenue to communities through community-based enterprises (CCAB, 2020). Indigenous Economic Development Corporations provide financing support and mentorship, training, and preferred supplier relationships and agreements to community entrepreneurs (CCAB, n.d.). According to the CCAB, the most common source of revenue for IEDCs is own-source revenue, i.e. revenue raised by a government from taxes, fees, business and other income (CCAB, 2020). Own-source revenue allows First Nations governments more control over the financing of their own community-owned enterprises and projects.

First Nations Finance Authority (FNFA)

FNFA is a not-for-profit financial organization owned and controlled by Indigenous Peoples to raise financing (short-term and long-term) for its members; all First Nations in Canada can be members. An example of how the FNFA supports Indigenous businesses is the $250 million loan secured through the FNFA by the Mi'kmaq Coalition[4] to pursue 100% ownership of all Clearwater Canadian lobster fishing quotas (FNFA, 2020). FNFA financing also supports a better investment environment, infrastructure, better transportation systems, and sustainable power sources, which in turn support First Nations businesses and entrepreneurs.

Future research agenda

This chapter does not attempt a complete inventory of current financial resources available to Indigenous businesses in Canada. Rather, it sets out a framework of existing Indigenous financial resources. Within this evolving landscape, the growing number and strength of Indigenous-owned and led financial institutions is evident. Research on Indigenous Entrepreneurship shows that Indigenous people, in all their diversity, have a collective inclination and generally engage in entrepreneurship to improve their social and economic conditions and build their communities and nations (Anderson, 1999; Dana, 1995; Peredo and Anderson, 2006). These distinctive characteristics and cultural aspirations for self-determination seem built into the development of Indigenous Economic Development Corporations and community-controlled financial institutions such as credit unions and Aboriginal Financial Institutions.

The existence and function of these Indigenous-led organizations leads to a vital research question. Indigenous community-based organizations tend to be closer to the communities and offer lenders a broader mechanism such as training and other services. Should these community-based organizations, such as AFIs, just act as a bridge between Indigenous businesses and mainstream commercial banks? Is their role in helping Indigenous entrepreneurs "transition" and thus provide a clientele to mainstream banks? Or should Indigenous entrepreneurs mobilize their resources to strengthen their own financial institutions or create new Indigenous

---

4 Membertou, Potlotek, Pictou Landing, Sipekne'katik, Miawpukek, Paqtnkek and We'kowma'q represent participating First Nations in the Mi'kmaq Coailition.

financial institutions? What are the barriers to supporting their own institutions? Is there a need to build larger Indigenous financial institutions? What are the implications of these two routes? Is there a third route in partnering with non-Indigenous community-owned organizations such as credit unions? Which route(s) would help Indigenous Peoples to achieve their goals for self-determination and decolonization? Ultimately, what does Indigenous inclusion really mean in the context of Indigenous peoples accessing financial services?

This brings to the surface a further and fundamental question that confronts scholars who discuss Indigenous entrepreneurship and economic life: Is Indigenous entrepreneurship and economic life distinct in ways that matter to Indigenous peoples and worth preserving in that form, or is it simply a pathway for Indigenous populations to enter more fully into the established economic life of the settler populations around them (Peredo and Anderson, 2006)? For those who believe that Indigenous economic life is distinctive in its dynamic and goals (e.g. Peredo & McLean, 2013), there are aspects of the landscape of Indigenous business financing that raise questions. When funding comes from government organizations, is there a risk that dependency and the goals established by settler appropriation of traditional Indigenous resources may be perpetuated by systems of grants and special loans, or can that risk be addressed in appropriate ways? When the source of funds is conventional, profit-oriented institutions operating in the mainstream market economy, can the requirements of those sources be reconciled with the collective and multi-goal inclination of many Indigenous enterprises? Will those features be swallowed up in the process of accessing those funds? A similar set of questions face even those organizations organized, owned and run by Indigenous people if they are immersed in a profit-based, market environment. If they wish to engage, how can they maintain distinctive Indigenous interests and their integrity while avoiding co-option and assimilation?

Answers to these two questions should serve as background for a further set of questions concerning the role of mainstream organizations in the colonial setting. To what extent should governments, mainstream banks and credit unions be expected to adapt to the distinctive goals and expectations that Indigenous communities often have, perhaps even bearing extra costs and enjoying lower financial returns? Or should they help those communities to adapt to the market priorities and learn to thrive by those standards? To what extent should these matters be governed by regulation or by conditions attached to accreditation?

Conclusion

The OECD (2020, p. 11) has commented, "Entrepreneurship and business growth is fundamental to creating opportunities for [Canadian] Indigenous peoples". Financial support is obviously crucial for supporting this growth in enterprise. In this chapter, we have explored Indigenous entrepreneurial finance in the Canadian context, using that context to explore the literature and identify some gaps to be filled in future research.

Our overview suggests that the landscape in Canada is more extensive and more diverse than many would have expected, and the response from Indigenous individuals and communities has reached new levels in recent years; though it remains true that yet more numerous and imaginative financing solutions are called for to address the circumstances of Indigenous populations in Canada and globally.

Our survey has highlighted the variety in kinds of funding that are directed at Indigenous venturing. To begin with, there are sources funded by the Government of Canada and/or its agencies, often in partnership with Indigenous organizations. Second, there is the mainstream layer of financing services offered through commercial banks, many of whom have launched programs geared to what are seen as Indigenous circumstances. An important variation on this is community-owned credit unions, which have also directed special lending opportunities to Indigenous initiatives. The landscape changes dramatically with the visibility of financial organizations owned and led by the Indigenous peoples themselves. Here, too, there is variety in organizational form and sources of funds. There are Indigenous banks and trusts that are Indigenous-owned and operated. There is a group of Indigenous-owned "Aboriginal Financial Institutions" that are organized under the National Aboriginal Capital Corporation Association to provide funding and other forms of support for Indigenous venturing. More regionally and locally, there are credit unions and co-operatives that are themselves Indigenous initiatives. An interesting development that runs like a network through Indigenous-initiated enterprise is the web of locally-owned and operated Indigenous Economic Development Corporations, funding local Indigenous ventures in a variety of ways. First Nations Finance Authority provides short- and long-term financing opportunities that support First Nations enterprises and contribute to stronger First Nations economies by creating better investment environments, more First Nations generated own-source revenue, and enhanced infrastructure that all contribute to supporting First Nations entrepreneurs.

The full delineation of these promising developments, and their accompanying challenges, constitutes a vital research program. We hope to have given some idea of the landscape that program might survey.

References

Aboriginal Financial Officers Association of British Columbia. (2011). *First Nations Financial Fitness: Your Guide for Getting Healthy, Wealthy and Wise.* Retrieved from: http://www.afoabc.org/wp-content/uploads/2015/06/financial-literacy-handbook.pdf (accessed April 30, 2021)

Alfred, T. (1999). Peace, power, righteousness: an Indigenous manifesto. Don Mills, Ontario: Oxford University Press.

Alvi, F. H. (2021). Social impact investing as a neoliberal construction: Ego and altruism in the post-colonial space of Oaxaca, Mexico. Critical Perspectives on International Business.

Amato, D. (2020). *Indigenous Entrepreneurship in Canada: The Impact and the Opportunity.* Retrieved from: https://discover.rbcroyalbank.com/indigenous-entrepreneurship-in-canada-the-impact-and-the-opportunity/ (accessed September 14, 2021)

Anderson, R. B. (1999). Economic Development among the Aboriginal Peoples of Canada: Hope for the Future. Captus University Press. Anderson, R.B., Kayseas, B., Dana, L.P. & Hindle, K. (2004). Indigenous land claims and

Anderson, R. B., Giberson, R., & McGillivray, S. (2003). The Nk'Mip Cellars: Wine and Wine Tourism with an Indigenous Flavour. In 2003 Wine Marketing Colloquium and Annual Conference.

Anderson, R. B., Camp II, R., Dana, L. P., Honig, B., Nkongolo-Bakenda, J.-M., & Peredo, A. M. (2005). Indigenous land rights in Canada: The foundation for development? International Journal of Entrepreneurship and Small Business, 2(2), 104–133.

Anderson, A. K., Yamaguchi, Y., Grabski, W., & Lacka, D. (2006). Emotional memories are not all created equal: evidence for selective memory enhancement. Learning & Memory, 13(6), 711–718.

ANZ (2017) *Te Tirohanga Whanui Iwi.* ANZ Document Cloud, July. Available at: https://assets.docu mentcloud.org/documents/3897022/Te-Tirohanga-Wh%C4%81Nui-Iwi-Investment-Insights -2017.pdf (accessed May 24, 2021)

Baker, R., Schneider, B., Anderson, R. (2015). Accountability and Control: Canada's First Nations Reporting Requirements. Issues in Social and Environmental Accounting, vol.9, no.2

Bank of Montreal. (2021). Serving Indigenous Communities. Retrieved from: https://www.bmo. com/assets/main/business/Indigenous /branches_en.pdf (accessed May 21, 2021)

Bank of Montreal. (2021). *Indigenous Banking.* Retrieved from: https://www.bmo.com/main/per sonal/Indigenous-banking/ (accessed May 2, 2021)

Bargh, M. (2020). Indigenous finance: Treaty settlement finance in Aotearoa New Zealand. In J. K. Gibson-Graham & K. Dombroski (Eds.), The Handbook of Diverse Economies (pp. 362–369). Edward Elgar Publishing.

Bishop, J. D. (1999). The Lockean basis of Iroquoian land ownership. Journal of Aboriginal Economic Development, 1, 35–43.

Berkes, F., & Adhikari, T. (2006). Development and conservation: Indigenous businesses and the UNDP Equator Initiative. *International Journal of Entrepreneurship and Small Business*, 3(6), 671–690.

Business Development Canada. (2021). Indigenous Entrepreneur. Retrieved from: https://www. bdc.ca/en/i-am/Indigenous-entrepreneur (accessed May 6, 2021).

Canadian Imperial Banking Corporation. (2021). Indigenous Banking Philosophy. Retrieved from: https://www.cibc.com/en/business/Indigenous-banking/Indigenous-banking-philosophy. html (accessed May 21, 2021)

Canadian Council for Aboriginal Business. (2011). Promise and Prosperity: the Aboriginal Business Survey. Retrieved from: http://ceric.ca/wp-content/uploads/2012/10/CCAB-businessurvey-F2 -singles1.pdf (accessed May 21, 2021).

Canadian Council for Aboriginal Business. (n.d.). Community and Commerce: A Survey of Aboriginal Economic Development Corporations. Retrieved from: http://www.nadf.org/upload/docu ments/community-and-commerce-final-report.pdf (accessed August 4, 2021).

Canadian Council for Aboriginal Business. (2020). Aboriginal Economic Development Corporation Capacity. Canadian Council for Aboriginal Business. Retrieved from: https://www.ccab.com/ wp-content/uploads/2020/02/CCAB-Report-1-web.pdf (accessed May 21, 2021).

Carter, S. (1990). Lost Harvests: Prairie Indian Reserve Farmers and Government Policy. London: McGill Queen's University Press.

Clarence Campeau Development Fund. (2021). About Us. Retrieved from: https://clarencecampeau. com/about-us/ (accessed May 21, 2021)

Chapman Tripp (2018) Te Ao Māori: Insights and Trends. Auckland: Chapman Tripp.

Community Futures Network of Canada. (2020). 2019–20 Annual Report. Retrieved from: https:// 2019-2020.annualreviewcfnc.ca/ (accessed May 6, 2021)

Conference Board of Canada. (2020). Indigenous Entrepreneurship in Northern and Remote Communities. Retrieved from: https://www.conferenceboard.ca/e-library/abstract.aspx?did= 10677 (accessed August 16, 2021).

Cooper, T. (2016). "Finance and Banking." In K. Brown, M. Doucette, and J. Tulk, eds., *Indigenous Business in Canada*, pp. 161–176. Sydney, NS: Cape Breton University Press.

Cooper, T. and Ulnooweg Development Group. (2011). Strategic Risks and Opportunities for First Nations Financial Institutions: Findings from a Market Demand Study. In White, J., Peters, J., Beavon, D., and Dinsdale, P. (Eds). Aboriginal Policy Research: Voting, Governance, and Research Methodology, Vol. 10. Toronto: Thompson Educational Publishing.

Cornell, S. and Kalt, J. 2007. Two Approaches to the Development of Native Nations: One Works, the Other Doesn't. In Rebuilding Native Nations: Strategies for Governance and Development. Tucson: University of Arizona Press.

Craig R, Taonui R and Wild S (2013). The concept of Taonga in Māori culture: Insights for accounting. Accounting, Auditing & Accountability Journal 25: 1025–1047.

Craig R, Taonui R, Wild S, et al. (2018). Accountability reporting objectives of Māori organizations. Pacific Accounting Review 30: 433–443.

Credit Union Central of Canada. (2012). Deepening Relationships: Credit Union and Aboriginal Peoples Case Studies. Retrieved from: https://nacca.ca/wpcontent/uploads/2017/04/CCUA_ DeepeningRelationshipsCreditUnionAboriginalPeoples_Jan2012.pdf (accessed May 21, 2021)

Dana, L. P. (1995). Entrepreneurship in a remote sub-Arctic community. Entrepreneurship Theory and Practice, 20(1), 57–72.

Dana, L. P., & Anderson, R. B. (2007). A multidisciplinary theory of entrepreneurship as a function of cultural perceptions of opportunity. International handbook of research on indigenous entrepreneurship, 1, 595–603.

Dahiwale, S. M. (2007). Aboriginal businesses and entrepreneurship in Canada: Towards economic self-sufficiency. Sociological bulletin, 56(2), 7–32.

DesBrisay, D. (1994). The impact of major resource development projects on aboriginal communities: a review of the literature. Ottawa: Royal Commission on Aboriginal Peoples.

Dyck, Noel and Tonio Sadik. "Indigenous Political Organization and Activism in Canada". The Canadian Encyclopedia, 04 December 2020, Historical Canada. Retrieved from: https://www.the canadianencyclopedia.ca/en/article/aboriginal-people-political-organization-and-activism.

Economic development: The Canadian experience. American Indian Quarterly, 28 (3/4), pp. 634–648.

Els, G. (2007). Unpacking'ethno-finance': An introduction to Indigenous ' financial knowledge systems. South African Journal of Information Management, 9(1).

First Nations Bank of Canada. (2020). 2019–20 Annual Report: CEO Letter. Retrieved from: https:// fnbcannualreport.ca/ceo-letter/ -(accessed May 21, 2021).

First Nations Bank of Canada. (2021). "Who We Are: FNBC at A Glance." Retrieved from: https://www.fnbc.ca/AboutUs/WhoWeAre/FNBCataGlance/ (accessed May 21, 2021).

First Nations Bank of Canada. (2017b). "Who We Are." Retrieved from: https://www.fnbc.ca/AboutUs/WhoWeAre/ (accessed May 21, 2021).

First Nations Finance Authority. (2020). FNFA Annual Report 2020/2021. Retrieved from: https://www.fnfa.ca/wp-content/uploads/2021/07/FNFA-Annual-report-2020-21-English-Web.pdf (accessed August 4, 2021).

Galbraith, C. S., & Stiles, C. H. (2003). Expectations of Indian reservation gaming: Entrepreneurial activity within a context of traditional land tenure and wealth acquisition. Journal of Developmental Entrepreneurship, 8(2), 93–112.

Heidrick, T. and Nichol, T. (2002). Financing SMEs in Canada: barriers faced by women, youth, aboriginal and minority entrepreneurs in accessing capital – phase 1: literature review research paper prepared for the small business policy branch as part of the Small and Medium-Sized Enterprise (SME) financing data initiative. Available at: www.ic.gc.ca/eic/site/061.nsf/vwapj/FinancingSMEsinCanadaPhase1_e.pdf/$FILE/FinancingSMEsinCanadaPhase1_e.pdf

Henriques, I., Colbourne, R., Peredo, A. M., & Anderson, R. B. (2020). Relational and social aspects of Indigenous entrepreneurship: The Hupacasath case. In R. Colbourne & R. B. Anderson (Eds.), Indigenous Wellbeing and Enterprise (pp. 313–340). Routledge.

Hindle, K., & Moroz, P. (2010). Indigenous entrepreneurship as a research field: Developing a definitional framework from the emerging canon. International Entrepreneurship and Management Journal, 6(4), 357–385.

Indian Business Corporation. (n.d.). Social Finance: Unlocking the Potential of Developmental Lending. Retrieved from: http://www.indianbc.ca/reports/potential.pdf (accessed August 13, 2021).

Indigenous Services Canada. (2021a). Aboriginal Entrepreneurship Program: Access to Capital. Retrieved from: https://www.isc-sac.gc.ca/eng/1375201178602/1610797286236 (accessed May 6, 2021)

Indigenous Services Canada. (2021b). Aboriginal Entrepreneurship Program: Access to Business Opportunities. Retrieved from: https://www.isc-sac.gc.ca/eng/1582037564226/1610797399865 (accessed May 6, 2021)

Indigenous and Northern Affairs Canada. (2016). Evaluation of Business Capital and Support Services. Retrieved from: https://www.rcaanc-cirnac.gc.ca/DAM/DAM-CIRNAC-RCAANC/DAM-AEV/STAGING/texte-text/ev_bcs_1491917187529_eng.pdf (accessed May 6, 2021)

Jansen, R. (2020). How Indigenous Communities are Regaining Economic Independence. Retrieved from: https://www.cpacanada.ca/en/news/pivot-magazine/2020-09-02-indigenous-communities-financial-autonomy (accessed May 6, 2021).

Jones, C. (2016). New Treaty, New Tradition: Reconciling New Zealand and Maori Law, Vancouver: University of British Columbia Press.

Joseph, B. (2016). 21 Things You May Not Know About the Indian Act. CBC News. Retrieved from: https://www.cbc.ca/news/Indigenous/21-things-you-may-not-know-about-the-indian-act-1.3533613 (accessed August 4, 2021)

Joseph, B. (2018). 21 Things You May Not Know About the Indian Act. Port Coquitlam, BC: Indigenous Relations Press.

Kayseas, B., Schneider, B., Pasap R., Gordon M. and Anderson R. (2017). Indigenous Rights Capital: The Basis for Sustainable Enterprise Creation. In Verbos, A., Henry, E., Peredo, A. (Eds.), Indigenous Aspirations and Rights: The Case for Responsible Business and Management. Salts Mill, UK: Greenleaf Publishing.

Ketilson, L. H., & MacPherson, I. (2001). A report on Aboriginal co-operatives in Canada: Current situation and growth potential. Centre for the Study of Co-operatives, University of Saskatchewan.

Ketilson, L.H. (2014, April). Partnering to Finance Enterprise Development in the Aboriginal Social Economy. Canadian Public Policy 40 (1), pp. S39–S49.

Lindsay, N. J. (2005). Toward a cultural model of indigenous entrepreneurial attitude. Academy of Marketing Science Review, 2005, 5, 206–213.

Loosemore, M., & Denny-Smith, G. (2016). Barriers to indigenous enterprise in the Australian construction industry. In Vol. 2 of Proc., 32nd Annual ARCOM Conf., edited by PW Chan and CJ Neilson (pp. 629–638).

Love T (2017). Māori values, care and compassion in organisations: A research strategy. Paper presented at the 33rd European group for organizational studies colloquium, Copenhagen Business School, Copenhagen, 6–8 July.

Macleod, K. (2016). "Pre-contact economies and the Fur-Trade." In *Indigenous Business in Canada*, eds. Keith G. Brown, Mary Beth Doucette and Janice Esther Tulk. Sydney, Nova Scotia: Cape Breton University Press.

Massie, M. (2008). "Trapping and Trapline Life." *Our Legacy*. Retrieved from: http://digital.scaa. sk.ca/ourlegacy/exhibit_trapping (accessed May 6, 2021).

Métis Economic Development Strategy. (2015). Retrieved from: https://economic.metisportals.ca/ wp-content/uploads/2019/10/MEDS-III-Report-3-Findings-Recommendations2.pdf (accessed May 6, 2021).

Métis Economic Development Fund. (2021). Financing. Retrieved from: https://www.medf.ca/financ ing (accessed August 4, 2021).

Mika JP, Warren L, Foley D, et al. (2017). Perspectives on Indigenous entrepreneurship, innovation and enterprise. Journal of Management and Organization 23: 767–773.

National Aboriginal Capital Corporation (NACCA). (2015). A Portrait of Aboriginal Financial Institutions. Retrieved from: https://nacca.ca/wp-content/uploads/2017/03/nacca_afi-portrait-2015-1.pdf (accessed May 21, 2021).

National Aboriginal Capital Corporation (NACCA). (2017). The AFI Story. https://nacca.ca/wp-content/uploads/2017/04/NACCA-TheAFIStory-Aug2017-WebVersion.pdf (accessed May 21, 2021).

National Aboriginal Capital Corporation (NACCA). (2020). NACCA and Aboriginal Financial Institutions Across the Country Roll Out Emergency Loans to Indigenous Businesses. Retrieved from: https://www.newswire.ca/news-releases/nacca-and-aboriginal-financial-institutions-across-the-country-roll-out-emergency-loans-to-Indigenous-businesses-807759631.html (accessed May 6, 2021).

National Aboriginal Capital Corporation (NACCA). (2021a). History of NACCA and AFIs. Retrieved from: https://nacca.ca/about/history/ (accessed May 6, 2021).

National Aboriginal Capital Corporation (NACCA). (2021b). Home. Retrieved from: https://nacca.ca (accessed May 21, 2021).

National Aboriginal Capital Corporation (NACCA). (2021c). List and Types of AFIs. Retrieved from: https://nacca.ca/aboriginal-financial-institutions/list-and-types-of-afis/(accessed May 21, 2021).

National Aboriginal Capital Corporation (NACCA). (2021d). About Us. Retrieved from: https://nacca. ca/about/ (accessed May 6, 2021).

National Aboriginal Capital Corporation (NACCA). (2021e). Membership Value for AFIs. Retrieved from: https://nacca.ca/membership-value-for-afis/ (accessed May 21, 2021).

National Aboriginal Capital Corporation (NACCA). (2021f). Indigenous Growth Fund Raises 150m in First Round to Support Indigenous Entrepreneurs in Canada. Retrieved from: https://www.

newswire.ca/news-releases/Indigenous-growth-fund-raises-150m-in-first-round-to-support-
Indigenous-entrepreneurs-in-canada-878961650.html (accessed May 6, 2021).

Nelson, R. (2019). Beyond Dependency: Economic Development, Capacity Building, and
Generational Sustainability for Indigenous People in Canada. SAGE Open, 9(3).

Northern Development Ministers Forum (2010). Aboriginal youth entrepreneurship: success factors
and challenges. Available at: www.focusnorth.ca/documents/english/library/2010/aborigi
nal_youth_entrepreneurship.pdf

NZIER (2005) Māori Business and Economic Performance: Report to Ministry of Māori Development.
Wellington: NZIER.

OECD. (2020). Linking Indigenous Communities with Regional Development in Canada: Policy
Recommendations. Paris: OECD Publishing. Retrieved from https://www.oecd.org/regional/re
gionaldevelopment/PH-Indigenous-Canada.pdf

Peace Hills Trust. (2021). Home. Retrieved from: https://www.peacehills.com/Personal/AboutUs/
CorporateProfile/. (accessed May 21, 2021).

Peredo, A. M., & Chrisman, J. J. (2006). Toward a theory of community-based enterprise. Academy
of management Review, 31(2), 309–328.

Peredo, A. M., & Anderson, R. B. (2006). Indigenous Entrepreneurship Research: Themes and
Variations. In C. S. Galbraith & C. H. Stiles (Eds.), Developmental Entrepreneurship: Adversity,
Risk, and Isolation (pp. 253–273). Elsevier.

Peredo, A. M., & Chrisman, J. J. (2017). Conceptual foundations: community-based enterprise and
community development. In Entrepreneurial Neighbourhoods (pp. 151–178). Edward Elgar
Publishing.

Peredo, A. M., McLean, M., & Tremblay, C. (2019). Indigenous Social Innovation: What Is
Distinctive? And a Research Agenda. In G. George, T. Baker, P. Tracey, & H. Joshi (Eds.),
Handbook of Inclusive Innovation: The Role of Organizations, Markets and Communities In
Social Innovation (pp. 107–128). Edward Elgar.

Peredo, A. M., & McLean, M. (2013). Indigenous development and the cultural captivity of
entrepreneurship. Business & Society, 52(4), 592–620.

Peredo, A.M. and McLean, M. (2010). Indigenous development and the cultural captivity of
entrepreneurship. Business & Society, Vol. 52 No. 4, pp. 592–620.

Pinto, L.E. and Blue, L. (2015). Pushing the entrepreneurial prodigy: Canadian Aboriginal
entrepreneurship education initiatives. Critical Studies in Education, pp. 1–18.

Pinto, L. E., & Blue, L. E. (2017). Aboriginal entrepreneurship financing in Canada: Walking the fine
line between self-determination and colonization. Journal of Entrepreneurship in Emerging
Economies.

Ponting, J. R., & Voyageur, C. J. (2001). Challenging the deficit paradigm: Grounds for optimism
among first nations in Canada. Canadian Journal of Native Studies, 21(2), 275–307.

Poyser, A., Scott, A., & Gilbert, A. (2021). Indigenous investments: Are they different? Lessons from
Iwi. Australian Journal of Management, 46(2), 287–303.

PWC (2012) Forming an Investment Strategy and Investment Policy for Iwi. Auckland: PWC.

Redpath, L., & Nielsen, M. O. (1997). A comparison of native culture, non-native culture and new
management ideology. Canadian Journal of Administrative Sciences/Revue Canadienne des
Sciences de l'Administration, 14(3), 327–339.

Royal Bank of Canada. (2021). A Chosen Journey: RBC Indigenous Partnership Report. Retrieved:
https://www.rbc.com/Indigenous/_assets-custom/pdfs/Indigenous-Report-2020_ENG.pdf
(accessed May 21, 2021).

Sayers (Kekinusuqs), J., & Peredo, A. M. (2017). Hupacasath First Nation: Roadmap to a sustainable
economy. In A. K. Verbos, E. Henry, & A. M. Peredo (Eds.), Indigenous Aspirations and Rights
(pp. 156–168). Routledge.

Schecter. B. (2015). An 'emerging market' at home: Canada's banks making a big push into aboriginal communities. Retrieved from: https://financialpost.com/news/fp-street/an-emerging-market-at-home-how-canadian-banks-are-making-a-big-push-into-aboriginal-banking (accessed May 6, 2021).

Schneider, B. (2009). Reclaiming Economic Sovereignty: Native and Aboriginal Financial Institutions. ISBN: 9781109217360 (micro).

Schneider, B. and Saylor A. (2018). Financial Empowerment: Personal Finance for Indigenous and Non-Indigenous People. Regina: University of Regina Press.

Scotiabank. (2021). Indigenous Financial Services. Retrieved from: https://www.scotiabank.com/ca/en/commercial-banking/industries/aboriginal.html (accessed May 6, 2021).

Sengupta, U. (2015). Indigenous co-operatives in Canada: The complex relationship between co-operatives, community economic development, colonization, and culture. Journal of Entrepreneurial and Organizational Diversity, 4(1), 121–152.

Standing Senate Committee on Aboriginal Peoples. 2007. "Sharing Canada's Prosperity: A Hand Up, Not a Hand Out.." Retrieved from: https://sencanada.ca/content/sen/Committee/391/abor/rep/rep06-e.pdf

Statistics Canada. (2016). Census Profile: 2016 Census. Retrieved from: https://www12.statcan.gc.ca/census-recensement/2016/dp-pd/prof/index.cfm?Lang=E

Te Pumautanga o Te Arawa (2017). Annual Report, Rotorua: Te Pumautanga o Te Arawa.

TDB Advisory (2017) Iwi Investment Report 2017. Wellington: TDB Advisory.

TDB Advisory (2018) Iwi Investment Report 2018. Wellington: TDB Advisory.

TDB Advisory (2019) Iwi Investment Report 2019. Wellington: TDB Advisory.

Toronto-Dominion. (2019). TD and Indigenous Communities in Canada 2019 Report. Retrieved from: https://www.td.com/document/PDF/corporateresponsibility/TD_Indigenous_Communities_Report2019-WEB.pdf (accessed May 21, 2021).

Tully, J. (1994). Aboriginal property and western theory: Recovering a middle ground. Social Philosophy and Policy, 11(02), 153–180.

UBC Sauder Centre for Social Innovation Impact Investing (2018). Impact Investing in the Indigenous Context: A Scan of the Canadian Marketplace. Vancouver, BC, Canada: The University of British Columbia.

Vancity. (2020). Vancity's investment in Indigenous communities. Retrieved from: https://www.vancity.com/AboutVancity/News/Backgrounders/AboriginalCommunities/ https://co-operativesfirst.com/blog/2018/07/20/context-and-opportunity-a-brief-survey-ofIndigenous-co-ops-in-canada/,K. (1993).

Warden, K (1993) "Indian Act: Permit to control a culture." Windspeaker. Retrieved from: https://ammsa.com/publications/windspeaker/indian-act-permit-control-culture (accessed May 6, 2021).

White, K. (2021). A brief survey of Indigenous Co-ops in Canada. Retrieved from https://co-operativesfirst.com/blog/2018/07/20/context-and-opportunity-a-brief-survey-of-Indigenous-co-ops-in-canada/

Rebecca Namatovu

18 Financing entrepreneurs in post-conflict and disaster zones

Abstract: There is substantial evidence that entrepreneurship occurs in crisis, disaster, and post-conflict contexts. Scholars examining post-conflict and disaster zones commonly see entrepreneurship as a solution to such adverse contexts. Central to the entrepreneurship solution is the financing of entrepreneurial businesses. Firms are successful in entrepreneurial financing when they integrate asymmetric information and signal the right investors and funders. Taking a demand-side perspective, we conduct an integrative review of literature in management, entrepreneurial financing economics and entrepreneurship in post-conflict and disaster contexts and identify research opportunities. We then propose future areas of inquiry to address gaps in our understanding. Besides highlighting research gaps, our paper sheds light on the interplay between institutions, entrepreneurial financing and context.

Keywords: entrepreneurial finance, entrepreneurship, post-conflict, disaster zones, research agenda

Introduction

There is substantial evidence that entrepreneurship occurs in crisis, disaster, and post-conflict contexts (Naudé, 2007, 2009). As we begin this piece, we need to bring some clarity to the domains we examine by defining three important concepts: (1) crisis, (2) disaster and (3) post-conflict, upfront. Scholars have recognised that it is a crisis when a community of people – an organization, a town, or a nation – perceives an urgent threat to core values or life-sustaining functions, which must be dealt with under conditions of uncertainty (Boin & 't Hart, 2007, p. 42). Crises arise from a wide variety of threats including health crises, wars, refugee crises, political revolutions, major acts of terrorism, economic depressions and other unexpected events (Rodríguez, Quarantelli, & Dynes, 2007). On the other hand a disaster is a "serious disruption of the functioning of a community or a society involving widespread human, material, economic or environmental losses and impacts, which exceeds the ability of the affected community or society to cope using its own resources" (Correa et al., 2011, p. 138). Agents of disasters may vary from natural forces (e.g floods, landslides, volcanic eruptions, hurricanes, tsunamis, and earthquakes) to

Rebecca Namatovu, Copenhagen Business School

https://doi.org/10.1515/9783110726312-023

other catastrophes such as terrorism, hostage-takings, ethnic conflicts, and financial and technological breakdowns. Although the two concepts, (i.e. crisis and disaster) are not the same, they can be related. For instance, a crisis with a devastating ending is a disaster (Boin, 2005). In this piece we focus on disaster.

A post-conflict context is "conceptualized as a transitional period bounded by past war and future peace"(Cunningham, 2017, p. 1).Post-conflict zones grapple with recovering their economy while at the same time reducing the likely of recurring conflict (Collier et al., 2008). This means that the term post-conflict applies to those areas where conflict has indeed subsided, but not necessarily to all parts of a nation's territory(Hamre & Sullivan, 2002, p. 90).

An underlying assumption of this chapter is that, post-conflict and disaster zones heighten the level of risk and uncertainty. Unlike uncertainty, risk has well defined probabilities and possible outcomes (Knight, 1921; Sarasvathy, 2001). For example, risk could include all types of insurance, gaming of various types and some areas of the stock market while uncertainty may include global warming, environmental pollution and commercialization of radical innovations among other things. We could argue that disasters are mostly uncertain and post-conflict zones are largely risky. Therefore, disaster cause chronic uncertainty, which affects the availability of entrepreneurial finance for start-ups (Brown et al., 2020), and entrepreneurial firms situated in post-conflict zones are risky because they lack collateral and stable cash flows (Brück et al., 2011; De Castro et al., 2014).

Scholars examining post-conflict and disaster zones commonly see entrepreneurship as a key part of the solution to such adverse contexts (Brown & Rocha, 2020). Central to the entrepreneurship solution is the financing of entrepreneurial businesses (Bruton et al., 2015). In particular, scholars view entrepreneurs' access to financing as important to their ability to start business in post-conflict and disaster zones. However, most studies of entrepreneurial financing in post-conflict and disaster zones have addressed the effects and after-effects of adversity on funding options (Bilau et al., 2017; Block & Sandner, 2009; Brown & Rocha, 2020; Cowling et al., 2018). We know that the level of equity investments slumps after a crisis(Brown & Rocha, 2020; Brown et al., 2020) and supporting angel investors has a positive impact on start-up activity in austerity economies (Bilau et al., 2017). Although our knowledge of effects of risky and uncertain contexts on entrepreneurial financing has grown, scholars believe we still have few theoretical and empirical studies exploring entrepreneurship processes in post-conflict and disaster zones(Tobias et al., 2013). We need to focus on entrepreneurial financing in post-conflict and disaster zones because in such contexts financial intermediation is largely absent and individuals do not have enough interest-bearing financial assets to access traditional forms (e.g. loans) of financing (Sanders & Weitzel, 2013). Brown et al (2020) argue that in post-conflict and disaster zones, firms are exposed to investment and growth challenges greater and different from those they would face in more stable economic environments. On the one hand, entrepreneurs in these settings face once-off shocks such as personnel injuries and disruption of markets and on the other hand, they contend with the pernicious impact of destroyed infrastructure, technological regress and massive income decreases (Brück et al., 2011). Thus scholars widely argue that such contexts warrant a greater need for understanding entrepreneurial financing (Block et al., 2021).

Most scholars view firms as successful in entrepreneurial financing when they can integrate asymmetric information and signal the right investors and funders (Berns et al., 2020; Block et al., 2018; Busenitz et al., 2014; Colombo, 2021). These actions represent key behaviours in entrepreneurial financing that have the potential to affect entrepreneurship in adverse contexts. Yet the scholarship on entrepreneurial finance has considered extensively the supply side dynamics of entrepreneurial financing, leaving our understanding of the entrepreneurial financing from the firm perspective (demand side) limited. As a result, with this chapter, we are interested in highlighting opportunities for future research to illuminate our understanding of entrepreneurial finance- from a demand side perspective – in post- conflict and disaster zones. The research question we address here is what research opportunities exist for entrepreneurial finance in post-conflict or disaster zones and how do we move forward the understanding of this context in entrepreneurial financing?

To answer these questions, we review the literature in management, entrepreneurial financing, economics and entrepreneurship in post-conflict and disaster contexts. Accordingly, we suggest future areas of inquiry-based on uncertainty and risk (information asymmetry)-based theories. Specifically, we highlight sources of entrepreneurial finance and the signaling of investors in post-conflict and disaster zones. Post-conflict and disaster zones pose disparate institutional setup and contexts with a distinctive set of participants (e.g. non-profits, individual and communities) in the entrepreneurial ecosystem. Moreover, the motivation and objectives of entrepreneurs and entrepreneurial ventures vary significantly from conventional ones in these settings. Accordingly, we highlight that sourcing and signaling of investors are especially important for entrepreneurs in post-conflict or disaster zones. Since investors (supply) tend to have specific funding objectives, entrepreneurs evaluate how appropriate the available options are. Those start-ups that perceive the supply of finance as poor get discouraged and rely on internal funding, i.e. savings, family and friends, trade credit and angel finance to some extent(Bruton et al., 2021). Therefore, disaster zones firms' pecking order is skewed to internal finance, because external financing is complex or the institutional setting is too challenging. For those firms that perceive external funding as appropriate, their objective is to position themselves as investor-ready. They must align themselves with funders' objectives and requirements and portray the right signals to the available investors.

Besides highlighting research gaps, we believe our paper provides insight into entrepreneurial financing and entrepreneurial practices in post-conflict and disaster zones thus shedding light on the interplay between institutions, entrepreneurial financing and context (Collier, 2009; Collier et al., 2008). Moreover, by comparing different streams of literature (e.g., management, entrepreneurial finance and development economics), we contribute to synthesizing the literature around post-conflict and disaster environments.

Literature review

Theoretical framework: Risk and uncertainty

Post-conflict contexts are volatile and pose high levels of risk (Collier et al., 2008; Naudé, 2009) while disaster zones are complex, making it harder to predict(Brown & Rocha, 2020). In the field of management, Milliken (1987) posited that uncertainty is categorized into three forms: state, effect and response uncertainty. Milliken argued that state uncertainty, akin to environmental uncertainty, is when actors perceive the organizational environment or components of the environment to be unpredictable. State uncertainty implies that one does not know how the environment will be changing or how other components in the environment interrelate or interact. However, it is a perceptual experience of uncertainty and not an objective state of the world. Therefore, firms are unable to appropriate the right predictions for future events. Typically, actors perceive it as a more complex environment to situate.

Effect uncertainty relates to how an individual can ably predict what the environmental changes will have on his or her organization. Knowing that a disaster (war, volcanic eruption, or earthquake) is happening does not mean you know how your enterprise or organization will be affected. Effect uncertainty relates to existing organizations, specifically their evaluation of the intensity, nature and timing of the disaster. Therefore, effect uncertainty is due to a lack of understanding of the cause-effect relationships. Response uncertainty relates to a lack of knowledge of response actions and their value or utility. Response uncertainty evaluates response options, the likely outcomes of each, and the value/utility associated with them. It is the uncertainty that is experienced when an immediate decision is needed.

To summarize, all states of uncertainty lack information, but in varying degrees. State uncertainty lacks information about the environment, effect uncertainty has a shortage of information on how the environment will affect the organization, and response uncertainty has limited information about the organizations' response options and the value of each. We expect that when state uncertainty is high, start-ups (actors) use the "garbage can" approach and not linear steps to formulate strategy. However, when effect and response uncertainty is high, start-ups spend more time and resources scanning the environments and forecasting. Therefore effect and response uncertainty is more associated with risk because some predictions and probabilities can be estimated.

Being cognizant of the varied types of uncertainty that actors may experience as they respond to disaster and post-conflict we attempt to categorize them based on the inherent uncertainty and speculate possible sources of entrepreneurial finance as shown in Table 18.1. Moreover, these different types of uncertainty elicit varied responses and so attract entrepreneurial financing differently.In post- conflict and disaster zones, entrepreneurs fulfil three broad aspects of a) sustain conflict/peace, b) overcoming adversity caused by the conflict/ disaster and c) exploiting new opportunities to gain profit (Naudé, 2009). In post-conflict environments, the absence of resources and key infrastructure triggers entrepreneurial activity. The actors respond to new opportunities and threats with varied resources and urgency.

Table 18.1: Context, type of uncertainty, strategy and possible entrepreneurial financing options.

Context	Uncertainty	Strategy	Possible sources of entrepreneurial finance
Post-conflict	Response uncertainty (risk)	a) Scanning and Forecasting to sustain peace b) Exploiting new opportunities to gain profit	State grants, Social capital, informal financing, crowd funding and impact investors.
Disaster e.g. natural forces such as floods, landslides, volcanic eruptions, hurricanes, tsunamis, and earthquakes)	State Uncertainty	Garbage can approach to overcome adversity	Savings, boot strapping, Family, friends and informal finance.
Disaster e.g. other catastrophes such as terrorism, war, hostage-takings, ethnic conflicts, financial and technological breakdowns.	Effect uncertainty	Scanning	Family, friends, angel investors, informal finance, crowd funding etc.

What we know about entrepreneurial financing in disaster and post-conflict zones

Entrepreneurs and entrepreneurial organizations in post-conflict and disaster contexts endure financial hardships, which push them to construct new entrepreneurial responses. Cowling et al (2012) highlighted a significant decline in debt and equity flows to SMEs after the 2008 financial crisis. In the absence of aid, entrepreneurs in post-conflict Africa could not access credit to grow their ventures(Naudé, 2007). Yet, in Sri Lanka, after the 2004 tsunami, loans obtained from microfinance institutions had a positive significant effect on the change in real income of SMEs (Becchetti & Castriota, 2011). Entrepreneurs in disaster and post-conflict zones struggle to identify appropriate funders(Guglielmetti, 2011). Funding gaps have always existed; the complex issue is disentangling how constrained funding supply interacts with crisis environments. How do start-ups and individuals with no record of accomplishment, collateral and known business commitment access funding? How do agency problems, information asymmetry and lack of internal cash flows affect firms' ability to raise funds? How do traditional or new types of funders and funding initiatives support or constrain entrepreneurship (e.g. crowdfunding, boot strapping, NGOs, microfinance, venture capitalists)? In post-conflict settings, where market disruption is high, asymmetric information-based theories are appropriate to explain the demand for financing. We cannot ignore the fact that entrepreneurial objectives, control and risk perception account for their financing decisions. The role of entrepreneurial cognition and perception in financing decisions is crucial in uncertain or risky settings.

Entrepreneurs' perceptions of the source of financing will affect where they consequently source financing (Fraser, Bhaumik, & Wright, 2015). For instance, entrepreneurs perceived debt as a poor financing option after the financial crisis, (Brown & Rocha, 2020). Therefore, new and alternative sources have since been more enticing for entrepreneurs. While there is a promise from micro-lending, crowdfunding and peer-to-peer funding to bridge funding gaps in a crisis environment, there is still a need for funding options that are contextually cognizant of the stressed crisis, post-crisis, and disaster environments. In disaster zones, entrepreneurs seek meagre resources to build their resilience but not for high growth projects(Brück et al., 2011; Kwong, Cheung, Manzoor, & Rashid, 2019). They seek financing from less risky providers or low requirement (cheaper) options (Dinger, Conger, Hekman, & Bustamante, 2020). Commonly, start-up financing is from their savings or contributions from family, friends and well-wishers (Desai, Naudé, & Stel, 2021; Salvato, Sargiacomo, Amore, & Minichilli, 2020). At the onset of the post-disaster phase, entrepreneurial venturing is small or micro, mainly needed to sustain resilience (Bullough, Renko, & Myatt, 2014). After a passage of time, entrepreneurial firms will desire to grow their ventures and seek financing from more formal sources like microfinance, banks and impact investors (Williams & Vorley, 2017). The choice of the financing source depends on the entrepreneur's cognitive judgement (Simon, Houghton, & Aquino, 2000). Entrepreneurs evaluate funders' terms, mission and affordability of the finances. With affordability, they assess asset (e.g. collateral or business registration) requirements and complexity. Since enterprises in disaster zones tend to be micro and small, with few assets, it turns out that some of the available funding is evaluated as poor because it is expensive or complicated (Naudé, 2007).

When entrepreneurs opt for external funding, they need to reorganize their ventures to send the right signals to the potential funders. In disaster zones, entrepreneurs' and funders' missions and objectives are not always aligned. Therefore, as entrepreneurs seek financing they have to review the available options critically. Funders regularly drift the mission of ventures (Karlan & Goldberg, 2006). The ventures with strict objectives are more likely to struggle to find the right funder (Kwong, Tasavori, & Cheung, 2017). The ventures with flexible objectives often pivot to respond to funders' requirements. Langevang and Namatovu (2020) show how youth entrepreneurs operating in the post-war zone of northern Uganda formed groups to attract funding from NGOs in the community. Funders select projects or enterprises from which they expect an improved performance (e.g. increase in assets, profitability and outreach). The challenge remains for those enterprises with strict objectives that do not align with the funders in the ecosystem. Such enterprise may seek financing outside the disaster zones. In this case, they will have to signal the "external" investors appropriately.

In disaster zones, the entrepreneurs have relatively limited capabilities and do not employ sophisticated business models. Therefore, venture capitalists, angel investors are not easily attracted by their ideas, but crowdfunding campaigns (including gifting and rewards and loans) and other platform funding may be worthwhile options. However, the firms need to improve their signalling skills significantly to attract investment. Typically, they hire professionals or collaborate with others outside the disaster zones to signal large investors(Lyon, Sepulveda, & Syrett, 2007). For instance, impact investors target projects or enterprises that can potentially scale and address grand challenges (Block, Hirschmann, & Fisch, 2021). While impact investors are likely funders, they demand extensive objective information such as estimates of the market share/outreach, and sustainability plans. Such objective information is out of reach for start-ups in disaster and post-conflict zones because they don't have hard data (uncertainty) and estimates/probabilities (risk) are difficult to model.

The response of entrepreneurs and start-ups in conflict and disaster zones

In the aftermath of disaster and conflict, actors emerge in response to opportunities that alleviate suffering (Shepherd & Williams, 2014). Actors develop entrepreneurial intentions to grow from adversity (Bullough, Renko, & Myatt, 2014) and organize in varied forms. These forms range from individuals (Desai, Naudé, & Stel, 2021; Kwong, Cheung, Manzoor, & Rashid, 2019), to community groups (Bullough & Renko, 2017; Langevang & Namatovu, 2019), social enterprises (Dinger, Conger, Hekman, & Bustamante, 2020; Farny, Kibler, & Down, 2019) and institutional or civil support organisations (Collier, 2009; Williams & Vorley, 2017). Depending on the actors' interaction with affected communities and their capabilities, new businesses are created (Kwong et al., 2019) or previous/ struggling businesses are revamped and rebuilt (Williams & Shepherd, 2016). The formation objective of these

start-ups will affect the resultant economic outcome. Regardless of economic outcome, though, entrepreneurial action in post-conflict and disaster zones is largely
viewed as relief from emotional (Farny et al., 2019; Wolfe & Shepherd, 2015), economic (Lyon, Sepulveda, & Syrett, 2007; Shepherd, Saade, & Wincent, 2020), and
political (Brück et al., 2013) adversity. Therefore, divergent actors initiate entrepreneurial action because it is crucial for a sustained recovery in post-conflict or disaster zones. However, actors differ in size, goal, capabilities, and form.

Since post-conflict and disaster zones lack the appropriate institutional support
structures (Naudé, 2009), governments focus on building infrastructure to overcome adversity. They support existing and new enterprises. Other emergent organizations build infrastructure to gain a profit or to facilitate resilience. However, they
struggle to access, utilize and rearrange meagre resources around them. In post-
conflict and disaster zones that are impoverished, the enterprise setup and business
models adopted are somewhat peculiar as (Salvato et al., 2020, p.603) state "small
and micro firms often represent instances of lifestyle entrepreneurship and thus
may follow a different logic from that of larger firms when making decisions about
business continuity". Social enterprises (SE), loosely described as ventures with a
social mission (Stevens, Moray, & Bruneel, 2015), are a dominant form of organization in disaster zones. Yet, the SE business models combine economic activity with
social mission in a variety of ways (Aldairany et al., 2018; Langevang & Namatovu,
2019; Seelos & Mair, 2005). For social enterprises to become sustainable, they
actively involve the community in their economic activity (Farny et al., 2019). Therefore, social entrepreneurial activity is an interaction of development and other civil
society organizations which support victims and individual within disaster zones
(Collier et al., 2008; Desai et al., 2021).

Entrepreneurial firms ranging from social to commercial enterprises are often
active participants in disaster zones. Their scope and size vary ranging from micro
to small to medium to large local and multinationals (Brück et al., 2011; Brück
et al., 2013). Depending on how firms perceive the conflict or evaluate its effect on
their activities, their response is often an imitation of what other actors are doing.
New firms emerge in such contexts to facilitate resource investment (Muñoz et al.,
2019), create jobs across business stages and industries (Shepherd, 2003), and support a torn social fabric (Langevang & Namatovu, 2019). For example, Williams &
Shepherd (2016) found that after the 2010 Haitian earthquake, emergent organizations either focussed on providing individuals with basic needs for the long-term
(sustaining) or helped individuals transition toward being self-reliant (transforming). Blattman et al., (2011) found that internally displaced youth-led enterprises in
post-conflict northern Uganda invested in vocational skills and tools. In developing
countries, entrepreneurial firms include informal firms, self-employment and small-
holder farmers.

Individuals in post-conflict and disaster zones such as refugees, immigrants
and internally displaced people have actively engaged in entrepreneurship (Desai

et al., 2021; Griffin-el & Olabisi, 2018; Levent & Kundak, 2009; Naudé et al., 2017). Venturing and entrepreneurial action affect how individuals respond to adversity (Shepherd et al., 2020; Williams & Shepherd, 2016), because recovery fundamentally depends on local practices (Muñoz et al., 2019). Moreover, the outcome of their entrepreneurial actions is dependent on social interaction with those within and outside their context. Therefore, individual participation resolves adversity. In host communities (i.e. communities hosting refugees), as was the case in war-torn Afghanistan, individuals developed entrepreneurial intentions to grow from adversity (Bullough et al., 2014). Entrepreneurial action also facilitated the integration of refugees into their new localities (Shepherd et al., 2020). In Pakistan, internally displaced entrepreneurs deployed strategies to start new endeavours in their host locations (Kwong et al., 2019). After Hurricane Katrina, self-employed persons supported the labour market recovery (Zissimopoulos & Karoly, 2010). Entrepreneurship creates new opportunities for those directly and indirectly affected by disaster and crises. For example, refugees have established sophisticated networks that have facilitated entrepreneurial start-up activity and business growth (Shepherd, Saade, & Wincent, 2020). In other instances, refugees have contributed remittances and funded start-up activity in home countries (Lyon et al., 2007). However, de facto barriers continue to impede the velocity and form of entrepreneurship for persons in disaster and post-conflict zones (Cheung & Kwong, 2017; Harmeling & Sarasvathy, 2013).

Communities and societies also initiate entrepreneurial activity in response to opportunities that will alleviate suffering in the aftermath of a natural disaster. The local communities are often nested in broader communities (Shepherd et al., 2020) and can tap into the resources beyond their meagre resource troves. Communities' resilience and desire to purge suffering coupled with local knowledge is highly effective in remedying broken infrastructure (Shepherd & Williams, 2014), customizing innovations to the needs of the victims (Collier, 2009) and re-assembling pre-existing systems (Langevang & Namatovu, 2019). Communities influence social and community identities, which change over the course of recovery (Dinger et al., 2020). For instance, communities living around the Chilean Calbuco volcano in 2015 and 2016, used entrepreneurial preparedness to react to continuous natural disasters (Muñoz et al., 2019).

Some ideas on where we should be heading next- research agenda

Confronting research in conflict or warzones tends to evoke divergent responses from scholars of varying backgrounds. It is a lightning rod for input from scholars in sociology, entrepreneurship, development economics and strategic management.

It is thus an exciting and valuable issue ripe for interdisciplinary inquiry. There is an extensive scope. Several research questions arising at different levels of analysis ranging from individuals to firms to industries to communities are interesting. Without a broader agenda that defies traditional disciplines, researchers may struggle to make progress on central questions about the interplay between different actors and their missions.

An example of the potential research to provide distinct conceptual advances concerning entrepreneurship in disaster or conflict zones is to explore the research potential concerning sourcing/selecting funders. A first question is: how do actors in the face of conflict and disaster zones source financing? In particular, how do actors organize to signal appropriate funders? These questions are relevant from diverse disciplinary orientations, including those that take a critical perspective such as investigating the role of gender, equality and inclusion. Research questions that seek to explain or display the dynamics and social interactions that actors undertake are insightful.

A second set of research questions is: how and why do some actors select certain funders over others? There is evidence that actors have varying capabilities and needs. What capabilities are crucial for signalling funders? Some entities have specific missions. Therefore, investors that address that mission are sought (e.g., smart agriculture with climate financing), while others re-invent themselves over time to suit funding opportunities. Studies can interrogate these issues with disciplinary lenses. Studies using theories on cognition, gender, ethics and social entrepreneurship are useful to provide nuances on factors that influence the uptake of financing.

The issue is important for practitioners and scholars alike. Policymakers must evaluate which funding options are most sought by actors in post-crisis and disaster and identify programs to support them. They need to identify crucial investors, ecosystem builders and matchmakers. They have to devise means to support these actors to participate in high risk and uncertain environments. Development partners also deal with this question, as they are important players in rebuilding disenfranchised communities. Often development partners have resources to support rebuilding but have little knowledge about what works, how it works, what is sustainable (or not)? Occasionally actors in disaster zones appeal to entrepreneurial institutions but fail to capture the resultant achievements (e.g. refugees setting up microfinancing projects to facilitate their entrepreneurial activity). More evidence regarding the interactions of entrepreneurs, entrepreneurial institutions and funding initiatives will help shed light on our understanding of entrepreneurial financing.

In essence, there are several pathways to interrogate how entities source financing and what signals are useful for external funders. While studies delineated by discipline may be insightful, those that are multidisciplinary can potentially bring into play interesting theoretical advancements. In this respect, we believe future research should address among others, the key issues below.

Development economics: How do fragile states respond to challenges of financing entrepreneurship and small businesses during violent conflicts? Under what circumstances does lack of entrepreneurial finance increase economic stagnation and collapse in economic states that experienced violent conflict?

Sociology: What kinds of actors operate more effectively in post-conflict and disaster zones? What are the social relationships between actors, communities and funders? What institutions are complementary or antagonistic in these settings?

Organizational theory and design: How do organizations expose themselves to information about funders? What routines and activities are crucial in fund mobilization? Under what circumstances can firms recombine new and old routines to find the most suitable funder?

Technology and digitization: How do firms use, adopt or deploy new technologies to source funders outside the post-conflict zones? How does gender, location and social networks address the digital divide and financing gaps?

Conclusion

In sum, the leading research issues of entrepreneurial finance in post-conflict and disaster contexts are interdisciplinary. We learn more about these issues by focussing on the phenomenon from multiple disciplinary perspectives. Probing such research questions can significantly improve our understanding of financing sources, suitable options and useful signals for funders in post-conflict and disaster zones. A better understanding of the link between sources of financing and responding to adversity can inform scholars and policymakers. It can guide decisions on the prioritization of policies and infrastructures for relevant entrepreneurial activity and attendant financing options.

References

Aldairany, S., Omar, R., & Quoquab, F. (2018). Systematic review: entrepreneurship in conflict and post conflict. *Journal of Entrepreneurship in Emerging Economies*, *10*(2), 361–383. https://doi.org/10.1108/JEEE-06-2017-0042

Berns, J. P., Figueroa-Armijos, M., da Motta Veiga, S. P., & Dunne, T. C. (2020). Dynamics of Lending-Based Prosocial Crowdfunding: Using a Social Responsibility Lens. *Journal of Business Ethics*, *161*(1), 169–185. https://doi.org/10.1007/s10551-018-3932-0

Becchetti, L., & Castriota, S. (2011). Does microfinance work as a recovery tool after disasters? Evidence from the 2004 tsunami. World Development, 39(6), 898–912.

Bilau, J., Mason, C., Botelho, T., & Sarkar, S. (2017). Angel investing in an austerity economy–the take-up of government policies in Portugal. *European Planning Studies*, *25*(9), 1516–1537. https://doi.org/10.1080/09654313.2017.1328045

Blattman, C., Fiala, N., & Martinez, S. (2011). *Employment Generation in Rural Africa : Mid-term Results from an Experimental Evaluation of the Youth Opportunities Program in Northern Uganda*. (December).

Block, J. H., Colombo, M. G., Cumming, D. J., & Vismara, S. (2018). New players in entrepreneurial finance and why they are there. *Small Business Economics*, *50*(2), 239–250. https://doi.org/10.1007/s11187-016-9826-6

Block, J. H., Fisch, C., & Hirschmann, M. (2021). The determinants of bootstrap financing in crises: evidence from entrepreneurial ventures in the COVID-19 pandemic. *Small Business Economics*. https://doi.org/10.1007/s11187-020-00445-6

Block, J. H., Hirschmann, M., & Fisch, C. (2021). Which criteria matter when impact investors screen social enterprises? *Journal of Corporate Finance*, *66*(February 2020). https://doi.org/10.1016/j.jcorpfin.2020.101813

Block, J., & Sandner, P. (2009). What is the effect of the financial crisis on venture capital financing? Empirical evidence from US Internet start-ups. *Venture Capital*, *11*(4), 295–309. https://doi.org/10.1080/13691060903184803

Boin, A., & Hart, P. T. (2007). The crisis approach. In Handbook of disaster research (pp. 42–54). Springer, New York, NY.

Boin, A. (2005). Disaster research and future crises: Broadening the research agenda. *International Journal of Mass Emergencies and Disasters*, *23*(3), 199.

Brown, R., & Rocha, A. (2020). Entrepreneurial uncertainty during the Covid-19 crisis: Mapping the temporal dynamics of entrepreneurial finance. *Journal of Business Venturing Insights*, *14*(May), 1–10. https://doi.org/10.1016/j.jbvi.2020.e00174

Brown, R., Rocha, A., & Cowling, M. (2020). Financing entrepreneurship in times of crisis: Exploring the impact of COVID-19 on the market for entrepreneurial finance in the United Kingdom. *International Small Business Journal: Researching Entrepreneurship*, *38*(5), 380–390. https://doi.org/10.1177/0266242620937464

Brück, T., Naudé, W., & Verwimp, P. (2011). Small Business, Entrepreneurship and Violent Conflict in Developing Countries. *Journal of Small Business and Entrepreneurship*, *24*(2), 161–178. https://doi.org/10.1080/08276331.2011.10593532

Brück, T., Naudé, W., & Verwimp, P. (2013). Business under Fire: Entrepreneurship and Violent Conflict in Developing Countries. *Journal of Conflict Resolution*, *57*(1), 3–19. https://doi.org/10.1177/0022002712464846

Bruton, G. D., Nuhu, N., & Qian, J. J. (2021). Informal Finance in settings of poverty: establishing an genda for future entrepreneurship research. *Journal of Developmental Entrepreneurship*, *26*(2). https://doi.org/10.1142/S1084946721500114

Bruton, G., Khavul, S., Siegel, D., & Wright, M. (2015). New Financial Alternatives in Seeding Entrepreneurship: Microfinance, Crowdfunding, and Peer-to-Peer Innovations. *Entrepreneurship: Theory and Practice*, 9–26. https://doi.org/10.1111/etap.12143

Bullough, A., & Renko, M. (2017). A different frame of reference: Entrepreneurship and gender differences in the perception of danger. Academy of Management Discoveries, 3(1), 21–41.

Bullough, A., Renko, M., & Myatt, T. (2014). Danger zone entrepreneurs: The importance of resilience and self-efficacy for entrepreneurial intentions. *Entrepreneurship: Theory and Practice*, *38*(3), 473–499. https://doi.org/10.1111/etap.12006

Busenitz, L. W., Plummer, L. A., Klotz, A. C., & Rhoads, K. (2014). Entrepreneurship Research (1985–2009) and the emergence of Opportunities. *Entrepreneurship: Concepts, Theory and Perspective*, (405), 1–20. https://doi.org/10.1111/etap.12120

Cheung, C. W. M., & Kwong, C. (2017). Path-and place-dependence of entrepreneurial ventures at times of war and conflict. *International Small Business Journal, 35*(8), 903–927.

Collier, P. (2009). Post-conflict recovery: How should strategies be distinctive?. *Journal of African Economies, 18*(suppl_1), i99–i131.

Collier, P., Hoeffler, A., & Söderbom, M. (2008). Post-conflict risks. *Journal of Peace Research*, *45*(4), 461–478. https://doi.org/10.1177/0022343308091356

Colombo, O. (2021). The Use of Signals in New-Venture Financing: A Review and Research Agenda. *Journal of Management, 47*(1), 237–259. https://doi.org/10.1177/0149206320911090

Correa, E., Ramírez, F., & Sanahuja, H. (2011). Populations at Risk of Disaster A Resettlement Guide. In *World Bank Populations at risk of Disaster A resettlement Guide*. Retrieved from http://reliefweb.int/sites/reliefweb.int/files/resources/Full_Report_2501.pdf

Cowling, M., Liu, W., & Ledger, A. (2012). Small business financing in the UK before and during the current financial crisis. *International Small Business Journal, 30*(7), 778–800.

Cowling, M., Liu, W., & Zhang, N. (2018). Did firm age, experience, and access to finance count? SME performance after the global financial crisis. *Journal of Evolutionary Economics*, *28*(1), 77–100. https://doi.org/10.1007/s00191-017-0502-z

Cunningham, A. J. (2017). Post-conflict contexts and humanitarian organizations: the changing relationship with states. *Journal of International Humanitarian Action*, *2*(1), 2–7. https://doi.org/10.1186/s41018-017-0022-3

De Castro, J. O., Khavul, S., & Bruton, G. D. (2014). Shades of grey: How do informal firms navigate between macro and meso institutional environments? *Strategic Entrepreneurship Journal*. https://doi.org/10.1002/sej.1172

Desai, S., Naudé, W., & Stel, N. (2021). Refugee entrepreneurship: context and directions for future research. *Small Business Economics*, *56*(3), 933–945. https://doi.org/10.1007/s11187-019-00310-1

Dinger, J., Conger, M., Hekman, D., & Bustamante, C. (2020). Somebody that I used to know: The immediate and long-term effects of social identity in post-disaster business communities. *Journal of Business Ethics*, *166*(1), 115–141. https://doi.org/10.1007/s10551-019-04131-w

Farny, S., Kibler, E., & Down, S. (2019). Collective emotions in institutional creation work. *Academy of Management Journal*, *62*(3), 765–799. https://doi.org/10.5465/amj.2016.0711

Fraser, S., Bhaumik, S. K., & Wright, M. (2015). What do we know about entrepreneurial finance and its relationship with growth? *International Small Business Journal, 33*(1), 70–88.

Finfgeld-Connett, D., & Johnson, E. D. (2013). Literature search strategies for conducting knowledge-building and theory-generating qualitative systematic reviews. *Journal of Advanced Nursing*, *69*(1), 194–204. https://doi.org/10.1111/j.1365-2648.2012.06037.x

Griffin-el, E. W., & Olabisi, J. (2018). Breaking Boundaries: Exploring the Process of Intersective Market Activity of Immigrant Entrepreneurship in the Context of High Economic Inequality. *Journal of Management Studies*, *55*(3), 457–485. https://doi.org/10.1111/joms.12327

Guglielmetti, C. (2011). Measuring the business environment for entrepreneurship in fragile states. In *Entrepreneurship and Economic Development* (pp. 124–143). Palgrave Macmillan, London.

Hamre, J. J., & Sullivan, G. R. (2002). Toward Postconflict Reconstruction. *Washington Quarterly*, *25*(4), 83–96. https://doi.org/10.1162/016366002760252554

Harmeling, S. S., & Sarasvathy, S. D. (2013). When Contingency Is a Resource: Educating Entrepreneurs in the Balkans, the Bronx, and Beyond. *Entrepreneurship: Theory and Practice*, *37*(4). https://doi.org/10.1111/j.1540-6520.2011.00489.x

Karlan, D., & Goldberg, N. (2006). *The Impact of Microfinance : A Review of Methodological Issues Nathanael Goldberg*.

Knight, F. H. (1921). Risk, Uncertainty, and Profit. *Library of Economics*, 1–18.

Kwong, C. C. Y., Cheung, C. W. M., Manzoor, H., & Rashid, M. U. (2019). Entrepreneurship through bricolage: a study of displaced entrepreneurs at times of war and conflict. *Entrepreneurship & Regional Development, 31*(5–6), 435–455. https://doi.org/10.1080/08985626.2018.1541592

Kwong, C., Tasavori, M., & Cheung, C. W. (2017). Bricolage, collaboration and mission drift in social enterprises. *Entrepreneurship & Regional Development : An International Journal, 29*(7–8), 609–638. https://doi.org/10.1080/08985626.2017.1328904

Langevang, T., & Namatovu, R. (2019). Social bricolage in the aftermath of war. *Entrepreneurship and Regional Development, 31*(9–10), 785–805. https://doi.org/10.1080/08985626.2019.1595743

Levent, T. B., & Kundak, S. (2009). Motivation and driving forces of Turkish entrepreneurs in Switzerland. *Innovation-The European Journal of Social Science Research, 22*(3), 283–308. https://doi.org/10.1080/13511610903383710

Lyon, F., Sepulveda, L., & Syrett, S. (2007). Enterprising refugees: Contributions and challenges in deprived urban areas. *Local Economy, 22*(4), 362–375. https://doi.org/10.1080/02690940701736769

Milliken, F. J. (1987). Three Types of Perceived Uncertainty About the Environment: State, Effect, and Response Uncertainty. *Academy of Management Review, 12*(1), 133–143. https://doi.org/10.5465/amr.1987.4306502

Muñoz, P., Kimmitt, J., Kibler, E., & Farny, S. (2019). Living on the slopes: entrepreneurial preparedness in a context under continuous threat. *Entrepreneurship and Regional Development, 31*(5–6), 413–434. papers2://doi.org/10.1080/08985626.2018.1541591

Naudé, W. (2007). *WIDER Discussion Paper 2007–02 Peace, Prosperity, and Pro-Growth Entrepreneurship*. Retrieved from https://publication/uuid/220092C1-73AF-4403-99B7-BAB824A165C1

Naudé, W. (2008). *WIDER Research Paper 2008/20 Entrepreneurship in Economic Development*. Retrieved from www.econstor.eu

Naudé, W. (2009). Entrepreneurship, Post-Conflict. In *Making Peace Work* (pp. 251–252).

Naudé, W., Siegel, M., & Marchand, K. (2017). Migration, entrepreneurship and development: critical questions. *IZA Journal of Migration, 6*(1). https://doi.org/10.1186/s40176-016-0077-8

Rodríguez, H., Quarantelli, E. L., & Dynes, R. (2007). Handbook of Disaster Research. In *The SAGE Dictionary of Social Research Methods*. https://doi.org/10.4135/9780857020116.n52

Salvato, C., Sargiacomo, M., Amore, M. D., & Minichilli, A. (2020). Natural disasters as a source of entrepreneurial opportunity: Family business resilience after an earthquake. *Strategic Entrepreneurship Journal, 14*(4), 594–615. https://doi.org/10.1002/sej.1368

Sanders, M., & Weitzel, U. (2013). Misallocation of entrepreneurial talent in postconflict environments. *Journal of Conflict Resolution, 57*(1), 41–64.

Sarasvathy, S. D. (2001). Causation and Effectuation: Toward a Theoretical Shift from Economic inevitability to Entrepreneurial contigency. *Academy of Management Review, 26*(2), 243–263.

Seelos, C., & Mair, J. (2005). Social entrepreneurship : Creating new business models to serve the poor. *Business Horizons, 48*, 241–246. https://doi.org/10.1016/j.bushor.2004.11.006

Shepherd, D. A. (2003). Learning from business failure: Propositions of grief recovery for the self-employed. *Academy of management Review, 28*(2), 318–328.

Shepherd, D. A., & Williams, T. A. (2014). Local venturing as compassion organizing in the aftermath of a natural disaster: The role of localness and community in reducing suffering. *Journal of Management Studies, 51*(6), 952–994.

Shepherd, D. A., Saade, F. P., & Wincent, J. (2020). How to circumvent adversity? Refugee-entrepreneurs' resilience in the face of substantial and persistent adversity. *Journal of Business Venturing, 35*(4), 105940. https://doi.org/10.1016/j.jbusvent.2019.06.001

Simon, M., Houghton, S., & Aquino, K. (2000). Cognitive biases, risk perception, and venture formation: How individuals decide to start companies. *Journal of Business Venturing*, *9026*(98), 113–134. Retrieved from http://www.sciencedirect.com/science/article/pii/S0883902698000032

Stevens, R., Moray, N., & Bruneel, J. (2015). The Social and Economic Mission of Social Enterprises: Dimensions, Measurement, Validation, and Relation. *Entrepreneurship: Theory and Practice*, *39*(5). https://doi.org/10.1111/etap.12091

Tobias, J. M., Mair, J., & Barbosa-Leiker, C. (2013). Toward a theory of transformative entrepreneuring: Poverty reduction and conflict resolution in Rwanda's entrepreneurial coffee sector. *Journal of Business Venturing*, *28*(6), 728–742. https://doi.org/10.1016/j.jbusvent.2013.03.003

Williams, N., & Vorley, T. (2017). Fostering productive entrepreneurship in post-conflict economies: the importance of institutional alignment. *Entrepreneurship and Regional Development*, *29*(5–6), 444–466. https://doi.org/10.1080/08985626.2017.1297853

Williams, T. A., & Shepherd, D. A. (2016). Building resilience or providing sustenance: Different paths of emergent ventures in the aftermath of the Haiti earthquake. *Academy of Management Journal*, *59*(6), 2069–2102. https://doi.org/10.5465/amj.2015.0682

Wolfe, M. T., & Shepherd, D. A. (2015). "Bouncing back" from a loss: Entrepreneurial orientation, emotions, and failure narratives. *Entrepreneurship Theory and Practice, 39*(3), 675–700.

Zissimopoulos, J., & Karoly, L. a. (2010). Employment and self-employment in the wake of hurricane katrina*. *Demography, 47*(2), 345–367.

Yves Fassin

19 Ethics and entrepreneurial finance

Abstract: Entrepreneurs are confronted to a variety of ethical issues at the different phases of the life cycle of their ventures: from start-up to growth and maturity stage. Despite large scandals of unethical behaviour by some entrepreneurs and investors, academic literature has drawn limited attention to the intersection of entrepreneurship and ethics. More recently, a few studies on the dark side in business have examined the opportunistic behaviour from both the entrepreneur's side or the venture investor's side. This chapter treats with the themes of ethical issues in entrepreneurship literature, the reasons that can explain unethical behaviour and its process: rationalization and the slippery slope. It further analyzes issues of information asymmetry, communication, incentives and conflicts of interests. It also examines specific ethical issues in social enterprises and in family business and the social responsibilities of entrepreneurs for the economy of the region. It suggests an agenda for future research.

Keywords: ethics, fairness, governance, conflict of interests, investor, social responsibility

Introduction

Ethics refers to the system of values and principles. Ethics is concerned with judgements involved in moral decisions: it is about the conception of what is right or wrong, and what is fair conduct or behavior (Vallaster, Kraus, Lindahl and Nielsen, 2019). Business ethics is the application of ethics to the business context. "Business ethics is about doing the correct things, and doing the things correctly; doing honourable business, and doing business honourably" (Fassin, 2005, p. 273). Different approaches in business ethics offer different perspectives and ethical principles that can inform decision-making: Kantian deontology, utilitarianism, virtue ethics. Ethical decision-making has to take into account the action itself, the consequences of the action, and the intent of the decision (Mele, 2012). There is a difference between what is ethical and what is legal. Ethics goes beyond compliance (Fassin, 2005).

Entrepreneurship and business ethics research have developed in the last decades as relatively new fields of academic research in business and management studies (Vallaster et al. 2019). These themes were conducted in different streams of research, in parallel, with little interaction between both themes. Only recently have a limited number of scholars started to investigate the interconnections between

Yves Fassin, University of Ghent

https://doi.org/10.1515/9783110726312-024

entrepreneurship and ethics. Unethical behaviour has been witnessed from both sides: from the entrepreneur's and from the investor's side. A few cases have reached the headlines of the news: how the founder of the medical instrument start-up Theranos managed to raise funds from a lot of reputed investors, while the firm launched misleading information and hid technical failures (Carreyrou, 2018). Less publicized in the media have been cases where investors unfairly diluted and sometimes eliminated the founder-CEO, in desperate need of new funds to save their firm.

While originally management research has mainly focused on the study of management processes, organization and structure in large companies, new streams of research have developed on other forms of companies. Small business and especially, family firms indeed represent the most dominant business model around the world. Many of these firms are entrepreneurial, either due to their newness, their orientation or their size. Acknowledging the importance of entrepreneurship and small business to local economies in most economies, researchers also started the study of those small and medium-sized enterprises (SMEs), start-ups and family firms. Specific attention went to the study of venture creation and to the essential role of start-ups and their central actors, the entrepreneur, defined as the man/woman who transforms the idea to a concrete project and mobilizes resources to realize his project, his dream.

Entrepreneurship studies have investigated the typical characteristics of entrepreneurial ventures, and this at the different phases of their life cycle: from start-up to growth and maturity stage. The increasing importance of technology in new entrepreneurial ventures has stimulated research on innovation, specifically technological innovation in new high technology-based firms, but also broader aspects such as innovation in services. Entrepreneurship research has devoted particular attention to the venture capital phenomenon that plays an essential role in the financing of those innovative companies. This led to the recent stream of entrepreneurial finance, which has since expanded to include other financing sources such as business angels and more recently, crowdfunding.

In parallel, a similar process occurred in business ethics research. Originating from philosophy, ethics was applied to business situation, principally in large companies. Researchers analyzed the behavior of business people in their organizations and in their relations with different stakeholders. While originally business ethicists focused on larger companies, also here new scholars focused on the smaller business firms and on various forms of entrepreneurship. The combined study of business ethics and entrepreneurship leads to the special focus in entrepreneurial finance ethics.

Academic literature at the intersection of entrepreneurship and ethics has grown: by 2021, data in the Web of Science listed 1450 common articles of which 750 in the categories of business or management, comprising 0.1% of the papers on entrepreneurship while 0.03% of the papers on ethics address the theme of ethics and entrepreneurship.

These statistics indicate that business ethics has been neglected for a long time in entrepreneurship research. In fact, the management and entrepreneurship literatures have been traditionally rather neutral with relation to ethics. It has focused on 'technical' issues as liability of newness, funds raising and growth. Most management scholars implicitly assumed that people behave in an ethical way, and so do the majority, as in all professional categories.

However, entrepreneurship research has been characterized by a rather more idealistic view, emphasizing the positive aspects of entrepreneurship, its contribution to job creation and to the regional economy, and the heroic, visionary role of entrepreneurs. In entrepreneurship finance, venture capital scholars (most originating from finance departments) have been predominantly positive in their ethical treatment of the phenomenon. Influenced by the dominant shareholder view, they have obfuscated unethical practices and opportunistic behavior.

On the other hand, there is some naivete and idealism in the mind of some philosophers, who sometimes lack a sense of business reality and have an insufficient knowledge of economics and management. It is easy to judge situations from a normative point of view, from the ivory tower, without experiencing the stress of pressures from different origins that founders of start-ups experience.

However, the philosophical perspective is not the reality of entrepreneurship and entrepreneurial finance, and unfortunately, there is also a dark side to these areas that causes much harm (Shepherd, 2019).

A brief literature study on entrepreneurial ethics

Research at the intersection of entrepreneurship and ethics is scarce, except a few articles (Hannafey, 2003; Fassin, 2005; Harris, Sapienza and Bowie, 2009; Morris, Schindehutte, Walton and Allen, 2002; Fassin and Drover, 2017). Vallaster et al. (2019) recently presented a bibliometric analysis of the field. While entrepreneurship studies have widely studied the financing of firms, especially start-ups and venture capital, research on entrepreneurial finance – just as the academic discipline of finance – have often neglected ethical issues. The rare articles on finance ethics by Boatright (1999, 2000, 2010) draw attention to the fiduciary duties of the managers and investors.

A stream of research has discussed problems of conflicts between actors and other stakeholders in the entrepreneurial venture; without mention of the ethical dimension, they describe conflict in a process of cooperation and work on solutions to solve those conflicts through negotiation. Higashide and Birley (2002) and Yitshaki (2008) utilized the conflict perspective between VC or business angels investors and entrepreneurs. In a neutral way, scholars (e.g. Payne, Davis, Moore and Bell 2009; De Clercq, Fried, Lehtonen and Sapienza 2006) have examined information asymmetries and the imbalance of power. Corporate governance articles treat the topic of agency relation between entrepreneurs and investors. Other scholars have concentrated on the role of procedural justice and fairness in their relationships (Sapienza and Korsgaard 1996).

Some studies on the dark side in business have analyzed the opportunistic behaviour from both the entrepreneur's side (Gorman and Sahlman 1989) or the venture investor's side (Cable and Shane 1997; Fassin 2000; Fried and Ganor 2006). Only a few specific articles extend this analysis of the dark side to its ethical dimension: a few treat the ethics in venture capital (Fassin 1993, 2000; Useem 2000; Collewaert and Fassin 2013). Bazerman et al. (2000) highlights the ethical aspects in every negotiation process; and funds raising for entrepreneurial ventures is a negotiation exercise with asymmetries of information and power. Other studies have sought after the reasons for unethical behaviour in entrepreneurship with a particular attention to the context with pressures from all sides (Fassin, 2005) and psychological motivation such as rationalization (Bandura, 1999).

Drover, Wood and Fassin (2014) point to the importance of the investors' ethical reputation while Pollack and Bosse (2014) investigate the effect of investors forgiveness to entrepreneurs for lying. Also exits pose ethical problems (Fassin and Drover, 2017). Successful entrepreneurial ventures often go public through IPOs. This exercise also merits more attention from an ethical perspective (Fassin, 2000), while Lam and Seidel (2020) question the hypergrowth exit mindset where entrepreneurs' basic objective is to exit quickly.

More recently new forms of funds raising as crowdfunding have emerged, with a few first articles on its ethical dimensions (Shneor and Torjesen, 2020).

Themes of ethical issues in entrepreneurship

Research on the ethics of individual entrepreneurs is concerned with the moral situations encountered by entrepreneurs and their organizations. Entrepreneurs face uniquely complex moral problems related to basic fairness, personnel and customer relationships, distribution dilemmas, and other challenges (Hannafey 2003, p. 99).

There is an enormous heterogeneity in entrepreneurial business in function of origin, context, sector, technology, market, phase in lifecycle and size. There are significant differences among entrepreneurs and their ventures, with the range from shop-owner, mom and pop shops, small business owner-managers, more established family business to high-technology based start-ups. All those different businesses may be confronted to different ethical problems, although a lot of ethical issues are in common. Studies have analysed the distinction between the ethics of entrepreneurs and managers. differences in ethical perceptions of small firms compared with large companies (Longenecker et al. 1989).

Context shapes the ethical judgement of entrepreneurs: the individual socio-cultural, organizational and social context (Vallaster et al. 2019). An individual entrepreneur's ethical standard is influenced by their personal background and experience, including religion and educational curriculum. Core values imprinted by family, teachers, and mentors early in life may heavily determine later behaviour.

Some publications have focused on the identification of ethical problems, issues at stake and ethical dilemmas involved. Dees and Starr (1992) suggest the ethical challenges encountered by entrepreneurs can be categorized into: promoter dilemmas (e.g., pragmatic versus moral considerations), relationship dilemmas (e.g., transactional ethics), innovator dilemmas (e.g., avoiding responsibility for one's creation) and other dilemmas (e.g., conflict between personal and business goals) (Morris et al. 2002).

As in business, also in entrepreneurship, some cases of unfair practices occur, unethical practices in different gradation forms. Fassin (2005) distinguishes classes of unethical practices: unfair competition, unfair communication, non-respect of agreements, unfair treatment of stakeholders, besides corruption, bribery and fraud. Entrepreneurial ventures are confronted to two major forms of unfair attitude towards stakeholders: abuse of power and conflict of interests (Fassin, 2005).

Different sets of ethical principles have lead to different but complementary approaches in business ethics – Kantian deontology, utilitarianism, virtue ethics. A multiple perspective approach can help to inform decision-making. Applying the different view on what is ethically acceptable conduct to the entrepreneurial context, helps to understand how both the entrepreneur and the investors may experience some actions differently. However, one should realize that ethics is about perceptions (Singhapakdi 1999; Carlson and Kacmar 1997), ethical judgments can do differ from the perspective of the various actors. (Forsyth 1992), who form differing views and perceptions of what constitutes ethical and unethical conduct.

Legal aspects and subjective perceptions are important considerations for the role of ethics in entrepreneurial finance. There is a difference between the legal and the ethical analyses. What is legally accepted is not necessarily ethical. Where illegal practices are not ethical, legal actions are not always ethical. In business, many questionable practices occur at the limit of what is legally acceptable, but ethically dubious. Ethical is broader than legal. Besides the letter of the law, there is the spirit of the law. Besides the legal contract, there is spirit of the agreement. Some severe actions from the investor such as firing a founder or excessive dilution may be seen as completely legal by the investor, as in compliance with the contract, but may be perceived as opportunistic and unethical by the entrepreneur.

Reasons for unethical behavior and its process

Entrepreneurs who want to create their venture need finance. Many discussions and conflicts between partners or stakeholders are originating from financial reasons.

Business is about money. The leadership and management of large companies is about vision and strategy and implementation through team work, but is also about power, ego and money. Growing high-tech firms are about technological advancement and realizing a dream but also about big money. Entrepreneurs deploy rent-seeking activities and strive for profit generation. There is also a dark side in entrepreneurship (Shepherd, 2019). Opportunistic behavior of some business people and entrepreneurs leads to the temptation to take shortcuts. Unethical behavior by entrepreneurs is not necessarily intentional, but can also be due to circumstances. Pressures from all sides can lead some good people to take unethical decisions and behave unethically. In his social cognitive theory of moral agency, Bandura (1999) explains how, in ambiguous situations, disengagement of internal control allows people to engage in morally or socially questionable behaviour without self-reproach. This phenomenon can follow different paths: moral justification or rationalization, using comparisons, displacing of responsibility, minimizing or ignoring adverse consequences or even blaming the victim (Bandura, 1999).

But not only financial reasons can motivate unethical behaviour; especially for start-up entrepreneurs, other major drivers are the drive to succeed, the drive to make his or her dream come true. Pressures from all sides can be immense, especially in periods close to the threat of failure, often just before the crucial point of breakthrough.

Rationalization leads to the phenomenon of the slippery slope: how a series of small indiscretions gradually can lead to larger transgressions (Welsh, Ordóñez, Snyder and Christian, 2015). When people engage in the minor infractions up to a certain level of severity, and are not caught and thus not punished for this behaviour, they are tempted to repeat the unethical act at a higher level, when placed in similar situation.

A typical example of the slippery slope occurs in the accounting fraud cases, with differed income statements. The following case illustrates the gradual advancement of the process. A company has obtained a new contract, but the signature is delayed to January, after the end of the book year. If the contract would have been realized in December, it could have ameliorated the results of the year. And if the company is in negotiation for a round of capital increase, this could have improved the results, and so the valuation of the company. The entrepreneurs or founders would receive better conditions for the shares they sell. Now, the next year, the same problem occurs, but at a higher level, for example five to ten times more. Once again, the entrepreneur who rationalizes this as only a temporary problem, slightly adapt his accounts and results. If this happens a few times, and without problems, and if nobody notices, the entrepreneur does not even realize the ethical problem, until the company really gets into trouble, when the new funds are really necessary to cover past losses, and not to finance future investments. And so have happened a few fraud cases, where billions of sales have been anticipated, and then happen to be inexistent or insufficient, with losses for the investor as a consequence.

Unethical behavior from a minority of entrepreneurs have led to increase the clauses in legal contracts to protect investors. But the pendulum has been too far. Investment contracts have been written to protect the investor from all kinds of misbehavior from the entrepreneur; in many cases, the entrepreneur signs a contract that allows the investor to fire them in case of poor results or no attaining the milestones. In the name of compliance, clauses are added to give all power to the investor. While these clauses were meant to be used in exceptional situation, the legal contract often allows the investor to intervene faster, and some venture investors have made use of these unbalanced articles of the contract to take the power in some ventures.

Ethical issues at successive stages of venture development

The entrepreneurial context can also be expected to change as the company develops and grows. An extensive body of literature on the concept of the organizational life cycle attempts to model the stages companies move through as they evolve from start-up to mature organization. There are different stages in the development of an innovation and of the venture that is commercializing that innovation. Most successful innovations derive from some basic idea from an inventor, who brings it to a practical realisation in his garage or in his company. In high technology, the idea often comes from university laboratories. Further development and testing lead to a prototype, then to a pre-industrial product, and later, to a product that can be launched on the market. The product has to pass several hurdles: technical hurdles with feasibility studies and cost reducing programs to be able to sell it to an affordable price. Then follow phases of upscaling, marketing and internationalization.

At every step in this process, there are ethical issues involved of different kind (Fassin, 2000). First question that arises especially in start-ups, is about the idea or concept: how is the technology? Is it safe? Especially for emerging new technologies as biotechnology, robotics and artificial intelligence: are there no problems of dual use? In case of external or scientific discoveries, issues of intellectual property have to be addressed with proper acknowledgements of parties involved.

Once at the production stage, safety issues emerge for the consumer and for the workers in the factories. In the commercialization phase, other ethical issues come up related to marketing and in case of start-ups, ethical issues of raising funds.

Start-ups need finance to grow. Different groups of financiers join in different steps, traditionally the entrepreneur and his team, friends, fools and family; in a following step, crowd-funding and venture capital. Later for larger companies follow an IPO to attract a large group of subscribers by a public listing on the stock exchange.

While many start-ups have been developed in new technologies, new forms of raising funds have been recently developed thanks to the information technology.

Crowdfunding platforms propose a large number of small ventures of all kind, also social enterprises and philanthropic or cultural activities with the aim to reach a larger group of small investors. Crowdfunding makes use of the pooling of small financial contributions from multiple backers via the Internet, and often without financial intermediaries and analysts (Shneor and Torjesen, 2020). Unlike IPOs, there is less regulation and only a brief description but no full disclosure prospectus. A few malicious investors have disappeared with the money raised.

While there have been many cases of dubious IPOs on stock markets, and mainly on the Chinese stock markets, the hypergrowth exit minded model also raises ethical question. The short-term vision of some entrepreneurs who strive for a quick exit notwithstanding the negative societal impacts does not correspond to the various ethical principles (Lam and Seidel 2020).

A recent phenomenon in exit is even worrying: the SPAC, a special purpose acquisition vehicle. In a SPAC, a sponsor takes the initiative to raise money in order to acquire a company, but without precise information on the target. In fact, the sponsor first raises funds and then searches for a company. The track record of the lead investor is therefore crucial.

Information asymmetry

At all these steps arises the difficult exercise of valuation of the company. The more developed the product, application, the lower the risk, the higher the value of the project. The larger the turnover, the higher the market and the potential of the market, the higher the valuation (Fassin, 2000). But valuation impacts on the entrepreneur: he gives shares away; realizing a capital increase is a negotiation exercise for any entrepreneur. Valuation is based on information and subjective elements as hypotheses of growth described on the business plan. There is the problem of information and power asymmetry.

Funds raising for a company needs disclosure of information, sometimes sensitive information. And there is asymmetry of information and power in those negotiation process. In most cases, the entrepreneur has more knowledge about the technology and the market. Although professional private equity players who have read dozens of business plans may have more knowledge than the entrepreneur. In some dubious cases, some VCs have misused the information received from the entrepreneur, despite confidentiality and non-disclosure agreements. In other cases, entrepreneurs have misled the investors on the technology and on the market, sometimes unwillingly, with overoptimism, sometimes due to negligence and some other times really misleading.

The problem of information asymmetry results in a conflict of interest.

Conflicts of interests – remuneration and incentives

In any collaborative endeavour, there is a search for a balance between incentives and fair treatment. The remuneration and incentive policy of both entrepreneurs and financial investors can pose problems of conflicts of interests.

Entrepreneurs or the founder's team deserve a decent part of the financial rewards in case of success. They negotiate a premium for financial partners who join the venture at a later stadium. In addition, in many ventures, bonuses and stock options are foreseen. The attribution of those extra remuneration should be determined in transparency following corporate governance rules.

Venture capital managers have a carried interest of 20% on the added value, before distribution to their investors. In a perfect legal construction, they play with other people's money without much personal risk; in case of failure, they do not lose but in case of success they have a huge reward. In addition, as all financial institutions, those private equity investors, take a fee, a few percentages on the capital they raise and a yearly percentage to cover their operational expenses and salaries.

There is an agency issue. The high upside of the rent, or commission in one or other form, constitutes a conflict of interest. From an ethical perspective of utilitarianism, does this system brings a fair share of returns to all parties involved? From a legal perspective, one could argue that all parties know the system and the rules of the game which are mentioned in the contract. But the asymmetry of risks poses problem.

As for venture capital investors, the sponsor lead investor of a SPAC often has a considerable leverage: once the target identified and acquired, the lead investor benefits from a double premium: they receive 20% of the target company for a symbolic sum, and they can exercise warrants to convert additional stock. While the whole operation is perfectly legal and transparent, the system is extracting rent from the whole operations. Even if legally without problems, it questions the ethical aspects of those agreements.

Communication

Closely related to information and information disclosure, is communication. A major business task for entrepreneurs is to promote their new venture to different publics – especially to potential investors. Some practices such as bending or breaking rules, creatively interpreting the facts, are presented by some as clever manifestations of the entrepreneurial spirit (see Bhide and Stevenson, 1990, in Morris 2002; Brenkert, 2009). Exaggerating the benefits of the new technology and promising more than one is currently able to deliver are questionable practices that are too often used in new ventures.

There is sometimes a huge difference between the communication of the entrepreneur and the reality behind. This issue situates the problem of sales people and is linked to marketing ethics: to present your product in a nice packaging while the reality is concealed. A similar problem of information asymmetry with conflict of interests exists from the entrepreneur's perspective. She has more knowledge on the internal value of the firm and has to convey a positive message in order to attract entrepreneurs. Entrepreneurs can make use of small or larger lies or deception in their pitch presentation or in their business plan: exaggerate the benefits of the new product, or the size the market. Although it should also be said that some venture capitalist investors want to see an aggressive business plan with high and rapid growth or decline to study the project. Even if the investors will often forgive some lies for best-will to their entrepreneurs (Pollack and Bosse, 2014), it later can lead to loss of trust.

Conversely, there are also ethical questions raised by the investors' attitude concerning the treatment of entrepreneurs in whose firms they have invested. While they advertise that they help companies to grow, and add value by their hands-on management, the reality often is different. Most private equity indeed appoint a board member but not always add the services they promised to the entrepreneur. Often the reality is experienced as a hard control and pressure, certainly with the contracts that stipulate some milestones; in case of not reaching the milestones, the entrepreneur can be fired. The venture capitalist investor will tell him that this was signed in the contract; however, entrepreneur who start have not the same experience, and in their optimistic view they think they will be able to realize the ambitious business plan. The investor with more experience better knows that business plans are seldom met, and have to be adapted, more often to extend the period; realizations of growth and further development often take more time than originally anticipated.

For IPOs, there is more regulation with information in the prospectus. Although mostly, they mention all possible risks as a matter of compliance. Not all stock markets have the same level of regulation. The recent phenomenon of SPAC is worrying as the fund raisers collect funds for a potential target company that they even do not have identified themselves.

Negative consequences of the incentive scheme

The remuneration packages of VC-investors with incentives as commissions on fee and carried interests on sales have other negative consequences. A result of this principle of percentage, is that venture capital and private equity investors who were originally investing in start-ups have moved to other markets as buyouts, and to larger deals. They raised larger funds to acquire large companies, often in buyout, as the total potential of profit is much higher than for smaller deals, while monitoring takes about similar time investment, even more; companies in problems need much more time to monitor, advise or coach. And time is the critical component of private investors. They consequently tend to concentrate on the promising companies, aligning their priorities with their incentives.

In buyouts also, there are huge conflicts of interests. The buyout deal tries to align the managers incentive to those of the venture capitalist investor: they all want to increase the value of the company. However, this is often at the cost of the company and its employees who are placed under a higher stress to perform. The company has to cut costs, sometimes delay investments in R&D, to increase its profitability in order to reimburse the loans. And the private investors who are temporary shareholders push towards a sale of their assets.

While the tactics of those investors can be explained as a good application of the stock market, and attention to shareholder value, it poses questions of corporate responsibility issues, especially social responsibility or CSR. The tactic presented as good corporate governance poses questions of the fair treatment of other stakeholders. The company is treated as a product, to buy and sale, without considerations for the people who are working in the firm, and the firm's other stakeholders. From an ethical point of view, the firm's employees are treated as a means which does not correspond to deontological ethical approach. This discourse enters into the debate between stakeholder management and shareholder value maximization.

Besides the action itself and the consequences of the action, an ethical analysis has also to analyse the intent. Now the intent is clear: the pursue of profit, in a classic shareholder value approach. However, the ethical problem that often appears lies in the story-telling and in the selling arguments. Venture capitalist claim to help companies to grow, claim to advise and coach entrepreneurs. However, their interventions are often seen as instrumental where companies are treated as means, and not as a collective of people. The message is to create more value, but is mainly to increase shareholder value (and thus their share in the value) not value for all stakeholders.

Social enterprises

A special category of entrepreneurship merits more discussion. A social enterprise is a business with specific social objectives that combine maximizing benefits to society and to the environment with profits to be principally used to fund social programs.

Their benevolent approach and specific contribution to social and sustainability issues have drawn the special attention of journalists but also many academic scholars who have presented them as positive role models against the capitalist entrepreneur. In the same confusion in terminology between social responsibility and ethics, social entrepreneurs have been classified as ethical with the same idealistic approach that some scholars had to CSR and to socially responsible investments designated as SRI funds with their synonym of ethical funds.

However, while many social entrepreneurs do a serious job and are honest, not all are that ethical. Some of them make use of unethical practices just as some 'normal' entrepreneurs. Having a social objective and responding to environmental needs is fine, but ethics also implies fair practices in the daily operations and an ethical treatment of all stakeholders, customers, personnel, supply chain.

Family and entrepreneurship

Family firms are the most important form of entrepreneurship, with most small and medium-sized firms and al mom and pops shops life-way ventures, but also large companies with several generations tradition. While there exist numerous definitions of family firms, two major criteria emerge: control and often also management are exercised by family members, and more than one generation is or has been active in the firm.

Family firms are confronted to additional ethical issues, with consequences on decision-making and governance of the company. Traditional conflicts exist between the unequal treatment of family members and external managers, and between active family members and non-active family members (Signori and Fassin, 2021). Non-family members may experience more difficulties to get promotion while family members with less competencies may obtain better paid and higher positions in the family firm, because of their belonging/heir. The objective of the family company is not only shareholder maximization as in most large non family companies, also non-financial benefits are important such as prestige and status. Rather than pure financial motives and shareholder maximization, family firms tend to preserve socio-emotional wealth and transgenerational succession.

A classic ethical dilemma in management is the agency problem, the tension between the personal benefit of the manager versus the company's objective. Some managers tend to serve their financial needs and extract rent from the company. Some family managers not always make the difference between their pocket and the company's assets, and make use of the firm's asset for private use. This problem occurs in larger families when several members of the next generation want to enter the company: all expect to receive a job position with sufficient status, which increases the cost for the firm; or when more non-active family members receive all kinds of fringe benefit. If this inflation of family benefits cannot be bear by the firm at a certain point, it can bring the firm into danger. Many larger family firms have declined and ultimately failed as a result of this poor management decision-making. The family firms fails to serve its social responsibility.

Through the different phases of financing of start-ups entrepreneurs can encounter ethical problems and relationships dilemmas, as roles and relationships change when friends or family become co-investors in the venture (Dees and Starr, 1992).

Economy of the region

There are philosophical and ethical issues at a higher level of the economy analysis. Besides the ethics of individual entrepreneurs, there are also issues of the role of entrepreneurship in society. "Entrepreneurship is a creative and dynamic activity that brings together labour, capital, and business know-how . . . to carry out activities which improve material well-being" (Hannafey, 2003).

Entrepreneurs play an important role in the life of society and the development of the regional economy through creation of new employment. A small number of start-ups realize breakthroughs that create new products, new production processes. Regional economy increasingly counts on the contribution of scientific discoveries and on technology transfer from the university labs to industry or more to new university spinoff companies.

Sometimes innovation and new ventures also threaten existing businesses and cause social harm in terms of loss of employment in traditional businesses. Often in innovation, there is what Schumpeter (1934) has called creative destruction: a new concept, or a new approach, may lead to destruction of other existing companies: digital cameras eliminating the silver film manufacturers; sometimes new business initiatives can replace and destroy some parts of the economy creating tensions: examples are the tensions between large warehouses versus individual local shopkeeper, and more recently e-business versus traditional shops.

Entrepreneurial ethics focuses on the lower level of the individual company. Closely related to business ethics, there are different streams of research that focused on issues as social responsibility, stakeholder management and corporate governance issues. The new concepts of CSR (corporate social responsibility), sustainability or responsible innovation, better posit the ethical issues of innovation at macro-economic level. In this respect, recently, the European Union has included the societal benefits of innovation as a criterion in its R&D programmes.

Future research agenda

What could be a future agenda for entrepreneurial ethics? Ethical issues are difficult to study because there is a lack of data. Where a few high-level fraud cases reach the press, or the court, the majority of cases of unethical behaviour in entrepreneurial ventures, as in business in general, are known by a few insiders, but generally not divulgated. Researchers have no access, except if they have personal connections; In most cases, people who were treated in an unethical way, do not tell that to a broad audience, in some cases, they are afraid of retaliation by the more powerful party, who threat with legal action if they publicize the case. Some researchers who published cases therefore had to change the name of the company involved.

The larger cases reach the press. But in ethical issues in business, there are a lot of different kinds of unethical behaviour in different order of magnitude. There is gradation in unethicality. A more in depth-study through anonymous survey could bring the different issues and investigate what is the kind of unethical actions entrepreneurs and investors are confronted with, as well as their frequency.

Very important is to have a better insight how this phenomenon increases; as awareness of the unethical act is the starting point. Some people start with some small indelicate action, not even thinking to the unethical part of it. Gradually, when circumstances force them to act, they will be tempted to repeat their unethical action, but at a higher level, and once trapped – as with the example of the accounting fraud case – they will be tempted or forced to continue. More research should be done to unravel the process of the slippery slope through gradual repetition and increase of unethical behaviour. This should help entrepreneurs and investors to distinguish between what is acceptable and what is not and formulate lessons to learn on how to detect this mechanism in order to avoid it.

A more realistic picture of entrepreneurship; not as a hero, but not as villain. Some reality also implies to study the difficulties entrepreneurs and small business encounter. Entrepreneurship as business, involves trial and error. Entrepreneurship is also about failure, the downside of entrepreneurship. Besides the loss of financial capital social and human losses, there are also consequences at the personal level. When an entrepreneur gets bankrupt, she/he loses her capital, his income, his status, and sometimes her family. The entrepreneur in trouble suffers and also her family suffers (Shepherd, 2019). This can explain why honest entrepreneurs sometimes are tempted to take unethical actions (in the expectance that they can survive and get to better times soon afterwards. Shepherd recently plead for more exploratory research; case studies on failures and on the dark and downside of business should help.

The implications of the IPO process also merit more attention from an ethical perspective, as well as the new forms of financing by crowdfunding and SPACs.

Another theme to investigate is around the ethics of collaborative agreements. In finance, where the dominant Anglo-Saxon view prevails, a signature is primordial for an agreement. The legal aspects are privileged. However, besides the signed documents, promises are made between partners, and there is also some tacit component in any collaborative agreement, based on good faith. More than the letter of the contract, it is the spirit of the agreement that counts. Partners in ventures should realize the psychological contract and the social contract that is implicit in those collaborative agreements.

Entrepreneurship is about collaboration in a fair and ethical way. "Business ethics is about the fair treatment of all stakeholders" (Fassin, 2005). Entrepreneurs and investors should take this principle of fairness into account.

References

Bandura, A. (1999). Moral disengagement in the perpetration of inhumanities. Personality and Social Psychology Review, 3, 193–209.

Bazerman, M. H., Curhan, J. R., Moore, D. A., & Valley, K. L. (2000). Negotiation. Annual Review of Psychology, 51(1), 279–314.

Bhide, A., & Stevenson, H. H. (1990). Why be honest if honesty doesn't pay. Harvard Business Review, September-October, 121–129.

Boatright, J. (1999). Ethics in finance. Malden: Blackwell Publishing.

Boatright, J. (2000). Conflicts of interests in financial services. Business and Society Review, 105 (2), 201–219.

Boatright, J. (Ed.). (2010). Finance ethics – critical issues in theory and practice. Hoboken: Kolb Series in Finance, Wiley.

Brenkert, G. 2009. Innovation, rule breaking and the ethics of entrepreneurship, Journal of Business Venturing, Volume 24, Issue 5, p. 448–464

Cable, D., & Shane, S. (1997). A prisoner's dilemma to entrepreneur-venture capitalist relationships. Academy of Management Review, 22, 142–176.

Carlson, D., & Kacmar, M. (1997). Perceptions of ethics across situations: A view through three different lenses. Journal of Business Ethics, 16(2), 147–160.

Carreyrou, J. (2018). Bad blood: Secrets and lies in a Silicon Valley startup. New York: Knopf.

Collewaert, V., & Fassin, Y. (2013). Conflicts between entrepreneurs and investors: the impact of perceived unethical behavior. Small Business Economics, 40(3), 635–649.

Crane A., & Matten, D. (2004). Business ethics: A European perspective. Oxford: Oxford University Press.

De Clercq, D., Fried, V., Lehtonen, O., & Sapienza, H. (2006). An entrepreneur's guide to the venture capital galaxy. Academy of Management Perspectives, 20, 90–112.

Dees, J. G. and J. A. Starr: 1992, 'Entrepreneurship Through an Ethical Lens: Dilemmas and Issues for Research and Practice', in D. L. Sexton and J. D. Kasarda (eds.), The State of the Art of Entrepreneurship (PWS-Kent, Boston), pp. 89–116.

Drover, W., Wood, M., & Fassin, Y. (2014). Take the money or run? Take the money or run? Investors' ethical reputation and entrepreneurs' Willingness to partner. Journal of Business Venturing, 29(6), 723–740.

Fassin, Y. (1993). Ethics and venture capital. Business Ethics A European Review, 2(3), 124–131.

Fassin, Y. (2000). Innovation and ethics: Ethical considerations in the innovation business. Journal of Business Ethics, 27(1–2), 193–203.

Fassin, Y. (2005). The reasons behind non-ethical behaviour in business and entrepreneurship. Journal of business ethics, 60(3), 265–279.

Fassin, Y., & Drover, W. (2017). Ethics in entrepreneurial finance: Exploring problems in venture partner entry and exit. Journal of Business Ethics, 140(4), 649–672.

Forsyth, D. (1992). Judging the morality of business practices: The influence of personal moral philosophies. Journal of Business Ethics, 11(5/6), 461–470.

Fried, J., & Ganor, M. (2006). Agency costs of venture capital control in startups. New York University Law Review, 81, 967–1025.

Gorman, M., & Sahlman, W. A. (1989). What do venture capitalists do? Journal of Business Venturing, 4(4), 231–248.

Hannafey, F. (2003). Entrepreneurship and ethics: A literature review. Journal of Business Ethics, 46, 99–110.

Harris, J., Sapienza, H., & Bowie, N. (2009). Ethics and entrepreneurship. Journal of Business Venturing, 24(5), 407–418.

Higashide, H., & Birley, S. (2002). The consequences of conflict between the venture capitalist and the entrepreneurial team in the United Kingdom from the perspective of the venture capitalist. Journal of Business Venturing, 17(1), 59–81.

Lam, L., & Seidel, M. D. L. (2020). Hypergrowth Exit Mindset: Destroying Societal Wellbeing through Venture Capital Biased Social Construction of Value. Journal of Management Inquiry, 29(4), 471–474.

Longenecker, J. G., J. A. McKinney and C. W. Moore: 1989, 'Ethics in Small Business', Journal of Small Business Management 27, 27–31.

Mele, D. (2012). Management ethics – placing ethics at the core of good management. London: Palgrave.

Morris, M. H., Schindehutte, M., Walton, J., & Allen, J. (2002). The ethical context of entrepreneurship: Proposing and testing a developmental framework. Journal of Business ethics, 40(4), 331–361.

Payne, G. T., Davis, J., Moore, C., & Bell, G. (2009). The deal structuring stage of the venture capitalist decision-making process: Exploring confidence and control. Journal of Small Business Management, 47(2), 154–179.

Pollack, J., & Bosse, D. A. (2014). When do investors forgive entrepreneurs for lying? Journal of Business Venturing, 29(6), 741–754.

Sapienza, H. J., & Korsgaard, M. A. (1996). Procedural justice in entrepreneur-investor relations. Academy of Management Journal, 39, 544–574.

Schumpeter, Joseph A. 1934. The Theory of Economic Development: An Inquiry into Profits, Capital, Credit, Interest, and the Business Cycle. Cambridge: Harvard University Press.

Shepherd, D. A. (2019). Researching the dark side, downside, and destructive side of entrepreneurship: It is the compassionate thing to do!. Academy of Management Discoveries, 5(3), 217–220.

Shneor, R., & Torjesen, S. (2020). Ethical Considerations in Crowdfunding. In Advances in Crowdfunding (pp. 161–182). Palgrave Macmillan, Cham.

Signori, S. & Fassin, Y. (2021). Family members' salience in family business: An identity-based stakeholder approach. Journal of Business Ethics, published online, 1–21.

Singhapakdi, A. (1999). Perceived importance of ethics and ethical decisions in marketing. Journal of Business Research, 45(1), 89–99.

Useem, J. (2000). New ethics or no ethics? Fortune, 141, 81–86.

Vallaster, C., Kraus, S., Lindahl, J. M. M., & Nielsen, A. (2019). Ethics and entrepreneurship: A bibliometric study and literature review. Journal of Business Research, 99, 226–237.

Welsh, D. T., Ordóñez, L. D., Snyder, D. G., & Christian, M. S. (2015). The slippery slope: How small ethical transgressions pave the way for larger future transgressions. Journal of Applied Psychology, 100(1), 114.

Yitshaki, R. (2008). Venture capitalist-entrepreneur conflicts: An exploratory study of determinants and possible resolutions. International Journal of Conflict Management, 19(3), 262–292.

David Lingelbach
Conclusion

In this conclusion, I will focus on three major themes. First, I will briefly review the research on topics not addressed in the earlier chapters: decentralized entrepreneurial finance, including crowdfunding and initial coin offerings; big data in entrepreneurial finance; behavioral economics; and recent innovation, such as special purpose acquisition companies (SPACs). Second, I will briefly consider the impact of the COVID-19 pandemic on entrepreneurial finance as a field. Third, I will look at the impact that entrepreneurial finance research is having beyond the field itself. I will close with some final thoughts.

Research not addressed in earlier chapters

Decentralized entrepreneurial finance

While no formalized definition exists, decentralized finance generally involves one or more of the following five elements: decentralization, distributed ledger technology and blockchain, smart contracts, disintermediation, and open banking (Zetzsche, Arner & Buckley, 2020). In essence, decentralized finance seeks to partially or entirely replace expertise with the wisdom of crowds.

There has been an explosion of academic interest in various aspects of decentralized finance as it relates to entrepreneurial finance. Part of this interest is due to scientific motivations to study the rapid expansion of various types of decentralized finance, such as blockchain technology, and part of the interest is due to non-scientific reasons such as career advancement and various socio-psychological drivers. Given the recency of this research, it is too early to determine if this emerging research stream is an academic fad that will fade away, or a permanent addition to the entrepreneurial finance research stream (Le Pendeven, Bardon & Manigart, 2021). However, the relative ease of data availability in comparison to other entrepreneurial finance phenomena likely ensures that research in decentralized entrepreneurial finance will remain a significant feature of the literature for the foreseeable future.

A recent special issue of *Small Business Economics* explored two phenomena within decentralized finance of relevance to entrepreneurial finance: crowdfunding and initial coin offerings (ICOs). Both are seen as "matchmakers in the digital entrepreneurial ecosystem:" (Block et al., 2021, p. 866).

Crowdfunding has been defined as ". . . a form of fundraising, via the Internet, whereby people pool money, usually small individual contributions, to support a

https://doi.org/10.1515/9783110726312-025

particular goal" (Ahlers, Cumming, Günther & Schweizer, 2015, p. 955). Crowdfunding and ICOs are distinct segments; the crowdfunding market is estimated at approximately $14B in 2019, while the ICO market is estimated at $22B in 2018 (Block et al., 2021). These phenomena have also been the "topic of the majority of the most frequently cited papers published in the past five years in the top entrepreneurship journals" (Block et al., 2021, p. 866). Interestingly, given the dominance of American data in many other research streams within entrepreneurial finance, Europe is empirical setting for most crowdfunding papers (Block et al., 2021).

Crowdfunding can be divided into two sub-segments: reward-based (for example, Kickstarter and Indiegogo) and equity (for example, Seedrs, Crowdcube, and Wefunder). Reward-based crowdfunding emerged first (2008–2009), while equity crowdfunding developed later (approximately 2013–2014).

ICO research is less developed than that focused on crowdfunding. ICOs have been defined as ". . . an event where a venture sells tokens to a crowd using distributed ledger technologies (DLTs), such as blockchain technology. Tokens are units of value and can provide utility (utility tokens) or resemble securities (security tokens). The former offers the right to use the products or services of the venture, whereas the latter makes the buyer a debt or equity holder and allows her to participate in the value increase of the venture or provides other financial incentives (e.g., interest or preferred dividends) (Block et al., 2021, p. 866). Given its relatively underdeveloped state, future ICO research should focus on 1) sort(ing) out and differentiat(ing) the supply of versus the demand for ICO funding, taking geography and regulation into account, 2) advocating for global analyses over country-specific ones, 3) replicating studies across different time windows to establish robustness, and 4) research emphasizing agent-based modeling appropriate for relatively unexplored phenomena, where variable relationships are potentially nonlinear, and change dynamic and frequent (Bellavitis, Fisch & Wiklund, 2021)

Big data in entrepreneurial finance

The advances in information technology that facilitated the development of decentralized entrepreneurial finance have also opened up new research opportunities for the broader field (Schwab & Zhang, 2019), even as the resultant massive data sets have raised fundamental philosophical, social, and economic concerns (Zuboff, 2019).

Big data have begun to transform the practice of entrepreneurial finance. For example, algorithms are being used in the deal flow screening and portfolio management processes in venture capital (Chen, 2021). In one study, algorithm-based angel investing significantly outperformed against individual investors' decisions (Blohm et al., 2020).

An important challenge for big data-based academic research in entrepreneurial finance is the lack of informed consent provided by the ultimate data providers.

Behavioral economics and its impact on entrepreneurial finance

One of the most significant advances in entrepreneurship research has been the incorporation of cognitive psychology as a theoretical perspective. How entrepreneurs – and those who finance them – make decisions has been a central research question in this endeavor. Some models of entrepreneurial decision-making – such as effectuation (Sarasvathy, 2001) – explicitly recognize the limits to rationality in that process, proposing a model that enables boundedly rational founders to navigate successfully the world of high uncertainty in which startups live. Other research streams investigate entrepreneurial cognition and the entrepreneurial mindset (e.g., Shepherd & Patzelt, 2018).

Behavioral economics has considered the question of why so many entrepreneurs choose to start new ventures when the expected utility of such ventures is negative, even for VC-backed firms (Hall & Woodward, 2010). Possible explanations for such behavior include risk preference, overconfidence, and nonpecuniary benefits (Åsterbro, Herz, Nanda & Weber, 2014). These explanations have implications for the shape that entrepreneurial finance takes. For example, overconfident entrepreneurs are more likely to demand short-term debt finance for their ventures (Landier & Thesmar, 2009).

However, behavioral economics and finance continues to be underexploited as a theoretical perspective in entrepreneurial finance, particularly on the supply side. In particular, the decision-making behaviors of key actors such as VCs, angels, and participants in crowdfunding remains relatively unexplored by this literature.

Recent innovation in entrepreneurial finance

Despite the historical nature of risk capital, the examples of crowdfunding and ICOs demonstrate that entrepreneurial finance practice continues to be innovative. One recent innovation is the special purpose acquisition company (SPAC). SPACs are defined as "shells initiated with the sole intent of acquiring a single privately held company" (Cumming, Hass & Schweizer, 2014, p. 198). While a significant research stream has not yet developed on this phenomenon, one important finding is that SPACs underperform in comparison to the market, the industry, and comparable IPO firms (Kolb & Tykvová, 2016, p. 80).

The COVID-19 pandemic and entrepreneurial finance

At the time that I am writing this conclusion (late January 2022), the COVID-19 pandemic continues to be one of the most significant factors in global economic, political, and social life. It remains challenging to predict when the pandemic will wane and what its ultimate consequences might be.

However, it is reasonable to state that the pandemic has already had a larger impact on the global economy than any event since at least World War II. Therefore, it seems likely that the pandemic has impacted both entrepreneurship and entrepreneurial finance. Business models are being revised across a wide range of industries, some central banks are supporting national economies through monetary easing (although this has reversed recently in the face of rising inflation), and supply chain disruptions have become more frequent. These developments represent both challenges and opportunities for entrepreneurs and those who fund them.

How have these developments impacted entrepreneurial finance? In the United Kingdom, one recent study found that the volume of new equity transactions has decreased significantly during the pandemic. This study found that seed financing was most heavily impacted (Brown, Rocha & Cowling, 2020). These findings are similar to those observed in China (Brown & Rocha, 2020).

More broadly, the pandemic could have an impact on both research and practice in entrepreneurial finance. Extreme contexts such as pandemics have the potential to help develop new theoretical perspectives (Yin, 2017) and clarify our understanding of the difference between risky, emergency, and disrupted contexts (Hällgren, Rouleau & de Rond, 2018; Rouleau, Hällgren & de Rond, 2021). With respect to practice, the pandemic may cause VCs to revisit the hypergrowth exit mindset underlying many of the industry's practices (Lam & Seidel, 2020).

Entrepreneurial finance's impact on other fields

As academic disciplines and theoretical perspectives develop, they are able to impact other fields. Perhaps the best example of this is Darwin's theory of natural selection, a biological perspective that has had a significant impact on many other academic disciplines, including entrepreneurship (Aldrich et al., 2008).

Has entrepreneurial finance had a significant impact on other fields? Let's start by looking at entrepreneurship and finance, the field's root disciplines. In order to assess intellecutal impact, total citations are used as a primary measure. Looking at the ten most cited publications in entrepreneurial finance, Table C.1 depicts those heavily cited publications that cited these publications and the fields with which those publications are associated.

Table C.1: The Impact of Entrepreneurial Finance on Other Fields.

Entrepreneurial Finance Publication	Heavily Cited Publications* Citing This Publication	Fields of These Publications
Sahlman (1990)	Jensen (1993); Shane (2003); Berger & Udell (1998); Ritter & Welch (2002)	Finance, Entrepreneurship
Mollick (2014)	None	Not applicable
Gompers & Lerner (2004)	Drucker (2014); Shane (2003); Chesbrough, Vanhaverbeke & West (2006); Mollick (2014)	Entrepreneurship, Innovation, Entrepreneurial Finance
Belleflamme, Lambert & Schwienbacher (2014)	Mollick (2014)	Entrepreneurial Finance
Kaplan & Stromberg (2003)	Shane (2003)	Entrepreneurship, Accounting
Kortum & Lerner (2001)	Chesbrough, Vanhaverbeke & West (2006); Allen, Qian & Qian (2005); Mollick (2014); Chesbrough (2006)	Innovation, Finance, Entrepreneurial Finance
Gompers & Lerner (2001)	Loughran & Ritter (2004)	Finance
Gompers (1996)	Drucker (2014); Berger & Udell (1998)	Entrepreneurship, Innovation, Finance
Bygrave & Timmons (1992)	Drucker (2014); Baldwin, Clark & Clark (2000); Shane (2003); Stuart, Hoang & Hybels (1999); Schulze, Lubatkin, Dino & Buchholtz (2001); Black & Gilson (1998); Sorenson & Stuart (2001); Hellman & Puri (2000)	Entrepreneurship, Innovation, Design, Management, Entrepreneurial Finance
Ahlers, Cumming, Günther & Schweizer (2015)	Belleflamme, Lambert & Schwienbacher (2014)	Entrepreneurial Finance

Note: *Defined as publications with more citations that the publication it cites.

What is evident from this table is that, while entrepreneurial finance has had an impact on its root disciplines of entrepreneurship and finance, its impact on other disciplines in business and management studies (and beyond) has remained quite limited to date.

How could entrepreneurial finance have a greater impact in business and management studies?

What follows in this section is necessarily speculative. But it seems that, if entrepreneurial finance is to continue to develop, it must begin to have a greater impact on other disciplines in business and management studies. Aside from the many research avenues suggested by the contributors, I suggest five additional avenues through which it might do so: uncertainty, the dark side of entrepreneurship, process studies, weak institutional environments, and engaged scholarship.

Exploiting uncertainty

Uncertainty has been of significant and growing interest to business and management researchers (Milliken, 1987; McMullen & Shepherd, 2006; Block & Sandner, 2009; Packard, Clark & Klein, 2017; Conti, Dass, De Lorenzo & Graham, 2019; Rindova & Courtney, 2020). One condition that differentiates entrepreneurship from other business activities is the high level of uncertainty faced by its actors (Knight, 1921). The relational nature of startup equity investments may mean that they are more impacted by uncertainty (Brown & Rocha, 2020).

Uncertainty has become an increasingly significant condition facing other business activities (Buchanan & Denyer, 2013; Wenzel, Stanske & Lieberman, 2020), including from COVID-19 (Baker, Bloom, Davis & Terry, 2020).

Entrepreneurial finance has developed structures, strategies, and practices that enable its successful practitioners to exploit the high levels of uncertainty they face. As such, entrepreneurial finance may offer insights into how actors in other parts of business and society can exploit uncertainty. One example of this cross-fertilization is venture philanthropy (Gordon, 2014).

The dark side of entrepreneurial finance

Baumol (1990) asserted that there are three varieties of entrepreneurship – productive, unproductive, and destructive. This contentio has been subsequently confirmed (Sobol, 2008). More recently, Shepherd (2019) has called for greater research attention to two of the Baumol (1990) dimensions understudied in entrepreneurship – unproductive and destructive – which have been labeled "dark." Examples of unproductive entrepreneurship include rent-seeking activities such as lobbying and lawsuits, while destructive entrepreneurship includes activities such as organized crime.

How does entrepreneurial finance relate to the dark side of entrepreneurship? In at least two ways. First, entrepreneurial finance may provide resources to startups that engage in unproductive or destructive activities. Second, the activities of entrepreneurial finance may themselves be unproductive or destructive.

Researchers have asserted that some of the most successful startups in modern economic history have engaged in unproductive or destructive activities. For example, Zuboff (2019) asserts that several VC-fund tech startups – notably Google and Facebook – have created large market capitalizations at the expense of human privacy.

Entrepreneurial finance activities may be directly unproductive or destructive. For example, Lam and Seidel (2020) argue that VCs' hypergrowth exit mindset (a key feature in their ability to exploit the uncertainty of startup investment) has destroyed social welfare. The recent example of WeWork has called attention to the central role of VCs in enabling mismanagement in order to facilitate exit (Brown & Farrell, 2021). One industry observer stated that "V.C.s seem to embody the cynical shape of modern capitalism, which too often rewards crafty middlemen and bombastic charlatans rather than hardworking employees and creative businesspeople" (Duhigg, 2020, p. 47). As a technology enabling some types of decentralized entrepreneurial finance, blockchain technology has been exploited by actors outside of entrepreneurial finance for criminal purposes. Some have also argued that it may be an artificially inflated source of value and could lead to the defrauding of investors, startups, or both. It is an open question as to whether blockchain is a productive, unproductive, or destructive form of entrepreneurial finance.

Process studies and entrepreneurial finance

Process research addresses the "how" question of business and management studies research. Entrepreneurship teaching and, to a lesser extent, research has begun to incorporate a process approach (McMullen and Dimov, 2013). Yet with few exceptions (e.g., Li, Chen, Kotha & Fisher, 2017) research on entrepreneurial finance continues to take mainly a variance approach, focused on the "what" questions of the field. There seems considerable scope for additional process research in the field, especially now that top-tier journals are regularly publishing process studies.

Weak institutional environments and entrepreneurial finance

As developing countries have become an increasingly significant feature of the global economy (Radelet, 2015), entrepreneurial finance research has increasingly focused on these weak institutional environments (Ahlstrom & Bruton, 2006; Lingelbach, 2015, 2013; Groh & Wallmeroth, 2016). These studies have focused on venture capital, and limited research to date has been conducted on the other types of entrepreneurial finance.

Engaged scholarship and entrepreneurial finance

Engaged scholarship is "a participative form of research for obtaining the advice and perspectives of key stakeholders (researchers, users, clients, sponsors, and practitioners) to understand a complex social problem" (Van de Ven, 2007, p. ix). It can be conducted in a variety of ways, including (ranging from least to most engaged) informed basic research, collaborative research, design/evaluation research, and action/intervention research. Such engagement is more likely to make significant contributions to research and practice than the alternative of routine academic research (Van de Ven, 2007).

Engaged scholarship is not without its challenges in entrepreneurial finance. For example, finding willing practitioners with whom to collaborate can be difficult, given confidentiality concerns in many financial activities.

Summing up

This book began with a tale about Mu Tha and her efforts in entrepreneurial finance in a hypothetical 2030 Bogotá. That story was meant to signal that the future of entrepreneurial finance as both an academic discipline and professional practice is not predetermined. Our contributors have suggested in their work the many possible directions in which the literature might move in the future, and the book more generally indicates how the practice of entrepreneurial finance may move in the years ahead. We live in uncertain times, and entrepreneurial finance seems prepared to respond to that uncertainty and contribute to a better understanding of it.

I wish each of our readers all the best on the journey that lies ahead.

References

Ahlers, G.K.C., Cumming, D., Günther, C. & Schweizer, D. (2015). Signaling in equity crowdfunding. *Entrepreneurship Theory & Practice, 39*(4), 955–80.

Ahlstrom, D. & Bruton, G.D. (2006). Venture capital in emerging economies: Networks and institutional change. *Entrepreneurship Theory & Practice, 30*(2), 299–320.

Aldrich, H.E., Hodgson, G.M., Hull, D.L., Knudsen, T., Mokyr, J. & Vanberg, V.J. (2008). In defense of generalized Darwinism. *Journal of Evolutionary Economics, 18,* 577–96.

Åsterbro, T., Herz, H., Nanda, R. & Weber, R.A. (2014). Seeking the roots of entrepreneurship: Insights from behavioral economics. *Journal of Economics Perspectives, 28*(3), 49–70.

Baker, S.R., Bloom, N., Davis, S.J. & Terry, S.J. (2020). COVID-induced economic uncertainty. *NBER Working Paper 26983,* April.

Baumol, W.J. (1900). Entrepreneurship: Productive, unproductive, and destructive. *The Journal of Political Economy*, *98*(5), 893–921.

Bellavitis, C., Fisch, C. & Wiklund, J. (2021). A comprehensive review of the global development of initial coin offerings (ICOs) and their regulation. *Journal of Business Venturing Insights, 15*, https://doi.org/10.1016/j.jbvi.2020.e00213

Block, J.H., Groh, A., Hornuf, L., Vanacker, T. & Vismara, S. (2021). The entrepreneurial finance markets of the future: A comparison of crowdfunding and initial coin offerings. *Small Business Economics, 57*, 865–82.

Block, J. & Sandner, P. (2009). What is the effect of the financial crisis on venture capital financing? Empirical evidence from US Internet start-ups. *Venture Capital: An International Journal of Entrepreneurial Finance*, *11*(4), 295–309.

Blohm, I., Antretter, T., Sirén, C., Grichnik, D. & Wincent, J. (2020). It's a peoples game, isn't it?! A comparison between the investment returns of business angels and machine learning algorithms. *Entrepreneurship Theory & Practice*, https://doi.org/10.1177/1042258720945206

Brown, E. & Farrell, M. (2021). *The cult of We: WeWork, Adam Neumann, and the great startup delusion*. Crown.

Brown, R. & Rocha, A. (2020). Entrepreneurial uncertainty during the COVID-19 crisis: Mapping the temporal dynamics of entrepreneurial finance. *Journal of Business Venturing Insights, 14*, https://doi.org/10.1016/j.jbvi.2020.e00174

Brown, R., Rocha, A. & Cowling, M. (2020). Financing entrepreneurship in times of crisis: Exploring the impact of COVID-19 on the market for entrepreneurial finance in the United Kingdom. *International Small Business Journal*, *38*(5), 380–90.

Buchanan, D.A. & Denyer, D. (2013). Researching tomorrow's crisis: Methodological innovations and wider implications. *International Journal of Management Reviews*, *15*(2), 205–24.

Chen, X.J. (2021). How AI is transforming venture capital. BRINK. https://www.brinknews.com/how-ai-is-transforming-venture-capital/.

Conti, A., Dass, N., Di Lorenzo, F. & Graham, S.J.H. (2019). Venture capital investment strategies under financing constraints: Evidence from the 2008 financial crisis. *Research Policy*, *48*(3), 799–812.

Cumming, D., Hass, L.H. & Schweizer, D. (2014). The fast track IPO – Success factors for taking firms public with SPACs. *Journal of Banking & Finance*, *47*, 198–213.

Duhigg, C. (2020). The enablers. *The New Yorker*, *96*(38), 38–47.

Gordon, J. (2014). A stage model of venture philanthropy. *Venture Capital: An International Journal of Entrepreneurial Finance*, *16*(2), 85–107.

Groh, A.P. & Wallmeroth, J. (2016). Determinants of venture capital investment in emerging markets. *Emerging Markets Review*, *29*, 104–32.

Hall, R.E. & Woodward, S.E. (2010). The burden of the nondiversifiable risk of entrepreneurship. *American Economic Review*, *100*(3), 1163–94.

Hällgren, M., Rouleau, L. & de Rond, M. (2018). A matter of life or death: How extreme context research matters for management and organization studies. *The Academy of Management Annals*, *12*(1), 111–53.

Knight, F.H. (1921). *Risk, Uncertainty and Profit*. Houghton Mifflin.

Kolb, J. & Tyková, T. (2016). Going public via special purpose acquisition companies: Frogs do not turn into princes. *Journal of Corporate Finance*, *40*, 80–96.

Lam, L. & Seidel, M. (2020). Hypergrowth exit mindset: Destroying societal wellbeing through venture capital biased social construction of value. *Journal of Management Inquiry*, *29*(4), 471–74.

Landier, A. & Thesmar, D. (2009). Financial contracting with optimistic entrepreneurs. *Review of Financial Studies*, *22*(1), 117–50.

Le Pendeven, B., Bardon, T. & Manigart, S. (2021). Explaining academic interest in crowdfunding as a research topic. *British Journal of Management*, published online March 9, https://doi.org/10.1111/1467-8551.12486.

Li, J., Chen, X-P., Kotha, S. & Fisher, G. (2017). Catching fire and spreading it: A glimpse into displayed entrepreneurial passion in crowdfunding campaigns. *Journal of Applied Psychology*, *102*(7), 1075–90.

Lingelbach, D. (2015). Developing venture capital when institutions change. *Venture Capital: An International Journal of Entrepreneurial Finance*, *17*(4), 327–63.

Lingelbach, D. (2013). Paradise postponed? Venture capital emergence in Russia. *critical perspectives on international business*, *9*(1/2), 204–25.

McMullen, J.S. & Dimov, D. (2013). Time and the entrepreneurial journey: The problems and promise of studying entrepreneurship as a process. *Journal of Management Studies*, *50*(8), 1481–1512.

McMullen, J.S. & Shepherd, D.A. (2006). Entrepreneurial action and the role of uncertainty in the theory of the entrepreneur. *The Academy of Management Review*, *31*(1), 132–52.

Milliken, F.J. (1987). Three types of perceived uncertainty about the environment: State, effect, and response uncertainty. *The Academy of Management Review*, *12*(1), 133–43.

Obschonka, M. & Audretsch, D.B. (2020). Artificial intelligence and big data in entrepreneurship: A new era has begun. *Small Business Economics*, *55*, 529–39.

Packard, M.D., Clark, B.B. & Klein, P.G. (2017). Uncertainty types and transitions in the entrepreneurial process. *Organization Science*, *28*(5), 840–56.

Radelet, S. (2015). *The Great Surge*. Simon & Schuster.

Rindova, V. & Courtney, H. (2020). To shape or adapt: Knowledge problems, epistemologies and strategic postures under Knightian uncertainty. *Academy of Management Review, 45* (4), 787–807.

Rouleau, L., Hällgren, M. & de Rond, M. (2021). Covid-19 and our understanding of risk, emergencies, and crises. *Journal of Management Studies*, *58*(1), 245–48.

Sarasvathy, S.D. (2001). Causation and effectuation: Toward a theoretical shift from economic inevitability to entrepreneurial contingency. *The Academy of Management Review*, *26*(2), 243–63.

Schwab, A. & Zhang, Z. (2019). A new methodological frontier in entrepreneurship research: Big data studies. *Entrepreneurship Theory & Practice*, *43*(5), 843–54.

Shepherd, D.A. (2019). Researching the dark side, downside, and destructive side of entrepreneurship: It is the compassionate thing to do! *Academy of Management Discoveries*, *5*(3), 217–20.

Shepherd, D.A. & Patzelt, H. (2018). *Entrepreneurial cognition: Exploring the mindset of entrepreneurs*. Palgrave Macmillan.

Sobel, R.S. (2008). Testing Baumol: Institutional quality and the productivity of entrepreneurship. *Journal of Business Venturing*, *23*, 641–55.

Van de Ven, A.H. (2007). *Engaged scholarship: A guide for organizational and social research*. Oxford.

Wenzel, M., Stanske, S. & Lieberman, M.B. (2020). *Strategic Management Journal*. Published online April 2.

Yin, R.K. (2017). *Case Study Research and Applications: Design and Methods*. SAGE.

Zetzsche, D.A., Arner, D.W. & Buckley, R.P. (2020). Decentralized finance. *Journal of Financial Regulation*, *6*, 172–203.

Zuboff, S. (2019). *The age of surveillance capitalism: The fight for a human future at the new frontier of power*. PublicAffairs.

List of figures

https://doi.org/10.1515/9783110726312-026

List of tables

https://doi.org/10.1515/9783110726312-027

Index

https://doi.org/10.1515/9783110726312-028